Nineteenth-Century Women Poets

Nineteenth-Century Women Poets

An Oxford Anthology

EDITED BY
ISOBEL ARMSTRONG
AND
JOSEPH BRISTOW
WITH
CATH SHARROCK

CLARENDON PRESS · OXFORD
1996

Oxford University Press, Great Clarendon Street, Oxford OX2 6DP
Oxford New York
Athens Auckland Bangkok Bogota Bombay
Buenos Aires Calcutta Cape Town Dar es Salaam
Delhi Florence Hong Kong Istanbul Karachi
Kuala Lumpur Madras Madrid Melbourne
Mexico City Nairobi Paris Singapore
Taipei Tokyo Toronto
and associated companies in
Berlin Ibadan

Oxford is a trade mark of Oxford University Press

Published in the United States by
Oxford University Press Inc., New York

British Library Cataloguing in Publication Data
Data available

Library of Congress Cataloging in Publication Data
Nineteenth-century women poets: an Oxford anthology/ edited by Isobel Armstrong and Joseph Bristow with Cath Sharrock.
Includes bibliographical references and indexes.
1. English poetry—Women authors. 2. English poetry—19th century.
I. Armstrong, Isobel. II. Bristow, Joseph. III. Sharrock, Cath.
PR1177.N56 1996 821'.80809287—dc20 96-345522
ISBN 0-19-811290-4

1 3 5 7 9 10 8 6 4 2

Typeset by Pure Tech India Ltd., Pondicherry
Printed in Great Britain by
Bookcraft Ltd,
Midsomer Norton, Somerset

ACKNOWLEDGEMENTS

THIS anthology has been some years in the making, and in the course of our editorial work, we have accumulated a great number of debts. Financial support came from several sources. The British Academy made us two awards: a small grant for research in the humanities to Joseph Bristow in 1987, and a major research grant to Isobel Armstrong in 1990. A generous award from the Wingate Foundation enabled Joseph Bristow to take study leave from Sheffield City Polytechnic for one term in 1990. The Birkbeck College Resource Centre D Research Priority Fund made a grant to Isobel Armstrong to cover the huge cost of photocopying. In particular, Professor David Wells, Head of the Resource Centre, must be thanked for his help in this matter. St John's College, University of Oxford, awarded Joseph Bristow a summer vacation scholarship in 1990, providing a sustained period of access to an important research library.

A project as large as this one draws on a broad range of printed sources, and the staffs of many libraries have often gone out of their way to assist us in locating materials. We should like to thank the following: the London Library; University of London Library, Senate House; the Bodleian Library, University of Oxford; Cambridge University Library; the Friends Library, London; the Mary Badland Library, Sheffield Hallam University (formerly Sheffield City Polytechnic); and the J. B. Morrell Library, University of York. Throughout the course of our work, we have constantly drawn upon the many services of the British Library, London, and we are indebted to its professionalism. Special acknowledgements must be made to the staff of the Department of Reprographic Services at the British Library.

The following colleagues and research students kindly drew our attention to materials and information that we might otherwise have missed: Diana Clarke, Ian Delaney, Emma Francis, Tricia Green, Gill Gregory, Barry Harkison, Druuske Hawkridge, Elizabeth Heaps, Anne Janowitz, John Kelly, Roger Lonsdale, Jane Rendall, Helen Rogers, Anira Rowanchild, Michael Sanders, T. V. Sathyamurthy, Cynthia Scheinberg, Michael Slater, and Glennis Stephenson. Cynthia Lawford gave us invaluable advice on the dating of poems by L. E. L. (Letitia Elizabeth Landon).

The editing of this anthology drew to a close when a notable conference, 'Rethinking Women's Poetry, 1730–1930', was held at Birkbeck College, University of London. Our thanks go to all participants in this stimulating event, especially to Laurel Brake and to all plenary speakers—Virginia Blain, Stuart Curran, Margaret Anne Doody, Cora Kaplan, Angela Leighton, Anne K. Mellor, Menakshee Mukherjee, and

Cheryl Walker. Warren Chernaik, Head of the Centre for English Studies at the University of London, gave encouragement, as well as material support, to the conference. Virginia Blain was a positive inspiration for the conference, and this anthology has benefited immeasurably from her advice. She allowed us to draw upon her knowledge of the whole field of nineteenth-century women poets, while invaluable guidance on our selection of poets came from *The Feminist Companion to Literature in English*, which she jointly edited.

We must thank those scholars whose research has drawn our attention to the richness and complexity of the field. Especially helpful have been studies and editions by Lucy Bland, R. W. Crump, Stuart Curran, J. R. de J. Jackson, Linda K. Hughes, Elizabeth Kraft, Angela Leighton, William McCarthy, and Margaret Reynolds. In addition, we learned much from the three parts of *Minor British Poets,* 1789–1918 (Davis, CA: The Library, 1986), whose anonymous bibliographers provided vital pieces of information that on many occasions would have proved difficult to obtain by other means.

The assistant editor, Cath Sharrock, would like to thank Sabina Sharkey and Deirdre Toomey for their generous advice on sources for identifying Irish poets. Clyde Binfield and Alan Cass made helpful suggestions about tracing Methodist writers. Maurice Hepworth, at Barnsley Central Library, provided her with detailed information about Louisa A. Horsfield.

Our own students helped us immeasurably by reading the poetry of women poets with full enthusiasm, in particular students of the Bread Loaf School of English, Middlebury College, Vermont.

'Thoughts on my Sick-Bed' and 'When Shall I Tread Your Garden Path?' by Dorothy Wordsworth are reproduced courtesy of the Wordsworth Trust. 'True Love', 'Dead Love', 'He and She and Angels Three', and 'Love and Hate' by Elizabeth Siddal are reproduced courtesy of the Ashmolean Museum. 'Cormacan Sings (Cormacan an Eigeas, 10th Century)', 'A Song of Freedom', 'When I Was a Little Girl', and 'The Dark Palace (The Palace of Aileach, Seat of the O'Neill)' by Alice Milligan are reproduced courtesy of Gill & Macmillan Ltd. Every effort has been made to clear the necessary permissions. Any omission will be rectified in future editions.

August 1995

I. M. A.
J. E. B.

CONTENTS

NOTE ON THE TEXTS

NINETEENTH-CENTURY poems were published in many different contexts. They appeared, for example, in newspapers, coterie magazines, periodicals, pamphlets, annuals, and albums books, as well as anthologies and single volumes. On a great number of occasions, poems were printed in volume form after they had appeared in periodicals. For the most part, we have taken our copy-texts from the first volume in which a poem was collected. Just to give one case, the work of Adelaide Anne Procter was printed in a number of periodical sources, such as *Household Words* and *English Woman's Journal*. These poems were subsequently collected in three later volumes, *Legends and Lyrics* (1858), *Legends and Lyrics*, Second Series (1861), and *A Chaplet of Verses* (1862). The texts by Procter we have chosen to reprint are taken from these collected volumes.

Given that a large proportion of our selections appeared in periodicals or in single volumes, we have been concerned to date them as clearly as possible. Our practice has been as follows. At the end of each poem, we present either one or two dates. Wherever we have given a single date, this means that the text has been reprinted in its earliest published form, or the earliest published form that we have been able to find. The earliest appearance of a poem is given in arabic numerals. Dates in italics refer to the collection from which we have reprinted the poem if it differs from the first appearance of a poem. For example, Joanna Baillie's 'A Winter's Day' was first published in 1790 and collected (with some textual changes) in 1851. Since we have used the 1851 collected version as our copy-text, two dates appear after this poem: 1790 *1851*. Similarly, Helen Maria Williams's 'To Sensibility' appeared first in 1786 but was collected in 1823, the edition we use. Thus 1786 *1823* appear under her poem. Amelia Opie's 'Consumption', however, is followed by one date in arabic numerals, 1802, because this is the earliest published text of the poem so far as we are aware and it is the text we have used.

Full details of our texts are given in the list of Sources and Notes (pp. 797–807). In some instances, we have discovered the dates of composition, and we have included this information when it was significant in the notes detailing the selections we have made from the work of each poet. Bibliographical research in the dating of nineteenth-century women's poetry is at an early stage. Future scholarship is bound to fill in what is incomplete in our current knowledge. Spelling and punctuation in our copy-texts have not been modified, even when there would appear to be inconsistencies in the work of the same poet. This means that some words—such as 'Christian' and 'christian'—at times appear in variant forms. In one or two places, there are lacunae in the original poems, and these have been preserved. Where space has allowed, we have retained the original annotation to our chosen poems, except in the case of lengthy footnotes, such as those accompanying Charlotte Smith's *Beachy Head* and Lucy Aikin's *Epistles on Women*. Glosses have been supplied on ancient Greek words. On almost every occasion, we have reprinted poems in their entirety. Where we have taken extracts, the title of the original poem has been retained. Brief comments have been supplied in italics when it has proved necessary to put excerpted passages in context.

I. M. A.
J. E. B.

INTRODUCTION

I

OVER the last two decades, researchers have gradually begun to rediscover the work of women poets of the nineteenth and earlier centuries. This process of rediscovery has been one of the most intellectually exciting developments within the field of literary history, and its significance cannot be underestimated. As a consequence, the contours of the literary past begin to change as new relations emerge, both between newly read poems and the largely male canon, and between women poets themselves. The poets in the present anthology vary from militant feminist radicals to conservative women of High Church principle. They wrote in a wide range of genres and styles, from the expressive lyric to strident polemic. We have reprinted works by over one hundred poets writing in England, Ireland, Scotland, and Wales, as well as the colonies. Our selection of writings indicates the breadth, ambition, and diversity of women's poetry and its distinctive contribution to nineteenth-century culture.

The century from which we have chosen poems begins in the aftermath of the French Revolution, continues through the Napoleonic wars, and ends with a decisive imperial conflict, the second Anglo-Boer War. The period starts with a poetry in dialogue with the dominant ideology of gender still informed by Edmund Burke's understanding that femininity belongs to the non-rational. In other words, the feminine is at this time associated with the aesthetic qualities of the beautiful, which are somatically ordered by the passive female body, rather than the sublime. By the close of the century, the figure of the New Woman has emerged as an icon, if not a reality. Equipped with higher education and demanding equality in personal relationships with men, the New Woman was the forerunner of the suffragists whose campaigns would lead to the most spectacular forms of organized feminist politics in the Edwardian age. So *Nineteenth-Century Women Poets* opens with late-Romantic poetry and closes with works from the Victorian *fin de siècle*.

Although this collection covers poetry published between 1800 and 1900, we have not been doctrinaire about our terminal dates. If the balance of a poet's work falls within the century, and if we have felt that work to be significant, then we have chosen material that allows a fair representation of the writer's œuvre, even if the selection has meant reprinting poetry that falls slightly outside the designated period. For example, although Mary Robinson wrote some magnificent poems in 1800, she died in that year, and the bulk of her work undoubtedly belongs to the eighteenth century. By comparison, Helen Maria

Williams, who also published a substantial body of poetry in the eighteenth century, brought out a collection four years before her death in 1823. This volume by Williams was prefaced with a notable essay that perhaps intimated renewed stirrings of the political radicalism with which she was in sympathy. So we have not represented Robinson but have given space to Williams. Similarly, some of the very late eighteenth-century poems of Anna Laetitia Barbauld have been included, together with her major work, *Eighteen Hundred and Eleven* (1812), which we have reprinted in full. Barbauld's niece, Lucy Aikin, brought out an edition of her aunt's work in 1825 which made Barbauld a figure to be reckoned with in that decade. At the other end of the century, we have made comparable decisions. Born in 1869, Charlotte Mew is often seen as one of the 'last Victorians'. But most of her poetry was produced after the turn of the twentieth century. Mew came to attention with her first book, *The Farmer's Bride*, in 1915. Alice Meynell, however, presents a rather different case. Although a large proportion of her work appeared after 1900, Meynell published notable volumes in 1875 and 1893. We have, therefore, selected from her earlier poems.

Anthologies can have a number of uses. Some collections indicate a sequence of publication over a given period, while others offer samplings of material that can be followed up and extended beyond the covers of the book. Another editorial strategy aims to preserve simply the bare minimum of typical poems that might ensure a lasting place for particular poets. Yet another is to publish works sufficiently ample for readers to reach independent conclusions about them. Since much of the poets' work presented here is not easily available elsewhere, we believe that this last alternative is the most satisfying. Accordingly, we have allocated substantial space to thirty out of our hundred or so poets whose achievements are unquestionable. Smaller samples have been taken from writers who were noted for particular types of poetry, including the popular song, the evangelical hymn, the legend, and the lullaby. In several instances, we represent works by sorely neglected writers, such as Eliza Keary, whose poetry took significant formal and intellectual risks. Wherever possible, we have reprinted poems in full. Since many nineteenth-century poems are lengthy (such as ballads, metrical tales, and novels in verse), we have on occasions taken self-contained extracts from larger works. Publishing passages that were to a large degree self-standing, so long as their context was clear, seemed preferable to omitting them altogether. The only form of poetic writing that we have not been able to represent is closet drama. This omission is disappointing, since many nineteenth-century women poets—notably, Joanna Baillie, George Eliot, Menella Bute Smedley, and Augusta Webster—produced some of their finest work in this genre.

We have, however, been able to print sufficient material to enable a reader to understand the ambitions of women poets. As a matter of convention, a chronological arrangement of poets according to their birth dates has been adopted. But, given this framework, we have chosen material that allows a multiplicity of thematic cross-connections to emerge. In this Introduction, we discuss, first of all, how a reader might trace some of these relationships. Then we describe the political formations and cultural groupings to which various poets belonged, and which make deeper sense of the woman poet's themes. Lastly, we consider how styles and genres change in the century.

II

Factory conditions and industrial labour; slavery and abolitionism; marriage and its discontents; motherhood (its pleasures, as well as its pressures); passion (both sexual and religious); the 'fallen' woman and the prostitute; militarism and the rise of nationalism; colonial experience, particularly in Ireland and India—these, to name the most obvious, are topics that can be traced across the work of many nineteenth-century women poets. Take, for example, the recurrent factory poem. One can set Caroline Bowles's 'The Father's Tale' (1836)—a subtle critique of bourgeois complacency about poverty, where a working-class man mourns a dead child—against Caroline Norton's conservative poem, *A Voice from the Factories* (1833), which does not envisage social change. The subject-matter of these poems compares with Elizabeth Barrett Browning's appeal for compassionate understanding in 'The Cry of the Children' (1843) or the radicalism of Christina Rossetti's 'A Royal Princess' (written in 1851, and published in 1863 in a collection sold to raise funds for 'Relief of Distress in the Cotton Districts').

Equally conflicted are the many poems on marriage, not surprising in a century when women lost their legal identity in marriage and when political campaigning led to the Divorce Act in 1857. Consider 'The Marriage Vow' (1841) by L.E.L. (the initials under which Letitia Elizabeth Landon published). Her poem, with its shudder of horror at the finality of the bond, compares with Helen Maria Williams's *The Charter* (1819), which virtually renegotiates the terms of nineteenth-century marriage. Much later in the period many dissident voices on this topic can be heard. Christina Rossetti's work, for instance, frequently places a stronger value on religious and familial sisterhood than loving relationships with men. By comparison, Amy Levy's iconoclastic lesbian satire, 'A Ballad of Religion and Marriage' (published posthumously in 1915), brilliantly attacks the institution altogether. Perhaps this intense concern with marriage is connected with a virtual obsession with Indian suttee (widow-burning) that persists until mid-century, such as Maria Jane Jewsbury's exploration of this disturbing phenomenon.

Numerous poems on the 'fallen woman' and the prostitute are all part of this ceaseless dialectic on marriage. But it is important to note that the mood and approach of these writings alter as social attitudes to such women begin to harden, notably with the increasing influence of evangelical morality and rigorous codes of moral respectability. In the early part of the period, compassionate narratives of betrayal are permissible. Consider, for example, Caroline Bowles's *Ellen Fitzarthur* (1820) and Caroline Norton's 'The Sorrows of Rosalie' (1829). By the time of Elizabeth Barrett Browning's *Aurora Leigh* (1856) and Christina Rossetti's 'Under the Rose' (1865), a far more intense politics has emerged. One only has to recall the vociferous attacks on the prostitute, such as those by William Acton, to see how decisively women poets felt they had to resist hypocrisy. Even Sarah Stickney Ellis—in many ways, a conventional thinker—regards the prostitute with compassion in *Janet: One of Many* (1862). In 'A Castaway' (1870) by Augusta Webster, one hears the bitter words of an upper-class prostitute who knows only too well what her poorer sisters who walk the streets have to do to earn their living. 'Magdalen' (1884) by Amy Levy is a poignant anatomy of suffering spoken from the confines of a lock-hospital. Under the terms of the Contagious Diseases Acts imposed in the 1860s, even women suspected of working as prostitutes could be thrown into prisons of this kind. Such poems were written in the context of Josephine Butler's feminist campaign against these laws.

Sensitivity to oppression relates not just to the subordination of women. Right up until the American Civil War, poems on slavery abound. One might almost say that slavery is pre-eminently the woman poet's theme. Anne Laetitia Barbauld, Hannah More, Helen Maria Williams, L.E.L., Amelia Opie, Ann Hawkshaw, and Elizabeth Barrett Browning—all write on this emotive and urgent issue, only to reach different conclusions. Just as with exploration of marriage, this too is a preoccupation that discloses contradictions. The numerous poems on slavery veer between radical and conservative thinking. Both Hannah More and Helen Maria Williams assert the fundamental humanity of the slave in long poems on this issue. Yet, in another work, 'The Sorrows of Yamba, or, The Negro Woman's Lamentation' (*c.* 1800), More's conservatism finds it necessary to convert a suicidal female slave to Christianity—since to her mind, if the master is a sinner, the slave must recognize that she is one as well. The gravitas of the poem that opens this anthology, Barbauld's 'Epistle to William Wilberforce, ... 1791', is quite unlike the deeply riven drama of the female runaway slave in Barrett Browning's poem who has murdered her 'too white' child.

Similar moral fracturing appears in poems that explore national identity. Early in the century, the woman's body—frequently imaged as a repository of virtue—becomes, rather like Britannia, an emblem of the ideal nation-state, notably in the poetry of Felicia Hemans. But such presentations of national identity are far from unambiguous. Eliza Cook, an influential editor, celebrates national power in 'The Englishman' (1838), expressing a staunch populist unity through an English spirit that transcends class. At the same time, Cook is aware of cultural difference in 'Song of the Red Indian' (1845), demonstrating a generous understanding that is radical for her time in urging respect for Native American customs, beliefs, and rituals. It is worth comparing Cook's poem with Lucy Aikin's unexamined Eurocentrism, despite her radicalism, in her 'Epistles on the Character and Condition of Women in Various Ages and Nations' (1810). Even Helen Maria Williams, with the Revoutionary sympathies that motivate her attack on colonial violence, asserts the superiority of Christianity in *Peruvian Tales* (1784). Faced with the large number of poems about Italian nationalism, we wondered if this passionate cause displaced women's anxieties about an implicitly oppressive and violently masculine British nation-state. Elizabeth Barrett Browning repeatedly turns to Italy as a motherland that must be liberated from tyranny. Likewise, Harriet Eleanor Hamilton King writes with unbounded exuberance on the heroes of the Risorgimento in their campaigns for national autonomy.

The power of women in national histories, whether of Britain itself or those of other European countries, preoccupies many poets. Joan of Arc is a popular icon. This fascination with women exercising power over the nation-state presents itself in numerous poems about Queen Victoria. L.E.L., Elizabeth Barrett Browning, Caroline Norton, and Eliza Cook write arrestingly about Victoria. 'Remember,' writes Cook in her address to Victoria, 'much of weal or woe | To millions rest alone with thee'. The millions, of course, grew with the expansion of empire. In the face of imperial rule, writers from the colonies make strong claims for their respective cultural identities, whether in the Irish nationalist poems of 'Speranza' (Jane Francesca Wilde), or the myth-making poets who followed her later in the century, such as Ethna Carbery and Alice Milligan. Conflicting outlooks on colonial experience can be found in many areas of the anthology. Emma Roberts was fascinated by Indian culture, travelling widely to research many different aspects of the subcontinent. The poems of the Indo-Anglian writer, Toru Dutt—a gifted translator of French poetry into English—make a stark contrast with the Anglo-Indian hauteur that one finds in the work of Laurence Hope (Adela Florence Nicolson), whose volumes were well received at the turn of the twentieth century.

With empire came war, and with war came many poems by women on the carnage of military conflict. So numerous are these poems that one feels women poets were more aware of bloodshed than their male contemporaries. Joanna Baillie, Anna Laetitia Barbauld, Charlotte Smith, and Felicia Hemans responded to the long-standing Revolutionary and Napoleonic wars. Barbauld's *Eighteen Hundred and Eleven* hauntingly conveys a civilian society crumbling under the pressure of the Peninsular War and its bloodshed. Hemans incessantly returns to the ethics of battle and the place of women in a warring society. In just the same way, the Crimean War with its slaughter at Alma, Balaclava, and Sebastopol prompted eloquent poems by Adelaide Anne Procter and Louisa Shore. Highly praised when it appeared in the *Spectator* in 1854, Shore's 'War Music' makes a disturbing connection between poetry and militarism: 'The merest soldier is to-day | The poet of his art, | Though he can neither sing nor say | The transports of his heart.' Left outside the realities of active service, women were forced to explore the 'transports of the heart', as if to compensate for this exclusion. The language of the 'heart' lies at the centre of women's writing of this period. Of course, women were often confined to what was commonly termed the 'poetry of the affections', but they could use this idiom in an empowering way. The 'heart' empowers because it enables the woman poet to mount a critique of masculine values.

Women belonged to a poetic culture that welcomed and celebrated intense passions. There are many love poems in this anthology, and yet it is often difficult to classify them as such. The signification of love extended to many forms of passion that we would no longer recognize. Love poems encompass both sexual and religious experience. An era unembarrassed by affective emotions could move between the erotic and the devotional as if they belonged to a continuum. In the poems of Christina Rossetti, Dora Greenwell, and Jean Ingelow, one sees a characteristically nineteenth-century lyric emerging, in which desires for divine and human love are fused. But there are always anxieties around sexual love, and even love of God. For both are at the heart of patriarchy. Countless poems reveal female speakers who have been betrayed in love, while others question paternalistic religion. The short extract from Eliza Keary's massive dialogic poem, 'Christine and Mary: A Correspondence' (1874), suggests how trenchantly religious values could be challenged. The huge range of religious poetry, which includes hymns and didactic poems—by, for instance, Hannah More, Felicia Hemans, Ann Taylor and Jane Taylor, A. L. Waring, and Frances Ridley Havergal—demonstrates that this was a living discourse, with all the complexities and contradictions that entails. Fuelled by tumultuous passion, Christina Rossetti's work constantly tests the limits of religious language. Religious poems are almost always concurrently poems about a woman's sexuality because the drama of religious devotion calls up adjacent emotions of sexual longing. It is not surprising, therefore, to find that a sophisticated religious poetry exists side by side with the questioning of sexual experience. Eliza Mary Hamilton's 'A Young Girl Seen in Church' (1838) delicately explores one woman's voyeuristic gaze at another.

By the end of the century, however, religious and sexual discourses had diverged. New challenges to orthodox female sexuality come into their own. In the erudite, sensual works of Michael Field, lesbian desire is coded through a scrupulous dramatization of Sappho's legend. This poetry has few equals in its representation of women's love for one another. A distinctive lesbian voice sounds in Amy Levy's ambitious poetry of the 1880s, which expresses anger at the taboo against erotic relations between women. New Woman poets, May Kendall and Constance Naden, drew on a fund of decisive wit to deal with the shortcomings of male lovers who could not accept women's intellectual power. Kendall and Naden turn no longer to God but to what they see as the evolutionary wisdom of Charles Darwin.

III

Now we move to the groupings and networks that give further meaning to the thematic cross-connections that have just been discussed. The majority of poets included in this anthology are middle-class writers. We have, however, brought together a number of working-class poets—Charlotte Richardson (a cook), Mary Colling (a servant), Ellen Johnston and Louisa Horsfield (industrial workers), an anonymous 'Factory Girl' who wrote on temperance and its virtues, Marianne Farningham (an educator), and Ruth Wills (a warehouse employee). But given their educational opportunities, few working-class poets had access to the print culture which reached middle-class readers. Middle-class poets tend to speak for the experience of the working classes. Such writings as the admonitory anti-Jacobin and anti-Revolutionary propaganda of Hannah More's 'Will Chip's *True* Rights of Man' (*c.* 1800), and Mary Sewell's later advocation of the domestic virtues in 'The Bad Manager' (1858) are deliberate attempts to control and direct working-class experience. On the other side, there are Anna Laetitia Barbauld's protest against manipulative and dishonest anti-Jacobin writing, 'To the Poor' (1794), and Mary Leman Grimstone's petition on behalf of working-class women's education, 'The Poor Woman's Appeal to Her Husband' (1834).

The hegemony of the middle classes was being established both before and after the French Revolution, and continued to be consolidated and defined in relation to the state throughout Victoria's reign.

But it scarcely needs saying that the middle classes were not homogeneous. They represented a multiplicity of religious and political cultures, from dissenting radicals to Anglican conservatives. True, the women represented here had access to education, however unofficial, and however much they struggled for it. They had access to the publishing media, even when they depended on male professionals to negotiate for them. They could circulate and even market their own writing, making use of their cultural capital. During this time, a shift took place from the patronage of the privately subscribed volume, where publication was financed by a group of wealthy (often aristocratic) individuals, to commercial publishing more or less as we currently know it. A diverse periodical press sprang up, serving both small ideological coteries and a mass market. Women poets exploited the possibilities of these forms of dissemination. Early periodicals, for instance, range from minority journals, such as the radical *Cambridge Intelligencer* and the dissenting *Monthly Repository*, to hugely popular emollient album books and annuals—often ruthlessly making use of aristocratic connections, and catering for a more conservative middle-class readership—such as *The Amulet, The Gem, Fisher's Drawing-Room Scrapbook, Friendship's Garland*, and *Heath's Book of Beauty*. Poets depended on these very different periodicals for the circulation of their work. Anna Laetitia Barbauld, for example, published poems in both of the radical journals just mentioned. By comparison, Felicia Hemans, Caroline Norton, and L.E.L.—all younger poets without the same radical ambitions—used album books as main outlets for their work. Both Hemans and L.E.L. needed money to support families, children in one case, and mother and brother in the other. L.E.L. edited several volumes of *Fisher's*. In later decades, publishing patterns changed. Periodicals diversified, becoming more specialised, a particular example being the *English Woman's Journal* (1858–62), devoted to a feminist agenda. The little magazine, such as the Decadent *Yellow Book* (1894), emerged, and publication in small single volumes became increasingly the norm. Although Augusta Webster was closely involved with the periodical press—she worked for some time as poetry editor of the *Athenaeum*—her reputation rested on the many single volumes she brought out with Macmillan and with Kegan Paul from the mid-1860s onwards. Later poets, such as Rosamund Marriott Watson and A. Mary F. Robinson developed their profile by placing slender volumes of tightly controlled poetry with publishers, including John Lane and T. Fisher Unwin, who served the literary avant-garde in the 1890s.

A glance at patterns of publication suggests that there were particular affiliations, networks, and groupings throughout the whole of this period. In our select bibliography, we mention the scholars who have begun to map these relationships (see p. 809). But it has taken time to comprehend the intricate connections between women poets whose reputations were well established in their own day. A perceptive late-nineteenth-century editor of women's poetry, Elizabeth Sharp, made a significant early attempt to describe and chart the influences that shaped and defined groups of writers. Looking back on the achievements of women writers whose reputations were established at different points in the nineteenth century, Sharp's comments show how decisively critical opinion had changed about the strengths of poetry by women. Her remarks reveal how several important aspects of the works of poets coming to prominence in the early part of the century were no longer meaningful to someone of her generation. In *Women Poets of the Victorian Era* (1890), Sharp certainly recognizes that there were significant personal and professional links between individual poets. For example, she puts Hannah More and Anna Laetitia Barbauld together as powerful intellectuals. Likewise, she relates Felicia Hemans and L.E.L. as lyrical writers, although she finds L.E.L. a 'sentimental' poet, far beneath the 'poetic energy, variety, and rhythmic power' of Hemans. Sharp understands that Charlotte Smith and the early, radical William Wordsworth belonged to the same political group, and acknowledges that Mary Tighe's *Psyche* (1805) powerfully influenced John Keats. But there are limitations to her analysis. Sharp cannot find a place, except as a 'Shakespearean' figure, for Joanna Baillie, and she misunderstands both Hannah More's conservatism and Barbauld's radicalism. She was right to see that Hemans and L.E.L.—album book writers who explored an affective rhetoric that appeared to conform to a quintessential feminine experience of home, family, and love—did not belong to these earlier traditions. Yet Hemans, writing in Wales outside metropolitan literary culture, came from a fastidious conservative Anglican network that included Maria Jane Jewsbury, who dedicated a volume to Hemans in 1829. Hemans's associates included Bishop Heber and the later reactionary Wordsworth. L.E.L., by contrast, perpetually disavowing indiscretion, belonged to a scandal-ridden group of society writers in London, who ranged from conservative subversives, such as William Maginn of *Fraser's Magazine*, to the Whig affiliations of the Lady Blessington circle.

Sharp was right, in some ways, to put More and Barbauld together (though she is tart about More's limitations) because this pairing recognizes the great vitality of provincial cultures, such as those of Bristol, Norwich, and Warrington, that were formative environments for these two poets. She does not, however, see that the post-Revolutionary radical formation to which Barbauld belonged was extraordinarily powerful at the beginning of the century. More was conservative and anti-Revolutionary, High Church, and Tory, and instinctively a Burkean traditionalist. But she represents an older bluestocking tradition.

Barbauld, though she was part of a second wave of the bluestocking group, was affiliated with a vigorous dissenting counter-culture, which was committed to Revolutionary ideals (though not to violence) and claimed that men and women could enter civic life on equal terms. Consequently, her work engaged with the dialectic between the masculine sublime and the feminine beautiful. (One might compare the same dialectic in Charlotte Smith's poetry, which also challenges Burke's paradigm.) Barbauld resisted the reactionary thought of Thomas Malthus and made a critique of advanced political economy, such as Adam Smith's work. Her affiliations are with the radical political circle of William Godwin and Mary Wollstonecraft—although as we can see from 'The Rights of Woman' (written *c*.1793), a poem written in response to Wollstonecraft's polemical prose work of the same name, they had their differences. Barbauld's poem, 'On the Expected General Rising of the French Nation in 1792' (first published as 'To a Great Nation'), was in all probability sent to Paris in 1792, together with funds subscribed by English radicals who supported Revolutionary ideas. Although she sent her anti-slavery poem to Hannah More, a cause that united women intellectuals, and was acquainted with More in London, her work is best associated with other provincial dissenters. Poets slightly younger than she, such as Joanna Baillie (of Scottish descent), and Helen Maria Williams (of Welsh descent), were both dissenters, and formed part of the same democratic tradition.

Baillie not only challenged the male sublime, which she associated with political reaction, but also sought a new poetry of common life and democratic experience. 'Homely subjects, in simple diction,' she wrote in her Preface to *Fugitive Verses* (1840), 'can be read with "relish"' by those taxed by an increasingly technological culture, 'coursing through the air in a balloon', for instance, or 'ploughing' the ocean in a steamship. Helen Maria Williams's records of the French Revolution, which extended to the Napoleonic period, in works such as *Letters, containing a sketch of the politics of France* (1795) and *A Narrative of the Events Which have Taken Place in France* (1815), are perhaps some of the most remarkable writings by a woman of that time. If we juxtapose Hannah More's distrustful poem, 'Sensibility', with Williams's ode of the same title, which celebrates passion as a form of knowledge, the divide between the two formations represented by each woman becomes apparent. It would not be an exaggeration to say that for one relatively short period a radical network dominated literary life. Barbauld knew the younger poet, Amelia Opie, through Norwich connections when she moved to East Anglia after her marriage. In London, Williams met her senior, Charlotte Smith, another poet with Revolutionary sympathies. Smith was praised by Wordsworth in his Revolutionary period but, like him, drew back from the violence of events in France. Baillie was a member of the congregation ministered to by Barbauld's husband in Hampstead. Barbauld's niece, Lucy Aikin, was a close friend of Joanna Baillie.

A questioning dissenting tradition moves through the century. It can be seen in the work of Sarah Flower Adams, who was associated with the Unitarian and Utilitarian *Monthly Repository*, to which Barbauld also contributed. The outspoken participation of this journal in politics is behind the work of Elizabeth Barrett Browning. Although Anglican, Barrett Browning was well acquainted with the *Repository* through Richard Hengist Horne, who edited the journal for a brief period. She married one of its contributors, Robert Browning. The social preoccupations of the radical tradition colour the poetry of Adelaide Anne Procter, whose father edited a collection of Robert Browning's poetry. They colour the poetry of George Eliot too. They reappear, through the Benthamite tradition, in the works of Augusta Webster, Emily Pfeiffer, Louisa Shore, and L. S. Bevington. But, interestingly, Elizabeth Barrett Browning recalls a quite different tradition in *Aurora Leigh* (1856), which begins by alluding to L.E.L.'s *The Improvisatrice* (1824). Affiliations change, shift, and blur as the century progresses, accounting for some of Elizabeth Sharp's misprisions. L.E.L., who died tragically and mysteriously in 1838 in West Africa after her marriage, was acknowledged as a precursor both by Barrett Browning and by Christina Rossetti. The Rossetti circle, tending towards High Anglicanism and Roman Catholicism, and hardly at all to dissent, included Adelaide Anne Procter, Dora Greenwell, and Jean Ingelow. These writers met regularly through the Portfolio Society, a London-based group that circulated poems to one another on a mutually supportive basis. Some of these women, including Rossetti herself, were activists among urban and destitute women. Such work, it may appear, would not have encouraged an assent to the 'sentimental' values of album book poetry. Nevertheless, this sentimental tradition clearly spoke to women of later generations. Christina Rossetti's brother, William Michael Rossetti, edited the poems of Felicia Hemans in 1873. Fascinatingly, two almost identical drawings by Charlotte Brontë and Emily Brontë turn out to have been copied from an engraving, entitled 'The Disconsolate', by H. Corbould in the *Forget Me Not* annual published in 1831 with a poem by L.E.L.

The political energies of the earlier radicals gave place to a concerted feminist propaganda that promoted professional opportunities for women, and campaigned for the development of a women's literary culture. The shift towards this politics occurs in the 1850s with the founding, by Bessie Rayner Parkes (herself a poet) and Barbara Leigh Smith (an artist), of the *English Woman's Journal*. Both Parkes and Smith came from Unitarian backgrounds, and their periodical remained unmatched in its avant-garde belief in the urgent need for increased democraticization at mid-century. Poetry was prominent in its pages. Two poets, in particular, were of note. The first was Isa Craig, a self-taught poet, who was at the centre of the Langham Place group that published the journal. The second, Adelaide Anne Procter, was a commercially successful poet. Although a popular figure in the pages of Charles Dickens' *Household Words* and *All the Year Round*, Procter was a committed feminist; the proceeds of her third collection of poetry were used to fund a night refuge for homeless women and children in London.

Many later poets became active in those campaigns for the suffrage that had first been mounted by the women of Langham Place. Prominent figures include Emily Pfeiffer, who, like Barrett Browning before her, was at times castigated in the press for her forthright views. Her vigorous 'Ode to the Teuton Women' (1876) makes her political position clear. The Unitarian and Utilitarian impulse that inspired the *Monthly Repository* and the founding editors of the *English Woman's Journal* was sustained by another influential periodical, the *Westminster Review*. The *Westminster*, which had George Eliot on its staff for several years, was the pre-eminent organ of advanced thought for much of the mid- and late-nineteenth century. Open to progressive intellectual currents, this imposing periodical brought within its pages supportive reviews of works by women poets, such as Augusta Webster, whose dazzling monologues articulate powerful voices of female discontent. To this same journal, one of the earliest women poets to absorb Darwinian thought, L. S. Bevington, would contribute a principled and tightly argued two-part essay on atheism and evolutionary theory in 1869. Bevington is perhaps a revealing example of the different channels into which radical thought flowed. In her last years, she wrote for anarchist journals. An equally gifted contributor to the *Westminster* was Mathilde Blind, whose essay on the radical poet, Percy Bysshe Shelley, appeared there in 1870. Not coincidentally, Blind published one of the earliest biographies of George Eliot. Also an evolutionist, Blind was closely associated with one of the most eminent of the New Women to come to public attention in the 1890s. This was Mona Caird, author of a polemical and much publicized article on the deplorable state of modern marriage published by the *Westminster* in 1889.

Elizabeth Sharp dedicated *Women Poets of the Victorian Era* to Mona Caird, and many of the poets that Sharp gathered together in her 1890 anthology belonged to a network that was establishing a women's literary culture as never before. This powerful grouping included Emily Pfeiffer, Harriet Eleanor Hamilton King, and Rosamund Marriott Watson (then known as Graham R. Tomson). Many of the late-Victorian women poets selected by Sharp were closely involved with literary journalism, and the proliferation of specialized periodicals at this time provided for many an income that could not be derived simply from publishing poetry. For several years, Watson served as poetry editor of the *Athenaeum*. The work of these later poets is often characterized by a concise lyricism, and it is this style that Sharp favours above all.

IV

In her introduction, Elizabeth Sharp praised the lyrical energy of a 'virile' poetry by women who came into prominence at the end of the century. She made a similar claim in the preface to an earlier anthology, published in 1887, that represented selections from the works of women poets from the seventeenth century to the Victorian *fin de siècle*. There she suggests that women's poetry decisively progressed through this long span of time, demonstrating a 'steady development in intellectual power, certainly not unaccompanied by artistic faculty—a fact which gives further sanction to the belief that still finer work will be produced in the future by women-poets'. Other commentators expressed similar views, drawing out the implicit criticism of the limits to women's poetry in Sharp's analysis. Many Victorians saw the language of the 'heart'—sometimes called the 'poetry of the affections'—simply as a consolidation of domestic virtues and a celebration of the women's sphere of home, love, and duty. In *The Newcomes* (1855), for example, William Makepeace Thackeray has Barnes Newcome make a bid to restore his political position by giving a lecture on Felicia Hemans, in which he unscrupulously and cynically exploits the clichés of the domestic sphere; this is how Newcome's performance is described:

> Our lecturer then makes a distinction between man's poetry and woman's poetry, charging considerably in favour of the latter. We show that to appeal to the affections is after all the true office of the bard; to decorate the homely threshold, to wreathe flowers round the domestic hearth, the delightful duty of the Christian singer. We glance at Mrs Hemans's biography, and state where she was born, and under what circumstances she must at first, &c &c.

Maria Abdy, an album book contributor whose sentimentality achieved extraordinary stamina, similarly believed that Hemans's 'duties were joys, her sphere was home'. This was overwhelmingly the dominant view of the nature of women's poetry, and it persisted for many decades afterwards. In a singularly unsympathetic essay entitled 'Poetesses', appearing in the *Saturday Review* in 1868, it was said that 'women, in writing poetry, draw their style from other women, and thus miss that largeness and universality which alone compels attention and preserves a work through all changes of sentiment and opinion'. A few years earlier, the same journal made the following demeaning remarks about 'Authoresses':

> Quick feminine perception gives an insight into the little trivialities and mannerisms, but cannot give the power of judging their value and the relation which

they bear to the sum total of character itself. A woman's judgement of those she meets is usually formed in a peculiar and an unsatisfactory manner . . . Her view of character generally is made up of vast and sweeping deductions, based on absurdly minute data.

It was precisely this view that Elizabeth Barrett Browning satirizes in *Aurora Leigh*, a poem about the professional ambitions of a woman poet, like the author herself. Romney Leigh, cousin of the protagonist, sneers at the woman poet for representing all experience with the immediacy of sensation—what he condemns as 'the personal pang'. The woman poet, he declares, is incapable of generalizing. In his view, she will write 'of factories and of slaves' with empathy but without the capacity for abstract thought and systematic analysis. But there is a contradiction here. He foists the *duty* of empathy upon the woman poet while simultaneously belittling her for it. In other words, the woman poet was expected to sustain the social conscience of her culture through the language of the 'heart'. And yet a fierce masculine rationality despised this feminine writing.

In some ways, then, Sharp was correct. The language of the 'heart' was the prevailing idiom among women poets writing in the earlier part of the period. And this prolix and discursive style was gradually superseded by the concise and philosophical lyric that achieved the formal compression and economy with which readers of literary Modernism are familiar. There certainly was a gradual move from extended narrative to the complexities of drama—especially the dramatic monologue. In recognizing this shift, however, it is not necessary to adopt Sharp's 'Whig' progressivism. Her evolutionary version of events—one that charts the developing maturity of women's poetry from weak sentimentality (what might be stigmatized as the heavily perfumed language of marketed sensibility) to the terseness of proto-Modernism—obscures the very real intellectual possibilities allowed by an earlier form of highly emotive writing. This wealth of feeling would surge forth in many different poetic forms. The women closest to the Revolutionary epoch showed that they could readily adopt the genres of privileged male discourse—satire (Anna Laetitia Barbauld's *Eighteen Hundred and Eleven* (1812)), epistles (Lucy Aikin's 'Epistles' on women (1810)), the sublime (Joanna Baillie's 'London' (*c.* 1790)), the discursive prospect poem (Charlotte Smith's 'Beachy Head' (1807)), the ode (Helen Maria Williams's 'The Bastille, A Vision' (1790)). But in whatever forms they worked, these works were also placed in a dynamic relation with these primarily male genres, transforming them through the language of sensibility and a tendency towards energetically discursive narrative.

Since no critical categories exist to classify such works, we have used a vocabulary of our own making to describe the two principal poetic genres of the early and mid-century in which women poets excelled. We call these very different forms 'monumental legend' and 'oceanic monody'. Legends and their cognate genres—the lay, the romance, the ballad, the story, the tale, the epillyon (or short epic)—were ubiquitous. Such narratives often summon up a primordial, distant, and indeterminate history, often presented as a simulacrum of the oral poem. 'The Phantom Bride' (1824) by L.E.L.; 'The Sword of the Tomb. A Northern Legend' (1825) by Felicia Hemans; 'The Lady Magdalene' (1835) by Mary Howitt; 'The Legend of Santarem' (1836) by Caroline Bowles; 'A Tomb in Ghent' (1853) by Adelaide Anne Procter; *The Lay of the Stork* (1856) by Louisa Stuart Costello; 'Orinda: A Ballad' (1880) by Anne Evans—these poems are typical of the genre. The mock orality of Christina Rossetti's 'Goblin Market' (1862) is an extraordinary example of the form. These poems are steeped in legend, but frequently not in any known legend. They were sometimes the result of antiquarian research and scholarship of a sophisticated kind. Metrical romances are strangely porous, occasionally recording familiar historical events and known places, but withdrawing into the archaic mystery of their fictional worlds as real history soaks out of the walls of the narrative. Such poems refuse myth—which abstracts and patterns its materials in such an insistent manner that it loses touch with the immediacy of particular experience—but they are never realist forms. Metrical romances rely instead on repetition and the recurrence of events to chart the experiences of their protagonists. It is, we think, appropriate to describe such works as 'monumental legends', by adopting Julia Kristeva's term for the non-linear temporality that belongs to a way of experiencing life as cyclical rather than goal-directed.

In these 'monumental legends', the sediment of modern history has, as it were, been washed away from the narrative and deposited elsewhere. Take, for example, 'The Warrior's Return' by Amelia Opie (1808). This is a medievalized tale of the Holy Wars. Sir Walter returns to his home expecting to greet his wife and fifteen-year-old boy, born while he was fighting for his land, only to find that he has killed his son in battle. There appears to be no contemporary reference in this tale. The fifteen-year-old son, however, should alert us to the fifteen years of Revolutionary wars with France, which were receiving a new impulse in the Peninsular War of 1808, the date when Opie's poem was published. 'The Warrior's Return' masks this relationship with contemporary history. But it is there. This 'monumental legend' is not simply a naïve attack on the culture of war. The son fails to recognize his father in battle because Sir Walter has changed his armour with that of a friend. The father does not recognize a scarf, a token given to her son by his wife, until it is too late. What this configuration of actions seems to suggest is that war not only sets father against son, but also creates a traumatic break in cultural experience that fatally impairs the continuities which enable generations to communicate with one another. Moreover, the significance of the wife's scarf, a token of domestic love, cannot have meaning on the battlefield. For that is what the scarf is—a mere token.

Frequent is the melodrama where a young woman has been incarcerated in a convent or prison, so that she can be prevented from marrying or joining a husband. L.E.L.'s 'The Phantom Bride' and Felicia Hemans's 'Arabella Stuart' (1828) create situations where the issue is not only a lack of choice enforced by parents who assume the power of the law, but also a bizarre and distorted spiritualization of the young woman's body. The agency of the young woman is always an issue in the 'monumental legend'. The outstanding example is Hemans's 'Joan of Arc in Rheims', which first appeared in the *New Monthly Magazine* in 1826, and was collected two years later in *Records of Woman* (1828). Here Hemans manages to suggest analogues with contemporary historical events, without making her work a straightforward and banal allegory of her time. She creates a kind of virtual past—one that is always already over. Yet her Joan of Arc, who is the means by which a king reasserts 'sublime' power, is relevant to the resurgence of monarchy in France after Napoleon's death in 1821. Her poem hints at the responsibilities of women in sustaining hierarchical societies. Robert Southey's long epic poem on Joan of Arc, published in 1796, which warns against aristocratic power, is implicitly recalled by Hemans's legend.

The 'monumental legend' is a populist—not just popular—form. It gestures towards community, to shared experience, to common indigenous experience and memory, even if it recalls a 'shared' past in a narrative unknown until its telling appears in album books or periodicals. The appeal of such legends to common memory and the unifying bonds of the past assuages division, or at least appears to circumvent it. That this appeal to communality was a deliberate and often sophisticated move is testified by Maria Jane Jewsbury in an essay published in *Phantasmagoria* (1825). Recalling Friedrich Schiller's distinction between the naïve and the sentimental poet, and praising her close friend Hemans for being a truly modern 'sentimental' poet, Jewsbury encourages her contemporaries to rediscover the ballad and legend, urging them to recast these forms for the present. In other words, the apparent naïvety of the manifest narrative is to be informed by the latent meaning created by the reflective and sophisticated thought of modern civilization.

The 'monumental legend' gradually gave way to dramatic poetry. Likewise, what we call 'oceanic monody' is eventually displaced by the compressed lyric. We use the term 'oceanic monody' to describe a group of poems in which an expansive language of highly expressive emotion and feeling prevails. The 'oceanic monody' takes a loosely organized lyric form, rather than meticulously obeying the conventions of particular genres. Its characteristic is ceaseless flow, to the point of being visceral. But in its impetuous fluency it becomes an exact analytical tool, and often achieves considerable virtuosity. Examples of this kind of writing include Charlotte Smith's 'Beachy Head', Maria Jane Jewsbury's 'Oceanides' (1832–3), Amelia Opie's 'St Michael's Mount' (1834), Eliza Mary Hamilton's 'Lines Composed at Sea' (1838), and Jean Ingelow's 'Gladys and Her Island' (1867). In each of these poems, the sea has a function that goes beyond simple descriptive presence. Images of tidal flows and rapidly pulsating currents register flux and change, representing not just inner psychological experience, but also the pressure upon the social body as it strives to stabilize the world it inhabits, only to find itself rocked from side to side. Whether aboard ship, undertaking some distant journey, or casting one's gaze across an expanse of ocean, the speakers of these poems experience the present as a force that presses in upon them as they strive to control it. Unlike the 'monumental legend', which absorbs readers back into an unverifiable past, the 'oceanic monody' tends to be prospective, anticipatory, and more fearful than hopeful about the future. Consider, for example, the metaphysical power that Jewsbury exacts from the kinaesthetic motion of the sea:

> Swinging in my cot at ease,
> Yet a wanderer o'er the seas,
> Seas that never lead may sound,—
> Seas that have for man no ground;—
> Depths whose wonders call for faith,
> Never known till known in death, . . .
>
> ('Oceanides', II)

This opening sentence continues to flow, recreating itself anew, just when it seems to be reaching closure. Such language exists with sensation at one boundary, and psychic experience at the other. It is always close to the visceral but always negotiates its opposite, the transcendence of the physical. Ultimately, in poems of this kind, the language of affect is an epistemological language because it probes knowledge—both of the body and the mind.

How did the dramatic monologue and dramatized lyric come to replace these genres? Despite the distinctions between them, there is no sharp break between narrative and drama. Drama, in any case, is always implicit in narrative precisely because narrative unfolds actions and events, and often creates multiple centres of consciousness. Multiple consciousnesses and experiences viewed from many perspectives are the essence of drama. Events seen from different points of view create a profoundly social literary form. The dramatic poetry of the later period absorbs a number of features that are prominent earlier—the presentation of scenes and the use of dialogue. This dramatic poetry can be best understood as an extension and modification of the earlier rhetoric of the affections. That earlier rhetoric, after all, arises from the immediacy of sensation, and imprints sensation through pictures and almost painterly descriptions of individual scenes. Like drama, the rhetoric of the 'heart' is a pictorial or presentational form. Poems that draw on its affective resources often appear as an illustration of illustration, accompanying pictures in albums. They use descriptive tableau and are hypersensitive to sight. The beginning of any poem by Hemans or L.E.L. shows these features. It is a only a short step from this style of writing to the moving picture and the dramatized scene. Consider the title of Augusta Webster's impressive collection of dramatic monologues, *Portraits* (1870). These poems clearly differentiate the speaker from the poet's persona. Here, for example, Webster makes the mythical Circe speak. Always drawn to dramatic styles, the two women writing as Michael Field stage the legend of Sappho through a series of powerful lyrics. In the same spirit, Field animates the stories told in well-known paintings by quattrocento and cinquecento artists.

By virtue of this gradual shift towards dramatic poetry, the lyric no longer remains a vehicle for the spontaneous expression of emotion. Since the speakers of late-Victorian lyrics reflect critically on their own voices, the form presents itself as a condensed analytical mode. A poem such as Amy Levy's 'At a Dinner Party' (1889) would be best called a dramatized lyric, rather than either a monologue or an expressive lyric. In two precisely drawn stanzas, the poem hints at a subtext that requires the reader's understanding of an interplay between the speaker—who is not necessarily the poet's self—and an unidentified addressee:

With fruit and flowers the board is deckt,
   The wine and laughter flow;
I'll not complain—could one expect
   So dull a world to know?

You look across the fruit and flowers,
   My glance your glances find.—
It is our secret, only ours,
   Since all the world is blind.

Here the private lyric voice is staged in a recognizably social arena. One of the significant aspects of the dramatized lyric is that it constantly refuses clear-cut distinctions between private and public worlds. Since the individual monologic voice has virtually disappeared by this point, the dramatized lyric is a deeply sceptical form. By questioning shared knowledge and experience, the poem does not lay claim to a unified and authoritative subjectivity. The best-known form of dramatized lyric from this period is the sonnet sequence. Elizabeth Barrett Browning's celebrated 'Sonnets from the Portuguese' (1850) and Christina

Rossetti's 'Monna Innominata' (1881)—both noted for their gendered critique of the genre—have their antecedents in sonnets by Mary Tighe and Helen Maria Williams. The titles of other sequences, such as George Eliot's 'Brother and Sister' (dating from 1869) and Augusta Webster's long, meditative, and regrettably incomplete sequence, *Mother and Daughter* (published posthumously in 1895), show how this form was exploited to take up and occupy different subject positions.

The dramatized lyric emerged from a context in which it was no longer possible to sustain the communality assumed by the 'monumental legend', which idealized a shared history based on consensus. In other words, the 'monumental legend' attempted to maintain the myth of a socially unifying literary culture. Elizabeth Sharp praises early nineteenth-century women's poetry for its capacity to assuage social division. The obliteration of class and cultural difference on which this populism depended, however, became an impossible project, as British society was increasingly riven by class, and racial theory did away with the universal subject. Advanced radical post-Revolutionary women were buoyed by the hope that both men and women of all classes might be capable of achieving the social and intellectual identity that would entitle them to a 'universal' subjecthood, in which gender and class distinctions fall away or become unimportant. But quite soon neither the high conservative sense of duty to inferiors that made Caroline Bowles, for example, respond to the suffering of the poor, nor the radical hopes of social equality that motivated the work of dissenting women could be sustained. By the mid-century, the poetry of ballad and lay was under strain because this hope had died. The women poets of the later generation were forced to confront the fractured experience that came from social rifts which could simply not be healed. The partial and many-sided positions of dramatic poetry register this crisis. Women poets had to search for a form that would accommodate the fragmented world they inhabited. Earlier in the century, women poets were exploring what possibilities there could be for the feminine experience of affect and the rhetoric of the 'heart' within the given social order. The next generation begins to redefine feminine experience and consider ways of reconstructing the accepted order.

INTRODUCTION

ANNA LAETITIA BARBAULD
(1743–1825)

Anna Laetitia Aikin (later Barbauld) was a radical in politics and a highly prominent literary figure. She was born in Kibworth, Leicestershire, the only daughter and eldest child of the Revd John Aikin, a Unitarian minister, who later became a classics tutor at the Dissenting Academy in Warrington, and of Jane (née Jennings). Said to have been able to read by the age of 3, Anna Laetitia Barbauld was educated by her parents. In 1774, she married Rochement Barbauld, a Unitarian minister who had himself been educated at Warrington Academy. The couple moved to Palgrave, in Suffolk, where they set up and ran for eleven years a boarding-school for boys. Stress and ill-health forced them to close the school and, having spent almost a year in France and Switzerland, they returned to live in Hampstead from 1786. Here she devoted herself to writing and befriended the poet, Joanna Baillie. In 1802, they moved to Stoke Newington, London, where she was to remain for the rest of her life. Her husband, whose insanity had become increasingly evident, was eventually put under restraint and died (possibly by suicide) in 1808. An intense period of mostly editorial work followed the move to London, and she produced, among other things, a massive fifty-volume edition of *The British Novelists* (1810), the first volume of which includes her essay, 'On the Origins and Progress of Novel-Writing'.

Joseph Priestley, whom the poet had met through her father, claims in his *Memoirs* (1806) that 'it was the perusal of some verses of mine that first induced [Anna Laetitia Barbauld] to write anything in verse'. She is said to have been encouraged by her brother, John Aikin, to publish her first volume, *Poems*, in 1773. This was so successful that four more editions were brought out in the same year. In 1792 a new and enlarged edition appeared, to which was added her anti-slavery poem, 'Epistle to William Wilberforce Esq.' Her radical politics also found expression in three anonymous political essays, which included her *Sins of Government, Sins of the Nation* (1793), signed 'A Volunteer'. In this particular essay, she advocates the legislative power of the people. In *An Address to the Opposers of the Repeal of the Corporation and Test Acts* (1790), she argues for religious liberty: 'What you call toleration, we call the exercise of a natural and unalienable right.' The year 1812 produced her forceful and prophetic poem about the demise of British (and European) hegemony: *Eighteen Hundred and Eleven*. The aggressive discussion of this poem by John Wilson Croker in the *Quarterly Review* (June 1812) is thought to have discouraged her from further writing. She did, however, contribute five poems and a few other pieces to the radical Unitarian journal, the *Monthly Repository* between 1828 and 1845.

Barbauld's other publications had included *Lessons for Children* (1787–88) and *Hymns in Prose for Children* (1781), both of which she had written for the nephew, Charles Rochement Aikin, whom she and her husband had adopted. These volumes were enormously popular, the latter being translated into many European languages. Again writing for children, she collaborated with her brother on *Evenings at Home; or, The Juvenile Budget Opened* between 1792 and 1796. A memoir by her niece, the poet Lucy Aikin, accompanied the two-volume *The Works of Anna Laetitia Barbauld* in 1825. Although she suffered from some bad press, her work was mostly highly acclaimed and won the praise of William Wordsworth and Samuel Taylor Coleridge, among many others. Her large circle of friends included Hannah More, Mary Wortley Montagu, Maria Edgeworth, and Sir Walter Scott.

1 *Epistle to William Wilberforce Esq. on the Rejection of the Bill for Abolishing the Slave Trade, 1791*

CEASE, Wilberforce, to urge thy generous aim!
Thy Country knows the sin, and stands the shame!
The Preacher, Poet, Senator in vain
Has rattled in her sight the Negro's chain;
With his deep groans assailed her startled ear,
And rent the veil that hid his constant tear;
Forced her averted eyes his stripes to scan,
Beneath the bloody scourge laid bare the man,
Claimed Pity's tear, urged Conscience' strong controul,
And flashed conviction on her shrinking soul.
The Muse too, soon awaked, with ready tongue
At Mercy's shrine applausive pæans rung;
And Freedom's eager sons in vain foretold
A new Astrean reign, an age of gold:
She knows and she persists—Still Afric bleeds,
Unchecked, the human traffic still proceeds;
She stamps her infamy to future time,
And on her hardened forehead seals the crime.

In vain, to thy white standard gathering round,
Wit, Worth, and Parts and Eloquence are found:
In vain, to push to birth thy great design,
Contending chiefs, and hostile virtues join;
All, from conflicting ranks, of power possesst
To rouse, to melt, or to inform the breast.
Where seasoned tools of Avarice prevail,
A Nation's eloquence, combined, must fail:
Each flimsy sophistry by turns they try;
The plausive argument, the daring lie,
The artful gloss, that moral sense confounds,
The' acknowledged thirst of gain that honour wounds;
Bane of ingenuous minds!—the' unfeeling sneer,
Which sudden turns to stone the falling tear:
They search assiduous, with inverted skill,
For forms of wrong, and precedents of ill;
With impious mockery wrest the sacred page,
And glean up crimes from each remoter age:
Wrung Nature's tortures shuddering, while you tell,
From scoffing fiends bursts forth the laugh of hell;
In Britain's senate, Misery's pangs give birth
To jests unseemly, and to horrid mirth—
Forbear!—thy virtues but provoke our doom,

And swell the' account of vengeance yet to come;
For, not unmarked in Heaven's impartial plan,
Shall man, proud worm, contemn his fellow-man!
And injured Afric, by herself redresst,
Darts her own serpents at her tyrant's breast.
Each vice, to minds depraved by bondage known,
With sure contagion fastens on his own;
In sickly languors melts his nerveless frame,
And blows to rage impetuous Passion's flame:
Fermenting swift, the fiery venom gains
The milky innocence of infant veins;
There swells the stubborn will, damps learning's fire,
The whirlwind wakes of uncontrouled desire,
Sears the young heart to images of woe,
And blasts the buds of Virtue as they blow.

Lo! where reclined, pale Beauty courts the breeze,
Diffused on sofas of voluptuous ease;
With anxious awe her menial train around
Catch her faint whispers of half-uttered sound;
See her, in monstrous fellowship, unite
At once the Scythian and the Sybarite!
Blending repugnant vices, misallied,
Which frugal nature purposed to divide;
See her, with indolence to fierceness joined,
Of body delicate, infirm of mind,
With languid tones imperious mandates urge;
With arm recumbent wield the household scourge;
And with unruffled mien, and placid sounds,
Contriving torture, and inflicting wounds.

Nor, in their palmy walks and spicy groves,
The form benign of rural Pleasure roves;
No milk-maid's song, or hum of village talk,
Soothes the lone poet in his evening walk:
No willing arm the flail unwearied plies,
Where the mixed sounds of cheerful labour rise;
No blooming maids and frolic swains are seen
To pay gay homage to their harvest queen:
No heart-expanding scenes their eyes must prove
Of thriving industry and faithful love:
But shrieks and yells disturb the balmy air,
Dumb sullen looks of woe announce despair,
And angry eyes through dusky features glare.
Far from the sounding lash the Muses fly,
And sensual riot drowns each finer joy.

Nor less from the gay East, on essenced wings,
Breathing unnamed perfumes, Contagíon springs;
The soft luxurious plague alike pervades
The marble palaces and rural shades;
Hence thronged Augusta builds her rosy bowers,
And decks in summer wreaths her smoky towers;
And hence, in summer bowers, Art's costly hand
Pours courtly splendours o'er the dazzled land:
The manners melt;—one undistinguished blaze
O'erwhelms the sober pomp of elder days;
Corruption follows with gigantic stride,
And scarce vouchsafes his shameless front to hide:
The spreading leprosy taints every part,
Infects each limb, and sickens at the heart.
Simplicity, most dear of rural maids,
Weeping resigns her violated shades:
Stern Independence from his glebe retires,
And anxious Freedom eyes her drooping fires;
By foreign wealth are British morals changed,
And Afric's sons, and India's, smile avenged:

For you, whose tempered ardour long has borne
Untired the labour, and unmoved the scorn;
In Virtue's fasti be inscribed your fame,
And uttered yours with Howard's honoured name;
Friends of the friendless—Hail, ye generous band!
Whose efforts yet arrest Heaven's lifted hand,
Around whose steady brows, in union bright,
The civic wreath and Christian's palm unite:
Your merit stands, no greater and no less,
Without, or with the varnish of success:
But seek no more to break a nation's fall,
For ye have saved yourselves—and that is all.
Succeeding times your struggles, and their fate,
With mingled shame and triumph shall relate;
While faithful History, in her various page,
Marking the features of this motley age,
To shed a glory, and to fix a stain,
Tells how you strove, and that you strove in vain.

(1792 *1825*)

2 *On the Expected General Rising of the French Nation in 1792*

RISE, mighty nation, in thy strength,
And deal thy dreadful vengeance round;
Let thy great spirit, roused at length,
Strike hordes of despots to the ground!

Devoted land! thy mangled breast
Eager the royal vultures tear;
By friends betrayed, by foes opprest,—
And Virtue struggles with Despair.

The tocsin sounds! arise, arise!
Stern o'er each breast let Country reign;
Nor virgin's plighted hand nor sighs
Must now the ardent youth detain:

Nor must the hind who tills thy soil
The ripened vintage stay to press,
Till Rapture crown the flowing bowl,
And Freedom boast of full success.

Briareus-like extend thy hands,
That every hand may crush a foe;
In millions pour thy generous bands,
And end a warfare by a blow!

Then wash with sad repentant tears
Each deed that clouds thy glory's page;
Each phrensied start impelled by fears,
Each transient burst of headlong rage:

Then fold in thy relenting arms
Thy wretched outcasts where they roam;
From pining want and war's alarms,
O call the child of misery home!

Then build the tomb—O not alone
Of him who bled in Freedom's cause;
With equal eye the martyr own
Of faith revered and ancient laws.

Then be thy tide of glory staid;
Then be thy conquering banners furled;
Obey the laws thyself hast made,
And rise the model of the world!

(1793 *1825*)

3 *To Dr Priestley, December 29, 1792*

STIRS not thy spirit, Priestley! as the train
With low obeisance, and with servile phrase,
File behind file, advance, with supple knee,
And lay their necks beneath the foot of power?
Burns not thy cheek indignant, when thy name,
On which delighted Science loved to dwell,
Becomes the bandied theme of hooting crowds?
With timid caution, or with cool reserve,
When e'en each reverend brother keeps aloof,
Eyes the struck deer, and leaves thy naked side
A mark for Power to shoot at? Let it be.
'On evil days though fallen and evil tongues,'
To thee, the slander of a passing age
Imports not. Scenes like these hold little space
In his large mind, whose ample stretch of thought
Grasps future periods.—Well canst thou afford
To give large credit for that debt of fame
Thy country owes thee. Calm thou canst consign it
To the slow payment of that distant day,—
If distant,—when thy name, to Freedom's joined,
Shall meet the thanks of a regenerate land.

(1793 *1825*)

4 *The Rights of Woman*

YES, injured Woman! rise, assert thy right!
Woman! too long degraded, scorned, opprest;
O born to rule in partial Law's despite,
Resume thy native empire o'er the breast!

Go forth arrayed in panoply divine;
That angel pureness which admits no stain;
Go, bid proud Man his boasted rule resign,
And kiss the golden sceptre of thy reign.

Go, gird thyself with grace; collect thy store
Of bright artillery glancing from afar;
Soft melting tones thy thundering cannon's roar,
Blushes and fears thy magazine of war.

Thy rights are empire: urge no meaner claim,—
Felt, not defined, and if debated, lost;
Like sacred mysteries, which withheld from fame,
Shunning discussion, are revered the most.

Try all that wit and art suggest to bend
Of thy imperial foe the stubborn knee;
Make treacherous Man thy subject, not thy friend,
Thou mayst command, but never canst be free.

Awe the licentious, and restrain the rude;
Soften the sullen, clear the cloudy brow:
Be, more than princes' gifts, thy favours sued;—
She hazards all, who will the least allow.

But hope not, courted idol of mankind,
On this proud eminence secure to stay;
Subduing and subdued, thou soon shalt find
Thy coldness soften, and thy pride give way.

Then, then, abandon each ambitious thought,
Conquest or rule thy heart shall feebly move,
In Nature's school, by her soft maxims taught,
That separate rights are lost in mutual love.

(1825)

5 *Inscription for an Ice-House*

STRANGER, approach! within this iron door
Thrice locked and bolted, this rude arch beneath
That vaults with ponderous stone the cell; confined
By man, the great magician, who controuls
Fire, earth and air, and genii of the storm,
And bends the most remote and opposite things
To do him service and perform his will,—
A giant sits; stern Winter; here he piles,
While summer glows around, and southern gales
Dissolve the fainting world, his treasured snows
Within the rugged cave.—Stranger, approach!
He will not cramp thy limbs with sudden age,
Nor wither with his touch the coyest flower
That decks thy scented hair. Indignant here,
Like fettered Sampson when his might was spent
In puny feats to glad the festive halls
Of Gaza's wealthy sons; or he who sat
Midst laughing girls submiss, and patient twirled
The slender spindle in his sinewy grasp;
The rugged power, fair Pleasure's minister,
Exerts his art to deck the genial board;
Congeals the melting peach, the nectarine smooth,
Burnished and glowing from the sunny wall:
Darts sudden frost into the crimson veins

Of the moist berry; moulds the sugared hail:
Cools with his icy breath our flowing cups;
Or gives to the fresh dairy's nectared bowls
A quicker zest. Sullen he plies his task,
And on his shaking fingers counts the weeks
Of lingering Summer, mindful of his hour
To rush in whirlwinds forth, and rule the year.

(1825)

6 *To the Poor*

CHILD of distress, who meet'st the bitter scorn
Of fellow-men to happier prospects born,
Doomed Art and Nature's various stores to see
Flow in full cups of joy—and not for thee;
Who seest the rich, to heaven and fate resigned,
Bear *thy* afflictions with a patient mind;
Whose bursting heart disdains unjust controul,
Who feel'st oppression's iron in thy soul,
Who dragg'st the load of faint and feeble years,
Whose bread is anguish, and whose water tears;
Bear, bear thy wrongs—fulfill thy destined hour,
Bend thy meek neck beneath the foot of Power;
But when thou feel'st the great deliverer nigh,
And thy freed spirit mounting seeks the sky,
Let no vain fears thy parting hour molest,
No whispered terrors shake thy quiet breast:
Think not their threats can work thy future woe,
Nor deem the Lord above like lords below;—
Safe in the bosom of that love repose
By whom the sun gives light, the ocean flows;
Prepare to meet a Father undismayed,
Nor fear the God whom priests and kings have made.[1]

(1825)

[1] These lines, written in 1795, were described by Mrs. B., on sending them to a friend, as 'inspired by indignation on hearing sermons in which the poor are addressed in a manner which evidently shows the design of making religion an engine of government.'

7 *To a Little Invisible Being Who Is Expected Soon to Become Visible*

GERM of new life, whose powers expanding slow
For many a moon their full perfection wait,—
Haste, precious pledge of happy love, to go
Auspicious borne through life's mysterious gate.

What powers lie folded in thy curious frame,—
Senses from objects locked, and mind from thought!
How little canst thou guess thy lofty claim
To grasp at all the worlds the Almighty wrought!

And see, the genial season's warmth to share,
Fresh younglings shoot, and opening roses glow!
Swarms of new life exulting fill the air,—
Haste, infant bud of being, haste to blow!

For thee the nurse prepares her lulling songs,
The eager matrons count the lingering day;
But far the most thy anxious parent longs
On thy soft cheek a mother's kiss to lay.

She only asks to lay her burden down,
That her glad arms that burden may resume;
And nature's sharpest pangs her wishes crown,
That free thee living from thy living tomb.

She longs to fold to her maternal breast
Part of herself, yet to herself unknown;
To see and to salute the stranger guest,
Fed with her life through many a tedious moon.

Come, reap thy rich inheritance of love!
Bask in the fondness of a Mother's eye!
Nor wit nor eloquence her heart shall move
Like the first accents of thy feeble cry.

Haste, little captive, burst thy prison doors!
Launch on the living world, and spring to light!
Nature for thee displays her various stores,
Opens her thousand inlets of delight.

If charmed verse or muttered prayers had power,
With favouring spells to speed thee on thy way,
Anxious I'd bid my beads each passing hour,
Till thy wished smile thy mother's pangs o'erpay.

(1825)

8 *To Mr S. T. Coleridge: 1797*

MIDWAY the hill of science, after steep
And rugged paths that tire the' unpractised feet,
A grove extends; in tangled mazes wrought,
And filled with strange enchantment:—dubious shapes
Flit through dim glades, and lure the eager foot
Of youthful ardour to eternal chase.
Dreams hang on every leaf: unearthly forms
Glide through the gloom; and mystic visions swim
Before the cheated sense. Athwart the mists,
Far into vacant space, huge shadows stretch,
And seem realities; while things of life,
Obvious to sight and touch, all glowing round,
Fade to the hue of shadows—Scruples here,
With filmy net, most like the autumnal webs
Of floating gossamer, arrest the foot
Of generous enterprise; and palsy hope
And fair ambition with the chilling touch
Of sickly hesitation and blank fear.
Nor seldom Indolence these lawns among
Fixes her turf-built seat; and wears the garb
Of deep philosophy, and museful sits,
In dreamy twilight of the vacant mind,
Soothed by the whispering shade; for soothing soft
The shades; and vistas lengthening into air,
With moonbeam rainbows tinted.—Here each mind
Of finer mould, acute and delicate,
In its high progress to eternal truth
Rests for a space, in fairy bowers entranced;
And loves the softened light and tender gloom;
And, pampered with most unsubstantial food,
Looks down indignant on the grosser world,
And matter's cumbrous shapings. Youth beloved
Of Science—of the Muse beloved,—not here,
Not in the maze of metaphysic lore,
Build thou thy place of resting! lightly tread
The dangerous ground, on noble aims intent;
And be this Circe of the studious cell
Enjoyed, but still subservient. Active scenes
Shall soon with healthful spirit brace thy mind;
And fair exertion, for bright fame sustained,
For friends, for country, chase each spleen-fed fog
That blots the wide creation.—
Now Heaven conduct thee with a parent's love!

(1799 *1825*)

9 Eighteen Hundred and Eleven; A Poem

STILL the loud death drum, thundering from afar,
O'er the vext nations pours the storm of war:
To the stern call still Britain bends her ear,
Feeds the fierce strife, the' alternate hope and fear;
Bravely, though vainly, dares to strive with Fate,
And seeks by turns to prop each sinking state.
Colossal power with overwhelming force
Bears down each fort of Freedom in its course;
Prostrate she lies beneath the Despot's sway,
While the hushed nations curse him—and obey.

Bounteous in vain, with frantic man at strife,
Glad Nature pours the means—the joys of life;
In vain with orange-blossoms scents the gale,
The hills with olives clothes, with corn the vale;
Man calls to Famine, nor invokes in vain,
Disease and Rapine follow in her train;
The tramp of marching hosts disturbs the plough,
The sword, not sickle, reaps the harvest now,
And where the soldier gleans the scant supply,
The helpless peasant but retires to die;
No laws his hut from licensed outrage shield,
And war's least horror is the' ensanguined field.

Fruitful in vain, the matron counts with pride
The blooming youths that grace her honoured side;
No son returns to press her widowed hand,
Her fallen blossoms strew a foreign strand.
—Fruitful in vain, she boasts her virgin race,
Whom cultured arts adorn and gentlest grace;
Defrauded of its homage, Beauty mourns,
And the rose withers on its virgin thorns.
Frequent, some stream obscure, some uncouth name,
By deeds of blood is lifted into fame;
Oft o'er the daily page some soft one bends
To learn the fate of husband, brothers, friends,
Or the spread map with anxious eye explores,
Its dotted boundaries and penciled shores,
Asks where the spot that wrecked her bliss is found,
And learns its name but to detest the sound.

And think'st thou, Britain, still to sit at ease,
An island queen amidst thy subject seas,
While the vext billows, in their distant roar,
But soothe thy slumbers, and but kiss thy shore?
To sport in wars, while danger keeps aloof,
Thy grassy turf unbruised by hostile hoof?
So sing thy flatterers;—but, Britain, know,
Thou who hast shared the guilt must share the woe.
Nor distant is the hour; low murmurs spread,
And whispered fears, creating what they dread;
Ruin, as with an earthquake shock, is here,
There, the heart-witherings of unuttered fear,
And that sad death, whence most affection bleeds,
Which sickness, only of the soul, precedes.
Thy baseless wealth dissolves in air away,
Like mists that melt before the morning ray:
No more on crowded mart or busy street
Friends, meeting friends, with cheerful hurry greet;
Sad, on the ground thy princely merchants bend
Their altered looks, and evil days portend,
And fold their arms, and watch with anxious breast
The tempest blackening in the distant West.

Yes, thou must droop; thy Midas dream is o'er;
The golden tide of Commerce leaves thy shore,
Leaves thee to prove the' alternate ills that haunt
Enfeebling Luxury and ghastly Want;
Leaves thee, perhaps, to visit distant lands,
And deal the gifts of Heaven with equal hands.
Yet, O my Country, name beloved, revered,
By every tie that binds the soul endeared,
Whose image to my infant senses came
Mixt with Religion's light and Freedom's holy flame!
If prayers may not avert, if 'tis thy fate
To rank amongst the names that once were great,
Not like the dim, cold Crescent shalt thou fade,
Thy debt to Science and the Muse unpaid;
Thine are the laws surrounding states revere,
Thine the full harvest of the mental year,
Thine the bright stars in Glory's sky that shine,
And arts that make it life to live are thine.
If westward streams the light that leaves thy shores,
Still from thy lamp the streaming radiance pours.
Wide spreads thy race from Ganges to the pole,
O'er half the western world thy accents roll:
Nations beyond the Apalachian hills
Thy hand has planted and thy spirit fills:

Soon as their gradual progress shall impart
The finer sense of morals and of art,
Thy stores of knowledge the new states shall know,
And think thy thoughts, and with thy fancy glow;
Thy Lockes, thy Paleys shall instruct their youth,
Thy leading star direct their search for truth;
Beneath the spreading platan's tent-like shade,
Or by Missouri's rushing waters laid,
'Old father Thames' shall be the poet's theme,
Of Hagley's woods the' enamoured virgin dream,
And Milton's tones the raptured ear enthrall,
Mixt with the roaring of Niagara's fall;
In Thomson's glass the' ingenuous youth shall learn
A fairer face of Nature to discern;
Nor of the bards that swept the British lyre
Shall fade one laurel, or one note expire.
Then, loved Joanna[1], to admiring eyes
Thy storied groups in scenic pomp shall rise;
Their high-souled strains and Shakespear's noble rage
Shall with alternate passion shake the stage.
Some youthful Basil from thy moral lay
With stricter hand his fond desires shall sway;
Some Ethwald, as the fleeting shadows pass,
Start at his likeness in the mystic glass;
The tragic Muse resume her just controul,
With pity and with terror purge the soul,
While wide o'er transatlantic realms thy name
Shall live in light, and gather all its fame.

Where wanders Fancy down the lapse of years
Shedding o'er imaged woes untimely tears?
Fond moody power! as hopes—as fears prevail,
She longs, or dreads, to lift the awful veil,
On visions of delight now loves to dwell,
Now hears the shriek of woe or Freedom's knell:
Perhaps, she says, long ages past away,
And set in western waves our closing day,
Night, Gothic night, again may shade the plains
Where Power is seated, and where Science reigns;
England, the seat of arts, be only known
By the grey ruin and the mouldering stone;
That Time may tear the garland from her brow,
And Europe sit in dust, as Asia now.

Yet then the' ingenuous youth whom Fancy fires
With pictured glories of illustrious sires,

[1] Joanna Baillie, dramatist and poet. Barbauld's ensuing references are to two of Baillie's plays: *Basil: A Tragedy* (1798) and *Ethwald: A Tragedy* (1802). Eds.

With duteous zeal their pilgrimage shall take
From the Blue Mountains, or Ontario's lake,
With fond adoring steps to press the sod
By statesmen, sages, poets, heroes trod;
On Isis' banks to draw inspiring air,
From Runnymede to send the patriot's prayer;
In pensive thought, where Cam's slow waters wind,
To meet those shades that ruled the realms of mind;
In silent halls to sculptured marbles bow,
And hang fresh wreaths round Newton's awful brow.
Oft shall they seek some peasant's homely shed,
Who toils, unconscious of the mighty dead,
To ask where Avon's winding waters stray,
And thence a knot of wild flowers bear away;
Anxious inquire where Clarkson, friend of man,
Or all-accomplished Jones his race began;
If of the modest mansion aught remains
Where Heaven and Nature prompted Cowper's strains;
Where Roscoe, to whose patriot breast belong
The Roman virtue and the Tuscan song,
Led Ceres to the black and barren moor
Where Ceres never gained a wreath before:[1]
With curious search their pilgrim steps shall rove
By many a ruined tower and proud alcove,
Shall listen for those strains that soothed of yore
Thy rock, stern Skiddaw, and thy fall, Lodore;
Feast with Dun Edin's classic brow their sight,
And 'visit Melross by the pale moonlight.'

But who their mingled feelings shall pursue
When London's faded glories rise to view?
The mighty city, which by every road,
In floods of people poured itself abroad;
Ungirt by walls, irregularly great,
No jealous drawbridge, and no closing gate;
Whose merchants (such the state which commerce brings)
Sent forth their mandates to dependent kings;
Streets, where the turban'd Moslem, bearded Jew,
And woolly Afric, met the brown Hindu;
Where through each vein spontaneous plenty flowed,
Where Wealth enjoyed, and Charity bestowed.
Pensive and thoughtful shall the wanderers greet
Each splendid square, and still, untrodden street;
Or of some crumbling turret, mined by time,
The broken stairs with perilous step shall climb,

[1] The Historian of the age of Leo has brought into cultivation the extensive tract of Chatmoss.

Thence stretch their view the wide horizon round,
By scattered hamlets trace its ancient bound,
And, choked no more with fleets, fair Thames survey
Through reeds and sedge pursue his idle way.

With throbbing bosoms shall the wanderers tread
The hallowed mansions of the silent dead,
Shall enter the long isle and vaulted dome
Where Genius and where Valour find a home;
Awe-struck, midst chill sepulchral marbles breathe,
Where all above is still, as all beneath;
Bend at each antique shrine, and frequent turn
To clasp with fond delight some sculptured urn,
The ponderous mass of Johnson's form to greet,
Or breathe the prayer at Howard's sainted feet.

Perhaps some Briton, in whose musing mind
Those ages live which Time has cast behind,
To every spot shall lead his wondering guests
On whose known site the beam of glory rests:
Here Chatham's eloquence in thunder broke,
Here Fox persuaded, or here Garrick spoke;
Shall boast how Nelson, fame and death in view,
To wonted victory led his ardent crew,
In England's name enforced, with loftiest tone,[1]
Their duty,—and too well fulfilled his own:
How gallant Moore,[2] as ebbing life dissolved,
But hoped his country had his fame absolved.
Or call up sages whose capacious mind
Left in its course a track of light behind;
Point where mute crowds on Davy's lips reposed,
And Nature's coyest secrets were disclosed;
Join with their Franklin, Priestley's injured name,
Whom, then, each continent shall proudly claim.

Oft shall the strangers turn their eager feet
The rich remains of ancient art to greet,
The pictured walls with critic eye explore,
And Reynolds be what Raphael was before.
On spoils from every clime their eyes shall gaze,
Egyptian granites and the' Etruscan vase;
And when midst fallen London, they survey
The stone where Alexander's ashes lay,
Shall own with humbled pride the lesson just
By Time's slow finger written in the dust.

[1] Every reader will recollect the sublime telegraphic dispatch, 'England expects every man to do his duty'.

[2] 'I hope England will be satisfied,' were the last words of General Moore.

There walks a Spirit o'er the peopled earth,
Secret his progress is, unknown his birth;
Moody and viewless as the changing wind,
No force arrests his foot, no chains can bind;
Where'er he turns, the human brute awakes,
And, roused to better life, his sordid hut forsakes:
He thinks, he reasons, glows with purer fires,
Feels finer wants, and burns with new desires:
Obedient Nature follows where he leads;
The steaming marsh is changed to fruitful meads;
The beasts retire from man's asserted reign,
And prove his kingdom was not given in vain.
Then from its bed is drawn the ponderous ore,
Then Commerce pours her gifts on every shore,
Then Babel's towers and terraced gardens rise,
And pointed obelisks invade the skies;
The prince commands, in Tyrian purple drest,
And Egypt's virgins weave the linen vest.
Then spans the graceful arch the roaring tide,
And stricter bounds the cultured fields divide.
Then kindles Fancy, then expands the heart,
Then blow the flowers of Genius and of Art;
Saints, heroes, sages, who the land adorn,
Seem rather to descend than to be born;
Whilst History, midst the rolls consigned to fame,
With pen of adamant inscribes their name.

The Genius now forsakes the favoured shore,
And hates, capricious, what he loved before;
Then empires fall to dust, then arts decay,
And wasted realms enfeebled despots sway;
Even Nature's changed; without his fostering smile
Ophir no gold, no plenty yields the Nile;
The thirsty sand absorbs the useless rill,
And spotted plagues from putrid fens distill.
In desert solitudes then Tadmor sleeps,
Stern Marius then o'er fallen Carthage weeps;
Then with enthusiast love the pilgrim roves
To seek his footsteps in forsaken groves,
Explores the fractured arch, the ruined tower,
Those limbs disjointed of gigantic power;
Still at each step he dreads the adder's sting,
The Arab's javelin, or the tiger's spring;
With doubtful caution treads the echoing ground,
And asks where Troy or Babylon is found.

And now the vagrant Power no more detains
The vale of Tempe, or Ausonian plains;
Northward he throws the animating ray,
O'er Celtic nations bursts the mental day:
And, as some playful child the mirror turns,
Now here now there the moving lustre burns;
Now o'er his changeful fancy more prevail
Batavia's dykes than Arno's purple vale,
And stinted suns, and rivers bound with frost,
Than Enna's plains or Baia's viny coast;
Venice the Adriatic weds in vain,
And Death sits brooding o'er Campania's plain;
O'er Baltic shores and through Hercynian groves,
Stirring the soul, the mighty impulse moves;
Art plies his tools, and Commerce spreads her sail,
And wealth is wafted in each shifting gale.
The sons of Odin tread on Persian looms,
And Odin's daughters breathe distilled perfumes.
Loud minstrel bards, in Gothic halls, rehearse
The Runic rhyme, and 'build the lofty verse':
The Muse, whose liquid notes were wont to swell
To the soft breathings of the' Æolian shell,
Submits, reluctant, to the harsher tone,
And scarce believes the altered voice her own.
And now, where Caesar saw with proud disdain
The wattled hut and skin of azure stain,
Corinthian columns rear their graceful forms,
And light varandas brave the wintry storms,
While British tongues the fading fame prolong
Of Tully's eloquence and Maro's song.
Where once Bonduca whirled the scythed car,
And the fierce matrons raised the shriek of war,
Light forms beneath transparent muslins float,
And tutored voices swell the artful note.
Light-leaved acacias and the shady plane
And spreading cedar grace the woodland reign;
While crystal walls the tenderer plants confine,
The fragrant orange and the nectared pine;
The Syrian grape there hangs her rich festoons,
Nor asks for purer air, or brighter noons:
Science and Art urge on the useful toil,
New mould a climate and create the soil,
Subdue the rigour of the northern Bear,
O'er polar climes shed aromatic air,
On yielding Nature urge their new demands,
And ask not gifts but tribute at her hands.

London exults:—on London Art bestows
Her summer ices and her winter rose;
Gems of the East her mural crown adorn,
And Plenty at her feet pours forth her horn;
While even the exiles her just laws disclaim,
People a continent, and build a name:
August she sits, and with extended hands
Holds forth the book of life to distant lands.

But fairest flowers expand but to decay;
The worm is in thy core, thy glories pass away;
Arts, arms and wealth destroy the fruits they bring;
Commerce, like beauty, knows no second spring.
Crime walks thy streets, Fraud earns her unblest bread,
O'er want and woe thy gorgeous robe is spread,
And angel charities in vain oppose:
With grandeur's growth the mass of misery grows.
For see,—to other climes the Genius soars,
He turns from Europe's desolated shores;
And lo, even now, midst mountains wrapt in storm,
On Andes' heights he shrouds his awful form;
On Chimborazo's summits treads sublime,
Measuring in lofty thought the march of Time;
Sudden he calls:—' 'Tis now the hour!' he cries,
Spreads his broad hand, and bids the nations rise.
La Plata hears amidst her torrents' roar;
Potosi hears it, as she digs the ore:
Ardent, the Genius fans the noble strife,
And pours through feeble souls a higher life,
Shouts to the mingled tribes from sea to sea,
And swears—Thy world, Columbus, shall be free.

(1812 *1825*)

10 *The Snowdrop*

ALREADY now the snowdrop dares appear,
The first pale blossom of th'unripen'd year;
As Flora's breath, by some transforming power,
Had chang'd an icicle into a flower,
Its name and hue the scentless plant retains,
And winter lingers in its icy veins.

(1835)

HANNAH MORE
(1745–1833)

THE daughter of Mary (née Grace), Hannah More was born in Stapleton, Gloucestershire, and educated at home by her schoolmaster father, Jacob More. In about 1757, one of her four sisters set up a boarding-school in Bristol, where More continued her education and taught briefly, until an annuity settled upon her by a Mr Turner (whose offer of marriage she had declined at the age of 22) helped finance her entrance into writing.

She began her literary career as a dramatist in 1773 and had two plays produced by her close friend, David Garrick, at Drury Lane: *Percy* (1777) and *The Fatal Falsehood* (1779). After his death in 1779, she abandoned the theatre, later only to publish her *Sacred Dramas* (1782), to which her poem, 'Sensibility', was added. An Anglican, who was accused of leaning towards Methodism, More's religious persuasions produced diverse political effects. Having first met William Wilberforce in 1776, she became an active supporter of the abolitionist movement and timed the publication of the first of her anti-slavery poems, *Slavery; A Poem*, to coincide with Wilberforce's submissions to Parliament in 1788. She was, however, also anti-Revolutionary and, using the persona of 'Will Chip', wrote a prose dialogue, *Village Politics* (1792), which was intended as an antidote to Tom Paine's *The Rights of Man* (1791–92). More's philanthropy led to the production of her *Cheap Repository Tracts* (1795–98), which consisted mostly of ballads and stories aimed at and affordable by, the working poor. Her philanthropy, however, was also tinged with a conservative concern to keep the poor in their place, and this was most evident in her patronage of the labouring-class poet, Ann Yearsley, between 1784–85. Her numerous other publications include *Strictures on the Modern System of Female Education* (1799) and the popular didactic novel, *Coelebs in Search of a Wife* (1808).

Her visits to London led to her friendships with many prominent figures: Lady Mary Wortley Montagu, Edmund Burke, Joshua Reynolds, Samuel Johnson, and Horace Walpole. More spent most of her life in Bristol and died in Clifton.

11 *from Sensibility*

SWEET SENSIBILITY! Thou secret pow'r
Who shed'st thy gifts upon the natal hour,
Like fairy favours; art can never seize,
Nor affectation catch thy pow'r to please:
Thy subtile essence still eludes the chains
Of definition, and defeats her pains.
Sweet SENSIBILITY! thou keen delight!
Unprompted moral! sudden sense of right!
Perception exquisite! fair virtue's seed!
Thou quick precursor of the lib'ral deed!
Thou hasty conscience! reason's blushing morn!
Instinctive kindness e'er reflexion's born!

Prompt sense of equity! to thee belongs
The swift redress of unexamin'd wrongs!
Eager to serve, the cause perhaps untried,
But always apt to chuse the suff'ring side!
To those who know thee not no words can paint,
And those who know thee, know all words are faint!
She does not feel thy pow'r who boasts thy flame,
And rounds her every period with thy name;
Nor she who vents her disproportion'd sighs
With pining *Lesbia* when her sparrow dies:
Nor she who melts when hapless *Shore* expires,
While real mis'ry unreliev'd retires!
Who thinks *feign'd* sorrows all her tears deserve,
And weeps o'er WERTER while her children starve.
As words are but th' external marks to tell
The fair ideas in the mind that dwell;
And only are of things the outward sign,
And not the things themselves they but define;
So exclamations, tender tones, fond tears,
And all the graceful drapery FEELING wears;
These are her garb, not her, they but express
Her form, her semblance, her appropriate dress;
And these fair marks, reluctant I relate,
These lovely symbols may be counterfeit.
There are, who fill with brilliant plaints the page,
If a poor linnet meet the gunner's rage;
There are, who for a dying fawn deplore,
As if friend, parent, country, were no more;
Who boast quick rapture trembling in their eye,
If from the spider's snare they snatch a fly;
There are, whose well sung plaints each breast inflame,
And break all hearts—but his from whom they came!
He, scorning life's low duties to attend,
Writes odes on friendship, while he cheats his friend.
Of jails and punishments he weeps to hear,
And pensions 'prison'd virtue with a tear;
While unpaid bills his creditor presents,
And ruin'd innocence his crime laments.
Not so the tender moralist of Tweed,
His gen'rous *man of feeling* feels indeed.
O LOVE DIVINE! sole source of Charity!
More dear one genuine deed perform'd for thee,
Than all the periods FEELING e'er cou'd turn,
Than all thy touching page, perverted STERNE!

(1782 *1816*)

12 *from The Black Slave Trade*

WHAT strange offence, what aggravated sin?
They stand convicted—of a darker skin!
Barbarians, hold! th' opprobrious commerce spare,
Respect HIS sacred image which they bear.
Tho' dark and savage, ignorant and blind,
They claim the common privilege of *kind;*
Let Malice strip them of each other plea,
They still are men, and men shou'd still be free.
Insulted Reason loaths th' inverted trade—
Loaths, as she views the human purchase made;
The outrag'd Goddess, with abhorrent eyes,
Sees MAN the traffic, SOULS the merchandize!
Man, whom fair Commerce taught with judging eye,
And liberal hand, to barter or to buy,
Indignant Nature blushes to behold,
Degraded Man himself, truck'd, barter'd, sold;
Of ev'ry native privilege bereft,
Yet curs'd with ev'ry wounded feeling left.
Hard lot! each brutal suff'ring to sustain,
Yet keep the sense acute of human pain.
Plead not, in reason's palpable abuse,
Their sense of feeling[1] callous and obtuse:
From heads to hearts lies Nature's plain appeal,
Tho' few can reason, all mankind can feel.
Tho' wit may boast a livelier dread of shame,
A loftier sense of wrong refinement claim;
Tho' polish'd manners may fresh wants invent,
And nice distinctions nicer souls torment;
Tho' these on finer spirits heavier fall,
Yet natural evils are the same to all.
Tho' wounds there are which reason's force may heal,
There needs no logic sure to make us feel.
The nerve, howe'er untutor'd, can sustain
A sharp, unutterable sense of pain;
As exquisitely fashion'd in a slave,
As where unequal fate a sceptre gave.
Sense is as keen where Gambia's waters glide,
As where proud Tiber rolls his classic tide.
Tho' verse or rhetoric point the feeling line,
They do not whet sensation, but define.
Did ever wretch less feel the galling chain,
When Zeno prov'd there was no ill in pain?

[1] Nothing is more frequent than this cruel and stupid argument, that they do not *feel* the miseries inflicted on them as Europeans would do.

In vain the sage to smooth its horror tries;
Spartans and Helots see with different eyes;
Their miseries philosophic quirks deride,
Slaves groan in pangs disown'd by Stoic pride.
  When the fierce Sun darts vertical his beams,
And thirst and hunger mix their wild extremes;
When the sharp iron[1] wounds his inmost soul,
And his strain'd eyes in burning anguish roll;
Will the parch'd Negro own, ere he expire,
No pain in hunger, and no heat in fire?
  For him, when agony his frame destroys,
What hope of present fame or future joys?
For *that* have Heroes shorten'd nature's date;
For *this* have Martyrs gladly met their fate;
But him, forlorn, no Hero's pride sustains,
No Martyr's blissful visions sooth his pains;
Sullen, he mingles with his kindred dust,
For he has learn'd to dread the Christian's trust;
To him what mercy can that GOD display,
Whose servants murder, and whose sons betray?
Savage! thy venial error I deplore,
They are *not* Christians who infest thy shore.

(1788 *1816*)

13 *Will Chip's* True *Rights of Man, in Opposition to the* New *Rights of Man*

Written for the Volunteers of Somersetshire, when there was an Alarm of Invasion on that Coast.

By a Journeyman Carpenter.

WHAT follies, what falsehoods were uttered in vain
To destroy our repose by that jacobin, Paine!
But if, for a while, a few fools were perplext,
The crimes of the French have explain'd Tommy's text.

That the rich do not work, some pretend to complain,
While they hint that the poor do but labour in vain;
But is there no labour then, let me demand,
But the march of the foot, or the work of the hand?

[1] This is not said figuratively. The writer of these lines has seen a complete set of chains, fitted to every separate limb of these unhappy, innocent, men; together with instruments for wrenching open the jaws, contrived with such ingenious cruelty as would gratify the tender mercies of an inquisitor.

'Tis the head that directs, 'tis the heart that supplies
Life, vigour, and motion to hands, feet and eyes.
Though diff'rent our stations, some great and some small,
One labours for each, and each labours for all.

That some *must* be poorer, this truth I will sing,
Is a law of my Maker, and not of my king.
And the *true Rights of Man*, and the life of his cause,
Is not equal POSSESSIONS, but equal, just LAWS.

If accus'd, I am try'd—to my peers I appeal;
Not smuggled, unheard, to some dismal Bastile.
Nor, like the new French, popp'd off to Cayenne,
Without any chance to be heard of again.

If I'm wrong, to the laws I am bound to submit;
If I'm right, oh, how glad are those laws to acquit!
If the right to correct to my judges belong,
I've a right to avoid it—by doing no wrong.

If sickness o'ertake me, the laws of the land
Hold out to my wants a compassionate hand;
Should some churlish churchwarden presume to oppress,
At the next Justice-meeting, I straight get redress.

If I scrape up but forty good shillings a year,
I help govern the land, as I'll make it appear;
For the makers of laws, my brave lads, do you see,
Are elected by folks not much richer than me.

From the parliament man, if he prove a turncoat,
I've a right to withhold, as to give him my vote;
And if British laws I'm oblig'd to respect,
Those laws, in return, will my substance protect.

As long as I work I've a right to full pay,
I've a right to my Bible, to read and to pray;
Then I'll pray with such fervour and fight with such glee,
As if the whole contest depended on me.

Equal rights, equal freedom all Britons possess,
The richest not more, and the poorest not less;
But all rights have their bounds, for the right to do evil
Is no rights of man, but the rights of the devil!

Then away with contention, no other we'll know,
But who'll have the honour to strike the first blow;
And let each true Briton join chorus with me,
We will die with the brave, or we'll live with the free.

(*c.* 1792 *1816*)

14 *The Sorrows of Yamba, or, the Negro Woman's Lamentation*

In St Lucia's distant isle,
Still with Afric's love I burn;
Parted many a thousand mile,
Never, never to return.

Come, kind death! and give me rest;
Yamba has no friend but thee;
Thou canst ease my throbbing breast;
Thou canst set the Prisoner free.

Down my cheeks the tears are dripping,
Broken is my heart with grief;
Mangled my poor flesh with whipping,
Come, kind death! and bring relief.

Born on Afric's golden coast,
Once I was as blest as you;
Parents tender I could boast,
Husband dear, and children too.

Whity man he came from far,
Sailing o'er the briny flood;
Who, with help of British Tar,
Buys up human flesh and blood.

With the baby at my breast
(Other two were sleeping by)
In my hut I sat at rest,
With no thought of danger nigh.

From the bush at even-tide,
Rush'd the fierce man-stealing crew;
Seiz'd the children by my side,
Seiz'd the wretched Yamba too.

Then for love of filthy gold,
Strait they bore me to the sea,
Cramm'd me down a Slave ship's hold,
Where were hundreds stow'd like me.

Naked on the platform lying,
Now we cross the tumbling wave;
Shrieking, sickening, fainting, dying;
Deed of shame for Britons brave!

At the savage Captain's beck,
Now, like brutes, they make us prance;
Smack the eat about the deck,
And in scorn they bid us dance.

Nauseous horse-beans they bring nigh,
  Sick and sad we cannot eat,
Cat must cure the sulks, they cry,
  Down their throats we'll force the meat.

I, in groaning pass'd the night,
  And did roll my aching head;
At the break of morning light,
  My poor child was cold and dead.

Happy, happy, there she lies;
  Thou shalt feel the lash no more;
Thus full many a Negro dies,
  Ere we reach the destin'd shore.

Thee, sweet infant, none shall sell;
  Thou hast gain'd a wat'ry grave;
Clean escap'd the tyrants fell,
  While thy mother lives a slave.

Driven like cattle to a fair,
  See, they sell us, young and old;
Child from mother too they tear,
  All for love of filthy gold.

I was sold to Massa hard,
  Some have Massas kind and good:
And again my back was scarr'd,
  Bad and stinted was my food.

Poor and wounded, faint and sick,
  All expos'd to burning sky,
Massa bids me grass to pick,
  And I now am near to die.

What, and if to death he send me,
  Savage murder tho' it be,
British laws shall ne'er befriend me,
  They protect not slaves like me.

Mourning thus my wretched state
  (Ne'er may I forget the day)
Once in dusk of evening late,
  Far from home I dar'd to stray.

Dar'd, alas! with impious haste,
  Tow'rds the roaring sea to fly;
Death itself I long'd to taste,
  Long'd to cast me in and die.

There I met upon the Strand,
   English Missionary good;
He had Bible book in hand;
   Which poor me no understood.

Led by pity from afar,
   He had left his native ground;
Thus, if some inflict a scar,
   Others fly to cure the wound.

Strait he pull'd me from the shore,
   Bid me no self-murder do;
Talk'd of State when life is o'er,
   All from Bible good and true.

Then he led me to his cot,
   Sooth'd and pity'd all my woe;
Told me 'twas the Christian's lot
   Much to suffer here below.

Told me then of God's dear Son,
   (Strange and wond'rous is the Story)
What sad wrong to him was done,
   Tho' he was the Lord of Glory.

Told me too, like one who knew him,
   (Can such love as this be true?)
How he died for them that slew him,
   Died for wretched Yamba too.

Freely he his mercy proffer'd,
   And to Sinners he was sent;
E'en to Massa pardon's offer'd:
   O, if Massa would repent!

Wicked deed full many a time,
   Sinful Yamba too hath done;
But she wails to God her crime,
   But she trusts his only Son.

O, ye slaves whom Massas beat,
   Ye are stain'd with guilt within;
As ye hope for Mercy sweet,
   So forgive your Massas' sin.

And with grief when sinking low,
   Mark the road that Yamba trod;
Think how all her pain and woe
   Brought the Captive home to God.

Now let Yamba, too, adore
 Gracious Heaven's mysterious plan;
Now I'll count my mercies o'er,
 Flowing through the guilt of man.

Now I'll bless my cruel capture,
 (Hence I've known a Saviour's name)
Till my grief is turn'd to rapture,
 And I half forget the blame.

But tho' here a convert rare,
 Thanks her God for Grace divine;
Let not man the glory share,
 Sinner still the guilt is thine.

Here an injur'd Slave forgives,
 There a host for vengeance cry;
Here a single Yamba lives,
 There a thousand droop and die.

Duly now baptiz'd am I,
 By good Missionary man:
Lord, my nature purify,
 As no outward water can!

All my former thoughts abhorr'd,
 Teach me now to pray and praise;
Joy and glory in my Lord,
 Trust and serve him all my days.

Worn, indeed, with grief and pain,
 Death I now will welcome in:
O, the heavenly prize to gain!
 O, to 'scape the power of Sin!

True of heart, and meek, and lowly,
 Pure and blameless let me grow!
Holy may I be, for holy
 Is the place to which I go.

But tho' death this hour may find me,
 Still with Afric's love I burn;
(There I've left a spouse behind me)
 Still to native land I turn.

And when Yamba sinks in death,
 This my latest prayer shall be,
While I yield my parting breath,
 O, that Afric might be free.

Cease, ye British sons of murder!
  Cease from forging's Afric's chain.
Mock your Saviour's name no further,
  Cease your savage lust of gain.

Ye that boast '*Ye rule the waves*,'
  Bid no Slave-ship soil the sea;
Ye, that '*never will be slaves*,'
  Bid poor Afric's land be free.

Where ye gave to war its birth,
  Where your traders fix'd their den,
There go publish '*Peace on Earth*,'
  Go, proclaim, '*good-will to men*.'

Where ye once have carried slaughter,
  Vice, and slavery, and sin;
Seiz'd on Husband, Wife, and Daughter,
  Let the Gospel enter in.

Thus, where Yamba's native home,
  Humble hut of rushes stood;
Oh, if there should chance to roam,
  Some dear Missionary good;

Tho' in Afric's distant land,
  Still shalt see the man I love;
Join him to the Christian band,
  Guide his soul to realms above.

There no fiend again shall sever
  Those whom God hath join'd and blest;
There they dwell with him for ever,
  There '*the weary are at rest*.'

(*c*. 1800 *1823*)

ANNA SEWARD
(?1747–1809)

KNOWN as 'The Swan of Lichfield', Anna Seward was born in Eyam, Derbyshire, and later moved with her family to Lichfield in 1754, where she was to remain for the rest of her life. She was the elder of the two surviving daughters of Thomas Seward, rector of Eyam and then canon of Lichfield and Salisbury, and Elizabeth (née Hunter), whose father had taught Dr Johnson. She was encouraged in her literary interests by her father (who co-edited the works of Beaumont and Fletcher) and by Erasmus Darwin, the physician and poet, about whom she was to publish a memoir in 1804.

A regular contributor to the *Gentleman's Magazine*, Seward expressed her dislike of Dr Johnson in letters published her under the signature of 'Benvolio' (1787). The patronage of Lady Anne Miller enabled her earliest poetry to be published in the *Batheaston Miscellany* (dates not known). Her poetic novel, *Louisa* (1784), was well received and went through five editions. This was followed by her *Llangollen Vale, with Other Poems* (1796), written after a visit to Lady Eleanor Butler and Sarah Ponsonby, and her *Original Sonnets, on Various Subjects* (1799), which also contains odes paraphrased from Horace. In 1807, she met the poet and novelist, Sir Walter Scott, to whom she bequeathed her literary works and remains. At her request, he published *The Poetical Works of Anna Seward, with Extracts from Her Literary Correspondence* (1810), but he refused to publish the whole of her correspondence on the grounds that he did not like to perpetuate gossip. The task was left to Archibald Constable, who edited the six-volume collection of her letters in 1811.

15 *The Ghost of Cuchullin*

From Ossian

ON Dora's hill, the fires of parting day,
With soften'd lustre, shed the yellow ray;
Yet scarce they sunk behind the mountain's breast
Ere gathering storms the fading scene invest.
Loud hollow gales fell murmuring on the floods,
And shook Temora through his bending woods.
One ample cloud a sable curtain rear'd,
And faint, behind its edge, a red star peer'd,
And in its shade a tall, unreal form
Stalk'd through the air, and mourn'd amid the storm.
His lengthen'd steps o'er the vast mountain pass'd,
And his broad shield a pale effulgence cast.
Too well Cuchullin's faded form I knew,
Yet, ere my lips could breathe their last adieu,
Swift, on his howling blast, away he strode,
And night, and horror, gather'd on the wood.

(1810)

CHARLOTTE SMITH
(1749–1806)

ALTHOUGH best known as a novelist, Charlotte Turner (later Smith) had already secured a reputation as a poet before she embarked upon the writing of fiction. The direction of her literary career was in part determined by the financial demands of her married life. She had been born into a wealthy family in Stoke House, Surrey, and was the eldest daughter of Nicholas Turner and Ann (née Towers). When she was only 3 years old, her mother died and she was left in the care of an aunt, who sent her off to be poorly educated at Chichester and Kensington. Her schooling, such as it was, finished entirely in her twelfth year. After her father's second marriage in 1764, her aunt's apparent dislike of stepmothers pushed her 15-year-old niece into a marriage of convenience to Benjamin Smith, the second son of a wealthy West Indian merchant and director of the East India Company. Despite requests from her father-in-law that she assist him in business, he eventually helped her move to Lys Farm in Hampshire. Her life with her husband proved both unhappy and impecunious, the latter owing mostly to his financial excesses, but no doubt also to the expense of maintaining their family of twelve children. Their financial resources were further drained by long-standing litigation over a complex will left by her father-in-law in 1776. By 1784 Benjamin Smith was imprisoned for debt, taking his wife with him for several months. They were to separate (though not legally), but she continued to give her husband financial assistance until his death in 1806. It was while in prison that she determined upon a writing career for financial support.

Having already written a number of sonnets, she presented these to publishers, eventually persuading her friend the poet, William Hayley, to become involved. He allowed her to dedicate a quarto volume to him, which was published at her own expense: *Elegaic Sonnets and Other Essays* (1784). So successful was this publication that a second edition was brought out in the same year and an enlarged, fifth edition in 1789. The list of subcribers to the 1789 volume demonstrates the considerable acclaim that she had already received, as it includes William Cowper, Horace Walpole, Mrs Siddons, and Charles James Fox. Although one poet, Anna Seward, was critical of these sonnets for their non-Petrarchan form, they were greatly admired by William Lisle Bowles, Samuel Taylor Coleridge, and William Wordsworth. The book was later reissued with a second volume in 1797 as *Elegaic Sonnets, with Additional Sonnets and Other Poems*. She went on to produce two more books of poetry, though neither as successful as the first, including her posthumous *Beachy Head: With Other Poems Now First Published* in 1807. The title poem of this collection (unfinished) focuses upon the defeat of the English and Dutch fleets by the French at Beachy Head on 30 June 1690.

She regarded herself primarily as a poet and was disdainful of the practice of novel-writing: 'I love Novels *No more than a Grocer does figs*' (Letter to J. C. Walker, 9 October 1793). However, her first novel, *Emmeline, or, The Orphan of the Castle* (1788) was so successful that her publisher supplemented her advance. It was followed by four more, with her last, *The Old Manor House* (1793) being considered her best. Many of her novels expressed her early pro-Republican stance, but her attitude was to change with the Terror, and her *The Emigrants: A Poem* (1793) marks this shift in sympathy.

Her other publications include a translation of Abbé Prévost's novel, *Manon Lescaut* (1785) and of stories based on French criminal trials, *The Romance of Real Life* (1787). Both of these were written during a brief period away in France. She also wrote moralistic work for children.

16 *Elegaic Sonnets, No. 44. Written in the Church Yard at Middleton in Sussex*

PRESS'D by the Moon, mute arbitress of tides,
While the loud equinox its power combines,
The sea no more its swelling surge confines,
But o'er the shrinking land sublimely rides.
The wild blast, rising from the Western cave,
Drives the huge billows from their heaving bed;
Tears from their grassy tombs the village dead,
And breaks the silent sabbath of the grave!
With shells and sea-weed mingled, on the shore
Lo! their bones whiten in the frequent wave;
But vain to them the winds and waters rave;
They hear the warring elements no more:
While I am doom'd—by life's long storm opprest,
To gaze with envy, on their gloomy rest.

(1784 *1789*)

17 *Elegaic Sonnets, No. 70. On Being Cautioned against Walking on an Headland Overlooking the Sea, because It Was Frequented by a Lunatic*

IS there a solitary wretch who hies
To the tall cliff, with starting pace or flow,
And, measuring, views with wild and hollow eyes
Its distance from the waves that chide below;
Who, as the sea-born gale with frequent sighs
Chills his cold bed upon the mountain turf,
With hoarse, half utter'd lamentation, lies
Murmuring responses to the dashing surf?
In moody sadness, on the giddy brink,
I see him more with envy than with fear;
He has no *nice felicities* that shrink
From giant horrors; wildly wandering here,
He seems (uncursed with reason) not to know
The depth or the duration of his woe.

(1797)

18 *Elegaic Sonnets, No. 77. To the Insect of the Gossamer*

SMALL, viewless Æronaut, that by the line
Of Gossamer suspended, in mid air
Float'st on a sun beam—Living Atom, where
Ends thy breeze-guided voyage;—with what design
In Æther dost thou launch thy form minute,
Mocking the eye?—Alas! before the veil
Of denser clouds shall hide thee, the pursuit
Of the keen Swift may end thy fairy sail!—
Thus on the golden thread that Fancy weaves
Buoyant, as Hope's illusive flattery breathes,
The young and visionary Poet leaves
Life's dull realities, while sevenfold wreaths
Of rainbow light around his head revolve.
Ah! soon at Sorrow's touch the radiant dreams dissolve!

(1797)

19 *Fragment. Descriptive of the Miseries of War; from a Poem Called 'The Emigrants', Printed in 1793*

TO a wild mountain, whose bare summit hides
Its broken eminence in clouds; whose steeps
Are dark with woods; where the receding rocks
Are worn with torrents of dissolving snow;
A wretched woman, pale and breathless, flies,
And, gazing round her, listens to the sound
Of hostile footsteps:—No! they die away—
Nor noise remains, but of the cataract,
Or surly breeze of night, that mutters low
Among the thickets, where she trembling seeks
A temporary shelter—Clasping close
To her quick throbbing heart her sleeping child,
All she could rescue of the innocent group
That yesterday surrounded her—Escaped
Almost by miracle!—Fear, frantic Fear,
Wing'd her weak feet; yet, half repenting now
Her headlong haste, she wishes she had staid
To die with those affrighted Fancy paints
The lawless soldiers' victims—Hark! again
The driving tempest bears the cry of Death;
And with deep, sudden thunder, the dread sound

Of cannon vibrates on the tremulous earth;
While, bursting in the air, the murderous bomb
Glares o'er her mansion—Where the splinters fall
Like scatter'd comets, its destructive path
Is mark'd by wreaths of flame!—Then, overwhelm'd
Beneath accumulated horror, sinks
The desolate mourner!

. . . .

The feudal Chief, whose Gothic battlements
Frown on the plain beneath, returning home
From distant lands, alone, and in disguise,
Gains at the fall of night his castle walls,
But, at the silent gate no porter sits
To wait his lord's admittance!—In the courts
All is drear stillness!—Guessing but too well
The fatal truth, he shudders as he goes
Thro' the mute hall; where, by the blunted light
That the dim Moon thro' painted casement lends,
He sees that devastation has been there;
Then, while each hideous image to his mind
Rises terrific, o'er a bleeding corse
Stumbling he falls; another intercepts
His staggering feet—All, all who us'd to rush
With joy to meet him, all his family
Lie murder'd in his way!—And the day dawns
On a wild raving Maniac, whom a fate
So sudden and calamitous has robb'd
Of reason; and who round his vacant walls
Screams unregarded, and reproaches Heaven!

(1793 *1797*)

20 *Beachy Head*

ON thy stupendous summit, rock sublime!
That o'er the channel rear'd, half way at sea
The mariner at early morning hails,
I would recline; while Fancy should go forth,
And represent the strange and awful hour
Of vast concussion; when the Omnipotent
Stretch'd forth his arm, and rent the solid hills,
Bidding the impetuous main flood rush between
The rifted shores, and from the continent
Eternally divided this green isle.
Imperial lord of the high southern coast!
From thy projecting head-land I would mark

Far in the east the shades of night disperse,
Melting and thinned, as from the dark blue wave
Emerging, brilliant rays of arrowy light
Dart from the horizon; when the glorious sun
Just lifts above it his resplendent orb.
Advances now, with feathery silver touched,
The rippling tide of flood; glisten the sands,
While, inmates of the chalky clefts that scar
Thy sides precipitous, with shrill harsh cry,
Their white wings glancing in the level beam,
The terns, and gulls, and tarrocks, seek their food,
And thy rough hollows echo to the voice
Of the gray choughs, and ever restless daws,
With clamour, not unlike the chiding hounds,
While the lone shepherd, and his baying dog,
Drive to thy turfy crest his bleating flock.

The high meridian of the day is past,
And Ocean now, reflecting the calm Heaven,
Is of cerulean hue; and murmurs low
The tide of ebb, upon the level sands.
The sloop, her angular canvas shifting still,
Catches the light and variable airs
That but a little crisp the summer sea,
Dimpling its tranquil surface.

Afar off,
And just emerging from the arch immense
Where seem to part the elements, a fleet
Of fishing vessels stretch their lesser sails;
While more remote, and like a dubious spot
Just hanging in the horizon, laden deep,
The ship of commerce richly freighted, makes
Her slower progress, on her distant voyage,
Bound to the orient climates, where the sun
Matures the spice within its odorous shell,
And, rivalling the gray worm's filmy toil,
Bursts from its pod the vegetable down;
Which in long turban'd wreaths, from torrid heat
Defends the brows of Asia's countless casts.
There the Earth hides within her glowing breast
The beamy adamant, and the round pearl
Enchased in rugged covering; which the slave,
With perilous and breathless toil, tears off
From the rough sea-rock, deep beneath the waves.
These are the toys of Nature; and her sport
Of little estimate in Reason's eye:
And they who reason, with abhorrence see

Man, for such gaudes and baubles, violate
The sacred freedom of his fellow man—
Erroneous estimate! As Heaven's pure air,
Fresh as it blows on this aërial height,
Or sound of seas upon the stony strand,
Or inland, the gay harmony of birds,
And winds that wander in the leafy woods;
Are to the unadulterate taste more worth
Than the elaborate harmony, brought out
From fretted stop, or modulated airs
Of vocal science.—So the brightest gems,
Glancing resplendent on the regal crown,
Or trembling in the high born beauty's ear,
Are poor and paltry, to the lovely light
Of the fair star, that as the day declines,
Attendant on her queen, the crescent moon,
Bathes her bright tresses in the eastern wave.
For now the sun is verging to the sea,
And as he westward sinks, the floating clouds
Suspended, move upon the evening gale,
And gathering round his orb, as if to shade
The insufferable brightness, they resign
Their gauzy whiteness; and more warm'd, assume
All hues of purple. There, transparent gold
Mingles with ruby tints, and sapphire gleams,
And colours, such as Nature through her works
Shews only in the ethereal canopy.
Thither aspiring Fancy fondly soars,
Wandering sublime thro' visionary vales,
Where bright pavilions rise, and trophies, fann'd
By airs celestial; and adorn'd with wreaths
Of flowers that bloom amid elysian bowers.
Now bright, and brighter still the colours glow,
Till half the lustrous orb within the flood
Seems to retire: the flood reflecting still
Its splendor, and in mimic glory drest;
Till the last ray shot upward, fires the clouds
With blazing crimson; then in paler light,
Long lines of tenderer radiance, lingering yield
To partial darkness; and on the opposing side
The early moon distinctly rising, throws
Her pearly brilliance on the trembling tide.

The fishermen, who at set seasons pass
Many a league off at sea their toiling night,
Now hail their comrades, from their daily task
Returning; and make ready for their own,

With the night tide commencing:—The night tide
Bears a dark vessel on, whose hull and sails
Mark her a coaster from the north. Her keel
Now ploughs the sand; and sidelong now she leans,
While with loud clamours her athletic crew
Unload her; and resounds the busy hum
Along the wave-worn rocks. Yet more remote,
Where the rough cliff hangs beetling o'er its base,
All breathes repose; the water's rippling sound
Scarce heard; but now and then the sea-snipe's cry
Just tells that something living is abroad;
And sometimes crossing on the moonbright line,
Glimmers the skiff, faintly discern'd awhile,
Then lost in shadow.

Contemplation here,
High on her throne of rock, aloof may sit,
And bid recording Memory unfold
Her scroll voluminous—bid her retrace
The period, when from Neustria's hostile shore
The Norman launch'd his galleys, and the bay
O'er which that mass of ruin frowns even now
In vain and sullen menace, then received
The new invaders; a proud martial race,
Of Scandinavia the undaunted sons,
Whom Dogon, Fier-a-bras, and Humfroi led
To conquest: while Trinacris to their power
Yielded her wheaten garland; and when thou,
Parthenope! within thy fertile bay
Receiv'd the victors—

In the mailed ranks
Of Normans landing on the British coast
Rode Taillefer; and with astounding voice
Thunder'd the war song daring Roland sang
First in the fierce contention: vainly brave,
One not inglorious struggle England made—
But failing, saw the Saxon heptarchy
Finish for ever.—Then the holy pile,
Yet seen upon the field of conquest, rose,
Where to appease heaven's wrath for so much blood,
The conqueror bade unceasing prayers ascend,
And requiems for the slayers and the slain.
But let not modern Gallia form from hence
Presumptuous hopes, that ever thou again,
Queen of the isles! shalt crouch to foreign arms.
The enervate sons of Italy may yield;
And the Iberian, all his trophies torn

And wrapp'd in Superstition's monkish weed,
May shelter his abasement, and put on
Degrading fetters. Never, never thou!
Imperial mistress of the obedient sea;
But thou, in thy integrity secure,
Shalt now undaunted meet a world in arms.

England! 'twas where this promontory rears
Its rugged brow above the channel wave,
Parting the hostile nations, that thy fame,
Thy naval fame was tarnish'd, at what time
Thou, leagued with the Batavian, gavest to France
One day of triumph—triumph the more loud,
Because even then so rare. Oh! well redeem'd,
Since, by a series of illustrious men,
Such as no other country ever rear'd,
To vindicate her cause. It is a list
Which, as Fame echoes it, blanches the cheek
Of bold Ambition; while the despot feels
The extorted sceptre tremble in his grasp.

From even the proudest roll by glory fill'd,
How gladly the reflecting mind returns
To simple scenes of peace and industry,
Where, bosom'd in some valley of the hills
Stands the lone farm; its gate with tawny ricks
Surrounded, and with granaries and sheds,
Roof'd with green mosses, and by elms and ash
Partially shaded; and not far remov'd
The hut of sea-flints built; the humble home
Of one, who sometimes watches on the heights,
When hid in the cold mist of passing clouds,
The flock, with dripping fleeces, are dispers'd
O'er the wide down; then from some ridged point
That overlooks the sea, his eager eye
Watches the bark that for his signal waits
To land its merchandize:—Quitting for this
Clandestine traffic his more honest toil,
The crook abandoning, he braves himself
The heaviest snow-storm of December's night,
When with conflicting winds the ocean raves,
And on the tossing boat, unfearing mounts
To meet the partners of the perilous trade,
And share their hazard. Well it were for him,
If no such commerce of destruction known,
He were content with what the earth affords
To human labour; even where she seems
Reluctant most. More happy is the hind,

Who, with his own hands rears on some black moor,
Or turbary, his independent hut
Cover'd with heather, whence the slow white smoke
Of smouldering peat arises—A few sheep,
His best possession, with his children share
The rugged shed when wintry tempests blow;
But, when with Spring's return the green blades rise
Amid the russet heath, the household live
Joint tenants of the waste throughout the day,
And often, from her nest, among the swamps,
Where the gemm'd sun-dew grows, or fring'd buck-bean,
They scare the plover, that with plaintive cries
Flutters, as sorely wounded, down the wind.
Rude, and but just remov'd from savage life
Is the rough dweller among scenes like these,
(Scenes all unlike the poet's fabling dreams
Describing Aready)—But he is free;
The dread that follows on illegal acts
He never feels; and his industrious mate
Shares in his labour. Where the brook is traced
By crouding osiers, and the black coot hides
Among the plashy reeds, her diving brood,
The matron wades; gathering the long green rush
That well prepar'd hereafter lends its light
To her poor cottage, dark and cheerless else
Thro' the drear hours of Winter. Otherwhile
She leads her infant group where charlock grows
'Unprofitably gay,' or to the fields,
Where congregate the linnet and the finch,
That on the thistles, so profusely spread,
Feast in the desert; the poor family
Early resort, extirpating with care
These, and the gaudier mischief of the ground;
Then flames the high rais'd heap; seen afar off
Like hostile war-fires flashing to the sky.
Another task is theirs: On fields that shew
As angry Heaven had rain'd sterility,
Stony and cold, and hostile to the plough,
Where clamouring loud, the evening curlew runs
And drops her spotted eggs among the flints;
The mother and the children pile the stones
In rugged pyramids;—and all this toil
They patiently encounter; well content
On their flock bed to slumber undisturb'd
Beneath the smoky roof they call their own.
Oh! little knows the sturdy hind, who stands
Gazing, with looks where envy and contempt

Are often strangely mingled, on the car
Where prosperous Fortune sits; what secret care
Or sick satiety is often hid,
Beneath the splendid outside: *He* knows not
How frequently the child of Luxury
Enjoying nothing, flies from place to place
In chase of pleasure that eludes his grasp;
And that content is e'en less found by him,
Than by the labourer, whose pick-axe smooths
The road before his chariot; and who doffs
What *was* an hat; and as the train pass on,
Thinks how one day's expenditure, like this,
Would cheer him for long months, when to his toil
The frozen earth closes her marble breast.

Ah! who *is* happy? Happiness! a word
That like false fire, from marsh effluvia born,
Misleads the wanderer, destin'd to contend
In the world's wilderness, with want or woe—
Yet *they* are happy, who have never ask'd
What good or evil means. The boy
That on the river's margin gaily plays,
Has heard that Death is there—He knows not Death,
And therefore fears it not; and venturing in
He gains a bullrush, or a minnow—then,
At certain peril, for a worthless prize,
A crow's, or raven's nest, he climbs the boll
Of some tall pine; and of his prowess proud,
Is for a moment happy. Are *your* cares,
Ye who despise him, never worse applied?
The village girl is happy, who sets forth
To distant fair, gay in her Sunday suit,
With cherry colour'd knots, and flourish'd shawl,
And bonnet newly purchas'd. So is he
Her little brother, who his mimic drum
Beats, till he drowns her rural lovers' oaths
Of constant faith, and still increasing love;
Ah! yet a while, and half those oaths believ'd,
Her happiness is vanish'd; and the boy
While yet a stripling, finds the sound he lov'd
Has led him on, till he has given up
His freedom, and his happiness together.

I once was happy, when while yet a child,
I learn'd to love these upland solitudes,
And, when elastic as the mountain air,
To my light spirit, care was yet unknown
And evil unforeseen:—Early it came,

And childhood scarcely passed, I was condemned,
A guiltless exile, silently to sigh,
While Memory, with faithful pencil, drew
The contrast; and regretting, I compar'd
With the polluted smoky atmosphere
And dark and stifling streets, the southern hills
That to the setting Sun, their graceful heads
Rearing, o'erlook the frith, where Vecta breaks
With her white rocks, the strong impetuous tide,
When western winds the vast Atlantic urge
To thunder on the coast—Haunts of my youth!
Scenes of fond day-dreams, I behold ye yet!
Where 'twas so pleasant by thy northern slopes
To climb the winding sheep-path, aided oft
By scatter'd thorns: whose spiny branches bore
Small woolly tufts, spoils of the vagrant lamb
There seeking shelter from the noon-day sun;
And pleasant, seated on the short soft turf,
To look beneath upon the hollow way
While heavily upward mov'd the labouring wain,
And stalking slowly by, the sturdy hind
To ease his panting team, stopp'd with a stone
The grating wheel.

Advancing higher still
The prospect widens, and the village church
But little, o'er the lowly roofs around
Rears its gray belfry, and its simple vane;
Those lowly roofs of thatch are half conceal'd
By the rude arms of trees, lovely in spring,
When on each bough, the rosy-tinctur'd bloom
Sits thick, and promises autumnal plenty.
For even those orchards round the Norman farms,
Which, as their owners mark the promis'd fruit,
Console them for the vineyards of the south,
Surpass not these.

Where woods of ash, and beech,
And partial copses, fringe the green hill foot,
The upland shepherd rears his modest home,
There wanders by, a little nameless stream
That from the hill wells forth, bright now and clear,
Or after rain with chalky mixture gray,
But still refreshing in its shallow course,
The cottage garden; most for use design'd,
Yet not of beauty destitute. The vine
Mantles the little casement; yet the briar
Drops fragrant dew among the July flowers;

And pansies rayed, and freak'd and mottled pinks
Grow among balm, and rosemary and rue:
There honeysuckles flaunt, and roses blow
Almost uncultured: Some with dark green leaves
Contrast their flowers of pure unsullied white;
Others, like velvet robes of regal state
Of richest crimson, while in thorny moss
Enshrined and cradled, the most lovely, wear
The hues of youthful beauty's glowing check.—
With fond regret I recollect e'en now
In Spring and Summer, what delight I felt
Among these cottage gardens, and how much
Such artless nosegays, knotted with a rush
By village housewife or her ruddy maid,
Were welcome to me; soon and simply pleas'd.

An early worshipper at Nature's shrine,
I loved her rudest scenes—warrens, and heaths,
And yellow commons, and birch-shaded hollows,
And hedge rows, bordering unfrequented lanes
Bowered with wild roses, and the clasping woodbine
Where purple tassels of the tangling vetch
With bittersweet, and bryony inweave,
And the dew fills the silver bindweed's cups—
I loved to trace the brooks whose humid banks
Nourish the harebell, and the freckled pagil;
And stroll among o'ershadowing woods of beech,
Lending in Summer, from the heats of noon
A whispering shade; while haply there reclines
Some pensive lover of uncultur'd flowers,
Who, from the tumps with bright green mosses clad,
Plucks the wood sorrel, with its light thin leaves,
Heart-shaped, and triply folded; and its root
Creeping like beaded coral; or who there
Gathers, the copse's pride, anémones,
With rays like golden studs on ivory laid
Most delicate: but touch'd with purple clouds,
Fit crown for April's fair but changeful brow.

Ah! hills so early loved! in fancy still
I breathe your pure keen air; and still behold
Those widely spreading views, mocking alike
The Poet and the Painter's utmost art.
And still, observing objects more minute,
Wondering remark the strange and foreign forms
Of sea-shells; with the pale calcareous soil
Mingled, and seeming of resembling substance.
Tho' surely the blue Ocean (from the heights

Where the downs westward trend, but dimly seen)
Here never roll'd its surge. Does Nature then
Mimic, in wanton mood, fantastic shapes
Of bivalves, and inwreathed volutes, that cling
To the dark sea-rock of the wat'ry world?
Or did this range of chalky mountains, once
Form a vast bason, where the Ocean waves
Swell'd fathomless? What time these fossil shells,
Buoy'd on their native element, were thrown
Among the imbedding calx: when the huge hill
Its giant bulk heaved, and in strange ferment
Grew up a guardian barrier, 'twixt the sea
And the green level of the sylvan weald.

Ah! very vain is Science' proudest boast,
And but a little light its flame yet lends
To its most ardent votaries; since from whence
These fossil forms are seen, is but conjecture,
Food for vague theories, or vain dispute,
While to his daily task the peasant goes,
Unheeding such inquiry; with no care
But that the kindly change of sun and shower,
Fit for his toil the earth he cultivates.
As little recks the herdsman of the hill,
Who on some turfy knoll, idly reclined,
Watches his wether flock; that deep beneath
Rest the remains of men, of whom is left
No traces in the records of mankind,
Save what these half obliterated mounds
And half fill'd trenches doubtfully impart
To some lone antiquary; who on times remote,
Since which two thousand years have roll'd away,
Loves to contemplate. He perhaps may trace,
Or fancy he can trace, the oblong square
Where the mail'd legions, under Claudius, rear'd
The rampire, or excavated fossé delved;
What time the huge unwieldy Elephant
Auxiliary reluctant, hither led,
From Afric's forest glooms and tawny sands,
First felt the Northern blast, and his vast frame
Sunk useless; whence in after ages found,
The wondering hinds, on those enormous bones
Gaz'd; and in giants dwelling on the hills
Believed and marvell'd—

Hither, Ambition, come!

Come and behold the nothingness of all
For which you carry thro' the oppressed Earth,
War, and its train of horrors—see where tread
The innumerous hoofs of flocks above the works
By which the warrior sought to register
His glory, and immortalize his name—
The pirate Dane, who from his circular camp
Bore in destructive robbery, fire and sword
Down thro' the vale, sleeps unremember'd here;
And here, beneath the green sward, rests alike
The savage native, who his acorn meal
Shar'd with the herds, that ranged the pathless woods;
And the centurion, who on these wide hills
Encamping, planted the Imperial Eagle.
All, with the lapse of Time, have passed away,
Even as the clouds, with dark and dragon shapes,
Or like vast promontories crown'd with towers,
Cast their broad shadows on the downs: then sail
Far to the northward, and their transient gloom
Is soon forgotten.

But from thoughts like these,
By human crimes suggested, let us turn
To where a more attractive study courts
The wanderer of the hills; while shepherd girls
Will from among the fescue bring him flowers,
Of wonderous mockery; some resembling bees
In velvet vest, intent on their sweet toil,
While others mimic flies, that lightly sport
In the green-shade, or float along the pool,
But here seem perch'd upon the slender stalk,
And gathering honey dew. While in the breeze
That wafts the thistle's plumed seed along,
Blue bells wave tremulous. The mountain thyme
Purples the hassock of the heaving mole,
And the short turf is gay with tormentil,
And bird's foot trefoil, and the lesser tribes
Of hawkweed; spangling it with fringed stars.—
Near where a richer tract of cultur'd land
Slopes to the south; and burnished by the sun,
Bend in the gale of August, floods of corn;
The guardian of the flock, with watchful care,
Repels by voice and dog the encroaching sheep—
While his boy visits every wired trap
That scars the turf; and from the pit-falls takes
The timid migrants, who from distant wilds,
Warrens, and stone quarries, are destined thus

To lose their short existence. But unsought
By Luxury yet, the Shepherd still protects
The social bird, who from his native haunts
Of willowy current, or the rushy pool,
Follows the fleecy croud, and flirts and skims,
In fellowship among them.

Where the knoll
More elevated takes the changeful winds,
The windmill rears its vanes; and thitherward
With his white load, the master travelling,
Scares the rooks rising slow on whispering wings,
While o'er his head, before the summer sun
Lights up the blue expanse, heard more than seen,
The lark sings matins; and above the clouds
Floating, embathes his spotted breast in dew.
Beneath the shadow of a gnarled thorn,
Bent by the sea blast, from a seat of turf
With fairy nosegays strewn, how wide the view!
Till in the distant north it melts away,
And mingles indiscriminate with clouds:
But if the eye could reach so far, the mart
Of England's capital, its domes and spires
Might be perceived—Yet hence the distant range
Of Kentish hills, appear in purple haze;
And nearer, undulate the wooded heights,
And airy summits, that above the mole
Rise in green beauty; and the beacon'd ridge
Of Black-down shagg'd with heath, and swelling rude
Like a dark island from the vale; its brow
Catching the last rays of the evening sun
That gleam between the nearer park's old oaks,
Then lighten up the river, and make prominent
The portal, and the ruin'd battlements
Of that dismantled fortress; rais'd what time
The Conqueror's successors fiercely fought,
Tearing with civil feuds the desolate land.
But now a tiller of the soil dwells there,
And of the turret's loop'd and rafter'd halls
Has made an humbler homestead—Where he sees,
Instead of armed foemen, herds that graze
Along his yellow meadows; or his flocks
At evening from the upland driv'n to fold—

In such a castellated mansion once
A stranger chose his home; and where hard by
In rude disorder fallen, and hid with brushwood
Lay fragments gray of towers and buttresses,

Among the ruins, often he would muse—
His rustic meal soon ended, he was wont
To wander forth, listening the evening sounds
Of rushing milldam, or the distant team,
Or night-jar, chasing fern-flies: the tir'd hind
Pass'd him at nightfall, wondering he should sit
On the hill top so late: they from the coast
Who sought bye paths with their clandestine load,
Saw with suspicious doubt, the lonely man
Cross on their way: but village maidens thought
His senses injur'd; and with pity say
That he, poor youth! must have been cross'd in love—
For often, stretch'd upon the mountain turf
With folded arms, and eyes intently fix'd
Where ancient elms and firs obscured a grange,
Some little space within the vale below,
They heard him, as complaining of his fate,
And to the murmuring wind, of cold neglect
And baffled hope he told.—The peasant girls
These plaintive sounds remember, and even now
Among them may be heard the stranger's songs.

Were I a Shepherd on the hill
  And ever as the mists withdrew
Could see the willows of the rill
Shading the footway to the mill
  Where once I walk'd with you—

And as away Night's shadows sail,
  And sounds of birds and brooks arise,
Believe, that from the woody vale
I hear your voice upon the gale
  In soothing melodies;

And viewing from the Alpine height,
  The prospect dress'd in hues of air,
Could say, while transient colours bright
Touch'd the fair scene with dewy light,
  'Tis, that *her* eyes are there!

I think, I could endure my lot
  And linger on a few short years,
And then, by all but you forgot,
Sleep, where the turf that clothes the spot
   May claim some pitying tears.

For 'tis not easy to forget
  One, who thro' life has lov'd you still,
And you, however late, might yet
With sighs to Memory giv'n, regret
  The Shepherd of the Hill.

Yet otherwhile it seem'd as if young Hope
Her flattering pencil gave to Fancy's hand,
And in his wanderings, rear'd to sooth his soul
Ideal bowers of pleasure—Then, of Solitude
And of his hermit life, still more enamour'd,
His home was in the forest; and wild fruits
And bread sustain'd him. There in early spring
The Barkmen found him, e'er the sun arose;
There at their daily toil, the Wedgecutters
Beheld him thro' the distant thicket move.
The shaggy dog following the truffle hunter,
Bark'd at the loiterer; and perchance at night
Belated villagers from fair or wake,
While the fresh night-wind let the moonbeams in
Between the swaying boughs, just saw him pass,
And then in silence, gliding like a ghost
He vanish'd! Lost among the deepening gloom.—
But near one ancient tree, whose wreathed roots
Form'd a rude couch, love-songs and scatter'd rhymes,
Unfinish'd sentences, or half erased,
And rhapsodies like this, were sometimes found—

Let us to woodland wilds repair
  While yet the glittering night-dews seem
To wait the freshly-breathing air,
  Precursive of the morning beam,
That rising with advancing day,
Scatters the silver drops away.

An elm, uprooted by the storm,
  The trunk with mosses gray and green,
Shall make for us a rustic form,
  Where lighter grows the forest scene;
And far among the bowery shades,
Are ferny lawns and grassy glades.

Retiring May to lovely June
  Her latest garland now resigns;
The banks with cuckoo-flowers are strewn,
  The woodwalks blue with columbines,
And with its reeds, the wandering stream
Reflects the flag-flower's golden gleam.

There, feathering down the turf to meet,
  Their shadowy arms the beeches spread,
While high above our sylvan seat,
  Lifts the light ash its airy head;
And later leaved, the oaks between
Extend their bows of vernal green.

The slender birch its paper rind
  Seems offering to divided love,
And shuddering even without a wind
  Aspins, their paler foliage move,
As if some spirit of the air
Breath'd a low sigh in passing there.

The Squirrel in his frolic mood,
  Will fearless bound among the boughs;
Yaffils laugh loudly thro' the wood,
  And murmuring ring-doves tell their vows;
While we, as sweetest woodscents rise,
Listen to woodland melodies.

And I'll contrive a sylvan room
  Against the time of summer heat,
Where leaves, inwoven in Nature's loom,
  Shall canopy our green retreat;
And gales that 'close the eye of day'
Shall linger, e'er they die away.

And when a sear and sallow hue
  From early frost the bower receives,
I'll dress the sand rock cave for you,
  And strew the floor with heath and leaves,
That you, against the autumnal air
May find securer shelter there.

The Nightingale will then have ceas'd
  To sing her moonlight serenade;
But the gay bird with blushing breast,
  And Woodlarks still will haunt the shade,
And by the borders of the spring
Reed-wrens will yet be carolling.

The forest hermit's lonely cave
  None but such soothing sounds shall reach,
Or hardly heard, the distant wave
  Slow breaking on the stony beach;
Or winds, that now sigh soft and low,
Now make wild music as they blow.

And then, before the chilling North
  The tawny foliage falling light,
Seems, as it flits along the carth,
  The footfall of the busy Sprite,
Who wrapt in pale autumnal gloom,
Calls up the mist-born Mushroom.

Oh! could I hear your soft voice there,
  And see you in the forest green
All beauteous as you are, more fair
  You'ld look, amid the sylvan scene,
And in a wood-girl's simple guise,
Be still more lovely in mine eyes.

Ye phantoms of unreal delight,
  Visions of fond delirium born!
Rise not on my deluded sight,
  Then leave me drooping and forlorn
To know, such bliss can never be,
Unless   loved like me.

The visionary, nursing dreams like these,
Is not indeed unhappy. Summer woods
Wave over him, and whisper as they wave,
Some future blessings he may yet enjoy.
And as above him sail the silver clouds,
He follows them in thought to distant climes,
Where, far from the cold policy of this,
Dividing him from her he fondly loves,
He, in some island of the southern sea,
May haply build his cane-constructed bower
Beneath the bread-fruit, or aspiring palm,
With long green foliage rippling in the gale,
Oh! let him cherish his ideal bliss—
For what is life, when Hope has ceas'd to strew
Her fragile flowers along its thorny way?
And sad and gloomy are his days, who lives
Of Hope abandon'd!

                    Just beneath the rock
Where Beachy overpeers the channel wave,
Within a cavern mined by wintry tides
Dwelt one, who long disgusted with the world
And all its ways, appear'd to suffer life
Rather than live; the soul-reviving gale,
Fanning the bean-field, or the thymy heath,
Had not for many summers breathed on him;
And nothing mark'd to him the season's change,
Save that more gently rose the placid sea,

And that the birds which winter on the coast
Gave place to other migrants; save that the fog,
Hovering no more above the beetling cliffs
Betray'd not then the little careless sheep
On the brink grazing, while their headlong fall
Near the lone Hermit's flint-surrounded home,
Claim'd unavailing pity; for his heart
Was feelingly alive to all that breath'd;
And outraged as he was, in sanguine youth,
By human crimes, he still acutely felt
For human misery.

Wandering on the beach,
He learn'd to augur from the clouds of heaven,
And from the changing colours of the sea,
And sullen murmurs of the hollow cliffs,
Or the dark porpoises, that near the shore
Gambol'd and sported on the level brine
When tempests were approaching: then at night
He listen'd to the wind; and as it drove
The billows with o'erwhelming vehemence
He, starting from his rugged couch, went forth
And hazarding a life, too valueless,
He waded thro' the waves, with plank or pole
Towards where the mariner in conflict dread
Was buffeting for life the roaring surge;
And now just seen, now lost in foaming gulphs,
The dismal gleaming of the clouded moon
Shew'd the dire peril. Often he had snatch'd
From the wild billows, some unhappy man
Who liv'd to bless the hermit of the rocks.
But if his generous cares were all in vain,
And with slow swell the tide of morning bore
Some blue swol'n cor'se to land; the pale recluse
Dug in the chalk a sepulchre—above
Where the dank sea-wrack mark'd the utmost tide,
And with his prayers perform'd the obsequies
For the poor helpless stranger.

One dark night
The equinoctial wind blew south by west,
Fierce on the shore;—the bellowing cliffs were shook
Even to their stony base, and fragments fell
Flashing and thundering on the angry flood.
At day-break, anxious for the lonely man,
His cave the mountain shepherds visited,
Tho' sand and banks of weeds had choak'd their way—
He was not in it; but his drowned cor'se

By the waves wafted, near his former home
Receiv'd the rites of burial. Those who read
Chisel'd within the rock, these mournful lines,
Memorials of his sufferings, did not grieve,
That dying in the cause of charity
His spirit, from its earthly bondage freed,
Had to some better region fled for ever.

(1807)

JOANNA BAILLIE
(1762–1851)

JOANNA BAILLIE was a Scottish poet and dramatist, but lived for most of her life in Hampstead where, despite her own increasingly reclusive nature, she became the focal point of a literary coterie and close friend of the poets, Anna Laetitia Barbauld and her niece, Lucy Aikin. Born in Bothwell, Lanark, Joanna Baillie was the youngest child of Dorothea Baillie and James Baillie, the latter being a minister and later Professor of Divinity at Glasgow. She was educated at a boarding school in Glasgow. After her father's death in 1784, the family moved to London and lived in her brother, William Baillie's house. The apparently frugal life in Hampstead with her sister, the poet Agnes Baillie, began in 1802.

Her entrance into print was not propitious. In 1790 her first volume of poems, *Poems, Wherein It Is Attempted to Describe Certain Views of Nature and of Rustic Manners*, was published, but appears to have gone almost entirely unnoticed and no copies are known to have been purchased. Only when she turned to drama did she begin to meet with success. *A Series of Plays; in which it is attempted to delineate the stronger passions of the mind* came out between 1798 and 1812. (In a two-volume edition published in 1812, they were retitled *Plays on the Passions.*) This collection includes her play on hatred, *De Montfort*, which was performed at Drury Lane on 29 April 1800. Critical interest in the series was immediately aroused, with many reviewers mistaking these anonymously published pieces as the work of a man. For a while their authorship was ascribed to Sir Walter Scott. When her identity was revealed in the third edition of the plays, she and Sir Walter Scott began what was to become a lasting friendship. In a warm tribute to her in the third canto of his *Marmion* (1808), Scott described her as 'the Bold enchantress', and his active promotion of Baillie did much to secure her success as a dramatist and fame as a poet. He also contributed the prologue to her single most successful drama, *The Family Legend: A Tragedy* (1810). She, in turn, was to acknowledge her indebtedness to Scott's poetry in the preface to her second book of poems, the epic romance, *Metrical Legends of Exalted Characters*, in 1821. Her two-volume *Dramas*, published in 1836, which reproduces the earlier plays on the passions and adds new material, was less well received than her earlier edition.

The failed business of a friend prompted Baillie to produce, through subscription, *A Collection of Poems, Chiefly Manuscript and from Living Authors* (1823). The list of contributors includes Sir Walter Scott, Robert Southey, William Wordsworth, Felicia Hemans, and Anna Laetitia Barbauld. More of her own poetry followed later with *Fugitive Verses* (1840), *Ahalya Baee: A Poem*

(1849), an ambitions poem set in India which includes an account of a widow-burning, and *The Dramatic and Poetical Works of Joanna Baillie* in 1851. She also became extremely popular as a writer of songs, with the musician, George Thomson, eagerly collecting her work.

A Unitarian, she expressed her religious views in a work published in her seventieth year, *A View of the General Tenour of the New Testament regarding the Nature and Dignity of Jesus Christ*. She continued writing until she was almost 80 years old.

21 *A Winter's Day*

THE cock, warm roosting 'mid his feather'd mates,
Now lifts his beak and snuffs the morning air,
Stretches his neck and claps his heavy wings,
Gives three hoarse crows, and glad his task is done,
Low chuckling turns himself upon the roost,
Then nestles down again into his place.
The labouring hind,[1] who, on his bed of straw
Beneath his home-made coverings, coarse but warm,
Lock'd in the kindly arms of her who spun them,
Dreams of the gain that next year's crop should bring;
Or at some fair, disposing of his wool,
Or by some lucky and unlook'd-for bargain,
Fills his skin purse with store of tempting gold;
Now wakes from sleep at the unwelcome call,
And finds himself but just the same poor man
As when he went to rest.
He hears the blast against his window beat,
And wishes to himself he were a laird,
That he might lie a-bed. It may not be:
He rubs his eyes and stretches out his arms;
Heigh oh! heigh oh! he drawls with gaping mouth,
Then, most unwillingly creeps from his lair,
And without looking-glass puts on his clothes.
  With rueful face he blows the smother'd fire,
And lights his candle at the reddening coal;
First sees that all be right among his cattle,
Then hies him to the barn with heavy tread,
Printing his footsteps on the new-fall'n snow.
From out the heap'd-up mow he draws his sheaves,
Dislodging the poor red-breast from his shelter

[1] Hind does not perfectly express the condition of the person here intended, who is somewhat above a common labourer, the tenant of a very small farm, which he cultivates with his own hands; a few cows, perhaps a horse, and some six or seven sheep, being all the wealth he possessed. A class of men very common in the west of Scotland, ere political economy was thought of.

Where all the live-long night he slept secure;
But now, affrighted, with uncertain flight,
Flutters round walls, and roof, to find some hole
Through which he may escape.
Then whirling o'er his head, the heavy flail
Descends with force upon the jumping sheaves,
While every rugged wall and neighbouring cot
The noise re-echoes of his sturdy strokes.

The family cares call next upon the wife
To quit her mean but comfortable bed.
And first she stirs the fire and fans the flame,
Then from her heap of sticks for winter stored
An armful brings; loud crackling as they burn,
Thick fly the red sparks upward to the roof,
While slowly mounts the smoke in wreathy clouds.
On goes the seething pot with morning cheer,
For which some little wistful folk await,
Who, peeping from the bed-clothes, spy well pleased
The cheery light that blazes on the wall,
And bawl for leave to rise.
Their busy mother knows not where to turn,
Her morning's work comes now so thick upon her.
One she must help to tie his little coat,
Unpin another's cap, or seek his shoe
Or hosen lost, confusion soon o'er-master'd!
When all is o'er, out to the door they run
With new-comb'd sleeky hair and glistening faces,
Each with some little project in his head.
His new-soled shoes one on the ice must try;
To view his well-set trap another hies,
In hopes to find some poor unwary bird
(No worthless prize) entangled in his snare;
While one, less active, with round rosy cheeks,
Spreads out his purple fingers to the fire,
And peeps most wistfully into the pot.

But let us leave the warm and cheerful house
To view the bleak and dreary scene without,
And mark the dawning of a Winter day.
The morning vapour rests upon the heights,
Lurid and red, while growing gradual shades
Of pale and sickly light spread o'er the sky.
Then slowly from behind the southern hills
Enlarged and ruddy comes the rising sun,
Shooting athwart the hoary waste his beams
That gild the brow of every ridgy bank,
And deepen every valley with a shade,

The crusted window of each scatter'd cot,
The icicles that fringe the thatched roof,
The new-swept slide upon the frozen pool,
All keenly glance, new kindled with his rays;
And e'en the rugged face of scowling Winter
Looks somewhat gay. But only for a time
He shows his glory to the brightening earth,
Then hides his face behind a sullen cloud.

The birds now quit their holes and lurking sheds,
Most mute and melancholy, where through night,
All nestling close to keep each other warm,
In downy sleep they had forgot their hardships;
But not to chant and carol in the air,
Or lightly swing upon some waving bough,
And merrily return each other's notes;
No; silently they hop from bush to bush,
Can find no seeds to stop their craving want,
Then bend their flight to the low smoking cot,
Chirp on the roof, or at the window peck,
To tell their wants to those who lodge within.
The poor lank hare flies homeward to his den,
But little burthen'd with his nightly meal
Of wither'd coleworts from the farmer's garden;
A wretched scanty portion, snatch'd in fear;
And fearful creatures, forced abroad by hunger,
Are now to every enemy a prey.

The husbandman lays by his heavy flail,
And to the house returns, where for him wait
His smoking breakfast and impatient children,
Who, spoon in hand, and ready to begin,
Toward the door cast many an eager look
To see their dad come in.
Then round they sit, a cheerful company;
All quickly set to work, and with heap'd spoons
From ear to ear besmear their rosy cheeks.
The faithful dog stands by his master's side
Wagging his tail and looking in his face;
While humble puss pays court to all around,
And purs and rubs them with her furry sides,
Nor goes this little flattery unrewarded.
But the laborious sit not long at table;
The grateful father lifts his eyes to heaven
To bless his God, whose ever bounteous hand
Him and his little ones doth daily feed,
Then rises satisfied to work again.

The varied rousing sounds of industry
Are heard through all the village.
The humming wheel, the thrifty housewife's tongue,
Who scolds to keep her maidens to their work,
The wool-card's grating, most unmusical!
Issue from every house.
But hark! the sportsman from the neighbouring hedge
His thunder sends! loud bark the village curs;
Up from her cards or wheel the maiden starts
And hastens to the door; the housewife chides,
Yet runs herself to look, in spite of thrift,
And all the little town is in a stir.

Strutting before, the cock leads forth his train,
And chuckling near the barn-door 'mid the straw,
Reminds the farmer of his morning's service.
His grateful master throws a liberal handful;
They flock about it, while the hungry sparrows
Perch'd on the roof, look down with envious eye,
Then, aiming well, amidst the feeders light,
And seize upon the feast with greedy bill,
Till angry partlets peck them off the field.
But at a distance, on the leafless tree,
All woe-begone, the lonely blackbird sits;
The cold north wind ruffles his glossy feathers;
Full oft he looks, but dares not make approach,
Then turns his yellow beak to peck his side
And claps his wings close to his sharpen'd breast.
The wandering fowler from behind the hedge,
Fastens his eye upon him, points his gun,
And firing wantonly, as at a mark,
Of life bereaves him in the cheerful spot
That oft hath echo'd to his summer's song.

The mid-day hour is near, the pent-up kine
Are driven from their stalls to take the air.
How stupidly they stare! and feel how strange!
They open wide their smoking mouths to low,
But scarcely can their feeble sound be heard,
Then turn and lick themselves, and step by step,
Move, dull and heavy, to their stalls again.

In scatter'd groups the little idle boys,
With purple fingers moulding in the snow
Their icy ammunition, pant for war;
And drawing up in opposite array,
Send forth a mighty shower of well-aim'd balls,
Each tiny hero tries his growing strength,

And burns to beat the foe-men off the field.
Or on the well-worn ice in eager throngs,
After short race, shoot rapidly along,
Trip up each other's heels, and on the surface
With studded shoes draw many a chalky line.
Untired and glowing with the healthful sport
They cease not till the sun hath run his course,
And threatening clouds, slow rising from the north,
Spread leaden darkness o'er the face of heaven;
Then by degrees they scatter to their homes,
Some with a broken head or bloody nose,
To claim their mother's pity, who, most skilful!
Cures all their troubles with a bit of bread.

The night comes on apace—
Chill blows the blast and drives the snow in wreaths;
Now every creature looks around for shelter,
And whether man or beast, all move alike
Towards their homes, and happy they who have
A house to screen them from the piercing cold!
Lo, o'er the frost a reverend form advances!
His hair white as the snow on which he treads,
His forehead mark'd with many a care-worn furrow,
Whose feeble body bending o'er a staff,
Shows still that once it was the seat of strength,
Though now it shakes like some old ruin'd tower.
Clothed indeed, but not disgraced with rags,
He still maintains that decent dignity
Which well becomes those who have served their country.
With tottering steps he gains the cottage door;
The wife within, who hears his hollow cough,
And pattering of his stick upon the threshold,
Sends out her little boy to see who's there.
The child looks up to mark the stranger's face,
And, seeing it enlighten'd with a smile,
Holds out his tiny hand to lead him in.
Round from her work the mother turns her head,
And views them, not ill pleased.
The stranger whines not with a piteous tale,
But only asks a little to relieve
A poor old soldier's wants.
The gentle matron brings the ready chair
And bids him sit to rest his weary limbs,
And warm himself before her blazing fire.
The children, full of curiosity,
Flock round, and with their fingers in their months
Stand staring at him, while the stranger, pleased,

Takes up the youngest urchin on his knee.
Proud of its seat, it wags its little feet,
And prates and laughs and plays with his white locks.
But soon a change comes o'er the soldier's face;
His thoughtful mind is turn'd on other days,
When his own boys were wont to play around him,
Who now lie distant from their native land
In honourable but untimely graves:
He feels how helpless and forlorn he is,
And big, round tears course down his wither'd cheeks.
His toilsome daily labour at an end,
In comes the wearied master of the house,
And marks with satisfaction his old guest,
In the chief seat, with all the children round him.
His honest heart is fill'd with manly kindness,
He bids him stay and share their homely meal,
And take with them his quarters for the night.
The aged wanderer thankfully accepts,
And by the simple hospitable board,
Forgets the by-past hardships of the day.

When all are satisfied, about the fire
They draw their seats and form a cheerful ring.
The thrifty housewife turns her spinning-wheel;
The husband, useful even in his hour
Of ease and rest, a stocking knits, belike,
Or plaits stored rushes, which with after skill
Into a basket form'd may do good service,
With eggs or butter fill'd at fair or market.

Some idle neighbours now come dropping in,
Draw round their chairs and widen out the circle;
And every one in his own native way
Does what he can to cheer the social group.
Each tells some little story of himself,
That constant subject upon which mankind,
Whether in court or country, love to dwell.
How at a fair he saved a simple clown
From being trick'd in buying of a cow;
Or laid a bet on his own horse's head
Against his neighbour's bought at twice his cost,
Which fail'd not to repay his better skill;
Or on a harvest day bound in an hour
More sheaves of corn than any of his fellows,
Though ere so stark, could do in twice the time;
Or won the bridal race with savoury broose
And first kiss of the bonny bride, though all
The fleetest youngsters of the parish strove

In rivalry against him.
But chiefly the good man, by his own fire,
Hath privilege of being listen'd to,
Nor dares a little prattling tongue presume
Though but in play, to break upon his story.
The children sit and listen with the rest;
And should the youngest raise its lisping voice,
The careful mother, ever on the watch,
And ever pleased with what her husband says,
Gives it a gentle tap upon the fingers,
Or stops its ill-timed prattle with a kiss.
The soldier next, but not unask'd, begins
His tale of war and blood. They gaze upon him,
And almost weep to see the man so poor,
So bent and feeble, helpless and forlorn,
Who has undaunted stood the battle's brunt
While roaring cannons shook the quaking earth,
And bullets hiss'd round his defenceless head.
Thus passes quickly on the evening hour,
Till sober folks must needs retire to rest;
Then all break up, and, by their several paths,
Hie homeward, with the evening pastime cheer'd
Far more, belike, than those who issue forth
From city theatre's gay scenic show,
Or crowded ball-room's splendid moving maze.
But where the song and story, joke and gibe,
So lately circled, what a solemn change
In little time takes place!
The sound of psalms, by mingled voices raised
Of young and old, upon the night air borne,
Haply to some benighted traveller,
Or the late parted neighbours on their way,
A pleasing notice gives, that those whose sires
In former days on the bare mountain's side,
In deserts, heaths, and caverns, praise and prayer,
At peril of their lives, in their own form
Of covenanted worship offered up,
In peace and safety in their own quiet home
Are—(as in quaint and modest phrase is termed)
Engaged now in *evening exercise*.[1]

[1] In the first edition of the *Winter Day*, nothing regarding family worship was mentioned: a great omission, for which I justly take shame to myself. 'The Evening exercise', as it was called, prevailed in every house over the simple country parts of the West of Scotland, and I have often heard the sound of it passing through the twilight air, in returning from a late walk.

But long accustom'd to observe the weather,
The farmer cannot lay him down in peace
Till he has look'd to mark what bodes the night.
He lifts the latch, and moves the heavy door,
Sees wreaths of snow heap'd up on every side,
And black and dismal all above his head.
Anon the northern blast begins to rise,
He hears its hollow growling from afar,
Which, gathering strength, rolls on with doubled might,
And raves and bellows o'er his head. The trees
Like pithless saplings bend. He shuts his door,
And, thankful for the roof that covers him,
Hies him to bed.

(1790 *1851*)

22 *A Summer's Day*

THE dark-blue clouds of night, in dusky lines
Drawn wide and streaky o'er the purer sky,
Wear faintly morning purple on their skirts.
The stars, that full and bright shone in the west,
But dimly twinkle to the steadfast eye,
And seen and vanishing and seen again,
Like dying tapers winking in the socket,
Are by degrees shut from the face of heaven;
The fitful lightning of the summer cloud,
And every lesser flame that shone by night;
The wandering fire that seems, across the marsh,
A beaming candle in a lonely cot,
Cheering the hopes of the benighted hind,
Till, swifter than the very change of thought,
It shifts from place to place, eludes his sight,
And makes him wondering rub his faithless eyes;
The humble glow-worm and the silver moth,
That cast a doubtful glimmering o'er the green,—
All die away.
For now the sun, slow moving in his glory,
Above the eastern mountains lifts his head;
The webs of dew spread o'er the hoary lawn,
The smooth, clear bosom of the settled pool,
The polish'd ploughshare on the distant field,
Catch fire from him, and dart their new-gain'd beams
Upon the gazing rustic's dazzled sight.

The waken'd birds upon the branches hop,
Peck their soft down, and bristle out their feathers,

Then stretch their throats and trill their morning song;
While dusky crows, high swinging over head,
Upon the topmost boughs, in lordly pride,
Mix their hoarse croaking with the linnet's note,
Till in a gather'd band of close array,
They take their flight to seek their daily food.
The villager wakes with the early light,
That through the window of his cot appears,
And quits his easy bed; then o'er the fields
With lengthen'd active strides betakes his way,
Bearing his spade or hoe across his shoulder,
Seen glancing as he moves, and with good will
His daily work begins.
The sturdy sun-burnt boy drives forth the cattle,
And, pleased with power, bawls to the lagging kine
With stern authority, who fain would stop
To crop the tempting bushes as they pass.
At every open door, in lawn or lane,
Half naked children half awake are seen,
Scratching their heads and blinking to the light,
Till, rousing by degrees, they run about,
Roll on the sward and in some sandy nook
Dig caves, and houses build, full oft defaced
And oft begun again, a daily pastime.
The housewife, up by times, her morning cares
Tends busily; from tubs of curdled milk
With skilful patience draws the clear green whey
From the press'd bosom of the snowy curd,
While her brown comely maid, with tuck'd-up sleeves
And swelling arm, assists her. Work proceeds,
Pots smoke, pails rattle, and the warm confusion
Still more confused becomes, till in the mould
With heavy hands the well-squeezed curd is placed.

So goes the morning till the powerful sun,
High in the heavens, sends down his strengthen'd beams,
And all the freshness of the morn is fled.
The idle horse upon the grassy field
Rolls on his back; the swain leaves off his toil,
And to his house with heavy steps returns,
Where on the board his ready breakfast placed
Looks most invitingly, and his good mate
Serves him with cheerful kindness.
Upon the grass no longer hangs the dew;
Forth hies the mower with his glittering scythe,
In snowy shirt bedight and all unbraced.
He moves athwart the mead with sideling bend,

And lays the grass in many a swathey line;
In every field, in every lawn and meadow
The rousing voice of industry is heard;
The hay-cock rises, and the frequent rake
Sweeps on the fragrant hay in heavy wreaths.
The old and young, the weak and strong are there,
And, as they can, help on the cheerful work.
The father jeers his awkward half-grown lad,
Who trails his tawdry armful o'er the field,
Nor does he fear the jeering to repay.
The village oracle and simple maid
Jest in their turns and raise the ready laugh;
All are companions in the general glee;
Authority, hard favour'd, frowns not there.
Some, more advanced, raise up the lofty rick,
Whilst on its top doth stand the parish toast
In loose attire, with swelling ruddy cheek.
With taunts and harmless mockery she receives
The toss'd-up heaps from fork of simple youth,
Who, staring on her, takes his aim awry,
While half the load falls back upon himself.
Loud is her laugh, her voice is heard afar;
The mower busied on the distant lawn,
The carter trudging on his dusty way,
The shrill sound know, their bonnets toss in the air,
And roar across the field to catch her notice:
She waves her arm to them, and shakes her head,
And then renews her work with double spirit.
Thus do they jest and laugh away their toil
Till the bright sun, now past his middle course,
Shoots down his fiercest beams which none may brave.
The stoutest arm feels listless, and the swart
And brawny-shoulder'd clown begins to fail.
But to the weary, lo—there comes relief!
A troop of welcome children o'er the lawn
With slow and wary steps approach, some bear
In baskets oaten cakes or barley scones,
And gusty cheese and stoups of milk or whey.
Beneath the branches of a spreading tree,
Or by the shady side of the tall rick,
They spread their homely fare, and seated round,
Taste every pleasure that a feast can give.

A drowsy indolence now hangs on all;
Each creature seeks some place of rest, some shelter
From the oppressive heat; silence prevails;
Nor low nor bark nor chirping bird are heard.

In shady nooks the sheep and kine convene;
Within the narrow shadow of the cot
The sleepy dog lies stretch'd upon his side,
Nor heeds the footsteps of the passer-by,
Or at the sound but raises half an eye-lid,
Then gives a feeble growl and sleeps again;
While puss composed and grave on threshold stone
Sits winking in the light.
No sound is heard but humming of the bee,
For she alone retires not from her labour,
Nor leaves a meadow flower unsought for gain.

Heavy and slow, so pass the sultry hours,
Till gently bending on the ridge's top
The dropping seedy grass begins to wave,
And the high branches of the aspen tree
Shiver the leaves and gentle rustling make.
Cool breathes the rising breeze, and with it wakes
The languid spirit from its state of stupor.
The lazy boy springs from his mossy lair
To chase the gaudy butterfly, which oft
Lights at his feet as if within his reach,
Spreading upon the ground its mealy wings,
Yet still eludes his grasp, and high in air
Takes many a circling flight, tempting his eye
And tiring his young limbs.
The drowsy dog, who feels the kindly air
That passing o'er him lifts his shaggy ear,
Begins to stretch him, on his legs half-raised,
Till fully waked, with bristling cock'd-up tail,
He makes the village echo to his bark.

But let us not forget the busy maid,
Who by the side of the clear pebbly stream
Spreads out her snowy linens to the sun,
And sheds with liberal hand the crystal shower
O'er many a favourite piece of fair attire,
Revolving in her mind her gay appearance,
So nicely trick'd, at some approaching fair.
The dimpling half-check'd smile and muttering lip
Her secret thoughts betray. With shiny feet,
There, little active bands of truant boys
Sport in the stream and dash the water round,
Or try with wily art to catch the trout,
Or with their fingers grasp the slippery eel.
The shepherd-lad sits singing on the bank
To while away the weary lonely hours,
Weaving with art his pointed crown of rushes,

A guiltless easy crown, which, having made,
He places on his head, and skips about,
A chaunted rhyme repeats, or calls full loud
To some companion lonely as himself,
Far on the distant bank; or else delighted
To hear the echo'd sound of his own voice,
Returning answer from some neighbouring rock,
Or roofless barn, holds converse with himself.

Now weary labourers perceive well pleased
The shadows lengthen, and the oppressive day
With all its toil fast wearing to an end.
The sun, far in the west, with level beam
Gleams on the cocks of hay, on bush or ridge,
And fields are checker'd with fantastic shapes,
Or tree or shrub or gate or human form,
All lengthen'd out in antic disproportion
Upon the darken'd ground. Their task is finish'd,
Their rakes and scatter'd garments gather'd up,
And all right gladly to their homes return.

The village, lone and silent through the day,
Receiving from the fields its merry bands,
Sends forth its evening sound, confused but cheerful;
Yelping of curs, and voices stern and shrill,
And true-love ballads in no plaintive strain,
By household maid at open window sung;
And lowing of the home-returning kine,
And herd's dull droning trump and tinkling bell,
Tied to the collar of the master-sheep,
Make no contemptible variety
To ears not over nice.
With careless lounging gait the favour'd youth
Upon his sweetheart's open window leans,
Diverting her with joke and harmless taunt.
Close by the cottage door, with placid mien,
The old man sits upon his seat of turf,
His staff with crooked head laid by his side,
Which oft some tricky youngling steals away,
And straddling o'er it shows his horsemanship
By raising clouds of sand; he smiles thereat,
But seems to chide him sharply:
His silver locks upon his shoulders fall,
And not ungraceful is his stoop of age.
No stranger passes him without regard,
And neighbours stop to wish him a good e'en,
And ask him his opinion of the weather.
They fret not at the length of his remarks

Upon the various seasons he remembers;
For well he knows the many divers signs
That do foretell high winds, or rain, or drought,
Or aught that may affect the rising crops.
The silken-clad, who courtly breeding boast,
Their own discourse still sweetest to their ear,
May at the old man's lengthen'd story fret,
Impatiently, but here it is not so.

From every chimney mounts the curling smoke,
Muddy and grey, of the new evening fire;
On every window smokes the family supper,
Set out to cool by the attentive housewife,
While cheerful groups, at every door convened,
Bawl 'cross the narrow lane the parish news,
And oft the bursting laugh disturbs the air.
But see who comes to set them all agape;
The weary-footed pedlar with his pack;
Stiffly he bends beneath his bulky load,
Cover'd with dust, slip-shod and out at elbows;
His greasy hat set backwards on his head;
His thin straight hair, divided on his brow,
Hangs lank on either side his glist'ning cheeks,
And woe-begone yet vacant is his face.
His box he opens and displays his ware.
Full many a varied row of precious stones
Cast forth their dazzling lustre to the light
And ruby rings and china buttons, stamp'd
With love devices, the desiring maid
And simple youth attract; while streaming garters,
Of many colours, fasten'd to a pole,
Aloft in air their gaudy stripes display,
And from afar the distant stragglers lure.
The children leave their play and round him flock;
Even sober, aged grandame quits her seat,
Where by the door she twines her lenthen'd threads,
Her spindle stops, and lays her distaff by,
Then joins with step sedate the curious throng.
She praises much the fashions of her youth,
And scorns each useless nonsense of the day;
Yet not ill-pleased the glossy riband views,
Unroll'd and changing hues with every fold,
Just measured out to deck her grandchild's head.

Now red but languid the last beams appear
Of the departed sun, across the lawn,
Gilding each sweepy ridge on many a field,
And from the openings of the distant hills

A level brightness pouring, sad though bright;
Like farewell smiles from some dear friend they seem,
And only serve to deepen the low vale,
And make the shadows of the night more gloomy.
The varied noises of the cheerful village
By slow degrees now faintly die away,
And more distinctly distant sounds are heard
That gently steal adown the river's bed,
Or through the wood come on the ruffling breeze.
The white mist rises from the meads, and from
The dappled skirting of the sober sky
Looks out with steady gleam the evening star.
The lover, skulking in some neighbouring copse,
(Whose half-seen form, shown through the dusky air
Large and majestic, makes the traveller start,
And spreads the story of a haunted grove,)
Curses the owl, whose loud ill-omen'd hoot
With ceaseless spite takes from his listening ear
The well-known footsteps of his darling maid,
And fretful chases from his face the night-fly,
That, buzzing round his head, doth often skim
With fluttering wings across his glowing cheek
For all but him in quiet balmy sleep
Forget the toils of the oppressive day;
Shut is the door of every scatter'd cot.
And silence dwells within.

(1790 *1851*)

23 *To a Child*

WHOSE imp art thou, with dimpled cheek,
    And curly pate, and merry eye,
And arm and shoulder round and sleek,
    And soft and fair?—thou urchin sly!

What boots it who with sweet caresses
    First call'd thee his,—or squire or hind?
Since thou in every wight that passes,
    Dost now a friendly play-mate find.

Thy downeast glances, grave, but cunning,
    As fringed eye-lids rise and fall;
Thy shyness, swiftly from me running,
    Is infantine coquetry all.

But far a-field thou hast not flown;
With mocks and threats, half lisp'd, half spoken,
I feel thee pulling at my gown,
Of right good will thy simple token.

And thou must laugh and wrestle too,
A mimic warfare with me waging;
To make, as wily lovers do,
Thy after-kindness more engaging.

The wilding rose, sweet as thyself,
And new-cropt daisies are thy treasure:
I'd gladly part with worldly pelf
To taste again thy youthful pleasure.

But yet, for all thy merry look,
Thy frisks and wiles, the time is coming,
When thou shalt sit in cheerless nook,
The weary spell or horn-book thumbing.

Well; let it be!—through weal and wo,
Thou knowst not now thy future range;
Life is a motley, shifting show,
And thou a thing of hope and change!

(1840 *1851*)

24 *London*

It is a goodly sight through the clear air,
From Hampstead's heathy height to see at once
England's vast capital in fair expanse,
Towers, belfries, lengthen'd streets, and structures fair.
St. Paul's high dome amidst the vassal bands
Of neighb'ring spires, a regal chieftain stands,
And over fields of ridgy roofs appear,
With distance softly tinted, side by side,
In kindred grace, like twain of sisters dear,
The Towers of Westminster, her Abbey's pride;
While, far beyond, the hills of Surrey shine
Through thin soft haze, and show their wavy line.
View'd thus, a goodly sight! but when survey'd
Through denser air when moisten'd winds prevail,
In her grand panoply of smoke array'd,
While clouds aloft in heavy volumes sail,
She is sublime.—She seems a curtain'd gloom
Connecting heaven and earth,—a threat'ning sign of doom.
With more than natural height, rear'd in the sky

'Tis then St. Paul's arrests the wondering eye;
The lower parts in swathing mist conceal'd,
The higher through some half spent shower reveal'd,
So far from earth removed, that well, I trow,
Did not its form man's artful structure show,
It might some lofty alpine peak be deem'd,
The eagle's haunt, with cave and crevice seam'd.
Stretch'd wide on either hand, a rugged screen,
In lurid dimness, nearer streets are seen
Like shoreward billows of a troubled main,
Arrested in their rage. Through drizzly rain,
Cataracts of tawny sheen pour from the skies,
Of furnace smoke black curling columns rise,
And many tinted vapours, slowly pass
O'er the wide draping of that pictured mass.

So shows by day this grand imperial town,
And, when o'er all the night's black stole is thrown,
The distant traveller doth with wonder mark
Her luminous canopy athwart the dark,
Cast up, from myriads of lamps that shine
Along her streets in many a starry line:—
He wondering looks from his yet distant road,
And thinks the northern streamers are abroad.
'What hollow sound is that?' approaching near,
The roar of many wheels breaks on his ear.
It is the flood of human life in motion!
It is the voice of a tempestuous ocean!
With sad but pleasing awe his soul is fill'd,
Scarce heaves his breast, and all within is still'd,
As many thoughts and feelings cross his mind,—
Thoughts, mingled, melancholy, undefined,
Of restless, reckless man, and years gone by,
And Time fast wending to Eternity.

(1840 *1851*)

25 *Lines to a Teapot*

ON thy carved sides, where many a vivid dye
In easy progress leads the wandering eye,
A distant nation's manners we behold,
To the quick fancy whimsically told.

The small-eyed beauty and her Mandarin,
Who o'er the rail of garden arbour lean,
In listless ease; and rocks of arid brown,
On whose sharp crags, in gay profusion blown,

The ample loose-leaved rose appears to grace
The skilful culture of the wondrous place;
The little verdant plat, where with his mate
The golden pheasant holds his gorgeous state,
With gaily crested pate and twisted neck,
Turn'd jauntily his glossy wings to peck;
The smooth-streak'd water of a paly gray,
O'er which the checker'd bridge lends ready way,
While, by its margin moor'd, the little boat
Doth with its oars and netted awning float;
A scene present all soft delights to take in,
A paradise for grave Grandee of Pekin.
With straight small spout, that from thy body fair
Diverges with a smart vivacious air,
And round, arch'd handle with gold tracery bound,
And dome-shaped lid with bud or button crown'd,
Thou standst complete, fair subject of my rhymes,
A goodly vessel of the olden times!

But far less pleasure yields this fair display
Than that enjoy'd upon thy natal day,
When round the potter's wheel their chins upraising,
An urchin group in silent wonder gazing,
Stood and beheld, as, touch'd with magic skill,
The whirling clay was fashion'd to his will,—
Saw mazy motion stopp'd, and then the toy
Complete before their eyes, and grinn'd for joy;
Clapping their naked sides with blythe halloo,
And curtail'd words of praise, like *ting, tung, too!*
The brown-skinn'd artist, with his unclothed waist
And girded loins, who, slow and patient, traced,
Beneath his humble shed, this fair array
Of pictured forms upon thy surface gay,
I will not stop in fancy's sight to place,
But speed me on my way with quicken'd pace.
Pack'd in a chest with others of thy kind,
The sport of waves and every shifting wind,
The Ocean thou hast cross'd, and thou mayst claim
The passing of the Line to swell thy fame,
With as good observation of the thing
As some of those who in a hammock swing.

And now thou'rt seen in Britain's polish'd land,
Held up to public view in waving hand
Of boastful auctioneer, whilst dames of pride
In morning farthingals, scarce two yards wide,
With collar'd lap-dogs snarling in their arms,
Contend in rival keenness for thy charms.

And certes well they might, for there they found thee
With all thy train of vassal cups around thee,
A prize which thoughts by day, and dreams by night,
Could dwell on for a week with fresh delight.

Our pleased imagination now pourtrays
The glory of thy high official days,
When thou on board of rich japan wast set,
Round whose supporting table gaily met
At close of eve, the young, the learn'd, the fair,
And e'en philosophy and wit were there.
'Midst basons, cream-pots, cups and saucers small,
Thou stoodst the ruling chieftain of them all;
And e'en the kettle of Potosi's ore,
Whose ample cell supplied thy liquid store,
Beneath whose base the sapphire flame was burning,
Above whose lid the wreathy smoke was turning,
Though richly chased and burnish'd it might be,
Was yet, confess'd, subordinate to thee.
But O! when beauty's hand thy weight sustain'd,
The climax of thy glory was attain'd!
Back from her elevated elbow fell
Its three-tired ruffle, and display'd the swell
And gentle rounding of her lily arm,
The eyes of wistful sage or beau to charm—
A sight at other times but dimly seen
Through veiling folds of point or colberteen.
With pleasing toil, red glow'd her dimpled cheek,
Bright glanced her eyes beneath her forehead sleek,
And as she pour'd the beverage, through the room
Was spread its fleeting, delicate perfume.
Then did bright wit and cheerful fancy play
With all the passing topics of the day.
So delicate, so varied, and so free
Was the heart's pastime, then inspired by thee,
That goblet, bowl, or flask could boast no power
Of high excitement, in their reigning hour,
Compared to thine;—red wildfire of the fen,
To summer moonshine of some fairy glen.

But now the honours of thy course are past,
For what of earthly happiness may last!
Although in modern drawing-room, a board
May fragrant tea from menial hands afford,
Which, pour'd in dull obscurity hath been,
From pot of vulgar ware, in nook unseen,
And pass'd in hasty rounds our eyes before,
Thou in thy graceful state art seen no more.

And what the changeful fleeting crowd, who sip
The unhonour'd beverage with contemptuous lip,
Enjoy amidst the tangled, giddy maze,
Their languid eye—their listless air betrays.
What though at times we see a youthful fair
By white clothed board her watery drug prepare,
At further corner of a noisy room,
Where only casual stragglers deign to come,
Like tavern's busy bar-maid; still I say,
The honours of thy course are pass'd away.

Again hath auctioneer thy value praised,
Again have rival bidders on thee gazed,
But not the gay, the young, the fair, I trow!
No; sober connoisseurs, with wrinkled brow
And spectacles on nose, thy parts inspect,
And by grave rules approve thee or reject.
For all the bliss which china charms afford,
My lady now has ceded to her lord.
And wisely too does she forego the prize,
Since modern pin-money will scarce suffice
For all the trimmings, flounces, beads and lace,
The thousand needful things that needs must grace
Her daily changed attire.—And now on shelf
Of china closet placed, a cheerless elf,
Like moody statesman in his rural den,
From power dismiss'd—like prosperous citizen,
From shop or change set free—untoward bliss!
Thou rest'st in most ignoble uselessness.

(1840 *1851*)

26 *Address to a Steamvessel*

FREIGHTED with passengers of every sort,
A motley throng, thou leav'st the busy port:
Thy long and ample deck,—where scatter'd lie
Baskets and cloaks and shawls of crimson dye;
Where dogs and children through the crowd are straying,
And on his bench apart the fiddler playing,
While matron dames to tressel'd seats repair,—
Seems, on the glassy waves, a floating fair.

Its dark form on the sky's pale azure cast,
Towers from this clustering group thy pillar'd mast;
The dense smoke, issuing from its narrow vent,
Is to the air in curly volumes sent,

Which coiling and uncoiling on the wind,
Trail, like a writhing serpent, far behind.
Beneath, as each merged wheel its motion plies,
On either side the white-churn'd waters rise,
And newly parted from the noisy fray,
Track with light ridgy foam thy recent way,
Then far diverged, in many a lustrous line
On the still-moving distant surface shine.

Thou holdst thy course in independent pride;
No leave ask'st thou of either wind or tide.
To whate'er point the breeze inconstant veer,
Still doth thy careless helmsman onward steer;
As if the stroke of some magician's wand
Had lent thee power the ocean to command.
What is this power which thus within thee lurks
And all unseen, like a mask'd giant works?
E'en that which gentle dames at morning tea,
From silver urn ascending, daily see
With tressy wreathings borne upon the air
Like loosen'd ringlets of a lady's hair;
Or rising from th' enamell'd cup beneath,
With the soft fragrance of an infant's breath:
That which within the peasant's humble cot
Comes from the uncover'd mouth of savoury pot,
As his kind mate prepares his noonday fare,
Which cur and cat and rosy urchins share;
That which, all silver'd by the moon's pale beam
Precedes the mighty Geyser's up-cast stream,
What time, with bellowing din, exploded forth,
It decks the midnight of the frozen north,
While travellers from their skin-spread couches rise
To gaze upon the sight with wondering eyes.

Thou hast to those 'in populous city pent'
Glimpses of wild and beauteous nature lent,
A bright remembrance ne'er to be destroy'd,
That proves to them a treasure long enjoy'd,
And for this scope to beings erst confined,
I fain would hail thee with a grateful mind.
They who had nought of verdant freshness seen,
But suburb orchards choked with coleworts green,
Now, seated at their ease, may glide along,
Loch Lomond's fair and fairy Isles among;
Where bushy promontories fondly peep
At their own beauty in the nether deep,
O'er drooping birch and rowan red that lave

Their fragrant branches in the glassy wave:
They who on higher objects scarce have counted
Than church-spire with its gilded vane surmounted,
May view within their near, distinctive ken
The rocky summits of the lofty Ben;
Or see his purple shoulders darkly lower
Through the dim drapery of a summer shower.
Where, spread in broad and fair expanse, the Clyde
Mingles his waters with the briny tide,
Along the lesser Cumbray's rocky shore,
With moss and crusted lichens flecker'd o'er,
He who but warfare held with thievish cat,
Or from his cupboard chaced a hungry rat,
The city cobbler,—scares the wild sea-mew
In its mid-flight with loud and shrill halloo;
Or valiantly with fearful threatening shakes
His lank and greasy head at Kittywakes.[1]
The eyes that have no fairer outline seen,
Than chimney'd walls with slated roofs between,
Which hard and harshly edge the smoky sky,
May Arran's softly-vision'd peaks descry,
Coping with graceful state her steepy sides
O'er which the cloud's broad shadow swiftly glides,
And interlacing slopes that gently merge
Into the pearly mist of ocean's verge.
Eyes which admired that work of sordid skill,
The storied structure of a cotton mill,
May wondering now behold the unnumber'd host
Of marshall'd pillars on fair Ireland's coast,
Phalanx on phalanx ranged with sidelong bend,
Or broken ranks that to the main descend,
Like Pharaoh's army on the Red Sea shore,
Which deep and deeper sank, to rise no more.

Yet ne'ertheless, whate'er we owe to thee,
Rover at will on river, lake, and sea,
As profit's bait or pleasure's lure engage,
Offspring of Watt, that philosophie sage,
Who in the heraldry of science ranks
With those to whom men owe high meed of thanks
For genius usefully employ'd, whose fame
Shall still be link'd with Davy's splendid name;
Dearer to fancy, to the eye more fair
Are the light skiffs, that to the breezy air
Unfurl their swelling sails of snowy hue

[1] The common or vulgar name of a bird frequenting that coast.

Upon the moving lap of ocean blue:
As the proud swan on summer lake displays,
With plumage brightening in the morning rays,
Her fair pavilion of erected wings,
They change, and veer, and turn like living things.

With ample store of shrouding, sails, and mast,
To brave with manly skill the winter blast
Of every clime,—in vessels rigg'd like these
Did great Columbus cross the western seas,
And to the stinted thoughts of man reveal'd
What yet the course of ages had conceal'd:
In such as these, on high adventure bent,
Round the vast world Magellan's comrades went.
To such as these are hardy seamen found
As with the ties of kindred feeling bound,
Boasting, while cans of cheering grog they sip,
The varied fortunes of 'our gallant ship':
The offspring these of bold sagacious man,
Ere yet the reign of letter'd lore began.

In very truth, compared to these, thou art
A daily labourer, a mechanic swart,
In working weeds array'd of homely gray,
Opposed to gentle nymph or lady gay,
To whose free robes the graceful right is given
To play and dally with the winds of heaven.
Beholding thee, the great of other days
And modern men with all their alter'd ways,
Across my mind with hasty transit gleam,
Like fleeting shadows of a feverish dream:
Fitful I gaze, with adverse humours teased,
Half sad, half proud, half angry, and half pleased.

(1840 *1851*)

27 *Volunteer's Song, Written in 1803*

YE who Britain's soldiers be,—
Freemen, children of the free,
Who quickly come at danger's call,
From shop and palace, cot and hall,
And brace ye bravely up in warlike gear,
For all that ye hold dear;

Blest in your hands be sword and spear!
There is no banded Briton here
On whom some fond mate hath not smiled,
Or hung in love some lisping child,
Or aged parent, grasping his last stay,
With locks of honour'd gray.

Such men behold with steady pride,
The threaten'd tempest gathering wide,
And list with onward form inclined
To sound of foe-men on the wind,
And bravely act amid the battle's roar,
In scenes untried before.

Let veterans boast, as well they may,
Nerves steel'd in many a bloody day;
The generous heart, who takes his stand
Upon his free and native land,
Doth, with the first sound of the hostile drum,
A fearless man become.

Then come, ye hosts, that madly pour
From wave-toss'd floats upon our shore!
If fell or gentle, false or true,
Let those inquire, who wish to sue:
Nor fiend nor hero from a foreign strand,
Shall lord it in our land.

Come, then, ye hosts that madly pour
From wave-toss'd floats upon our shore!
An adverse wind or breezeless main
Lock'd in their ports our tars detain,
To waste their eager spirits, vainly keen,
Else here ye had not been.

Yet ne'ertheless, in strong array,
Prepare ye for a well-fought day.
Let banners wave and trumpets sound,
And closing cohorts darken round,
And the fierce onset raise its mingled roar,
New sound on England's shore!

Freemen, children of the free,
Are brave alike on land or sea;
And every rood of British ground,
On which a hostile spear is found,
Proves under their firm tread and vigorous stroke,
A deck of royal oak.

(1840 *1851*)

HELEN MARIA WILLIAMS
(1762–1827)

HELEN MARIA WILLIAMS's reputation as an admired poet of the 1780s was to suffer from adverse reaction to her pro-Revolutionary writings of the 1790s onwards. She continued to adhere to her Revolutionary principles, while condemning Jacobin extremism, when even most liberals were turning away in horror from the Terror. The *Gentleman's Magazine* of December 1795 registers a perceived impropriety in her position: 'she has debased her sex, her heart, her feelings, her talents, in recording such a tissue of horror and villainy.'

She was born in London, the second of three daughters. Her father was a Welsh army officer and her mother, Helen (née Hays) came from Scotland. After her father's death, the family moved to Berwick-on-Tweed, and she was there educated at home. She was, however, later to feel hampered by 'the disadvantages of a confined education' (Preface to *Poems, by Helen Maria Williams*, 1786). In 1781, she moved to London, where she was later joined by her mother and sister and there met Andrew Kippis, an advocate of social and political reform and prominent Dissenting minister. Through him she came into contact with several literary women, including Elizabeth Montagu and Fanny Burney, and she was later to befriend radicals such as Dr Richard Price, Joseph Priestley, and William Godwin. Andrew Kippis helped her to publish her first book of poetry, *Edwin and Eltruda* (1782), an anti-war poem, which received some favourable reviews. Two more poems followed, both published by subscription: *An Ode on the Peace* (1783), celebrating the end of the American war, and *Peru, A Poem. In Six Cantos* (1784), which expresses her libertarian views. Her abolitionist poem, 'A Poem on the Bill Lately Passed for Regulating the Slave Trade', was published in 1788. The poems were reissued, along with new material, in her two-volume *Poems* (1786). A complimentary review of her next piece of work, a novel, *Julia* (1790), is believed to have been written by Mary Wollstonecraft, as it is affixed with the signature, 'M', used by Wollstonecraft at this time (*Analytical Review*, May 1790). The novel contains a poem by the author, 'The Bastille, A Vision', in which she publicly supports the French Revolution for the first time.

Helen Maria Williams moved to France in 1790 and was to stay there for most of her life, except for a brief period in Switzerland in 1794, where she had fled in fear of attacks upon her for her anti-Jacobin writing. Between 1792 and 1816 she produced numerous books recording the events in France as she witnessed them, beginning with her best-known *Letters from France 1792–6*.

As a poet, she is also known for her sonnets. Some of these first appeared in her translation of her friend, Jacques-Henri Bernardin de St Pierre's novel, *Paul and Virginia* (1795). They were later reprinted in her *Poems, Moral, Elegant and Pathetic: and Original Sonnets by Helen Maria Williams* (1796). A 'Sketch of the Influence of the Revolution on French Poetry' is offered in the introduction to her *Poems on Various Subjects with Introductory Remarks on the Present State of Science and Literature* (1823). The volume includes previously unpublished poems, as well as reprinting (in the case of *Peru*, with a revised title) the poems from the 1780s which, as she says, have 'reference to public events'.

28 *from Peruvian Tales. Tale II, Alzira*

Pizarro lands with the Forces—His meeting with Ataliba—
Its unhappy consequences—Zorai dies—Ataliba imprisoned,
and strangled—Despair of Alzira.

FLUSH'D with impatient hope, the martial band,
By stern Pizarro led, approach the land;
No terrors arm his hostile brow, for guile
Seeks to betray with candour's open smile.
Too artless for distrust, the Monarch springs
To meet his latent foe on friendship's wings.
On as he moves, with dazzling splendour crown'd,
His feather'd chiefs the golden throne surround;
The waving canopy its plume displays,
Whose waving hues reflect the morning rays;
With native grace he hails the warrior train,
Who stood majestic on PERUVIA'S plain,
In all the savage pomp of armour drest,
The frowning helmet, and the nodding crest.
Yet themes of joy PIZARRO'S lips impart,
And charm with eloquence the simple heart;
Unfolding to the monarch's wond'ring thought
All that inventive arts the rude have taught.
And now he bids the musing spirit rise
Above the circle of surrounding skies;
Presents the page that sheds Religion's light
O'er the dark mist of intellectual night:
While, thrill'd with awe, the monarch trembling stands,
He dropp'd the hallow'd volume from his hands.
Sudden,[1] while frantic zeal each breast inspires,
And shudd'ring demons fan the rising fires,
The bloody signal waves, the banners play,
The naked sabres flash their streaming ray;
The trumpet rolls its animating sound,
And the loud cannon rend the vault around;

[1] Pizarro, who during a long conference had with difficulty restrained his soldiers, eager to seize the rich spoils of which they had now so near a view, immediately gave the signal of assault. At once the martial music struck up, the cannon and muskets began to fire, the horse sallied out fiercely to the charge, the infantry rushed on sword in hand. The Peruvians, astonished at the suddenness of an attack which they did not expect, and dismayed with the destructive effects of the fire-arms, fled with universal consternation on every side. Pizarro, at the head of his chosen band, advanced directly towards the Inca; and though his nobles crowded around him with officious zeal, and fell in numbers at his feet, while they vied one with another in sacrificing their own lives that they might cover the sacred person of their sovereign, the Spaniards soon penetrated to the royal seat; and Pizarro, seizing the Inca by the arm, dragged him to the ground, and carried him a prisoner to his quarters. (*Robertson's History of America.*)

While fierce in sanguine rage, the sons of Spain
Rush on Peru's unarm'd, defenceless train!
The fiends of slaughter urg'd their dire career,
And virtue's guardian spirits dropped a tear!
Mild ZORAI fell, deploring human strife,
And clos'd with prayer his consecrated life!—
In vain PERUVIA'S chiefs undaunted stood,
Shield their lov'd Prince, and bathe his robes in blood;—
Touch'd with heroic ardour, cling around,
And high of soul, receive each fatal wound;
Dragg'd from his throne, and hurried o'er the plain,
The wretched Monarch swells the captive train;
With iron grasp the frantic Prince they bear,
And feel their triumph in his wild despair.—
Deep in the gloomy dungeon's lone domain,
Lost ATALIBA wore the galling chain;
The earth's cold bed refus'd oblivious rest,
While throbb'd the woes of thousands at his breast;
ALZIRA'S desolating moan he hears,
And with the monarch's blends the lover's tears.
Soon had ALZIRA felt affliction's dart
Pierce her soft soul, and rend her bleeding heart;
Its quick pulsations paus'd, and chill'd with dread,
A livid hue her fading cheek o'erspread;
No tear the mourner shed, she breath'd no sigh,
Her lips were mute, and clos'd her languid eye;
Fainter, and slower heav'd her shiv'ring breast,
And her calm'd passions seem'd in death to rest.—
At length reviv'd, 'mid rising heaps of slain,
She prest with hurried step the crimson plain;
The dungeon's gloomy depth she fearless sought,
For love with scorn of danger arm'd her thought:
She reach'd the cell where ATALIBA lay,
Where human vultures haste to seize their prey.—
In vain her treasur'd wealth Peruvia gave,
This dearer treasure from their grasp to save;
ALZIRA! lo, the ruthless murd'rers come,
This moment seals thy ATALIBA'S doom.
Ah, what avails the shriek that anguish pours?
The look that mercy's lenient aid implores?
Torn from thy clinging arms, thy throbbing breast,
The fatal cord his agony suppress!—
In vain the livid corpse she firmly clasps,
And pours her sorrows o'er the form she grasps,
The murd'rers soon their struggling victim tear
From the lost object of her soul's despair!
The swelling pang unable to sustain,

Distraction throbb'd in every beating vein;
Its sudden tumults seize her yielding soul,
And in her eye distemper'd glances roll—
'They come!' the mourner cried with panting breath,
'To give the lost ALZIRA rest in death!
One moment more, ye bloody forms, bestow,
One moment more for ever cures my woe—
Lo! where the purple evening sheds her light
On blest remains! O! hide them, pitying night!
Slow in the breeze I see the verdure wave,
That shrouds with tufted grass my lover's grave;
Hark! on its wand'ring wing in mildness blows
The murm'ring gale, nor wakes his deep repose—
And see, you hoary form still lingers there!
Dishevell'd by rude winds his silver hair;
O'er his chill'd bosom falls the winter rain,
I feel the big drops on my wither'd brain.
Not for himself that tear his bosom steeps,
For his lost child it flows—for me he weeps!
No more the dagger's point shall pierce thy breast,
For calm and lovely is thy silent rest;
Yet still in dust these eyes shall see thee roll,
Still the sad thought shall waste ALZIRA's soul—
What bleeding phantom moves along the storm?
It is my ATALIBA's well-known form!
Approach! ALZIRA's breast no terrors move,
Her fears are all for ever lost in love.
Safe on the hanging cliff I now can rest,
And press its pointed pillow to my breast—
He weeps! in heaven he weeps!—I feel his tear—
It chills my trembling heart, yet still 'tis dear.
To him all joyless are the realms above,
That pale look speaks of pity and of love!
Ah come, descend in yonder bending cloud,
And wrap ALZIRA in thy misty shroud!'
As roll'd her wand'ring glances wild around,
She snatch'd a reeking sabre from the ground;
Firmly her lifted hand the weapon prest,
And deep she plung'd it in her panting breast!
''Tis but a few short moments that divide'—
She falt'ring said—then sunk on earth and died!

(1784 *1823*)

29 *To Sensibility*

In SENSIBILITY'S lov'd praise
I tune my trembling reed,
And seek to deck her shrine with bays,
On which my heart must bleed!

No cold exemption from her pain
I ever wish to know;
Cheer'd with her transport, I sustain
Without complaint her woe.

Above whate'er content can give,
Above the charm of ease,
The restless hopes and fears, that live
With her, have power to please.

Where, but for her, were Friendship's power
To heal the wounded heart,
To shorten sorrow's ling'ring hour,
And bid its gloom depart?

'Tis she that lights the melting eye
With looks to anguish dear;
She knows the price of every sigh,
The value of a tear.

She prompts the tender marks of love,
Which words can scarce express;
The heart alone their force can prove,
And feel how much they bless.

Of every finer bliss the source!
'Tis she on love bestows
The softer grace, the boundless force,
Confiding passion knows;

When to another, the fond breast
Each thought for ever gives;
When on another leans for rest,
And in another lives!

Quick, as the trembling metal flies
When heat or cold impels,
Her anxious heart to joy can rise,
Or sink where anguish dwells!

Yet though her soul must griefs sustain
Which she alone can know,
And feel that keener sense of pain
Which sharpens every woe;

Though she, the mourners' grief to calm,
  Still shares each pang they feel,
And, like the tree distilling balm,
  Bleeds others' wounds to heal;

Though she, whose bosom, fondly true,
  Has never wish'd to range,
One alter'd look will trembling view,
  And scarce can bear the change;

Though she, if death the bands should tear
  She vainly thought secure,
Through life must languish in despair,
  That never hopes a cure;

Though wounded by some vulgar mind,
  Unconscious of the deed,
Who never seeks those wounds to bind,
  But wonders why they bleed;—

She oft will heave a secret sigh,
  Will shed a lonely tear,
O'er feelings nature wrought so high,
  And gave on terms so dear.

Yet who would hard INDIFFERENCE choose,
  Whose breast no tears can steep?
Who, for her apathy, would lose
  The sacred power to weep?

Though in a thousand objects pain
  And pleasure tremble nigh,
Those objects strive to reach in vain
  The circle of her eye.

Cold as the fabled god appears
  To the poor suppliant's grief,
Who bathes the marble form in tears,
  And vainly hopes relief.

Ah, GREVILLE! why the gifts refuse
  To souls like thine allied?
No more thy nature seem to lose,
  No more thy softness hide.

No more invoke the playful sprite
  To chill, with magic spell,
The tender feelings of delight,
  And anguish sung so well;

That envied ease thy heart would prove
  Were sure too dearly bought
With friendship, sympathy, and love,
  And every finer thought.

(1786 *1823*)

30 *from On the Bill which Was Passed in England for Regulating the Slave Trade; a Short Time before Its Abolition*

  The hollow winds of night no more
In wild, unequal cadence pour,
On musing fancy's wakeful ear,
The groan of agony severe
From yon dark vessel, which contains
The wretch new bound in hopeless chains!
Whose soul with keener anguish bleeds,
As AFRIC's less'ning shore recedes—
No more where Ocean's unseen bound
Leaves a drear world of waters round,
Between the howling gust, shall rise
The stifled captive's latest sighs!—
No more shall suffocating death
Seize the pent victim's sinking breath;
The pang of that convulsive hour,
Reproaching man's insatiate power;
Man! who to AFRIC's shore has past,
Relentless, as the annual blast
That sweeps the Western Isles, and flings
Destruction from its furious wings!—
And woman, she, too weak to bear
The galling chain, the tainted air,—
Of mind too feeble to sustain
The vast, accumulated pain,—
No more, in desperation wild,
Shall madly strain her gasping child;
With all the mother at her soul,
With eyes where tears have ceas'd to roll,
Shall catch the livid infant's breath,
Then sink in agonizing death!
BRITAIN! the noble, blest decree
That soothes despair, is fram'd by thee!
Thy powerful arm has interpos'd,
And *one* dire scene for ever clos'd;
Its horror shall no more belong
To that foul drama, deep with wrong.

O, first of EUROPE'S polish'd lands
To ease the captive's iron bands;
Long, as thy glorious annals shine,
This proud distinction shall be thine!
Not first alone when valour leads
To rush on danger's noblest deeds;
When mercy calls thee to explore
A gloomy path, untrod before,
Thy ardent spirit springs to heal,
And, greatly gen'rous, dares to feel!—
Valour is like the meteor's light,
Whose partial flash leaves deeper night;
While Mercy, like the lunar ray,
Gilds the thick shade with softer day.
 Blest deed! that met consenting minds
In all but those whom av'rice binds,—
Who creep in interest's crooked ways,
Nor ever pass her narrow maze;
Or those whom hard indiff'rence steels
To every pang another feels.
For *them* has fortune round their bowers
Twin'd, partial nymph! her lavish flowers;
For *them* from unsunn'd caves, she brings
Her summer ice; for *them* she springs
To climes where hotter suns produce
The richer fruit's delicious juice;
While *they*, whom wasted blessings tire,
Nor leave *one* want to feed desire,
With cool, insulting ease demand
Why, for yon hopeless, captive band,
Is ask'd, to mitigate despair,
The mercy of the common air?
The boon of larger space to breathe,
While coop'd that hollow deck beneath?
A lengthen'd plank, on which to throw
Their shackled limbs, while fiercely glow
The beams direct, that on each head
The fury of contagion shed?—
And dare presumptuous, guilty man,
Load with offence his fleeting span?
Deform creation with the gloom
Of crimes that blot its cheerful bloom?
Darken a work so perfect made,
And cast the universe in shade?—
Alas! to AFRIC'S fetter'd race
Creation wears no form of grace!

(1788 *1823*)

31 *The Bastille, A Vision*

I

'DREAR cell! along whose lonely bounds,
Unvisited by light,
Chill silence dwells with night,
Save where the clanging fetter sounds!
Abyss, where mercy never came,
Nor hope the wretch can find;
Where long inaction wastes the frame,
And half annihilates the mind!

II

'Stretch'd helpless in this living tomb,
O haste, congenial death!
Seize, seize this ling'ring breath,
And shroud me in unconscious gloom.
BRITAIN! thy exil'd son no more
Thy blissful vales shall see—
Why did I leave thy hallow'd shore,
Ah, land ador'd, where all are free?'

III

BASTILLE! within thy hideous pile,
Which stains of blood defile,
Thus rose the captive's sighs,
Till slumber seal'd his weeping eyes.
Terrific visions hover near!
He sees an awful form appear!
Who drags his step to deeper cells,
Where stranger, wilder horror dwells!

IV

'O! tear me from these haunted walls,
Or these fierce shapes controul!
Lest madness seize my soul!
That pond'rous mask of iron[1] falls,
I see—' 'Rash mortal, ha! beware,
Nor breathe that hidden name!
Should those dire accents wound the air,
Know death shall lock thy stiff'ning frame.

[1] Alluding to the prisoner who has excited so many conjectures in Europe.

V

'Hark! that loud bell which sullen tolls!
  It wakes a shriek of woe
  From yawning depths below;
Shrill through this hollow vault it rolls!
  A deed was done in this black cell
Unfit for mortal ear—
  A deed was done when toll'd that knell,
No human heart could live and hear!

VI

'Arouse thee from thy numbing glance,
Near yon thick gloom advance;
The solid cloud has shook;
Arm all thy soul with strength to look—
Enough!—thy starting locks have rose—
Thy limbs have fail'd—thy blood has froze!—
On scenes so foul, with mad affright,
I fix no more thy fasten'd sight.

VII

'Those troubled phantoms melt away!
  I lose the sense of care—
  I feel the vital air—
I see—I see the light of day!
  Visions of bliss!—eternal powers!
What force has shook those hated walls?
  What arm has rent those threat'ning towers?
It falls—the guilty fabric falls!'

VIII

'Now, favour'd mortal, now behold!
  To soothe thy captive state
  I hope the book of fate;
Mark what its registers unfold:
  Where this dark pile in chaos lies,
With nature's execrations hurl'd,
  Shall Freedom's sacred temple rise,
And charm an emulating world!

IX

‘’Tis her awak’ning voice commands
Those firm, those patriot bands;
  Arm’d to avenge her cause,
  And guard her violated laws!—
Did ever earth a scene display
More glorious to the eye of day,
Than millions with according mind,
Who claim the rights of human kind?

X

‘Does the fam’d Roman page sublime
  An hour more bright unroll,
  To animate the soul,
Than this lov’d theme of future time?—
  Posterity, with rapture meet,
The consecrated act shall hear;
  Age shall the glowing tale repeat,
And youth shall drop the burning tear!

XI

‘The peasant, while he fondly sees
  His infants round the hearth
  Pursue their simple mirth,
Or emulously climb his knees,
  No more bewails their future lot,
By tyranny’s stern rod opprest;
  While freedom cheers his straw-roof’d cot,
And tells him all his toils are blest!

XII

‘Philosophy! O, share the meed
Of freedom’s noblest deed!
’Tis thine each truth to scan,
And dignify the rank of man!
’Tis thine all human wrongs to heal,
’Tis thine to love all nature’s weal;
To give our frail existence worth,
And shed a ray from heav’n on earth.’

(1790 *1823*)

32 *Sonnet to the Strawberry*

THE Strawberry blooms upon its lowly bed,
Plant of my native soil!—the Lime may fling
More potent fragrance on the zephyr's wing,
The milky Cocoa richer juices shed,
The white Guava lovelier blossoms spread—
But not, like thee, to fond remembrance bring
The vanished hours of life's enchanting spring;
Short calendar of joys for ever fled!
Thou bid'st the scenes of childhood rise to view,
The wild wood-path which fancy loves to trace;
Where, veil'd in leaves, thy fruit of rosy hue
Lurk'd on its pliant stem with modest grace.
But ah! when thought would later years renew,
Alas, successive sorrows crowd the space!

(1795 *1823*)

33 *Sonnet to the Curlew*

SOOTH'D by the murmurs on the sea-beat shore,
His dun-grey plumage floating to the gale,
The Curlew blends his melancholy wail
With those hoarse sounds the rushing waters pour.
Like thee, congenial bird! my steps explore
The bleak lone sea-beach, or the rocky dale,—
And shun the orange bower, the myrtle vale,
Whose gay luxuriance suits my soul no more.
I love the ocean's broad expanse, when drest
In limpid clearness, or when tempests blow:
When the smooth currents on its placid breast
Flow calm, as my past moments us'd to flow;
Or when its troubled waves refuse to rest,
And seem the symbol of my present woe.

(1795 *1823*)

34 The Charter, Lines Addressed by Helena Maria Williams, to Her Nephew Athanase C. L. Coquerel, On His Wedding Day

CHILD of my heart! while others hail
This festive morn' when joys prevail,
With careless wishes they may last,
Spite of all annals of the past;

As if for thee alone, secure,
Their fleeting nature would endure,
With roses strewing all thy way,
And life were but a bridal day;—
For me, by pensive thoughts opprest,
The future fills my anxious breast;
And flowers that fade, and joys that flee
Are not the things I ask, for thee!—
My heart for thee has learn'd to prove
The throbbings of a mother's love,
Since on thy cradle fell the tear
That mourn'd a sister's early bier;
And sure that angel's sainted prayer
Has shed sweet influence o'er my care;
To sorrow doomed in all the rest,
And only in her children blest!—
While now you sign with hope elate,
The civic register of fate;
Or, at the holy altar bow,
To ratify the plighted vow,
Which made aright, or breath'd amiss,
Includes all future woe, or bliss;
While kneeling youth, and weeping beauty
Hear the grave ritual of their duty,
And the stern rubrick well approve
That charges to be true to love;—
This compact that for ever binds
In holy links two kindred minds,
Their happiness the mutual barter,
This solemn league we'll call a CHARTER;
Th'allusion never can be wrong,
White omens to the name belong;
Palladium that has all withstood,
And harbinger of boundless good.—
And ever may its hallow'd law
Your willing hearts together draw!
Ah! may no *ultra* thirst of power
Embitter life's domestic hour;
No principles of feudal sway
Teach without loving, to obey;
The heart such joyless hommage slights,
And wedlock claims its bill of rights—
May you to virtue nobly just,
Disdain the whisper of mistrust;
Your truth her dark *police* may brave,
Made for the tyrant, and the slave.—
May discord pass with sullen tread,

Far from the threshold of your shed;
With accents that on harshness border,
And words that love would call to order,
Or VETO he would pine to hear,
Protesting only by a tear.—
Nor when true fondness with submission
Her right asserting of petition,
Shall meekly hint at some abuse,
Or some reform of gen'ral use,
Unheeding all that she may say,
Pass to the order of the day.—
Nor, bidding every blessing fade,
Let jealousy your peace invade;
Whose shadow clings to all that's dear,
And adds the lengthning shapes of fear;
Whose mind with sickly colours ting'd,
Discerns in all, the code infring'd;
Reads violations in the eye,
And marks the treason of a sigh;
Or loads a tear with false aspersion,
Mistaking sorrow for aversion;
Or construes into acts of guile
The tender pleadings of a smile;
Condemns unheard, with *ultra* fury,
Nor suffers love to call a jury,
Where innocence with pride appears,
Safe, in a trial by her peers.—
　Thus, having ne'er from duty swerv'd,
The faith of treaties well observ'd;
When time your destin'd lot shall fling
Of sorrow from his loaded wing;
For you, of other good bereft,
Unchanging love will still be left;
Not like the world he then will roam,
But rest, the morning star of home.
Not yours, their bitter fate, who know
That agony of lonely woe,
An altered heart was bound to share,
Nor find defence, nor charter there!—
　For you, to every duty true,
The Charter held in rev'rence due,
Each tender clause shall habit seal,
With no suggestion of repeal;
Firm to the law of true election,
And treating change with stern rejection;
Tho' time the graceful form has worn
To which fidelity was sworn.

For not alone with blooming youth
Is made that league of lasting truth;
The compact sign'd with beauty now,
Includes wan age, with wrinkled brow,
With tresses gray, with visage pale,
And eyes whose liquid lustre fail;
For then the hand, that shrivel'd thing,
Shall still display the nuptial ring,
Pledge of your faith, and cherish'd token
Of vows, thro' lengthen'd years unbroken;
When all that's left of passion's flame
Is friendship, with a dearer name!
Thus be the Charter'd code imprest
With all its statutes, on your breast;
No duty it enjoins forsook,
Till time at length, shall close the book;
And hope shall frame, for worlds to come,
A treaty that survives the tomb.

(1819)

CAROLINA NAIRNE
(1766–1845)

Lady Carolina Nairne was a Scottish poet, whose songs were to become hugely popular both during and after her lifetime. She was born in Gask, Perthshire, the daughter of Margaret (née Robertson) and a Jacobite laird, Laurence Oliphant. The Jacobitism that she inherited, in fact, came from both sides of her family, and she was to marry her Jacobite cousin, William Murray Nairne, an army Major, and live with him in Edinburgh. After his death (1830) and that of their son in 1837, she travelled widely across Europe and lived for some time in France.

Throughout her song-writing, she was at pains to conceal her identity. Her first songs were circulated anonymously and she went on to compose lyrics for traditional airs under the pseudonym of 'Mrs Bogan of Bogan' for the *Scottish Minstrel* between 1821–24. The alternative signature 'B.B.' also allowed her to hide her sex, recognizing that, as she put it, 'the balance is in favour of the lords of creation'. Not until after her death was her real name attached to her writing. In 1846 her songs were published as *Lays of Strathearn. The Life* and *Songs of the Baroness Nairne* (1869) went into two further and enlarged editions (1869; 1872), and it includes her most popular song, 'The Land O' the Leal'.

35 *Cradle Song*

Baloo, loo, lammy, now baloo my dear;
Now, baloo loo, lammy, ain minnie is here.
What ails my sweet bairnie? what ails it this nicht?
What ails my wee lammy? is bairnie no richt?

Baloo, loo, lammy, now baloo, my dear,
Does wee lammy ken that its daddie's no here?
Ye're rockin' fu' sweetly on mammie's warm knee,
But daddie's a-rockin' upon the saut sea.

Now hush-a-ba, lammy; now hush-a my dear;
Now hush-a-ba, lammy; ain minnie is here:
The wild wind is ravin', and mammie's heart's sair.
The wild wind is ravin', and ye dinna care.

Sing, baloo loo, lammy, sing baloo, my dear;
Sing, baloo loo, lammy, ain minnie is here:
My wee bairnie's dozin', it's dozin now fine,
And oh! may its wauk'nin' be blyther than mine.

(1869)

AMELIA OPIE
(1769–1853)

ALTHOUGH she is usually thought of as a novelist, Amelia Alderson (later Opie) had begun contributing poetry to journals, principally the *Monthly Magazine*, when only a teenager. She was born and lived for most of her life in Norwich, then a prosperous commercial city with a large dissenting community. Both her mother, Amelia (née Briggs) and father, James Alderson, a physician, were Unitarians. Her father was also a radical in politics and renowned for his generous approach to poorer patients. Amelia Opie received only a cursory education, although she learned a little French through private tuition. After the death of her mother in 1784, she was left to take over the charge of the household.

During her many visits to London in the 1790s she met John Opie, a painter, whom she was to marry in 1798. He is thought to have encouraged her writing. She had published a novel anonymously in 1790, but *The Father and Daughter: A Tale* (1801) was her first acknowledged and very successful piece of fiction. The novel also contained her poem, 'The Maid of Corinth'. In the same year she began publishing volumes of poetry. Both *An Elegy to the Memory of the Duke of Bedford* and *Poems* came out in 1802. The latter contains her two most popular poems, 'The Orphan Boy' and 'The Felon's Address to his Child'. It was an immediate success and continued to be reprinted until its sixth edition in 1811. *The Warrior's Return, and Other Poems* followed in 1808.

Amelia Opie's own radical politics were first publicly expressed in her attending the 1794 trials of the Jacobins, Horne Tooke and William Holcroft. In London she also moved amid literary and radical circles, which included Anna Laetitia Barbauld, Elizabeth Inchbald, William Godwin, and William Holcroft. She had first met Godwin in Norwich in 1793 and, although she was said also to admire Mary Wollstonecraft, her most famous novel, *Adeline Mowbray, or, The Mother and Daughter* (1805), in part modelled on the feminist's life, attacks Godwinian views on marriage.

Returning to Norwich after her husband's death in 1807, the poet was to convert to the Quaker religion in about 1814, which put an end to her novel writing. Along with her philanthropic work, she became active within the abolitionist movement, attending the London Anti-slavery Convention of 1840 as the Norwich delegate. Her anti-slavery poem, *The Black Man's Lament*, had been published in 1826. After taking up the Quaker faith, however, most of her literary energy was devoted to books on morality and her devotional poems, *Lays for the Dead*, were published in 1834.

36 *The Negro Boy's Tale*

'HASTE! hoist the sails! fair blows the wind!
Jamaica, sultry land, adieu!...
Away! and loitering Anna find!
I long dear England's shores to view!'

The sailors gladly haste on board,
Soon is Trevannion's voice obeyed,
And instant, at her father's word,
His menials seek the absent maid.

But where was 'loitering Anna' found? . . .
Mute, listening to a Negro's prayer,
Who knew that sorrow's plaintive sound
Could always gain her ready ear; . . .

Who knew, to sooth the slave's distress
Was gentle Anna's dearest joy,
And thence, an earnest suit to press,
To Anna flew the Negro boy.

'Missa,' poor Zambo cried, 'sweet land
Dey tell me dat you go to see,
Vere, soon as on de shore he stand,
De helpless Negro slave be free.

'Ah! dearest missa, you so kind!
Do take me to dat blessed shore,
Dat I mine own dear land may find,
And dose who love me see once more.

'Oh! ven no slave, a boat I buy,
For me a letel boat vould do,
And over wave again I fly
Mine own loved negro land to view.

'Oh! I should know it quick like tink,
No land so fine as dat I see,
And den perhaps upon de brink
My moder might be look for me! . . .

'It is long time since lass ve meet,
Ven I was take by bad vite man,
And moder cry, and kiss his feet,
And shrieking after Zambo ran.

'O missa! long, how long me feel
Upon mine arms her lass embrace!
Vile in de dark, dark ship I dwell,
Long burn her tear upon my face.

'How glad me vas she did not see
De heavy chain my body bear;
Nor close, how close ve crowded be,
Nor feel how bad, how sick de air!

'Poor slaves!... but I had best forget.
Dey say (but teaze me is deir joy)
Me grown so big dat ven ve meet
My moder vould not know her boy.

'Ah! sure 'tis false! But yet if no,
Ven I again my moder see,
Such joy I at her sight vould show
Dat she vould tink it must be me.

'Den, kindest missa, be my friend;
Yet dat indeed you long become;
But now one greatest favour lend,...
O find me chance to see my home!

'And ven I'm in my moder's arms,
And tell de vonders I have know,
I'll say, Most best of all de charms
Vas she who feel for negro's woe.

'And she shall learn for you dat prayer
Dey teach to me to make me good;
Though men who sons from moders tear,
She'll tink, teach goodness never could.

'Dey say me should to oders do
Vat I vould have dem do to me;...
But, if dey preach and practise too,
A negro slave me should not be.

'Missa, dey say dat our black skin
Be ugly, ugly to de sight;
But surely if dey look vidin,
Missa, de negro's heart be vite.

'Yon cocoa nut so smooth as silk,
But rough and ugly is de rind;
Ope it, sweet meat and sweeter milk
Vidin dat ugly coat ve find.

'Ah missa! smiling in your tear,
I see you know vat I'd impart;
De cocoa husk de skin I vear,
De milk vidin be Zambo's heart.

'Dat heart love you, and dat good land
Vere every negro slave be free, . . .
Oh! if dat England understand
De negro wrongs, how wrath she be!

'No doubt dat ship she never send
Poor harmless negro slave to buy,
Nor vould she e'er de wretch befriend
Dat dare such cruel bargain try.

'O missa's God! dat country bless!'
(Here Anna's colour went and came,
But saints might share the pure distress,
For Anna blushed at others' shame.)

'But, missa, say; shall I vid you
To dat sweet England now depart,
Once more mine own good country view,
And press my moder on my heart?'

Then on his knees poor Zambo fell,
While Anna tried to speak in vain:
The expecting boy she could not tell[1]
He'd ne'er his mother see again.

But, while she stood in mournful thought,
Nearer and nearer voices came;
The servants 'loitering Anna' sought,
The echoes rang with Anna's name.

Ah! then, o'ercome with boding fear,
Poor Zambo seized her trembling hand,
'Mine only friend,' he cried, 'me fear
You go, and me not see my land.'

Anna returned the artless grasp:
'*I* cannot grant thy suit,' she cries;
'But I my father's knees will clasp,
Nor will I, till he hears me, rise.

'For, should thine anxious wish prove vain,
And thou no more thy country see,
Still, pity's hand might break thy chain,
And lighter bid thy labours be.

'Here wanton stripes, alas! are thine,
And tasks, far, far beyond thy powers;
But I'll my father's heart incline
To bear thee to more friendly shores.

[1] 'I could not tell the imp he had no mother.' Vide Series of Plays on the Passions, by Miss Baillie, . . . Count Basil, page III.

'Come! to the beach! for me they wait!'
Then, grasping Zambo's sable hand,
Swift as the wind, with hope elate,
The lovely suppliant reached the sand.

But woe betides an ill-timed suit:
His temper soured by her delay,
Trevannion bade his child be mute,
Nor dare such fruitless hopes betray.

'I know,' she cried, 'I cannot free
The numerous slaves that round me pine;
But one poor negro's friend to be,
Might (blessed chance!) might now be mine.'

But vainly Anna wept and prayed,
And Zambo knelt upon the shore;
Without reply, the pitying maid
Trevannion to the vessel bore.

Mean while, poor Zambo's cries to still,
And his indignant grief to tame,
Eager to act his brutal will,
The negro's scourge-armed ruler came.

The whip is raised . . . the lash descends . . .
And Anna hears the sufferer's groan;
But while the air with shrieks she rends,
The signal's given . . . the ship sails on.

That instant, by despair made bold,
Zambo one last great effort tried;
He burst from his tormentor's hold, . . .
He plunged within the foaming tide.

The desperate deed Trevannion views,
And all his weak resentment flies:
'See, see! the vessel he pursues!
Help him, for mercy's sake!' he cries:

'Out with the boat! quick! throw a rope!
Wretches, how tardy is your aid!'
While, pale with dread, or flushed with hope,
Anna the awful scene surveyed.

The boat is out, . . . the rope is cast, . . .
And Zambo struggles with the wave, . . .
'Ha! he the boat approaches fast!
O father, we his life shall save!'

'But low, my child, and lower yet
His head appears; . . . but sure he sees
The succour given. . . . and seems to meet
The opposing waves with greater ease: . . .

'See, see! the boat, the rope he nears!
I see him now his arm extend! . . .
My Anna, dry those precious tears;
My child shall be *one negro's friend!*'

Ah! Fate was near, that hope to foil: . . .
To reach the rope poor Zambo tries; . . .
But, ere he grasps it, faint with toil,
The struggling victim sinks, and dies.

Anna, I mourn thy virtuous woe;
I mourn thy father's keen remorse;
But from my eyes no tears would flow
At sight of Zambo's silent corse: . . .

The orphan from his mother torn,
And pining for his native shore, . . .
Poor tortured slave . . . poor wretch forlorn . . .
Can I his early death deplore? . . .

I pity those who live, and groan:
Columbia countless Zambos sees; . . .
For swelled with many a wretch's moan
Is Western India's sultry breeze.

Come, Justice, come! in glory drest,
O come! the woe-worn negro's friend, . . .
The fiend-delighting trade arrest,
The negro's chains asunder rend!

(1802)

37 *Consumption*

CONSUMPTION, fairest of Death's craving brood!
But, ah! most treacherous too! thou smiling fate,
Hence! I conjure thee, hence from those I love!
For on the heart's best feelings thou canst play
A dread variety of hopes and fears.
Thy flattering hand paints the poor victim's cheek
With roses emulous of health's rich glow,
And to the sinking eye such lustre gives
As fills the eager glance of joy and love.
Thy long-devoted prey by thee is decked

With bright attractions ne'er till then its own,
As victims were of old with flowers adorned
Before they bled in pagan sacrifice:...
And as the schoolboy, whose expected sport
Adown some favourite stream or well-known walk
Thick gathering clouds and falling rains prevent,
If he of sunshine see one partial beam,
Fancies (fond dreamer!) general splendor near,...
So anxious friends thy beauteous seemings watch,
As o'er thy victim's restless couch they hang,
And hail them pledges that all danger's past;...
Pledges as sure as to the Patriarch's eye
Was the bright arch of ever-mingling hues:
But, in that very moment, (treacherous power!)
Upon security Death softly steals,
And on thy conquest lays his icy hand,
Smiling amidst the beauty thou hast made.

Ye who have watched beside a fading friend,
Unconscious that the cheek's luxuriant red
Bloomed like the nightshade with unwholesome beauty,
And that the bright dilated eye but owed,
Like mouldering wood, its lustre to decay,...
Ye who have wept, then smiled amidst your tears,
And checked forebodings which ill-founded seemed,...
Ye who have hoped even in death's dread presence,
And then been summoned, O heart-freezing call!
Affection's last sad duties to perform,
And hear upon the narrow dwelling's lid
The first earth thrown, (sound deadliest to the soul!...
For, strange delusion! then, and then alone,
Hope seems for ever fled, and separation,
The final separation, to begin)...
Ye who have felt all this... will on my verse
Drop, as you read, a sympathetic tear,
And, sighing, own the mournful picture just.

(1802)

38 *The Despairing Wanderer*

OH! 'tis an hour to misery dear!
No noise but dashing waves I hear,
Save hollow blasts that rush around,
For Midnight reigns with horrors crowned.

Lo! clouds in swarthy grandeur sweep
Portentous o'er the troubled deep:
O'er the tall rocks' majestic heads,
Lo! billowy vapour slowly spreads,
While Fancy, as she marks its swell,
Around it throws her magic spell:...
And see! fantastic shapes seem near,
The rocks with added height appear,
And from the mist, to seek the tide,
Gigantic figures darkly glide;
While, with quick step and hurried mien,
Pale Terror leads the shadowy scene.
Again loud blasts I shuddering hear,
Which seem to Fancy's listening ear
To toll some shipwrecked sailor's knell!
Of fear, of grief, of death, they tell.
Perhaps they bade yon foaming tide
Unheard-of misery scatter wide.

Hail! dread idea, fancy-taught,...
To me with gloomy pleasure fraught!
I should rejoice the world to see
Distressed, distracted, lost, like me.

Oh! why is phrensy called a curse?
I deem the sense of misery worse:
Come, Madness, come! though pale with fear
Be joy's flushed cheek when thou art near,
On thee I eager glances bend;
Despair, O Madness, calls thee friend!
Come, with thy visions cheer my gloom,...
Spread o'er my cheek thy feverish bloom,
To my weak form thy strength impart,
From my sunk eye thy lightnings dart!
O come, and on the troubled air
Throw rudely my disordered hair;
Arm me with thy supporting pride,
Let me all ills, all fears deride!
O bid me roam in tattered vest,
Bare to the wintry wind my breast,
Horrors with dauntless eye behold,
And stalk in fancied greatness bold!
Let me, from yonder frowning rock,
With thy shrill scream the billows mock;
With fearless step ascend the steep,
That totters o'er the encroaching deep;
And while the swelling main along
Blue lightning's awful splendors throng,...

And while upon the foaming tide
Danger and Death in triumph ride,
And thunder rends the ear of Night,
Rousing the form of pale Affright, . . .
Let me the mountain torrent quaff,
And midst the war of nature . . . laugh!

(1802)

39 *The Warrior's Return*

SIR WALTER returned from the far Holy Land,
And a blood-tinctured falchion he bore;
But such precious blood as now darkened his sword
Had never distained it before.

Fast fluttered his heart as his own castle towers
He saw on the mountain's green height;
'My wife, and my son!' he exclaimed, while his tears
Obscured for some moments his sight.

For terror now whispered, the wife he had left
Full fifteen long twelvemonths before,
The child he had claspt in his farewel embrace,
Might both, *then*, alas! be no more.

Then, sighing, he thought of his Editha's tears
As his steed bore him far from her sight,
And her accents of love, while she fervently cried,
'Great God! guard his life in the fight!'

And then he remembered, in language half formed
How his child strove to bid him adieu;
While scarcely he now can believe, as a man,
That infant may soon meet his view.

But should he not live! . . . To escape from that fear,
He eagerly spurred his bold steed:
Nor stopped he again, till his own castle moat
Forbade on the way to proceed.

'Twas day-break: yet still past the windows he saw
Busy forms lightly trip to and fro:
'Blest sight! that she lives,' he exclaimed with a smile,
'Those symptoms of housewifery show:

'For, stranger to sloth, and on business intent,
The dawn calls her forth from her bed;
And see, through the castle, all busy appear,
By her to their duty still led.'

That instant the knight by the warder was seen,
  For far flamed the cross on his breast;
And while loud blew the horn, now a smile, now a tear,
  Sir Walter's mixt feelings expressed.

''Tis I, my loved vassals!' the warrior exclaimed,...
  The voice reached his Editha's ears;
Who, breathless and speechless, soon rushed to his arms,
  Her transport betraying by tears.

'And dost thou still love me?' he uttered, when first
  A silence so rapturous he broke;
She tried to reply, but in vain... while her sobs
  A volume of tenderness spoke.

'Behold how I'm changed! how I'm scarred!' he exclaimed,
  'Each charm that I boasted is o'er:'...
'Thou hast bled for THY GOD,' she replied, 'and each scar
  Endears thee, my warrior, the more.'

'But where is my child?' he cried, pale with alarm,
  'Thou namest not my Alfred... my boy!'...
'And comes he not with you?' she said;... 'then some woe
  Embitters our beverage of joy.'

'What meanest thou, my love?'... 'When to manhood he grew,
  And heard of his father's great name,
"O let me", he cried, "to the Holy Land go,
  To share my sire's dangers, and fame.

' "Perchance my young arm, by the cause nerved with strength,
  May lower the Pagan's proud crest:
And the brave Christian knights, in reward of my zeal,
  May bind the red cross on my breast"...

' "And think'st thou," I said, "with the son I can part,
  Till the father be safe in my arms?
No... hope not I'll add to the fears of the wife
  The mother's as poignant alarms."

'I ceased... and his head on my bosom reclined,
  While his golden hair shaded his cheek;
When, parting his ringlets, I saw the big tears
  His heart's disappointment bespeak.

'The sight overcame me: "Most loved," I exclaimed,
  "Go, share in thy father's renown!
Thy mother will gladly, to dry up *thy* tears,
  Endure an increase of *her own*."

'He kissed me . . . he thanked me . . . I armed him myself,
  And girt his pure sword on his side;
So lovely he looked, that the mother's fond fears
  Were lost in the mother's fond pride.'

'He went then? . . . How long has my warrior been gone?'
  'A twelvemonth, my Walter, and more.'
'Indeed! . . . then he scarcely could reach the far land
  Until the last battle was o'er.'

'I told him, my Walter, what armour was yours,
  And what the device on your shield,
In hopes of your meeting.' . . . 'Alas!' he returned,
  'My armour I changed on the field!

'A friend whom I loved from the dawning of youth,
  For conquest and courage renowned,
Fell, fighting beside me, and thus he exclaimed,
  While life issued fast from the wound:

' "And must I then die ere the flag of the Cross
  Waves proudly o'er Saracen towers?
But grant me, loved Walter, this dying request,
  For victory must surely be ours:

' "My armour well tried, and my falchion, my shield,
  In memory of me deign to wear!
'Twould sooth me to know, when the victory comes on,
  That something of mine will be there!"

'I granted his wish, and his arms I assumed,
  While yet he the action could see,
And marked with delight that his last closing look
  Was fixt with fond pleasure on me.

'Yet now, this remembrance so dear to my heart
  Is clouded by anxious regret;
Since, but for this change on the field of the fight,
  The father and son would have met!'

'But if he has fought, and has fallen, my love!' . . .
  'Suppress,' cried the knight with a frown,
'A fear so ill-founded; . . . if Alfred had died,
  He'd have fallen a *child of renown*.'

Yet vainly he strove by the father's proud hopes
  To conquer the father's fond fears;
He feared for the life of his boy, though with smiles
  He answered his Editha's tears.

And more and more forced grew the smile on his lip,
His brow more o'erclouded with thought;
At length he exclaimed, 'From the field of renown
One mournful memorial I've brought.

'I grieve that I won it! . . . A Saracen chief
Fell bleeding before me in fight,
When lo! as I claimed him my prisoner and prize,
A warrior disputed my right.

' "I'm new to the battle," he cried, "and this prize
Will wreathe my young brow with renown,
Nor will I the conquest resign but with life: . . .
That chief by *this* arm was o'erthrown."

'His daring enraged me, . . . for mine seemed the stroke
Which laid the proud Saracen low; . . .
Besides, from his bosom depended no cross,
His right to such daring to show.'

'But surely, my Walter, the daring bespoke
A soul nobly eager for fame:
So many *your* laurels, that one you could spare, . . .
O tell me you granted his claim!'

'No, Editha, no! . . . martial pride steeled my heart,
The youth I to combat defied;
He fought like a hero! but *vainly* he fought, . . .
Beneath my strong falchion he died.'

'O ill-fated youth! how I bleed for his fate!
Perhaps that *his* mother, like me,
Had armed him, and blest him, and prays for his life,
As *I* pray, my Alfred, for thee! . . .

'But never again shall he gladden her eyes,
And haste her fond blessing to crave!
O Walter! I tremble lest you in return
Be doomed to the sorrow you gave!

'Say, did not the cross, when your victim he fell,
Lie heavy and cold on your breast; . . .
That symbol of him full of meekness and love,
Whose deeds *mercy* only expressed?'

'Yes . . . pity, shame, penitence seized on my soul;
So sweet too his voice was in tone!
Methought as he lay, and in agony groaned,
His accents resembled thine own.

'His casque I unlaced, and I chafed his cold brow,
And fain every wound would have healed;
So young, and so lovely he seemed, that I wept
As by him I tenderly kneeled.

'He saw my distress, and his last dying grasp
Forgiveness and kindness expressed;
And then, with a look I shall never forget,
He breathed his last sigh on my breast.'

'But what's this memorial?' with cheek deadly pale
His Editha falteringly cried: . . .
'This scarf from his bosom!' . . . he uttered no more,
For Editha sunk by his side.

Ah then in her danger, her pale look of death,
He forgot all the laurels he'd won.
'O father accurst!' she exclaimed, 'in that youth
You slaughtered your Alfred . . . your son!'

(1808)

40 *The Mad Wanderer, A Ballad*

(*Written to a Provincial Tune, and published by Mr Biggs.*)

THERE came to Grasmere's pleasant vale
A stranger maid in tatters clad,
Whose eyes were wild, whose cheek was pale,
While oft she cried, 'Poor Kate is mad!'

Four words were all she'd ever say,
Nor would she shelter in a cot;
And e'en in winter's coldest day
She still would cry, 'My brain is hot'.

A look she had of better days;
And once, while o'er the hills she ranged,
We saw her on her tatters gaze,
And heard her say, 'How Kate is changed!'

Whene'er she heard the death-bell sound,
Her face grew dreadful to behold;
She started, trembled, beat the ground,
And shuddering cried, 'Poor Kate is cold!'

And when to church we brought the dead,
She came in ragged mourning drest;
The coffin-plate she trembling read,
Then laughing cried, 'Poor Kate is blest!'

But when a wedding peal was rung,
With dark revengeful leer she smiled,
And, curses muttering on her tongue,
She loudly screamed, 'Poor Kate is wild!'

To be in Grasmere church interred,
A corpse one day from far was brought;
Poor Kate the death-bell sounding heard,
And reached the aisle as quick as thought:

When on the coffin looking down,
She started, screamed, and back retired,
Then clasped it . . . breathing such a groan!
And with that dreadful groan expired.

(1808)

Sketches of Saint Michael's Mount

Gratefully inscribed to
the Lord de Dunstanville
and
Sir John St Aubyn, Bart.

41 *Sketch the First*

Boast of Cornubia's shores, I bid thee hail!
Hail to thy castled brow! thy lofty head
Pointed like pyramid! Yes, there the tower,
And there the ramparts rise! But, needless they,
And powerless e'en the utmost art of man
To add to thee or dignity, or grace,
Undeck'd, uncastled, in thy native charms
More awfully sublime! for turrets then
Thou hadst thy rugged peaks—for battlements,
Crags of rough granite—for thy dungeon-keep,
The green recesses in you beetling crags—
For drawbridge, yonder causeway's rocky sand,
Which it would foil all mortal power to raise,
Or to let fall again—that pathway, left
By the kind waves at morn, or noon, or eve,
Which, with resistless force resume their own,
And who can stay them?—In that distant age
It was, ere building dared presume to clothe
Thy naked grandeur, that some pious men
First sought thy rock, on holy purpose bent;[1]

[1] 'When it was first consecrated to religious purposes is unknown; but the earliest time it appears on record, as a place of devotion, is the fifth century. . . . Edward the Confessor

And gave the bright angelic vision birth.
Whence comes thy name, oh, fearful phantasy?
How did the brain, which could conceive, survive
The grand appalling image fancy drew?
What says tradition? Did the vision come
In day's bright hour—and in what garb array'd?
Look'd the archangel[1] terrible as when
He with dark demons awful conflict held,
Meek, yet victorious? Was the lofty crest
Upon his casque of sunbeams fashion'd? No.
Twilight's mysterious hour, or darkest night
Would better suit such advent—gathering mists
Through which the moon would force some slanting rays,
Would easier image such a being forth.
Methinks that through his wide transparent wings
The stars of heaven were seen, and his tall spear
Was tipt with moonbeams! while afraid to gaze
Upon the o'erwhelming vision, to the earth
Appall'd the trembling hermit bow'd his head;
Then to the bright creation *added voice*.

What said the warrior angel? of his words
Do holy legends record bear? Suffice,
That soon upon the mountain's rugged brow
Rose the dark monastery—soon, alas!
To fortress chang'd—but not for works like these[2]
Would heavenly form descend. Not come to lure
Man, social man, from love's endearing ties,
And life's blest duties—and still less to change -
The home of cloister'd peace to scenes of war;
To stain thy verdant turf with human blood,
And for the hymn of praise, bid the loud drum

founded on it a priory of Benedictine monks, on whom he bestowed the property of the mount.... At the dissolution, its revenues were valued at £110 12s. per annum, and were bestowed, together with the government of the mount, then a military fort, on Humphrey Arundell, Esq.... In the first year of Elizabeth, it was granted by patent to Thomas Bellett and John Budden, who afterwards conveyed it to Robert Earl of Salisbury, from whose family it passed to Francis Basset, Esq. (the ancestor of Lord de Dunstanville) but previous to the last century, was sold to Sir John St Aubyn, whose descendant, Sir John St Aubyn, bart, still possesses it' (see *Beauties of England and Wales*).

[1] Jude 1: 9.

[2] 'The earliest transaction of a military nature, recorded to have happened at this mount, was in the reign of Richard I... The civil contentions, in the reign of Charles I, were the cause of the fortifications of the mount being encreased, till (in a chronicle of the proceedings of the time) the works were styled "impregnable and almost inaccessible"... They were, however, reduced, after being vigorously defended by the king's adherents, in the month of April, 1646, by Colonel Hammond... This was the *last* transaction of a military description that happened on this romantic spot' (see *Beauties of England and Wales*).

And din of arms the echoes round awake.
But, be thy rock convent- or castle-crown'd,
If mailed warrior, or if hooded monk
Be ruler of thy walls, and pace along
The weary length of their dark corridor,
Or youthful beauties smile away its gloom,
Telling of softer rule and brighter scenes,
Thou art so varied, wild, romantic, grand,
One gazes on thee with untired delight!—

How oft on eager feet I wandered forth
From my lone dwelling, on the terrac'd beach,
To gaze upon thee, in thy varied robe,
At morn, at noon, at twilight, and at eve;
And watch thy various tints, and light, and shade,
Which ever round thee like a garment hang.
Sometimes I've seen the brightly-bounding waves,
Like liquid emeralds, clasp thy frowning base,
By shadows veil'd—then climbing up thy sides,
Retreating thence—then rushing on again,
Seeming resolved to sport away thy gloom—
As playful children, half afraid, yet bold,
Clasp the lov'd parent's knees, whose brows are dark
With frowns unwonted, then, abash'd retire,
But, since uncheck'd, the bold caress renew—
And I have seen thee when thy verdant sides
Were clothed in yellow radiance—and again,
When to the west, on the deep crimson sky
Outlined in dark magnificence, thy form
Stood boldly forth! next, in a gorgeous stole
Of roseate hue, reflected from that sky,
I saw thee clad! then, thou wast dark again,
Save that the sinking sun, as parting gift,
Threw on thy loftiest height a coronal
Of golden rays, which brightest seem'd, methought,
When vanishing. The dying christian thus
In his last hour, sometimes distinctly gains
A glimpse of opening heaven, and sheds around
A brightning radiance, as his soul departs!

(1834)

42 *Sketch the Second*

MUCH had I heard of thee, thou sea-girt rock!
And I had seen thy wondrous heights portray'd
By him I lov'd—and I had oft admired
Thy grandeur on his canvass—but I found
The real mountain might indeed defy
Art's power to paint—but, till I near thee came
I could not feel thy vastness;[1] and at length
Around thy rocky base with weary feet[2]
I won my arduous way; full oft alarm'd
Lest the fierce wintry wind, which round me blew,
Should sweep me to the waves, or loose the crags
Of massy granite ever beetling forth,
As if about to hurl destruction wide;
And as I upward look'd, athwart me came
Such sense of thy dread magnitude, I felt
My admiration swallow'd up in awe;
And when I laboured up thy steep ascent,
And found, that though the storm was howling round,
And the wide waters roll'd in snow-white foam,
While not a boat could dare their fury brave,
In safety I upon thy brow could stand
Unconscious of their motion—I, secure,
On that tumultuous sea, as on the shore,
Because my feet on thee were planted; then
The thought of Him, the Rock of ages, came
Athwart my mind, whose type thou art, and prayer
To my full heart was given,—to have my faith
On that great Rock secure, as on thy heights
I felt my stedfast feet; and while I prayed,
A calm, a solemn calm, came o'er my soul,
And on the midnight air thanksgiving rose!

(1834)

43 *Sketch the Third*

THE time was midnight; and the wintry wind
Howl'd o'er the bosom of the foaming deep,
Which to its voice in louder roar replied,
When on the ramparts of that castled rock,
Sea-girt, which bears the great archangel's name,

[1] 'The distant view of the mount excites ideas of impressive grandeur, but the effect is considerably encreased when traversing its base, ascending its craggy sides, as slowly winding beneath its immense masses of pendant rock' (see *Beauties of England and Wales*).

[2] It is said that the mountain is more than a mile round the base.

I held my lonely watch—and held it, awe struck!
For ever and anon upon the blast,
Already terrible to hear, was borne
The fearful notice of the minute gun,
Distant, yet audible, and asking aid
For drowning wretches—ask'd perhaps, in vain;
And fancy, shuddering at the scene she drew,
Portray'd the vessel sinking in the deep!
Saw the blue lights hung on the shivering mast
In desperate haste, and vainly!—doom'd to serve
Only as funeral torches, to their grave
To light the struggling victims! on the blast
She hears a dread variety of sounds
At that dread moment! wild appalling oaths
From desperate lips! and there the mortal plunge,
Scarce heard amidst the waters' roar—and then,
The short, shrill, fruitless prayer for help! then comes
The fearful shriek of agonized despair!
But happier thoughts stole on me as the wind
Ceas'd its wild roar—and round the castle walls
I took my solitary walk, and hoped
The dark Atlantic heav'd with gentler swell
Its mighty billows—while the eastern waves
Began to wear a soft and pallid hue,
As yet, the source unseen—that unseen source,
The cause that led me to my midnight watch
On that tall rock, braving the driving storm;
For I was come to see the beauteous moon
In cloudless majesty her state assume;
But I was forced to wait upon her smile
As courtiers watch the smile of earthly queen,
And long I waited, on the battlements
Leaning with folded arms—with pensive eye
Marking the scene below—wide, billowy, dark,
Save where from lowly cottages which lay
Scattered around the mountain's foot below,
And from the dwellings on the distant shores,
As yet some lights put forth faint twinkling rays;
But when the distant clock, upon the wind,
Gave solemn notice of the midnight hour,
Lo! one by one I saw those welcome lights
Fade from the view, till not a single beam
Was left to tell that in the dark expanse,
And near that wilderness of waters then,
Another eye than mine a vigil kept;
But *I, alone*, seem'd waking!—Thus methought,
As life advances, one by one we mark

Our dearest friends and relatives expire!
No eye of love remains to cheer our age,
And we are left alone!

(1834)

44 *Sketch the Fourth*

STILL, darkness reign'd—and visionary forms
Of those long-lov'd, the distant, and the dead,
Floated before me on the mists of night.
And wrapt me in forgetfulness of all
I came to gaze upon! till with the clouds
On which my fancy sketch'd them, suddenly
They vanished! then, still slowly stealing forth,
The moon appeared, bidding each object wear
Her pallid livery; while distinctness spread
O'er hill and rampart, and the granite rocks
Below me threw upon their modest gray
A vest of warmer hue; but still night's queen
Delay'd her bright career; for rebels still
Remained to conquer, as dark-frowning clouds
And driving rain cross'd rudely o'er her path,
Till, like successful troops in war's red field,
The winds came rushing on, and, in a trice,
Drove rain, and mist, and rebel clouds away,
Like soldiers charging on a flying foe;
Then to her throne in undisputed power
The smiling queen arose, and round her shed
Her showers of diamonds—of recovered sway
The brilliant tokens—and with varied gems
Decking her subject waves—but still she had,
Like earthly queen, her favourites; and her gifts
She in one corner of the wide expanse
Heap'd so profusely, that the light they gave,
Made me discern e'en the green turf that sheaths
The rock's rough base, and there with mimic day
The sea, the shore, the crags, and mountain shone.
The scene, the sights I coveted, were mine.
From that steep eminence my eyes beheld
Three seas uniting[1] their deep waters roll,
Clasping the mountain in one glorious zone;
While, as their radiant ruler rose at length
To her supreme dominion; soon she mov'd
Her silver sceptre o'er her subject tides;

[1] The Atlantic, the British, and the Irish.

And beauty's magic spell around them threw,
Till, hush'd to calmness was each rebel wave;
And as it gently bow'd its shining head,
Seem'd softly murmuring peace, allegiance, love.

So may the light of gospel truth arise
To full and cloudless sway o'er every land,
Those mingling waters lave, and shine at length
To earth's remotest bounds! May that pure light,
As yon fair moon the subjugated waves,
Soothe each rebellious passion; drive away
All party bitterness, all bigot zeal,
Till every shore is in truth's radiance steeped;
Till on the mountains, vallies, rocks, and plains,
Love—Christian love—one general anthem pours.
And as those oceans meet around yon rock,
So round the Rock of ages, from whose side
Flow healing fountains, may the nations meet,
And in eternal blessed union join,
Till earth appears a prototype of heaven.

(1834)

45 *The Skeleton*

Some years ago, when Sir John St Aubyn was enlarging the chapel at St Michael's Mount, a wall resisted for some time the efforts of the workmen. At last, being desired by Sir John to persevere, they resumed their labours, and discovered a narrow cell, in which was the skeleton of a large man, who had evidently been bricked up to starve and die! A punishment in former times resorted to by monkish communities.

HAIL! once again, huge rock! whose front sublime
New graces gathers from the hand of time.
Hail! matchless mount! by him immortal made,
Who the sad death of Lycidas portray'd;
Whose magic muse, fresh from Castalia's fount,
Sung 'the great vision of the guarded mount';[1]
And gave the meed of 'a melodious tear'
To the young poet on 'his watery bier.'
The wondrous legends of those ancient days,
Were themes befitting Milton's classic lays:[2]

[1] Where 'the great vision of the guarded mount Looks towards Numania's and Bayona's hold.'

[2] The mount has been sung by other bards—by Sir Humphrey Davy, in his poem, called 'Mount's Bay', and by W. Lisle Bowles, a name also well known to fame.

And well might fancy, on the midnight storm,
Trace on thy crags th' archangel's shadowy form!
While such traditions, spite of reason, throw
A more than human grandeur round thy brow.

But to thy masses hanging o'er the deep,
From the green turf that clothes thy rocky steep,
Thy gothic chapel, and the social hall,
Whose carvings rude the antique chase recall;
Oh! not on these alone my feelings dwell,
My haunted memory sees the *secret cell.*

What stops yon workman in his eager toil?
Why does yon wall his utmost labour foil?
St Aubyn bids, and he renews his toils;
And see, no more he from the task recoils—
The harden'd mortar yields—the wall gives way,
The dark interior is disclos'd to day.
But horror-struck, behold him now retreat—
What object chains his late impatient feet?
In that small space, before his shrinking sight,
A ghastly skeleton's disclos'd to light!
But curiosity o'ercame alarm,
E'en o'er that object mystery threw a charm.
How came it there? is soon the general cry;
And just suspicion gives but *one* reply:—
Brick'd up within those suffocating walls,
Whose sight the gazer's shuddering eye appals,
In all the horrors of a living death
That human victim drew his parting breath!
What was his crime? it undivulg'd remains—
His cruel sentence that dark cell explains,
And shews what tortures, fiend-delighting plan!
Man once inflicted on his fellow-man.
To feel devouring thirst and hunger's pain,
With burning eye-balls, and with throbbing brain;
To feel life's powers by gradual pangs decay,
And pine in lingering agonies away;
Vainly to watch upon the stifling air,
To catch one pitying sound to check despair.
Appalling picture! scene, alas! too true;
Though o'er it truth may shed this soft'ning hue:—
What though fond mourners watch the dying bed,
And veils of kindness o'er death's image spread,
Still, where's the power that can this truth conceal?
We, for *ourselves*, death's closing strife must feel:
'Give me thy pangs,' devoted love may cry,
'Would I for thee could suffer them and die.'

But vain—how vain the wish to fondness true,
(Alas! that love can then so *little* do!)
Love can indeed await the parting sigh;
Can close with pious hand the sightless eye:
And having clos'd those eyes, whose cheerful rays
Shone the soft sunshine of our dearest days,
It starts, it mourns, to feel its tasks are o'er,
And weeps, that tenderest love can do *no more*.
And thou, poor victim of that cruel fate,
By fancied justice will'd or fiend-like hate,
Must still, though love had watch'd thy closing eye,
Have for thyself perform'd the *task to die*.
And though stern vengeance from thy breast might tear
The cross, the rosary to thy feelings dear,
In life's last hour, if he, whose pangs surpast
Whate'er of suffering is on mortals cast;
He, whose lov'd form was pictur'd on thy cross,
Bade thee the gold distinguish from the dross;
Taught that chang'd heart its inmost sins to feel,
And while he wounded, deign'd thy wound to heal;
Bade faith in him despair's dread power controul,
And whisper'd pardon to thy trembling soul,
Then, e'en the tenants of the grandest dome,
Death's call awaiting in the proudest home;
If toss'd on doubt's and fear's tempestuous sea,
Stretch'd on their beds of down might envy thee.

Peace to thy bones! within you hallow'd ground,
Where monks and warriors mouldering lie around,
And near, perhaps, thy judges and thy foes,
The castle's lord bade thy remains repose:
His pious care a Christian burial gave,
And thy pale relics found, at last, *a grave*.

Theme of my mournful lay, a long farewell!
Yet oft in memory shall I view thy cell:
Shall still that scene of pictur'd crime recall;
While fancy dares to lift oblivion's pall,
Still seem to stand within thy living tomb;
Still paint thy spectral figure on the gloom;
Still deem, whate'er thy crime, thy fate unjust,
And breathe a requiem to thy nameless dust!

(1834)

DOROTHY WORDSWORTH
(1771–1855)

BORN in Cockermouth in the Lake District of England, Dorothy Wordsworth was the third child of Ann (née Cookson) and John Wordsworth, an attorney and law-agent to Sir James Lowther. After the death of her mother in 1778, Wordsworth moved to the home of Elizabeth Threlkeld, in Halifax, Yorkshire, where she stayed until 1787. During this period, she was educated for a short time at a boarding-school in nearby Hipperholme, and subsequently at a day-school in Halifax. Her father's death in 1783 meant that the orphaned Wordsworth was left in the care of her guardians, Richard Wordsworth and Christopher Cookson. For a period of fourteen years, she lived with various relatives, until joining her brother William at Alfoxden House, Somerset, in 1797. It was during her stay there that she wrote her Alfoxden journal; it was also where the future Laureate, William, composed 'Tintern Abbey', his major poetic tribute to her. Thereafter, she remained for most of her life in William's company, travelling with him to Germany before settling into Dove Cottage at Grasmere, where she maintained a detailed journal between 1799 and 1803. On many occasions, Wordsworth frequently accompanied her brother, who married in 1802, on visits across England and in continental Europe. In addition, she occasionally worked as his amanuensis, writing out a copy of his poems for their friend, the poet and essayist Samuel Taylor Coleridge, to take to Malta in 1804.

Although most of Wordsworth's activity as an author was devoted to her highly regarded journals, she began writing poetry in 1805, and three of her poems appear anonymously in William's *Poems* (1815). Later, additional unsigned poems would appear in his collections of 1836 and 1842. Apart from time spent writing, much of her adult life was devoted to the upkeep of the family household. Childcare, as well as local charitable work, absorbed much of her attention. She was not, however, entirely dependent on her brother and his family. In 1822, she undertook a seven-week tour of Scotland with her friend, Joanna Hutchinson. Characteristically, she kept a journal of this tour. But on the advice of the poet, Samuel Rogers, she decided to dedicate herself to revising the diary she kept of her previous tour of Scotland in 1803. Wordsworth clearly hoped to make an income from her writing. This distinguished journal was not published in her lifetime, the first edition appearing in 1876. In 1829, Wordsworth experienced her first serious period of illness, and for the last twenty years of her life she would seem to have been suffering from senile dementia, even though there were periods of lucidity when she could turn her hand to letter-writing.

Although some of her correspondence was published in William A. Knight's *Memorials of Coleorton* (1887), it took until the 1930s before a substantial portion of her letters came to the public's notice in Ernest de Selincourt's three distinguished editions of *The Letters of William and Dorothy Wordsworth*. A two-volume edition of some of her journals was published in 1904, and a selection of poems taken from the journals came out in 1940. Again, it was de Selincourt who provided careful insights into these writings, and his edition of 1952 provided the basis for the numerous scholarly reprints of her prose works that are inspiring in their detailed accounts of nature. A number of previously unpublished poems by Wordsworth were printed in *The Wordsworth Circle* in

1978, and these have been the subject of pioneering feminist criticism by Margaret Homans.

46 *Thoughts on my Sick-Bed*

And has the remnant of my life
Been pilfered of this sunny Spring?
And have its own prelusive sounds
Touched in my heart no echoing string?

Ah! say not so—the hidden life
Couchant within this feeble frame
Hath been enriched by kindred gifts,
That, undesired, unsought-for, came.

With joyful heart in youthful days
When fresh each season in its Round
I welcomed the earliest Celandine
Glittering upon the mossy ground;

With busy eyes I pierced the lane
In quest of known and *un*known things,
—The primrose a lamp on its fortress rock,
The silent butterfly spreading its wings,

The violet betrayed by its noiseless breath,
The Daffodil dancing in the breeze,
The carolling thrush, on his naked perch,
Towering above the budding trees.

Our cottage-hearth no longer our home,
Companions of Nature were we,
The Stirring, the Still, the Loquacious, the Mute—
To all we gave our sympathy.

Yet never in those careless days
When spring-time in rock, field, or bower
Was but a fountain of earthly hope,
A promise of fruits & the *splendid* flower,

No—then I never felt a bliss
That might with *that* compare
Which, piercing to my couch of rest
Came on the vernal air,

When loving Friends an offering brought,
The first flowers of the year,
Culled from the precincts of our home,
From nooks to Memory dear.

With some sad thoughts the work was done,
Unprompted and unbidden,
But joy it brought to my *hidden* life,
To consciousness no longer hidden.

I felt a Power unfelt before,
Controlling weakness, languor, pain;
It bore me to the Terrace walk
I trod the Hills again;—

No prisoner in this lonely room,
I *saw* the green Banks of the Wye,
Recalling thy prophetic words,
Bard, Brother, Friend from infancy!

No need of motion, or of strength,
Or even the breathing air:
—I thought of Nature's loveliest scenes;
And with Memory I was there.

(composed 1832 *1978*)

47 *'When Shall I Tread Your Garden Path?'*

When shall I tread your garden path?
Or climb your sheltering hill?
When shall I wander, free as air,
And track the foaming rill?

A prisoner on my pillowed couch
Five years in feebleness I've lain,
Oh! shall I e'er with vigorous step
Travel the hills again?

(composed 1835 *1978*)

MARY TIGHE
(1772–1810)

BORN into a wealthy family in County Wicklow, Mary Tighe was the daughter of Theodosia (née Rosanna), a prominent member of the Methodist movement in Ireland, who claimed descent from Edward Hyde, first Earl of Clarendon. Her father, William Blachford, was a clergyman and librarian of Marsh's and St Patrick's libraries in Dublin. After his death in Mary Tighe's first year, her mother devoted herself to educating her daughter and her son, John. Mary Tighe received a classical education that was to inform her poetry, and she was also to become well read in French, Italian, and German literature. In 1793 she entered into an unhappy marriage with her cousin, Henry Tighe of Woodstock, County Wicklow, who was a member of the Irish Parliament from 1790 until the Act of Union. They were to spend most of their first eight years together in London.

Mary Tighe's poetry was not widely known during her lifetime. The only poem of hers to be circulated before her death was *Psyche; Or, The Legend of Love*, which was privately printed in 1805. The poem was written in Spenserian stanzas and narrates the story of Cupid and Psyche. In the Preface, she acknowledges her debt to Apuleius for the first two cantos. A posthumous volume of *Psyche* was brought out in 1811, which included some previously unpublished poems and was edited by her brother-in-law, William Tighe. Some of these additional poems were taken from her autobiographical novel in manuscript, *Selena*, which was written between 1801 and 1803, and is held in the National Library of Ireland. *Psyche* received mixed reviews, but was keenly received by the public, running through numerous editions in both Britain and America until 1853. It is said to have inspired John Keats's 'Ode to Psyche'. Mary Tighe is the subject of Felicia Hemans' poem, 'Grave of a Poetess'. The 1827 edition of the *Amulet* published two poems by Mary Tighe that had not appeared in the editions of *Psyche*: 'The Old Maid's Prayer to Diana' and 'On a Night-Blowing Cereus'.

In her early thirties, Tighe developed consumption and she was to be afflicted by this until her death in 1810. Her *Mary: a series of reflections during twenty years* was edited by her brother-in-law, William Tighe, and privately printed in 1811.

48 *from* Psyche, *Canto I*

[The poem portrays the trials of Psyche, who has earned the displeasure of Venus. After Cupid has accidentally pierced himself with the love dart intended for Psyche alone (Canto I), he accompanies her on her travels in disguise. Her trials allegorise the troubles that beset a young, sexually vulnerable and inexperienced young woman first entering the social world. She is, for instance, deceived by Vanity and Ambition (Canto III), and overcome by Glacella, or coldness, or insensibility to the sufferings of others (Canto VI), before she can achieve happiness. Eds.]

AND in the grassy centre of the isle,
Where the thick verdure spreads a damper shade,
Amid their native rocks concealed awhile,
Then o'er the plains in devious streams displayed,
Two gushing fountains rise; and thence conveyed,
Their waters through the woods and vallies play,
Visit each green recess and secret glade,
With still unmingled, still meandering way,
Nor widely wandering far, can each from other stray.

But of strange contrast are their virtues found,
And oft the lady of that isle has tried
In rocky dens and caverns under ground,
The black deformed stream in vain to hide;
Bursting all bounds her labours it defied;
Yet many a flowery sod its course conceals

Through plains where deep its silent waters glide,
Till secret ruin all corroding steals,
And every treacherous arch the hideous gulph reveals.

Forbidding every kindly prosperous growth,
Where'er it ran, a channel bleak it wore;
The gaping banks receded, as though loth

To touch the poison which disgraced their shore:
There deadly anguish pours unmixed his store
Of all the ills which sting the human breast,
The hopeless tears which past delights deplore,
Heart-gnawing jealousy which knows no rest,
And self-upbraiding shame, by stern remorse opprest.

Oh, how unlike the pure transparent stream,
Which near it bubbles o'er its golden sands!
The impeding stones with pleasant music seem
Its progress to detain from other lands;
And all its banks, inwreathed with flowery bands,
Ambrosial fragrance shed in grateful dew:
There young Desire enchanted ever stands,
Breathing delight and fragrance ever new,
And bathed in constant joys of fond affection true.

But not to mortals is it e'er allowed
To drink unmingled of that current bright;
Scarce can they taste the pleasurable flood,
Defiled by angry Fortune's envious spite;
Who from the cup of amorous delight
Dashes the sparkling draught of brilliant joy,
Till, with dull sorrow's stream despoiled quite,
No more it cheers the soul nor charms the eye,
But 'mid the poisoned bowl distrust and anguish lie.

Here Cupid tempers his unerring darts,
And in the fount of bliss delights to play;
Here mingles balmy sighs and pleasing smarts,
And here the honied draught will oft allay
With that black poison's all-polluting sway,
For wretched man. Hither, as Venus willed,
For Psyche's punishment he bent his way:
From either stream his amber vase he filled,
For her were meant the drops which grief alone distilled.

His quiver, sparkling bright with gems and gold,
From his fair plumed shoulder graceful hung,
And from its top in brilliant chords enrolled
Each little vase resplendently was slung:

Still as he flew, around him sportive clung
His frolic train of winged Zephyrs light,
Wafting the fragrance which his tresses flung:
While odours dropped from every ringlet bright,
And from his blue eyes beamed ineffable delight.

Wrapt in a cloud unseen by mortal eye,
He sought the chamber of the royal maid;
There, lulled by careless soft security,
Of the impending mischief nought afraid,
Upon her purple couch was Psyche laid,
Her radiant eyes a downy slumber sealed;
In light transparent veil alone arrayed,
Her bosom's opening charms were half revealed,
And scarce the lucid folds her polished limbs concealed.

A placid smile plays o'er each roseate lip,
Sweet severed lips! why thus your pearls disclose,
That slumbering thus unconscious she may sip
The cruel presage of her future woes?
Lightly, as fall the dews upon the rose,
Upon the coral gates of that sweet cell
The fatal drops he pours; nor yet he knows,
Nor, though a God, can he presaging tell
How he himself shall mourn the ills of that sad spell!

Nor yet content, he from his quiver drew,
Sharpened with skill divine, a shining dart:
No need had he for bow, since thus too true
His hand might wound her all exposed heart;
Yet her fair side he touched with gentlest art,
And half relenting on her beauties gazed;
Just then awaking with a sudden start
Her opening eye in humid lustre blazed,
Unseen he still remained, enchanted and amazed.

The dart which in his hand now trembling stood,
As o'er the couch he bent with ravished eye,
Drew with its daring point celestial blood
From his smooth neck's unblemished ivory:
Heedless of this, but with a pitying sigh
The evil done now anxious to repair,
He shed in haste the balmy drops of joy
O'er all the silky ringlets of her hair;
Then stretched his plumes divine, and breathed celestial air.

Unhappy Psyche! soon the latent wound
The fading roses of her cheek confess,
Her eyes bright beams, in swimming sorrows drowned,
Sparkle no more with life and happiness
Her parents fond exulting heart to bless;

She shuns adoring crowds, and seeks to hide
The pining sorrows which her soul oppress,
Till to her mother's tears no more denied,
The secret grief she owns, for which she lingering sighed.

(1805 *1811*)

49 *from* Psyche, *Canto III*

YET though the knight close wrapt in slumber lay,
Her steps, at distance, still the page pursued,
Fearful that danger might befal her way,
Or lest, entangled in the mazy wood,
Returning she should miss the pathway rude.
The lark now hails the sun with rapturous song,
The cheerful earth resounds with gratitude,
O'er the gay scene, as Psyche tript along,
She felt her spirits rise, her lightened heart grow strong.

And hark, soft music steals upon the ear!
'Tis woman's voice most exquisitely sweet!
Behold two female forms approaching near
Arrest with wonder Psyche's timid feet;
On a gay car, by speckled panthers fleet
Is drawn in gallant state a seeming queen,
And at her foot on low but graceful seat
A gentle nymph of lovely form is seen,
In robe of fairest white, with scarf of pleasant green.

In strains of most bewitching harmony,
And still adapted to her sovereign's praise,
She filled the groves with such sweet melody,
That, quite o'ercome with rapture and amaze,
Psyche stood listening to the warbled lays;
Yet with a sullen, scarce approving ear
Her mistress sits, but with attentive gaze,
Her eyes she fixes on a mirror clear
Where still by fancy's spell unrivalled charms appear.

And, as she looked with aspect ever new,
She seemed on change and novel grace intent,
Her robe was formed of ever varying hue,
And whimsically placed each ornament;
On her attire, with rich luxuriance spent,
The treasures of the earth, the sea, the air,
Are vainly heaped her wishes to content;
Yet were her arms and snowy bosom bare,
And both in painted pride shone exquisitely fair.

Her braided tresses in profusion drest,
Circled with diadem, and nodding plumes,
Sported their artful ringlets o'er her breast,
And to the breezes gave their rich perfumes;
Her cheek with tint of borrowed roses blooms:
Used to receive from all rich offerings,
She quaffs with conscious right the fragrant fumes
Which her attendant from a censer flings,
Who graceful feeds the flame with incense while she sings.

Soon as her glance fair Psyche's form had caught,
Her soft attendant smiling she addressed:
'Behold, Lusinga! couldst thou e'er have thought
'That these wild woods were so in beauty blest?
'Let but that nymph in my attire be drest
'And scarce her loveliness will yield to mine!
'At least invite her in our bower to rest,
'Before her eyes let all my splendor shine,
'Perhaps to dwell with us her heart we may incline.'

With softest smile applauding all she heard,
Lusinga bowing left her golden seat,
And Psyche, who at first in doubt had feared
While listening to the lay so silver sweet,
Now passive followed with unconscious feet;
Till Constance, all alarmed, impatient flew,
And soft his whispers of the maid entreat
To fly the Syren's song, for well he knew
What lurking dangers hence would to his Lord ensue.

'Oh, do not trust her treacherous lips,' he cried,
'She is the subtle slave of Vanity,
'Her queen, the child of folly, and of pride,
'To lure thee to her power each art will try,
'Nor ever will release thee peaceably.'
He spoke, but spoke in vain, for lo! from far,
Of giant port they fast approaching spy
A knight, high mounted on a glittering car,
From whose conspicuous crest flames wide a dazzling star.

'Psyche, escape! Ambition is at hand!'
The page exclaims: while swift as thought he flies;
She would have followed, but with parley bland
Lusinga soon her terrors pacifies.
'Fair nymph, ascend my car,' the sovereign cries,
'I will convey thee where thy wishes lead,
'Haply the safest course I may advise
'How thou thy journey mayst perform with speed;
'For ne'er in woods to dwell such beauty was decreed.'

So gently urgent her consent they wooed
With much persuasion of the stranger knight,
That yielding Psyche now no more withstood,
But pointing out to her observant sight
The humble cot where she had passed the night,
She prayed her kind conductress there to turn,
And promised to herself what vast delight
Her wondering knight would feel at her return,
And with what blushing shame the timid page would burn.

But scarcely had she climbed the fatal car
When swifter than the wind the panthers flew,
The traversed plains and woods, receding far,
Soon shut from trembling Psyche's anxious view
The spot where she had left her guardian true;
With desperate efforts, all in vain she tries
To escape the ills which now too sure she knew
Must from her ill-placed confidence arise:
Betrayed—Ah! self-betrayed, a wretched sacrifice.

She strove to quit the car with sudden bound,
Ah, vain attempt! she now perceived too late
A thousand silken trammels, subtly wound
O'er her fair form, detained her as she sate:
Lost in despair she yields to her sad fate,
And silent hears but with augmented fright
The queen describe her brother's splendid state,
Who now outstripped them by his rapid flight,
And prest his foaming steeds to gain the arduous height.

High o'er the spacious plain a mountain rose,
A stately castle on its summit stood:
Huge craggy cliffs behind their strength oppose
To the rough surges of the dashing flood;
The rocky shores a boldly rising wood
On either side conceals; bright shine the towers
And seem to smile upon the billows rude.
In front the eye, with comprehensive powers,
Sees wide extended plains enriched with splendid bowers.

Hither they bore the sad reluctant fair,
Who mounts with dizzy eye the awful steep;
The blazing structure seems high poised in air,
And its light pillars tremble o'er the deep:
As yet the heavens are calm, the tempests sleep,
She knows not half the horrors of her fate:
Nor feels the approaching ruin's whirlwind sweep:
Yet with ill-boding fears she past the gate,
And turned with sickening dread from scenes of gorgeous state.

In vain the haughty master of the hall
Invites her to partake his regal throne,
With cold indifference she looks on all
The gilded trophies, and the well-wrought stone
Which in triumphal arches proudly shone:
And as she casts around her timid eye,
Back to her knight her trembling heart is flown,
And many an anxious wish, and many a sigh
Invokes his gallant arm protection to supply.

Sudden the lurid heavens obscurely frown,
And sweeping gusts the coming storm proclaim;
Flattery's soft voice the howling tempests drown,
While the roofs catch the greedy lightning's flame.
Loud in their fears, the attendant train exclaim
The light built fabric ne'er can stand the blast
And all its insecure foundations blame:
Tumultuously they rush: the chief aghast
Beholds his throne o'erturned, his train dispersing fast.

Psyche dismayed, yet thoughtful of escape,
In anxious silence to the portal prest;
And freedom would have hailed in any shape
Though seen in death's tremendous colours drest:
But ah! she feels the knight's strong grasp arrest
Her trembling steps. 'Think not,' he cries, 'to fly
'With yon false crowd who by my favours blest,
'Can now desert me when with changeful eye
'Inclement fortune frowns from yon dark angry sky.'

While yet he spoke loud bursts the groaning hall,
With frightful peal the thundering domes resound,
Disjointed columns in wild ruin fall,
While the huge arches tremble to the ground.
Yet unappalled amid the crush is found
The daring chief: his hold he firm maintains
Though hideous devastation roars around;
Plunged headlong down his prey he stills sustains,
Who in his powerful grasp in death-like swoon remains.

Down sinks the palace with its mighty lord,
Hurled from the awful steep with vehemence
Even to the floods below, which angry roared
And gaping wide received the weight immense:
Indignant still, with fearless confidence
He rose, high mounting o'er the heaving waves;
Against their rage one arm is his defence,
The other still his lovely burden saves,
Though strong the billows beat, and fierce the tempest raves.

The blazing star yet shone upon his brow,
And flamed triumphant o'er the dashing main;
He rides secure the watery waste, and now
The sheltering shore he might in safety gain;
The sheltering shore he shuns with proud disdain,
And breasts the adverse tide. Ah, rash resource!
Yon vessel, Prince, thou never shalt attain!
For plunging 'mid the deep, with generous force,
See where the lion's lord pursues thy hardy course!

(1805 *1811*)

50 *from* Psyche, *Canto VI*

ALMOST unconscious they their course pursue,
So smooth the vessel cuts the watery plain;
The wide horizon to their boundless view
Gives but the sky, and Neptune's ample reign:
Still the unruffled bosom of the main
Smiles undiversified by varying wind;
No toil the idle mariners sustain,
While, listless, slumbering o'er his charge reclined,
The pilot cares no more the unerring helm to mind.

With light exulting heart glad Psyche sees
Their rapid progress as they quit the shore:
Yet weary languor steals by slow degrees
Upon her tranquil mind; she joys no more
The never changing scene to wander o'er
With still admiring eye; the enchanting song
Yields not that lively charm it knew before,
When first enraptured by his tuneful tongue
She bad her vocal knight the heavenly strain prolong.

A damp chill mist now deadens all the air,
A drowsy dullness seems o'er all to creep,
No more the heavens their smile of brightness wear,
The winds are hushed, while the dim glassy deep
Oppressed by sluggish vapours seems to sleep;
See his light scarf the knight o'er Psyche throws,
Solicitous his lovely charge to keep
From still increasing cold; while deep repose
Benumbs each torpid sense and bids her eye-lids close.

Now as with languid stroke they ply the oars,
While the dense fog obscures their gloomy way;
Hymen, well used to coast these dangerous shores,
Roused from the dreaming trance in which he lay,
Cries to the knight in voice of dread dismay,
'Steer hence they bark, oh! yet in time beware;
'Here lies Petrea, which with baneful sway
'Glacella rules, I feel the dank cold air,
'I hear her chilling voice, methinks it speaks despair!'

Even while he speaks, behold the vessel stands
Immoveable! in vain the pilot tries
The helm to turn; fixed in the shallow strands,
No more obedient to his hand, it lies,
The disappointed oar no aid supplies
While sweeping o'er the sand it mocks their force.
The anxious knight to Constance now applies,
To his oft tried assistance has recourse,
And bids his active mind design some swift resource.

Debating doubtfully awhile they stood,
At length on their united strength rely,
To force the bark on the supporting flood;
They rouse the seamen, who half slumbering lie,
Subdued and loaded by the oppressive sky.
Then wading mid the fog, with care explore
What side the deepest waters may supply,
And where the shallows least protect the shore,
While through their darksome search the star sheds light before.

Mean time deep slumbers of the vaporous mist
Hang on the heavy eye-lids of the fair;
And Hymen too, unable to resist
The drowsy force of the o'erwhelming air,
Laid at her feet at length forgets his care.
When lo! Glacella's treacherous slaves advance,
Deep wrapt in thickest gloom; the sleeping pair
They seize, and bear away in heedless trance,
Long ere her guardian knight suspects the bitter chance.

Thus the lorn traveller imprudent sleeps
Where his high glaciers proud Locendro shews;
Thus o'er his limbs resistless torpor creeps,
As yielding to the fatal deep repose
He sinks benumbed upon the Alpine snows,
And sleeps no more to wake; no more to view
The blooming scenes his native vales disclose,
Or ever more the craggy path pursue,
Or o'er the lichened steep the chamois chase renew.

Lo! to their queen they bear their sleeping prey,
Deep in her ice-built castle's gloomy state,
There on a pompous couch they gently lay
Psyche, as yet unconscious of her fate,
And when her heavy eyes half opening late
Dimly observe the strange and unknown scenes,
As in a dream she views her changed estate,
Gazing around with doubtful, troubled mien,
Now on the stupid crowd, now on their dull proud queen.

With vacant smile, and words but half exprest,
In one ungracious, never-varying tone,
Glacella welcomes her bewildered guest,
And bids the chief supporter of her throne
Approach and make their mighty mistress known.
Proud Selfishness, her dark ill-favoured lord!
Her gorgeous seat, which still he shared alone,
He slowly leaves obedient to her word,
And ever as he moved the cringing train adored.

Nought of his shapeless form to sight appears,
Impenetrable furs conceal each part;
Harsh and unpleasing sounds in Psyche's ears
That voice which had subdued full many a heart;
While he, exerting every specious art,
Persuades her to adore their queen's control;
Yet would he not Glacella's name impart,
But with false title, which she artful stole
From fair Philosophy, deludes the erring soul.

'Rest, happy fair!' he cries, 'who here hast found
'From all the storms of life a safe retreat,
'Sorrow thy breast henceforth no more shall wound
'Nor care invade thee in this quiet seat:
'The voice of the distressed no more shall meet
'Thy sympathising ear; another's woes
'Shall never interrupt the stillness sweet,
'Which here shall hush thee to serene repose,
'Nor damp the constant joys these scenes for thee disclose....'

(1805 *1811*)

51

The Lily

MAY, 1809

How withered, perished seems the form
Of yon obscure unsightly root!
Yet from the blight of wintry storm,
It hides secure the precious fruit.

The careless eye can find no grace,
No beauty in the scaly folds,
Nor see within the dark embrace
What latent loveliness it holds.

Yet in that bulb, those sapless scales,
The lily weeps her silver vest,
'Till vernal suns and vernal gales
Shall kiss once more her pregnant breast.

Yes, hide beneath the mouldering heap
The undelighting slighted thing;
There in the cold earth buried deep,
In silence let it wait the spring.

Oh! many a stormy night shall close
In gloom upon the barren earth,
While still, in undisturbed repose,
Uninjured lies the future birth;

And Ignorance, with sceptic eye,
Hope's patient smile shall wondering view;
Or mock her fond credulity,
As her soft tears the spot bedew.

Sweet tear of hope, delicious tear!
The sun, the shower indeed shall come;
The promised verdant shoot appear,
And nature bid her blossoms bloom.

And thou, O virgin Queen of Spring!
Shalt, from thy dark and lowly bed,
Bursting thy green sheath's silken string,
Unveil thy charms, and perfume shed;

Unfold thy robes of purest white,
Unsullied from their darksome grave,
And thy soft petals silvery light
In the mild breeze unfettered wave.

So Faith shall seek the lowly dust
  Where humble Sorrow loves to lie,
And bid her thus her hopes entrust,
  And watch with patient, cheerful eye;

And bear the long, cold, wintry night,
  And bear her own degraded doom,
And wait till Heaven's reviving light,
  Eternal Spring! shall burst the gloom.

(1811)

CHARLOTTE RICHARDSON
(1775–1850?)

Born into a working-class family called Smith, in York, and receiving only a cursory education at a Grey-coat school, Charlotte Richardson went into service at 16 years of age. In 1802 she married a shoemaker, Mr Richardson. Both her husband and their two-month old baby contracted pulmonary consumption; only the child survived.

One of her poems was presented to Catharine Cappe, who, on inquiring further, received a book of manuscript poems by the same hand. A selection of these verses were then edited by Catharine Cappe and printed by subscription as *Poems Written on Different Occasions* in 1806. Four more books of Charlotte Richardson's poetry were published between 1809 and 1823, including *Waterloo, A Poem, on the late Victory* (1815). She also wrote a story in verse (1817) and a two-volume novel in 1821.

52 *Ode on Visiting the Retreat near York; a House Erected by the Society of Friends, for the Reception of Insane Persons*

Hail to these tranquil shades, this calm retreat,
  Scenes sacred to the children of Despair!
Here mild Benevolence has fix'd her seat,
  And here, the social Virtues oft repair.
    Compassion tries each soothing art,
  And Sympathy, with pitying eye
    Pours balm into the bleeding heart,
  And breathes the sorrowing sigh;
    Here modest Meekness dwells, and here
    Humanity dispels each fear;
  Attentive, they by every method strive,
  The glimmering spark of reason to revive.

In safety here, the maniac wildly roves,
No curious eyes his wand'ring steps descry,
As swift he paces through these shady groves,
Or on the landscape casts his vacant eye.
Here, melancholy, pensive child,
Sits list'ning to the wood-lark's strains,
Or in sad accents, sweetly wild,
Of all her fancied woe complains.
That downcast look, that head reclin'd,
Those tresses waving from the wind,
The ruin of her lovely form,
Her dress neglected and forlorn,
All speak a mind by anguish torn—
While oft beneath the spreading shade,
Of yonder weeping willow laid,
She weaves fresh garlands for her lover's head
Then starts, and breathless listens for his well-known tread.
—Ye mourning relatives, suppress your fears,
For they whose fate, incessant you deplore,
Shall soon return to wipe away your tears,
And happiness again to you restore—
For lo, to calm the tumult of the breast,
Which madness had too long possesst;
To chase away the fiend, Despair,
To clear the brow of gloomy Care;
Bid pensive Melancholy cease to mourn,
Calm reason re-assume her seat;
Each intellectual power return,
Heaven bade this structure rise, and call'd it the retreat.

(1806)

53 *The Negro, Sept. 1806*

WHENCE that agonizing groan?
Whence those shrieks that rend the air?
'Tis the sable negro's moan,
'Tis the language of despair.
See the hapless mourner stand,
Hear him all his woes deplore,
Stolen from his native land,
Never to behold it more!

Yet, though dear his native lot,
Higher griefs his bosom swell,

For in yon far distant spot,
His love'd wife and children dwell.
Far from wife and children torn,
All his bosom held most dear,
Can he cease his loss to moan?
Can he dry the flowing tear?

Fancy oft before his eyes
Brings the objects of his love;
Bids his native valleys rise,
Tow'ring hill and orange grove.
Soon the whip's heart-rending sound
Wakes him from his pleasing dream;
Hark! the echoing strokes rebound—
Stop, monsters! see that crimson stream!

Blush, ye Britons! blush for shame,
Let compunction seize your mind;
Dare ye boast the Christian name,
While ye prey on human kind?
Is it thus the Faith ye spread?
Thus advance your Saviour's cause?
While you on his precepts tread,
Will you disobey his laws?

Rise ye noble friendly band,[1]
In whose hearts compassion glows;
Rise, ye patriots of our land,
Ye who feel for Afric's woes.
Wilberforce shall lead the way,
His exertions ne'er shall cease,
Till Oppression yields her sway,
And the oppressed, taste of peace.

(1809)

[1] Alluding to the Society of Friends, whose humane endeavours to ameliorate the evils of slavery, while it exists, and to procure the total abolition of that most inhuman traffic, are well known.

LUCY AIKIN
(1781–1864)

DAUGHTER of John Aikin, author and physician, and Martha (née Jennings), and niece of Anna Laetitia Barbauld, Lucy Aikin was born in Warrington. She was educated mostly at home by her father, following his historical and biographical interests and learning French, Italian, and Latin. Having moved to Yarmouth in 1784, the family then lived in Hampstead from 1822, after the death of her father. Lucy Aikin remained in Hampstead for most of her life and there became a close friend of Joanna Baillie.

She began writing as a translator, moving on to edit a collection of *Poetry for Children* (1803) and produce her major poetical work, *Epistles on Women* (1810), of which we print the first, which her biographer defined as 'moral and didactic poetry of which Pope had given the moral' (1864). This volume included miscellaneuous poems, mostly drawn from her earlier contributions to journals, such as the *Athenaeum*. Her fiction, *Lorimer: A Tale* (1814), was followed by the four historical works for which she was best known; these were written between 1818 and 1843, concluding with her *Life of Addison*, which was reviewed somewhat critically by Thomas Macaulay for the *Edinburgh Review* (July 1843). Aikin was a liberal and a feminist. Her Unitarian beliefs, along with her views on politics, philosophy, and literature, are expressed in her letters to the Revd Dr W. E. Channing, a Unitarian minister of Boston (1826–42). These letters were collected posthumously in the *Memoirs, Miscellanies and Letters of... Lucy Aikin* (1864), edited by her friend, P. H. Le Breton. Aikin wrote a memoir of her father (1823) and one of Anna Laetitia Barbauld (1825), with whose poetry she had been familiar since childhood.

54 *Epistles on the Character and Condition of Women, in Various Ages and Nations, I*

Argument of Epistle

Subject proposed—the fame of man extended over every period of life—that of woman transient as the beauty on which it is founded—Man renders her a trifler, then despises her, and makes war upon the sex with Juvenal and Pope. A more impartial view of the subject to be attempted. Weakness of woman, and her consequent subserviency. General view of various states of society undertaken. Birth of Eve—Angels prophesy the doom of the sex—description of Adam before he sees her—a joyless, hopeless, indolent creature. Meeting of Adam and Eve—Change produced in both—their mutual happiness and primary equality. Reflections. Conclusion.

HEAR, O my friend, my Anna, nor disdain
My sober lyre and moralizing strain!
I sing the Fate of Woman:... Man to man
Adds praise, and glory lights his mortal span;

Creation's lord, he shines from youth to age,
The blooming warrior or the bearded sage;
But she, frail offspring of an April morn,
Poor helpless passenger from love to scorn,
While dimpled youth her sprightly cheek adorns
Blooms a sweet rose, a rose amid the thorns;
A few short hours, with faded charms to earth
She sinks, and leaves no vestige of her birth.
E'en while the youth, in love and rapture warm,
Sighs as he hangs upon her beauteous form,
Careless and cold he views the beauteous mind,
For virtue, bliss, eternity designed.
'Banish, my fair,' he cries, 'those studious looks;
Oh! what should beauty learn from crabbed books?
Sweetly to speak and sweetly smile be thine;
Beware, nor change that dimple to a line!'

Well pleased she hears, vain triumph lights her eyes;
Well pleased, in prattle and in smiles complies;
But eyes, alas! grow dim, and roses fade,
And man contemns the trifler he has made.
The glass reversed by magic power of Spleen,
A wrinkled idiot now the fair is seen;
Then with the sex his headlong rage must cope,
And stab with Juvenal, or sting with Pope.
Be mine, while Truth with calm and artless grace
Lifts her clear mirror to the female face,
With steadier hand the pencil's task to guide,
And win a blush from Man's relenting pride.

No Amazon, in frowns and terror drest,
I poise the spear, or nod the threatening crest,
Defy the law, arraign the social plan,
Throw down the gauntlet in the face of man,
And, rashly bold, divided empire claim,
Unborrowed honours, and an equal's name:
No, Heaven forbid! I touch no sacred thing,
But bow to Right Divine in man and king;
Nature endows him with superior force,
Superior wisdom then I grant, of course;
For who gainsays the despot in his might,
Or when was ever weakness in the right?
With passive reverence too I hail the law,
Formed to secure the strong, the weak to awe,
Impartial guardian of unerring sway,
Set up by man for woman to obey.

In vain we pout or argue, rail or chide,
He mocks our idle wrath and checks our pride;
Resign we then the club and lion's skin,
And be our sex content to knit and spin;
To bow inglorious to a master's rule,
And good and bad obey, and wise and fool;
Here a meek drudge, a listless captive there,
For gold now bartered, now as cheap as air;
Prize of the coward rich or lawless brave,
Scorned and caressed, a plaything and a slave,
Yet taught with spaniel soul to kiss the rod,
And worship man as delegate of God.

Ah! what is human life? a narrow span
Eked out with cares and pains to us and man;
A bloody scroll that vice and folly stain,
That blushing Nature blots with tears in vain,
That frowning Wisdom reads with tone severe,
While Pity shudders with averted ear.
Yet will I dare its varying modes to trace
Through many a distant tribe and vanisht race;
The sketch perchance shall touch the ingenuous heart,
And hint its moral with a pleasing art.
Aid me, Historic Muse! unfold thy store
Of rich, of various, never-cloying lore;
Thence Fancy flies with new-born visions fraught,
There old Experience lends his hoards to Thought.

When slumbering Adam pressed the lonely earth,...
Unconscious parent of a wondrous birth,...
As forth to light the infant-woman sprung,
By pitying angels thus her doom was sung:
'Ah! fairest creature! born to changeful skies,
To bliss and agony, to smiles and sighs:
Beauty's frail child, to thee, though doomed to bear
By far the heavier half of human care,
Deceitful Nature's stepdame-love assigned
A form more fragile, and a tenderer mind;
More copious tears from Pity's briny springs,
And, trembling Sympathy! thy finest strings:
While ruder man she prompts, in pride of power,
To bruise, to slay, to ravage, to devour;
On prostrate weakness turn his gory steel,
And point the wounds not all thy tears can heal.
Poor victim! stern the mandate of thy birth,
Ah dote not, smile not, on the things of earth!
Subdue thyself; those rapturous flutterings still!
Armed with meek courage and a patient will,

With thoughtful eye pursue thy destined way,
Adore thy God, and hope a brighter day!'
In solemn notes thus flowed the prescient strain,...
In smiling wonder fixt, the new-born bride
Drank the sweet gale, the glowing landscape eyed,
And murmured untried sounds, and gazed on every side.
With look benign the boding angels view
The fearless innocent, and wave adieu:
Too well thy daughters shall our strain believe;
Too short thy dream of bliss, ill-fated Eve.'

Prophetic spirits! that with ken sublime
Sweep the long windings of the flood of time,
Joyless and stern, your deep-toned numbers dwell
On rocks, on whirlpools, and the foaming swell,
But pass unmarked the skiffs that gaily glide
With songs and streamers down the dimpling tide:
Else rapturous notes had floated on the wind,
And hailed the stranger born to bless her kind,
To bear from heaven to earth the golden ties,
Bind willing man, and draw him to the skies.

See where the world's new master roams along,
Vainly intelligent and idly strong;
Mark his long listless step and torpid air,
His brow of densest gloom and fixt infantile stare!
Those sullen lips no mother's lips have prest,
Nor drawn, sweet labour! at her kindly breast;
No mother's voice has touched that slumbering ear,
Nor glistening eye beguiled him of a tear;
Love nursed not him with sweet endearing wiles,
Nor woman taught the sympathy of smiles;
Vacant and sad his rayless glances roll,
Nor hope nor joy illumes his darkling soul;
Ah! hapless world that such a wretch obeys!
Ah! joyless Adam, though a world he sways!

But see!... they meet,... they gaze,... the new-born pair;...
Mark now the wakening youth, the wondering fair:
Sure a new soul that moping idiot warms,
Dilates his stature, and his mien informs!
A brighter crimson tints his glowing cheek;
His broad eye kindles, and his glances speak.
So roll the clouds from some vast mountain's head,
Melt into mist, and down the valleys spread;
His crags and caves the bursting sunbeams light,
And burn and blaze upon his topmost height;
Broad in full day he lifts his towering crest,

And fire celestial sparkles from his breast.
Eve too, how changed!... No more with baby grace
The smile runs dimpling o'er her trackless face,
As painted meads invite her roving glance,
Or birds with liquid trill her ear intrance:
With downcast look she stands, abasht and meek,
Now pale, now rosy red, her varying cheek;
Now first her fluttering bosom heaves a sigh,
Now first a tear stands trembling in her eye;
For hark! the youth, as love and nature teach,
Breathes his full bosom, and breaks forth in *speech:*
His quivering lips the winged accents part,
And pierce, how swift! to Eve's unguarded heart.

Now rose complete the mighty Maker's plan,
And Eden opened in the heart of Man;
Kindled by Hope, by gentle Love refined,
Sweet converse cheered him, and a kindred mind;
Nor deem that He, beneficent and just,
In woman's hand who lodged this sacred trust,
For man alone her conscious soul informed,
For man alone her tenderer bosom warmed;
Denied to her the cup of joy to sip,
But bade her raise it to his greedy lip,
Poor instrument of bliss, and tool of ease,
Born but to serve, existing but to please:...
No;... hand in hand the happy creatures trod,
Alike the children of no partial God;
Equal they trod till want and guilt arose,
Till savage blood was spilt, and man had foes:
Ah! days of happiness,... with tearful eye
I see you gleam, and fade, and hurry by:
Why should my strain the darkening theme pursue?
Be husht, my plaintive lyre! my listening friend, adieu!

(1810)

ANN TAYLOR (1782–1866)
AND
JANE TAYLOR (1783–1824)

Ann Taylor and Jane Taylor grew up in a family of writers, artists, and engravers. Both parents, Isaac Taylor and Ann (née Martin) Taylor were Nonconformists, the father becoming a minister. The two sisters were born in London and educated by their father in their childhood home in Suffolk. In their twenties, they began to work collaboratively and produced collections of hymns for children. Their *Original Poems for Infant Minds* (1805) went into fifty editions in England and was published in other countries.

Separate careers were also established. Ann Taylor, who married a tutor at a Congregational College in 1813, moved to Marborough, near Rotherham, and produced more hymns and poetry for children. Her autobiography was published in 1874 and edited by her son, Josiah Gilbert. Their *Rhymes for the Nursery* (1806) includes Jane Taylor's 'The Star' ('Twinkle, twinkle little star') and this was followed by her more ambitious *Essays in Rhyme, on Morals and Manners* (1816). Her *Poetical Remains* were published posthumously in 1825. Most of the essays in her *The Contributions of Q.Q.* (1824) had been previously printed in the *Youth's Magazine* between 1816 and 1822, and they were admired by Robert Browning. It was during the compilation of this book that Jane Taylor suffered from the cancer that was to prove fatal.

55 *The Star*

TWINKLE, twinkle, little star,
How I wonder what you are!
Up above the world so high,
Like a diamond in the sky.

When the blazing sun is gone,
When he nothing shines upon,
Then you show your little light,
Twinkle, twinkle, all the night.

Then the trav'ller in the dark,
Thanks you for your tiny spark
He could not see which way to go,
If you did not twinkle so.

In the dark blue sky you keep,
And often thro' my curtains peep,
For you never shut your eye,
Till the sun is in the sky.

'Tis your bright and tiny spark,
Lights the trav'ller in the dark,—
Though I know not what you are,
Twinkle, twinkle, little star.

(1806)

56 *A Child's Hymn of Praise*

I THANK the goodness and the grace
Which on my birth have smil'd,

And made me, in these christian days,
A happy English child.

I was not born, as thousands are,
Where GOD was never known;
And taught to pray a useless pray'r,
To blocks of wood and stone.

I was not born a little slave,
To labour in the sun,
And wish I were but in the grave,
And all my labour done!

I was not born without a home,
Or in some broken shed;
A gipsy baby; taught to roam,
And steal my daily bread.

My GOD, I thank thee, who hast plann'd
A better lot for me,
And plac'd me in this happy land,
And where I hear of thee.

(1810)

57 *The Folly of Finery*

SOME poor little ignorant children delight,
In wearing fine ribbons and caps;
But this is a very ridiculous sight,
Though they do not know it perhaps.

Clean hands, and clean faces, and neatly-combed hair,
And garments made decent and plain,
Are better than all the fine things they can wear,
Which make them look vulgar and vain.

A girl who will keep herself tidy and clean,
(As every child easily may,)
Needs not be afraid or ashamed to be seen,
Whoever may come in her way.

Then children, attend to the words you repeat,
And always remember this line:
'Tis a *credit* to any good girl to be neat,
But quite a *disgrace* to be fine.

(1816)

CAROLINE BOWLES (LATER SOUTHEY) (1786–1854)

CAROLINE BOWLES was the second wife of the poet, Robert Southey, and only child of Captain Charles Bowles of the East India Company's Service and Anne (née Burrard). Her father seems to have retired soon after his daughter's birth at Buckland Cottage, in Buckland, Hampshire. Her married years, 1839–1843, were troubled by the mental instability of her husband, and she was left less wealthy after his death than she had been before it. The £2,000 bequeathed to her by her husband in no way compensated for the loss of an annuity, forfeited by marriage, that had been settled upon her by a Colonel Bruce (her father's adopted son). In 1852, however, she was to receive a Civil List Pension of £200 per year. The *Athenaeum* obituary of 5 August 1854 offers a rather bleak perspective upon her life. Having contracted smallpox, the poet is said to have been for many years disabled and confined to the house, living the life of a recluse. She certainly removed herself from the public domain by ceasing to write after the death of her husband.

Her writing career seems, in part, to have been motivated by financial concerns. By 1816 both her parents had died and she then suffered the loss of much of her property through the dishonesty of a guardian. Her fear of poverty prompted her to earn her living by her pen. She had already published numerous poems in magazines and journals, often signed under the initial 'C', but it was not until 1820 that she collected any of her verses into volumes. Having sent a copy of a manuscript poem to Robert Southey, he forwarded it to the publisher, Robert Murray. Though Murray declined to publish it, it was eventually brought out anonymously through Longman's as *Ellen Fitzarthur: A Metrical Tale in Five Cantos* (1820). Two more anonymous poetry volumes followed in 1822 and 1826, and it was not until her one and only collection in prose, *Chapters on Churchyards* (1829)—a book of what she called 'pathetic novelettes'—that she was to put her name to her work. Her *The Birthday; A Poem, in Three Parts* (1836) was well received, winning for her the title of 'the Cowper of our modern Poetesses' from H. N. Coleridge (*Quarterly Review*, September 1840).

In 1833 she produced *Tales of the Factories: Respectfully Inscribed to Mr Sadler*. This work anticipated Caroline Norton's *A Voice from the Factories* (1836) and Elizabeth Barrett Browning's 'The Cry of the Children' (1843). In dedicating her volume to Michael Sadler, Bowles was identifying her writing with his political campaigning for the prevention of child labour and the limiting of the hours of the working day; this was parliamentary work later taken over by Lord Ashley. The propagandist nature of *Tales of the Factories* is further heightened by her reprinting with it, by way of an appendix, the 'Address' from a labourers' meeting in Bradford, as well as the minutes from the 'Factories' Labour Regulation Bill', which includes interviews with the workers. Extracts from Robert Southey's 'The Manufacturing System' from his *Sir Thomas More: or, Colloquies on the Progress and Prospects of Society* (1829) conclude her volume.

Bowles and Robert Southey had unsuccessfully tried to write a poem together, which was eventually published after their deaths as *Robin Hood: A Fragment. With other fragments and poems by Robert Southey and Caroline Southey* (1847). *The Poetical Works of Caroline Bowles Southey* (1867) and the Southeys' correspondence (1881) were also published posthumously.

58 *from* Ellen Fitzarthur: A Metrical Tale

[*Ellen has been persuaded to elope from her father's rural cottage. In the city, her lover tires of her and deserts her when she becomes pregnant. The marriage was a deception and she is left alone. The poem ends with her death at the end of an arduous journey back to the country, when she discovers that her father has died of grief. Eds.*]

THRO' many a long and lonely day,
That tender hope was Ellen's stay;
Thro' those sad hours of solitude
One patient labour she pursued;
Her needle's busy skill was plied
(Fond preparation!) to provide
For the expected one, whose smile
Would soon repay her willing toil;
And sometimes, thro' dejection's shade,
Hope's rays, like slanting sun-beams played,
Fair, flatt'ring heralds of a light
That soon might break thro' sorrow's night.
'Yes, that dear precious babe might prove
The pledge of re-awakened love:—
Oh! when a father's arms should press
His infant's tender helplessness,
The father's feelings might renew
The husband's lost affections too:—
Yes—it might prove the harbinger
Of better days—of peace to her,
Of pardon, long in vain implored.—
Oh! she would teach the earliest word
Its lisping accents could attain,
To say, "Forgive!" and not in vain,
Oh! not in vain, such voice would plead;
With her dear father 'twould succeed:
He could not look upon her child
With heart unmoved, unreconciled;
He could not fold unto his heart
Her child, and bid his own depart.'

It came, the hour of suff'ring came,
And Ellen bore a mother's name,
And to a mother's throbbing breast,
A second, dearer self was prest.—
No voice of soothing love was near
In the dark hour of pain and fear;
No sympathising heart was there

A parent's new-born hopes to share;
No father with impatient claim,
Assuming proud that sacred name,
Was there with grateful tenderness
The mother and her child to bless:
Poor babe! to this dark world of cares
Welcomed with sighs, baptized in tears.
Long, long and ling'ring were the days
Of Ellen's weakness,—cold delays,
That chill the heart—and hope deferred;
Conjecture, whose vague thoughts still erred,
And still surmised as fruitlessly—
And contrast sad of days gone by,
When, if her finger did but ache,
Some heart was anxious for her sake,
And love devised such tender care,
'Twas almost sweet the pain to bear.
Thoughts such as these, in Ellen's breast,
The healthful spring of youth deprest,
Like nipping frost's ungenial breath,
That ling'ring hangs on April's wreath.

Day after day, and not a word,—
Day after day, and still deferred,—
Oh! yes—at last a letter came—
Impatience thrilled her feeble frame,
And almost marred its wish—so shook,
Like quiv'ring leaf upon the brook,
Her eager hand—at length she read—
And soon her eyes' bright lustre fled,
And from her cheek the heightened hue,
Emotion's crimson flush withdrew,
And pale and motionless she grew—
Pale as her white robe's stainless fold,
Like sculptured marble pale and cold.—
Alas! that cruel letter, well
Might work such life-benumbing spell:—
De Morton's last farewell it bore,
The veil was rent—the dream was o'er—
De Morton would return no more!
A dream, indeed! a mockery,
All he had said, and seemed to be—
A dream, indeed! his very name,
No wedded right had she to claim—
Assumed t'elude the holy rite
That, he had seemed with hers to plight.

(1820)

59 *The Father's Tale*

'Shall I not visit for these things, saith the Lord?'
JEREMIAH 5: 29

COME near, my children! till the hour of prayer
  Close we, with serious talk, the Sabbath-day;
Come clust'ring round us—round your mother's chair
  And mine: Methinks I'd have you so alway,
But so it cannot be. Soon far and wide
In this world must your several paths divide.

But work ye to one end, and with one mind,
  Unto His glory, whose redeemed ye are,
Doing his pleasure—rend'ring to your kind
  As ye'd receive again. Though sundered far,
Your earthly portions, bright or overcast,
Doubt not ye all shall meet in Heaven at last.

And we—whose treasure and whose trust ye are,
  If faithful found at the great reckoning day,
Shall back receive ye, each a living star
  Wreathed in one crown of glory. Lo! the way
Is plain before us; let us but endure
Our time appointed, and the end is sure.

But oh! beloved ones—full many a snare
  And treacherous pitfall in your path doth lie;
Be constant still in watchfulness and prayer,
  Search out your secret hearts continually;
Lest, from the root of evil set therein,
Shoot up and flourish some triumphant sin.

At first 'a little one,'—and so excused—
  Or for a while in virtue's semblance drest—
Till moral sense and feeling, self-abused,
  Are lulled at last to deep and deadly rest;
And the whole heart, corrupted to the core,
To work the Tempter's will, is given o'er.

Oh, my dear children! I have seen to-day,
  Have heard and seen what made my blood run cold.
There is a moral leprosy—I say
  A *plague* among us—yea, the love of gold;
And rank and foul idolaters we see,
As e'er to ruthless Moloch bent the knee.

Ye've read (and shuddered) of those rites accurst,
  Of Jaggernaut, the Indian demon god,
Whose maddened votaries struggle to be first,
  When yearly his dread chariot comes abroad,
Headlong themselves or tender babes to dash
Before the horrid wheels, as on they crash.

Shudd'ring ye've read—but all in pity too
  For those poor fanatics have wept the while;
Those blinded ones, who 'know not what they do.'
  But here in England, in our *Christian* isle,
Baptized men, for love of cursed gain,
Heap Mammon's altar with their infant slain.

Marvel not, children! that ye see me so
  In spirit moved for poor humanity—
This morning, as is oft my wont, you know,
  Being awake, and stirring with the bee,
I took my way to visit that small mound
Ye wot of, in our parish burying-ground—

That low green grave, where your young sister lies,
  Whom late, with many tears, ye saw laid there—
Kiss off those drops from your fond mother's eyes—
  Children! ye see how dear to us ye are.
But God, who gave, required his own again—
We wept, and yielded up our little Jane.

But oh! with what an agony of prayer
  That *one* dear lamb selected from our fold
For his good pleasure, he the rest would spare;
  Even with like pleadings that may not be told,
This very morn, my precious ones! I prayed
By that green mound beneath the lime-tree's shade.

While thus I stood, smote heavy on mine ear
  The funeral-bell; and, turning, I espied
An open grave, planked loosely over, near,
  That scarce a few short paces did divide
From that of mine own child; and it must be,
Methought, for one as early called as she.

Once—twice again (no more) that sullen sound
  Jarred with uneven stroke—and, at the call
Appeared, within the consecrated ground,
  No funeral pomp of mourners—plume and pall;
But minister and clerk—and, huddling nigh,
A squalid group—one wretched family.

Foremost, a man of wasted frame, and weak,
  But tall and bony—bowed, but not by years;
Grizzled his thick black locks—his sallow cheek
  Dug out, as if by long corroding tears;
But the deep sunken caves were parch'd and dry,
And glazed and meaningless his hollow eye.

With him came step for step, with shambling gait,
  A pale-faced boy, whose swollen and feeble knees
Bowed out and bent beneath his starveling weight;
  They two between them, slung with careless ease,
A little coffin, of the roughest boards
And rudest framing Parish help affords.

And close behind, with stupid looks agape,
  Two sickly, shivering girls, dragged shuffling on
A long-armed, withered creature, like an ape,
  From whose bleared eyeballs reason's light was gone;
The idiot gibbered in his senseless glee,
And the man turned—and cursed him bitterly.

Alas, my children! But the Judge of all
  Tries not the heart by superficial sign;
And when *we* think his thunderbolt must fall
  On some offender, oft the hand divine
Reserves its wrath the guiltier wretch to slay
Who led, or drove him from the righteous way.

Bareheaded, by the grave of mine own dead
  I stood, while his, that wretched Man's, was lowered
Into the narrow house. His shaggy head
  Sank on his breast; but when the earth was poured
Upon the coffin lid, there stirred in him
No visible change or tremor, face or limb.

And so he stood, while all was finished—
  The grave filled in—the daisied turf smooth'd o'er;
Till one cried—'Father!' Then he raised his head
  With such a look!—I see it to this hour—
And turning, stampt down hard the new-laid sod,
Mutt'ring with half-clenched teeth, 'One's gone—thank God!'

'One's gone!' I echoed, glancing where mine own
  Slept in *her* grave; 'and thou can'st tread *that spot*
So rudely—speak those words in such a tone!
  Art *thou* a father?' 'Would that I were not!'
Facing quick round his questioner to scan,
Made answer stern, that miserable Man.

Dark scowling from beneath his close-knit brow,
His gloomy eye full fixt on mine, he said,
'Children may be good gifts to thee, and thou
Mayst love them living, and lament them dead;
But mine are born to slavery and despair—
They're better off in Heaven, or—anywhere!'

'Ye're of the Fact'ries,' I began, but he
Broke in with horrid laugh—'Aye, who can doubt
That same that sees us? Fact'ry hands are we—
Their mark's upon us—and it don't wear out.'
And dragging forward one poor girl—'Look there!'
He shouted out, and laid her shoulders bare,

Tearing the ragged shawl off—'*That's* fresh done!
They sent her home scored black and blue last night,
To serve as mourning for the little one—
We've no black rags.—And *that's* a goodly sight
For parents' eyes—that poor demented thing!
He was born straight and healthy—Duke or King

'Might have been proud of him; sharp-witted too—
Aye, 'cutest of 'em all—till his time came
For the curst Mill. They strapped him on to do
Beyond his strength: He fell against a frame
Struck backward—Hurt his spine, the doctors say,
And grew deformed and foolish from that day.

'Sir! when *your* young ones are in bed, asleep,
Mine must slave on—in dust, and steam, and flue:
You may with *yours* the Lord's day holy keep
In his own house. 'Tis more than I can do,
(Brute as you think me,) from their rest that day,
Poor little wretches! to drag mine away.

''Tis somewhere written in the Bible book,
How that Christ loves young children, and for foes
Counts all who wrong them. Think ye, does *he* look
In suchwise on our little ones, and those
Who rack their tender limbs, their sinews strain,
And coin out their young lives in cursed gain!

'There came a man to me but yesternight,
Collecting pennies, towards setting free
Poor Negro slaves abroad! I laughed outright.
Master! says I, no need to cross the sea
For your good work; on *this* side the salt waves,
No lack of Slavery, nor of *Infant Slaves*.

'Your pardon, sir!' he said, with softened tone
  Deep lowered; and touched his hat in act to go—
'But if I *have* forgot myself, you'll own
  Wrongs such as mine may make a man do so.
I've loved my children—God *he* knows how well—
But my heart's hardened—and my thoughts are hell.

'I've been myself, a wretched Fact'ry boy—
  Untaught—uncared for—a poor foundling too;
I never felt the feeling *you* call joy,
  Nor leapt, nor laughed, as happy children do;
But I got on, and married like the rest
In reckless folly.—And I say 'tis best

'To die a sinless child, as mine lies there'—
  With aching pity, tenderly I strove
To soothe the wretched man in his despair:
  I talked to him of seeking strength above—
He shook his head—Of comfort found in prayer—
   He groaned out, pointing to the grave, 'There! there!'

But we must seek him in his home distrest,
  Where ague-struck his helpless partner lies,
Nursing a wailing baby at her breast,
  That drains her life-blood with its scant supplies:
And we must try what Christian love can do,
For the sick soul, and sinking body too.

And oh, my children! fervent be our prayer,
  This night before we sleep, and day by day,
That from our country, this good land and fair!
  The moral plague-spots may be wiped away.
Ere from her heights, like guilty Tyre, she's hurled,
The wonder and opprobrium of a world.

(1833)

60 *from The Birthday, Book I*

[*The growth of a woman poet's mind, to adapt the subtitle of William Wordsworth's* The Prelude, *might well describe this three-part poem. The formative experiences of family are its theme. Elizabeth Barrett Browning's* Aurora Leigh *at times echoes Bowles's poem. The first passage concerns the death of a grandmother. Eds.*]

ALREADY changed!—already clouded o'er
With the Death-shadow that fair morning sky—
The kindred band is broken. One goes hence,
The very aged. Follows soon, too soon,

Another most endeared, the next in age.
Then fell from childhood's eyes the earliest tears
Shed for Man's penal doom. Unconscious half,
Incomprehensive of the awful truth;
But flowing faster, when I looked around
And saw that others wept; and faster still,
When clinging round my Nurse's neck, with face
Half-buried there, to hide the bursting grief,
I heard her tell how in the churchyard cold,
In the dark pit, the form I loved was laid.
Bitter exceedingly the passionate grief
That wrings to agony the infant heart:
The *first* sharp sorrow:—ay, the breaking up
Of that deep fountain, never to be sealed,
Till we with Time close up the great account.
But that first outbreak, by its own excess
Exhausted soon; exhausting the young powers:
The quivering lip relaxes into smiles,
As soothing slumber, softly stealing on;
Less and less frequent comes the swelling sob,
Till like a summer breeze it dies away;
While on the silken eyelash, and the cheek
Flushed into crimson, hang the large round drops—
Well I remember, from that storm of grief
Diverted soon, with what sensations new
Of female vanity—inherent sin!
I saw myself arrayed in mourning frock
And long crape sash—Oh, many a riper grief
Forgets itself as soon before a glass
Reflecting the becomingness of weeds!

[Learning to read. Eds.]

Soon came the days when fond parental care
'Gan mingle easy tasks with childish play.
Right welcome lessons! conned with willing mind:
For it was told me, by such labour won,
And exercise of patience, I should gain
Access to countless treasures hid in books.
'What! shall I read myself, and *when I will*,
All those fine stories Jane can tell sometimes
When she's good-natured?—but not half so well—
Oh, no! not half—as Cousin Marianne.
What! shall I read about the sea of glass
The lady walked on to the ivory hill?
And all about those children at the well
That met the fairy, and the toads, and frogs,
And diamonds; and about the talking bird,
And dancing water, and the singing bough,

And Princess Fairstar? Shall I read all that,
And more, and *when I will*, in printed books?
Oh, let me learn!'—And never student's brain,
Fagging for college prize, or straining hard,
In prospect of tremendous little go,
To fetch up Time's leeway in idlesse lost,
Applied with such intensity as mine.

And soon attained, and sweet the fruit I reaped.
Oh, never ending, ever new delight!
Stream swelling still to meet the eager lip!
Receiving as it flows fresh gushing rills
From hidden sources, purer, more profound.
Parents! dear parents! if the latent powers
Called into action by your early cares—
God's blessing on them!—had attained no more
Than that acquaintance with His written will,
Your first most pious purpose to instil,
How could I e'er acquit me of a debt
Might bankrupt Gratitude? If scant my stores
Of human learning;—to my mother tongues,
A twofold heritage, wellnigh confined
My skill in languages;—if adverse Fate—
Heathenish phrase!—if *Providence* has fixed
Barriers impassable 'cross many a path
Anticipation with her Hope-winged feet,
Youthfully buoyant, all undoubting trod;—
If in the mind's infirmity, erewhile,
Thoughts that are almost murmurs whisper low
Stinging comparisons, suggestions sad,
Of what I *am*, and what I *might have* been—
This Earth, so wide and glorious! I fast bound,
A human lichen, to one narrow spot—
A sickly, worthless weed! Such brave bright spirits,
Starring this nether sphere, and I—lone wretch!
Cut off from oral intercourse with all—
'The day far spent', and oh, how little known!—
The night at hand, alas! and nothing done;—
And neither 'word, nor knowledge, nor device,
Nor wisdom, in the grave whereto I go.'

* * *

When thoughts like these arise, permitted tests,
Proving my frailty, and Thy mercy, Lord,
Let but Thy ministering angel draw mine eyes
To yonder *Book*; and, lo! this troublous world
Fades from before me like a morning mist,

And, in a spirit *not* mine own, I cry,
'Perish all knowledge but what leads to Thee!'

And, was it chance, or thy prevailing taste,
Beloved instructress! that selected first,
Part of my daily task, a portion short,
Culled from thy 'Seasons,' Thomson?—Happy choice,
Howe'er directed, happy choice for me!
For as I read, new thoughts, new images,
Thrilled through my heart with undefined delight,
Awakening so th' incipient elements
Of tastes and sympathies that with my life
Have grown and strengthened; often on its course,
Yea, on its darkest moments, shedding soft
That rich warm glow they only can impart—
A sensibility to Nature's charms
That seems its living spirit to infuse,
A breathing soul, in things inanimate,
To hold communion with the stirring air,
The breath of flowers, the ever-shifting clouds,
The rustling leaves, the music of the stream,
To people solitude with airy shapes,
And the dark hour, when Night and Silence reigns,
With immaterial forms of other worlds;
But best and noblest privilege, to feel
Pervading Nature's all-harmonious whole,
The Great Creator's presence, in His works.

. . . .

[Dolls. Eds.]

Lo! what a train like Bluebeard's wives appear,
So many headless, half dismembered some,
With battered faces—eyeless—noseless—grim
With cracked enamel, and unsightly scars—
Some with bald pates, or hempen wigs unfrizzed,
And ghastly stumps, like Greenwich pensioners;
Others mere Torsos—arms, legs, heads, all gone!
But precious all. And chief that veteran doll,
She from whose venerable face is worn
All prominence of feature; shining brown,
Like chestnut from its prickly coating freed,
With equal polish as the wigless skull—
Well I remember, with what bribery won
Of a fair rival—one of waxen mould—
Long coveted possession!—I was brought
The mutilated favourite to resign.
The blue-eyed fair one came—perfection's self!
With eager joy I clasped her waxen charms;

But then—the stipulated sacrifice!
'And must we part?' my piteous looks expressed—
Mute eloquence! 'And *must* we part, dear Stump!'
'Oh! might I keep ye both!'—and both I kept.

Unwelcome hour, I ween, that tied me down
Restless, reluctant, to the sempstress' task!
Sight horrible to me, th' allotted seam
Of stubborn Irish, or more hateful length
Of handkerchief, with folded edge tacked down,
All to be hemmed; ay, *selvidge sides* and all.
And so they were in tedious course of time,
With stitches long and short, 'cat's teeth' yclept;
Or jumbled thick and thin, oblique, transverse,
At last, in sable line imprinted grim.
But less distasteful was the sampler's task;
There green and scarlet vied; and fancy claimed
Her privilege to crowd the canvass field
With hearts and zigzags, strawberries and leaves,
And many a quaint device; some moral verse,
Or Scripture text, enwrought; and, last of all,
Last, though not least, the self-pleased artist's name.

And yet, with more alacrity of will,
I fashioned various raiment; caps, cloaks, gowns;
Gay garments for the family of dolls;
No matter how they fitted—they were *made;*
Ay, and applauded, and rewarded too
With silver thimble. Precious gift! bestowed
By a kind aunt; one ever kind and good,
Mine early benefactress! Since approved
By time and trial mine unchanging friend;
Yet most endeared by the affecting bond
Of mutual sorrows, mutual sympathies.
. . . .

[Learning to write. Eds.]

A day to be remembered well was that,
When, by my father taught, I first essayed
The early rudiments of penmanship.
Long-wished-for lesson! by prudential love—
Wisely considerate of my infant years—
Withheld, till granted slow in fair exchange
For some relinquished pleasure; 'twas received
A twofold grant—a boon and a reward.
So I began, long rigorously confined
To rows of sloping strokes. Not *sloping* all;
At first in straggling piles they jostled rude,

Like raw recruits, till into order drilled,
Maintaining equal distance on their march,
Even and close they ranged like veteran troops,
In ranks symmetrical; and *then* at last
My long restrained ambition was indulged
In higher flights, with nicer art to shape
The involutions of the alphabet.
Unsteady and perplexed the first attempts—
Great A's, that with colossal strides encroached
On twice the space they should have occupied,
And I's like T's, and R's whose lower limbs
Beyond the upper bulged unseemly out,
And sprawling W's, and V's, and Y's,
Gaping prodigiously, like butter-boats.
But soon succeeded to those shapeless scrawls
Fair capitals and neat round characters,
Erelong in words and sentences combined;
At first restrained between two guiding lines,
Then ranged on one—that one continued long,
Spite of ambitious daring, that would fain
Have strayed, from limit and restriction free;
For ardently I longed to scrawl at will
The teeming fancies of a busy brain,
Not half content, not satisfied, albeit
My father, with a kind and ready pen,
Vouchsafed assistance to the infant muse.

(1836 *1867*)

61 *from The Birthday, Book II*

My poor old Chloe! gentle playfellow!
Most patient, most enduring was thy love;
To restless childhood's teasing fondness proof,
And its tormenting ingenuity.
Methinks I see thee in some corner stuck,
In most unnatural posture, bolt upright,
With rueful looks and drooping ears forlorn,
Thy two fore-paws, to hold my father's cane—
Converted to a musket—cramped across.
Then wert thou posted like a sentinel
Till numbers ten were slowly counted o'er—
That welcome tenth! the signal sound to thee
Of penance done and liberty regained!
Down went the cane, and from thy corner forth,
With uproar wild and madly frolic joy,
Bounding aloft, and wheeling round and round

With mirth-inviting antics, didst thou spring.
And the grave teacher—grave no longer—shared
The boisterous pupil's loud unbridled glee.
Then were there dismal outcries, shrill complaints,
From angry Jane, of frocks and petticoats
All grim with muddy stains and ghastly rents.
''Twas all in vain,' the indignant damsel vowed—
''Twas all in vain to toil for such a child—
For such a Tom-boy! Climbing up great trees—
Scrambling through brake and bush, and hedge and ditch,
For paltry wild-flowers. Always without gloves,
Grubbing the earth up like a little pig
With her own nails, and, just as bad as *he*,
Racing and romping with that dirty beast.'
Then followed serious—'But the time will come
You'll be ashamed, Miss, of such vulgar ways:
You a young lady!—Not much like one now.'
Too oft unmoved by the pathetic zeal
Of such remonstrance, pertly I replied,
'No, Mistress Jane! that time will never come.
When I'm grown up I'll romp with Chloe still,
As I do now; and climb and scramble too
After sweet wild-flowers just as much as now;
And "grub the earth", and "never put on gloves."
Then if I dirt my hands and tear my frock,
You'll not dare scold when I'm a woman grown;
For who would mind your scolding, Mistress Jane?'

. . . .

Bid them turn—
Those sentimental chymics, who extract
The essence of imaginary griefs
From overwrought refinement,—bid them turn
To some poor cottage—not a bower of sweets
Where woodbines cluster o'er the neat warm thatch,
And mad Marias sing fantastic ditties,
But to some wretched hut, whose crazy walls,
Crumbling with age and dripping damps, scarce prop
The rotten roof, all verdant with decay;
Unlatch the door, those starting planks that ill
Keep out the wind and rain, and bid them look
At the *home-comforts* of the scene within.
There on the hearth a few fresh-gathered sticks,
Or smouldering sods, diffuse a feeble warmth,
Fanned by that kneeling woman's labouring breath
Into a transient flame, o'erhanging which
Cowers close, with outspread palms, a haggard form,
But yesterday raised up from the sick-bed

Of wasting fever, yet to-night returned
From the resumption of his daily toil.
'Too hastily resumed—imprudent man!'
Ay, but his famished infants cried for bread;
So he went forth and strove, till nature failed,
And the faint dews of weakness gathered thick
In the dark hollows of his sallow cheek,
And round his white-parched lips. Then home he crawled
To the cold comforts of that cheerless hearth,
And of a meal whose dainties are set out
Invitingly—a cup of coarse black tea,
With milk unmingled, and a crust of bread.
No infant voices welcome his return
With joyous clamour, but the piteous wail,
'Father! I'm hungry—father! give me bread!'
Salutes him from the little huddled group
Beside that smoky flame, where one poor babe,
Shaking with ague-chills, creeps shuddering in
Between its mother's knees—that most forlorn,
Most wretched mother, with sad lullaby
Hushing the sickly infant at her breast,
Whose scanty nourishment yet drains her life.

Martyrs of sensibility! look there!
Relieve in acts of charity to those
The exuberance of your feelings.
'Ay, but those
Are horrid objects—squalid, filthy, low
Disgusting creatures—sentiment turns sick
In such an atmosphere at such a sight.
True cottage children are delightful things,
With rosy dimpled cheeks, and clustering curls;
It were an interesting task to dress
Such pretty creatures in straw cottage-bonnets,
And green stuff gowns, with little bibs and aprons
So neat and nice! and every now and then,
When visitors attend the Sunday school,
To hear them say their catechism and creed.
But those!—oh heaven! what feelings could endure
Approach or contact with those dirty things?
True—they *seem* starving; but 'tis also true
The parish sees to all those vulgar wants;
And when it does not, doubtless there must be—
Alas! too common in this wicked world—
Some artful imposition in the case.'

Martyrs of sensibility! farewell!
I leave ye to your earwigs and your flies.

(1836 *1867*)

62 *from The Birthday, Book III*

That was a lovely brook, by whose green marge
We two, the patient angler and his child,
Loitered away so many summer days!
A shallow sparkling stream, it hurried, now
Leaping and glancing among large round stones,
With everlasting friction chafing still
Their polished smoothness, on a gravelly bed
Then softly slipped away with rippling sound,
Or all inaudible where the green moss
Sloped down to meet the clear reflected wave
That lipped its emerald bank with seeming show
Of gentle dalliance; in a dark, deep pool
Collected now, the peaceful waters slept,
Embayed by rugged headlands, hollow roots
Of huge old pollard willows. Anchored there,
Rode safe from every gale a sylvan fleet
Of milk-white water-lilies, every bark
Worthy as those on his own sacred flood
To waft the Indian Cupid. Then the stream
Brawling again o'er pebbly shallows ran,
On, on to where a rustic, rough-hewn bridge,
All bright with mosses and green ivy wreaths,
Spanned the small channel with its single arch;
And underneath the bank on either side
Shelved down into the water, darkly green
With unsunned verdure, or whereon the sun
Looked only when his rays at eventide
Obliquely glanced between the blackened piers
With arrowy beams of orient emerald light
Touching the river and its velvet marge.
'Twas there, beneath the archway, just within
Its rough misshapen piles, I found a cave,
A little secret cell—one large flat stone
Its ample floor, imbedded deep in moss,
And a rich tuft of dark blue violet;
And fretted o'er with curious groining dark,
Like vault of Gothic chapel, was the roof
Of that small cunning cave—'The Naiad's Grot'
I named it learnedly, for I had read
About Egeria, and was deeply versed
In heathenish stories of the guardian tribes
In groves, and single trees, and sylvan streams
Abiding co-existent. So methought
The little Naiad of our brook might haunt
That cool retreat, and to her guardian care

My wont was ever, at the bridge arrived,
To trust our basket, with its simple store
Of home-made, wholesome cates, by one at home
Provided for our banquet-hour at noon.

A joyful hour! anticipated keen,
With zest of youthful appetite I trow,
Full oft expelling unsubstantial thoughts
Of Grots and Naiads, sublimated fare.
The busy, bustling joy, with housewife airs—
Directress, handmaid, lady of the feast—
To spread that 'table in the wilderness'!
The spot selected with deliberate care,
Fastidious from variety of choice,
Where all was beautiful: some pleasant nook
Among the fringing alders, or beneath
A single spreading oak, or higher up
Within the thicket, a more secret bower,
A little clearing, carpeted all o'er
With creeping strawberry, and greenest moss
Thick veined with ivy. There unfolded smooth
The snowy napkin, carefully secured
At every corner with a pebbly weight,
Was spread prelusive—fairly garnished soon
With the contents, most interesting then,
Of the well-plenished basket: simple viands,
And sweet brown bread, and biscuits for dessert,
And rich, ripe cherries; and two slender flasks,
Of cyder one, and one of sweet new milk,
Mine own allotted beverage, tempered down
To wholesome thinness by admixture pure
From the near streamlet. Two small silver cups
Set out our grand buffet—and all was done.
But there I stood immovable, entranced,
Absorbed in admiration, shifting oft
My ground contemplative to reperuse
In every point of view the perfect whole
Of that arrangement, mine own handiwork.
Then glancing skyward, if my dazzled eyes
Shrank from the sunbeams, vertically bright,
Away, away, toward the river's brink
I ran to summon from his silent sport
My father to the banquet, tutored well,
As I approached his station, to restrain
All noisy outbreak of exuberant glee,
Lest from their quiet haunts the finny prey
Should dart far off to deeper solitudes.

The gentle summons met observance prompt,
Kindly considerate of the famished child:
And all in order left; the mimic fly
Examined and renewed, if need required,
Or changed for other sort, as time of day,
Or clear or clouded sky, or various signs
Of atmosphere or water, so advised
The experienced angler; the long line afloat,
The rod securely fixed, then into mine
The willing hand was yielded, and I led
With joyous exultation that dear guest
To our green banquet-room. Not Leicester's self,
When to the hall of princely Kenilworth
He led Elizabeth, exulted more
With inward gratulation at the show
Of his own proud magnificence, than I,
When full in view of mine arrangèd feast,
I held awhile my pleased companion back,
Exacting wonder, admiration, praise,
With pointing finger, and triumphant 'There!'

Our meal concluded—or, as Homer says,
'Soon as the rage of hunger was appeased'—

And by the way, our temperate sylvan feast
Deserved poetic illustration more
Than those vast hecatombs of filthy swine,
Where Trojans, Greeks, and half-immortals gorged,
Sharpening their wits for council. Process strange!
But most effectual, doubtless, as we see
Clearly illustrated in this our day,
In this our favoured isle, where all affairs
(Glory to Britain's intellectual age!)
Begin and end with feasting. Statesmen meet
To eat and legislate; to eat and hang
Judges assemble; chapters congregate
To eat and order spiritual affairs;
Philhellenists to eat and free the Greeks;
Committees of Reform, Relief, Conversion,
Eat with amazing unction: and so on,
Throughout all offices, sects, parties, grades,
Down to the Parish worthies, who assemble
In conclave snug to eat, and starve the poor.

(1836 *1867*)

63 *The Legend of Santarem*

COME listen to a monkish tale of old,
  Right Catholic, but puerile some may deem,
Who all unworthy their high notice hold
  Aught but grave truth, or lofty learnèd theme;
Too wise for simple fancies, smiles, and tears,
Dreams of our earliest, purest, happiest years.

Come, listen to my legend; for of them
  Surely thou art not: and to thee I'll tell
How on a time in holiest Santarem
  Strange accident miraculous befell
Two little ones, who to the sacred shrine
Came daily to be schooled in things divine.

Twin sisters—orphan innocents were they:
  Most pure, I ween, from all but the olden taint,
Which only Jesu's blood can wash away:
  And holy, as the life of holiest saint,
Was his, that good Dominican's, who fed
His Master's lambs, with more than daily bread.

The children's custom, while that pious man
  Performed the various duties of his state
Within the spacious church, as sacristan,
  Was on the altar steps to sit and wait,
Nestling together ('twas a lovely sight!)
Like the young turtle-doves of Hebrew rite.

A small rich chapel was their sanctuary,
  While thus abiding;—with adornment fair
Of curious carvèd work, wrought cunningly,
  In all quaint patterns and devices rare:
And over them, above the altar, smiled
From Mary-Mother's arms, the Holy Child:

Smiled on His infant guests, as there below,
  On the fair altar steps, those young ones spread—
Nor aught irreverent in such act, I trow—
  Their simple morning meal of fruit and bread.
Such feast not ill beseemed the sacred dome—
Their Father's house is the dear children's home.

At length it chanced, upon a certain day,
  When Frey Bernardo to the chapel came,
Where patiently was ever wont to stay
  His infant charge, with vehement acclaim,
Both lisping creatures forth to meet him ran,
And each to tell the same strange tale began.

'Father!' they cried, as, hanging on his gown
  On either side, in each perplexèd ear
They poured their eager tidings—'He came down—
  Menino Jesu has been with us here!—
We asked Him to partake our fruit and bread;
And He came down—and sate with us—and fed.'

'Children! my children! know ye what ye say?'
  Bernardo hastily replied. 'But hold!—
Peace, Briolanja!—rash art thou alway:
  Let Inez speak.' And little Inez told,
In her slow silvery speech, distinctly o'er,
The same strange tidings he had heard before.

'Blessed are ye, my children!' with devout
  And deep humility the good man cried.
'Ye have been highly favoured. Still to doubt
  Were gross impiety and sceptic pride.
Ye have been highly favoured. Children dear!
Now your old master's loving counsel hear.

'Return to-morrow with the morning light,
  And, as before, spread out your simple fare
On the same table; and again invite
  Menino Jesu to descend and share:
And if He come, say, "Bid us, blessed Lord!
We and our master, to Thy heavenly board."

'Forget not, children of my soul! to plead
  For your old master:—Even for *his* sake
Who fed ye faithfully: and He will heed
  Your innocent lips; and I shall so partake
With His dear lambs. Beloved! with the sun
Return to-morrow.—Then—His will be done.'

'To-night! to-night! Menino Jesu saith
  We shall sup with Him, Father! we and thee,'
Cried out both happy children in a breath,
  As the good Father entered anxiously,
About the morrow's noon, that holy shrine,
Now consecrate by special grace divine.

'He bade us come alone; but then we said
  We could not, without thee, our master dear.
At that, He did not frown, but shook His head
  Denyingly: Then straight with many a tear
We prayed so sore, He could not but relent,
And so He smiled at last, and gave consent.'

'Now, God be praised!' the old man said, and fell
  In prayer upon the marble floor straightway,
His face to earth: and so, till vesper-bell,
  Entrancèd in the spirit's depths he lay;
Then rose like one refreshed with wine, and stood
Composed among the assembling brotherhood.

The mass was said; the evening chant was o'er;
  Hushed its long echoes through the lofty dome:
And now Bernardo knew the appointed hour
  That he had prayed for, of a truth was come.
Alone he lingered in the solemn pile,
Where darkness gathered fast from aisle to aisle;

Except that through a distant doorway streamed
  One slanting sunbeam, gliding whereupon
Two angel spirits—so in sooth it seemed
  That loveliest vision—in hand came on,
With noiseless motion. 'Father! we are here,'
Sweetly saluted the good Father's ear.

A hand he laid on each fair sun-bright head,
  Rayed like a seraph's with effulgent light,
And—'Be ye blest, ye blessed ones,' he said,
  'Whom Jesu bids to His own board to-night.
Lead on, ye chosen; to the appointed place
Lead your old master.' So, with steadfast face,

He followed where those young ones led the way,
  To that small chapel. Like a golden clue
Streamed on before that long bright sunset ray,
  Till at the door it stopt. Then passing through,
The master and the pupils, side by side,
Knelt down in prayer before the Crucified.

Tall tapers burnt before the holy shrine;
  Chalice and paten on the altar stood,
Spread with fair damask. Of the crimson wine
  Partaking first alone, the living food
Bernardo next with his dear children shared—
Young lips, but well for heavenly food prepared.

And there we leave them. Not for us to see
  The feast made ready, that first act to crown;
Nor to peruse the solemn mystery
  Of the divine Menino's coming down
To lead away the elect, expectant three,
With Him that night at His own board to be.

Suffice it that with Him they surely were
That night in Paradise; for those who came
Next to the chapel found them as in prayer,
Still kneeling, stiffened every lifeless frame,
With hands and eyes upraised as when they died,
Toward the image of the Crucified.

That mighty miracle spread far and wide,
And thousands came the feast of death to see;
And all beholders, deeply edified,
Returned to their own homes more thoughtfully,
Musing thereon: with one great truth imprest—
That 'to depart and be with Christ is best.'

(1836 *1867*)

MARY RUSSELL MITFORD
(1787–1855)

THE only child of George Mitford, a Whig, who trained as a physician, and of an heiress, Mary Russell, Mary Russell Mitford was born in Alresford, Hampshire. She was educated at school in London and, on its completion in 1802, was to live with her parents until the death of her mother in 1830 and that of her father in 1842. The family's move to the outskirts of London and then to the rural setting of Three Mile Cross, near Reading, in 1820 marked the family's declining prosperity: the result of her father's extravagance and gambling. Mary Russell Mitford's writing career was, in part, to be determined by the need to support her family.

She began writing as a poet, with her first collection, *Poems*, being published in 1810. Although this was not generally well-received, she was encouraged to continue writing by Samuel Taylor Coleridge. Further poems followed until 1813, with her *Watlington Hall. A Poem* (1812) being the most favourably reviewed. Not until 1827 was she to produce another volume of poems, *Dramatic Scenes, Sonnets and Other Poems*. The continuing need to support her parents had led her to pursue a more lucrative path and turn away, reluctantly, from what she called 'the lofty steep of Tragic Poetry to the every-day path of Village Stories'. Drawing from her own experience at Three Mile Cross, Mary Russell Mitford began to write the rural sketches in prose for which she was to become best-known, both in Britain and America. These began to appear in *The Lady's Magazine* from 1829. Their success encouraged her to recoup the loss of £40 that she sustained after the departure of the magazine's editor by continuing to publish them in volume form: *Our Village: Sketches of Rural Character and Scenery* (1824–1832). A year before the first of these appeared, she had also begun to write for the stage. Of her four tragedies, the most successful was *Rienzi*, which was performed at Drury Lane in October, 1828, was frequently republished and further established her popularity in America. Her one volume of fiction, *Atherton and Other Tales* (1854), received a complimentary review from the novelist, Geraldine Jewsbury (*Athenaeum*, 15 April 1854) and her collected works (both prose and verse) were published in 1841, to be followed by her *Dramatic Works* in 1854. It was only in the last years of her life that she achieved some degree of financial security through her literary works.

Her many literary acquaintances ranged across Britain and America and included Felicia Hemans, John Ruskin and Nathaniel Hawthorne, but her closest and most long-standing friendship was with Elizabeth Barrett Browning.

64 *To a Yellow Butterfly, April 8th, 1808*

HAIL! loveliest insect of the spring!
Sweet buoyant child of Phoebus, hail!
High soaring on thy downy wing,
Or sporting in the sunny vale!

Oh! lovely is thy airy form,
That wears the primrose hue so fair,
It seems as if some passing storm
Had rais'd the beauteous flow'r in air.

Far diff'rent from the spotted race,
The sultry June's bright suns unfold;
That seek in her fair flow'rs their place,
And proud display their wings of gold.

For brilliant is their varying dye,
And, basking in the the fervid ray,
They in the new-blown roses lie,
Or round the gay carnation play.

But thou, with April's modest flow'r,
Her violet sweet of snowy hue,
Tranquil shalt pass the noon-tide hour,
And sip content the ev'ning dew.

Oh! may no frosts thy beauties chill!
No storms thy little frame destroy!
But, sporting gay beside the rill,
May'st thou thy transient life enjoy!

(1810)

CHARLOTTE ELLIOTT
(1789–1871)

One of the most prominent hymn writers of the Victorian period, Charlotte Elliott came to prominence with 'Just as I am', published for the first time in the *Invalid's Hymn Book* (1834). Born in Clapham, South London, she was the third of of a large family of eight children. Her parents, Charles Elliott and Eling Elliott (née Venn), were members of the Clapham Sect, a group of notable evangelicals, philanthropists, and social reformers whose influence was felt throughout the nineteenth century. Troubled constantly by ill-health, Elliott focused her adult life on spiritual and devotional matters, reading little other than Scripture. From 1834 to 1859, she edited the *Christian Remembrancer Pocket Book*, as well as the sixth edition of the *Invalid's Hymn Book* (1854). Many collections of her poetry appeared throughout her lifetime, including *Hours of Sorrow; or, Thoughts in Verse, Chiefly Adapted to Seasons of Sickness* (1836). Her sister, Eleanor Babington, furnished a memoir for her *Selections from the Poems* (1873), and a year later extracts from her published journals appeared in one volume. Much of Elliott's adult life was spent in Torquay (1845–57). From 1857, she lived at Brighton, where she died at the age of 82.

65 *'Just as I am'*

'Him that cometh to Me I will in no wise cast out.'
John 6: 37

Just as I am—without one plea
But that Thy blood was shed for me,
And that Thou bid'st me come to Thee—
O Lamb of God, I come!

Just as I am—and waiting not
To rid my soul of one dark blot,
To Thee, whose blood can cleanse each spot—
O Lamb of God, I come!

Just as I am—though toss'd about,
With many a conflict, many a doubt,
Fightings and fears within, without—
O Lamb of God, I come!

Just as I am—poor, wretched, blind;
Sight, riches, healing of the mind,
Yea, all I need, in Thee to find—
O Lamb of God, I come!

Just as I am—Thou wilt receive,
Wilt welcome, pardon, cleanse, relieve,
Because Thy promise I believe—
O Lamb of God, I come!

Just as I am—Thy love unknown
Has broken every barrier down;
Flow to be Thine, yea, Thine alone—
O Lamb of God, I come!

Just as I am—of that free love,
The breadth, length, depth, and height to probe,
Here, for a season, then above—
O Lamb of God, I come!

(1834 *1873*)

EMMA ROBERTS
(*c*.1794–1840)

EMMA ROBERTS, who wrote extensively and knowledgeably about the Indian subcontinent, was the posthumous daughter of Capt. William Roberts, who had at one time served in the Russian service, afterwards acting as paymaster to a British regiment. Born near Leeds, she grew up with her mother in Bath. From an early age, she showed scholarly inclinations, and her most significant literary contact was L.E.L. (Letitia Elizabeth Landon), whom she met while undertaking research in the British Museum. Roberts' first book was a historical study, *Memoirs of the Rival Houses of York and Lancaster* (1827). Her later writing, however, is almost exclusively devoted to Indian history and culture.

In 1828, Roberts travelled to India with her sister and her brother-in-law, Capt. Robert Adair McNaughton of the 61st Bengal Infantry. She lived with them at a number of hill stations at Agra, Cawnpore, and Etawah until 1830. After her sister's death, she settled for some time in Calcutta, where she wrote for the *Oriental Observer*. *Oriental Scenes, Dramatic Sketches and Tales, with Other Poems* was privately printed there in 1830.

On her return to England in 1832, Roberts set to work on *Scenes and Characteristics of Hindustan, with Sketches of Anglo-Indian Society*, which appeared in 1835. Much of this writing is notable for its criticism of Anglo-Indian attitudes. In 1839, she returned to the East, planning to write a study of British India's development in the course of the decade. After settling in Bombay, she edited the *Bombay United Service Gazette*. Although her ambitious study of British India was never brought to completion, Roberts managed to produce a substantial manuscript before her death. This was published in 1841 as *Notes of an Overland Journey through France and Egypt to Bombay*, which is prefaced with a memoir of her life. She died at Poona, after being taken seriously ill with stomach pains.

66 *A Scene in the Doaab*

In tangled depths the jungles spread
  Around the solitary scene,
The lurking panther's sullen tread
  Marks the wild paths of the ravine;

Here too the fierce hyena prowls,
  Haunting the dark *Jheel's* broad lagoon,
And here, at eve, the wolf-cub howls,
  And famished jackals bay the moon.

Its scorching breath the hot wind pours
  Along the arid waste; and loud,
The storm-fiend of the desert roars,
  When bursts the sable thunder-cloud,

A crumbling mosque—a ruined fort—
  Hastening alike to swift decay,
Where owls and vampire bats resort,
  And vultures hide them from the day,

Alone remain to tell the tale
  Of Moslem power, and Moslem pride,
When shouts of conquest filled the gale
  And swords in native blood were dyed.

They sleep—the slayer and the slain—
  A lowly grave the victor shares
With the weak slave who wore the chain
  None save a craven spirit wears.

Yet had the deeds which they have done
  Lived in the power's deathless song,
These nameless *spahis* would have won
  All that to valour's hopes belong.

They brought their faith from distant lands,
  They reared the Moslem badge on high,
And swept away with reeking brands
  The reliques of idolatry.

Where'er they spread their prophet's creed
  The guilty rite of Brama fled;
No longer shrinking victims bleed,
  Nor sleeps the living with the dead.

The frantic shrieks of widowed brides
  From burning piles resound no more,
Nor Ganges' desecrated tides
  Bear human offerings from its shore.

Their wreaths have faded—lizards bask
  Upon the marble pavement, where
'Twas erst the dark-eyed beauty's task
  To crown with flowers her raven hair.

Unheeded now the scorpion crawls,
  And snakes unscathed in silence glide,
Where once the bright *Zenana's* halls
  To woman's feet were sanctified.

No trace remains of those gay hours
  When lamps, in golden radiance bright,
Streamed o'er these now deserted towers
  The sunshine of their perfumed light.

The maiden's song, the anklet's bells
  So sweetly ringing o'er the floor,
And eyes as soft as the gazelle's
  Are heard, and seen, and felt no more.

Now all is silent; the wild cry
  Of savage beasts alone is heard,
Or wrathful temepest hurrying by,
  Or moanings of some desert bird.

(1830)

JANET HAMILTON
(1795–1873)

One of the most admired self-taught poets of the mid-nineteenth century, Janet Hamilton was well known for her incisive and polemical writings on the lives of working women, the evils of the Sunday railway, and the terrible consequences of the demon drink. Born in 1795 in Shotts, Lanarkshire, Janet Thomson was raised in a family of few means. Her father was originally a shoemaker. In her early childhood, she moved with her parents to Hamilton, and then to Langloan, where they worked as farm labourers. Her mother taught her to spin and to read, and she learned how to work a tambour-frame.

It was during her mid-teens that she began writing poems of a religious character, which were influenced by her Calvinist upbringing. But marriage and subsequent reponsibilities for her ten children absorbed much of her time. One of her proudest achievements was to have taught each of her sons and daughters to read and spell by the age of 5. It was only at the age of 54 that Hamilton returned to writing, publishing her work in Cassell's *Working Man's Friend*. Three volumes, bringing together her poems, ballads, and prose works, were published in the 1860s: *Poems and Essays* (1863), *Poems of Purpose and Sketches in Prose* (1865), and *Poems and Ballads* (1868). The last of these collections was prefaced with an 'Introductory Paper' by the eminent Scottish literary critic, George Gilfillan, who remarked:

The self-taught strugglers with narrow circumstances, learn usually a certain hardihood of spirit, a contempt for petty difficulties and for puling semintimentalities... Belonging, though she does, to the softer sex, she displays a manlike purpose, a rugged independence of spirit, and a contempt for all 'mealy-mouthedness' and gilded humbug, which make her seem almost an incarnation of the better nature of Burns.

In old age, Hamilton enjoyed some celebrity. In 1868, after a petition to Benjamin Disraeli, Hamilton received a grant of £50 from the Royal Bounty Fund. An ardent supporter of Italian campaigns for national liberation, Hamilton received a visit from a general of one of her long-standing heroes, Garibaldi.

67 *Civil War in America—Expostulation*

No darker record on the roll of time
Was e'er inscribed to country, age, or clime,
By the red hand of war—so barbarous, frantic;
The war you wage—mad cousins transatlantic.

Your glorious land of men and gold you drain—
And seas of blood and festering hills of slain.
Bankrupt and beggar'd: in your every state
These are your gains, you'll sum them up too late.

Sons of the Union—ah! a mighty change
Your words and deeds have wrought—beyond the range
Of British sympathy your cause you place;
We almost blush to own your kindred race.

Your freedom's dead. Her last expiring groan
Comes o'er the waters wild; a shudd'ring moan
Wails through your forests, echoes round your hills,
We hear, and Britain's heart with horror thrills.

Yes, freedom of the press! the tongue, the mind,
Henceforth ye must be deaf, and dumb, and blind:
Lincoln and Seward wills it. Kiss your chains,
And sing of conquest in triumphant strains.

And 'Stowe,' thou gifted daughter of the North,
Friend of the Southern slave, we call thee forth:
Let truth and candour guide thy graphic pen;
Denounce white slavery in the Northern men.

Columbian dames! do ye sustain your part?
The weeping, blushing blood of woman's heart,
Say—does it pulse your veins and dye with shame
Your blushing cheeks at Butler's branded name?

Of braggart speech that spurns at check or rule,
Like 'idiot's tale of sound and fury full';
You feed on lies that fail you at your need,
Nor heaven nor earth will bid your cause God-speed.

(1863)

68 *Lines Addressed to Mrs H. B. Stowe, on the Occasion of Her Visit to Glasgow, April 13, 1853*

LADY, to thee, to fortune, and to fame,
I, all unknown, would yet aspiring claim
A right to love thee, and admire from far
Thy pure and tender light. Benignant star,
Bright in Columbian heavens we see thee rise,
Herald of freedom's dawn in Southern skies.
Far on the dim horizon she appears
Struggling through blood, red clouds bedewed with tears,
The dews of anguish, wrung from hearts and eyes—
Crush'd, blasted, sever'd from all human ties.
Dark exhalations rise her form to shroud,
And wrathful demons glare from every cloud.
In vain shall Slavery's vile Draconian code
Of lawless laws, that flout the laws of God—
Her blood-hounds, scourges, chains—exclude the day.
No; things of darkness, hence! avaunt! away!
  Day breaks. Aside the murky vapours roll'd,
Mid roseate draperies, rich with orient gold,
Appears the goddess, shouts the applauding world,
The striped and starry flag she holds unfurl'd.
From the proud blazonry wipes out the name—
The curse of slavery and the brand of shame.
  Lady, my land breeds not nor barters slaves,
But she has ruined homes and drunkards' graves.
Here mad Intemperance clanks her Bedlam chain,
And plies her scourge of snakes, shame, ruin, pain—
The fangs of fell remorse, and fierce despair,
Sink in the victim's heart and quiver there.
  O gifted lady! from mine island strand
I gaze far sea-ward, wave the beckoning hand.
Thou comest—Oh, welcome guest!—and worthless, I
Shall meet thee—not on earth; our goal's the sky.

(1863)

69 *The Sunday Rail—I. On the Opening of the North British Railway for Running Sunday Trains, September 3, 1865*

NOW range up the carriages, feed up the fires!
To the rail, to the rail, now the pent up desires
Of the pale toiling million find gracious reply.
On the pinions of steam they shall fly, they shall fly,
The beauties of nature and art to explore,
To ramble the woodlands and roam by the shore.
The city spark here with his smart smirking lass
All peg-topp'd and crinolined, squat on the grass:
While with quips and with cranks, and soft-wreathed smiles,
Each nymph with her swain the dull Sabbath beguiles.
Here mater and pater familias will come
With their rollicking brood from their close city home.
How they scramble and scream, how they scamper and run,
While pa and mamma are enjoying the fun.
And the urchins bawl out, Oh how funny and jolly,
Dear ma, it is thus to keep Sabbath-day holy!
Now for pipe and cigar, and the snug pocket flask,
What's the rail on a Sunday without them, we ask?
What the sweet-scented heather and rich clover blooms
To the breath of the weed as it smoulders and fumes!
So in courting and sporting, in drinking and smoking,
Walking and talking, in laughter and joking,
They while the dull hours of the Sabbath away.
What a Sabbath it is! Who is lord of the day?
Son of man, Son of God, in the sacred record?
'Tis written that thou art of Sabbath the Lord.
But impious man hath reversed the decree,
And declares himself lord of the Sabbath to be.

In a world without souls it might not be amiss
The Sabbath to spend in such fashion as this;
But men having souls, if aware of the fact,
Should remember the Sabbath to keep it intact.
For souls are immortal, and bodies are clay,
And life but a vapour that fleeteth away,
To the soul and to God in His worship be given,
Oh, is it too much?—'tis but one day in seven.

(1868)

70 *A Lay of the Tambour Frame*

BENDING with straining eyes
  Over the tambour frame,
Never a change in her weary routine—
  Slave in all but the name.
Tambour, ever tambour,
  Tambour the wreathing lines
Of 'broidered silk, till beauty's robe
  In rainbow lustre shines.

There, with colourless cheek;
  There, with her tangling hair;
Still bending low o'er the rickety frame,
  Seek, ye will find her there.
Tambour, ever tambour,
  With fingers cramped and chill;—
The panes are shattered, and cold the wind
  Blows over the eastern hill.

Why quail, my sisters, why,
  As ye were abjects vile,
When begging some haughty brother of earth
  'To give you leave to toil?'
It is tambour you must,
  Naught else you have to do;
Though paupers' dole be of higher amount
  Than pay oft earned by you.

No union strikes for you;—
  Unshielded and alone,
In the battle of life—a battle it is,
  Where virtue is oft o'erthrown.
O working men! O why
  Pass ye thus careless by,
Nor give to the working woman's complaint
  One word of kind reply?

Selfish, unfeeling men!
  Have ye not had your will?
High pay, short hours; yet your cry, like the leech,
  Is Give us, Give us still.
She who tambours—tambours
  For fifteen hours a day—
Would have shoes on her feet, and dress for church
  Had she a third of your pay.

Sisters, cousins, and aunts
  Are they; yet, if not so,
Say, are they not sisters by human ties,
  And sympathy's kindly flow?
To them how dear the boon
  From brother's hand that came!
It would warm the heart and brighten the eyes,
  While bending o'er the frame.

Raise ye a fund to aid
  In times of deep distress;
While man helps man, to their sisters in need
  Brothers can do no less.
Still the tambourer bends
  Wearily o'er the frame.
Patterns oft vary, for fashions will change—
  She is ever the same.

(1868)

FELICIA HEMANS
(1795–1835)

Felicia Dorothea Browne (later Hemans) was the best-selling poet of the nineteenth century. Although the writer of her obituary in the *Athenaeum* (23 May 1835) was to draw attention to a received sense of the 'essentially feminine' nature of her poetry, her verses range from lyrics to a most unfeminine preoccupation with wars. The diversity and sheer volume of her poetic output is remarkable, with books of verse being produced on an almost annual basis from her first published volume in 1808 until her death.

She was born into a large family in Liverpool. Her father, George Browne, came from Ireland, having moved to Liverpool in the 1780s and her mother, Felicity (née Wagner), was of Italian and German descent. The daughter's education at home was facilitated by her access to an extensive library. As her mother was chiefly responsible for supervising her education, she became fluent in German, French, and Italian. By 1818, when she produced her *Translations from Camoens and Other Poets*, she had also added Spanish and Portugese to her list. When she was about 7 years old, the commercial setbacks experienced by her father (he had set up in a wine-making partnership with his father-in-law) led to the family's removal to Wales, where they stayed until 1809. In 1812, much to her family's disapproval, she married a man fifteen years her senior, a Captain Hemans. They were effectively separated in 1818. He moved to Italy, supposedly for the sake of his health, leaving his wife behind to look after their five sons. She then lived with her mother and sister until, after her mother's death in 1828, returning to Liverpool. Her final years were spent in Dublin.

At the age of only 15 she published her first book of poetry: *Poems, by Felicia Dorothea Browne*. Despite hostile criticism, she went on to produce another poem in the same year, 'England and Spain, or Valour and Patriotism, a Poem', which was inspired by her two brothers' involvement in the Peninsula War. She was to return to the subject of war, this time the Napoleonic wars, in her next book, misleadingly entitled *The Domestic Affections, and Other Poems* (1812). Critical success was first achieved with *The Restoration of the Works of Art to Italy: A Poem* (1816). Despite Lord Byron's private criticism of her *Modern Greece: A Poem* (1817), on the grounds that it was 'good for nothing; written by some one who has never been there' (Letter to John Murray, 4 September 1817), her poetry continued from this point to receive general acclaim. Her *Dartmoor: A Poem* (1821) won the Royal Society of Literature's prize for the year, and she was to go on to publish the highly popular *The Forest Sanctuary; and Other Poems* (1825), the second edition of which included the much anthologized poem, 'Casabianca'. It is reputed that she wrote most of *The Forest Sanctuary* in the laundry since this was the only quiet space in her household. An essay on Felicia Hemans's work by her closest friend, the poet Maria Jane Jewsbury, for the *Athenaeum* (5 February 1831) singles out 'The Forest Sanctuary' as 'our favourite'; it is also said to be the work that Felicia Hemans herself thought to be her best. However, the most successful of her works was still to come: *Records of Woman: with Other Poems* (1828). This collection of poems about legendary and historical women contained both previously published and new material. 'Joan of Arc in Rheims' (1826), for instance, followed 'Indian Woman's Death-Song' and both were preceded by 'Properzia Rossi'. 'Arabella Stuart' was placed first in the volume. Her reputation was equally well established in America, with a two-volume *Poems by Mrs Hemans* (1826) being edited by Andrews Norton in Boston and a second edition following in the next year. Further American publications include *The Poetical Works* in 1836. In Edinburgh a seven-volume edition of her works was published, again posthumously, in 1839. Her writing had, in fact, extended beyond the boundaries of poetry with her prose contributions to the *Edinburgh Monthly Magazine* in the 1820s and her play, *The Vespers of Palermo: A Tragedy, in Five Acts*, which was performed at the Theatre Royal, Covent Garden, on 12 December 1823 and published in the same year. Her friend, Sir Walter Scott, had written the epilogue to this piece. Other literary friends included Mary Howitt, Joanna Baillie, Mary Mitford, and William Wordsworth.

71 *England's Dead*

SON of the Ocean Isle!
Where sleep your mighty dead?
Show me what high and stately pile
Is reared o'er Glory's bed.

Go, stranger! track the deep—
Free, free the white sail spread!
Wave may not foam, nor wild wind sweep,
Where rest not England's dead.

On Egypt's burning plains,
By the pyramid o'erswayed,
With fearful power the noonday reigns,
And the palm-trees yield no shade;—

But let the angry sun
From heaven look fiercely red,
Unfelt by those whose task is done!—
There slumber England's dead.

The hurricane hath might
Along the Indian shore,
And far by Ganges' banks at night
Is heard the tiger's roar;—

But let the sound roll on
It hath no tone of dread
For those that from their toils are gone,—
There slumber England's dead.

Loud rush the torrent-floods
The Western wilds among,
And free, in green Columbia's woods,
The hunter's bow is strung;—

But let the floods rush on!
Let the arrow's flight be sped!
Why should *they* reck whose task is done?—
There slumber England's dead.

The mountain-storms rise high
In the snowy Pyrenees,
And toss the pine boughs through the sky
Like rose-leaves on the breeze;—

But let the storm rage on!
Let the fresh wreaths be shed!
For the Roncesvalles' field is won,—
There slumber England's dead.

On the frozen deep's repose
'Tis a dark and dreadful hour,
When round the ship the ice-fields close,
And the northern night-clouds lower;—

But let the ice drift on!
Let the cold-blue desert spread!
Their course with mast and flag is done—
Even there sleep England's dead.

The warlike of the isles,
The men of field and wave!
Are not the rocks their funeral piles,
The seas and shores their grave?

Go, stranger! track the deep—
Free, free the white sails spread!
Wave may not foam, nor wild wind sweep,
Where rest not England's dead.

(1823 *1839*)

72 *The Sword of the Tomb. A Northern Legend*

The idea of this ballad is taken from a scene in *Starkother*, a tragedy by the Danish poet Ochlenschlager. The sepulchral fire here alluded to, and supposed to guard the ashes of deceased heroes, is frequently mentioned in the Northern Sagas. Severe sufferings to the departed spirit were supposed by the Scandinavian mythologists to be the consequence of any profanation of the sepulchre.—See Ochlenschlager's *Plays*.

'VOICE of the gifted elder time!
Voice of the charm and the Runic rhyme!
Speak! from the shades and the depths disclose
How Sigurd may vanquish his mortal foes;
Voice of the buried past!

'Voice of the grave! 'tis the mighty hour
When night with her stars and dreams hath power,
And my step hath been soundless on the snows,
And the spell I have sung hath laid repose
On the billow and the blast.'

Then the torrents of the North
And the forest pines were still,
While a hollow chant came forth
From the dark sepulchral hill.

'There shines no sun midst the hidden dead,
But where the day looks not the brave may tread;
There is heard no song, and no mead is poured,
But the warrior may come to the silent board
In the shadow of the night.

'There is laid a sword in thy father's tomb,
And its edge is fraught with thy foeman's doom;
But soft be thy step through the silence deep,
And move not the urn in the house of sleep,
For the viewless have fearful might!'

Then died the solemn lay,
As a trumpet's music dies,
By the night-wind borne away
Through the wild and stormy skies.

The fir-trees rocked to the wailing blast,
As on through the forest the warrior passed—
Through the forest of Odin, the dim and old—
The dark place of visions and legends, told
By the fires of Northern pine.

The fir-trees rocked, and the frozen ground
Gave back to his footstep a hollow sound;
And it seemed that the depths of those awful shades,
From the dreary gloom of their long arcades,
Gave warning with voice and sign.

But the wind strange magic knows,
To call wild shape and tone
From the grey wood's tossing boughs,
When Night is on her throne.

The pines closed o'er him with deeper gloom,
As he took the path to the monarch's tomb:
The Pole-star shone, and the heavens were bright
With the arrowy streams of the Northern light
But his road through dimness lay!

He passed, in the heart of that ancient wood,
The dark shrine stained with the victim's blood.
Nor paused till the rock, where a vaulted bed
Had been hewn of old for the kingly dead,
Arose on his midnight way.

Then first a moment's chill
Went shuddering through his breast,
And the steel-clad man stood still
Before that place of rest.

But he crossed at length, with a deep-drawn breath,
The threshold-floor of the hall of Death,
And looked on the pale, mysterious fire
Which gleamed from the urn of his warrior-sire
With a strange and solemn light.

Then darkly the words of the boding strain
Like an omen rose on his soul again—
'Soft be thy step through the silence deep,
And move not the urn in the house of sleep;
For the viewless have fearful might!'

But the gleaming sword and shield
Of many a battle-day
Hung o'er that urn, revealed
By the tomb-fire's waveless ray;

With a faded wreath of oak-leaves bound,
They hung o'er the dust of the far-renowned,
Whom the bright Valkyriur's warning voice
Had called to the banquet where gods rejoice,
    And the rich mead flows in light.

With a beating heart his son drew near,
And still rang the verse in his thrilling ear—
'Soft be thy step through the silence deep,
And move not the urn in the house of sleep;
    For the viewless have fearful might!'

      And many a Saga's rhyme,
      And legend of the grave,
      That shadowy scene and time
      Called back to daunt the brave.

But he raised his arm—and the flame grew dim,
And the sword in its light seemed to wave and swim,
And his faltering hand could not grasp it well—
From the pale oak-wreath, with a clash it fell
    Through the chamber of the dead!

The deep tomb rang with the heavy sound,
And the urn lay shivered in fragments round;
And a rush, as of tempests, quenched the fire,
And the scattered dust of his warlike sire
    Was strewn on the champion's head.

      One moment—and all was still
      In the slumberer's ancient hall,
      When the rock had ceased to thrill
      With the mighty weapon's fall.

The stars were just fading one by one,
The clouds were just tinged by the early sun,
When there streamed through the cavern a torch's flame,
And the brother of Sigurd the valiant came
    To seek him in the tomb.

Stretched on his shield, like the steel-girt slain,
By moonlight seen on the battle-plain,
In a speechless trance lay the warrior there;
But he wildly woke when the torch's glare
    Burst on him through the gloom.

      'The morning wind blows free,
      And the hour of chase is near:
      Come forth, come forth with me!
      What dost thou, Sigurd, here?'

'I have put out the holy sepulchral fire,
I have scattered the dust of my warrior-sire!
It burns on my head, and it weighs down my heart;
But the winds shall not wander without their part
    To strew o'er the restless deep!

'In the mantle of death he was here with me now—
There was wrath in his eye, there was gloom on his brow;
And his cold still glance on my spirit fell
With an icy ray and a withering spell—
    Oh! chill is the house of sleep!'

        'The morning wind blows free,
        And the reddening sun shines clear;
        Come forth, come forth with me!
        It is dark and fearful here!'

'He is there, he is there, with his shadowy frown!
But gone from his head is the kingly crown—
The crown from his head, and the spear from his hand—
They have chased him far from the glorious land
    Where the feast of the gods is spread!

'He must go forth alone on his phantom steed,
He must ride o'er the grave-hills with stormy speed!
His place is no longer at Odin's board,
He is driven from Valhalla without his sword;
    But the slayer shall avenge the dead!'

        That sword its fame had won
        By thc fall of many a crest;
        But its fiercest work was done
        In the tomb, on Sigurd's breast!

(1825 *1839*)

73 *from The Forest Sanctuary*

[*The narrator discovers that a long lost friend is one of the victims of an execution by the Spanish Inquisition. He flees to the New World in self-imposed exile. Eds.*]

XIV

SILENCE upon the mountains! But within
The city's gate a rush, a press, a swell
Of multitudes, their torrent-way to win;
And heavy boomings of a dull deep bell,
A dead pause following each—like that which parts
The dash of billows, holding breathless hearts
Fast in the hush of fear—knell after knell;
And sounds of thickening steps, like thunder rain
That plashes on the roof of some vast echoing fane!

XV

What pageant's hour approached? The sullen gate
Of a strong ancient prison-house was thrown
Back to the day. And who, in mournful state,
Came forth, led slowly o'er its threshold-stone?
They that had learned, in cells of secret gloom,
How sunshine is forgotten! They to whom
The very features of mankind were grown
Things that bewildered! O'er their dazzled sight
They lifted their wan hands, and cowered before the light!

XVI

To this, man brings his brother! Some were there,
Who, with their desolation, had entwined
Fierce strength, and girt the sternness of despair
Fast round their bosoms, even as warriors bind
The breastplate on for fight; but brow and cheek
Seemed *theirs* a torturing panoply to speak!
And there were some, from whom the very mind
Had been wrung out; they smiled—oh, startling smile,
Whence man's high soul is fled! Where doth it sleep the while?

XVII

But onward moved the melancholy train,
For their false creeds in fiery pangs to die.
This was the solemn sacrifice of Spain—
Heaven's offering from the land of chivalry!
Through thousands, thousands of their race they moved—
Oh! how unlike all others!—the beloved,
The free, the proud, the beautiful! whose eye
Grew fixed before them, while a people's breath
Was hushed, and its one soul bound in the thought of death!

XVIII

It might be that, amidst the countless throng,
There swelled some heart with pity's weight oppressed:
For the wide stream of human love is strong;
And woman, on whose fond and faithful breast
Childhood is reared, and at whose knee the sigh
Of its first prayer is breathed—she, too, was nigh.
But life is dear, and the free footstep blessed,
And home a sunny place, where each may fill
Some eye with glistening smiles,—and therefore all were still.

XIX

All still,—youth, courage, strength!—a winter laid,
A chain of palsy cast, on might and mind!
Still, as at noon a southern forest's shade,
They stood, those breathless masses of mankind,
Still, as a frozen torrent! But the wave
Soon leaps to foaming freedom; they, the brave,
Endured—they saw the martyr's place assigned
In the red flames—whence is the withering spell
That numbs each human pulse? They saw, and thought it well.

XX

And I, too, thought it well! That very morn
From a far land I came, yet round we clung
The spirit of my own. No hand had torn
With a strong grasp away the veil which hung
Between mine eyes and truth. I gazed, I saw
Dimly, as through a glass. In silent awe
I watched the fearful rites; and if there sprung
One rebel feeling from its deep founts up,
Shuddering, I flung it back, as guilt's own poison-cup.

XXI

But I was wakened as the dreamers waken,
Whom the shrill trumpet and the shriek of dread
Rouse up at midnight, when their walls are taken,
And they must battle till their blood is shed
On their own threshold floor. A path for light
Through my torn breast was shattered by the might
Of the swift thunder-stroke; and freedom's tread
Came in through ruins, late, yet not in vain,
Making the blighted place all green with life again.

XXII

Still darkly, slowly, as a sullen mass
Of cloud o'ersweeping, without wind, the sky,
Dream-like I saw the sad procession pass,
And marked its victims with a tearless eye.
They moved before me but as pictures, wrought
Each to reveal some secret of man's thought,
On the sharp edge of sad mortality;
Till in his place came one—oh! could it be?
My friend, my heart's first friend!—and did I gaze on thee!

XXIII

On thee! with whom in boyhood I had played,
At the grape-gatherings, by my native streams;
And to whose eye my youthful soul had laid
Bare, as to heaven's, its glowing world of dreams;
And by whose side midst warriors I had stood,
And in whose helm was brought—oh, earned with blood!—
The fresh wave to my lips, when tropic beams
Smote on my fevered brow! Ay, years had passed,
Severing our paths, brave friend!—and *thus* we met at last!

XXIV

I see it still—the lofty mien thou borest!
On my pale forehead sat a sense of power—
The very look that once thou brightly worest,
Cheering me onward through a fearful hour,
When we were girt by Indian bow and spear,
Midst the white Andes—even as mountain deer,
Hemmed in our camp; but through the javelin shower
We rent our way, a tempest of despair!
And thou—hadst thou but died with thy true brethren there!

XXV

I call the fond wish back—for thou hast perished
More nobly far, my Alvar!—making known
The might of truth; and be thy memory cherished
With theirs, the thousands that around her throne
Have poured their lives out smiling, in that doom
Finding a triumph, if denied a tomb!
Ay, with their ashes hath the wind been sown,
And with the wind their spirit shall be spread,
Filling man's heart and home with records of the dead.

XXVI

Thou Searcher of the soul! in whose dread sight
Not the bold guilt alone that mocks the skies,
But the scarce-owned unwhispered thought of night,
As a thing written with the sunbeam lies;
Yet a dim awfulness was on the brow—
No! not like sleep to look upon art thou,
Death, Death! She lay a thing for earth's embrace,
To cover with spring-wreaths. For earth's?—the wave
That gives the bier no flowers, makes moan above her grave!

(1825 *1839*)

74 *Joan of Arc in Rheims*

[*When 'Joan of Arc in Rheims' was printed in* Records of Woman *(1828) it followed no. 78, 'Indian Woman's Death-Song'. Both were preceded by 'Arabella Stuart' (no. 76) and 'Properzia Rossi' (no. 77). Eds.*]

Jeanne d'Arc avait eu la joie de voir à Chalons quelques amis de son enfance. Une joie plus ineffable encore l'attendait à Rheims, au sein de son triomphe: Jacques d'Arc, son père, y se trouva, aussitôt que de troupes de Charles VII. y furent entrées; et comme les deux frères de notre héroine l'avaient accompaguée, elle se vit pour un instant au milieu de sa famille, dans les bras d'un père vertueux.

Vie de Jeanne d'Arc

Thou hast a charmèd cup, O Fame!
  A draught that mantles high,
And seems to lift this earth-born frame
  Above mortality:
Away! to me—a woman—bring
Sweet waters from affection's spring!

THAT was a joyous day in Rheims of old,
When peal on peal of mighty music rolled
Forth from her thronged cathedral; while around,
A multitude, whose billows made no sound,
Chained to a hush of wonder, though elate
With victory, listened at their temple's gate.
And what was done within? Within, thc light,
  Through the rich gloom of pictured windows flowing
Tinged with soft awfulness a stately sight—
  The chivalry of France their proud heads bowing
In martial vassalage! While midst that ring,
And shadowed by ancestral tombs, a king
Received his birthright's crown. For this, the hymn
  Swelled out like rushing waters, and the day
With the sweet censer's misty breath grew dim,
  As through long aisles it floated o'er the array
Of arms and sweeping stoles. But who, alone
And unapproached, beside the altar stone,
With the white banner forth like sunshine streaming,
And the gold helm through clouds of fragrance gleaming,
Silent and radiant stood? The helm was raised,
And the fair face revealed, that upward gazed,
Intensely worshiping—a still, clear face,
Youthful, but brightly solemn! Woman's cheek
And brow were there, in deep devotion meek,
Yet glorified, with inspiration's trace
On its pure paleness; while, enthroned above,

The pictured Virgin, with her smile of love,
Seemed bending o'er her votaress. That slight form!
Was that the leader through the battle storm?
Had the soft light in that adoring eye
Guided the warrior where the swords flashed high?
'Twas so, even so!—and thou, the shepherd's child,
Joanne, the lovely dreamer of the wild!
Never before, and never since that hour,
Hath woman, mantled with victorious power,
Stood forth as *thou* beside the shrine didst stand,
Holy amidst the knighthood of the land,
And, beautiful with joy and with renown,
Lift thy white banner o'er the olden crown,
  Ransomed for France by thee!
                                        The rites are done.
Now let the dome with trumpet-notes be shaken,
And bid the echoes of the tomb awaken,
  And come thou forth, that heaven's rejoicing sun
May give thee welcome from thine own blue skies,
  Daughter of victory! A triumphant strain,
A proud rich stream of warlike melodies,
  Gushed through the portals of the antique fane,
And forth she came. Then rose a nation's sound:
Oh! what a power to bid the quick heart bound,
The wind bears onward with the stormy cheer
Man gives to glory on her high career!
Is there indeed such power?—far deeper dwells
In one kind household voice, to reach the cells
Whence happiness flows forth! The shouts that filled
The hollow heaven tempestuously, were stilled
One moment; and in that brief pause, the tone,
As of a breeze that o'er her home had blown,
Sank on the bright maid's heart. 'Joanne!'—Who spoke
  Like those whose childhood with *her* childhood grew
Under one roof? 'Joanne!'—*that* murmur broke
  With sounds of weeping forth! She turned—she knew
Beside her, marked from all the thousands there,
In the calm beauty of his silver hair,
The stately shepherd; and the youth, whose joy,
From his dark eye flashed proudly; and the boy,
The youngest born, that ever loved her best:—
'Father! and ye, my brothers!' On the breast
Of that grey sire she sank—and swiftly back,
Even in an instant, to their native track
Her free thoughts flowed. She saw the pomp no more,
The plumes, the banners: to her cabin-door,
And to the Fairy's Fountain in the glade,

Where her young sisters by her side had played,
And to her hamlet's chapel, where it rose
Hallowing the forest unto deep repose,
Her spirit turned. The very wood-note, sung
  In early spring-time by the bird, which dwelt
Where o'er her father's roof the beech leaves hung,
  Was in her heart; a music heard and felt,
Winning her back to nature. She unbound
  The helm of many battles from her head,
And, with her bright locks bowed to sweep the ground,
  Lifting her voice up, wept for joy and said—
'Bless me, my father! bless me! and with thee,
To the still cabin and the beechen tree,
Let me return!'
                    Oh! never did thine eye
Through the green haunts of happy infancy
Wander again, Joanne! Too much of fame
Had shed its radiance on thy peasant name;
And bought alone by gifts beyond all price—
The trusting heart's repose, the paradise
Of home, with all its loves—doth fate allow
The crown of glory unto woman's brow.

(1826 *1839*)

75 *The Homes of England*

Where's the coward that would not dare
To fight for such a land?
Marmion

THE stately homes of England,
  How beautiful they stand,
Amidst their tall ancestral trees,
  O'er all the pleasant land!
The deer across their greensward bound,
  Through shade and sunny gleam;
And the swan glides past them with the sound
  Of some rejoicing stream.

The merry homes of England!
  Around their hearths by night,
What gladsome looks of household love
  Meet in the ruddy light!
There woman's voice flows forth in song,
  Or childhood's tale is told,
Or lips move tunefully along
  Some glorious page of old.

The blessed homes of England!
How softly on their bowers
Is laid the holy quietness
That breathes from Sabbath hours!
Solemn, yet sweet, the church-bell's chime
Floats through their woods at morn;
All other sounds, in that still time.
Of breeze and leaf are born.

The cottage homes of England!
By thousands on her plains,
They are smiling o'er the silvery brooks,
And round the hamlet fanes.
Through glowing orchards forth they peep,
Each from its nook of leaves;
And fearless there the lowly sleep,
As the bird beneath their eaves.

The free, fair homes of England!
Long, long, in hut and hall,
May hearts of native proof be reared
To guard each hallowed wall!
And green for ever be the groves,
And bright the flowery sod,
Where first the child's glad spirit loves
Its country and its God!

(1827 *1839*)

76 *Arabella Stuart*

[*This poem was placed first in* Records of Woman *(1828). Eds.*]

'THE LADY ARABELLA', as she has been frequently entitled, was descended from Margaret, eldest daughter of Henry VII, and consequently allied by birth to Elizabeth as well as James I. This affinity to the throne proved the misfortune of her life, as the jealousies which it constantly excited in her royal relatives, who were anxious to prevent her marrying, shut her out from the enjoyment of that domestic happiness which her heart appears to have so fervently desired. By a secret but early discovered union with William Seymour, son of Lord Beauchamp, she alarmed the cabinet of James, and the wedded lovers were immediately placed in separate confinement. From this they found means to concert a romantic plan of escape; and having won over a female attendant, by whose assistance she was disguised in male attire, Arabella, though faint from recent sickness and suffering, stole out in the night, and at last reached an appointed spot, where a boat and servants were in waiting. She embarked, and at break of day a French vessel engaged to receive her was discovered and gained. As Seymour, however, had not yet arrived, she was desirous that the vessel should lie at anchor for him; but this wish was overruled by her companions, who, contrary to her entreaties, hoisted sail, 'which', says D'Israeli, 'occasioned so fatal a termination to this romantic adventure. Seymour, indeed, had escaped from the Tower; he reached the wharf, and found his confidential man waiting with a boat, and arrived at Lee. The time passed; the waves were rising; Arabella was not there; but in the distance he descried a vessel. Hiring a fisherman to take him on board, he discovered, to his grief, on hailing it, that it was not the French ship charged with his Arabella; in despair and confusion he found another ship from Newcastle, which for a large sum altered its course, and landed him in Flanders.' Arabella, meantime, whilst imploring her attendants to linger, and earnestly looking out for the expected boat of her husband, was overtaken in Calais Roads by a vessel in the king's service, and brought back to a captivity, under the suffering of which her mind and constitution gradually sank. 'What passed in that dreadful imprisonment cannot perhaps be recovered for authentic history, but enough is known—that her mind grew impaired, that she finally lost her reason, and, if the duration of her imprisonment was short, that it was only terminated by her death. Some effusions, often begun and never ended, written and erased, incoherent and rational, yet remain among her papers' (*D'Israeli's Curiosities of Literature*).

The following poem, meant as some record of her fate, and the imagined fluctuations of her thoughts and feelings, is supposed to commence during the time of her first imprisonment, whilst her mind was yet buoyed up by the consciousness of Seymour's affection, and the cherished hope of eventual deliverance.

And is not love in vain
Torture enough without a living tomb?
Byron

Fermossi al fin il cor che balzò tanto.
Pindemonte

I

'TWAS but a dream! I saw the stag leap free,
  Under the boughs where early birds were singing;
I stood o'ershadowed by the greenwood tree,
  And heard, it seemed, a sudden bugle ringing
Far through a royal forest. Then the fawn
Shot, like a gleam of light, from grassy lawn
To secret covert; and the smooth turf shook,
And lilies quivered by the glade's lone brook,
And young leaves trembled, as, in fleet career,
A princely band, with horn, and hound, and spear,
Like a rich masque swept forth. I saw the dance
Of their white plumes, that bore a silvery glance
Into the deep wood's heart; and all passed by
Save one—I met the smile of *one* clear eye,
Flashing out joy to mine. Yes, *thou* wert there,
Seymour! A soft wind blew the clustering hair
Back from thy gallant brow, as thou didst rein
Thy courser, turning from that gorgeous train,
And fling, methought, thy hunting spear away,
And, lightly graceful in thy green array,
Bound to my side. And we, that met and parted

Ever in dread of some dark watchful power,
Won back to childhood's trust, and fearless-hearted,
Blent the glad fulness of our thoughts that hour
Even like the mingling of sweet streams, beneath
Dim woven leaves, and midst the floating breath
Of hidden forest-flowers.

II

'Tis past! I wake,
A captive, and alone, and far from thee,
My love and friend! Yet fostering, for thy sake,
A quenchless hope of happiness to be;
And feeling still my woman-spirit strong,
In the deep faith which lifts from earthly wrong
A heavenward glance. I know, I know our love
Shall yet call gentle angels from above,
By its undying fervour, and prevail—
Sending a breath, as of the spring's first gale,
Through hearts now cold; and, raising its bright face,
With a free gush of sunny tears, erase
The characters of anguish. In this trust,
I bear, I strive, I bow not to the dust,
That I may bring thee back no faded form,
No bosom chilled and blighted by the storm,
But all my youth's first treasures, when we meet,
Making past sorrow, by communion, sweet.

III

And thou too art in bonds! Yet droop thou not,
O my beloved! there is *one* hopeless lot.
But one, and that not ours. Beside the dead
There sits the grief that mantles up its head,
Loathing the laughter and proud pomp of light,
When darkness, from the vainly doting sight
Covers its beautiful! If thou wert gone
To the grave's bosom, with thy radiant brow—
If thy deep-thrilling voice, with that low tone
Of earnest tenderness, which now, even now
Seems floating through my soul, were music taken
For ever from this world—oh! thus forsaken
Could I bear on? Thou livest, thou livest, thou'rt mine!
With this glad thought I make my heart a shrine,
And by the lamp which quenchless there shall burn,
Sit a lone watcher for the day's return.

IV

And lo! the joy that cometh with the morning,
  Brightly victorious o'er the hours of care!
I have not watched in vain, serenely scorning
  The wild and busy whispers of despair!
Thou hast sent tidings, as of heaven—I wait
  The hour, the sign, for blessèd flight to thee.
Oh! for the skylark's wing that seeks its mate
  As a star shoots!—but on the breezy sea
We shall meet soon. To think of such an hour!
  Will not my heart, o'erburdened by its bliss,
Faint and give way within me, as a flower
  Borne down and perishing by noontide's kiss?
Yet shall I *fear* that lot—the perfect rest,
The full deep joy of dying on thy breast,
After long suffering won? So rich a close
Too seldom crowns with peace affection's woes.

V

Sunset! I tell each moment. From the skies
  The last red splendour floats along my wall,
Like a king's banner! Now it melts, it dies!
  I see one star—I hear—'twas not the call,
The expected voice; my quick heart throbbed too soon
I must keep vigil till yon rising moon
Shower down less golden light. Beneath her beam
Through my lone lattice poured, I sit and dream
Of summer-lands afar, where holy love,
Under the vine or in the citron grove,
May breathe from terror.
                    Now the night grows deep,
And silent as its clouds, and full of sleep.
I hear my veins beat. Hark! a bell's slow chime!
My heart strikes with it. Yet again—'tis time!
A step!—a voice!—or but a rising breeze?
Hark!—haste!—I come, to meet thee on the seas!

* * *

VI

Now never more, oh! never, in the worth
Of its pure cause, let sorrowing love on earth
Trust fondly—never more! The hope is crushed
That lit my life, the voice within me hushed
That spoke sweet oracles; and I return
To lay my youth, as in a burial urn,

Where sunshine may not find it. All is lost!
No tempest met our barks—no billow tossed;
Yet were they severed, even as we must be,
That so have loved, so striven our hearts to free
From their close-coiling fate! In vain—in vain!
The dark links meet, and clasp themselves again,
And press out life. Upon the deck I stood
And a white sail came gliding o'er the flood,
Like some proud bird of ocean; then mine eye
Strained out, one moment earlier to descry
The form it ached for, and the bark's career
Seemed slow to that fond yearning: it drew near
Fraught with our foes! What boots it to recall
The strife, the tears? Once more a prison wall
Shuts the green hills and woodlands from my sight,
And joyous glance of waters to the light,
And thee, my Seymour!—thee!
I will not sink
Thou, *thou* hast rent the heavy chain that bound thee!
And this shall be my strength—the joy to think
That thou mayest wander with heaven's breath around thee,
And all the laughing sky! This thought shall yet
Shine o'er my heart a radiant amulet,
Guarding it from despair. Thy bonds are broken;
And unto me, I know, thy true love's token
Shall one day be deliverance, though the years
Lie dim between, o'erhung with mists of tears.

VII

My friend! my friend! where art thou? Day by day,
Gliding like some dark mournful stream away,
My silent youth flows from me. Spring, the while,
Comes and rains beauty on the kindling boughs
Round hall and hamlet; summer with her smile
Fills the green forest; young hearts breathe their vows,
Brothers long parted meet; fair children rise
Round the glad board; hope laughs from loving eyes:
All this is in the world!—These joys lie sown,
The dew of every path! On *one* alone
Their freshness may not fall—the stricken deer
Dying of thirst with all the waters near.

VIII

Ye are from dingle and fresh glade, ye flowers!
By some kind hand to cheer my dungeon sent;
O'er you the oak shed down the summer showers,

And the lark's nest was where your bright cups bent,
Quivering to breeze and raindrop, like the sheen
Of twilight stars. On you heaven's eye hath been.
Through the leaves pouring its dark sultry blue
Into your glowing hearts; the bee to you
Hath murmured, and the rill. My soul grows faint
With passionate yearning, as its quick dreams paint
Your haunts by dell and stream—the green, the free,
The full of all sweet sound—the shut from me!

IX

There went a swift bird singing past my cell—
O Love and Freedom! ye are lovely things!
With you the peasant on the hills may dwell,
And by the streams. But I—the blood of kings,
A proud unmingling river, through my veins
Flows in lone brightness, and its gifts are chains!
Kings!—I had silent visions of deep bliss,
Leaving their thrones far distant; and for this
I am cast under their triumphal car,
An insect to be crushed! Oh! Heaven is far—
Earth pitiless!

Dost thou forget me, Seymour? I am proved
So long, so sternly! Seymour, my beloved!
There are such tales of holy marvels done
By strong affection, of deliverance won
Through its prevailing power! Are these things told
Till the young weep with rapture, and the old
Wonder, yet dare not doubt; and thou! oh, thou!
Dost thou forget me in my hope's decay?—
Thou canst not! Through the silent night, even now,
I, that need prayer so much, awake and pray
Still first for thee. O gentle, gentle friend!
How shall I bear this anguish to the end?

Aid!—comes there yet no aid? The voice of blood
Passes heaven's gate, even ere the crimson flood
Sinks through the greensward! Is there not a cry
From the wrung heart, of power, through agony,
To pierce the clouds? Hear, Mercy!—hear me! None
That bleed and weep beneath the smiling sun
Have heavier cause! Yet hear!—my soul grows dark!—
Who hears the last shriek from the sinking bark
On the mid seas, and with the storm alone,
And bearing to the abyss, unseen, unknown,
Its freight of human hearts? The o'ermastering wave

Who shall tell how it rushed—and none to save!
Thou hast forsaken me! I feel, I know,
There would be rescue if this were not so.
Thou'rt at the chase, thou'rt at the festive board,
Thou'rt where the red wine free and high is poured,
Thou'rt where the dancers meet! A magic glass
Is set within my soul, and proud shapes pass,
Flushing it o'er with pomp from bower and hall;
I see one shadow, stateliest there of all—

Thine! What dost *thou* amidst the bright and fair,
Whispering light words, and mocking my despair?
It is not well of thee! My love was more
Than fiery song may breathe, deep thought explore;
And there thou smilest, while my heart is dying,
With all its blighted hopes around it lying:
Even thou, on whom they hung their last green leaf—
Yet smile, smile on! too bright art thou for grief!

Death! What! is death a locked and treasured thing,
Guarded by swords of fire? a hidden spring,
A fabled fruit, that I should thus endure,
As if the world within me held no cure?
Wherefore not spread free wings—Heaven, heaven control
These thoughts!—they rush—I look into my soul
As down a gulf, and tremble at the array
Of fierce forms crowding it! Give strength to pray!
So shall their dark host pass.

The storm is stilled.
  Father in Heaven thou, only thou, canst sound
The heart's great deep, with floods of anguish filled,
  For human line too fearfully profound.
Therefore, forgive, my Father! if thy child,
Rocked on its heaving darkness, hath grown wild
And sinned in her despair! It well may be
That thou wouldst lead my spirit back to thee,
By the crushed hope too long on this world poured—
The stricken love which hath perchance adored
A mortal in thy place! Now let me strive
With thy strong arm no more! Forgive, forgive!
Take me to peace!

And peace at last is nigh.
  A sign is on my brow, a token sent
The o'erwearied dust from home: no breeze flits by,
  But calls me with a strange sweet whisper, blent
Of many mysteries.

Hark! the warning tone

Deepens—its word is *Death!* Alone, alone,
And sad in youth, but chastened, I depart,
Bowing to heaven. Yet, yet my woman's heart
Shall wake a spirit and a power to bless,
Even in this hour's o'ershadowing fearfulness,
Thee, its first love! O tender still, and true!
Be it forgotten if mine anguish threw
Drops from its bitter fountain on thy name,
Though but a moment!

Now, with fainting frame,
With soul just lingering on the flight begun,
To bind for thee its last dim thoughts in one,
I bless thee! Peace be on thy noble head,
Years of bright fame, when I am with the dead!
I bid this prayer survive me, and retain
Its might, again to bless thee, and again!
Thou hast been gathered into my dark fate
Too much; too long, for my sake, desolate
Hath been thine exiled youth: but now take back,
From dying hands, thy freedom, and re-track
(After a few kind tears for her whose days
Went out in dreams of thee) the sunny ways
Of hope, and find thou happiness! Yet send
Even then, in silent hours, a thought, dear friend!
Down to my voiceless chamber; for thy love
Hath been to me all gifts of earth above,
Though bought with burning tear! It is the sting
Of death to leave that vainly-precious thing
In this cold world! What were it, then, if thou,
With thy fond eyes, wert gazing on me now?
Too keen a pang. Farewell! and yet once more,
Farewell! The passion of long years I pour
Into that word! Thou hearest not—but the woe
And fervour of its tones may one day flow
To thy heart's holy place: there let them dwell.
We shall o'ersweep the grave to meet. Farewell!

(1828 *1839*)

77 *Properzia Rossi*

[One of the sequence of poems comprising Records of Woman *(1828). Eds.]*

Properzia Rossi, a celebrated female sculptor of Bologna, possessed also of talents for poetry and music, died in consequence of an unrequited attachment. A painting, by Ducis, represents her showing her last work, a basso-relievo of Ariadne, to a Roman knight, the object of her affection, who regards it with indifference.

'Tell me no more, no more
Of my soul's lofty gifts! Are they not vain
To quench its haunting thirst for happiness?
Have I not loved, and striven, and failed to bind
One true heart unto me, whereon my own
Might find a resting-place, a home for all
Its burden of affections? I depart,
Unknown, though Fame goes with me; I must leave
The earth unknown. Yet it may be that death
Shall give my name a power to win such tears
As would have made life precious.'

I

ONE dream of passion and of beauty more!
And in its bright fulfilment let me pour
My soul away! Let earth retain a trace
Of that which lit my being, though its race
Might have been loftier far. Yet one more dream!
From my deep spirit one victorious gleam
Ere I depart! For thee alone, for thee!
May this last work, this farewell triumph be—
Thou, loved so vainly! I would leave enshrined
Something immortal of my heart and mind,
That yet may speak to thee when I am gone,
Shaking thine inmost bosom with a tone
Of lost affection,—something that may prove
What she hath been, whose melancholy love
On thee was lavished; silent pang and tear,
And fervent song that gushed when none were near,
And dream by night, and weary thought by day,
Stealing the brightness from her life away—
While thou—Awake! not yet within me die!
Under the burden and the agony
Of this vain tenderness—my spirit, wake!
Even for thy sorrowful affection's sake,
Live! in thy work breathe out!—that he may yet,
Feeling sad mastery there, perchance regret
Thine unrequited gift.

II

It comes! the power
Within me born flows back—my fruitless dower
That could not win me love. Yet once again
I greet it proudly, with its rushing train
Of glorious images: they throng—they press—
A sudden joy lights up my loneliness—
I shall not perish all

The bright work grows
Beneath my hand, unfolded as a rose,
Leaf after leaf, to beauty; line by line,
I fix my thought, heart, soul, to burn, to shine,
Through the pale marble's veins. It grows!—and now
I give my own life's history to thy brow,
Forsaken Ariadne!—thou shalt wear
My form, my lineaments; but oh! more fair,
Touched into lovelier being by the glow
Which in me dwells, as by the summer light
All things are glorified. From thee my woe
Shall yet look beautiful to meet his sight,
When I am passed away. Thou art the mould,
Wherein I pour the fervent thoughts, the untold,
The self-consuming! Speak to him of me,
Thou, the deserted by the lonely sea,
With the soft sadness of thine earnest eye—
Speak to him, lorn one! deeply, mournfully,
Of all my love and grief! Oh! could I throw
Into thy frame a voice—a sweet, and low,
And thrilling voice of song! when he came nigh,
To send the passion of its melody
Through his pierced bosom—on its tones to bear
My life's deep feeling, as the southern air
Wafts the faint myrtle's breath—to rise, to swell,
To sink away in accents of farewell,
Winning but one, *one* gush of tears, whose flow
Surely my parted spirit yet might know,
If love be strong as death!

III

Now fair thou art,
Thou form, whose life is of my burning heart!
Yet all the vision that within me wrought,
I cannot make thee. Oh! I might have given
Birth to creations of far nobler thought;
I might have kindled, with the fire of heaven,

Things not of such as die! But I have been
Too much alone! A heart whereon to lean,
With all these deep affections that o'erflow
My aching soul, and find no shore below;
An eye to be my star; a voice to bring
Hope o'er my path like sounds that breathe of spring:
These are denied me—dreamt of still in vain.
Therefore my brief aspirings from the chain
Are ever but as some wild fitful song,
Rising triumphantly, to die ere long
In dirge-like echoes.

IV

Yet the world will see
Little of this, my parting work! in thee.
  Thou shalt have fame! Oh, mockery! give the reed
From storms a shelter—give the drooping vine
Something round which its tendrils may entwine—
  Give the parched flower a rain-drop, and the meed
Of love's kind words to woman! Worthless fame!
That in *his* bosom wins not for my name
The abiding place it asked! Yet how my heart,
In its own fairy world of song and art,
Once beat for praise! Are those high longings o'er?
That which I have been can I be no more?
Never! oh, never more! though still thy sky
Be blue as then, my glorious Italy!
And though the music, whose rich breathings fill
Thin air with soul, be wandering past me still;
And though the mantle of thy sunlight streams
Unchanged on forms, instinct with poet-dreams.
Never! oh, never more! Where'er I move,
The shadow of this broken-hearted love
Is on me and around! Too well *they* know
  Whose life is all within, too soon and well,
When there the blight hath settled! But I go
  Under the silent wings of peace to dwell;
From the slow wasting, from the lonely pain,
The inward burning of those words—'*in vain*,'
  Seared on the heart—I go. 'Twill soon be past!
Sunshine and song, and bright Italian heaven,
  And thou, oh! thou, on whom my spirit cast
Unvalued wealth—who knowest not what was given
In that devotedness—the sad, and deep,
And unrepaid—farewell! If I could weep
Once, only once, beloved one! on thy breast,

Pouring my heart forth ere I sink to rest!
But that were happiness!—and unto me
Earth's gift is *fame*. Yet I was formed to be
So richly blessed! With thee to watch the sky,
Speaking not, feeling but that thou wert nigh;
With thee to listen, while the tones of song
Swept even as part of our sweet air along—
To listen silently; with thee to gaze
On forms, the deified of olden days—
This had been joy enough; and hour by hour,
From its glad well-springs drinking life and power,
How had my spirit soared, and made its fame
  A glory for thy brow! Dreams, dreams!—the fire
Burns faint within me. Yet I leave my name—
  As a deep thrill may linger on the lyre
When its full chords are hushed—awhile to live,
And one day haply in thy heart revive
Sad thoughts of me. I leave it, with a sound,
A spell o'er memory, mournfully profound;
I leave it, on my country's air to dwell—
Say proudly yet—"*'Twas hers who loved me well!*"

(1828 *1839*)

78 *Indian Woman's Death-Song*

[*One of the poems comprising* Records of Woman *(1828), where it preceded 'Joan of Arc in Rheims.' Eds.*]

An Indian woman, driven to despair by her husband's desertion of her for another wife, entered a canoe with her children, and rowed it down the Mississippi towards a cataract. Her voice was heard from the shore singing a mournful death-song, until overpowered by the sound of the waters in which she perished. The tale is related in Long's 'Expedition to the Source of St Peter's River'.

Non, je ne puis vivre avec un cœur brisé. Il faut que je retrouve la joie, et que je m'unisse aux esprits libres de l'air.'

Bride of Messina—Translated by Madame de Stael

Let not my child be a girl, for very sad is the life of a woman.

The Prairie

DOWN a broad river of the western wilds,
Piercing thick forest-glooms, a light canoe
Swept with the current: fearful was the speed
Of the frail bark, as by a tempest's wing
Borne leaf-like on to where the mist of spray
Rose with the cataract's thunder. Yet within,

Proudly, and dauntlessly, and all alone,
Save that a babe lay sleeping at her breast,
A woman stood! Upon her Indian brow
Sat a strange gladness, and her dark hair waved
As if triumphantly. She pressed her child,
In its bright slumber, to her beating heart,
And lifted her sweet voice, that rose awhile
Above the sound of waters, high and clear,
Wafting a wild proud strain—a song of death.

'ROLL swiftly to the spirit's land, thou mighty stream and free!
Father of ancient waters, roll! and bear our lives with thee!
The weary bird that storms have tossed would seek the sunshine's calm,
And the deer that hath the arrow's hurt flies to the woods of balm.

'Roll on!—my warrior's eye hath looked upon another's face,
And mine hath faded from his soul, as fades a moonbeam's trace:
My shadow comes not o'er his path, my whisper to his dream,
He flings away the broken reed. Roll swifter yet, thou stream!

'The voice that spoke of other days is hushed within *his* breast,
But *mine* its lonely music haunts, and will not let me rest;
It sings a low and mornful song of gladness that is gone—
I cannot live without that light. Father of waves! roll on!

'Will he not miss the bounding step that met him from the chase?
The heart of love that made his home an ever-sunny place?
The hand that spread the hunter's board, and decked his couch of yore?—
He will not! Roll, dark foaming stream, on to the better shore!

'Some blessed fount amidst the woods of that bright land must flow,
Whose waters from my soul may lave the memory of this woe;
Some gentle wind must whisper there, whose breath may waft away
The burden of the heavy night, the sadness of the day.

'And thou, my babe! though born, like me, for woman's weary lot,
Smile!—to that wasting of the heart, my own! I leave thee not;
Too bright a thing art *thou* to pine in aching love away—
Thy mother bears thee far, young fawn! from sorrow and decay.

'She bears thee to the glorious bowers where none are heard to weep,
And where the unkind one hath no power again to trouble sleep;
And where the soul shall find its youth, as wakening from a dream;
One moment, and that realm is ours. On, on, dark rolling stream!'

(1828 *1839*)

79 *The Image in Lava*[1]

THOU thing of years departed!
  What ages have gone by
Since here the mournful seal was set
  By love and agony?

Temple and tower have mouldered,
  Empires from earth have passed,
And woman's heart hath left a trace
  Those glories to outlast!

And childhood's fragile image,
  Thus fearfully enshrined,
Survives the proud memorials reared
  By conquerors of mankind.

Babe wert thou brightly slumbering
  Upon thy mother's breast
When suddenly the fiery tomb
  Shut round each gentle guest?

A strange, dark fate o'ertook you,
  Fair babe and loving heart!
One moment of a thousand pangs—
  Yet better than to part!

Haply of that fond bosom
  On ashes here impressed,
Thou wert the only treasure, child?
  Whereon a hope might rest.

Perchance all vainly lavished
  Its other love had been,
And where it trusted, nought remained
  But thorns on which to lean.

Far better, then, to perish,
  Thy form within its clasp,
Than live and lose thee, precious one
  From that impassioned grasp.

Oh! I could pass all relics
  Left by the pomps of old,
To gaze on this rude monument
  Cast in affection's mould.

[1] The impression of a woman's form, with an infant clasped to the bosom, found at the uncovering of Herculaneum.

Love! human love! what art thou?
  Thy print upon the dust
Outlives the cities of renown
  Wherein the mighty trust!

Immortal, oh! immortal
  Thou art, whose earthly glow
Hath given these ashes holiness—
  It must, it *must* be so!

(1827 *1839*)

80 *Casabianca*[1]

THE boy stood on the burning deck
  Whence all but he had fled;
The flame that lit the battle's wreck
  Shone round him o'er the dead.

Yet beautiful and bright he stood,
  As born to rule the storm—
A creature of heroic blood,
  A proud, though child-like form.

The flames rolled on—he would not go
  Without his father's word;
That father, faint in death below,
  His voice no longer heard.

He called aloud:—'Say, father, say
  If yet my task is done!'
He knew not that the chieftain lay
  Unconscious of his son.

'Speak, father!' once again he cried,
  'If I may yet be gone!'
And but the booming shots replied,
  And fast the flames rolled on.

Upon his brow he felt their breath,
  And in his waving hair,
And looked from that lone post of death
  In still yet brave despair;

[1] Young Casabianca, a boy about thirteen years old, son to the Admiral of the Orient, remained at his post (in the Battle of the Nile) after the ship had taken fire, and all the guns had been abandoned; and perished in the explosion of the vessel, when the flames had reached the powder.

And shouted but once more aloud,
  'My father! must I stay?'
While o'er him fast, through sail and shroud,
  The wreathing fires made way.

They wrapt the ship in splendour wild,
  They caught the flag on high,
And streamed above the gallant child
  Like banners in the sky.

There came a burst of thunder-sound—
  The boy—oh! where was he?
Ask of the winds that far around
  With fragments strewed the sea!—

With mast, and helm, and pennon fair,
  That well had borne their part;
But the noblest thing which perished there
  Was that young faithful heart!

(1826 *1839*)

81 *The Shadow of a Flower*

La voilà telle que la mort nous l'a faite.
Bossuet

Never was a philosophical imagination more beautiful than that exquisite one of Kircher, Digby, and others, who discovered in the ashes of plants their primitive forms, which were again raised up by the power of heat. The ashes of roses, say they, will again revive in roses, unsubstantial and unodoriferous; they are not roses which grow on rose-trees, but their delicate apparitions, and, like apparitions, they are seen but for a moment.

Curiosities of Literature

'TWAS a dream of olden days,
  That Art, by some strange power
The visionary form could raise
  From the ashes of a flower.

That a shadow of the rose,
  By its own meek beauty bow'd,
Might slowly, leaf by leaf, unclose,
  Like pictures in a cloud.

Or the hyacinth, to grace,
  As a second rainbow, Spring;
Of Summer's path a dreary trace,
  A fair, yet mournful thing!

For the glory of the bloom
  That a flush around it shed,
And the soul within, the rich perfume,
  Where were they?—fled, all fled!

Nought but the dim faint line
  To speak of vanish'd hours—
Memory! what are joys of thine?
  —Shadows of buried flowers!

(1830)

MARIA ABDY
(*c*.1797–1867)

WELL known for her contributions to annuals, such as *The Keepsake*, Maria Abdy collected her often highly sentimental work in a volume simply entitled *Poetry*, which was reprinted on many occasions between 1834 and 1862. Born in London, she was the daughter of Richard Smith, a solicitor. It seems that she wrote poetry from a very early age. Her first literary appearance was in the *New Monthly Magazine*, to which she contributed several poems. Her poems were placed there at the encouragement of the Revd John Channing Abdy, Rector of St John's Southwark, whom she had married when young. Much later in life, she won first prize for her poem entitled 'An Appeal on Behalf of Governesses', entered into a competition held in 1856. The topic in question was one that preoccupied many writers in the early and mid-Victorian period, and it is taken up by the poem we have reprinted here.

82 *A Governess Wanted*

'OUR governess left us, dear brother,
  Last night, in a strange fit of pique,
Will you kindly seek out for another?
  We want her at latest next week:
But I'll give you a few plain credentials,
  The bargain with speed to complete;
Take a pen—just set down the essentials,
  And begin at the top of the sheet!

'With easy and modest decision,
  She ever must move, act, and speak;
She must understand French with precision,
  Italian, and Latin, and Greek:
She must play the piano divinely,
  Excel on the harp and the lute,
Do all sorts of needle-work finely,
  And make feather-flowers, and wax-fruit.

'She must answer all queries directly,
  And all sciences well understand,
Paint in oils, sketch from nature correctly,
  And write German text, and short-hand:
She must sing with power, science, and sweetness,
  Yet for concerts must sigh not at all,
She must dance with etherial fleetness;
  Yet never must go to a ball.

'She must not have needy relations,
  Her dress must be tasteful yet plain,
Her discourse must abound in quotations,
  Her memory all dates must retain:
She must point out each author's chief beauties,
  She must manage dull natures with skill,
Her pleasures must lie in her duties,
  She must never be nervous or ill!

'If she write essays, odes, themes, and sonnets,
  Yet be not pedantic or pert;
If she wear none but deep cottage bonnets,
  If she deem it high treason to flirt,
If to mildness she add sense and spirit,
  Engage her at once without fear;
I love to reward modest merit,
  And I give—forty guineas a year.'

'I accept, my good sister, your mission,
  To-morrow, my search I'll begin,—
In all circles, in every condition,
  I'll strive such a treasure to win;
And, if after years of probation,
  My eyes on the wonder should rest,
I'll engage her without hesitation,
  But not on the terms you suggest.

'Of a bride I have ne'er made selection,
  For my bachelor thoughts would still dwell
On an object so near to perfection,
  That I blushed half my fancies to tell;
Now this list that you kindly have granted,
  I'll quote and refer to through life,
But just blot out—"A Governess Wanted",
  And head it with—"Wanted a Wife!"'

(1838)

MARY SEWELL
(1797–1884)

Mary Sewell's great popularity as a ballad writer was the product of an intense literary output that began only later in life: it was not until she was nearly 60 years old that she was to become a writer. The daughter of Quaker parents, Ann Wright and John Wright, she was born in Sutton, Suffolk, and educated mostly by governesses. Moving with her family to Yarmouth, she there married Isaac Sewell, a businessman and one of the leading Friends in the area. They had two children, the daughter, Anna Sewell, being the author of the children's story, *Black Beauty* (1877).

Her ballads are often highly sentimental, especially *Mother's Last Words* (1860), which is reputed to have sold almost a million copies. However, many of the ballads are also motivated by philanthropic and political concerns. A book dedicated to 'The Working Man' (1867), proceeds of a later book directed to the 'Outcast Poor' of London (1883), and the writing of *Homely Ballads For the Working Man's Fireside* (1858) are such examples. She also exhorted women not to buy American cotton, the product of 'slaves' labour', in her essay, 'An Appeal to Englishwomen' (1863).

Having spent many years in and around London, she lived in various places in Britain, finally settling in Old Catton, Norfolk, to be near her widowed son.

83 *The Bad Manager*

'Oh, Fanny! my dear, what a beautiful pie!
  I declare that I never did see
A crust so delicious—and risen so high!
  And baked, as they say, to a T.

'It makes me feel hungry to see it, I own,
  And really it flavours the street;
That boy smack'd his lips, he would like to have one—
  Who would not enjoy such a treat?

'I cannot think how your good mother affords
  To feed you on victuals like this;
My father has just the same wages as yours,
  But doesn't give mother all his.

'You see sister Susan is so fond of dress,
  (She's older than me by three years;)
She will have her way, and I leave you to guess
  That sometimes we've little but tears.

''Twas only last week that she quite set her heart
  On a wreath of red roses and green,
To wear round her head like the ladies, you know;
  She said she would look like a queen.

'She's pretty, they say, I don't see it myself—
   I think she looks foolish and vain;
Be that as it may, she's no comfort to us—
   I'd rather by far she were plain.

'She determined to go to the dance t'other night,
   In the room at the "Hatchet and Wood";
She came home at midnight, and father was cross,
   And said she would come to no good.

'And so, you see, mother gets worried and plagued
   For money by night and by day,
And says, just for peace and for quietness sake,
   That Susan shall have her own way.

'But I can assure you, if you will believe,
   We often have nothing to eat;
And there's little Charley, the doctor has said,
   That he should have plenty of meat.

'But we are in debt to the butcher, I know,
   And the baker will trust us no more,
And the landlord has call'd for his rent many times,
   And says he'll soon show us the door.

'Then that beautiful shawl, that my mother would buy
   Last winter to go to the play;
The people won't wait any longer, you see,
   But say they'll compel her to pay.

'So father gets angry, as you may suppose,
   And isn't to blame, that I see;
For supper at night, he has often no more
   Than bread, with a poor cup of tea.

'So he takes up his hat, and flings out of the house,
   Like an angry and quarrelsome man,
And says, if he cannot find comfort at home,
   He'll go to a place where he can.

'And when he comes knocking late into the night,
   We tremble to open the door.
I'm sorry for father, it isn't his fault,
   He always was sober before.

'If mother and Susan would keep the house neat,
   Nor let such extravagance come,
We'd have a nice pie, just the print of your own,
   And father would keep to his home.

'But why should I keep you out here in the street,
Whilst I have my troubles to tell?
If you'll let me, Fanny, I'll come to your house,
To learn how you manage so well.'

(1858)

LOUISA STUART COSTELLO
(1799–1870)

AN Irish poet, Louisa Stuart Costello was the daughter of James Francis Costello, an army officer born into the barony of Costello, County Mayo. His early death left the family impoverished and they moved to Paris in 1814, where Costello worked as an artist to help support her mother and brother. With her brother, Dudley Costello, she copied illustrated manuscripts and, on her return to London a few years later, took up miniature painting as a profession. Her first collection of poems, *The Maid of the Cyprus Isle, and Other Poems* (1815), was followed by two others (including *Songs of a Stranger* (1825), which was dedicated to William Lisle Bowles), as well as *The Lay of the Stork* (1856): a poem which weaves a fantasy around the Crimean War. She edited collections of early French poetry (1835) and of translated Persian poetry (1845). Historical novels, travel narratives and memoirs of historical women were also written by her. A small competence was supplemented by a pension from the Burdett family and, in 1852, she was awarded a civil list annuity of £75. In about 1865 she moved to Boulogne where she was to die of cancer.

84 *The Maid of the Cyprus Isle. A Ballad*

PART I

I

THOUGH many, full many a tale has been told,
Of gallant young knights and of warriors bold;
And many a tale of a virgin divine,
In strains of a muse more exalted than mine.
Yet gentles give ear to my ballad awhile,
As I sing of the Maid of the Cyprus Isle.

II

Full dark was the night, and no cheering star shone—
Ah! who is yon maiden who wanders alone?
Her dark hair dishevelled, her cheek fair and pale,
And her long flowing garments that wave in the gale;
Who has traversed this mountain for many a mile?
It is the fair Maid of the Cyprus Isle!

III

What is it that makes her thus brave the rude storm,
And thus to the tempest expose her fair form?
What is it that makes her thus hasten along,
The gloomy and dark-shaded forests among?
'Tis Love—which e'en sorrow and fear can beguile,
That impels on the Maid of the Cyprus Isle.

IV

No maid was more happy, no maid was more fair,
Her young tender heart was a stranger to care;
She danced by the fountains, she sung in the hall,
Amidst her attendants the fairest of all.
Till Reginald's beauty—till Reginald's smile
Stole the heart of the Maid of the Cyprus Isle!

V

But he'd left her to fight in his country's cause,
And vainly she wished his return from the wars.
Now she hastens her steps to the goddess's shrine,
For him to solicit her favours divine.
This hope does the tedious journey beguile,
Of Ianthé, the Maid of the Cyprus Isle.

VI

The mountains she passed as the morning appeared,
The storm from the face of the heavens was cleared.
The myrtles, which glittered with dew-drops around,
Showed the maiden the Temple of Venus was found.
She rested, with fear and fatigue for awhile,
Then entered, the Maid of the Cyprus Isle.

VII

At the feet of the goddess she sunk on her knee,
And her gifts she presented, so costly to see.
A vase of pure silver, a myrtle of gold,
With berries of rubies, all fair to behold;
And these on the high marble altar were laid,
While thus, in soft accents, petitioned the maid.

VIII

'Oh, Venus, fair goddess! give ear to my prayer,
'Receive all the gifts which with hope I prepare!
'Let Reginald live! let my lover return:
'Ah, leave not, fair goddess, a maiden to mourn!
'For all that I ask is, his form once to view,
'To see him in safety!—to know he is true!'

IX

She ceased.—Lo! the statue its head gently bowed,
While the altar and gifts were immersed in a cloud.
Then suddenly blazing, they vanished in air:
Sure sign of assent from the goddess so fair.
O'erjoyed, the young maiden her gratitude poured;
And knelt at the shrine which she humbly adored.

PART II

X

Who is it that sits in her palace so gay,
Surrounded by maidens in bridal array?
Her hair graceful braided, her ringlets confined
By blossoms of jasmine, that waved in the wind.
Her robes white and scarlet, embroidered with gold,
Her sandals of purple, so fair to behold?

XI

What knight is it sits by the side of the maid,
In vesture of purple, so costly arrayed?
Whose gaze is so tender, who presses her hand;—
'Tis Reginald, come from a far distant land.
And she, whose fair cheek is adorned with a smile,
Is Ianthé, the Maid of the Cyprus Isle!

XII

He had fought and had conquered—attended by fame,
His valour rewarded, triumphant he came;
That morning he hail'd the fair maid as his bride,
And now in the palace he sat by her side;
With rapture her hand to his bosom he prest.
Ah! never were lovers before half so blest!

XIII

The sun shone full bright and the tempest was chain'd,
O'er nature the calm hand of silence still reigned:
The maid led her lover thro' grove and thro' shade,
To her favourite spot, where a rivulet played;
With sonnets of love they the minutes beguile,
Who so blest as the Maid of the Cyprus Isle?

XIV

When sudden, a shriek at a distance they hear.
The maid pressed his hand in emotion and fear,
For near to their bower a tall form stood revealed,
By long ebon locks were the features concealed:
In the white hand a dagger was raised in the air,
And sobs half suppressed, wrung the bosom so fair.

XV

'Oh! hear me, false Reginald!' loudly she cried,
'And think not to save from my fury, thy bride!
'Why, why faithless youth, did'st thou leave me to mourn?
'While constant I pined for thy promised return.
'And thus, of thy absence as vain I complained,
'I heard that Ianthé that false heart had gained!

XVI

'See now, oh, deceiver! Alcesta once fair,
'But chang'd by thy falsehood, by sorrow, and care!
'Prepare, oh, vain maid! now approaches thy doom,
'Thy lover's false heart has prepared thee a tomb!'
She said, tow'rds the maid in distraction she prest,
But the dagger sunk deep in her Reginald's breast!

XVII

The murderess shrieked, as with horror she view'd
Her hand in the blood of the false one imbrued;
She saw the cold dew on his cheek still so dear—
She saw the last spark from his eye disappear—
She caught the fell poignard, and wild with despair,
She plunged the red steel in her bosom so fair!

* * *

XVIII

Ah, who is yon maid with the dark flowing hair,
In robes white and scarlet, so pale and so fair?
Who ne'er quits the mountains, but warbles so sweet,
Sad notes from her dismal and lonely retreat?
Whose gestures now frantic, now mildly composed,
Denote that her bosom 'gainst reason is closed.

XIX

Who oft in her song sighs out Reginald's name,
Then lists to the echo's which answer the same:
Who is pitied by all, but approaches to none:
Each evening who watches the set of the sun:
Who is rare seen to weep, but is ne'er seen to smile?
It is the mad Maid of the Cyprus Isle!

(1815)

85 *On Reading the Account of the Battle of Waterloo*

OH! who can listen with delight
To tales of battles won?
And who can hear without affright
The news of war begun.
Oh when the glory does their hearts inspire,
Did they reflect what woes some bosoms fire?
Oh did their thoughts fly to the battle plain,
And mark the writhing agony and pain,
And hear the cries, and see the bleeding slain!
Ah! sure no more their hearts with joy would bound,
But shrink in horror from the vict'ry's sound.
While thro' the streets the news of conquest spread,
Each parent listens with consuming dread.
Those shouts of triumph breath'd from every tongue,
Some anxious heart with agony has wrung.
The meanest soldier sunk to death's repose,
Has caus'd *some* breast to feel affliction's throes:
How can they bear each joyful shout to hear,
Which still renews remembrances so dear!
Oh! long may battle's terrors cease!
Be war and vengeance fled;
That Europe, wrapt in lasting peace,
May rest her laurell'd head!

(1815)

86 *from* The Lay of the Stork

PLUNGED deep in Asian wilds remote
Where lances flash and banners float,
And the shrill trumpet's clamorous note
Frights nature's stillness,—and where roar
Loud thunders, that are not of Heaven!—
Where lightnings blast the forests hoar,
And torrents, from the mountains driven,
Sparkle and foam, not as of yore
By long accustomed tempests tost—
But roll full tides of crimson gore
And mangled forms, from either host,
Hurl'd down, and in abysses lost—

Khālid leads on: and never yet
Had chief a band more wildly brave,
Ardent and true, but who forget

Or scorn to pity or to save:
Bearing all ills with minds unmoved,
Making e'en famine's self a jest:
Casting by life, as if unloved,
And slaught'ring with untiring zest!
And he must urge, command—nay force
His victims to this desp'rate course,
With Lila's message in his breast,
Where beats a heart as soft and kind
As ever pitied the distrest,
And throbb'd to succour all mankind.

Oh accident! that chains us still
Who talk of power, and boast of will!

(1856)

MARY HOWITT
(1799–1888)

BORN at Coleford in Gloucestershire, Mary Howitt was the daughter of the Quaker, Samuel Botham, and Ann Wood, a Friend 'by convincement'. As a young woman, she attended Quaker schools in Croydon, Uttoxeter, and Sheffield. It was through the Society of Friends that she met William Howitt. They married in 1821. From 1822 onwards, they lived above William Howitt's chemist's shop in Nottingham. After losing three children during pregnancy, Mary Howitt gave birth to her daughter, Anna Mary, in 1824. Five more children followed. She and her husband published many joint volumes of poetry, including *The Forest Minstrel* (1823) and *The Desolation of Eyam* (1827). Her most ambitious work was *The Seven Temptations* (1834). During this period she contributed poems to many of the leading periodicals of the day, including *Tait's Edinburgh Magazine*, and also to the popular annuals, such as *The Winter's Wreath*, edited by William Chorley. Her oldest daughter, Anna Mary, became closely associated with members of the Langham Place group—notably Bessie Rayner Parkes and Barbara Leigh Smith (later Bodichon). The latter enlisted Mary Howitt's help in petitioning for the Married Woman's Property Committee. In the 1840s, Mary Howitt and William Howitt were at the forefront of many of the emancipatory and progressive campaigns of that turbulent decade: the Anti-Corn Law movement; the anti-enclosure acts; and the extension of the suffrage. By the 1850s, Mary Howitt became heavily involved in spiritualism, and she held 'open house' for eminent spiritualists such as Daniel Douglas Home (the figure satirized in Robert Browning's 'Mr Sludge, "The Medium"' (1864)). From 1870, the Howitts resided in Europe, principally in Italy. William Howitt died in 1879. She survived her husband by nine years. Although she converted to Roman Catholicism in 1883, she was buried by special dispensation in the Protestant Cemetery at Rome.

87 *The Spider and the Fly. An Apologue*

A New Version of an Old Story

'WILL you walk into my parlour?' said the Spider to the Fly,
' 'Tis the prettiest little parlour that ever you did spy;
The way into my parlour is up a winding stair,
And I've a many curious things to shew when you are there.'
'Oh no, no,' said the little Fly, 'to ask me is in vain,
For who goes up your winding stair can ne'er come down again.'

'I'm sure you must be weary, dear, with soaring up so high;
Will you rest upon my little bed?' said the Spider to the Fly.
'There are pretty curtains drawn around; the sheets are fine and thin,
And if you like to rest awhile, I'll snugly tuck you in!'
'Oh no, no,' said the little Fly, 'for I've often heard it said,
They never, never wake again, who sleep upon your bed!'

Said the cunning Spider to the Fly, 'Dear friend what can I do,
To prove the warm affection I've always felt for you?
I have within my pantry, good store of all that's nice;
I'm sure you're very welcome—will you please to take a slice?'
'Oh no, no,' said the little Fly, 'kind sir, that cannot be,
I've heard what's in your pantry, and I do not wish to see!'

'Sweet creature!' said the Spider, 'you're witty and you're wise,
How handsome are your gauzy wings, how brilliant are your eyes!
I've a little looking-glass upon my parlour shelf,
If you'll step in one moment, dear, you shall behold yourself.'
'I thank you, gentle sir,' she said, 'for what you're pleased to say,
And bidding you good morning now, I'll call another day.'

The Spider turned him round about, and went into his den,
For well he knew the silly Fly would soon come back again:
So he wove a subtle web, in a little corner sly,
And set his table ready, to dine upon the Fly.
Then he came out to his door again, and merrily did sing,
'Come hither, hither, pretty Fly, with the pearl and silver wing;
Your robes are green and purple—there's a crest upon your head;
Your eyes are like the diamond bright, but mine are dull as lead!'

Alas, alas! how very soon this silly little Fly,
Hearing his wily, flattering words, came slowly flitting by;
With buzzing wings she hung aloft, then near and nearer drew,
Thinking only of her brilliant eyes, and green and purple hue—
Thinking only of her crested head—poor foolish thing! At last,
Up jumped the cunning Spider, and fiercely held her fast.
He dragged her up his winding stair, into his dismal den,
Within his little parlour—but she ne'er came out again!

And now dear little children, who may this story read,
To idle, silly flattering words, I pray you ne'er give heed:
Unto an evil counsellor, close heart and ear and eye,
And take a lesson from this tale, of the Spider and the Fly.

(1834)

88 *The Lady Magdalene. A Legend of an English Hall*

PART I

In a large old house dwells Magdalene,
  And with her there are three:
A blithe old man the gardener;
  And good Dame Margery;

And a priest, who cometh now and then,
  With a high and shaven crown,
With a foot that treads so silently,
  And a long black camlet gown.

All up and down the galleries
  Went the Lady Magdalene,
A-looking at the pictures old,
  That on the walls were seen.

'And who is this, Dame Margery,
  With the gold chain and the sword?'
'That was thy father, Magdalene;
  He was a noble lord!'

'And who is this boy, Dame Margery,
  With the greyhound at his side?'
'That was thy brother, Magdalene;
  At four years old he died!'

'And tell me, I pr'ythee, Margery,
  Who's this with the downcast eye?
It troubles my heart, Dame Margery,
  And yet I know not why.'

No answer at all made Margery,
  For a little season's space;
And again the maiden, Magdalene,
  Looked up into her face.

'There are chambers many,' quoth Magdalene,
  'And many a stately bed;
And many a room so beautiful,
  All green, and gold, and red.

'How is it, I pray, Dame Margery,
  That all alone I dwell?
I have asked the question of myself,
  And I'm sure I cannot tell.

'In the village street, Dame Margery,
  Even in winter weather,
I see the children, sevens and eights,
  All playing there together:

'But in this large and grand old house,
  I pray, how may it be,
That I am thus alone, alone,
  With none for company?

'I look into the distant fields,
  On the terrace as I stand,
And see the mothers walking there,
  And children hand in hand.

'And now, I pray, Dame Margery,
  This mystery make clear;
What spell is it, so sad yet sweet,
  That ever draws me here?

'The face is very fair to see,
  And so is many another;
But the spell is like the yearning love
  Which bindeth child and mother.'

Sore troubled was Dame Margery,
  The tears were in her eye,
And she wiped them with her withered hand,
  As thus she made reply.

'Yes, she was fair, sweet Magdalene,
  Like an angel fair and mild!
And she *was* thy mother, Magdalene;
  I nursed her as a child.

'Ah me! I can remember well
  Those times for ever fled,
When there were children and friends enow
  To sleep in every bed.

'When the hall table was too small
  For those who sate to meat;
And serving-men went to and fro
  With rapid, noiseless feet.

'There were thirty horses then in stall,
  And grooms nigh half a score;
Even I was gay and handsome then—
  But all those times are o'er!

'The house, in troth, is silent now,
  And hath a look of gloom;
I can remember dance and song
  And lights in every room!

'The jackdaws now, and swallows, build
  In the chimneys cold and tall;
The ivy creeps o'er the window-glass,
  And green damps on the wall.

'I can remember, Magdalene,
  When the trees, that grow so wild
Along the shrubbery paths, were set;
  Thy mother was then a child.

'He thinks, old John the gardener,
  Those times may come again;
Mayhap they will, sweet Magdalene,—
  But ah! I know not when!'

PART II

ON the terrace broad walked Magdalene,
  With gentle steps and slow;
And blithe old John the gardener
  Was working down below.

And he sang, the blithe old gardener—
  'The bird upon the tree
Is merry in budding spring-time,
  And I'm as merry as he.'

He cut the leaves of the snowdrop down,
  And tied up the daffodilly;
And then he sang, as he bent to work,
  With a 'Heigho! willy, nilly!'

Down the broad stone steps went Magdalene,
  And stood by the old flower-bed:
Still at his work the old man bent,
  Nor once raised up his head.

''Tis a lonesome place!' said Magdalene,
  'A lonesome dreary place!'
The blithe old man he ceased his work,
  And gazed into her face.

'Ay, lone enough, my lady fair!'
  Said the cheerful gardener;
But I can remember yon terrace steps
  With children all astir.

'There was my Lady Isabel,
  With hair like the raven's wing;
And the second sister, Adeline,
  A wilful, proud young thing.

'There was Lord Francis, and Lady Jane,
  And your blessed lady-mother;
Two younger brothers besides, and he
  That was dearer than a brother.

'He was your father afterwards—
  Good lack! how time moves on!—
There were seven children then i' th'house,
  And now there is but one!
And all those happy children,
  Like flowers of spring, are gone!

'What troops of ladies I have seen
  Go walking up and down,
Each softly fanning of herself,
  In a shining silken gown!

'What gay and gallant gentlemen,
  All clad in velvet fine;
What riding in and out there was;
  What drinking of the wine!

'Ay, sure enough, the place is still—
  Stiller than it was then;
But perchance, my Lady Magdalene,
  It may be blithe again!'

With that he stooped down to his work,
  And harder worked than ever,
Nodding his head to his favourite song,
  'Let care drown in the river!'

And as he sang he cleared the leaves
  From the crocus, matted and wan;
The Lady Magdalene walked away,
  But he kept singing on.

PART III

In a stately room, at eventide,
  The old priest sate and read
In an old and large black-letter book,
  O'er which he bent his head.

In a painted oriel window stood
  Beside him Magdalene,
And o'er her streamed the sunset light,
  Rose-tinted, gold, and green.

'Put down thy books,' said Magdalene,
  'Thou must not read to-day;
Put down thy books, good father,
  And hearken what I say!'

Roused by her words, the grave old man
  His eyelids slowly raised,
And silently at Magdalene
  In calm surprise he gazed.

'Now, father good,' said Magdalene,
  'This hour, I pray thee, tell,
Why in this grand old house, alone,
  Year after year I dwell.

'Thou hast taught me both to read and write,
  Hast taught me all I know,
Yet kept me from my kind apart,
  I pray, why is it so?

'Why? when the lore which thou hast taught
  Is love in each degree,
From God down to the meanest thing
  Of his great family?

'Father, I've seen the children poor,
  Glad sisters with their brothers;
Have seen the joy within the heart
  Of lowly village mothers;

'Have seen, upon the Sabbath morn,
  How many a loving band
Of Christian people churchward go,
  And children hand in hand.

'Have seen them kneeling, side by side,
  Each to the other known,
Like groups of saints together set,
  But I kneel all alone!

'Oh, 'tis a pleasant sight to me!
And yet my heart doth ache,
To see such holy happiness
Which I cannot partake!

'Why is it thus? I pray thee tell
Why none with me abide.
Oh, for a loving sister
To worship at my side!

'Father, I scarce know who I am,
Save that my line is great,
And that some heavy household woe
Hath made me desolate.

'Thou art a righteous man and wise,
Thy teachings I revere;
But why I dwell in solitude,
I pray thee, let me hear!'

For a moment's space the grave old man
No answer made at all;
The tears were in his mild grey eyes,
Yet he no tear let fall.

'Hearken to me, my Magdalene,'
At length he calmly spake;
'Thou hast been nurtured in this wise
For thy well-being's sake.

'I can remember when this house
Was full of sons and daughters,
When its fortunes all seemed flourishing,
As willows by the waters.

'Daughters and sons, I mind me well
What a noble band was there;
The sons all goodly men of might,
The daughters wondrous fair.

'I can recall this solitude
An ever-changing crowd,
And the silence of these chambers vast
Was riot long and loud.

'I will not tell thee, Magdalene,
Of heartlessness and crime;
Enough, the wrath of Heaven hath scourged
The evil of that time.

'There was a blight upon the race,
They one by one did fall;
Sorrow and sin had stricken them,
And death consumed them all.

'There was but one of all her house
Whom folly did not win,
An angel in a woman's form,
Thy mother, Magdalene!

'And when upon her bed of death
In her bright youth she lay,
An angel to her native skies
About to pass away,

'She made me promise solemnly,
Before our imaged Lord,
That thou, my precious Magdalene,
Shouldst be my sacred ward.

'She gave me rules to guide my will,
Prescribed a course whereby
Thy heart should be enlarged by love,
Thy mind have purpose high.

'"Thou know'st the follies of this house,"
Said she, "its woe, its pride;
And through these errors of the past
Let her be sanctified!"

'She died! the place was desolate,
Her kindred all were gone,
There was but I, her ghostly friend,
And thou, her orphaned one!

'Their thriftless lives had made thee poor,
Their shame thy name had shent,
Sorely run out were all thy lands,
And mortgaged all thy rent.

'I trained thee in this sober wise,
And in this solitude,
That thou mightst grow up innocent,
Sedate, and wise, and good.

'Thy manors now lie far and wide,
Thy noble lands are free,
And young and old, my Magdalene,
Are looking up to thee.

'Ere long thou wilt have friends enow,
And, so Heaven give thee grace,
The sounds of joy may ring again
From this deserted place.

'It has been stripped and desolate,
Its want laid open wide,
But a youthful spirit's innocence
The place hath purified!

'Be patient yet, my Magdalene,
Please God the time draws near,
When blameless mirth and many friends
Shall gather round thee here!'

(1847)

MARY LEMAN GRIMSTONE
(?1800–1866)

THE daughter of Leman Thomas Rede, an English expatriate, Mary Leman (later Gillies and Grimstone) was born into a literary family in Tasmania. Moving to London in 1807, she began writing verses under the pseudonym, 'Oscar', and published two volumes, *Zayda* (1820) and *Cleone* (1821). The family went back to Hobart in 1826, where she contributed to the *Colonial Times*, her poetry then being reprinted from British periodicals in the Hobart press after her return to England in 1829. Her first novel, *Woman's Love* (1832), probably written while she was still in Tasmania (from amidst 'the small circle of a Colonial community', as she puts it), was followed by four others all written under her own name and receiving favourable reviews. During the 1830s she moved among the circle of women associated with Caroline Norton's magazine, *La Belle Assemblée*; this magazine commended the feminist import of her novel (July 1834), also entitled *Cleone* (1834). Her support of women's education and of social reform is also evident in her contributions to the radical dissenting journal, the *Monthly Repository* (1833–37), and Mary Howitt's *People's Journal* (1846–47). Twice married, she concluded her literary career by writing tales for children in the 1860s.

89 *The Poor Woman's Appeal to Her Husband*

YOU took me, Colin, when a girl, unto your home and heart,
To bear in all your after fate a fond and faithful part;
And tell me, have I ever tried that duty to forego—
Or pin'd there was not joy for me, when you were sunk in woe?
No—I would rather share *your* grief than any other's glee,
For though you're nothing to the world, you're all the world to me;

You make a palace of my shed—this rough-hewn bench a throne—
There's sunlight for me in your smile, and music in your tone.
I look upon you when you sleep, my eyes with tears grow dim,
I cry 'O Parent of the poor, look down from Heaven on him:
Behold him toil from day to day exhausting strength and soul—
Look down with mercy on him, Lord, for thou canst make him
whole!'
And when at last relieving sleep has on my eyelids smil'd,
How oft are they forbade to close in slumber, by my child;
I take the little murmurer, that spoils my span of rest,
And feel it is a part of *thee* I lull upon my breast.
There's only one return I crave,—I may not need it long,
And it may soothe thee when I'm where the wretched feel no
wrong!
I ask not for a kinder tone—for thou wert ever kind;
I ask not for less frugal fare—my fare I do not mind;
I ask not for more gay attire—if such as I have got
Suffice to make me fair to *thee*, for more I murmur not:
But I would ask some share of hours that you at clubs bestow—
Of knowledge that *you* prize so much, may *I* not something know?
Subtract from meetings among men, each eve, an hour for me—
Make me companion of your *soul*, as I may surely be!
If you will read, I'll sit and work; then think when you're away—
Less tedious I shall find the time, dear Colin, of your stay.
A meet companion soon I'll be for e'en your *studious* hours,—
And teacher of those little ones you call your cottage flowers;
And if we be not rich and great, we may be wise and kind;
And as my heart can warm your heart, so may my mind your mind.

(1834)

MARIA JANE JEWSBURY
(1800–1833)

MARIA JANE JEWSBURY (later Fletcher) is thought to have been born into a large family at Measham, Derbyshire, where she was educated at school until, at 14 years old, ill health led to her being taught at home by tutors. Her father, Thomas Jewsbury, was a cotton manufacturer and her sister, Geraldine Jewsbury, a well-known novelist. After the death of her mother, Maria (née Smith), the family moved to Manchester where Maria Jane Jewsbury assumed responsibility for looking after the family.

Her contributions to the *Manchester Courier* led to her being encouraged by the editor, Alaric A. Watts, to take up writing as a profession. *Phantasmagoria; or Sketches of Life and Literature* (1825) was her first published volume, consisting of poetry and prose. A great admirer of William Wordsworth's poetry, she dedicated this book to him. Their correspondence then developed into a lasting close friendship with him and Dorothy Wordsworth, and he later addressed his poem, 'Liberty', to her. Her next volume of poetry, *Lays of Leisure Hours* (1829), was dedicated to her friend, Felicia Hemans, and she was also to enter into correspondence with Letitia Elizabeth Landon (L.E.L.) in the 1830s. In 1825 she had begun contributing poetry and reviews to the *Athenaeum*, her 1830s work here being particularly noted. These reviews are a useful source for her ideas about literature. She writes: 'Imaginative Literature, even when second-rate, has a use, and a *national* use;—it helps to stave off barbarism'. She continues: 'A poem is not the place for controversy . . . the intention of poetry is to excite sympathy on points universally admitted, not to make proselytes, and not to propound theories' (30 April 1831). She also produced two books of essays: *Letters to the Young* (1828) and *The Three Histories* (1830).

An Anglican, she married the Revd William Kew Fletcher, a chaplain of the East India Company, in 1832. Travelling with him to India, she wrote twelve sections of 'Oceanides', perhaps her finest achievement, which were sent back to England and published in the *Athenaeum* in the successive months of her voyage during 1832–33. She died of cholera shortly after her arrival. Extracts from her travel diary were published in Francis Espinasse's *Lancashire Worthies* (2nd series, 1874–7).

90 *Joan of Arc*

Had Joan of Arc been a Spartan Matron, her countrymen would have erected statues to her while she lived, and instituted festivals in honour of her memory when she died. As it was, after having roused the degraded spirit of a whole nation, and served her King with the ability of a General, and the self-devotedness of a Woman, she endured perfidy in return for her services, and a barbarous death was her only recompence.

Anonymous

I

IN infancy, nor named, nor known;
  In youth a homeless thing;
And then the proudest rank her own,
  Amid the courtly ring!—
Ay, men might marvel at a change
Than eastern one more true, more strange
  Than all that poets sing!
For when hath saint and heroine stood
Concealed, beneath a peasant's hood?

II

The land was swept by alien hosts;
  An alien monarch reigned;
And France beheld, through all her coasts,—
  Her ancient lilies stained.
The maiden mused upon the wrong—
In midnight vigils lone and long—
  Self-dazzled! self-sustained!
Mused on the crown, the sword, the shrine,—
Then rose a spirit half divine.

III

I see her, as a vision, now,
  In all her glory's height!
See patriot ranks around her bow,
  And lilied banners bright!
I hear the shouts, that, oft renewed,
Burst rapturous from the multitude,
  Before that stirring sight!
While fear is on the alien hosts,
And gone their strength, and mute their boasts.

IV

She comes,—with brow and breast in mail—
  Like one to battles bred;
And firmly guides, while thousands hail,
  Her courser's stately tread.
Yet, 'mid the pomp and pageant high,
With lofty port, and quiet eye,
  Appears the warrior-maid,
As though to France the victory given,—
The glory, she resigned to heaven.

V

'Tis past,—and she who crowned a king,
  And bade a realm be free,
A hated, an accursed thing,
  To-morrow's dawn will be!
She comes,—and still the lofty port,
She bore amid a camp and court,
  Still, as of old, I see!
And hosts, as then around her ranged,
But all besides, how dark and changed!

VI

Nor helm, nor steed await her more;
  Nor victory, nor vow;
For those who hailed her, saint, before,
  As sorceress, greet her now.
I hear their curses round the stake;
I see the fiery column make
  The boldest shield his brow;—
I see, their victim, and their queen,
Die as she lived, severe, serene!

VII

Preserver of a realm and king!
  Was this a doom for thee?
This, the sole laurel they could bring
  To her who set them free?
Maiden, they could not quench thy fame!—
That rose, immortal, from the flame;
  And ages yet to be,
Shall tell how saint and heroine stood
Concealed, beneath a peasant's hood.

(1825)

91 *Song of the Hindoo Women, While Accompanying a Widow to the Funeral Pile of Her Husband*

On the decease of her husband, if his widow resolves to accompany him to the world of spirits, a Funeral Pile is erected, covered with an arbour of dry boughs, on which the dead body is placed: the living victim follows, dressed in her bridal jewels, surrounded by relations, priests, and musicians. After certain prayers and ceremonies, she takes off her jewels, and presenting them with her last blessing to her nearest relative, she ascends the funeral pile, enters the awful bower, and placing herself near the body of her husband, with her own hand generally sets fire to the pile, which, being constantly supplied with aromatic oils, the mortal frames are soon consumed, and the Hindoos entertain no doubt of the soul's re-union in purer realms. During the cremation, the noise of the trumpets and other musical instruments, overpowers the cries of the self-devoted victim, should her resolution fail her: but those who have attended this solemn sacrifice, assure us that they always observed even the youngest widows manifest the greatest composure and dignity throughout the awful scene.

Forbes' Oriental Memoirs

She who follows her husband to another world, shall dwell in a region of joy for so many years as there are hairs in the human body, or thirty-five millions.

The Laws of Unggira and Heerut.

I

NOT in grief to the Pile we go—
With looks of fear, or sounds of woe,
But timing our steps to the eager swell

Of Citarr[1] and Vin[2]—while each silver bell
That hangs on our dancers' feet, resembles
The Lotos white, when the dark wave trembles.
Proudly falls the raptured beam
Of the setting sun on our Goddess-stream;
And there, the tall ship meets his ray—
The gaudy Bolio's streamer gay—
The fabric slight—and the sail of snow
Of native boat, or Arab Dow—
And he smiles as the offerers fondly tell,
On each floating wreath, and gilded shell,
That brightly on the waters swell.

II

The groves that hang o'er the river's bank,
Each sculptured temple, and shaded tank,[3]
With Gunga's[4] festal lights are gleaming—
Through porch and lofty column streaming:—
Haste, Lillah haste, the rites are done,
Thy last bright thread of life is spun;
A moment—and its limit breaks—
A moment—and thy spirit wakes
From its earthly dream, in a land afar,
Higher, and brighter, than Sun or Star!
Each golden gate, and ruby key,
And curtain of light shall ope' for thee—
Till last, and brightest of the seven,[5]
Where Brahma dwells shall be thy heaven!

III

We have wreathed thy arms with bracelets bright,[6]
And with chains of gold thy ancles light—
Thy limbs are dewed with fragrant ghee,[7]
With many a balm from many a tree,

[1] [2] Musical Instruments.

[3] A lake or reservoir of water, often surrounded with strong masonry, and the banks adorned by mango and tamarind trees.

[4] Gunga is the goddess of the Ganges; during the festivals which commemorate her descent to earth, crowds of people assemble near the river, bringing offerings of rice, fruit, flowers, sweetmeats, &c. and hang garlands across the river, even where it is very wide. At some of these festivals the sides of the Ganges are in many places gaily illuminated.

[5] Some of the Hindoos (like the Mahommedans) believe their heaven and hell to be divided into different stages, which are peopled by different kinds of angels and gods, and in which exist various degrees of happiness and misery.

[6] The arms of the Hindoo women are covered with bracelets from the wrist to the elbow; they also wear chains round the ancles, and abundance of rings on their fingers and toes.

[7] Clarified butter.

And o'er them falls the light shalie.[8]
Thy dark and root-stained locks confined,[9]
No longer float upon the wind—
O'er them, each bright flower sheds its bloom,
The precious Attar its perfume;—
Thy hand the sacred grass[10] is bearing—
Thy head the bridal veil is wearing—
And every jewel on thy breast,
And every wreath upon thy vest,
Glows in that sunset-light afar,
Each flower a gem—each gem a star.

IV

The Gooroo,[11] and the wild Fakeer,[12]
Pilgrim, and Parsee[13] crowd thy bier,
And there, the Brahmin nobler far
With flowing robe and white zennaar,[14]
Is waiting with the sacred fire,
Lillah, the phœnix of the pyre!
Each precious gum and odorous bough,
Have grove and forest yielded now,
To rear a costlier shrine for thee,
Than blest the bird of Araby.
Haste then, with glittering fingers dress
The couch thy faithful limbs must press;
And scatter with a tearless eye
Thy flowers upon each passer by;—
While shouts of triumph to thy fame,
Shall mingle with the mounting flame
That bears thee as a chariot bright,
To Vishnoo's thousand halls of light:—
Haste, Lillah haste, the rites are done,
Thy last bright thread of life is spun!

(1825)

[8] The *shalie* is a light upper garment, generally composed of silk and cotton, and forms a very graceful drapery around the figure. 'All thy garments smell of myrrh, aloes and cassia' (Psalms 45: 8).

[9] The Hindoo women frequently stain the roots of their hair red, they also adorn it with wreaths of flowers and jewels, and those who are sufficiently wealthy, perfume it with attar of roses.

[10] The cusha grass is esteemed sacred; the hands of the bride and bridegroom are bound together with it when they are married, and the widow generally carries some of it in her hand when she walks to the funeral pile.

[11] A spiritual teacher.

[12] A religious mendicant.

[13] The Parsees are descendants of the Persian fire worshippers.

[14] The sacred thread composed of twisted cotton, worn by the Brahmins over the left shoulder.

92 *The First Sacrifice*

PART I

A small dell, open on one side to the surrounding country. An altar-mound of green turf.—Adam and Eve standing beside it, a lamb lying at their feet.

EVE

ADAM, the hour is nigh!
And this green mound,
Smooth in its surface as the o'erhanging sky,
And starred around
With flowers of all bright hues,
(Bright though not born in Paradise)
Seems meet for any sacrifice
Our God, and earth's, may choose!

ADAM

Oh! woman, proud to know, yet little knowing;
Blind to the ills from thy first error flowing;
Doting on whatsoe'er
Is in its aspect fair,
And even now, amidst thy spirit's grieving,
Visions of beauty weaving;
Dismiss that care;
With me, thy wretched lord of dust, prepare
Again to view that FORM,
(Not mild as when He woke me with his breath,
Again to hear that Voice,
(Oh! not to rejoice,)
A Voice as of the winds and waves in storm,
Speaking alone of Death!
The doom He comes to show,—
The apprehended woe,—
We faint because we know not, and yet fear to know.

EVE

Adam, look not so pale;
I know that He is strong, and we, I feel are weak,
Reeds that the elements of earth may break,
And he hath heavenly ones—but not to wreak
His vengeance on the fallen and the frail.
Adam, look not so pale!
This quiet, sunny dell,
Wherein, save we ourselves, but pure things dwell,
Gay glittering insects,—flowers with beauty bowed,
And trees that shelter them a stately crowd,

And yonder brook flowing so bright and fleet,
And this our offering Lamb that nestles at our feet,
May all thy fears dispel:—
Not for a work of wrath—not for despair,
He bade us wait him in a spot so fair.

ADAM

Thy language hath no echo. From the earth,
And from the clouds, yea, from mine own wrung soul,
And the bright watchers that around us roll,
There breaks no answering gleam, there comes not forth
One oracle of trust
To the poor child of dust!
I ask them of my doom yet unrevealed;
I bid them tell me what is death? and whence?
But the sweet stars are mute, the clouds are sealed,
Silent and happy in their innocence.
Eve, hear'st thou aught?

EVE

I hear the leaves stirred by the passing breeze,
As to a sound of showers;
I hear the brook make answer to the trees,
And the bee greet the flowers.
Murmurs of happy breath,
That whisper nought of death!

ADAM

Nor aught discern'st thou?

EVE

I see the firmament high, and stretched abroad
As if in likeness of the power of God!
I see the mountains rearing each tall brow,
Blue and far distant—at their feet a sea!
Midway, wide forests wrapt in gorgeous gloom,
Nearer, green plains smiling in sunny bloom,
And here, this dell and thee.

ADAM

Oh will not HE be seen!

EVE

(wildly)—I see—*She prostrates herself on the earth, Adam does the same.*

PART II

The same dell; the lamb lying on the altar-mound, dead and bleeding. Eve weeping over it.

ADAM

AND *this* is death! And now I look upon
What I must one day feel! The Lamb hath paid
Its innocent life for mine; but some day's sun
Will see me like it, in cold stillness laid.
I know that I am strong—that guilt and fear
Have not worn out my majesty of soul;—
King am I to the world's extremest sphere;
Sire shall I be of sons beyond control,
Save of the Mightiest! Wood and plain are mine,
And the plumed birds that cleave the golden air;—
But I must *die*—I—filled with breath divine—
Like the poor beast that poured its life-blood there!
Myriads will tread the earth I tread alone,
Fruitful, and fair, and glorious, and free,
They too will die—they too by sin o'erthrown,
Will breathe the curse of dying men on me!

EVE

But will all life *thus* close?
Must blood flow from each breast,
Mingled with groans, and sobs, and bitter throes,
Before it lies at rest?
Shall I o'er thee
As o'er this Lamb, weep for thy form defaced?
Wilt thou o'er me?
The flowers that Eden graced
Changed in their aspect and similitude;
Ev'n there the rose grew pale,
Its fair leaves fell, or floated on the gale,
And the far-scented violet drooped subdued!
The lily's silver bell
Became a silent cell,
Wherein no wild bee would its music pour;
And many another flower,
At night, or'neath a shower,
Shut its bright eye, and opened it no more!
Oh was not this too death?
A yielding up of life and breath
That nothing could restore?
As their's dropped from its stem
May not *our* being close?
May we not die like them,
In beauty?—in repose?

ADAM

'Twould be death still; the ending of all life,
Mournful or glad;
Less painful unaccompanied by strife,
But not less sad;—
Death, though disguised as sleep, yet bears from sight
All thought, all love, and love's sweet image light;
It is a bright path to a darksome land;
A violent deed done by a gentle hand;—
'Tis death! a night
Without a promised morrow!
Unblest—unbright—
Lacking ev'n hope, the single star of sorrow!

EVE

Adam, the sun hath set,
And half our task is unaccomplished yet.

Adam kindles a fire on the altar-mound, on which the lamb is gradually consumed.

ADAM

'Tis ended! and afar, beyond our gaze,
Floats off the smoke of our FIRST SACRIFICE,
The first of thousands that in after days
Will bleed and burn,
Telling the tale of our lost Paradise!
Bidding earth learn
By a perpetual rite, and penal sign,
The curse of sin, the power of wrath Divine:—
And multitudes discern,
A MEANING and a MYSTERY therein,
Yet deeper—and from that, strong comfort win!

(1829)

93 *Oceanides, I. The Outward-Bound Ship*

SHE is on her way, a goodly ship,
With her tacklings loosed, her pilot gone;
Behind, beneath, around, the deep,
And far the land where she beareth on:
Fading, fast fading, yonder lie
The last of her home, the hills of Devon,
And the brightness and calm of a Sabbath sky
Have made them shine like the gates of heaven.

To those who watch her from the strand,
She is but a cloud 'mid sea and air!
And having gazed, perchance the band
Move onward with a languid prayer.
Yet is she vast from deck to keel,
A city moving on the waters,
Freighted with business, woe and weal,
Freighted with England's sons and daughters.

The sea is round them: many a week
They o'er that deep salt sea must roam,
And yet the sounds of land will break
The spell, and send their spirits home;
The cry of prisoned household bird,
Shrill mingling with the boatswain's call;
With surge and sail, the lowing herd,
And hark—street music over all!

'Arouse thee', from the bugle's mouth,
And with the merry viol's aid,
Tunes gathered from the north and south,
For dance and dinner signals made:
Harsh music to the gifted ear,
Teasing, perhaps, heard day by day,
Yet often precious, often dear,
As waking dreams of—Far away.

Alas! the sea itself wakes more!
With its briny smell and heaving breast,
With its length and breadth without a shore,
With its circling line from east to west,
Telleth it not of home, of *earth*,
With her rills, and flowers, and steadfastness,
Till sick thoughts in the soul have birth,
And loath'd is the foaming wilderness?

No more, no more: we are on our way:
The tropics are gained, and who would pine
For the pallid sun of an English day?
For the glittering cold of its night's moon-shine?
No more, no more—why pine for flowers,
If DUTY our Indian amaranth be?
If we look to the land that shall soon be ours,
A land where is 'no more sea'!

OFF MADEIRA (1832)

94 *Oceanides, II. My Sea-Hermitage*

Inscribed to Capt. C. Biden, E.I.C.S. Commander of the ship *Victory*.

SWINGING in my cot at ease,
Yet a wanderer o'er the seas,
Seas that never lead may sound,—
Seas that have for man no ground;—
Depths whose wonders call for faith,
Never known till known in death,
Till, unto the drowner's eye
Knowledge blends with agony;
And too soon, too sadly, he
Fathometh the mystery,
One, one with Eternity!
O thou element, whose band
Is alone thy Maker's hand,
By thy fullness never spent,
But for Him, omnipotent!
By thy length and breadth of span,
By thy tides since Time began,
By thy heaving, and, oh! move,
By thy dread and solemn roar;
By thy depths that nought may stir,
Mighty, mighty sepulchre!—
By the ravage thou hast wrought,
By the sorrow thou hast brought
Unto human life and thought;—
Ay, by all thy power and pride,
When thou wast, and nought beside,
Save the heaven thou couldst not drown,
And the arm that kept thee down;—
Thee, I name, with spirit bent,
But for God, omnipotent!
Yet a wanderer o'er thy waves,
(Call them liquid land of graves)
Frail as feather in the breeze,
I am in my cot at ease!—
All thy dreaded storms forgot,
All thy strength as it were not,
Heaving with thee, as a child
With its mother's pulses mild,
Looking on thy billows' sway
As that child on lambs at play;
Not a shore from east to west,
Not a fear within my breast,
And my cabin full of all

That may lessen sense of thrall;
Books, read last amid green hills
With their poetry of rills;—
Miniatures of friends afar,
Each a fond memorial star;—
Birds that singing in their cage
Make my ocean-hermitage
Have a sound and look of hours,
That once trod on moss and flowers:
Tranquil I, and happy they,
Though the salt and booming spray
Is around us—night and day.
Yes, but better things than these
Make me have a heart at ease;
Better even than the knowing
That our ship is swiftly going,
With her frame and tackling good,
To the haven where we would:—
Better even than the knowing,
That her ruler's heart is glowing
With each brave and kindly thought
Tempered as a sailor's ought.
Yes 'tis something more than these
Maketh *home* upon the seas:—
Name it, ye who know the worth
Of the nearest friend on earth;
Name it; ye who know the love
Of the nearer friend above!

OFF TENERIFFE (1833)

95 *Oceanides, IV. The Sunken Rock.*

A GENTLE ship was sailing
  Upon the Indian seas,
O lovely looked she sailing,
  So fair were wave and breeze:
Yet sunken rocks were near her,
  And but one seaman grey
Of all who had to steer her,
  Knew the dangers of the way:
But they hearkened not the fearer,
  For a syren-song that day.

In air, the waves were flinging
 Their silver crowns of spray,
And these their words of singing,—
 'Away, bold ship, away;
To-day, all fair together
 We bear thee o'er the sea,
And who talks of stormy weather,
 A moody wight is he.

'So white the furrow streameth,
 As strewn with pearls are we,
And who of danger dreameth,
 A moody wight is he.
Light hearts are in thee dancing,
 Light steps are on thy deck,
The sun is cloudless glancing,—
 Sail on—who dreams of wreck?

'We are thine, bold ship, and bear thee
 Home, home,—trust us, not him;
Ay, home, bold ship, we bear thee,
 Trust us, trust us, not him:
The pilot's trade is caution,
 And with talk of rocks and sands,
He tells foul tales of ocean,
 And us, his wandering bands.

'Brave bark, bound on, and heed not,
 Let rocks be sunk or seen,
The chart and line they need not,
 Where once we've pilots been.
On, on, and end thy roaming,
 There are many look for thee,
Who will laugh to greet thy coming,
 Ay, kiss thy sides for glee.

'Thou hast never heard such laughter
 As that will greet thee soon;
Thou wilt never hear such after,
 Beneath the sun or moon.
We will love and leave thee never;
 We will tell our secrets thee;
And thou shalt be for ever,
 Our nursling of the sea!'

'Ha! ha! we have won! and the silly ship
  That braved us so long, is ours;
She sinks in our arms as if drunk or asleep;—
  Down with her, fathoms, fathoms deep,—
And laugh we, and leap, with conquering roar;
Her wreck hath displaced some waves a score.
And to all upon earth she's a name and no more!'

The waves were hushed, the song they spoke
  In cruel triumph o'er the waters;
And other, milder music broke,
  From other, milder ocean's daughters.

'Well, too well, the depths are cloven,
Soon, too soon, the work is done;
Many a weedy shroud is woven—
Many a mortal course is run!
Fathom deep their bodies lie,
Stiffened limb, and stony eye;
Wrapped about with slimy things,
Who were Beauty's queens and kings;
Wealth, with all his gold outspread,
Sleeps upon a rocky bed;
And the salt and hungry spray
Eateth Valour's sword away,
Once, as flashing as the day:
Wisdom charmeth now no longer,
Wcakcr brain is as thc strongcr,
And the man of giant size
With the little infant lies:
Whilst afar the taper burneth,
And the watcher's bosom yearneth,
Each, for one who ne'er returneth;
Buried by our father sea,
Where none know their graves, but we!
We are daughters of the deep,
Yet, because his daughters, weep
That the sound of human woe
Through our caverned halls should flow,
And that he, so calm to us
And the fragile nautilus,
Stern and full of death should be
To a mightier race than we!
We would save, but we are weak;
And when mighty tempests break,
And a ship with all her crew
Sink, as if a drop of dew
Fell upon an ocean weed,

We may pity their great need,
And, when hushed is foam and surge,
Sing, as now, their funeral dirge;
Hide awhile the limbs of youth
From some monster's ravening tooth,
Bind sea blooms round beauty's locks
Sadly floating on our rocks;
Or remove a hoary head
From its lacerating bed
Unto soft sea-weeds instead—
But 'tis all that we can do,
Mortals, yet our love is true!'
  Thus, upon the self-same seas,
  Sang the Oceanides!

(1833)

96 *Oceanides, IX. The Eden of the Sea.*

Inscribed to the Revd B. Bailey, Senior Chaplain of Ceylon.

A DREAM! a dream! Our billowy home
  Before me, as so late, so long,
The Ocean, with its sparkling foam;
  The Ocean, with its varying song:—
Our ship at rest, where late she rode,
  Furled every sail though fair the breeze,
And narrow walks and small abode
  Exchanged for roaming, land, and ease.

Short sojourn make we, yet how sweet
  The change, the unaccustomed air
Of all we see, and hear, and meet—
  Ceylon, thy wooded shores are fair!
I love the land left far behind,
  Its glorious oaks, and streamlets clear,
Yet wherefore should mine eye be blind,
  My heart be cold to beauty here?—

No, in a world as childhood new,
  Is it not well to be a child?—
As quick to ask, as quick to view,
  As promptly pleased, perchance as wild?
Deride who will as childish wit,
  My scorn to-day of graver things;
Let *them* be proud, but let *me* sit
  Enamoured of a beetle's wings.

Books for to-morrow: this calm shade
  (Yet mind and learning know the spot)
Suggests to me the primal hour
  When goodness was, and sin was not;
When the wild tenants of the wood
  Came trustingly at Adam's call,
Nor he nor they athirst for blood,
  The world one Paradise for all.

I know that creatures strange and fierce
  Here lurk, and here make man afraid;
But let the daring hunter pierce
  Their hidden lairs—in this bright shade,
Let me forget save what I greet,
  The air alive with glancing wings;
Tame creatures pecking near my seat;
  Resplendent flowers, and happy things.

The squirrel at his morning meal,
  And morning sport—so lithe and free,
No shadow o'er the grass may steal
  With lighter, quicker steps than he.
Racing along the cocoa leaf
  You see him through its ribs of green;
Anon, the little mime and thief
  Expanded on the trunk is seen.

These cocoa-trees—not fair in woods,
  But singly seen, and seen afar,
When sunset pours his yellow floods,
  A column, and its crown a star!
Yet, dowered with wealth of uses rare,
  Whene'er its plumy branches wave,
Some sorrow seems to haunt the air;
  Some vision of a desert grave!

Ceylon! Ceylon! 'tis nought to me
  How thou wert known or named of old,
As Ophir, or Taprobane,
  By Hebrew king, or Grecian bold:—
To me, thy spicy-wooded vales,
  Thy dusky sons, and jewels bright,
But image forth the far-famed tales—
  But seem a new Arabian Night.

And when engirdled figures crave,
  Heed to thy bosom's dazzling store—
I see Aladdin in his cave;
  I follow Sindbad on the shore.
Nor these, the least of all thy wealth,
  Thou heiress of the eastern isles!
Thy mountains boast of northern health;
  And Europe amid Asia smiles.

Were India not where I must wend,
  And England where I would return,
To thee my steps would soonest tend:
  Ev'n now, I feel my spirit yearn;
Not as the stranger of a day,
  Who soon forgets where late he dwelt,
But like a friend, who, far away,
  Feels ever what at first he felt.

(1833)

97 *Oceanides, XII. The Haven Gained*

Inscribed to Captain C. Biden, Commander of the ship *Victory*.

AND we are parting, glorious Sea!
  And thou art anchored, gallant ship!
Strange, that the hour which makes me free,
  Should be the one that tempts to weep;
Strange, strange that through my heart should flow,
Regrets, I never dreamed to know.

How often, in a wayward mood,
  Upon our thronged and sultry deck,
I've sat and longed for solitude
  And silence—fondly tracing back
The fresh and stilly evening air,
All that made England dear and fair.

How often have I looked with scorn
  On what I deemed my prison home;
Sick of the vastness daily born
  In ocean's circle, heaven's high dome,—
Turned from the sun with evil eye,
Nay, greeted moonlight with a sigh!

But this is over: long relieved,
  I have rejoiced in Night and Day;
Loved our sea-life, and only grieved
  That Time, like waters, lapsed away;
Not lately, Discontent, old Sea,
Hath bent a wrinkled brow on thee.

My cabin, that I thought a tomb,
  Despite its neat and bright array,
Seems now a smiling summer room
  Where only Peace hath leave
And Occupation's Eden-state,
Light, mirthful, earnest, and elate.

And I have learned to read the face
  Of many a rude yet kindly tar;
So loves the human eye to trace
  The lines of brotherhood afar;
So longs the human heart to love
Something, beneath, around, above.

But hark, that sound!—the boat is lowered,
  I never thought 'twould vex mine ear;
I thought not when I came on board
  To leave at last with sigh and tear;—
But then, I did not dream to find
Such friendship as I leave behind.

(1833)

CAROLINE CLIVE ('V') (1801–1873)

Caroline Clive was born in London and brought up in what the editor of her diary and papers calls the 'arcadian seclusion' of Shakenhurst, Worcestershire. She was the second daughter of Edmund Weysey Migley who acted as Recorder of Leicester, and served as a Member of Parliament until 1802. Her mother, Anna Maria Meysey, came from a gentry family that could trace its genealogy to William the Conqueror. At the age of 3 Clive contracted poliomyelitis which left her permanently disabled. Her recorded memories of her childhood are far from happy ones. She did everything within her power to ensure that serious disability did not impede her from living a very full and rewarding adult life, enjoying riding on horseback, even though her legs were in irons. Between 1829 and 1833, she ran the household of her brother, Edmund, who had inherited Malvern Hall, Solihull. Thereafter, she settled into Olton Hall, located in an adjacent parish, and which she had inherited in her own right. It was there that she met the Revd Archer Clive, Rector of Solihull, who was connected to a branch of the Clive family, the Earls of Powys, descended from Lord Clive of India. She married him in 1840, the year in which she pseudonymously published *IX Poems* under the cryptic letter 'V'. In the same year, this accomplished volume, which demonstrates a prosodically assured and rather eighteenth-century style, drew the praise of Hartley Coleridge in his extensive review of contemporary poetry by women, published in the *Quarterly Review*. Clive and her spouse moved to the rectory Archer Clive had built at Solihull, and one of the windows commissioned with her husband in 1872 for the church in Solihull is believed to represent her seven happy years in the parish. Olton Hall was sold was in 1844.

Caroline Clive bore two children, Meysey in 1842 and Alice the following year. On the death of his elder brother, Archer Clive inherited his family seat, Whitfield in Herefordshire, and it was with some reluctance that she moved there in 1847. It was during this period that she started work on what is generally considered to be the first Victorian 'sensation' novel, *Paul Ferroll*, published in 1855. This novel created a furore in its depiction of a man who not only murders his wife to marry his first love but also manages to escape punishment by emigrating with the help of his daughter by his second wife and the young woman's husband. This novel was followed by a notable sequel, *Why Paul Ferroll Killed His Wife*, in 1860. Her last novel, *John Greswold*, appeared in 1864, attracting far less attention.

The *IX Poems* were frequently praised throughout the Victorian period, and the volume passed into several editions over the course of fifty years. This collection was followed by longer and more ambitious works: *I Watched the Heavens* (1842), *The Queen's Ball* (1847), *The Valley of the Rea* (1851), and arguably her greatest work, *The Valley of the Morlas* (1853). She died in tragic circumstances in 1873 when her clothes caught fire in the family home. Her achievements were acknowledged by W. E. Gladstone when he was asked for his opinion of the most eminent nineteenth-century women poets.

98 *The Grave*

I STOOD within the grave's o'ershadowing vault;
  Gloomy and damp it stretch'd its vast domains;
Shades were its boundary; for my strained eye sought
  For the limit to its wealth in vain.

Faint from the entrance came a daylight ray,
  And distant sound of living men and things;
This, in th' encountering darkness pass'd away,
  That, took the tone in which a mourner sings.

I lit a torch at a sepulchral lamp,
  Which shot a thread of light amid the gloom;
And feebly burning 'gainst the rolling damp,
  I bore it through the regions of the tomb.

Around me stretch'd the slumbers of the dead,
  Whereof the silence ach'd upon mine ear;
More and more noiseless did I make my tread,
  And yet its echoes chill'd my heart with fear.

The former men of every age and place,
  From all their wand'rings gathered, round me lay;
The dust of withered Empires did I trace,
  And stood 'mid Generations pass'd away.

I saw whole cities that, in flood or fire,
  Or famine or the plague, gave up their breath;
Whole armies whom a day beheld expire,
  Swept by ten thousands to the arms of Death.

I saw the old world's white and wave-swept bones,
  A giant heap of creatures that had been;
Far and confus'd the broken skeletons
  Lay strewn beyond mine eye's remotest ken.

Death's various shrines—the Urn, the Stone, the Lamp—
    Were scatter'd round, confus'd, amid the dead;
Symbols and Types were mould'ring in the damp;
  Their shapes were waning and their meaning fled.

Unspoken tongues, perchance in praise or woe,
  Were character'd on tablets Time had swept;
And deep were half their letters hid below
  The thick small dust of those they once had wept.

No hand was here to wipe the dust away;
  No reader of the writing trac'd beneath;
No spirit sitting by its form of clay;
  No sigh nor sound from all the heaps of Death.

One place alone had ceas'd to hold its prey;
  A form had press'd it and was there no more;
The garments of the Grave beside it lay,
  Where once they wrapp'd him on the rocky floor.

He only with returning footsteps broke
  Th' eternal calm wherewith the Tomb was bound;
Among the sleeping Dead alone He woke,
  And bless'd with outstretch'd hands the host around.

Well is it that such blessing hovers here,
  To soothe each sad survivor of the throng
Who haunt the portals of the solemn sphere,
  And pour their woe the loaded air along.

They to the verge have follow'd what they love,
  And on th' insuperable threshold stand;
With cherish'd names its speechless calm reprove,
  And stretch in the abyss their ungrasp'd hand.

But vainly there they seek their soul's relief,
  And of th' obdurate Grave its prey implore;
Till Death himself shall medicine their grief,
  Closing their eyes by those they wept before.

All that have died, the Earth's whole race, repose
  Where Death collects his Treasures, heap on heap;
O'er each one's busy day the nightshades close;
  Its Actors, Sufferers, Schools, Kings, Armies—sleep.

(1840)

99 *Written in Illness*

MY bark floats on the sea of death,
  Of deepening waves the sport;
And dull disease, with heavy breath,
  Impels me from the port.

Wide and unknown, the ocean surge
  Outstretches to my ken;
Oh, when I reach yon cloudy verge,
  What sights will reach me then?

Thee, native world, full well I know;
  And as thy shores recede,
Mine eyes desert the onward prow,
  Thy well-known forms to read.

There shines the light that first I knew,
  The scenes that light displayed;
From which my soul the feelings drew
  Whereof itself was made.

There lie the shapes of joys and ills,
  Which mov'd erewhile my mind;
Like storms and suns upon the hills
  The traveller leaves behind.

But still receding, wafted on,
  All indistinct they grow;
The busy crowd that moves thereon
  To me is silent now.

Its glittering ray mine eye escapes,
  The mists are round me furl'd;
Farewell, farewell, ye human shapes!
  Farewell, my native world!

(1840)

100 *Former Home*

In scenes untrod for many a year,
  I stand again, the long estranged;
And gazing round me, ponder here
  On all that has, and has not changed.

The casual visitor would see
  Nought altered in the aspects round;
But long familiar shapes to me
  Are missing, which I fain had found.

Still stands the rock, still runs the flood,
  Which not an eye could pass unmov'd;
The airy copse, the fringing wood,
  Which e'en the passer mark'd and lov'd.

But when mine eyes' delighted pride
  Had dwelt the rock's high front upon,
I sought, upon its warmer side,
  A vine we train'd—and that was gone.

And though awhile content I gazed
  Upon the river quick and fair,
I sought ere long a seat we raised
  In childhood—but it was not there.

Stones lay around, I know not whether
  Its relics, or the winter's snow—
And sitting where we sate together,
  Again I watch'd the torrent flow.

So whirl'd the waves that form'd it then,
  In foam around yon jutting stone;
So arrowy shot they down the glen,
  When there we pass'd the hours long flown.

There in the waters dipp'd the tree
  From which, the day I parted hence,
I took a few green leaves, to be
  My solace still through time and chance.

Full many a spring the tree has shone
  In sunlight, air, and beauty here;
While I in cities gaz'd upon
  The wither'd leaves of that one year.

That year was fraught with heavy things,
  With deaths and partings, loss and pain;
And every object round me rings
  Its mournful epitaph again.

But most, those small familiar traits,
  Which only we have lov'd or known;
They flourish'd with our happier days—
  They wither'd because we were gone.

Their absence seems to speak of those
  Who're scatter'd far upon the earth;
At whose young hands they once arose,
  Whose eyes gazed gleeful on their birth.

Those hands since then have grasp'd the brand,
  Those eyes in grief grown dim and hot;
And wand'ring through a stranger's land,
  Oft yearn'd to this remember'd spot.

How chang'd are they!—how chang'd am I!
  I was a boy then—and 'tis gone;
Gone is each boyish vanity,
  But what in manhood have I won?

I know not—but while standing now,
  Where open'd first the heart of youth,
I recollect how high would glow
  Its thoughts of Glory, Faith, and Truth—

How full it was of good and great,
  How true to heaven, how warm to men;
Alas! I scarce forbear to hate
  The colder breast I bring again.

Hopes disappointed, sin and time
  Have moulded me, since here I stood;
Ah! paint old feelings, rock sublime,
  Speak life's fresh accents, mountain flood!

(1840)

SARA COLERIDGE
(1802–1852)

SARA COLERIDGE was born at Greta Hall, near Keswick, the daughter of Samuel Taylor Coleridge and Sarah Coleridge (née Fricker). As a girl, she lived under the care of her uncle, Robert Southey, through whom she met William Wordsworth, who wrote of her in his poem, 'The Triad'. In 1829 she married her cousin, Henry Nelson Coleridge, a barrister, with whom she lived in London and had two children. Her friends in London included Thomas Macaulay, the Carlyles and Aubrey de Vere.

With her husband, she edited the works of her father, becoming sole editor, after her husband's death in 1843, producing editions of Samuel Taylor Coleridge's *Biographia Literaria* (2nd edn., 1847), *Notes and Lectures Upon Shake-*

speare (1849) and *Essays on his Own Times* (1850) among others. She had begun her literary career with two translations, the first of which, Martin Dobrizhoffer's *Account of the Abipones* (1822), was undertaken to help defray the college expenses of her brother, Derwent, and to ease the financial difficulties produced by her father's excesses. In 1837, she published *Phantasmion: A Fairy Tale*, a prose tale with lyrics, which was said to be 'the product of the enforced leisure on a sick bed'. Although much praised by her nephew, Hartley Coleridge, in the *Quarterly Review* (September 1840), and republished in 1874, the book received little attention. Coleridge's own preference was for the Romantic rather than the Victorian poets, yet she admired Tennyson's *The Princess* (*Quarterly Review*, March 1848), identifying him with 'the School of Sensation', while considering Felicia Hemans and Letitia Elizabeth Landon (L.E.L.) to be only second-rate poets (*Letters*, 1873). Her letters and an incomplete memoir were edited posthumously by her daughter, Edith Coleridge, in 1873. Having been afflicted by bouts of nervous illness throughout her life, her health seriously declined in 1850, and she died, two years later, of breast cancer.

101 *'The Sun May Speed or Loiter on His Way'*

THE sun may speed or loiter on his way,
May veil his face in clouds or brightly glow;
Too fast he moved to bring one fatal day,
I ask not now if he be swift or slow.

I have a region, bathed in joyous beams,
Where he hath never gilded fruit or flower,
Hath ne'er lit up the glad perennial streams,
Nor tinged the foliage of an Autumn bower.

Then hail the twilight cave, the silent dell,
That boast no beams, no music of their own;
Bright pictures of the past around me dwell,
Where nothing whispers that the past is flown.

(1837 *1874*)

102 *'O Sleep, My Babe, Hear Not the Rippling Wave'*

O SLEEP, my babe, hear not the rippling wave,
Nor feel the breeze that round thee lingering strays
To drink thy balmy breath,
And sigh one long farewell.

Soon shall it mourn above thy wat'ry bed,
And whisper to me, on the wave-beat shore,
Deep murm'ring in reproach,
Thy sad untimely fate.

Ere those dear eyes had opened on the light,
In vain to plead, thy coming life was sold,
O! wakened but to sleep,
Whence it can wake no more!

A thousand and a thousand silken leaves
The tufted beech unfolds in early spring,
All clad in tenderest green,
All of the self same shape:

A thousand infant faces, soft and sweet,
Each year sends forth, yet every mother views
Her last not least beloved
Like its dear self alone.

No musing mind hath ever yet foreshaped
The face to-morrow's sun shall first reveal,
No heart hath e'er conceived
What love that face will bring.

O sleep, my babe, nor heed how mourns the gale
To part with thy soft locks and fragrant breath,
As when it deeply sighs
O'er autumn's latest bloom.

(1837 *1874*)

103 *'The Winds Were Whispering, the Waters Glistering'*

THE winds were whispering, the waters glistering,
A bay-tree shaded a sun-lit stream;
Blasts came blighting, the bay-tree smiting,
When leaf and flower, like a morning dream,
Vanished suddenly.

The winds yet whisper, the waters glister,
And softly below the bay-tree glide;
Vain is their cherishing, for, slowly perishing,
It doth but cumber the river side.
Leafless in summer-time.

(1837 *1874*)

L.E.L. (LETITIA ELIZABETH LANDON) (1802–1838)

HERALDED as a female Byron, Letitia Elizabeth Landon's highly successful poetic career was punctuated by scandal and concluded tragically early in mysterious circumstances. She was generally known by her initials: L.E.L. Born in London, the eldest of three children, her father, John Landon, was a partner in an army agency and her mother (formerly Bishop) was of Welsh extraction. L.E.L. was educated at the same school in Chelsea as the novelists and poets, Mary Mitford and Caroline Lamb. In about 1815 the family moved to Brompton and there became acquainted with William Jerdan, the editor of the *Literary Gazette*. Her mother having shown some of L.E.L.'s early poems to the editor, he then published her first printed poem, 'Rome', in his gazette, affixed with the signature, 'L', (March 1818). She was only twenty-one years old when he commissioned her to write a series of 'Poetical Sketches', again for the *Literary Gazette*, which were published without interruption between the summers of 1821 and 1824. She here used the signature of L.E.L. for the first time. These verses were so well received that she felt encouraged to publish in volume form and proceeded to do so at a prodigious rate. Five volumes of poetry followed between 1821 and 1828 alone. The first book, *The Fate of Adelaide, A Swiss Romantic Tale; and Other Poems* (1821) was financed, in part, by a family friend, the actress Mrs Siddons, to whom L.E.L. dedicated the work.

She acted as one of the main reviewers for Jerdan's gazette and was also to be taken on to the staff of *Fraser's Magazine*, contributing tales as well as poetry. Her intimacy with the editor of this magazine, William Maginn, as also with William Jerdan, led to the circulation of rumours which are said to have produced the breakdown of her engagement with the essayist and later biographer of Charles Dickens, John Forster. Her name was also romantically linked with the novelist, Edward Bulwer Lytton, who was to feature, with his wife, Rosanne, in one of L.E.L.'s novels, *Romance and Reality* (1831). Much to her friends' surprise, she eventually married the apparently less than congenial George Maclean, the Governor of Cape Coast, West Africa. After their marriage in 1838, they moved to Cape Coast and, within months of their arrival, L.E.L. had died from an overdose of prussic acid. It is not known whether the death was caused by accident, suicide, or murder.

Her intense literary activity was, in part, motivated by the need to support her family, which was impoverished firstly by her father's failing business and then his death in 1824. Along with her numerous contributions to further annuals and journals, including the *Drawing-Room Scrapbook*, the *Keepsake*, and *Friendship's Offering*, she also published three novels, the most successful being her last, *Ethel Churchill; or, The Two Brides* (1838). Her final piece of writing was the poem, 'Zenana', which was one of her longest contributions to Fisher's *Drawing-Room Scrapbook*. This poem was republished posthumously in *The Zenana, and Minor Poems of Letitia Elizabeth Landon* (1839). A *Poetical Works* was issued in 1873. L.E.L.'s late work, 'Subjects for Pictures', published in the *New Monthly Magazine* (1836), a series of poems on women in mythology, legend and history, which in some ways compares with Felicia Hemans's *Records of Woman* (1828), is a distinguished achievement. We have selected three poems (nos 111, 112 and 113) from this series. The two-volume *Life and Literary Remains of L.E.L.*, which was edited by Laman Blanchard, appeared in 1841.

104 *Different Thoughts; Suggested by a Picture by G. S. Newton, No. 16 in the British Gallery, and Representing a Girl Looking at Her Lover's Miniature*

WHICH is the truest reading of thy look?
Just one look before I sleep,
Just one parting glance, to keep
On my heart and on my brain
Every line and feature plain,
In sweet hopes that they may be
Present in those dreams to me,
Which the gentle night-hour brings
Ever on her starry wings.
I have heard the deep tolled chime
Of the moonlight vesper time—
Scarcely seems one hour-glass run,
Since beneath the setting sun
Hill and vale were red, and I
And OLAVE looked upon the sky,
And said, or ere the grapes, which now
Shone green gems in the sunset glow,
Might darken, that we two should be
Linked in gentlest unity;
And the soft twilight came on
Ere our pleasant words were done;
Stars were glancing overhead
When our last 'Good night!' was said:
Since, I've sat and watched this brow
(Not so beautiful as thou,
Yet thy shadow) in the light
Of the fair moon. Now, Good night!
By the dawn-blush I must wake,
OLAVE, if but for thy sake:
We have flowers to plant and cull,—
Our home must be beautiful;
Waking, I must dream no more,
Night has lovelier dreams in store.
Picture dear, farewell to thee,
Be thine image left with me!

* * *

Yes, every lineament of thine
Full well the painter's skill hath given;
That forehead the proud spirit's shrine,
The lightning of that eye's dark heaven.

Yes, here at least thou art the same
  As once thou wert in years departed,
When truth and love shone o'er thy name,
  Or ere I knew thee cold, false hearted!

How many a dark and bitter thought
  These pictured features now awaken!
There is no balm by memory brought,
  To hopes betrayed, to hearts forsaken.

Those whose life's Summer-path has been
  A fairy round of light and pleasure,
May well recall each vanished scene—
  To them remembrance is a treasure;

But those whose year has only known
  The clouds, the coldness of December,
Why should they pause on moments gone?
  'Tis searing wounds when they remember.

Drear was the hour of youth to me,
  My hopes were stars that fell when lightest;
But one sweet dream still clung to Thee,
  My first, my best, my last, my brightest!

Would I could live that time again,
  When life was but a void without thee!
To me 'twere worth an age of pain
  To feel once more I did not doubt thee.

But, like this picture-frame, thy heart
  Is but a gilded toy, concealing
A darker and a meaner part,
  Bright coloured, but cold and unfeeling!

Farewell to love for ever past,
  Farewell to the dear hopes that leave me!
I'd almost, could that bid them last,
  Wish that thou couldst again deceive me!

* * *

I must turn from this idol: I am kneeling
With vows and homage only made for heaven;
I must turn from this idol. I have been
Like to a child who plays with poisoned arrows,
And then is wounded by them. I have yielded,
Foolishly, fondly yielded, to the love
Which is a curse and sickness to me now.
I am as one who sleeps beneath the power
Of some wild dream; hopes, fears, and burning throbs
Of strange delight, dizzy anxieties,

And looks and words dwelt upon overmuch,
Fill up my feverish circle of existence.
My spirit wanders wildly: all in vain!
I would bring order to my troubled thoughts;
Like autumn leaves scattered by driving gales,
They wander round. Once my heart's sleep was calm
As a young bird's beneath its parent wing;
That quiet is no more! for Love hath breathed
Upon my heart, and with him came a train
Of visionary things:—impatient hope,
Sickening of its own vanity; and more
Than all, concealment preys upon me; life
But animate with emotion, which must yet
Be hidden fire. Oh, I must, I must
Turn from this idol! Our love is forbidden—
You are above me, and in loving you—
Oh God! I dare not think to what that leads:
I dare not think on all I have been told
Of all man's cruelty to woman—how
He will soothe, flatter, vow, till he has won,
And then repay her confidence with ruin,
Leaving her trusting heart a desolate place,
Herself an outcast with an unwept grave,
Perhaps unhallowed too—her last lone refuge.
I've more than loved,—oh I have worshipped you;
I have thought, spoken, dreamt of you alone,
And deep has been my misery! my cheek
Has burnt even to pain when you were named;
I have sat hours thinking o'er your last words,
Have sought my couch for solitude, not sleep,
And wept, I only know how bitterly.
I have no joy in pleasure: all I took
A pride in, once, has lost its interest now;
The days I see you not, to me are blanks,
And yet I shrink from meeting you! I have
Insulted heaven with prayers (prayers not to love you,)
And then have trembled lest they should be heard.
I most forget all this: the veins that throb
In agony will surely learn from time
A calm and quiet pulse; yet I will own,
Though woman's weakness is in the confession,
I never could have nerved my soul to this,
But that I know you wavering and weak,
Passionate, but unsteady; born to win
Hearts, but not keep them. Tell me not you love
Intensely, wholly, well, as I have done.
But oh, farewell, farewell! I give thy portrait

To the red flames,—it is a sacrifice
On which I swear forgetfulness!

(1823)

105 *The Phantom Bride*

AND over hill and over plain
He urged his steed with spur and rein,
Till the heat drops hung on his courser's hide,
And the foam of his speed with blood was dyed.
He saw a bird cut through the sky;
He longed for its wings as it fleeted by;
He looked on the mountain-river gushing,
He heard the wind of the forest rushing,
He saw a star from the heavens fall,
He thought on their swiftness, and envied them all.
  Well the young warrior may fiercely ride,
For to-night he must woo, and must win his bride—
The maiden, whose colours his helmet has borne,
Whose picture has still next his heart been worn.
And then he thought on the myrtle grove,
Where the villa stood he had built for his Love:
With its pillars and marble colonnade,
Its bright fountain beneath the palm-tree's shade;
Fair statues and pictured porticos,
Where the air came sweet from the gardens of rose;
Silver lamps; and vases filled
With perfumed waters, from odours distilled;
And the tapestry hung round each gorgeous room
Was the richest of Tyre's purple loom;
And all that his love, and all that his care,
Had had such pride in making fair:
And then he thought how life would glide,
In such a home, and with such a bride,
Like a glad tale told to the lute's soft tone,—
Never hath happiness dwelt alone.
And swifter he urged his courser's flight,
When he thought on who was waiting that night.
But once beneath a spreading shade,
  He stopped his panting steed for breath;
And as a flickering moon-beam played,
  He saw it was a place of death.
The lonely cypress-tree was keeping
The watch of its eternal weeping;
And at the head was a grey cross;

And scattered o'er the covering moss
Lay withered flower and faded wreath,
That told some maiden slept beneath.
The youth took one or two dried leaves—
Perhaps, thought he, some lover grieves
O'er her who rests, and now can know
No more of human joy or wo.
And answered to his thought a sound,
A murmur from the plaining ground—
He started! oh, it could but be
The wind that swept the cypress tree.
   And almost midnight's hour was come,
Ere he had reached his maiden's home.
All, saving one old slave, were sleeping—
Who, like some stealthy phantom creeping,
Silently and slowly led
The wondering stranger to his bed:
Just pointed to his supper fare,
And the piled wood, and left him there.
   It was a large and darksome room;
With all the loneliness and gloom
That hang round the neglected, walls
O'er which the spider's net-work falls;
And the murk air felt chill and damp,
And dimly burnt the one pale lamp;
And faint gleams from the embers broke
Thro' their dun covering of smoke,
And all felt desolate and drear—
And is this, he sighed, my welcome here?
'No—mine be thy welcome, from my lone home
To greet thee, and claim thee mine own, am I come.'
He heard no step, but still by his side
He saw her stand—his betrothed bride!
Her face was fair, but from it was fled
Every trace of its beautiful red:
And stains upon her bright hair lay
Like the dampness and earth-soil of clay;
Her sunken eyes gleamed with that pale blue light,
Seen when meteors are flitting at night;
And the flow of her shadowy garments' fall,
Was like the black sweep of a funeral pall.
   She sat her down by his side at the board,
And many a cup of the red wine poured;
And as the wine were inward light,
Her cheek grew red and her eye grew bright:—
'In my father's house no more I dwell,
But bid not, with them, to thee farewell.

They forced me to waste youth's hour of bloom
In a grated cell and a convent's gloom,
But there came a Spirit and set me free,
And had given me rest but for love of thee—
There was fire in my heart, and fire in my brain,
And mine eyes could not sleep till they saw thee again.
My home is dark, my home is low,
And cold the love I can offer now;
But give me one curl of thy raven hair,
And, by all thy hopes in heaven, swear
That, chance what may, thou wilt claim thy bride,
And thou to-morrow shalt lie by my side.'
He gave the curl, and wildly press'd
Her cold brow to his throbbing breast;
And kiss'd the lips, as his would share
With hers their warmth and vital air,—
As kiss and passionate caress
Could warm her wan chid loveliness.
And calm upon his bosom she lay,
Till the lark sang his morning hymn to the day;
And a sun-beam thro' the curtain shone,—
As passes a shadow—the maiden was gone!
That day the youth was told the tale,
How she had pined beneath the veil
And died, and then they show'd her grave—
He knew that cypress's green wave.—
That night, alone, he watched his bride—
The next they laid him by her side.

(1824)

106 *The Haunted Lake:*[1] *The Irish Minstrel's Legend*

ROSE up the young moon; back she flung
The veil of clouds that o'er her hung:
Thus would fair maiden fling aside
Her bright curls in their golden pride;
On pass'd she through the sky of blue,
Lovelier as she pass'd it grew;
At last her gentle smiles awake
The silence of the azure lake.
Lighted to silver, waves arise,

[1] *The Haunted Lake* is founded on the Irish tradition of O'Donoghue mentioned in one of Moore's charming melodies. I trust the slight liberties taken with the story will be pardoned on the plea of poetical variety.

As conscious of her radiant eyes.
Hark! floats around its music's tone,
Sweeter than mortal ear hath known:
Such, when the sighing night-wind grieves
Amid the rose's ruby leaves,
Conscious the nightingale is nigh,
  That too soon his reluctant wing
Must rival song and rival sigh
  To his own fair flower bring;
Such as the lute, touch'd by no hand
  Save by an angel's, wakes and weeps;
Such is the sound that now to land
  From the charmed water sweeps.
Around the snowy foam-wreaths break,
The spirit band are on the lake.
First, a gay train form'd of the hues
Of morning skies and morning dews:
A saffron-light around them play'd,
As eve's last cloud with them delay'd;
Such tints, when gazing from afar,
The dazed eye sees in midnight star.
They scatter'd flowers, and the stream
  Grew like a garden, each small billow
Shining with the crimson gleam
  The young rose flung upon its pillow;
And from their hands, and from their hair,
Blossoms and odours fill'd the air;
And some of them bore wreathed shells,
Blush-dyed, from their coral cells,
Whence the gale at twilight brought
The earliest lesson music caught:
And gave they now the sweetest tone,
That unto the sea-born lyre was known;
For they were echoes to the song
  That from spirit lips was fleeting,
And the wind bears no charm along
  Such as the shell and voices meeting.
On pass'd they to the lulling tune,
Meet pageant for the lady moon.
A louder sweep the music gave:
The chieftain of the charmed wave,
Graceful upon his steed of snow,
Rises from his blue halls below;
And rode he like a victor-knight
Thrice glorious in his arms of light.
But, oh! the look his features bear
Was not what living warriors wear;

The glory of his piercing eye
Was not that of mortality;
Earth's cares may not such calm allow,
Man's toil is written on his brow:
But here the face was passionless,
The holy peace of happiness,
With that grave pity spirits feel
In watching over human weal;
An awful beauty round him shone
But for the good to look upon.
Close by his side a maiden rode,
Like spray her white robe round her flow'd;
No rainbow hues about her clung,
Such as the other maidens flung;
And her hair hath no summer crown,
But its long tresses floating down
Are like a veil of gold which cast
A sunshine to each wave that past.
She was not like the rest: her cheek
  Was pale and pure as moonlight snows;
Her lip had only the faint streak
  The bee loves in the early rose;
And her dark eye had not the blue
  The others had, clear, wild, and bright;
But floating starry, as it drew
  Its likeness from the radiant night.
And more she drew my raised eye
Than the bright shadows passing by;
A meeker air, a gentler smile,
A timid tenderness the while,
Held sympathy of heart, and told
The lady was of earthly mould.
Blush'd the first blush of coming day,
Faded the fairy band away.
They pass'd, and only left behind
A lingering fragrance on the wind,
And on the lake their haunted home,
One long white wreath of silver foam.
Heard I in each surrounding vale
What was that mortal maiden's tale.
Last of her race, a lonely flower,
She dwelt within their ruin'd tower.
Orphan without one link to bind
Nature's affection to her kind;
She grew up a neglected child,
As pure, as beautiful, as wild,
As the field flowers which were for years

Her only comrades and compeers.
Time pass'd, and she, to woman grown,
Still, like a wood bird, dwelt alone.
Save that, beside a peasant's hearth,
Tales of the race which gave her birth
Would sometimes win the maiden's ear;
And once, in a worst hour of fear,
When the red fever raged around,
Her place beside the couch was found
Of sickness, and her patient care,
And soothing look, and holy prayer,
And skill in herbs, had power sublime
Upon the sufferer's weary time:
But, saving these, her winter day
Was passed within the ruins gray;
And ever summer noons were spent
  Beside the charmed lake, and there
Her voice its silver sweetness sent
  To mingle with the air.
Thus time pass'd on. At length, one day
Beside her favourite haunt she lay,
When rush'd some band who wish'd to make
Her prisoner for her beauty's sake.

She saw them ere they gain'd her seat.
  Ah! safety may she gain?
Though mountain deer be not more fleet,
  Yet here flight is in vain.
The lake—oh, it is there to save!
She plunges—is it to a grave?
Moons waned; again is come the night
When sprites are free for earthly sight.
They see the mortal Maiden ride
In honour by the Chieftain's side,
So beautiful, so free from sin,
Worthy was she such boon to win:
The spirit race that floated round
Were not more pure, more stainless found:
Her utmost loveliness and grace
Were sole signs of her human race;
Happy, thus freed from earthly thrall,
She skims the lake, fairest of all.

(1827 *1873*)

107 *Revenge*

Ay, gaze upon her rose-wreath'd hair,
  And gaze upon her smile;
Seem as you drank the very air
  Her breath perfumed the while;

And wake for her the gifted line,
  That wild and witching lay,
And swear your heart is as a shrine,
  That only owns her sway.

'Tis well: I am revenged at last;—
  Mark you that scornful cheek,—
The eye averted as you pass'd,
  Spoke more than words could speak.

Ay, now by all the bitter tears
  That I have shed for thee,—
The racking doubts, the burning fears,—
  Avenged they well may be—

By the nights pass'd in sleepless care,
  The days of endless woe;
All that you taught my heart to bear,
  All that yourself will know.

I would not wish to see you laid
  Within an early tomb;
I should forget how you betray'd,
  And only weep your doom:

But this is fitting punishment,
  To live and love in vain,—
O my wrung heart, be thou content,
  And feed upon his pain.

Go thou and watch her lightest sigh,—
  Thine own it will not be;
And bask beneath her sunny eye,—
  It will not turn on thee.

'Tis well: the rack, the chain, the wheel,
  Far better hadst thou proved;
Ev'n I could almost pity feel,
  For thou art not beloved.

(1829 *1873*)

108 *The Princess Victoria*

AND art thou a Princess?—in sooth, we may well
Go back to the days of the sign and the spell,
When a young queen sat on an ivory throne
In a shining hall, whose windows shone
With colours its crystals caught from the sky,
Or the roof which a thousand rubies dye;
Where the summer garden was spread around,
With the date and the palm and the cedar crowned;
Where fountains played with the rainbow showers,
Touched with the hues of their comrade flowers;
Where the tulip and rose grew side by side,
One like a queen, and one like a bride;
One with its own imperial flush,
The other reddening with love's sweet blush;
When silver stuffs for her step were unrolled,
And the citron was served on a plate of gold;
When perfumes arose from pearl caskets filled
With odours from all sweet things distilled;
When a fairy guarded the throne from ill,
And she knew no rule but her own glad will:
Those were the days for a youthful queen,
And such, fair Princess, thou should'st have been.

But now thou wilt fill a weary throne,
What with rights of the people, and rights of thy own:
An ear-trumpet now thy sceptre should be,
Eternal debate is the future for thee.
Lord Brougham will make a six-hours' oration,
On the progress of knowledge, the mind of the nation;
Lord Grey one yet longer, to state that his place
Is perhaps less dear to himself than his race;
O'Connell will tell Ireland's griefs and her wrongs,
In speech, the mac-adamized prose of Moore's songs:
Good patience! how weary the young queen will be
Of 'the flower of the earth, and the gem of the sea!'
Mr Hume, with his watchwords 'Retrenchment and Waste',
Will insist that your wardrobe in his care be placed;
The silk he will save! the blonde he will spare—
I wish he may leave Your Grace any to wear.
That feminine fancy, a will of your own,
Is a luxury wholly denied to a throne;
And this is your future—how soon time will trace
A change and a sign on that fair and young face!
Methinks the best wish to be offered thee now,
Is—God keep the crown long from that innocent brow!

(1832)

109 *The Pirate's Song off the Tiger Island*

OUR prize is won, our chase is o'er,
Turn the vessel to the shore.
Place yon rock, so that the wind,
Like a prisoner, howl behind;
Which is darkest—wave, or cloud?
One a grave, and one a shroud.
Though the thunder rend the sky,
Though the echoing wind reply,
Though the lightning sweep the seas,
We are used to nights like these;
Let it foam, the angry main—
Washing out the blood-red stain,
Which the evening conflict threw
O'er the waters bright and blue.
Though above the thunder break,
'Twill but drown our victims' shriek;
And the lightning's serpent coil,
Will but glimmer o'er our spoil:
Maidens, in whose orient eyes,
More than morning's sunshine lies—
Honour to the wind and waves,
While they yield us such sweet slaves—
Shawls the richest of Cashmere,
Pearls from Oman's bay are here;
And Golconda's royal mine
Sends her diamonds here to shine;
Let the stars at midnight glow,
We have brighter stars below;
Leave the planet of the pole
Just to guide us to our goal,
We'd not change for heaven's own stars,
Yon glad heap of red dinars;[1]
See the crimson silks unfold,
And the slender chains of gold,
Like the glittering curls descending,
When the bright one's head is bending;
And the radiant locks fall over,
Or her mirror or her lover,
On which face she likes to dwell,
'Twere a prophet's task to tell;
All those crystal flasks enclose
Sighs of the imprisoned rose;
And those porcelain urns are filled

[1] An Indian coin.

By sweet Indian wood distilled;
And behold those fragrant piles,
Spice from the Manilla isles,
Nutmegs, cloves, and cinnamon—
But our glorious task is done.
Little dreamed the merchant's care
Who his precious freight should share—
Fill the wine-cup to the brim,
Our first health shall be to him.

(1832)

110 *Hurdwar,*[1] *a Place of Hindoo Pilgrimage*

I LOVE the feeling which, in former days,
  Sent men to pray amid the desert's gloom,
  Where hermits left a cell, or saints a tomb;
Good springs alike from penitence and praise,
From aught that can the mortal spirit raise:
  And though the faith be false, the hope be vain,
  That brought the Hindoo to his idol fane;
Yet one all-sacred truth his deed conveys—
How still the heart doth its Creator own,
  Mid strange idolatry and savage rite,
A consciousness of power eternal shown,
  How man relies on some superior might.
The soul mid darkness feels its birth divine,
And owns the true God in the false god's shrine.

(1832)

[1] Hurdwar, or Haridwar, means the gate of Vishnoo, the Prinsir. The Hindoos perform this pilgrimage, to bathe in a particular spot of the Ganges,[2] at the time when the sun enters the sign Aries. A fair is then held, which, thanks to the precautions taken by the British government, has, of late years, gone off without bloodshed. 'At the annual fairs, it is supposed, from 200,000 to 300,000 persons are collected. Once in twelve years, when particular ceremonies are performed, the number of those present has been computed at one million' (*Hamilton's Gazetteer*).

[2] 'Parvati, the bride of Siva, ventured one day to cover his eyes with her hands. Thereupon all the functions of life were suspended—times stood—nay, the drops poured from Siva's brow, to think of the awful consequences arising from his almighty eye relaxing from its eternal watchfullness. From these drops the Ganges had its divine origin; hence the veneration of the Hindoos for the sacred river'—(Asiatic Researches).

111 *The Banquet of Aspasia and Pericles*

WAKEN'D by the small white fingers,
  Which its chords obey,
On the air the music lingers
  Of a low and languid lay
    From a soft Ionian lyre;—
Purple curtains hang the walls,
And the dying daylight falls
O'er the marble pedestals
    Of the pillars that aspire,
  In honour of Aspasia,
  The bright Athenian bride.

There are statues white and solemn,
  Olden gods are they;
And the wreath'd Corinthian column
  Guardeth their array.
    Lovely that acanthus wreath,
Drooping round the graceful girth:
All the fairest things of earth,
Art's creations have their birth—
    Still from love and death.
  They are gather'd for Aspasia,
  The bright Athenian bride.

There are gold and silver vases
  Where carved victories shine:
While within the sunlight blazes
  Of the fragrant Teian wine,
    Or the sunny Cyprian isle.
From the garlands on each brow
Take they early roses now;
And each rose-leaf bears a vow,
    As they pledge the radiant smile
  Of the beautiful Aspasia,
  The bright Athenian bride.

With the spoils of nations splendid
  Is that stately feast;
By her youthful slaves attended—
  Beauties from the East,
    With their large black dewy eyes.
Though their dark hair sweeps the ground,

Every heavy tress is wound
With the white sea-pearl around;
For no queen in Persia vies
With the proud Aspasia,
The bright Athenian bride.

One hath caught mine eye—the fairest;
'Tis a Theban girl:
Though a downcast look thou wearest,
And nor flower nor pearl
Winds thy auburn hair among:
With a white, unsandall'd foot,
Leaning languid on thy lute,
Weareth thy soft lip, though mute,
Smiles yet sadder than thy song.
Can grief come nigh Aspasia,
The bright Athenian bride?

On an ivory couch reclining
Doth the bride appear;
In her eyes the light is shining,
For her chief is near;—
And her smile grows bright to gaze
On the stately Pericles,
Lord of the Athenian seas,
And of Greece's destinies.
Glorious, in those ancient days,
Was the lover of Aspasia,
The bright Athenian bride.

Round her small head, perfume breathing
Was a myrtle stem,
Fitter for her bright hair's wreathing
Than or gold or gem;
For the myrtle breathes of love.
O'er her cheek so purely white,
From her dark eyes came such light
As is, on a summer night,
With the moon above.
Fair as moonlight was Aspasia,
The bright Athenian bride.

These fair visions have departed,
Like a poet's dream,
Leaving us pale and faint-hearted
By life's common stream,
Whence all lovelier light hath fled.
Not so: they have left behind
Memory to the kindling mind,

With bright fantasies combined.
Still the poet's dream is fed
By the beauty of Aspasia,
The bright Athenian bride.

(1836 *1873*)

112 *Calypso Watching the Ocean*

YEARS, years, have pass'd away,
Since to yonder fated bay
Did the Hero come.
Years, years, have pass'd the while
Since he left the lovely isle
For his Grecian home.
He is with the dead—but She
Weepeth on eternally
In the lone and lovely island
'Mid the far-off southern seas.

Downwards floateth her bright hair,
Fair—how exquisitely fair!
But it is unbound.
Never since that parting hour
Golden band or rosy flower
In it has been wound!
There it droopeth sadly bright,
In the morning's sunny light,
On the lone and lovely island
In the far-off southern seas.

Like a marble statue placed,
Looking o'er the watery waste,
With its white fixed gaze;
There the Goddess sits, her eye
Raised to the unpitying sky:
So uncounted days
Has she asked of yonder main,
Him it will not bring again
To the lone and lovely island
In the far-off southern seas.

To that stately brow is given,
Loveliness that sprung from heaven—
Is, like heaven, bright:
Never there may time prevail,
But her perfect face is pale;
And a troubled light

Tells of one who may not die,
Vex'd with immortality
In the lone and lovely island
'Mid the far-off southern seas.

Desolate beside that strand,
Bow'd upon her cold, white hand,
Is her radiant head;
Silently she sitteth there,
While her large eyes on the air
Traced the much-loved dead:
Eyes that know not tears nor sleep,
Would she not be glad to weep,
In the lone and lovely island
'Mid the far-off southern seas.

Far behind the fragrant pile,
Sends its odours through the isle;
And the winds that stir
In the poplars are imbued
With the cedar's precious wood,
With incense and with myrrh,
Till the azure waves beneath
Bear away the scented breath
Of the lone and lovely island
In the far-off southern seas.

But no more does that perfume
Hang around the purple loom
Where Calypso wove
Threads of gold with curious skill,
Singing at her own sweet will
Ancient songs of love;
Weary on the sea-wash'd shore,
She will sing those songs no more
In the lone and lovely island
'Mid the far-off southern seas.

From the large green leaves escape
Clusters of the blooming grape;
Round the shining throne
Still the silver fountains play,
Singing on through night and day,
But they sing alone:
Lovely in their early death,
No one binds a violet wreath,
In the lone and lovely island
'Mid the far-off southern seas.

Love and Fate—oh, fearful pair!
Terrible in strength ye are;
Until ye had been,
Happy as a summer night,
Conscious of its own sweet light,
Was that Island-queen.
Would she could forget to grieve,
Or that she could die and leave
The lone and lovely island
'Mid the far-off southern seas.

She is but the type of all,
Mortal or celestial,
Who allow the heart,
In its passion and its power,
On some dark and fated hour,
To assert its part.
Fate attends the steps of Love,—
Both brought misery from above
To the lone and lovely island
'Mid the far-off southern seas.

(1836 *1873*)

113 *A Supper of Madame de Brinvilliers*

SMALL but gorgeous was the chamber
Where the lady leant;
Heliotrope, and musk, and amber,
Made an element,
Heavy like a storm, but sweet.
Softly stole the light uncertain
Through the silken fold
Of the sweeping purple curtain;
And enwrought in gold
Was the cushion at her feet.
There he knelt to gaze on her—
He the latest worshipper.

From the table came the lustre
Of its fruit and flowers;
There were grapes, each shining cluster
Bright with sunny hours,—
Noon and night were on their hues.
There the purple fig lay hidden
'Mid its wide green leaves;
And the rose, sweet guest, was bidden,
While its breath receives

Freshness from the unshed dews.
Nothing marks the youth of these—
One bright face is all he sees.

With such colours as are dying
On a sunset sky;
With such odours as are sighing,
When the violets die,
Are the rich Italian wines.
Dark and bright they glow together,
In each graceful flask,
Telling of the summer weather,
And the autumn task,
When young maidens stripped the vines.
One small flask of cold pale green,
Only one, he has not seen.

When She woke the heart that slumber'd
In a poet's dream,
Few the summers he had number'd,
Little did he deem
Of such passion and such power;
When there hangs a life's emotion
On a word—a breath—
Like the storm upon the ocean,
Bearing doom and death.
Youth has only one such hour;
And its shadow now is cast
Over him who looks his last.

Does he love her?—Yes, to madness,
Fiery, fierce, and wild;
Touch'd, too, with a gentle sadness;
For his soul is mild,
Tender as his own sad song.
And that young wan cheek is wasted
With the strife within:
Well he knows his course has hasted
Through delicious sin,
Borne tumultuously along.
Never have the stars above
Chronicled such utter love.

Well the red robe folded round her
Suits her stately mien;
And the ruby chain has bound her
Of some Indian queen;—
Pale her cheek is, like a pearl.
Heavily the dusky masses

Of her night-black hair,
Which the raven's wing surpasses,
Bind her forehead fair;
Odours float from every curl.
He would die, so he might wear
One soft tress of that long hair.

Clear her deep black eyes are shining,
Large, and strangely bright;
Somewhat of the hid repining,
Gives unquiet light
To their wild but troubled glow.
Dark-fringed lids an eastern languor
O'er their depths have shed;
But the curved lip knoweth anger,
'Tis so fiercely red,—
Passion crimsons in its glow.
Tidings from that face depart
Of the death within her heart.

Does she love the boy who, kneeling,
Brings to her his youth,
With its passionate, deep feeling,
With its hope, its truth?
No; his hour has pass'd away!
Scarcely does she seek to smother
Change and scornful pride;
She is thinking of another,
With him at her side;—
He has had his day!
Love has darken'd into hate,
And her falsehood is his fate.

Even now, her hand extending,
Grasps the fated cup;
For her red lip o'er it bending,
He will drink it up,—
He will drink it to her name;
Little of the vial knowing
That has drugg'd its wave,
How its rosy tide is flowing
Onwards to the grave!
One sweet whisper from her came;
And he drank to catch her breath,—
Wine and sigh alike are death!

(1836 *1873*)

114 *The Factory*

'Tis an accursed thing!

THERE rests a shade above yon town,
  A dark funereal shroud:
'Tis not the tempest hurrying down,
  'Tis not a summer cloud.

The smoke that rises on the air
  Is as a type and sign;
A shadow flung by the despair
  Within those streets of thine.

That smoke shuts out the cheerful day
  The sunset's purple hues,
The moonlight's pure and tranquil ray,
  The morning's pearly dews.

Such is the moral atmosphere
  Around thy daily life;
Heavy with care, and pale with fear,
  With future tumult rife.

There rises on the morning wind
  A low appealing cry,
A thousand children are resign'd
  To sicken and to die!

We read of Moloch's sacrifice,
  We sicken at the name,
And seem to hear the infant cries—
  And yet we do the same;—

And worse–'twas but a moment's pain
  The heathen altar gave,
But we give years,—our idol, Gain,
  Demands a living grave!

How precious is the little one,
  Before his mother's sight,
With bright hair dancing in the sun,
  And eyes of azure light!

He sleeps as rosy as the south,
  For summer days are long;
A prayer upon the little mouth,
  Lull'd by his nurse's song.

Love is around him, and his hours
  Are innocent and free;
His mind essays its early powers
  Beside his mother's knee.

When afteryears of trouble come,
  Such as await man's prime,
How will he think of that dear home,
  And childhood's lovely time!

And such should childhood ever be,
  The fairy well; to bring
To life's worn, weary memory
  The freshness of its spring.

But here the order is reversed,
  And infancy, like age,
Knows of existence but its worst,
  One dull and darken'd page;—

Written with tears and stamp'd with toil,
  Crush'd from the earliest hour,
Weeds darkening on the bitter soil
  That never knew a flower.

Look on yon child, it droops the head,
  Its knees are bow'd with pain;
It mutters from its wretched bed,
  'O, let me sleep again!'

Alas! 'tis time, the mother's eyes
  Turn mournfully away;
Alas! 'tis time, the child must rise,
  And yet it is not day.

The lantern's lit–she hurries forth,
  The spare cloak's scanty fold
Scarce screens her from the snowy north,
  The child is pale and cold.

And wearily the little hands
  Their task accustom'd ply;
While daily, some 'mid those pale bands,
  Droop, sicken, pine, and die.

Good God! to think upon a child
  That has no childish days,
No careless play, no frolics wild,
  No words of prayer and praise!

Man from the cradle–'tis too soon
  To earn their daily bread,
And heap the heat and toil of noon
  Upon an infant's head.

To labour ere their strength be come,
  Or starve,—such is the doom
That makes of many an English home
  One long and living tomb!

Is there no pity from above,—
  No mercy in those skies;
Hath then the heart of man no love,
  To spare such a sacrifice?

O, England! though thy tribute waves
  Proclaim thee great and free,
While those small children pine like slaves,
  There is a curse on thee!

(1838 *1873*)

115 *The Marriage Vow*

THE altar, 'tis of death! for there are laid
The sacrifice of all youth's sweetest hopes.
It is a dreadful thing for woman's lip
To swear the heart away; yet know that heart.
Annuls the vow while speaking, and shrinks back
From the dark future that it dares not face.
The service read above the open grave
Is far less terrible than that which seals
The vow that binds the victim, not the will:
For in the grave is rest.

(1841 *1873*)

SUSANNA STRICKLAND (LATER MOODIE)
(1803–1885)

BEST known for her autobiographical narrative, *Roughing It in the Bush* (1852), Susanna Moodie (as she was named after her marriage) has exerted a powerful influence on later Canadian writers, notably Margaret Atwood, whose volume of poetry, *The Journals of Susanna Moodie*, appeared in 1970. Born in Bungay, Suffolk, the young Susanna Strickland was educated at home. Her father moved to Suffolk after working as the manager of the Greenland Dock in London. After his death, she and her sisters supported themselves through writing. Her first book, *Enthusiasm, and Other Poems*, was published in 1831; it collected a number of pieces that had already appeared in album books. At this time, she was in correspondence with the poet, Mary Russell Mitford, and her work bears some resemblance to this older poet's works. In the year that *Enthusiasm* went out on sale, she married Lt. John Wedderburn Dunbar Moodie, a half-pay officer. They lived together for some time in London, and then briefly at Southwold (where her father had purchased a property in 1808). Having decided to emigrate to Canada, they set sail in July 1832. They eventually settled on a farm near Peterborough, Ontario, to be close to her sister, Catherine Parr Traill. Her husband developed his career as a military officer and then as a farmer, before becoming the Sheriff of Belleville. In what were often difficult times, both her family and professional life flourished. Although Moodie was preoccupied with raising their seven children, she worked busily on her writing to add to the family income. From 1838 to 1852, she published poems and prose in *The Literary Garland*, the most highly regarded journal of its kind. Between 1847 and 1848, she edited the Canadian *Victoria Magazine*. The two volumes of *Roughing It in the Bush* proved highly successful, and they were rapidly followed by a sequel, *Life in the Clearings versus the Bush*, in 1853. Much of her later career from the 1850s onwards was devoted to writing fiction, including *The World before Them* (1868) and *George Leatrim; or, The Mother's Test* (1875).

116 *The Spirit of Motion*

SPIRIT of eternal motion!
Ruler of the stormy ocean,
Lifter of the restless waves,
Rider of the blast that raves
Hoarsely through yon lofty oak,
Bending to thy mystic stroke;
Man from age to age has sought
Thy secret—but it baffles thought!

Agent of the Deity!
Offspring of eternity,
Guider of the steeds of time
Along the starry track sublime,
Founder of each wondrous art,
Mover of the human heart;
Since the world's primeval day
All nature has confessed thy sway.

They who strive thy laws to find
Might as well arrest the wind,
Measure out the drops of rain,
Count the sands which bound the main,
Quell the earthquake's sullen shock,
Chain the eagle to the rock,
Bid the sun his heat assuage,
The mountain torrent cease to rage.
Spirit, active and divine—
Life and all its powers are thine!
Guided by the first great cause,

Sun and moon obey thy laws,
Which to man must ever be
A wonder and a mystery,
Known alone to him who gave
Thee sovereignty o'er wind and wave
And only chained thee in the grave!

(1831)

SARAH FLOWER ADAMS
(1805–1848)

SHE was born into an Unitarian family in Great Harlow, Essex. Her father, Benjamin Flower, a radical political journalist and editor of the *Cambridge Intelligencer*, and mother, Eliza (née Gould), were supporters of free speech and religious liberty. Sarah Flower (later Flower Adams) and her sister, Eliza, were educated at home by their father and schoolmasters. From 1820 onwards they lived in London, where the two sisters became acquainted with Robert Browning. After the death of her father in 1829, Flower Adams lived for five years with the family of William Johnson Fox, a Unitarian minister, political writer, and prominent member of the Anti-Corn Law League.

Best known as a writer of hymns (collaborating with her sister, a composer), including 'Nearer, my God, to Thee', she also contributed poems, stories, and essays to the radical, Unitarian journal, the *Monthly Repository* between 1832–36, while it was under Fox's editorship. Her belief in the power of art to ensure the spirituality of the people is expressed in some of these essays. In 1834, she married another contributor of poems and articles to the journal, William Bridges Adams, a civil engineer.

After a brief acting career in 1837, she concentrated on her writing, reviewing Elizabeth Barrett's *Poems* (1844) for the *Westminster Review* (December 1844), which she commended for their 'power of individualizing passion', but criticized for their melancholic 'pressure of strong thought and intense emotion'. Such a contrast between the two poets' sensibilities was noticed by Fox in his *Lectures Addressed Chiefly to the Working Classes* (Lecture IX, Vol. 4, 1849), where he also admires Flower Adams for being the more politically sensitive of the two. In his lecture, Fox focuses upon her principal work, *Vivia Perpetua* (1841), a blank verse drama about the martyrdom of a Christian woman in AD 204.

117 *A Dream*

METHOUGHT I wander'd through a wilderness;
And many a turn, and many a devious way
I traversed o'er, and many a form I met
That, like myself, seem'd bent upon some end
Which still they found not. Ever and anon
The tread of footsteps hurrying to and fro,
The busy hum of voices in dispute,
Throughout the maze, came sounding far and near:
At last from out this dreary labyrinth
We came upon a plain;—in the centre stood
A temple; high in pillar'd pomp it rose;
So that mine eye did wonder to behold
Such loftiness of marble majesty!
Towards this I hurried on—and many more,
Differing in age, in station, and degree,
Moved on by different paths across the plain.
But all seem'd hastening to one common end,—
To add themselves unto the gathering crowd,
That like a troubled ocean heav'd and swell'd
Around the mighty temple's open gate:
Still they increasing came, and still pour'd in,
Wave after wave, and yet no overflow.
I gain'd the thickening throng. Anon there came
A swarthy Oriental, by my side:
He had a face whereon each passion wild
Had deeply trac'd its darkest character;
A snowy turban mock'd his sallow brow;
And, in return, his eye sent forth such rays
As put to shame the flashing gems that serv'd
To fix its pliant folds:—beneath a vest
Of bloody red, you saw his sanguine heart
Leap up against his glittering armed belt
To claim a kindred with its native hue.
He spoke of war and murder, curse and crime,
Of heathen rite, and burning sacrifice;
And then his dark idolatry he made
A fit excuse for all his foul misdeeds,
And, like the bigots of a nearer clime,
All those who differed doom'd to agony;
Inflicted what he could; and when no more
He had the power to make them suffer here,
Liv'd in the hope of their eternal pangs—
But, as he pass'd beneath the stately arch,
His speech was stopp'd, his white and restless lips
Suddenly clos'd, leaving a lie half told:

We enter'd silently and stood within.
Thousands on thousands, in a circle vast,
Of every tongue, and tribe, and station, there
Mingled in mighty union—all arrayed
In the extremest pomp of their degree:—
Kings, in their coronation robes of state;—
Warriors, all armed as if for deadly fight;
Courtiers, in all their pride, and priests in theirs;—
And yet no sign was there of kingly rite,
Nor battle fierce, nor courtly pageant gay,
Nor that miscalled religious pomp which makes
The worship of the ever-blessed God
Naught but a sensual, soulless offering!
Each seemed unconscious of the other's being.
There was a Turk, who by a Christian sat
(A *Christian!*—such are called so oftentime)
They both were men whose eyes, if bent on each,
Would have flashed daggers of the deadliest hate,
But like the rest of that mass'd multitude,
They spoke not—stirr'd not:—Silence cast her spell
In such complete perfection o'er the whole,
That, with clos'd lids, you might have deem'd the place
A vast untrodden desert in a calm.
Lifted the curtains of the precious sense,
And looked upon that mighty moveless mass,
You would have thought them senseless, lifeless all,
But for the fixed intent in every eye;
And there her seat of empire life had made,
And in such bright, consummate glory shone,
As if she had deserted for a while
Each other sense, to reign triumphant there.
The gaze of all was fastened to one point,—
What seem'd a cloud—a small dense purple cloud—
And rose above the centre of the throng;
Anon it brighter grew, and then it glow'd
With ever-changing colours:—all sat by
In rapt expectancy,—when suddenly
A ray of heavenly light swift darted down,
And, like a golden wand, it touch'd the cloud,
Which, parting instantly, display'd to view
A radiant angel form—how dazzling bright!
How pure! how beautiful to look upon!
With snowy wings outspread, poised like a bird,
She seem'd to hover o'er the multitude
Like an embodied blessing from above;
I could have liv'd a long and blissful life
In gazing on her—but brief time had I,

For as the sever'd cloud dispers'd in air,
The spell that bound that deathly stilly throng
In silence, was dissolved, and there uprose
One universal, rending, deafening, shout—
One word was all I heard—that word was *Truth.*
And I awoke! Awoke unto a world
Where yet the angel form is veiled in clouds.
Oh! God our Father, when wilt thou send down
The blessed light from Heaven to pierce the gloom?
Thou wilt in thine own time,—thy will be done.

(1832)

118 *Songs of the Months.—No. 3, March. Winds and Clouds*

A WIZARD is he!
D'ye see, d'ye see?
Temples arise in the upper air;
Now they are gone,
And a troop comes on
Of plumed knights and ladies fair;
They pass—and a host of spirits grey
Are floating onward—away, away!

His sun-beams are light'ning,
The black clouds brightening,
Grand is the world in the heavens to see!
His winds are the thunder,
Scattering asunder
The world he has made—but what cares he?
In a chariot of storm he rolls along,
While the whirlwinds shout a triumphal song.

Blow, March, blow!
Your time is now;
Soon you must hush your noisy breath;
Soon we shall listen,
While rain-drops glisten,
To the airs that murmur of Spring's bright wreath;
Harm not the buds that dare to peep,
Lest April away her sweet life weep.

(1834)

119 *Nearer, My God, To Thee*

NEARER, my God, to Thee,
  Nearer to Thee!
E'en though it be a cross
  That raiseth me:
Still all my song shall be,
Nearer, my God! to Thee,
  Nearer to Thee.

Though, like the wanderer,
  The sun gone down,
Darkness be over me,
  My rest a stone;
Yet in my dreams I'd be
Nearer, my God, to Thee,
  Nearer to Thee.

Then let the way appear
  Steps unto heaven;
All that Thou sendest me
  In mercy given:
Angels to beckon me
Nearer, my God, to Thee,
  Nearer to Thee.

Then with my waking thoughts
  Bright with Thy praise,
Out of my stony griefs
  Bethel I'll raise;
So by my woes to be
Nearer, my God, to Thee,
  Nearer to Thee.

Or if on joyful wing,
  Cleaving the sky,
Sun, moon, and stars forgot,
  Upward I fly:
Still all my song shall be,
Nearer, my God, to Thee,
  Nearer to Thee.

(*c.*1834 *1868*)

MARY MARIA COLLING
(1805–?)

MARY MARIA COLLING was a working-class poet, born in Tavistock, and daughter of Edmund Colling, a husbandsman, and Anne Colling. She was able to read before she was 5 years old and her (often interrupted) school education lasted until she was 13, after which she went into service. Although she was not well read, her poetry is none the less informed by her knowledge of John Gay's *Fables* and of the entries on ancient mythology in the addenda to her dictionary. Her one collection of poetry, *Fables and Other Pieces in Verse* (1831), was published by subscription. Colling had given a few of her poems to Mrs Anne E. Bray, who then showed them to Robert Southey, through whom subscribers, such as William Wordsworth, were secured. Southey reviewed Colling's poetry for the *Quarterly Review*, describing it as 'an interesting little volume' (March 1832).

120 *The Moon and the Cloud*

FULL-ORB'D in her splendour the Moon rose on high,
And shed her pure light o'er the blue-vaulted sky,
While mountains, and vallies, and woodlands, and streams,
Were glowing with beauty beneath her fair beams.
But soon the bright orb by a Cloud was o'erspread,
Which sullied the lustre she kindly had shed:
While blackness it gather'd, and, prompted by spite,
Thus it sternly address'd the mild Queen of the night:
'How vain is the praise which thy radiance beguiles!
Though mountains and vallies are cheered by thy smiles,
Of thyself well thou know'st thou no beauty could'st render,
To the Sun thou'rt indebted for all thy famed splendour.'
The Moon thus replied, while more lovely she shone,
And scatter'd the darkness which veil'd her bright throne:
'Though thou may'st despise it, with joy I confess
That I owe to the Sun all the light I possess;
While cheer'd and adorn'd by his splendour benign,
In my course, as a spark of his glory, I shine,
And deem it an honour a debtor to be
To an orb that's so great and so glorious as he.'

(1831)

ELIZABETH BARRETT BROWNING
(1806–1861)

If one writer would leave an impression on succeeding generations of women poets, it was Elizabeth Barrett Browning. Born at Coxhoe Hall, Kelloe, County Durham, she was the eldest of eleven children. Both her parents were descended from families with slave-owning interests in the West Indies. Her father, Edward Barrett Moulton-Barrett, should have been a wealthy heir to a plantation estate in Jamaica; he spent, however, much of his adult life wrangling over the terms of his grandfather's will, which had been successfully challenged in 1801. Her mother, Mary Graham-Clarke, had married in 1805, and from 1806 until 1824 she was almost always in a state of childbearing. After a short period in County Durham, the family moved to London and Surrey, finally settling for many years at Hope End, a large house at Ledbury, Herefordshire. Somewhat contrary to convention, the young Elizabeth Barrett was allowed to receive lessons with her oldest brother, while he was being prepared for entry to Charterhouse. Soon she became proficient in Ancient Greek, and her reading ranged widely across many classical and modern literary works. It was at Hope End that she met the renowned elderly scholar, Uvedale Price, who encouraged her intellectul pursuits. More important, however, was the friendship she developed with Hugh Stuart Boyd, a classics scholar who had written Greek tragedies. Four years after her mother's death in 1828, her father suffered reverses, and Hope End was put up for auction. Thereafter, Elizabeth Barrett spent three years in Sidmouth, before her strong-willed father decided that it would be better to have his family under one roof in London. From 1835 until the time of her elopement in 1846, she resided at Wimpole Street. For most of her life in London, she remained reclusive, feeling too unwell to venture out of doors. The death of her favourite brother ('Bro') in a drowning accident at Torquay had a serious impact on her health.

In London, Elizabeth Barrett made several literary contacts that would enrich and develop her intellectual life. Perhaps her most supportive friendship was with the novelist and poet, Mary Russell Mitford, with whom she frequently corresponded. It was Mitford who made her a gift of lasting importance in the form of her dog, Flush. Such was the role that this much-loved pet played in Barrett's life that Virginia Woolf was moved to write *Flush* (1922), a biography that wittily charts the relationship between Elizabeth Barrett and Robert Browning from a dog's point of view. Equally important, in terms of her political outlook, were her links with Anna Jameson, a mid-Victorian feminist, and Richard Hengist Horne, a poet. She helped to edit Horne's *A New Spirit of the Age* (1844), which described up-and-coming literary writers of the period. In addition, she completed a poem for Horne's projected *Chaucer Modernized*. It was through Horne's work on parliamentary reports that Barrett became knowledgeable about the conditions of child labour in mines and factories. In 1845, she received the first of many letters from Robert Browning. Their eventual clandestine marriage at Marylebone Church, and subsequent escape to France and Italy, against her father's wishes, became a Victorian literary legend. Once settled in Florence, Barrett Browning wrote her finest poems, including the sequence that records the dramatic nature of her courtship, 'Sonnets from the Portuguese' (1850). Her growing passion for Louis Napoleon III appears to have caused some embarrassment to her husband; likewise, he found her interest in spiritualism rather disagreeable. Their marriage, however, was generally happy, and she gave birth to a son in 1849.

Barrett Browning published ambitious volumes of poetry from an early age. At her father's expense, *The Battle of Marathon* was brought out in 1820. This precocious work was followed by her *Essay on Mind* in 1826, and her accomplished translation of *Prometheus Bound* in 1833. Her fame grew with the next two collections, *The Seraphim and Other Poems* (1838) and *Poems* (1844). There is no doubt her poetry from the 1850s onwards is more technically assured, and certainly more modern in theme and style. *Casa Guidi Windows* (1851) reflects her growing intellectual involvement in Italian politics, a preoccupation that intensifies in *Poems before Congress* (1860). By far the most influential and polemical of her works was *Aurora Leigh*, published in late 1856. This narrative poem in nine books charts the career of an aspiring woman poet who, like Barrett Browning herself, was faced with conflicting views about Victorian womanhood. Many reviewers, such as Coventry Patmore and William Roscoe, were indignant at its outspokenness, not least its concern with inventing 'woman's figures' (that is, female forms of poetic expression). Since the 1970s, *Aurora Leigh* has been the subject of some of the finest feminist literary criticism available, notably Cora Kaplan's Introduction to the edition published by The Women's Press in 1979. Several of the poems contained in the posthumously published *Last Poems* (1862), especially 'A Musical Instrument', are regarded as her best. Although Barrett Browning commanded a great deal of respect during her lifetime (she was proposed for the position of Poet Laureate in 1850), her reputation went into serious decline for more than a century after her death in 1861. Recent important studies of Barrett Browning's work—by Helen Cooper, Deirdre David, Angela Leighton, and Dorothy Mermin—have done much to re-evaluate the significance of her contribution to mid-Victorian literary culture.

121 *The Cry of the Children*

'Φεῦ, φεῦ τί προσδέρκεσθέ μ' ὄμμασιν, τέκνα;[1]'
Medea

Do ye hear the children weeping, O my brothers,
Ere the sorrow comes with years?
They are leaning their young heads against their mothers,
And *that* cannot stop their tears.
The young lambs are bleating in the meadows;
The young birds are chirping in the nest;
The young fawns are playing with the shadows;
The young flowers are blowing toward the west—
But the young, young children, O my brothers,
They are weeping bitterly!
They are weeping in the playtime of the others,
In the country of the free.

[1] 'Alas, alack, why do ye gaze upon me with your eyes, my children?' Euripides, *Medea*, 1040. Eds.

Do you question the young children in the sorrow,
    Why their tears are falling so?—
The old man may weep for his to-morrow
    Which is lost in Long Ago—
The old tree is leafless in the forest—
  The old year is ending in the frost—
The old wound, if stricken, is the sorest—
  The old hope is hardest to be lost;
But the young, young children, O my brothers,
    Do you ask them why they stand
Weeping sore before the bosoms of their mothers,
    In our happy Fatherland!

They look up with their pale and sunken faces,
    And their looks are sad to see,
For the man's grief abhorrent draws and presses
    Down the cheeks of infancy.
'Your old earth,' they say, 'is very dreary';
  'Our young feet,' they say, 'are very weak!
Few paces have we taken, yet are weary—
  Our grave-rest is very far to seek!
Ask the aged why they weep, and not the children;
    For the outside earth is cold,—
And we young ones stand without, in our bewildering,
    And the graves are for the old.'

'True,' say the children, 'it may happen
    That we die before our time!
Little Alice died last year—the grave is shapen
    Like a snowball, in the rime.
We looked into the pit prepared to take her—
  Was no room for any work in the close clay!
From the sleep wherein she lieth none will wake her,
  Crying, "Get up, little Alice! it is day."
If you listen by that grave, in sun and shower,
  With your ear down, little Alice never cries!—
Could we see her face, be sure we should not know her,
  For the smile has time for growing in her eyes:
And merry go her moments, lulled and stilled in
    The shroud, by the kirk-chime!
It is good when it happens,' say the children,
    'That we die before our time!'

Alas, the wretched children! they are seeking
    Death in life, as best to have!
They are binding up their hearts away from breaking,
    With a cerement from the grave.
Go out, children, from the mine and from the city—
  Sing out, children, as the little thrushes do—
Pluck you handfuls of the meadow-cowslips pretty—
  Laugh aloud, to feel your fingers let them through!
But they answer, 'Are your cowslips of the meadows
    Like our weeds anear the mine?
Leave us quiet in the dark of the coal-shadows,
    From your pleasures fair and fine!

'For oh,' say the children, 'we are weary,
    And we cannot run or leap;
If we cared for any meadows, it were merely
    To drop down in them and sleep.
Our knees tremble sorely in the stooping—
  We fall upon our faces, trying to go;
And, underneath our heavy eyelids drooping,
  The reddest flower would look as pale as snow;
For, all day, we drag our burden tiring
    Through the coal-dark, underground—
Or, all day, we drive the wheels of iron
    In the factories, round and round.

'For, all day, the wheels are droning, turning,—
    Their wind comes in our faces,—
Till our hearts turn,—our head, with pulses burning,
    And the walls turn in their places:
Turns the sky in the high window blank and reeling,
  Turns the long light that droppeth down the wall—
Turn the black flies that crawl along the ceiling—
  All are turning, all the day, and we with all!—
And all day, the iron wheels are droning;
    And sometimes we could pray,
"O ye wheels" (breaking out in a mad moaning),
    "Stop! be silent for to-day!"'

Aye! be silent! Let them hear each other breathing
For a moment, mouth to mouth—
Let them touch each other's hands, in a fresh wreathing
Of their tender human youth!
Let them feel that this cold metallic motion
Is not all the life God fashions or reveals—
Let them prove their living souls against the notion
That they live in you, or under you, O wheels!—
Still, all day, the iron wheels go onward,
As if Fate in each were stark;
And the children's souls, which God is calling sunward,
Spin on blindly in the dark.

Now tell the poor young children, O my brothers,
To look up to Him and pray—
So the blessed One who blesseth all the others,
Will bless them another day.
They answer, 'Who is God that He should hear us,
While the rushing of the iron wheels is stirred?
When we sob aloud, the human creatures near us
Pass by, hearing not, or answer not a word!
And *we* hear not (for the wheels in their resounding)
Strangers speaking at the door:
Is it likely God, with angels singing round Him,
Hears our weeping any more?

'Two words, indeed, of praying we remember,
And at midnight's hour of harm,—
"Our Father," looking upward in the chamber,
We say softly for a charm.[1]
We know no other words, except "Our Father,"
And we think that, in some pause of angels' song,
God may pluck them with the silence sweet to gather,
And hold both within His right hand which is strong.
"Our Father!" If He heard us, He would surely
(For they call Him good and mild)
Answer, smiling down the steep world very purely,
"Come and rest with Me, My child."

[1] A fact rendered pathetically historical by Mr Horne's report of his Commission. The name of the poet of 'Orion' and 'Cosmo de' Medici' has, however, a change of associations, and comes in time to remind me that (with other noble instances) we have some brave poetic heat of literature still,—though open to the reproach, on certain points, of being somewhat gelid in our humanity.

'But, no!' say the children, weeping faster,
'He is speechless as a stone;
And they tell us, of His image is the master
Who commands us to work on.
Go to!' say the children,—'Up in Heaven,
Dark, wheel-like, turning clouds are all we find!
Do not mock us; grief has made us unbelieving—
We look up for God, but tears have made us blind.'
Do you hear the children weeping and disproving,
O my brothers, what ye preach?
For God's possible is taught by His world's loving,
And the children doubt of each.

And well may the children weep before you!
They are weary ere they run;
They have never seen the sunshine, nor the glory
Which is brighter than the sun:
They know the grief of man, without its wisdom;
They sink in man's despair, without its calm—
Are slaves, without the liberty in Christdom—
Are martyrs, by the pang without the palm,—
Are worn, as if with age, yet unretrievingly
No dear remembrace keep,—
Are orphans of the earthly love and heavenly:
Let them weep! let them weep!

They look up, with their pale and sunken faces,
And their look is dread to see,
For they mind you of their angels in their places,
With eyes turned on Deity;—
'How long,' they say, 'how long, O cruel nation,
Will you stand, to move the world, on a child's heart,—
Stifle down with a mailed heel its palpitation,
And tread onward to your throne amid the mart?
Our blood splashes upward, O our tyrants,
And your purple shows your path;
But the child's sob curseth deeper in the silence
Than the strong man in his wrath.'

(1843 *1844*)

122 *Bertha in the Lane*

PUT the broidery-frame away,
For my sewing is all done!
The last thread is used to-day,
And I need not join it on.
Though the clock stands at the noon
I am weary! I have sewn,
Sweet, for thee, a wedding-gown.

Sister, help me to the bed,
And stand near me, Dearest-sweet.
Do not shrink nor be afraid,
Blushing with a sudden heat!
No one standeth in the street?—
By God's love I go to meet,
Love I thee with love complete.

Lean thy face down! drop it in
These two hands, that I may hold
'Twixt their palms thy cheek and chin,
Stroking back the curls of gold.
'Tis a fair, fair face, in sooth—
Larger eyes and redder mouth
Than mine were in my first youth!

Thou art younger by seven years—
Ah!—so bashful at my gaze,
That the lashes, hung with tears,
Grow too heavy to upraise?
I would wound thee by no touch
Which thy shyness feels as such—
Dost thou mind me, Dear, so much?

Have I not been nigh a mother
To thy sweetness—tell me, Dear?
Have we not loved one another
Tenderly, from year to year,
Since our dying mother mild
Said with accents undefiled,
'Child, be mother to this child!

Mother, mother, up in heaven,
  Stand up on the jasper sea,
And be witness I have given
  All the gifts required of me,—
  Hope that blessed me, bliss that crowned,
  Love, that left me with a wound,
  Life itself, that turneth round!

Mother, mother, thou art kind,
  Thou art standing in the room,
In a molten glory shrined,
  That rays off into the gloom!
  But thy smile is bright and bleak
  Like cold waves—I cannot speak,
  I sob in it, and grow weak.

Ghostly mother, keep aloof
  One hour longer from my soul—
For I still am thinking of
  Earth's warm-beating joy and dole!
  On my finger is a ring
  Which I still see glittering,
  When the night hides everything.

Little sister, thou art pale!
  Ah, I have a wandering brain—
But I lose that fever-bale,
  And my thoughts grow calm again.
  Lean down closer—closer still!
  I have words thine ear to fill,—
  And would kiss thee at my will.

Dear, I heard thee in the spring,
  Thee and Robert—through the trees,—
When we all went gathering
  Boughs of May-bloom for the bees.
  Do not start so! think instead
  How the sunshine overhead
  Seemed to trickle through the shade.

What a day it was, that day!
  Hills and vales did openly
Seem to heave and throb away
  At the sight of the great sky;
  And the Silence, as it stood
  In the Glory's golden flood,
  Audibly did bud—and bud!

Through the winding hedgerows green,
  How we wandered, I and you,—
With the bowery tops shut in,
  And the gates that showed the view—
  How we talked there! thrushes soft
  Sang our praises out,—or oft
  Bleatings took them from the croft.

Till the pleasure grown too strong
  Left me muter evermore,
And, the winding road being long,
  I walked out of sight, before;
  And so, wrapt in musings fond,
  Issued (past the wayside pond)
  On the meadow-lands beyond.

I sate down beneath the beech
  Which leans over to the lane,
And the far sound of your speech
  Did not promise any pain;
  And I blessed you full and free,
  With a smile stooped tenderly
  O'er the May-flowers on my knee.

But the sound grew into word
  As the speakers drew more near—
Sweet, forgive me that I heard
  What you wished me not to hear.
  Do not weep so—do not shake—
  Oh,—I heard thee, Bertha, make
  Good true answers for my sake.

Yes, and HE too! let him stand
  In thy thoughts, untouched by blame.
Could he help it, if my hand
  He had claimed with hasty claim?
  That was wrong perhaps—but then
  Such things be—and will, again!
  Women cannot judge for men.

Had he seen thee, when he swore
  He would love but me alone?
Thou wert absent—sent before
  To our kin in Sidmouth town.
  When he saw thee who art best
  Past compare, and loveliest,
  He but judged thee as the rest.

Could we blame him with grave words,
  Thou and I, Dear, if we might?
Thy brown eyes have looks like birds,
  Flying straightway to the light:
  Mine are older.—Hush!—look out—
  Up the street! Is none without?
  How the poplar swings about!

And that hour—beneath the beech—
  When I listened in a dream,
And he said in his deep speech,
  That he owed me all *esteem*,—
  Each word swam in on my brain
  With a dim, dilating pain,
  Till it burst with that last strain.

I fell flooded with a Dark,
  In the silence of a swoon.
When I rose, still cold and stark,
  There was night,—I saw the moon:
  And the stars, each in its place,
  And the May-blooms on the grass,
  Seemed to wonder what I was.

And I walked as if apart
  From myself, when I could stand—
And I pitied my own heart,
  As if I held it in my hand,
  Somewhat coldly,—with a sense
  Of fulfilled benevolence,
  And a 'Poor thing' negligence.

And I answered coldly too,
  When you met me at the door;
And I only *heard* the dew
  Dripping from me to the floor;
  And the flowers I bade you see
  Were too withered for the bee,—
  As my life, henceforth, for me.

Do not weep so—Dear—heart-warm!
  All was best as it befell!
If I say he did me harm,
  I speak wild,—I am not well.
  All his words were kind and good—
  He esteemed me! Only, blood
  Runs so faint in womanhood.

Then I always was too grave,—
  Liked the saddest ballad sung,—
With that look, besides, we have
  In our faces, who die young.
  I had died, Dear, all the same—
  Life's long, joyous, jostling game
  Is too loud for my meek shame.

We are so unlike each other,
   Thou and I, that none could guess
We were children of one mother,
   But for mutual tenderness.
   Thou art rose-lined from the cold,
   And meant, verily, to hold
   Life's pure pleasures manifold.

I am pale as crocus grows
   Close beside a rose-tree's root;
Whosoe'er would reach the rose,
   Treads the crocus underfoot.
   I, like May-bloom on thorn-tree—
   Thou, like merry summer-bee!
   Fit, that *I* be plucked for *thee*.

Yet who plucks me?—no one mourns,
   I have lived my season out,
And now die of my own thorns
   Which I could not live without.
   Sweet, be merry! How the light
   Comes and goes! If it be night,
   Keep the candles in my sight.

Are there footsteps at the door!
   Look out quickly. Yea, or nay!
Some one might be waiting for
   Some last word that I might say.
   Nay! So best!—So angels would
   Stand off clear from deathly road,
   Not to cross the sight of God.

Colder grow my hands and feet.
   When I wear the shroud I made,
Let the folds lie straight and neat,
   And the rosemary be spread,
   That if any friend should come
   (To see *thee*, sweet!) all the room
   May be lifted out of gloom.

And, dear Bertha, let me keep
  On my hand this little ring,
Which at nights, when others sleep,
  I can still see glittering:
  Let me wear it out of sight,
  In the grave,—where it will light
  All the Dark up, day and night.

On that grave, drop not a tear!
  Else, though fathom-deep the place,
Through the woollen shroud I wear
  I shall feel it on my face.
  Rather smile there, blessed one,
  Thinking of me in the sun—
  Or forget me—smiling on!

Art thou near me? nearer? so!
  Kiss me close upon the eyes,—
That the earthly light may go
  Sweetly, as it used to rise,—
  When I watched the morning-grey
  Strike, betwixt the hills, the way
  He was sure to come that day.

So,—no more vain words be said!
  The hosannas nearer roll.
Mother, smile now on thy Dead,—
  I am death-strong in my soul!
  Mystic Dove alit on cross,
  Guide the poor bird of the snows
  Through the snow-wind above loss!

Jesus, Victim, comprehending
  Love's divine self-abnegation,
Cleanse my love in its self-spending,
  And absorb the poor libation!
  Wind my thread of life up higher,
  Up, through angels' hands of fire!—
  I aspire while I expire!—

(1844)

123

To George Sand

A DESIRE

THOU large-brained woman and large-hearted man,
Self-called George Sand! whose soul, amid the lions
Of thy tumultuous senses, moans defiance,
And answers roar for roar, as spirits can:
I would some mild miraculous thunder ran
Above the applauded circus, in appliance
Of thine own nobler nature's strength and science—
Drawing two pinions, white as wings of swan,
From thy strong shoulders, to amaze the place
With holier light! that thou to woman's claim,
And man's, mightst join beside the angel's grace
Of a pure genius sanctified from blame,—
Till child and maiden pressed to thine embrace,
To kiss upon thy lips a stainless fame.

(1844)

124

To George Sand

A RECOGNITION

TRUE genius, but true woman! dost deny
Thy woman's nature with a manly scorn,
And break away the gauds and armlets worn
By weaker women in captivity?
Ah, vain denial! that revolted cry
Is sobbed in by a woman's voice forlorn:—
Thy woman's hair, my sister, all unshorn,
Floats back dishevelled strength in agony,
Disproving thy man's name! and while before
The world thou burnest in a poet-fire,
We see thy woman-heart beat evermore
Through the large flame. Beat purer, heart, and higher,
Till God unsex thee on the heavenly shore,
To which alone unsexing, purely aspire.

(1844)

125 *L.E.L.'s Last Question*

'Do you think of me as I think of you?'
From HER POEM WRITTEN DURING THE VOYAGE TO THE CAPE.

'Do you think of me as I think of you,
My friends, my friends?'—She said it from the sea,
The English minstrel in her minstrelsy,
While, under brighter skies than erst she knew,
Her heart grew dark, and groped there, as the blind,
To reach, across the waves, friends left behind—
'Do you think of me as I think of you?'

It seemed not much to ask—As *I* of *you?*
We all do ask the same. No eyelids cover
Within the meekest eyes, that question over.
And little, in the world, the Loving do
But sit (among the rocks?) and listen for
The echo of their own love evermore—
'Do you think of me as I think of you?'

Love-learnèd she had sung of love and love,—
And like a child that, sleeping with dropt head
Upon the fairy-book he lately read,
Whatever household noises round him move,
Hears in his dream some elfin turbulence,—
Even so, suggestive to her inward sense,
All sounds of life assumed one tune of love.

And when the glory of her dream withdrew,
When knightly gestes and courtly pageantries
Were broken in her visionary eyes,
By tears the solemn seas attested true,—
Forgetting that sweet lute beside her hand
She asked not,—Do you praise me, O my land?—
But, 'Think ye of me, friends, as I of you?'

Hers was the hand that played for many a year
Love's silver phrase for England,—smooth and well!
Would God, her heart's more inward oracle

In that lone moment, might confirm her dear!
For when her questioned friends in agony
Made passionate response,—'We think of thee'—,
Her place was in the dust, too deep to hear.

Could she not wait to catch their answering breath?
Was she content,—content,—with ocean's sound,
Which dashed its mocking infinite around
One thirsty for a little love?—beneath
Those stars, content, where last her song had gone,—
They mute and cold in radiant life,—as soon
Their singer was to be, in darksome death?[1]

Bring your vain answers—cry, 'We think of *thee*!'
How think ye of her? warm in long ago
Delights?—or crowned with budding bays? Not so.
None smile and none are crowned where lieth she,—
With all her visions unfulfilled save one,—
Her childhood's—of the palm-trees in the sun—
And lo! their shadow on her sepulchre!

'Do ye think of me as I think of you?'—
O friends,—O kindred,—O dear brotherhood
Of all the world! what are we, that we should
For covenants of long affection sue?
Why press so near each other when the touch
Is barred by graves? Not much, and yet too much,
Is this 'Think of me as I think of you'.

But while on mortal lips I shape anew
A sigh to mortal issues,—verily
Above the unshaken stars that see us die,
A vocal pathos rolls; and HE who drew
All life from dust, and for all, tasted death,
By death and life and love, appealing, saith,
Do you think of me as I think of you?

(1844)

[1] Her lyric on the polar star, came home with her latest papers.

126 *The Runaway Slave at Pilgrim's Point*

I

I STAND on the mark beside the shore
  Of the first white pilgrim's bended knee,
Where exile turned to ancestor,
  And God was thanked for liberty.
I have run through the night, my skin is as dark,
I bend my knee down on this mark...
  I look on the sky and the sea.

II

O pilgrim-souls, I speak to you!
  I see you come out proud and slow
From the land of the spirits pale as dew...
  And round me and round me ye go!
O pilgrims, I have gasped and run
All night long from the whips of one
  Who in your names works sin and woe.

III

And thus I thought that I would come
  And kneel here where ye knelt before,
And feel your souls around me hum
  In undertone to the ocean's roar;
And lift my black face, my black hand,
Here, in your names, to curse this land
  Ye blessed in freedom's, evermore.

IV

I am black, I am black!
  And yet God made me, they say;
But if He did so, smiling back
  He must have cast His work away
Under the feet of His white creatures,
With a look of scorn,—that the dusky features
  Might be trodden again to clay.

V

And yet He has made dark things
  To be glad and merry as light:
There's a little dark bird sits and sings;
  There's a dark stream ripples out of sight;
And the dark frogs chant in the safe morass,

And the sweetest stars are made to pass
  O'er the face of the darkest night.

VI

But *we* who are dark, we are dark!
  Ah God, we have no stars!
About our souls in care and cark
  Our blackness shuts like prison-bars;
The poor souls crouch so far behind
That never a comfort can they find
  By reaching through the prison-bars.

VII

Indeed we live beneath the sky, . . .
  That great smooth Hand of God stretched out
On all His children fatherly,
  To save them from the fear and doubt
Which would be, if, from this low place,
All opened straight up to His face
  Into the grand eternity.

VIII

And still God's sunshine and His frost,
  They make us hot, they make us cold.
As if we were not black and lost:
  And the beasts and birds, in wood and fold,
Do fear and take us for very men!
Could the weep-poor-will or the cat of the glen
  Look into my eyes and be bold?

IX

I am black, I am black!—
  But, once, I laughed in girlish glee,
For one of my colour stood in the track
  Where the drivers drove, and looked at me,
And tender and full was the look he gave—
Could a slave look *so* at another slave?—
  I look at the sky and the sea.

X

And from that hour our spirits grew
  As free as if unsold, unbought:
Oh, strong enough, since we were two,
  To conquer the world, we thought!
The drivers drove us day by day;

We did not mind, we went one way,
  And no better a liberty sought.

XI

In the sunny ground between the canes,
  He said 'I love you' as he passed:
When the shingle-roof rang sharp with the rains,
  I heard how he vowed it fast:
While others shook he smiled in the hut
As he carved me a bowl of the cocoa-nut
  Through the roar of the hurricanes.

XII

I sang his name instead of a song,
  Over and over I sang his name—
Upward and downward I drew it along
  My various notes; the same, the same!
I sang it low, that the slave-girls near
Might never guess from aught they could hear,
  It was only a name.

XIII

I look on the sky and the sea—
  We were two to love, and two to pray,—
Yes, two, O God, who cried to Thee,
  Though nothing didst Thou say.
Coldly Thou sat'st behind the sun!
And now I cry who am but one,
  Thou wilt not speak to-day.—

XIV

We were black, we were black!
  We had no claim to love and bliss,
What marvel, if each turned to lack?
  They wrung my cold hands out of his,—
They dragged him . . . where? . . . I crawled to touch
His blood's mark in the dust! . . . not much,
  Ye pilgrim-souls, . . . though plain as *this!*

XV

Wrong, followed by a deeper wrong!
  Mere grief's too good for such as I;
So the white men brought the shame ere long
  To strangle the sob of my agony.
They would not leave me for my dull

Wet eyes!—it was too merciful
  To let me weep pure tears and die.

XVI

I am black, I am black!
  I wore a child upon my breast...
An amulet that hung too slack,
  And, in my unrest, could not rest:
Thus we went moaning, child and mother,
One to another, one to another,
  Until all ended for the best:

XVII

For hark! I will tell you low...low...
  I am black, you see,—
And the babe who lay on my bosom so,
  Was far too white...too white for me;
As white as the ladies who scorned to pray
Beside me at church but yesterday,
  Though my tears had washed a place for my knee.

XVIII

My own, own child! I could not bear
  To look in his face, it was so white;
I covered him up with a kerchief there;
  I covered his face in close and tight:
And he moaned and struggled, as well might be,
For the white child wanted his liberty—
  Ha, ha! he wanted the master-right.

XIX

He moaned and beat with his head and feet,
  His little feet that never grew—
He struck them out, as it was meet,
  Against my heart to break it through.
I might have sung and made him mild—
But I dared not sing to the white-faced child
  The only song I knew.

XX

I pulled the kerchief very close:
  He could not see the sun, I swear,
More, then, alive, than now he does
  From between the roots of the mangles... where?
...I know where. Close! a child and mother

Do wrong to look at one another,
  When one is black and one is fair.

XXI

Why, in that single glance I had
  Of my child's face, . . . I tell you all,
I saw a look that made me mad . . .
  The *master's* look, that used to fall
On my soul like his lash . . . or worse!—
And so, to save it from my curse,
  I twisted it round in my shawl.

XXII

And he moaned and trembled from foot to head,
  He shivered from head to foot;
Till, after a time, he lay instead
  Too suddenly still and mute.
I felt, beside, a stiffening cold . . .
I dared to lift up just a fold, . . .
  As in lifting a leaf of the mango-fruit.

XXIII

But *my* fruit . . . ha, ha!—there, had been
  (I laugh to think on't at this hour! . . .)
Your fine white angels, who have seen
  Nearest the secret of God's power, . . .
And plucked my fruit to make them wine,
And sucked the soul of that child of mine,
  As the humming bird sucks the soul of the flower.

XXIV

Ha, ha, the trick of the angels white!
  They freed the white child's spirit so.
I said not a word, but, day and night,
  I carried the body to and fro,
And it lay on my heart like a stone . . . as chill.
—The sun may shine out as much as he will;
  I am cold, though it happened a month ago.

XXV

From the white man's house, and the black man's hut,
  I carried the little body on;
The forest's arms did round us shut,
  And silence through the trees did run.
They asked no question as I went,—

They stood too high for astonishment,—
  They could see God sit on his throne.

XXVI

My little body, kerchiefed fast,
  I bore it on through the forest... on:
And when I felt it was tired at last,
  I scooped a hole beneath the moon.
Through the forest-tops the angels far,
With a white sharp finger from every star,
  Did point and mock at what was done.

XXVII

Yet when it was all done aright,...
  Earth, 'twixt me and my baby, strewed,...
All, changed to black earth,... nothing white,...
  A dark child in the dark!—ensued
Some comfort, and my heart grew young:
I sate down smiling there and sung
  The song I learnt in my maidenhood.

XXVIII

And thus we two were reconciled,
  The white child and black mother, thus;
For, as I sang it soft and wild,
  The same song, more melodious,
Rose from the grave whereon I sate!
It was the dead child singing that,
  To join the souls of both of us.

XXIX

I look on the sea and the sky!
  Where the pilgrims' ships first anchored lay
The free sun rideth gloriously;
  But the pilgrim-ghosts have slid away
Through the earliest streaks of the morn.
My face is black, but it glares with a scorn
  Which they dare not meet by day.

XXX

Ah!—in their 'stead, their hunter sons!
  Ah, ah! they are on me—they hunt in a ring—
Keep off! I brave you all at once—
  I throw off your eyes like snakes that sting!
You have killed the black eagle at nest, I think:

Did you never stand still in your triumph, and shrink
  From the stroke of her wounded wing?

XXXI

(Man, drop that stone you dared to lift!—)
  I wish you who stand there five a-breast,
Each, for his own wife's joy and gift,
  A little corpse as safely at rest
As mine in the mangles!—Yes, but *she*
May keep live babies on her knee,
  And sing the song she likes the best.

XXXII

I am not mad: I am black.
  I see you staring in my face—
I know you staring, shrinking back,
  Ye are born of the Washington-race,
And this land is the free America,
And this mark on my wrist . . . (I prove what I say)
  Ropes tied me up here to the flogging-place.

XXXIII

You think I shrieked then? Not a sound!
  I hung, as a gourd hangs in the sun;
I only cursed them all around
  As softly as I might have done
My very own child—From these sands
Up to the mountains, lift your hands,
  O slaves, and end what I begun!

XXXIV

Whips, curses; these must answer those!
  For in this UNION you have set
Two kinds of men in adverse rows,
  Each loathing each: and all forget
The seven wounds in Christ's body fair,
While HE sees gaping everywhere
  Our countless wounds that pay no debt.

XXXV

Our wounds are different. Your white men
  Are, after all, not gods indeed,
Nor able to make Christs again
  Do good with bleeding. *We* who bleed . . .
(Stand off!) we help not in our loss!

We are too heavy for our cross,
And fall and crush you and your seed.

XXXVI

I fall, I swoon! I look at the sky:
The clouds are breaking on my brain.
I am floated along, as if I should die
Of liberty's exquisite pain—
In the name of the white child, waiting for me
In the death-dark where we may kiss and agree,
White men, I leave you all curse-free
In my broken heart's disdain!

(1848 *1850*)

127 *Felicia Hemans*

TO. L.E.L., REFERRING TO HER MONODY ON THE POETESS

I

THOU bay-crowned living One, that o'er the bay-crowned Dead art bowing,
And o'er the shadeless moveless brow the vital shadow throwing;
And o'er the sighless songless lips the wail and music wedding;
And dropping o'er the tranquil eyes, the tears not of their shedding!—

II

Take music from the silent Dead, whose meaning is completer,
Reserve thy tears for living brows, where all such tears are meeter,
And leave the violets in the grass to brighten where thou treadest!
No flowers for her! no need of flowers—albeit 'bring flowers,' thou saidest.

III

Yes, flowers, to crown the 'cup and lute!' since both may come to breaking;
Or flowers, to greet the 'bride!' the heart's own beating works its aching;
Or flowers, to soothe the 'captive's' sight, from earth's free bosom gathered,
Reminding of his earthly hope, then withering as it withered!

IV

But bring not near the solemn corse, a type of human seeming!
Lay only dust's stern verity upon the dust undreaming.
And while the calm perpetual stars shall look upon it solely,
Her spherëd soul shall look on *them*, with eyes more bright and
holy.

V

Nor mourn, O living One, because her part in life was mourning.
Would she have lost the poet's fire for anguish of the burning?—
The minstrel harp, for the strained string? the tripod, for the
afflated
Woe? or the vision, for those tears in which it shone dilated?

VI

Perhaps she shuddered, while the world's cold hand her brow was
wreathing,
But never wronged that mystic breath which breathed in all her
breathing;
Which drew from rocky earth and man, abstractions high and
moving,
Beauty, if not the beautiful, and love, if not the loving.

VII

Such visionings have paled in sight: the Saviour she descrieth.
And little recks *who* wreathed the brow which on His bosom lieth:
The whiteness of His innocence o'er all her garments, flowing,
There, learneth she the sweet 'new song,' she will not mourn in
knowing.

VIII

Be happy, crowned and living One! and, as thy dust decayeth,
May thine own England say for thee, what now for Her it sayeth—
'Albeit softly in our ears her silver song was ringing,
The footfall of her parting soul is softer than her singing!'

(1850)

128 *Sonnets from the Portuguese, I*

I THOUGHT once how Theocritus had sung
Of the sweet years, the dear and wished for years,
Who each one in a gracious hand appears
To bear a gift for mortals, old or young:

And, as I mused it in his antique tongue,
I saw, in gradual vision through my tears,
The sweet, sad years, the melancholy years,...
Those of my own life, who by turns had flung
A shadow across me. Straightway I was 'ware,
So weeping, how a mystic Shape did move
Behind me, and drew me backward by the hair;
And a voice said in mastery while I strove,...
'Guess now who holds thee?'—'Death,' I said. But, there,
The silver answer rang,... 'Not Death, but Love.'

(1850)

129 *Sonnets from the Portuguese, V*

I LIFT my heavy heart up solemnly,
As once Electra her sepulchral urn,
And, looking in thine eyes, I overturn
The ashes at thy feet. Behold and see
What a great heap of grief lay hid in me,
And how the red wild sparkles dimly burn
Through the ashen greyness. If thy foot in scorn
Could tread them out to darkness utterly,
It might be well perhaps. But if instead
Thou wait beside me for the wind to blow
The grey dust up,... those laurels on thine head,
O My belovèd, will not shield thee so,
That none of all the fires shall scorch and shred
The hair beneath. Stand farther off then! go.

(1850)

130 *Sonnets from the Portuguese, XII*

INDEED this very love which is my boast,
And which, when rising up from breast to brow,
Doth crown me with a ruby large enow
To draw men's eyes and prove the inner cost,...
This love even, all my worth, to the uttermost,
I should not love withal, unless that thou
Hadst set me an example, shown me how,
When first thine earnest eyes with mine were crossed,
And love called love. And thus, I cannot speak
Of love even, as a good thing of my own.
Thy soul hath snatched up mine all faint and weak,
And placed it by thee on a golden throne,—
And that I love (O soul, we must be meek!)
Is by thee only, whom I love alone.

(1850)

131 *Sonnets from the Portuguese, XIV*

IF thou must love me, let it be for nought
Except for love's sake only. Do not say
'I love her for her smile... her look... her way
Of speaking gently,... for a trick of thought
That falls in well with mine, and certes brought
A sense of pleasant ease on such a day'—
For these things in themselves, Belovèd, may
Be changed, or change for thee,—and love, so wrought,
May be unwrought so. Neither love me for
Thine own dear pity's wiping my cheeks dry,—
A creature might forget to weep who bore
Thy comfort long, and lose thy love thereby.
But love me for love's sake, that evermore
Thou mayst love on through love's eternity.

(1850)

132 *Sonnets from the Portuguese, XXIX*

I THINK of thee!—my thoughts do twine and bud
About thee, as wild vines, about a tree,
Put out broad leaves, and soon there's nought to see
Except the straggling green which hides the wood.
Yet, O my palm-tree, be it understood
I will not have my thoughts instead of thee
Who art dearer, better! Rather instantly
Renew thy presence! As a strong tree should,
Rustle thy boughs, and set thy trunk all bare,
And let these bands of greenery which insphere thee,
Drop heavily down,... burst, shattered, everywhere!
Because, in this deep joy to see and hear thee
And breathe within thy shadow a new air,
I do not think of thee—I am too near thee.

(1850)

133 *Sonnets from the Portuguese, XLII*

HOW do I love thee? Let me count the ways.
I love thee to the depth and breadth and height
My soul can reach, when feeling out of sight
For the ends of Being and Ideal Grace.
I love thee to the level of everyday's
Most quiet need, by sun and candlelight.
I love thee freely, as men strive for Right;
I love thee purely, as they turn from Praise;

I love thee with the passion put to use
In my old griefs, and with my childhood's faith.
I love thee with a love I seemed to lose
With my lost saints,—I love thee with the breath,
Smiles, tears, of all my life!—and, if God choose,
I shall but love thee better after death.

(1850)

134 *from* Aurora Leigh, *First Book*

[*The following passage comes from the opening of the first book to Barrett Browning's novel-in-verse. Narrated by Aurora Leigh herself, these lines explain her upbringing, especially her relations with her English father, and her memory of her Italian mother. Eds.*]

Of writing many books there is no end;
And I who have written much in prose and verse
For others' uses, will write now for mine,—
Will write my story for my better self,
As when you paint your portrait for a friend,
Who keeps it in a drawer and looks at it
Long after he has ceased to love you, just
To hold together what he was and is.

I, writing thus, am still what men call young;
I have not so far left the coasts of life
To travel inland, that I cannot hear
That murmur of the outer Infinite
Which unweaned babies smile at in their sleep
When wondered at for smiling; not so far,
But still I catch my mother at her post
Beside the nursery-door, with finger up,
'Hush, hush—here's too much noise!' while her sweet eyes
Leap forward, taking part against her word
In the child's riot. Still I sit and feel
My father's slow hand, when she had left us both,
Stroke out my childish curls across his knee;
And hear Assunta's daily jest (she knew
He liked it better than a better jest)
Inquire how many golden scudi went
To make such ringlets. O my father's hand,
Stroke stroke it heavily;—the poor hair down,
Draw, press the child's head closer to thy knee!
I'm still too young, too young, to sit alone.

I write. My mother was a Florentine,
Whose rare blue eyes were shut from seeing me

When scarcely I was four years old, my life
A poor spark snatched up from a failing lamp
Which went out therefore. She was weak and frail;
She could not bear the joy of giving life—
The mother's rapture slew her. If her kiss
Had left a longer weight upon my lips
It might have steadied the uneasy breath,
And reconciled and fraternised my soul
With the new order. As it was, indeed,
I felt a mother-want about the world,
And still went seeking, like a bleating lamb
Left out at night, in shutting up the fold,—
As restless as a nest-deserted bird
Grown chill through something being away, though what
It knows not. I, Aurora Leigh, was born
To make my father sadder, and myself
Not overjoyous, truly. Women know
The way to rear up children, (to be just,)
They know a simple, merry, tender knack
Of tying sashes, fitting baby-shoes,
And stringing pretty words that make no sense,
And kissing full sense into empty words,
Which things are corals to cut life upon,
Although such trifles: children learn by such,
Love's holy earnest in a pretty play
And get not over-early solemnised,—
But seeing, as in a rose-bush, Love's Divine
Which burns and hurts not,—not a single bloom,—
Become aware and unafraid of Love.
Such good do mothers. Fathers love as well
—Mine did, I know,—but still with heavier brains,
And wills more consciously responsible,
And not as wisely, since less foolishly;
So mothers have God's licence to be missed.

My father was an austere Englishman,
Who, after a dry life-time spent at home
In college-learning, law, and parish talk,
Was flooded with a passion unaware,
His whole provisioned and complacent past
Drowned out from him that moment. As he stood
In Florence, where he had come to spend a month
And note the secret of Da Vinci's drains,
He musing somewhat absently perhaps
Some English question . . . whether men should pay
The unpopular but necessary tax
With left or right hand—in the alien sun

In that great square of the Santissima
There drifted past him (scarcely marked enough
To move his comfortable island scorn,)
A train of priestly banners, cross and psalm,
The white-veiled rose-crowned maidens holding up
Tall tapers, weighty for such wrists, aslant
To the blue luminous tremor of the air,
And letting drop the white wax as they went
To eat the bishop's wafer at the church;
From which long trail of chanting priests and girls,
A face flashed like a cymbal on his face
And shook with silent clangour brain and heart,
Transfiguring him to music. Thus, even thus,
He too received his sacramental gift
With eucharistic meanings; for he loved.

And thus beloved, she died. I've heard it said
That but to see him in the first surprise
Of widower and father, nursing me,
Unmothered little child of four years old,
His large man's hands afraid to touch my curls,
As if the gold would tarnish,—his grave lips
Contriving such a miserable smile
As if he knew needs must, or I should die,
And yet 'twas hard,—would almost make the stones
Cry out for pity. There's a verse he set
In Santa Croce to her memory,—
'Weep for an infant too young to weep much
When death removed this mother'—stops the mirth
To-day on women's faces when they walk
With rosy children hanging on their gowns,
Under the cloister, to escape the sun
That scorches in the piazza. After which,
He left our Florence and made haste to hide
Himself, his prattling child, and silent grief,
Among the mountains above Pelago;
Because unmothered babes, he thought, had need
Of mother nature more than others use,
And Pan's white goats, with udders warm and full
Of mystic contemplations, come to feed
Poor milkless lips of orphans like his own—
Such scholar-scraps he talked, I've heard from friends,
For even prosaic men, who wear grief long
Will get to wear it as a hat aside
With a flower stuck in't. Father, then, and child,
We lived among the mountains many years,
God's silence on the outside of the house,

And we, who did not speak too loud, within,
And old Assunta to make up the fire,
Crossing herself whene'er a sudden flame
Which lightened from the firewood, made alive
That picture of my mother on the wall.

The painter drew it after she was dead,
And when the face was finished, throat and hands,
Her cameriera carried him, in hate
Of the English-fashioned shroud, the last brocade
She dressed in at the Pitti; 'he should paint
No sadder thing than that,' she swore, 'to wrong
Her poor signora.' Therefore very strange
The effect was. I, a little child, would crouch
For hours upon the floor with knees drawn up,
And gaze across them, half in terror, half
In adoration, at the picture there,—
That swan-like supernatural white life
Just sailing upward from the red stiff silk
Which seemed to have no part in it, nor power
To keep it from quite breaking out of bounds.
For hours I sate and stared. Assunta's awe
And my poor father's melancholy eyes
Still pointed that way. That way, went my thoughts
When wandering beyond sight. And as I grew
In years, I mixed, confused, unconsciously,
Whatever I last read or heard or dreamed,
Abhorrent, admirable, beautiful,
Pathetical, or ghastly, or grotesque,
With still that face... which did not therefore change,
But kept the mystic level of all forms
Hates, fears, and admirations, was by turns
Ghost, fiend, and angel, fairy, witch, and sprite,
A dauntless Muse who eyes a dreadful Fate,
A loving Psyche who loses sight of Love,
A still Medusa with mild milky brows
All curdled and all clothed upon with snakes
Whose slime falls fast as sweat will; or, anon,
Our Lady of the Passion, stabbed with swords
Where the Babe sucked; or Lamia in her first
Moonlighted pallor, ere she shrunk and blinked
And shuddering wriggled down to the unclean;
Or, my own mother, leaving her last smile
In her last kiss, upon the baby-mouth
My father pushed down on the bed for that,—
Or my dead mother, without smile or kiss,
Buried at Florence. All which images,

Concentred on the picture, glassed themselves
Before my meditative childhood,... as
The incoherencies of change and death
Are represented fully, mixed and merged,
In the smooth fair mystery of perpetual Life.

(1856)

135 *from* Aurora Leigh, *First Book*

[*This passage, also from the first book, has often been noted as one of the most significant statements about the meaning and function of poetry by a Victorian poet. Here Aurora Leigh makes a powerful case for the 'essential truth' that only poets can convey in an increasingly industrialized age. Eds.*]

Books, books, books!
I had found the secret of a garret-room
Piled high with cases in my father's name,
Piled high, packed large,—where, creeping in and out
Among the giant fossils of my past,
Like some small nimble mouse between the ribs
Of a mastodon, I nibbled here and there
At this or that box, pulling through the gap,
In heats of terror, haste, victorious joy,
The first book first. And how I felt it beat
Under my pillow, in the morning's dark,
An hour before the sun would let me read!
My books!
At last because the time was ripe,
I chanced upon the poets.
As the earth
Plunges in fury, when the internal fires
Have reached and pricked her heart, and, throwing flat,
The marts and temples, the triumphal gates
And towers of observation, clears herself
To elemental freedom—thus, my soul,
At poetry's divine first finger touch,
Let go conventions and sprang up surprised,
Convicted of the great eternities
Before two worlds.
What's this, Aurora Leigh,
You write so of the poets, and not laugh?
Those virtuous liars, dreamers after dark,
Exaggerators of the sun and moon,
And soothsayers in a tea-cup?
I write so
Of the only truth-tellers now left to God—

The only speakers of essential truth,
Opposed to relative, comparative,
And temporal truths; the only holders by
His sun-skirts, through conventional grey glooms;
The only teachers who instruct mankind
From just a shadow on a charnel wall
To find man's veritable stature out
Erect, sublime,—the measure of a man,
And that's the measure of an angel, says
The apostle. Ay, and while your common men
Build pyramids, gauge railroads, reign, reap, dine,
And dust the flaunty carpets of the world
For kings to walk on, or our senators,
The poet suddenly will catch them up
With his voice like a thunder, . . . 'This is soul,
This is life, this word is being said in heaven,
Here's God down on us! what are you about?'
How all those workers start amid their work,
Look round, look up, and feel, a moment's space,
That carpet-dusting, though a pretty trade,
Is not the imperative labour after all.

My own best poets, am I one with you,
That thus I love you,—or but one through love?
Does all this smell of thyme about my feet
Conclude my visit to your holy hill
In personal presence, or but testify
The rustling of your vesture through my dreams
With influent odours? When my joy and pain,
My thought and aspiration, like the stops
Of pipe or flute, are absolutely dumb
Unless melodious, do you play on me
My pipers,—and if, sooth, you did not blow,
Would no sound come? or is the music mine,
As a man's voice or breath is called his own,
Inbreathed by the Life-breather? There's a doubt
For cloudy seasons!

But the sun was high
When first I felt my pulses set themselves
For concord; when the rhythmic turbulence
Of blood and brain swept outward upon words,
As wind upon the alders, blanching them
By turning up their under-natures till
They trembled in dilation. O delight
And triumph of the poet,—who would say
A man's mere 'yes,' a woman's common 'no,'
A little human hope of that or this,

And says the word so that it burns you through
With a special revelation, shakes the heart
Of all the men and women in the world,
As if one came back from the dead and spoke,
With eyes too happy, a familiar thing
Become divine i' the utterance! while for him
The poet, speaker, he expands with joy;
The palpitating angel in his flesh
Thrills inly with consenting fellowship
To those innumerous spirits who sun themselves
Outside of time.
O life, O poetry,
—Which means life in life! cognisant of life
Beyond this blood-beat,—passionate for truth
Beyond these senses!—poetry, my life,
My eagle, with both grappling feet still hot
From Zeus's thunder, who hast ravished me
Away from all the shepherds, sheep, and dogs,
And set me in the Olympian roar and round
Of luminous faces for, a cup-bearer,
To keep the mouths of all the godheads moist
For everlasting laughters,—I, myself
Half drunk across the beaker with their eyes!
How those gods look!
Enough so, Ganymede,
We shall not bear above a round or two.
We drop the golden cup at Heré's foot
And swoon back to the earth,—and find ourselves
Face-down among the pine-cones, cold with dew,
While the dogs bark, and many a shepherd scoffs,
'What's come now to the youth?' Such ups and downs
Have poets.
Am I such indeed? The name
Is royal, and to sign it like a queen,
Is what I dare not,—though some royal blood
Would seem to tingle in me now and then,
With sense of power and ache,—with imposthumes
And manias usual to the race. Howbeit
I dare not: 'tis too easy to go mad
And ape a Bourbon in a crown of straws;
The thing's too common.
Many fervent souls
Strike rhyme on rhyme, who would strike steel on steel
If steel had offered, in a restless heat
Of doing something. Many tender souls
Have strung their losses on a rhyming thread,
As children, cowslips:—the more pains they take,

The work more withers. Young men, ay, and maids,
Too often sow their wild oats in tame verse,
Before they sit down under their own vine
And live for use. Alas, near all the birds
Will sing at dawn,—and yet we do not take
The chaffering swallow for the holy lark.

(1856)

136 *from* Aurora Leigh, *Third Book*

[*In this section from the third book, Aurora Leigh tells of her first meeting with Marian Erle, a young working-class woman. At this point in the narrative, Marian Erle expects to marry Aurora's cousin, Romney Leigh. Renowned for his philanthropic designs upon the world, especially the 'phalanstery' he runs along communitarian and socialist lines, Romney Leigh has sought to extend his political sentiments to his personal life by offering his hand in marriage to a member of the working class. Here Aurora explains how she came to learn of the terrible hardship Marian suffered as a child, particularly when assaulted by her abusive father. This is not the only episode that reveals how Marian Erle has had to endure unimaginable violence from men. Once she has decided that the social gulf between herself and Romney Leigh is altogether too great for any marriage between them to succeed, Marian flees to France, only to be raped in a Parisian brothel. Readers may like to note that, ultimately, it is Aurora who will marry her cousin, even though at first she protests loudly against his condescending attitude towards her literary aspirations and achievements. For the moment, however, the assumption is that Marian will surely be his bride. Eds.*]

No wise beautiful
Was Marian Erle. She was not white nor brown,
But could look either, like a mist that changed
According to being shone on more or less:
The hair, too, ran its opulence of curls
In doubt 'twixt dark and bright, nor left you clear
To name the colour. Too much hair perhaps
(I'll name a fault here) for so small a head,
Which seemed to droop on that side and on this,
As a full-blown rose uneasy with its weight
Though not a wind should trouble it. Again,
The dimple in the cheek had better gone
With redder, fuller rounds; and somewhat large
The mouth was, though the milky little teeth
Dissolved it to so infantine a smile.
For soon it smiled at me; the eyes smiled too,
But 'twas as if remembering they had wept,
And knowing they should, some day, weep again.

We talked. She told me all her story out,
Which I'll re-tell with fuller utterance,
As coloured and confirmed in aftertimes
By others and herself too. Marian Erle
Was born upon the ledge of Malvern Hill
To eastward, in a hut, built up at night
To evade the landlord's eye, of mud and turf,
Still liable, if once he looked that way,
To being straight levelled, scattered by his foot,
Like any other anthill. Born, I say;
God sent her to his world, commissioned right,
Her human testimonials fully signed,
Not scant in soul—complete in lineaments;
But others had to swindle her a place
To wail in when she had come. No place for her,
By man's law! born an outlaw, was this babe;
Her first cry in our strange and strangling air,
When cast in spasms out by the shuddering womb,
Was wrong against the social code,—forced wrong.
What business had the baby to cry there?

I tell her story and grow passionate.
She, Marian, did not tell it so, but used
Meek words that made no wonder of herself
For being so sad a creature. 'Mister Leigh
Considered truly that such things should change.
They *will*, in heaven—but meantime, on the earth,
There's none can like a nettle as a pink,
Except himself. We're nettles, some of us,
And give offence by the act of springing up;
And, if we leave the damp side of the wall,
The hoes, of course, are on us.' So she said.
Her father earned his life by random jobs
Despised by steadier workmen—keeping swine
On commons, picking hops, or hurrying on
The harvest at wet seasons—or, at need,
Assisting the Welsh drovers, when a drove
Of startled horses plunged into the mist
Below the mountain-road, and sowed the wind
With wandering neighings. In between the gaps
Of such irregular work, he drank and slept,
And cursed his wife because, the pence being out,
She could not buy more drink. At which she turned,
(The worm) and beat her baby in revenge
For her own broken heart. There's not a crime
But takes its proper change out still in crime
If once rung on the counter of this world;

Let sinners look to it.
                                        Yet the outcast child,
For whom the very mother's face forewent
The mother's special patience, lived and grew;
Learnt early to cry low, and walk alone,
With that pathetic vacillating roll
Of the infant body on the uncertain feet,
(The earth being felt unstable ground so soon)
At which most women's arms unclose at once
With irrepressive instinct. Thus, at three,
This poor weaned kid would run off from the fold,
This babe would steal off from the mother's chair,
And, creeping through the golden walls of gorse,
Would find some keyhole toward the secrecy
Of Heaven's high blue, and, nestling down, peer out—
Oh, not to catch the angels at their games,
She had never heard of angels,—but to gaze
She knew not why, to see she knew not what,
A-hungering outward from the barren earth
For something like a joy. She liked, she said,
To dazzle black her sight against the sky,
For then, it seemed, some grand blind Love came down,
And groped her out, and clasped her with a kiss;
She learnt God that way, and was beat for it
Whenever she went home,—yet came again,
As surely as the trapped hare, getting free,
Returns to his form. This grand blind Love, she said,
This skyey father and mother both in one,
Instructed her and civilised her more
Than even Sunday-school did afterward,
To which a lady sent her to learn books
And sit upon a long bench in a row
With other children. Well, she laughed sometimes
To see them laugh and laugh and maul their texts;
But ofter she was sorrowful with noise
And wondered if their mothers beat them hard
That ever they should laugh so. There was one
She loved indeed,—Rose Bell, a seven years' child
So pretty and clever, who read syllables
When Marian was at letters; *she* would laugh
At nothing—hold your finger up, she laughed,
Then shook her curls down over eyes and mouth
To hide her make-mirth from the schoolmaster:
And Rose's pelting glee, as frank as rain
On cherry-blossoms, brightened Marian too,
To see another merry whom she loved.
She whispered once (the children side by side,

With mutual arms entwined about their necks)
'Your mother lets you laugh so?' 'Ay,' said Rose,
'She lets me. She was dug into the ground
Six years since, I being but a yearling wean.
Such mothers let us play and lose our time,
And never scold nor beat us! don't you wish
You had one like that?' There, Marian breaking off
Looked suddenly in my face. 'Poor Rose,' said she,
'I heard her laugh last night in Oxford Street.
I'd pour out half my blood to stop that laugh,—
Poor Rose, poor Rose!' said Marian.
She resumed.
It tried her, when she had learnt at Sunday-school
What God was, what he wanted from us all,
And how in choosing sin we vexed the Christ,
To go straight home and hear her father pull
The name down on us from the thunder-shelf,
Then drink away his soul into the dark
From seeing judgment. Father, mother, home,
Were God and heaven reversed to her: the more
She knew of Right, the more she guessed their wrong;
Her price paid down for knowledge, was to know
The vileness of her kindred: through her heart,
Her filial and tormented heart, henceforth,
They struck their blows at virtue. Oh, 'tis hard
To learn you have a father up in heaven
By a gathering certain sense of being, on earth,
Still worse than orphaned: 'tis too heavy a grief,
The having to thank God for such a joy!

And so passed Marian's life from year to year.
Her parents took her with them when they tramped,
Dodged lane and heaths, frequented towns and fairs,
And once went farther and saw Manchester,
And once the sea, that blue end of the world,
That fair scroll-finis of a wicked book,—
And twice a prison,—back at intervals,
Returning to the hills. Hills draw like heaven,
And stronger sometimes, holding out their hands
To pull you from the vile flats up to them.
And though perhaps these strollers still strolled back,
As sheep do, simply that they knew the way,
They certainly felt bettered unaware
Emerging from the social smut of towns
To wipe their feet clean on the mountain turf.
In which long wanderings, Marian lived and learned,
Endured and learned. The people on the roads

Would stop and ask her why her eyes outgrew
Her cheeks, and if she meant to lodge the birds
In all that hair; and then they lifted her,
The miller in his cart, a mile or twain,
The butcher's boy on horseback. Often too
The pedlar stopped, and tapped her on the head
With absolute forefinger, brown and ringed,
And asked if peradventure she could read,
And when she answered 'ay,' would toss her down
Some stray odd volume from his heavy pack,
A Thomson's Seasons, mulcted of the Spring,
Or half a play of Shakespeare's, torn across,
(She had to guess the bottom of a page
By just the top sometimes,—as difficult,
As, sitting on the moon, to guess the earth!)
Or else a sheaf of leaves (for that small Ruth's
Small gleanings) torn out from the heart of books,
From Churchyard Elegies and Edens Lost,
From Burns, and Bunyan, Selkirk, and Tom Jones.
'Twas somewhat hard to keep the things distinct,
And oft the jangling influence jarred the child
Like looking at a sunset full of grace
Through a pothouse window while the drunken oaths
Went on behind her; but she weeded out
Her book-leaves, threw away the leaves that hurt,
(First tore them small, that none should find a word)
And made a nosegay of the sweet and good
To fold within her breast, and pore upon
At broken moments of the noontide glare,
When leave was given her to untie her cloak
And rest upon the dusty roadside's bank
From the highway's dust. Or oft, the journey done,
Some city friend would lead her by the hand
To hear a lecture at an institute.
And thus she had grown, this Marian Erle of ours,
To no book-learning,—she was ignorant
Of authors,—not in earshot of the things
Out-spoken o'er the heads of common men
By men who are uncommon,—but within
The cadenced hum of such, and capable
Of catching from the fringes of the wind
Some fragmentary phrases, here and there,
Of that fine music,—which, being carried in
To her soul, had reproduced itself afresh
In finer motions of the lips and lids.

(1856)

137 *A Curse for a Nation*

PROLOGUE

I HEARD an angel speak last night,
And he said, 'Write!
Write a Nation's curse for me,
And send it over the Western Sea.'

I faltered, taking up the word:
'Not so, my lord!
If curses must be, choose another
To send thy curse against my brother.

'For I am bound by gratitude,
By love and blood,
To brothers of mine across the sea,
Who stretch out kindly hands to me.'

'Therefore,' the voice said, 'shalt thou write
My curse to-night.
From the summits of love a curse is driven,
As lightning is from the tops of heaven.'

'Not so, I answered. 'Evermore
My heart is sore
For my own land's sins: for little feet
Of children bleeding along the street:

'For parked-up honours that gainsay
The right of way:
For almsgiving through a door that is
Not open enough for two friends to kiss:

'For love of freedom which abates
Beyond the Straits:
For patriot virtue starved to vice on
Self-praise, self-interest, and suspicion:

'For an oligarchic parliament,
And bribes well-meant.
What curse to another land assign,
When heavy-souled for the sins of mine?'

'Therefore,' the voice said, 'shalt thou write
My curse to-night.
Because thou hast strength to see and hate
A foul thing done *within* thy gate.'

'Not so,' I answered once again.
'To curse, choose men.
For I, a woman, have only known
How the heart melts and the tears run down.'

'Therefore,' the voice said, 'shalt thou write
My curse to-night.
Some women weep and curse, I say
(And no one marvels,) night and day.

'And thou shalt take their part to-night,
Weep and write.
A curse from the depths of womanhood
Is very salt, and bitter, and good.'

So thus I wrote, and mourned indeed,
What all may read.
And thus, as was enjoined on me,
I send it over the Western Sea.

THE CURSE

I

BECAUSE ye have broken your own chain
With the strain
Of brave men climbing a Nation's height,
Yet thence bear down with brand and thong
On souls of others,—for this wrong
This is the curse. Write.

Because yourselves are standing straight
In the state
Of Freedom's foremost acolyte,
Yet keep calm footing all the time
On writhing bond-slaves,—for this crime
This is the curse. Write.

Because ye prosper in God's name,
With a claim
To honour in the old world's sight,
Yet do the fiend's work perfectly
In strangling martyrs,—for this lie
This is the curse. Write.

II

Ye shall watch while kings conspire
Round the people's smouldering fire,
And, warm for your part,
Shall never dare—O shame!
To utter the thought into flame
Which burns at your heart.
This is the curse. Write.

Ye shall watch while nations strive
With the bloodhounds, die or survive,
  Drop faint from their jaws,
Or throttle them backward to death,
And only under your breath
  Shall favor the cause.
      This is the curse. Write.

Ye shall watch while strong men draw
The nets of feudal law
  To strangle the weak,
And, counting the sin for a sin,
Your soul shall be sadder within
  Than the word ye shall speak.
      This is the curse. Write.

When good men are praying erect
That Christ may avenge His elect
  And deliver the earth,
The prayer in your ears, said low,
Shall sound like the tramp of a foe
  That's driving you forth.
      This is the curse. Write.

When wise men give you their praise,
They shall pause in the heat of the phrase,
  As if carried too far.
When ye boast your own charters kept true,
Ye shall blush;—for the thing which ye do
  Derides what ye are.
      This is the curse. Write.

When fools cast taunts at your gate,
Your scorn ye shall somewhat abate
  As ye look o'er the wall,
For your conscience, tradition, and name
Explode with a deadlier blame
  Than the worst of them all.
      This is the curse. Write.

Go, wherever ill deeds shall be done,
Go, plant your flag in the sun
  Beside the ill-doers!
And recoil from clenching the curse
Of God's witnessing Universe
  With a curse of yours.
      This is the curse. Write.

(1860)

138 *Lord Walter's Wife*

I

'But why do you go,' said the lady, while both sate under the yew,
And her eyes were alive in their depth, as the kraken beneath the
 seablue.

II

'Because I fear you,' he answered;—'because you are far too fair,
And able to strangle my soul in a mesh of your gold-coloured hair.'

III

'Oh, that,' she said, 'is no reason! Such knots are quickly undone,
And too much beauty, I reckon, is nothing but too much sun.'

IV

'Yet farewell so,' he answered;—'the sun-stroke 's fatal at times.
I value your husband, Lord Walter, whose gallop rings still from
 the limes.'

V

'Oh, that,' she said, 'is no reason. You smell a rose through a fence:
If two should smell it, what matter? who grumbles, and where's the
 pretence?'

VI

'But I,' he replied, 'have promised another, when love was free,
To love her alone, alone, who alone and afar loves me.'

VII

'Why, that,' she said, 'is no reason. Love's always free, I am told.
Will you vow to be safe from the head-ache on Tuesday, and think
 it will hold?'

VIII

'But you,' he replied, 'have a daughter, a young little child, who
 was laid
In your lap to be pure; so I leave you: the angels would make me
 afraid.'

IX

'Oh, that,' she said, 'is no reason. The angels keep out of the way;
And Dora, the child, observes nothing, although you should please me and stay.'

X

At which he rose up in his anger,—'Why, now, you no longer are fair!
Why, now, you no longer are fatal, but ugly and hateful, I swear.'

XI

At which she laughed out in her scorn.—'These men! Oh, these men overnice,
Who are shocked if a colour not virtuous, is frankly put on by a vice.'

XII

Her eyes blazed upon him—'And *you!* You bring us your vices so near
That we smell them! You think in our presence a thought 'twould defame us to hear!

XIII

'What reason had you, and what right,—I appeal to your soul from my life,—
To find me too fair as a woman? Why, sir, I am pure, and a wife.

XIV

'Is the day-star too fair up above you? It burns you not. Dare you imply
I brushed you more close than the star does, when Walter had set me as high?

XV

'If a man finds a woman too fair, he means simply adapted too much
To uses unlawful and fatal. The praise!—shall I thank you for such?

XVI

'Too fair?—not unless you misuse us! and surely if, once in a while,
You attain to it, straightway you call us no longer too fair, but too vile.

XVII

'A moment,—I pray your attention!—I have a poor word in my head
I must utter, though womanly custom would set it down better unsaid.

XVIII

'You grew, sir, pale to impertinence, once when I showed you a ring
You kissed my fan when I dropped it. No matter!—I've broken the thing.

XIX

'You did me the honour, perhaps, to be moved at my side now and then
In the senses—a vice, I have heard, which is common to beasts and some men.

XX

'Love's a virtue for heroes!—as white as the snow on high hills,
And immortal as every great soul is that struggles, endures, and fulfils.

XXI

'I love my Walter profoundly,—you, Maude, though you faltered a week,
For the sake of... what was it? an eye-brow? or, less still, a mole on a cheek?

XXII

'And since, when all's said, you're too noble to stoop to the frivolous cant
About crimes irresistible, virtues that swindle, betray and supplant,

XXIII

'I determined to prove to yourself that, whate'er you might dream or avow
By illusion, you wanted precisely no more of me than you have now.

XXIV

'There! Look me full in the face!—in the face. Understand, if you can,
That the eyes of such women as I am, are clean as the palm of a man.

XXV

'Drop his hand, you insult him. Avoid us for fear we should cost you a scar—
You take us for harlots, I tell you, and not for the women we are.

XXVI

'You wronged me: but then I considered . . . there's Walter! And so at the end,
I vowed that he should not be mulcted, by me, in the hand of a friend.

XXVII

'Have I hurt you indeed? We are quits then. Nay, friend of my Walter, be mine!
Come Dora, my darling, my angel, and help me to ask him to dine.'

(1862)

139 *A Musical Instrument*

I

WHAT was he doing, the great god Pan,
  Down in the reeds by the river?
Spreading ruin and scattering ban,
Splashing and paddling with hoofs of a goat,
And breaking the golden lilies afloat
  With the dragon-fly on the river.

II

He tore out a reed, the great god Pan,
  From the deep cool bed of the river:
The limpid water turbidly ran,
And the broken lilies a-dying lay,
And the dragon-fly had fled away,
  Ere he brought it out of the river.

III

High on the shore sate the great god Pan,
  While turbidly flowed the river;
And hacked and hewed as a great god can,
With his hard bleak steel at the patient reed,
Till there was not a sign of a leaf indeed
  To prove it fresh from the river.

IV

He cut it short, did the great god Pan
  (How tall it stood in the river!),
Then drew the pith, like the heart of a man,
Steadily from the outside ring,
And notched the poor dry empty thing
  In holes, as he sate by the river.

V

'This is the way,' laughed the great god Pan
  (Laughed while he sate by the river),
'The only way, since gods began
To make sweet music, they could succeed.'
Then, dropping his mouth to a hole in the reed,
  He blew in power by the river.

VI

Sweet, sweet, sweet, O Pan!
  Piercing sweet by the river!
Blinding sweet, O great god Pan!
The sun on the hill forgot to die,
And the lilies revived, and the dragon-fly
  Came back to dream on the river.

VII

Yet half a beast is the great god Pan,
  To laugh as he sits by the river,
Making a poet out of a man:
The true gods sigh for the cost and pain,—
For the reed which grows nevermore again
  As a reed with the reeds in the river.

(1862)

HELEN DUFFERIN
(1807–1867)

HELEN SELINA SHERIDAN (later Blackwood, Lady Dufferin and afterwards Hays, Countess of Gifford) was one of the most popular ballad writers of the nineteenth century. She is usually cited as an Irish poet, as she was of an Anglo-Irish family, but was probably born in London. Her Irish father, Thomas Sheridan, was the son of the dramatist, Richard Brinsley Sheridan, and her mother, Caroline Henrietta (née Callander, later Campbell) wrote novels. Helen Dufferin was the eldest daughter and one of her two sisters was the poet, Caroline Norton. In 1813 she was taken with her parents to the Cape of Good Hope, her father being in the colonial service. After his death in 1817, the remaining family returned to England and were granted residence in Hampton Court Palace. In 1825 she married Commander Price Blackwood, and they lived in Florence, to return to Thames Ditton in 1828. They had one son, Frederick Temple Hamilton Blackwood, and she was to devote herself to his education after her husband's death in 1841. She also travelled with her son, and their journey along the Nile led to her *Lispings from Low Latitudes. Or, Extracts from the Journal of the Hon. Impulshia Gushington* (1863): her son had published his *Letters from High Latitudes* in 1856. In London her literary friends included Henry Taylor, John Lockhart, Fanny Kemble, and the politician and novelist, Benjamin Disraeli. She was to marry George Hay, the Earl of Gifford on his deathbed in 1862.

She had begun writing verses as a child, but her reputation as a poet was first established through her enormously popular ballads, 'Terence's Farewell' (1840) and 'The Irish Emigrant' (*c.*1840). These were said to have been internationally known. The *Songs, Poems and Verses and Verses by Helen, Lady Dufferin (Countess of Gifford)* (1894) were published posthumously and edited, with a memoir, by her son.

140 *The Charming Woman*

So Miss Myrtle is going to marry?
  What a number of hearts she will break!
There's Lord George, and Tom Brown, and Sir Harry,
  Who are dying of love for her sake!
'Tis a match that we all must approve,—
  Let gossips say all that they can!
For indeed she's a charming woman,
  And he's a most fortunate man!

Yes, indeed, she's a charming woman,
  And she reads both Latin and Greek,—
And I'm told that she solved a problem
  In Euclid before she could speak!
Had she been but a daughter of mine,
  I'd have taught her to hem and to sew,—
But her mother (a charming woman)
  Couldn't think of such trifles, you know!

Oh, she's really a charming woman!
  But, perhaps, a little too thin;
And no wonder such very late hours
  Should ruin her beautiful skin!
And her shoulders are rather too bare,
  And her gown's nearly up to her knees,
But I'm told that these charming women
  May dress themselves just as they please!

Yes, she's really a charming woman!
  But, I thought, I observed, by the bye,
A something—that's rather uncommon,—
  In the flash of that very bright eye?
It may be a mere fancy of mine,
  Tho' her voice has a very sharp tone,—
But I'm told that these charming women
  Are inclined to have wills of their own!

She sings like a bullfinch or linnet,
  And she talks like an Archbishop too;
Can play you a rubber and win it,—
  If she's got nothing better to do!
She can chatter of Poor-laws and Tithes,
  And the value of labour and land,—
'Tis a pity when charming women
  Talk of things which they don't understand!

I'm told that she hasn't a penny,
  Yet her gowns would make Maradan stare;
And I feel her bills must be many,—
  But that's only her husband's affair!
Such husbands are very uncommon,
  So regardless of prudence and pelf,—
But they say such a charming woman
  Is a fortune, you know, in herself!

She's brothers and sisters by dozens,
  And all charming people, they say!
And several tall Irish cousins,
  Whom she loves in a sisterly way.
O young men, if you'd take my advice,
  You would find it an excellent plan,—
Don't marry a charming woman,
  If you are a sensible man!

(1835 *1894*)

ELIZA MARY HAMILTON
(1807–1851)

ELIZA (ELIZABETH) MARY HAMILTON was an Irish Protestant. She was born in Dublin, the fifth child of a Scottish father, Archibald Hamilton, an attorney, and Sarah (née Hutton). Her brother, Sir William Rowan Hamilton, was the President of the Royal Irish Academy and the Royal Astronomer of Ireland. He also contributed poems to magazines and had many literary friends, including William Wordsworth, Samuel Taylor Coleridge, Felicia Hemans, Robert Southey, and Maria Edgeworth. It is possible that Eliza Mary Hamilton met some of these people through him, as she and her sisters lived with her brother for some time before his marriage in 1833. She certainly knew Wordsworth, with whom she stayed at Rydal Mount, and he was familiar with some of her poetry and spoke favourably of it.

Her first published poems appeared in English and Irish journals, including the *Dublin University Magazine*, to which she contributed, as 'E.M.H.', between 1833 and 1851. She therefore continued to publish poetry after her one volume of verses, *Poems* (1838), came out under her name in Dublin. The *Poems* were dedicated to her brother, and were commended for their depth of feeling by a reviewer for the *Dublin University Magazine* (August 1838).

141 *The Moon Seen by Day*

THOU most companionless! what dost thou here
  Walking the bright but foreign fields of day?
Faint, as if weary of that golden sphere,
  Where little more than wonder greets thy ray,
Doing cold homage to thy daring flight,
  Weak, lovely rival of the unenvying sun!
Who only smiles to see his throne by right,—
  Where his supremacy will bow to none—
  By such a soft and meek-browed Being won,
As thee, thou shrinking stranger in a sky
Whose blaze seems weighing down thy modest eye,
And dulling its pure lustre; never made
To stand forth thus, without a single shade,
In the broad noon of daylight's loud domain,
Where heartless crowds thy nature so profane;
And they, who loved thee in thy deep-hushed home,
Feel thee another in that dazzling dome.

Sisterless spirit! palest of the pale!
  Like a white violet, beaten by the rain,—
A single one, that, strange as it is frail,
  Has sprung by chance, where every pencilled vein
Of its young heart lies open to the gaze
  Of each gay flower-group, in the sun-filled air;
Making it fear, its wet, wan cheek to raise,
  And meet the summer multitude's bright stare.
  Thou to me look'st heart-sick of all this glare,
And pining for thine own land's raven veil,
Through whose soft folds of stillness more avail
Thy dearer, holier smiles, and glistening hair
Flung down and streaming o'er the bosom bare
Of the clear waters, breathing their deep love;
While star-beams girdle thy pure zone above,
And every nearer cloud that wanders by
Catches a silent sweetness from thine eye.

What art thou like, oh! solitary thing?
  Something is in thee touches much my heart—
Bending its reeds of feeling with a wing
  Cold as the winds that have sad music's art,
Among those green, wild river-flutes, that taught
  The lip of man to imitate their sigh.—
What is in thee of bitterness, oh! what,
  Angel of silence in day's gaudy sky!
  To bow my spirit thus o'erwhelmingly,
Beneath the meaning of thy mournful smile?

What likeness, as I gaze, grows clear the while
In thine to other features,—of a fate
As high, as strange, as proudly desolate?
Which, as it diadems the drooping head
With light and sound, but dims, and maketh dead
The glory nature gave to her who wears
The sweeter power that no such sceptre bears.

Alas! too strong it grows,—the likeness mute!—
What is this lonely look, but the gilt shame
Twined round the sensitive ethereal lute,
(Along with all thy glorious laurels, Fame!)
When woman's veil is gone!—when song hath laid
(As it will ever lay) the bosom bare,
And she whose lip was of itself afraid,
Trembles to hear her own name fill the air—
A worthless echo! for which fewer care,
Than for the humblest, most ungifted breast,
Whose feelings but like moonlight are expressed
In the sweet silence of her natural home;
Not where the world's whole day-light crowds may come
To gaze on them: oh! what though many eyes
Will pause to bend on hers in gentlest guise,
A moment as they pass; she stands apart—
They cannot pay her for the thoughts that start.

Genius! whose snow-white wings show life's least stain,
Lonely enough on earth thou ever art,
But never half so lonely, or so vain,
As when thy burning breath disturbs the heart
Whose path should be but as a forest stream,
Whispering along, looked through by only heaven,
And the lone primrosed banks that edge its gleam,
Smiling back love for the green freshness given:—
Where never bough that curtains it is riven,
But casts its autumn-sorrows year by year,
Its yellow leaves upon that bosom clear,
Which sighs, and bears them out of thought away.
Oh! thou young queen, that vainly wouldst look gay,
In this, thy foreign realm! sad bride of light!
Dear star of peace! have I e'er wished such height?
Me, may but silence veil unto my grave,
And there, there only, the cold laurel wave!

(1838)

142 *Lines Composed at Sea*

'He leadeth me beside the still waters.'

'BESIDE still waters!' yes, how deeply still!
  E'en on this night I feel thee lead my soul,
Oh! gracious Guide! whose voice within my breast,
  With power its deeper ocean to control,
Is breathing now such all-unearthly rest,
  While the wild sea doth lift me, at its will,
High on its thundering, tempest-maddened roll,
  To the dread summit of each moving hill;
Then downward suddenly to valleys dark
  Bear me again; and with a heavy sound,
(Like that which, as they sank to death,
  Has sternly spoken to the drowned,)
Sweep o'er the quivering, struggling ship,
That still,—without companionship,—
While pants her noble heart for breath,
Right onward holds her way, like fixed intrepid Faith!
Hark to the fathomless Atlantic's call
From its far solitudes!—while all its bays
With a deep voice reply! The solemn hall
Of the sky's temple, and the assembled stars,
That nothing feel of earth or earth-born wars,
Methinks are listening, with their silent gaze,
To the strong winds; and to the music fierce
Of their loud worship. Hark! again they raise
Their choral anthem's awful swell of praise:
Again the waves pour forth their savage lays,
Responded to afar by cliff and cavern tall.
I listen too—yet walk in heart with Thee,
Where there is nothing but the summer sound
Of stillest streams:—my pillow is the sea,
That like a bosom stung with griefs profound,
Never from guilt's dark memories to be free,
Trembles and heaves 'neath my reposing cheek,
Convulsively: and yet I am at rest;
I only see a form of glory meek,
Treading the deep. Oh! high and heavenly Guest!
'The sea is thine, and thou hast made it,'—thou,
With that most sorrowful and gentle brow,
Crowned upon earth with thorns! I hear thee speak;
And at thy feet the mighty waters lie,
In adoration, dumb, confessing they are weak.
And should for me no earthly morning break,
Sweet are thy words that whisper, 'Fear not, it is I!'

(1838)

143 *A Young Girl Seen in Church*

WAS she an orphan?—can another grief
So wholly chasten?—can another woe
So sanctify?—for she was (as a leaf
Of hue funereal mid the Spring's young glow)
Robed in emphatic black:—the soul of night
Filled her rich simply-parted ebon hair,
And raven eye-lashes, and made her bright
With solemn lustre day can never wear.

Two younger buds, a sister at each side,
Like little moon-lit clouds beside the moon,
Which up the sky's majestic temple glide,
Clad darkly too, she led,—but music soon
Moved over her, and like a breeze of heaven,
Shook from her lips the fragrance of her soul,—
And then, the thoughts with which my heart had striven,
Spoke in my gaze, and would not brook control.

I bent upon her my astonished eye,
That glowed, I felt, with an expression full
Of all that love which dares to deify,—
That adoration of the beautiful
Which haunts the poet,—I forgot the sighs
Of whispered prayer around me, and the page
Of hope divine, and the eternal eyes
That look through every heart, in every place and age.
I gazed and gazed as though she were a star,
Unconscious and unfallen, which shone above, afar.-
But eloquently grave, a crimson cloud
Of deep disquietude her cheek o'erspread
With exquisite rebuke;—and then I bowed
Like hers my earnest looks and conscious head,
Ashamed to have disturbed the current meek
Of her translucent thoughts, and made them flow
Painfully earthward. But she veiled that cheek,—
Veiled even its sweet reproach and sacred glow,
Like those pure flowers too sensitive to brook
Noon's burning eye, and its oppressive look,
That shut, in beautiful displeasure, up
Each brilliant petal of their heart's deep cup.

(1838)

CAROLINE NORTON
(1808–1877)

CAROLINE SHERIDAN (later Norton) was to become an infamous figure in London society, a renowned beauty, popular writer, and also a tireless campaigner for the rights of the oppressed. She was born into an Anglo-Irish family in London, the daughter of Thomas Sheridan and granddaughter of the dramatist, Richard Brinsley Sheridan. Her mother, Caroline Henrietta (née Callander, later Campbell) wrote novels, and one of her sisters was the poet, Lady Helen Dufferin. After the death of the father in colonial service in 1817, the remaining family were granted residence in Hampton Court Palace. In 1827 she married the Honourable George Chapple Norton, a barrister, with whom she had three sons, but from whom she was to separate in 1836. Her experience of this notoriously unhappy marriage both motivated her campaigining on behalf of women's rights and was to inform the subject of her three semi-autobiographical novels: *Stuart of Dunleath* (1851), *Lost and Saved* (1863) and *Old Sir Douglas* (1867). Her husband having died in 1875, she was to marry Sir William Maxwell-Stirling only four months before her death.

A liberal, she supported the Whig 1832 Reform Bill, and through this she became acquainted with William Lamb, Lord Melbourne, and thus much antagonized her husband, who held the Tory seat of Guildford. It is reputed that her husband, in part motivated by a desire to bring down the Whig government, accused his wife of adultery with Lord Melbourne and brought a suit for £10,000 damages against him. His additional denial of visitation rights to his wife led to her campaigning for a reform of both the custody and divorce laws, with remarkable success. Under the pseudonym of 'Pearce Stevenson', she published *A Plain Letter to the Lord Chancellor on the Infant Custody Bill* (1839). Later, her essays, *English Laws for Women in the Nineteenth Century* (1854) and *A Letter to the Queen on Lord Chancellor Cranworth's Marriage and Divorce Bill* (1855), with Cranworth actually paraphrasing from the latter in his parliamentary speeches, helped to secure the eventual passing of the 1857 Divorce Act. She also wrote on behalf of the poor and disadvantaged, for example in her *A Voice from the Factories* (1836), in her many letters to *The Times* in 1841, and in a later poem, *The Child of the Islands* (1845). J.G. Lockhart identified the latter as a 'Condition-of-England-Question' piece (*London Quarterly Review*, June 1845). *A Voice* was published anonymously (presented as if by a man) and was dedicated to Lord Ashley, the parliamentarian who took over Michael Sadler's advocacy of a ten-hour working day. She was motivated in her politics not by a radical, egalitarian agenda, but by a belief in the inevitability of social (and sexual) hierarchies and the concomitant need of state protection for the vulnerable. Her anti-Chartist stance is thus curiously consistent with her more liberal campaigning. In *Letters to the Mob* (1848), she writes as 'Libertas':

> The Chartist dream of equality is the most cruel of all the temptations with which mob-traps are baited; for it is at once the most specious and the most false. There can be *no* equality, any more than there can be a sea without a shore! Superiority is not a thing of man's devising, but of God's appointing. Gradation is His Law.

Caroline Norton's writing career was enormously successful. She once boasted that she could earn £1,400 per year through her contributions of short stories and poems to journals. Her popularity extended also to her published volumes of poetry, which began with her anonymous 'The Sorrows of Rosalie' in 1829. Hartley Coleridge was to define her as 'the Byron of our modern poetesses' (*Quarterly Review*, September 1840).

144 *from The Sorrows of Rosalie, II*

[*Rosalie has been seduced by an upper-class man, Walter, who promises marriage. His servants turn her from his door when she bears his child. Eds.*]

XL

I PRESSED my baby to my throbbing breast,
In the wide world he was my only tie;
Others had parents, husbands, homes of rest,
Loved and were loved again—Oh! what had I?
No voice was there to soothe mine agony,
I wandered on 'mid crowds, alone, alone;
None bade me stay, none bade me cease to sigh;
By all unpitied, and to all unknown,
I had my love—my grief—my child:—all else was gone.

XLI

I reached his door—that door which once I thought
Had oped to welcome me as Arthur's bride;
Where oft in joyous fancy, I had brought
My poor old father, evermore beside
His couch to watch, and be his only guide!
Where were those buoyant hopes and feelings *now?*
Where was that vision, raised by youthful pride?
Fled with the pureness of that virgin brow
Which sorrow might have dimmed, but sin alone could bow.

XLII

I knocked—oh! louder knocked my beating heart!
When to the door a heavy footstep came;
The menial smiled, and bade me quick depart,
Muttering, 'hard travelling for so fair a dame,'
While indignation shook my trembling frame;
I shrank away, the ready tears gushed forth,
But pride forbade—I could not speak my name;
A moment's silence, and upon the earth
That pitying servant threw some coins of little worth.

XLIII

Yea, pity touched his heart—but oh! for *me*—
Was *this* my fate?—I was condemned to take

From Arthur's servant common charity?
I rose—I said, 'alas! for pity's sake
Let me see him—thy master—let me make
Myself appeal unto his hardened soul!
Some throb of dying mercy I might wake—
Some feeling interest *cannot* controul—
Some wish, the bitter grief he caused me, to console!'

(1829)

145 *from The Sorrows of Rosalie, III*

XVI

ON, on—through many a dark and mournful day
I lived, half conscious, in a dreamy land,
While many a vision came, and passed away,
And many a fairy scheme of bliss was planned,
And ever by me Arthur seemed to stand;
With *him* in sunny fields and bowers I ranged,
In scenes where we had wandered hand in hand;
And I was happy till the vision changed;
'Twas Arthur still, but oh! with heart and looks estranged!

XVII

And then, methought, beneath a stormy sky,
With his gray hair thin streaming on the wind,
My father stood in hopeless agony;
Reproached me as ungrateful and unkind;
And prayed that *I* as hard a fate might find;
Or on a lowly couch his form was lying,
Whispering sad words, which, still with head inclined,
I vainly strove to hear; and, he while dying,
Cast a reproachful glance at *me* for not replying.

XVIII

And then again it changed, and bound I stood
While demons tore my baby limb from limb,
And still the stream of gushing living blood
Came trickling on the earth, all fresh from him
Who might have mingled with the cherubim,
And been as bright as they: warm o'er my feet,
All seen too plain, though vision-like and dim,
Those crimson rivulets appeared to meet,
While powerless still I stood, unable to retreat.

XIX

At length I slept; and when I woke again
Those fevered dreams had fled, and left me weak,
With but the sense confused of grief and pain:
I gazed around, and feebly tried to speak;
And kindly eyes, that watched my slumber break,
Turned to the couch,—I asked them for my child,
And that young wife replied, in accents meek:
My babe was brought me—I was wan and wild;
And, shrinking back, it turned to that kind one, and smiled.

(1829)

146 *from The Undying One, Canto II*

SHE pointed to the river's surface, where
Our forms were pictured seated side by side;
I gazed on them, and her's was very fair,
And mine—was as thou seest it *now*, my bride.
But her's, though fair, was fading—wan and pale
The brow whose marble met the parting day.
Time o'er her form had thrown his misty veil,
And all her ebon curls were streak'd with grey:
But mine was youthful—yes! Such youth as glows
In the young tree by lightning scathed and blasted
That, joyless, waves its black and leafless boughs,
On which spring showers and summer warmth are wasted.
The lines upon my brow were those of age;
The hollow cheek might speak of time or woe;
But all the rest was as in life's first stage—
The tangled curls without one touch of snow.
Oh! wherefore do I thus describe old times?
Am I not here—the same accursed thing,
Stamp'd with the brand of darkness for my crimes—
Never to die—but ever withering?

(1830)

147 *'As When from Dreams Awaking'*

As when from dreams awaking
The dim forms float away
Whose visioned smiles were making
Our darkness bright as day;
We vainly strike, while weeping,
From their shining spirit track,
(Where they fled while we were sleeping,)
To call those dear ones back!

Like the stars, some power divides them
From a world of want and pain;
They *are* there, but daylight hides them,
And we look for them in vain.
For a while we dwell with sadness,
Or the beauty of that dream,
Then turn, and hail with gladness,
The light of morning's beam.

So, when memory's power is wringing
Our lonely hearts to tears,
Dim forms around us bringing
That brightened former years:
Fond looks and low words spoken,
Which those dreamy days could boast,
Rise; till the spell is broken,
We forget that they are lost!

But when the hour of darkness rolls
Like heavy night away;
And peace is stealing o'er our souls
Like the dawn of summer day:
The dim sweet forms that used to bless,
Seem stealing from us too;
We loved them—but joy's sunniness
Hath hid them from our view!

Oh could day beam eternally,
And memory's power cease,
This world, a world of light would be,
Our hearts were worlds of peace:
But dreams of joy return with night,
And dwell upon the past—
And every grief that clouds our light,
Reminds us of the last!

(1830)

148 *The Name*

'What's in a name?'
Shakespeare

THY name was once the magic spell, by which my thoughts were bound,
And burning dreams of light and love were wakened by that sound;
My heart beat quick when stranger tongues, with idle praise or blame,
Awoke its deepest thrill of life, to tremble at that name.

Long years—long years have passed away, and altered is thy brow;
And we who met so gladly once, must meet as strangers now:
The friends of yore come round me still, but talk no more of thee;
'Tis idle ev'n to wish it now—for what art *thou to me*?

Yet still thy name, thy blessed name, my lonely bosom fills,
Like an echo that hath lost itself among the distant hills,
Which still, with melancholy note, keeps faintly lingering on,
When the jocund sound that woke it once is gone—for ever gone.

(1830)

149 *from Recollections of a Faded Beauty*

I RECOLLECT the man who did declare
When I was *at* the *fair*, myself was *fair*:
(I had it in my album for three years
And often looked, and shed delicious tears.)
I didn't fall in love, however, *then*,
Because I never saw that man again.
And I remember Popkins—ah! too well!
And *all* who once in love with Chloe fell.
They called *me* Chloe, for they said my grace
Was nymph-like, as was also *half* my face.
My mouth was wide, but then I had a smile
Which might a demon of its tears beguile.—
As Captain Popkins said, or rather swore,
He liked me (ah! my Popkins!) all the more.
He couldn't bear a little mouth, for when
It laughed, it was like a long slit in a pen;
Or button-hole stretched on too big a button;
Or little cut for gravy in boiled mutton.
(Popkins was clever)—but I must proceed
More regularly, that my friends may read.
I didn't marry, for I couldn't get

A man I liked; I havn't got one yet;
But I had handsome lovers by the score:
Alas! Alas! I always sighed for more.

(1830)

150 *from* A Voice from the Factories

III

SEE the Stage-Wonder (taught to earn its bread
By the exertion of an infant skill),
Forsake the wholesome slumbers of its bed,
And mime, obedient to the public will.
Where is the heart so cold that does not thrill
With a vexatious sympathy, to see
That child prepare to play its part, and still
With simulated airs of gaiety
Rise to the dangerous rope, and bend the supple knee?

IV

Painted and spangled, trembling there it stands,
Glances below for friend or father's face,
Then lifts its small round arms and feeble hands
With the taught movements of an artist's grace:
Leaves its uncertain gilded resting-place—
Springs lightly as the elastic cord gives way—
And runs along with scarce perceptible pace—
Like a bright bird upon a waving spray,
Fluttering and sinking still, whene'er the branches play.

V

Now watch! a joyless and distorted smile
Its innocent lips assume; (the dancer's leer!)
Conquering its terror for a little while:
Then lets the truth of infancy appear,
And with a stare of numbed and childish fear
Looks sadly towards the audience come to gaze
On the unwonted skill which costs so dear,
While still the applauding crowd, with pleased amaze,
Ring through its dizzy ears unwelcome shouts of praise.

VI

What is it makes us feel relieved to see
That hapless little dancer reach the ground;
With its whole spirit's elasticity

Thrown into one glad, safe, triumphant bound?
Why are we sad, when, as it gazes round
At that wide sea of paint, and gauze, and plumes,
(Once more awake to sense, and sight, and sound,)
The nature of its age it re-assumes,
And one spontaneous smile at length its face illumes?

VII

Because we feel, for Childhood's years and strength,
Unnatural and hard the task hath been;—
Because our sickened souls revolt at length,
And ask what infant-innocence may mean,
Thus toiling through the artificial scene;—
Because at that word, Childhood, start to birth
All dreams of hope and happiness serene—
All thoughts of innocent joy that visit earth—
Prayer—slumber—fondness—smiles—and hours of rosy mirth.

VIII

And therefore when we hear the shrill faint cries
Which mark the wanderings of the little sweep;
Or when, with glittering teeth and sunny eyes,
The boy-Italian's voice, so soft and deep,
Asks alms for his poor marmoset asleep;
They fill our hearts with pitying regret,
Those little vagrants doomed so soon to weep—
As though a term of joy for all was set,
And that *their* share of Life's long suffering was not yet.

. . . .

XVIII

What is to be a slave? Is't not to spend
A life bowed down beneath a grinding ill?—
To labour on to serve another's end,—
To give up leisure, health, and strength, and skill—
And give up each of these *against your will?*
Hark to the angry answer:—'Theirs is not
A life of slavery; if they labour,—still
We *pay* their toil. Free service is their lot;
And what their labour yields, by us is fairly got.'

XIX

Oh, Men! blaspheme not Freedom! Are they free
Who toil until the body's strength gives way?
Who may not set a term for Liberty,

Who have no time for food, or rest, or play,
But struggle through the long unwelcome day
Without the leisure to be good or glad?
Such is their service—call it what you may.
Poor little creatures, overtasked and sad,
Your Slavery hath no name,—yet is its Curse as bad!

XX

Again an answer. ''Tis their parents' choice.
By *some* employ the poor man's child must earn
Its daily bread; and infants have no voice
In what the allotted task shall be: they learn
What answers best, or suits the parents' turn.'
Mournful reply! Do not your hearts inquire
Who tempts the parents' penury? They yearn
Toward their offspring with a strong desire,
But those who starve *will* sell, even what they most require.

XXI

We grant their class must labour—young and old;
We grant the child the needy parents' tool:
But still our hearts a better plan behold;
No bright Utopia of some dreaming fool,
But rationally just, and good by rule.
Not against TOIL, but TOIL'S EXCESS we pray,
(Else were we nursed in Folly's simplest school);
That so our country's hardy children may
Learn not to loathe, but bless, the well apportioned day.

(1836)

151 *Lines, Etc.*

'A WOMAN should not rule this realm';
Oh weak and brutal mind!
In which fierce ignorance of truth
With folly was combined:
Shall England, then, forget when most
Fair Commerce spread her sails,
While Peace and Plenty dwelt unharmed
Within her fertile vales?—
When, planted like our native oak,
To flourish evermore,
Religion rose in Majesty,
The storms of faction o'er,
And flung her holy ample shade

Along the quiet land,
Protected by the sceptred strength
Of Woman's Royal hand!
Shall we forget when most we grew
In glory and in might,
And one by one, like circling stars
That dawn upon the night,
Name after name of sterling worth
Claimed place in History's page,
To stamp that term of Woman's rule
As Britain's 'Golden Age'?
Brute strength and mail-clad force are past;
The barbarous times are gone,
When Richard Cœur de Lion fought
The field of Ascalon;
But not from England's crown is lost
What never can depart,
The courage of her Royal blood,
Though shrined in Woman's heart!
Not in a wild and Pagan land,
Not in the battle-strife,
The traitor's arm was lifted up
Against her sacred life;
To England's long-enduring shame,
Her own unworthy son
Taught us, a 'Lion-Heart' still holds
The sceptre and the throne.
She heard the bolt of death fly past
(Oh! moment dark and dread!)
Then fearlessly she raised again
Her young majestic head;
And on she went, with gracious smile,
All tranquil and serene,
She knew, tho' *one* rash traitor aimed,
The People loved their Queen!
She turned not with a woman's fear
To sheltering Palace wall,
Her guards were in her subjects hearts—
The hope, the star of all!
Was this a soul unfit to reign?
Was this, the bright young bride,
A girl irresolute and weak,
A mock to England's pride?
No! If to that high soul be joined
Fair face and feeble arm,
It doth but add, to thinking minds,
A glory and a charm:

And God shall bless the brave young Queen,
Who feared no traitor's might,
And guard our Cœur de Lion still,
In every sacred right!

(1840)

FRANCES ANNE KEMBLE
(1809–1893)

The daughter of Charles Kemble and the niece of Sarah Siddons, Frances Anne Kemble was born into one of the most distinguished theatrical families of the time. She was educated from an early age at French schools, first in Boulogne and then in Paris. When at home in London, she became acquainted with many of her father's influential literary associates, including the salon run by Anne Skepper Procter (the mother of the poet, Adelaide Anne Procter). Important figures in this group were Charles Dickens and William Charles Macready. Through her brother, John Mitchell Kemble, she came into contact with members of the Cambridge Apostles, including F. D. Maurice, Alfred Tennyson, and Richard Chenevix Trench. Although she had been writing poetry while at school, her ambitions as an author were overtaken when a crisis at Covent Garden almost bankrupted her family. To help alleviate debts, she turned to the stage, impressing audiences with her leading performance in *Romeo and Juliet* in 1829. Her successful career as an actress led to extensive tours in America during 1833, where she met her future husband, the plantation owner, Pierce Butler. They were married in Philadelphia in 1834. Her marriage took her away from the stage, and she settled into far from happy family life, with two children, at Butler's Island, Georgia. By this time, she had completed one play, *Francis I* (1832). In 1835, she published *Journal of a Residence in America* (1835), which makes notable points about slavery in the South.

By the early 1840s, it was obvious that her marriage was under considerable strain, and she took the opportunity to travel to England with her husband in 1842, renewing friendships and acquaintances. Since Butler was experiencing serious financial problems, they returned not to his plantation but to a boarding-house in Philadelphia. Butler was obviously not pleased with the modest monies that Kemble was obtaining through her contributions to journals. In 1845, she returned alone to England, and for a short period worked as an actress. Her greatest success, however, came through giving readings from Shakespeare's works at the great houses of the aristocracy. Once it became clear that her husband was to sue for divorce on the grounds of desertion, she made her way back to America. The subsequent divorce meant that she could only see her children for one month every year. Having resumed her maiden name, she lived for twenty years in Lennox, Massachusetts. At the time of the American Civil War, she published a journal that recalled her period of residence on Butler's plantation during 1838–39. In 1877, she returned to England for the last time, where she worked on three volumes of autobiography. Her canon of published writings is quite extensive. In 1882, she produced *Notes upon Some of Shakespeare's Plays*, and seven years later she brought out a novel, *Far Away and Long*

Ago. Kemble's poems, which first appeared in America in 1844, were reprinted (with various revisions and expansions) in 1866 and 1883.

152 *Lines on a Young Woman, Who, after a Short and Wretched Marriage, Went Mad and Died*

WEEP not, ye dear ones! for I am at rest;
Short was the season of my misery,
'Tis past, and I am now among the blest,
The blest for evermore—oh weep not ye!

Remember how my happy childhood fled,
Made bright by your fond love, and tender care;
Of the brief hours time numbered o'er my head
Many were those of joy—few of despair.

Think not of that sharp torture that is past—
Still I lay safe within my Father's arms,
Even through that dark eclipse He held me fast,
And bore me swiftly from all earthly harms.

I waged with woe no long protracted strife,
Nor dragged o'er disappointment's flinty path
Year after year my bleeding feet; for Life
Struck me but once—and gave me o'er to Death.

Mine eyes were not put out by ceaseless tears
Blinding them hour by hour, and day by day;
The hideous vision of my future years
Scared them but once—and all was swept away.

Happier than in my girlhood's early home,
Fairer than in the form that then I wore,
To God, my Father's mansions, am I come,
To dwell in peace and joy for evermore.

So think of me as at His feet I stand,
Led thither through how short an agony,
How brief a task-hour in Time's labor land
For one who rests through all eternity.

And weep not, weep not! hither shall ye come,
Soon as our Father calls—and find the love
Whose precious root was in our mortal home,
Immortal blooming in the realms above.

(1866)

LADY JOHN SCOTT
(1810–1900)

ALICIA ANNE SPOTTISWOODE was born into an ancient family of Berwickshire landowners. She was the eldest of four children. Much of her childhood was divided between periods on the family estate and in London, where her father conducted some of his business. Privately educated, she became fluent in French and Italian. In 1836, she married Lord John Scott, the only brother of the Duke of Buccleuch. They lived together at Cowdenknowes (1836–39), Newton Don (until 1841), and Stichill (until 1853). After her husband's death in 1859, most of her remaining life was spent at the family home of Spottiswoode.

153 *We've Lookit for Ye Lang*

WE've lookit for ye lang, Prince Charlie,
Thro' years o' disgrace and pain;
But the heather will bloom, and the thistle-top wave—
There's a Stuart in Scotland again!

Argyle's gi'en ower the crown and sceptre
(The fause traitor dog),
But he couldna' mak a King o' Scotland
Out o' a German Hog!

They've brak into our King's palace,
They've ripit his treasury,
An' he's climbed into our King's throne, who was
A bit crofter in Germanie!

He's ta'en place o' our lords and nobles,
As tho' he were head o' the state;
An' he's daured to ca' us his subjects—
My Faith! but he isna blate!

He may head us, an' he may hang us,
He may chain us within stane wa's;
But he canna gar a man in Scotland
Stir a fit in his beggarly cause!

Ae glance o' your eagle e'e,
Ae wave o' your yellow hair,
Ae tone o' your princely voice
Will lead us—we need nae mair.

There's a road thro' your foes, Prince Charlie!
A way that is sure an' fleet,
We'll ding down the usurpin' carlie,
An' fling him beneath your feet!

(composed 1873 *1904*)

MARY ANN BROWNE
(1812–1844)

BORN in Maidenhead, Berkshire, Mary Anne Browne spent much of her adult life in Ireland. It has proved difficult to establish many details about her life and career. In 1842, she married James Gray (a nephew of the Scottish writer, James Hogg), and they settled in Cork. Her poetry frequently appeared in the *Dublin University Magazine* from 1839 onwards. Her volumes of poetry include *Mont Blanc, and Other Poems* (1827), *Ada, and Other Poems* (1828), *The Coronal* (1833), *The Birth-day Gift* (1834), and *Ignatia, and Other Poems* (1838).

154 *Noon by the Sea Side*

QUIET is the broad Ocean—wide between
My footsteps and his ebbing tides, the sand
Lies damp, and glittering with dark wreaths of weed,
And little yeasty flakes of palest foam
Amidst them—disappearing in the glare
Of the hot sun, or scattered on the sand,
As some light, wanton breath of air awakes
A moment, then is still in sleep again.
Far off, beyond the line of yellow sand,
Lie the dark group of vessels, with their sails
Spread, ready to take prisoner the first wind
That, with the rising tide, shall come to bear
Them safe to harbour. In those vessels, now
All is at rest;—the seaman on the deck,
Whose heart leaped joyfully at thought of home,
Listlessly leans against the tapering mast,
Now gazing up towards the hot blue sky,
Marking the progress of the stately sun,
Now looking to the shadowy line of shore,
And with a quickened pulse again to heaven.
Yes—when the sun shall drop in yonder west,
The evening tide, and cool, fresh wind shall bring
In triumph to their homes, the weary crew.
How the sea glitters! as if all night's stars,
Driven from the heavens by the triumphant sun,
Had laid them there to sleep with open eyes,
To win the gaze of wanderers like me,
Down from the full proud blaze of day to them.

Quiet is all the shore—the fisher goes
Lazily on with his unladen creel,
Home from the town, marking the heavy sand
With slow, deep footsteps. Here a merry boy

Hath gathered up a heap of shining shells,
And builded him a fairy grotto, thatched
With dripping sea-weed; but o'erwearied now,
He hath stretched him on the sand beside his task,
Not yet quite finished; still one little hand
Is grasping the pink shells, and one is laid
Behind his head, its pillow; sleep hath come
And wooed him to be her's, and watches him,
Like an invisible spirit; the hot sunshine
Falls on his brow, but wakes him not. I gaze,
But I'll not wake him—the deep, even breath
Tells of the slumber of a heart unstilled
By aught save weariness of spirit—farewell!
Sleep, child! I would not wake thee for a world,
For few such slumbers more on earth are thine;
So beautiful, so peaceful, and so pure!

(1833)

155 *'My Baby! My Baby! They've Told Me He is Dead'*

My baby! my baby! They've told me he is dead;
That they've ta'en him to the church-yard, and the funeral rite is said;
They have told me that his blue eyes have closed in their last sleep,
That his lips are lying silent there, and worms may o'er them creep;
My baby! my baby! and then to comfort me,
They say 't is gone away to rest, where sorrow cannot be!
I heed not, I care not, lay ashes on my head;
Let me lie down in silence too, mine only child is dead!

Who dared to speak of comfort? I tell thee, he is gone,
And I shall never see him more, my dear, my precious one;
I tell thee that these arms have clasped his young limbs o'er and o'er,
And I tell thee that these empty arms shall never clasp him more.
Who art thou, with solemn brow, who wouldst whisper words of peace?
They fall on me like dew on rocks, I pray, I pray thee, cease!
Thou never wast a mother, or thou never couldst have said,
There is comfort for a mother, whose only babe is dead!

Oh let me speak of sorrow, and nurture it with tears;
Let me think of all the hope with which I looked to future years;
Let me number up the treasures that in him were stored for me,
And try to find the bound of this my burning agony;
Thus weave around my spirit, o'erwearied with its task,

A hollow cloud of comfort, a mocking, specious mask;
Till my soul, awakening with a start, recoileth in its dread,
As again it echoeth the words, 'My child, my child is dead!'

(1834)

SARAH STICKNEY ELLIS
(1812–1872)

SARAH STICKNEY (later Stickney Ellis) was born in Holderness, Yorkshire, the daughter of Quakers, William Stickney, a farmer, and Esther Richardson Stickney. She later became a member of the Congregational Church and married William Ellis, a missionary who worked in the South Sea Islands and Madagascar, in 1837. Before her marriage, she became well known for *The Poetry of Life* (1835), on the nature of poetry, and then went on to publish three volumes of poetry: *The Sons of the Soil* (1840); *The Island Queen* (1846); and *Janet: One of Many* (1862). She also befriended the poets, Mary Howitt and Mary Sewell. In addition, she wrote novels, expressing a firm belief in the moral efficacy of fiction in the Preface to the first of these, *Pictures of Private Life* (1833–37), and published *The Beautiful in Nature and Art* in 1866. However, her reputation was mostly built upon her highly popular conduct manuals for middle-class women (1839–43), beginning with the much reprinted *The Women of England.* Along with her promotion of temperance, she was concerned with the education of both middle- and working-class women, setting up a school, Rawdon House, in 1845, and teaching there for many years. She contracted her husband's fatal cold and died very shortly after him in Hoddesdon, Hertfordshire.

156 *from* The Island Queen, *I*

[*This poem is about the plight of the Queen of Tahiti and implicitly contrasts her fate with that of Queen Victoria. Eds.*]

WORK? There are millions working at the loom,
Mere tools of labour, thoughtless of their doom;
Thousands, who, every day when light begins,
Go forth and spend their lives in shaping pins;
And thousands more, whose utmost range of skill,
A brooch, a button, or a bead can fill.
We blame them not, nor grudge their scanty fare,
The sole reward of all their toil and care;
Still less despise, for in the eternal plan
'Tis moral worth alone ennobles man.
He who can stand where strong temptations plead,
Where famine points the hungry to his need;
He who can keep, by every friend bereft,
His heart from envy, and his hand from theft;
He who, oppressed, seeks not the oppressor's spoil,
But toils to live, and yet must starve and toil;

He who can meet his famished babes at night,
Nor turn appalled and sick'ning from the sight,
To snatch and wield rebellion's fiery brand—
The only weapon in the poor man's hand;
He is the hero, and our pride should be
To swell the fame of victories such as he
Wins every hour—unseen—unheard of—lost—
And least remembered in our country's boast.

(1846)

157 *from* Janet: One of Many

They met; for there was none to interfere.
  A widowed mother now was Janet's all;
And small her influence, by word, or tear,
  That wayward child from folly to recall.

They met; the student half forgot his books,
  Forgot the future in the present joy;
And gazing oft on Janet's varying looks,
  He almost wished himself a peasant boy.

This was the life then—empty all beside!
  The *real* life which all men must fulfil,
When good and evil ask them to decide,
  And they must answer with unflinching will.

He took his stand—*he* chose his portion, when,
With fond caress, he vowed to meet again.
Enough; it is a tale of common shame,
Of guilt, and tears, and woe, and mutual blame.

But not of mutual suffering. He went forth,
A man of learning and a man of worth.
So the world called him; and he questioned not,
For soon—too soon—are sins like his forgot.

He was not mean in giving. Maxwell gave
Enough in gold from present want to save.
The weeping mother took the sordid fee,
And promised all he asked her—secrecy.
She knew too well what misery was in store;
But, weak in purpose, only wept the more.

On Janet's part there had been little love,
Maxwell was not the man her heart to move.
It was a novelty, and woke her pride
To have him fond and flattering by her side.

And even now, the thought that he was gone
Brought less of pain, than to be left alone.
She did not like the cold dull blank that came
Around her like a frost; still less the blame.
For neighbours mocked, and said they always knew
He meant no good, and now their words were true.
And so, from many clouds, the dark days grew.

. . . .

[*Janet's life as a prostitute accounts for the coldness of Lady Ellen's husband. Eds.*]

The Lady Ellen sits alone,
She knows not where her lord is gone;
She will not ask, for changed is now
The very aspect of his brow,
That used to look so kind and true,
So bold, and yet so tender too.
Alone she waits his late return,
Oft trims her fire, and makes it burn
With fitful blaze, again to die;
Too like her own sad destiny.

Alone, she waits through half the night;
Alone, while stars are shining bright;
While all the world around her sleeps;
And no one sees her, if she weeps.
Alone, when skies are overcast,
She heeds not storm, nor raging blast;
Save as they sometimes wake a fear,
Lest when he comes she may not hear.

Ah! where is now that lady's pride,
Since flowed her life with backward tide?
And where is now the haughty brow,
And where the look exulting now,
That told of treasure prized too much;
Of bliss no human power might touch;
Of certain joys for years to come,
All safely garnered in her home?

Behold her then, with drooping head,
Her careless tresses loosely spread,
Her hand beneath her marble cheek,
Her lips, that scarce have power to speak,
Just breathing forth this murmuring strain,
So often sung, and sung in vain.

ELLEN'S SONG

They tell of cold and hunger,
  And the cry for food and fire;
But I know a want that is stronger.
  A more intense desire.
'Tis not for the morning breaking,
  Nor the song of summer birds;
But, oh! when the heart is aching
  For a few kind words!

'Tis not when the wintry shadows
  Lie dark upon the ground;
For the joy of purple meadows,
  Nor the streamlet's summer sound.
'Tis not for the spring returning,
  Nor the song of early birds;
But, oh! when the heart is yearning
  For a few kind words.

. . . . .

The girl is dying. Many die like her—
Uncared for, in their misery and despair,
A fevered flush burns in her hollow cheek,
Her flashing eyes a tale of frenzy speak;
While fitful laughter, sadder far than tears,
Rings out the knell of worse than wasted years.

The girl is dying; but she must be made
To look her best, ere falls the night of shade.
The painted victim, for a few more hours,
Must smile. The sacrifice, adorned with flowers,
Go forth again upon her downward way—
A curse by night, a shadow through the day.

The girl is dying; but that voice so sweet
They cannot spare, where light companions meet.
So, bent on pleasure for the passing hour,
A deeper draught into her cup they pour,
And half with flattering words, and half in scorn,
They cheer her on—poor jaded thing—till worn
With faint resistance she at length complies,
And sings a low, sad song, while tears are in her eyes.

JANET'S SONG

Happy man, to die and leave me!
  Father, father!
Glad I am I did not grieve thee,
  Death I would have welcomed rather.

Glad I am thou canst not hear me—
  Lover, lover!
Only once thou shouldst come near me,
  When the pale, dead face they cover.

But to thee my heart is crying—
  Mother, mother!
Just to lay my head in dying,
  On thy bosom, and no other.

'That is no song,' the gay companions cry;
'Who wants to hear of dying, or to die?'
Yet something strikes them strange in Janet's strain,
And, half afraid, they turn and look again.

For who, since first she came, has ever heard
Of home or friends, from her sad lips a word?
Outcast she might have been, with heart of stone;
A parent's sheltering roof might ne'er have known;
Still less have ever hushed a babe to rest,
Or stilled its cry upon that weary breast.
Nay, some have said she loathes the very touch
Of infant hands; and once was seen to clutch,
As if in hate, a little hand away,
That round her neck in gentle sport would play.
But greater still the wonder of that throng,
That thoughts of love should blend with Janet's song.
For never yet, in moments sad or gay,
Has love been known the burden of her lay.

What ails the girl? She seems bewildered, crazed—
See how she sits and stares, with eye-balls glazed!
As if she saw some distant world, unseen
By those around, where once her life had been.
And still her eyes are glistening—strange, and bright—
And still she laughs—oh, sickening sound and sight!
While half unconsciously she sings again;
Her hands pressed on her heart, with eager strain,
As if to keep the fluttering mischief there,
From its last throb of anguish and despair.

(1862)

ANN HAWKSHAW
(1813–1885)

VERY little is known about Ann Jackson's (later Hawkshaw's) life. She was born in Green Hamerton, Yorkshire, the daughter of the Revd James Jackson. In 1835 she married Sir John Hawkshaw (knighted in 1873), a railway engineer, who is said to have been the first person to have proposed a practical scheme for the Channel Tunnel. He was known to the circle associated with Elizabeth Gaskell, and Ann Hawkshaw is mentioned by Samuel Bamford, the Manchester working-class poet and radical, in one of the Prefaces to his poems (1843). Ann Hawkshaw may have been an Unitarian and probably lived for some time in Lancashire, but died in London.

Her first book of poetry, *Dionysius the Areopagite, with Other Poems*, was published in 1842. *Poems for my Children* (1847) and *Sonnets on Anglo-Saxon History* (1854) followed. She was best known for the children's poetry that she wrote under the name of 'Aunt Effie', whose two books of nursery rhymes were brought out in 1852 and 1854.

158 *The Mother to Her Starving Child*

OH! sleep; I dread to see those eyes
  To mine in silent grief appealing;
Sleep, and I will not breathe a sigh,
  Though down my cheeks the tears are stealing;
My breaking heart be still awhile,
He sleeps, and I may almost smile.

I might have born it if disease
  Had changed thee thus, and only wept,
As others oft have wept before,
  And in my heart thy memory kept,
And treasured there, like parting token,
Each lisped word that thou had'st spoken;
I should have dreamed of thee by night,
A blessed thing with wings of light;
I should have thought of thee by day,
And all that thou wouldst do or say;
I should have heard the very tone
  Of thy soft voice in every sound,
Then wept to know myself alone,
  And thou beneath the church yard ground:
But they had only been such tears
As memory keeps for by-gone years,
Softening the heart like summer's showers,
That bend, but do not break its flowers.

But now, my tears for thee will fall
  Like burning drops to scorch my heart;

Fancy nor memory e'er recall,
My child, why, how, we part.
There was a sound, long years ago,
By Rachael's grave,—a voice was heard
In Ramah,—'twas a cry of woe
From mothers' hearts to madness stirred;
A sorrow that refused relief,
And such, ay such, will be my grief!

(1842)

159 *Why Am I a Slave?*

One poor wretch died here (Isle of France) broken hearted, constantly exclaiming, 'Why am I a Slave?'

Bennet and Tyerman's Voyage Round the World

WHY do I bear that cursed name?
Why, why am I a slave?
Why doomed to drag a wretched life
In sorrow to the grave?
Born 'mid the mountain solitudes,
And as the lion free,
Who had a right to bind these limbs
And make a slave of me?

I looked—there stood the white man's home,
'Mid pleasant founts and flowers,
'Mid waving woods and waters clear,
Green vines and rosy bowers;
It had an air of loveliness
That suited not despair—
I turned away, for well I knew
That happy hearts were there.

I knew that happy hearts were there,
For voices full of glee
Came on the air, and from their tone
I knew that they were free;
Unlike the low faint murmuring sound,
That marks the wretched slave,
Words wrung from misery's quivering lips,
That sound as from the grave.

I turned—there stood my lonely hut,
I call it not my home,
For no beloved face is there,

And no familiar form,
No voice to break its solitude,
And none to soothe the woe
Of him who was but born to sigh,
Whose tears must ever flow.

Why does the rose bestrew his path,
And mine the pricking thorn?
Why was the white man born to smile,
And I to sigh and mourn?
I know not, only this I know,
Till in the silent grave
There is no hope, no joy for me,
I am a slave—a slave!

(1842)

GRACE AGUILAR
(1816–1847)

DESCENDED from a Sephardi family that retained oral traditions from both Spain and Portugal, Grace Aguilar was born and raised in Hackney, East London. Her father, Emanuel Aguilar, belonged to a family of merchants. Grace, the eldest of his three children, was brought up in a strictly observant religious household. Owing to her father's ill-health, Aguilar moved to Devon in 1828, and it was in this rural environment that she began to write the poems collected in *The Magic Wreath* (1835). Throughout this period of her life, Aguilar found herself defending her religious heritage in an overwhelmingly Christian society, and her epistolary work, *The Jewish Faith* (1846), features a young Jewish girl writing about her own confrontation with alien Christian beliefs.

Although Aguilar counted among the most prolific and widely-read of Anglo-Jewish writers in the nineteenth century, her work was frequently criticized for its tendency to present tenets of Judaism in language drawn from Christian texts. This is particularly true of the prose work, *The Spirit of Judaism*, published in 1842. Her biographer, Beth-Zion Lask Abrahams, observes: 'Her Jewish Protestantism, if one might call it that, led her sometimes to oppose the Bible to the traditions of the Rabbis and minimize the role of the Rabbis in the development and spirituality of Judaism'.

During the course of her brief life, Aguilar placed numerous stories and poems in album books and periodicals, including *The Belle Assemblée*, *The Keepsake*, and *The Ladies' Magazine*. Many of her most popular works were not related to specifically Jewish topics. *Home Influence: A Tale for Mothers and Daughters* came out in 1847, and by 1869 it had reached twenty-four editions. Two full-length works of fiction were published posthumously, *The Vale of Cedars* (1850), on the Spanish Inquisition, and *The Days of Bruce: A Story of Scottish History* (1852).

In 1847, Aguilar became seriously ill, and that summer she left England in search of a cure at a German spa. Three months later, she died, and was buried at the Jewish cemetery at Frankfurt. Eight volumes of her collected works were edited by her mother, Sarah Aguilar; these appeared in 1861.

160 *The Vision of Jerusalem*

WHILE LISTENING TO A BEAUTIFUL ORGAN IN ONE OF THE GENTILE SHRINES

I saw thee, oh my fatherland, my beautiful, my own!
As if thy God had raised thee from the dust where thou art strewn,
His glory cast around thee, and thy children bound to Him,
In links so brightly woven, no sin their light could dim.

Methought the cymbals' sacred sound came softly on my ear,
The timbrel, and the psaltery, and the harp's full notes were near;
And thousand voices chaunted, His glory to upraise,
More heavenly and thrillingly than e'en in David's days.

Methought the sons of Levi were in holy garments there,
Th' anointed one upon his throne, in holiness so fair,
That all who gazed on him might feel the promise be fulfill'd.
And sin, and all her baleful train, now he had come, were still'd.

And thousands of my people throng'd the pure and holy fane,
The curse removed from every brow, ne'er more to come again;
Th' Almighty hand from each, from all, had ta'en the scorching
brand,
And Israel, forgiven, knelt within our own bright band!

My country! oh my country! was my soul enrapt in thee
One passing moment, that mine eyes might all thy glory see?
What magic power upheld me there?—alas! alas! it past,
And darkness o'er my aspiring soul the heavy present cast.

I stood ALONE 'mid thronging crowds who fill'd that stranger shrine
For there were none who kept the faith I held so dearly mine:
An exile felt I, in that house, from Israel's native sod,—
An exile yearning for my *house*,—yet loved still by my God.

No exile from His love! No, no; though captive I may be,
And I must weep whene'er I think, my fatherland, on thee!
Jerusalem! my beautiful! my own! I feel thee still,
Though for our sins thy tainted sod the Moslem strangers fill.

Oh! that thy children all would feel what our sins have done.
And by our every action prove such guilt the exiles shun,
Until they seek their God in prayer, oh! will He turn to them,
And raise thee once again in life, my own Jerusalem!

'If they their own iniquity in humbleness confess,
And all their fathers' trespasses,—nor seek to make them less;[1]
If they my judgements say are right, and penintently own
They reap the chastisment of sin, whose seeds long years have sown:[2]

Then will I all my vows recall, and from them take my hand,
My covenant remember, and have mercy on their land'.[3]
So spake the Lord in boundless love to Israel His son;[4]
But can we, dare we say, these things we *do*, or we *have* done?

Alas, my country! thou must yet deserted rest and lone,
Thy glory, loveliness and life, a Father's gifts, are flown!
Oh that my prayers could raise thee radiant from the sod,
And turn from Judah's exiled sons their God's avenging rod!

And like an oak thou standest, of leaves and branches shorn;[5]
And we are like the wither'd leaves by autumn tempests torn
From parent stems, and scatter'd wide o'er hill, and vale, and sea,
And known as Judah's ingrate race wherever we may be.

Oh! blessed was that vision'd light that flash'd before mine eye;
But, oh, the quick awakening check'd my soul's ecstatic sigh!
Yet still, still wilt thou rise again, my beautiful, my home,
Our God will bring thy children back, ne'er, ne'er again to roam!

(1844)

CHARLOTTE BRONTË
(1816–1855)

CHARLOTTE BRONTË was the only one of the three literary Brontë sisters to be very successful in the nineteenth century. One of six children, she was deeply affected by the deaths of her two elder sisters, Elizabeth and Maria, in 1825. Charlotte Brontë had been born in Thornton, in the parish of Bradford, but from 1820 was brought up in Haworth parsonage, Yorkshire, where her father, Patrick Brontë, became curate. In 1821 her mother, Maria (née Branwell) died, leaving an aunt to supervise the household. Charlotte Brontë was formally educated at Cowan Bridge (1824–5), and then, from 1831, at Roehead, to where she was to return as an assistant teacher in 1835. After a few years back in Haworth, where she was taught by her father, the family's financial problems obliged her to become a governess in 1839 and 1841. Intent upon setting up her own school, she and her sister Emily gained further tuition at the Pensionnat Heger in Brussels in 1842. She was to marry Arthur Bell Nichols in 1854.

As early as 1826, she and her brother, Branwell Brontë, had begun to compose stories about a fictitious realm and this was to evolve, for Charlotte, into her 'Angria' tales (first published only in 1933). Her later discovery of some of

[1] Leviticus 36: 40. [2] Leviticus 36: 41. [3] Leviticus 36: 42, 45.
[4] Exodus 4: 22–23. [5] Isaiah 1: 29–30; 6: 13.

Emily Brontë's early manuscript poems suggested to her the possibility of co-publishing some of the poems that all three sisters had, in fact, been writing. *Poems by Currer, Ellis and Acton Bell* appeared, under pseudonyms, in 1846. The book was barely noticed. However, *The Poems of Charlotte Brontë* were published in 1882 and *The Complete Poems of Charlotte Brontë* in 1923.

1846 was also the year in which the three sisters submitted their first novels for publication, but Charlotte Brontë's *The Professor: a Tale* was rejected. Encouraged by the publishers to try again, *Jane Eyre: An Autobiography* came out in the October of 1847, again signed 'Currer Bell', and proved an immediate success. In 1850 she edited a volume which comprised a republication of Emily Brontë's *Wuthering Heights* and Anne Brontë's *Agnes Grey* and a further selection from their poetry. None of Charlotte Brontë's later novels—*Shirley: A Tale* (1849), *Villette* (1853) and the postponed *The Professor: A Tale* (1857)—were to create quite the same impact as her first, though each was well received. Her reputation was further enhanced by the publication of her friend, Elizabeth Gaskell's *The Life of Charlotte Brontë* in 1857.

161 *The Wife's Will*

SIT still—a word—a breath may break
(As light airs stir a sleeping lake,)
The glassy calm that soothes my woes,
The sweet, the deep, the full repose.
O leave me not! for ever be
Thus, more than life itself to me!

Yes, close beside thee, let me kneel—
Give me thy hand that I may feel
The friend so true—so tried—so dear,
My heart's own chosen—indeed is near;
And check me not—this hour divine
Belongs to me—is fully mine.

'Tis thy own hearth thou sitt'st beside,
After long absence—wandering wide;
'Tis thy own wife reads in thine eyes,
A promise clear of stormless skies,
For faith and true love light the rays,
Which shine responsive to her gaze.

Aye,—well that single tear may fall
Ten thousand might mine eyes recall,
Which from their lids, ran blinding fast,
In hours of grief, yet scarcely past,
Well may'st thou speak of love to me;
For, oh! most truly—I love thee!

Yet smile—for we are happy now.
Whence, then, that sadness on thy brow?
What say'st thou? 'We must once again,
Ere long, be severed by the main?'
I knew not this—I deemed no more,
Thy step would err from Britain's shore.

'Duty commands?' 'Tis true—'tis just;
Thy slightest word I wholly trust,
Nor by request, nor faintest sigh
Would I, to turn thy purpose, try;
But, William—hear my solemn vow—
Hear and confirm!—with thee I go.

'Distance and suffering,' did'st thou say?
'Danger by night, and toil by day?'
Oh, idle words, and vain are these;
Hear me! I cross with thee the seas.
Such risk as thou must meet and dare,
I—thy true wife—will duly share.

Passive, at home, I will not pine;
Thy toils—thy perils, shall be mine;
Grant this—and be hereafter paid
By a warm heart's devoted aid:
'Tis granted—with that yielding kiss,
Entered my soul unmingled bliss.

Thanks, William—thanks! thy love has joy,
Pure—undefiled with base alloy;
'Tis not a passion, false and blind,
Inspires, enchains, absorbs my mind;
Worthy, I feel, art thou to be
Loved with my perfect energy.

This evening, now, shall sweetly flow,
Lit by our clear fire's happy glow;
And parting's peace-embittering fear,
Is warned, our hearts to come not near;
For fate admits my soul's decree,
In bliss or bale—to go with thee!

(1846)

162 *The Teacher's Monologue*

THE room is quiet, thoughts alone
People its mute tranquillity;
The yoke put off, the long task done,—
I am, as it is bliss to be,
Still and untroubled. Now, I see,
For the first time, how soft the day
O'er waveless water, stirless tree,
Silent and sunny, wings its way.
Now, as I watch that distant hill,
So faint, so blue, so far removed,
Sweet dreams of home my heart may fill,
That home where I am known and loved:
It lies beyond; yon azure brow
Parts me from all Earth holds for me;
And, morn and eve, my yearnings flow
Thitherward tending, changelessly.
My happiest hours, aye! all the time,
I love to keep in memory,
Lapsed among moors, ere life's first prime
Decayed to dark anxiety.

Sometimes, I think a narrow heart
Makes me thus mourn those far away,
And keeps my love so far apart
From friends and friendships of to-day;
Sometimes, I think 'tis but a dream
I treasure up so jealously,
All the sweet thoughts I live on seem
To vanish into vacancy:
And then, this strange, coarse world around
Seems all that's palpable and true;
And every sight, and every sound,
Combines my spirit to subdue
To aching grief, so void and lone
Is Life and Earth—so worse than vain,
The hopes that, in my own heart sown,
And cherished by such sun and rain
As Joy and transient Sorrow shed,
Have ripened to a harvest there:
Alas! methinks I hear it said,
'Thy golden sheaves are empty air.'

All fades away; my very home
I think will soon be desolate;
I hear, at times, a warning come
Of bitter partings at its gate;

And, if I should return and see
The hearth-fire quenched, the vacant chair;
And hear it whispered mournfully,
That farewells have been spoken there,
What shall I do, and whither turn?
Where look for peace? When cease to mourn?

* * *

'Tis not the air I wished to play,
  The strain I wished to sing;
My wilful spirit slipped away
  And struck another string.
I neither wanted smile nor tear,
  Bright joy nor bitter woe,
But just a song that sweet and clear,
  Though haply sad, might flow.

A quiet song, to solace me
  When sleep refused to come;
A strain to chase despondency,
  When sorrowful for home.
In vain I try; I cannot sing;
  All feels so cold and dead;
No wild distress, no gushing spring
  Of tears in anguish shed;

But all the impatient gloom of one
  Who waits a distant day,
When, some great task of suffering done,
  Repose shall toil repay.
For youth departs, and pleasure flies,
  And life consumes away,
And youth's rejoicing ardour dies
  Beneath this drear delay;

And Patience, weary with her yoke,
  Is yielding to despair,
And Health's elastic spring is broke
  Beneath the strain of care.
Life will be gone ere I have lived;
  Where now is Life's first prime?
I've worked and studied, longed and grieved,
  Through all that rosy time.

To toil, to think, to long, to grieve,—
  Is such my future fate?
The morn was dreary, must the eve
  Be also desolate?
Well, such a life at least makes Death

A welcome, wished-for friend;
Then, aid me, Reason, Patience, Faith,
To suffer to the end!

(1846)

163 *Evening Solace*

THE human heart has hidden treasures,
In secret kept, in silence sealed;—
The thoughts, the hopes, the dreams, the pleasures,
Whose charms were broken if revealed.
And days may pass in gay confusion,
And nights in rosy riot fly,
While, lost in Fame's or Wealth's illusion,
The memory of the Past may die.

But, there are hours of lonely musing,
Such as in evening silence come,
When, soft as birds their pinions closing,
The heart's best feelings gather home.
Then in our souls there seems to languish
A tender grief that is not woe;
And thoughts that once wrung groans of anguish,
Now cause but some mild tears to flow.

And feelings, once as strong as passions,
Float softly back—a faded dream;
Our own sharp griefs and wild sensations,
The tale of others' sufferings seem.
Oh! when the heart is freshly bleeding,
How longs it for that time to be,
When, through the mist of years receding,
Its woes but live in reverie!

And it can dwell on moonlight glimmer,
On evening shade and loneliness;
And, while the sky grows dim and dimmer,
Feel no untold and strange distress—
Only a deeper impulse given
By lonely hour and darkened room,
To solemn thoughts that soar to heaven,
Seeking a life and world to come.

(1846)

FRANCES BROWNE
(1816–1879)

BORN into a Presbyterian family in Stranorlar, County Donegal, Frances Browne was to become known as 'The Blind Poetess of Ulster', having lost her eyesight through contracting smallpox at only eighteen months old. Her blindness, combined with the poverty of her large family (she was the seventh of twelve children), led to her being educated only by listening to her brothers and sisters. However, she was to earn her living through writing. Much of her literary life was spent away from Ireland, as she lived in Edinburgh from 1847 and then moved to London in 1852.

Her first poem was published in the *Irish Penny Journal* in 1840, and she then began to contribute to many other journals, including the *Athenaeum*, from 1841. Many of these poems were then reproduced in her two volumes of poetry: *The Star of Atteghei: The Vision of Schwartz* (1844), for which she was awarded an annual pension of £20, and *Lyrics and Miscellaneous Poems* (1848). Although these poems were well received, it was for her collection of children's fairy stories that she was to remain best known: *Granny's Wonderful Chair* (1857). She wrote many other tales and novels, as well as, in 1861, an autobiography.

164 *Words*

WORDS—household words!—that linger on
 When household love is past,
And keep our childhood's tender tone
 About us, to the last;—
Like pleasant streams that murmur yet
 Of valleys far and green,
And make the pilgrim's heart forget
 The deserts spread between:
For sin and sorrow have no part
In that bright Ennoe of the heart.

Words—words of hope!—oh! long believed,
 As oracles of old,
When stars of promise have deceived,
 And beacon-fires grown cold!
Though still, upon time's stormy steeps,
 Such sounds are faint and few,
Yet oft from cold and stranger lips
 Hath fallen that blessed dew,—
That, like the rock-kept rain, remained
When many a sweeter fount was drained.

Words—words of love!—the ocean-pearl
  May slumber far and deep,
Though tempests wake or breezes curl
  The wave that hides its sleep;
So, deep in memory's hidden cells,
  The winds of life pass o'er
Those treasured words, whose music swells,
  Perchance, for us no more,—
But, Memnon-like, its echoes fill
The early-ruined temples, still.

Words—mighty words!—we see your power,
  Where'er the sun looks down
On forest-tree or fortress-tower,
  Or desert bare and brown;—
The power that, by old Tiber's wave,
  Could rouse the Roman ire,
And wake to war the Indian brave,
  Beside his council fire,—
Or call the flower of Gothic shields,
To find their rest in Syrian fields.

That mystic power is with us, still,—
  To wake the waves of strife,
Or breathe in tones of love, that thrill
  The sweetest chords of life:—
But if from mortal lips be poured
  Such spells of wondrous might,
What glorious wisdom filled *His* word
  Who spake—and there was light!
Well may that mighty Word restore
The morning of the world once more!

(1844)

165 *The Last Friends*

Come to my country, but not with the hope
  That brighten'd my youth like the cloud-lighting bow—
For the vigour of soul that seem'd mighty to cope
  With Time and with Fortune, hath fled from me now;
And Love, that illumined my wanderings of yore,
  Hath perish'd, and left but a weary regret
For the star that can rise on my midnight no more;—
  But the hills of my country, they welcome me yet!

The hue of their verdure was fresh with me still,
  When my path was afar by the Tanais' lone track;
From the wide-spreading deserts and ruins, that fill
  The lands of old story, they summon'd me back;
They rose on my dreams through the shades of the West,
  They breath'd upon sands which the dew never wet,
For the echoes were hush'd in the home I loved best—
  But I knew that the mountains would welcome me yet!

The dust of my kindred is scatter'd afar—
  They lie in the desert, the wild, and the wave;
For, serving the strangers through wandering and war,
  The Isle of their memory could grant them no grave.
And I—I return with the memory of years,
  Whose hope rose so high, though in sorrow it set;
They have left on my soul but the trace of their tears—
  But our mountains remember their promises yet!

Oh! where are the brave hearts that bounded of old,
  And where are the faces my childhood hath seen?
For fair brows are furrow'd, and hearts have grown cold—
  But our streams are still bright, and our hills are still green;
Aye, green as they rose to the eyes of my youth,
  When, brothers in heart, in their shadows we met—
For the hills have no memory of sorrow or death,
  And their summits are sacred to liberty yet!

Like ocean retiring, the morning mists now
  Roll back from the mountains that girdle our land,
And sunlight encircles each heath-cover'd brow,
  For which Time hath no furrow and tyrants no brand:
Oh! thus let it be with the hearts of the Isle—
  Efface the dark seal that oppression hath set;
Give back the lost glory again to the soil,
  For the hills of my country remember it yet![1]

(1848)

[1] One of the United Irishmen, who lately returned to his country after many years of exile, being asked what had induced him to revisit Ireland when all his friends were gone, answered—'I came back to see the mountains.'

ELIZA COOK
(1818–1889)

Eliza Cook was a writer of predominantly sentimental verse on domestic themes, whose prose work expressed her feminist arguments. She was the youngest of eleven children and was born in Southwark, later to live for some time in Peckham. Her father, Joseph Cook, was a wealthy merchant and, on his retirement, the family moved to a small farm near Horsham, Sussex. As an adult, she was to dress in masculine clothing and form a very close intimacy with the actress, Charlotte Cushman, to whom she is thought to have sent love sonnets.

Despite her middle-class background, she was entirely self-educated and began writing poetry at the age of fifteen. Her first collection of verses, *Lays of a Wild Harp*, was published two years later (1835). The volume was well received and encouraged her to continue publishing poetry to journals, such as the *New Monthly Magazine*, the *Metropolitan*, and the *Literary Gazette*. From 1836 she began contributing to the *Weekly Dispatch* and was here to publish her most popular of sentimental poems, 'The Old Arm-Chair', about the death of her mother (1837). This was reprinted in her next volume of verses, which was also her most successful: *Melaia and Other Poems* (1838). It contained some satire (including the title poem) and went through many editions. A book of songs in 1850 was followed by her last book of poems, *New Echoes, and Other Poems* (1864).

Between May 1849 and May 1854, she produced a monthly journal, which appealed to a middle-class readership, although its price—1½*d*—also made it accessible to a less wealthy market. Published as *Eliza Cook's Journal*, her writing addressed issues from a feminist perspective, such as the education of girls, women's clothing, and the Property Act for married women. The enormous popularity of the journal was marked by its having outsold even Charles Dickens' *Household Words* and the fact that much of it was reissued in 1860 as *Jottings from My Journal*. Ill-health had forced her to give up the project, and she was seriously debilitated in later years, publishing only one new work, *Diamond Dust* (1865), a book of aphorisms. She was to live off the royalties from her work and a civil list pension of £100 per year, which had been awarded to her in 1863.

166 *Lines to the Queen of England*

Lady, perchance my untaught strain
  May little suit a royal ear;
But I would break my lyre in twain
  Ere aught it yield be insincere.

There's been enough of dulcet tone
  To praise thy charms and greet thy youth;
But I, though standing by thy throne,
  Would proudly dare to sing the truth.

I cannot join the minstrel throng
  Who pour idolatrous pretence;
Because I deem such fulsome song
  Must sadly pall upon thy sense.

Thou art a star, whose leading light
  Must beacon through a stormy way:
Shine out, and, if thou guid'st aright,
  Our hearts will bless the saving ray.

If thou would'st walk a better path
  Than regal steps have chiefly trod,
So sway thy sceptre, that it hath
  Some glorious attributes of God.

Peace, Mercy, Justice, mark *his* reign,
  And these should dwell with all who rule;
Beware! resist the poison bane
  Of tyrant, knave, or courtier fool.

Thou hast been train'd by goodly hand
  To fill thy place of mighty care;
And Heaven forbid that Faction's band
  Should turn our hopes to blank despair.

Lean on thy people, trust their love,
  Thou'lt never find a stronger shield;
The 'toiling herd' will nobly prove
  What warm devotion they can yield.

Remember, much of weal or woe
  To millions rests alone with thee;
Be firm, and let Old England show
  A nation happy, wise, and free.

(*c.*1837 *1838*)

167 *The Old Arm-Chair*

I LOVE it, I love it; and who shall dare
To chide me for loving that old Arm-chair?
I've treasured it long as a sainted prize;
I've bedewed it with tears, and embalmed it with sighs
'Tis bound by a thousand bands to my heart;
Not a tie will break, not a link will start.
Would ye learn the spell?—a mother sat there;
And a sacred thing is that old Arm-chair.

In Childhood's hour I lingered near
The hallowed seat with listening ear;
And gentle words that mother would give;
To fit me to die, and teach me to live.
She told me shame would never betide,
With truth for my creed and God for my guide;
She taught me to lisp my earliest prayer;
As I knelt beside that old Arm-chair.

I sat and watched her many a day,
When her eye grew dim, and her locks were grey:
And I almost worshipped her when she smiled,
And turned from her Bible, to bless her child.
Years rolled on; but the last one sped—
My idol was shattered; my earth-star fled:
I learnt how much the heart can bear,
When I saw her die in that old Arm-chair.

'Tis past, 'tis past, but I gaze on it now
With quivering breath and throbbing brow:
'Twas there she nursed me; 'twas there she died:
And Memory flows with lava tide.
Say it is folly, and deem me weak,
While the scalding drops start down my cheek;
But I love it, I love it; and cannot tear
My soul from a mother's old Arm-chair.

(1837 *1838*)

168 *Oh! Dear to Memory Are Those Hours*

Oh! dear to Memory are those hours
When every pathway led to flowers;
When sticks of peppermint possessed
A sceptre's power o'er the breast,
And heaven was round us while we fed
On rich ambrosial gingerbread.
I bless the days of Infancy,
When stealing from my mother's eye,
Elysian happiness was found
On that celestial field—the ground;
When we were busied, hands and hearts:
In those important things, dirt tarts.
Don't smile; for sapient, full-grown Man
Oft cogitates some mighty plan;
And, spell-bound by the bubble dream,
He labours till he proves the scheme

About as useful and as wise
As manufacturing dirt pies.
For many a change on Folly's bells
Quite equals dust and oyster-shells.

Then shone the meteor rays of Youth;
Eclipsing quite the lamp of Truth;
And precious those bright sunbeams were;
That dried all tears, dispersed all care;
That shed a stream of golden joy,
Without one shadow of alloy:
Oh! ne'er in mercy strive to chase
Such dazzling phantoms from their place
However trifling, mean, or wild,
The deeds may seem of youth or child;
While they still leave untarnished soul,
The iron rod of stern control
Should be but gentle in its sway;
Nor rend the magic veil away.

I doubt if it be kind or wise,
To quench the light in opening eyes:
By preaching fallacy and woe
As all that we can meet below.
I ne'er respect the ready tongue;
That augurs sorrow to the young;
That aptly plays a sibyl's part,
To promise nightshade to the heart.
Let them exult! their laugh and song
Are rarely known to last too long.
Why should we strive with cynic frown
To knock their fairy castles down?
We know that much of pain and strife
Must be the common lot of life:
We know the World *is* dark and rough
But Time betrays that soon enough.

(1838)

169 *The Englishman*

THERE's a land that bears a world-known name,
  Though it is but a little spot;
I say 'tis first on the scroll of Fame,
  And who shall say it is not?
Of the deathless ones who shine and live
  In Arms, in Arts, or Song;

The brightest the whole wide world can give,
  To that little land belong.
'Tis the star of earth, deny it who can;
The island home of an Englishman.

There's a flag that waves o'er every sea,
  No matter when or where;
And to treat that flag as aught but the free
  Is more than the strongest dare.
For the lion-spirits that tread the deck
  Have carried the palm of the brave;
And that flag *may* sink with a shot-torn wreck,
  But never float over a slave;
Its honour is stainless, deny it who can;
And this is the flag of an Englishman.

There's a heart that leaps with burning glow,
  The wronged and the weak to defend;
And strikes as soon for a trampled foe,
  As it does for a soul-bound friend.
It nurtures a deep and honest love;
  It glows with faith and pride;
And yearns with the fondness of a dove,
  To the light of its own fireside.
'Tis a rich, rough gem, deny it who can;
And this is the heart of an Englishman.

The Briton may traverse the pole or the zone,
  And boldly claim his right;
For he calls such a vast domain his own,
  That the sun never sets on his might.
Let the haughty stranger seek to know
  The place of his home and birth;
And a flush will pour from cheek to brow;
  While he tells his native earth.
For a glorious charter, deny it who can,
Is breathed in the words 'I'm an Englishman.'

(1838)

170 *Song of the Red Indian*

OH! why does the white man hang on my path,
  Like the hound on the tiger's track?
Does the flush of my dark skin awaken his wrath!
  Does he covet the bow at my back?
He has rivers and seas where the billow and breeze
  Bear riches for him alone;

And the sons of the wood never plunge in the flood
 That the white man calls his own.
Then why should he covet the streams where none
 But the red-skin dare to swim?
Oh! why should he wrong the hunter one
 Who never did harm to him?

The Father above thought fit to give
 To the white man corn and wine;
There are golden fields where he may live,
 But the forest shades are mine.
The eagle has its place of rest,
 The wild horse where to dwell;
And the Spirit who gave the bird its nest,
 Made me a home as well.
Then back, go back from the red-skin's track,
 For the hunter's eyes grow dim,
To find the white man wrongs the one
 Who never did harm to him.

Oh! why does the pale-face always call
 The red man 'heathen brute'?
He does not bend where the dark knees fall,
 But the tawny lip is mute.
We cast no blame on his creed or name,
 Or his temples, fine and high;
But he mocks at us with a laughing word
 When we worship a star-lit sky.
Yet, white man, what has thy good faith done,
 And where can its mercy be,
If it teach thee to hate the hunter one
 Who never did harm to thee?

We need no book to tell us how
 Our lives shall pass away;
For we see the onward torrent flow,
 And the mighty tree decay.
'Let thy tongue be true and thy heart be brave,'
 Is among the red-skins' lore;
We can bring down the swift wing and dive in the wave,
 And we seek to know no more.
Then back, go back, and let us run
 With strong, unfettered limb;
For why should the white man wrong the one
 Who never did harm to him?

We know there's a hand that has fixed the hill
 And planted the prairie plain;
That can fling the lightnings when it will.

And pour out the torrent rain.
Far away and alone, where the headlong tide
Dashes on with our bold canoe,
We ask and trust that hand to guide
And carry us safely through.
The Great Spirit dwells in the beautiful sun,
And while we kneel in its light,
Who will not own that the hunter one
Has an altar pure and bright?

The painted streak on a warrior's cheek
Appears a wondrous thing;
The white man stares at a wampum belt,
And a plume from the heron's wing.
But the red man wins the panthers' skins
To cover his dauntless form;
While the pale-face hides his breast in a garb
That he takes from the crawling worm.
And your lady fair, with her gems so rare,
Her ruby, gold, and pearl,
Would be as strange to other eyes
As the bone-decked Indian girl.

Then why does the cruel, white man come
With the war-whoop's yelling sound?
Oh! why does he take our wigwam home,
And the jungled hunting-ground?
The wolf-cub has its lair of rest,
The wild horse where to dwell,
And the Spirit who gave the bird its nest
Made me a place as well.
Then back, go back, from the red-skin's track;
For the hunter's eyes grow dim,
To find that the white man wrongs the one
Who never did harm to him.

(1845)

171 *Harvest Song*

I LOVE, I love to see
Bright steel gleam through the land:
'Tis a goodly sight, but it must be
In the reaper's tawny hand.

The helmet and the spear
Are twined with the laurel wreath;
But the trophy is wet with the orphan's tear,
And blood-spots rust beneath.

I love to see the field
  That is moist with purple stain;
But not where bullet, sword, and shield
  Lie strewn with the gory slain.

No, no; 'tis where the sun
  Shoots down his cloudless beams,
'Till rich and bursting juice-drops run
  On the vineyard earth in streams.

My glowing heart beats high
  At the sight of shining gold;
But it is not that which the miser's eye
  Delighteth to behold.

A brighter wealth by far,
  Than the deep mine's yellow vein,
Is seen around in the fair hills crowned
  With sheaves of burnished grain.

Look forth, thou thoughtless one,
  Whose proud knee never bends;
Take thou the bread that's daily spread,
  But think on Him who sends.

Look forth, by toiling men,
  Though little ye possess,—
Be glad that dearth is not on earth
  To make that little less.

Let the song of praise be poured
  In gratitude and joy,
By the rich man with his garners stood
  And the ragged gleaner boy.

The feast that Nature gives
  Is not for one alone;
'Tis shared by the meanest slave that lives
  And the tenant of a throne.

Then glory to the steel
  That shines in the reaper's hand,
And thanks to Him who has blest the seed,
  And crowned the harvest land.

(1845)

EMILY BRONTË
(1818–1848)

EMILY BRONTË'S considerable reputation as a novelist and poet was established only after her death. She was born at Thornton Parsonage, in the parish of Bradford, the fifth child of Patrick Brontë, a curate, and Maria (née Branwell). In 1820 the family moved to Haworth, where the father became perpetual curate. The mother died in the following year and her sister moved into the parsonage to look after the household. Emily Brontë had one brother, Branwell, whose addiction to alcohol and opium led to his death in 1848, and four sisters. Maria and Elizabeth died when still children, leaving her two remaining sisters, Charlotte and Anne, with whom she was first to enter into print. Her formal education was brief. She attended a school at Cowan Bridge until 1825 and another at Roe Head for only three months in 1835. She continued her education at home. Haworth Parsonage was to remain her home for the rest of her life, except for two short interludes. Obliged to earn her living as a governess, she taught for six months at Law Hill, near Halifax (1838–39) and attended the Pensionnat Heger in Brussels, with her sister, Charlotte, as a pupil in 1842.

Emily Brontë had begun writing when she was about 13 years old. She and her sister, Anne, following a practice already established by Branwell and Charlotte Brontë, began to write about an imaginary realm called Gondal in poetry, dialogues, and prose history. Emily Brontë transcribed the best of her poems into notebooks, one being entitled 'Gondal Poems', which she continued to develop throughout her life. Charlotte Brontë's chance discovery of her sister's poems led to the co-publishing, under pseudonyms, of the verses that each sister had been writing: *Poems by Currer, Ellis and Acton Bell* (1846). The book was barely noticed, with only a few reviews marking its existence. Sydney Dobell, writing for the *Athenaeum* (July 1846) considered the poems of 'Ellis Bell' (Emily Brontë) to be the only ones which 'may yet find an audience in the outer world'. Some of her poems were published in the 1850 volume of *Wuthering Heights* and *Agnes Grey*, edited by Charlotte Brontë. However, it was not until 1938 that the *Gondal Poems* were to be published from manuscript, and this was followed by *The Complete Poems of Emily Jane Brontë* in 1923 and 1941.

The manuscripts of the novels, *Wuthering Heights*, Charlotte Brontë's *The Professor* and Anne Brontë's *Agnes Grey* were submitted to publishers in 1846, under their pseudonyms. Emily Brontë's and Anne Brontë's works alone were accepted, but then not until the immediate success of Charlotte Brontë's *Jane Eyre* (1847) had aroused interest in the 'Bells'' work. *Wuthering Heights* (1847) met with consistently hostile criticism, the reviewers condemning it as a gloomy and even diabolical piece of writing. It was only after the novelist's death that critical appreciation of this work began to emerge.

172 *Stars*

AH! why, because the dazzling sun
  Restored our Earth to joy,
Have you departed, every one,
  And left a desert sky?

All through the night, your glorious eyes
  Were gazing down in mine,
And, with a full heart's thankful sighs,
  I blessed that watch divine.

I was at peace, and drank your beams
  As they were life to me;
And revelled in my changeful dreams,
  Like petrel on the sea.

Thought followed thought, star followed star,
  Through boundless regions, on;
While one sweet influence, near and far,
  Thrilled through, and proved us one!

Why did the morning dawn to break
  So great, so pure, a spell;
And scorch with fire, the tranquil cheek,
  Where your cool radiance fell?

Blood-red, he rose, and, arrow-straight,
  His fierce beams struck my brow;
The soul of nature, sprang, elate,
  But *mine* sank sad and low!

My lids closed down, yet through their veil,
  I saw him, blazing, still,
And steep in gold the misty dale,
  And flash upon the hill.

I turned me to the pillow, then,
  To call back night, and see
Your worlds of solemn light, again,
  Throb with my heart, and me!

It would not do—the pillow glowed,
  And glowed both roof and floor;
And birds sang loudly in the wood,
  And fresh winds shook the door;

The curtains waved, the wakened flies
  Were murmuring round my room,
Imprisoned there, till I should rise,
  And give them leave to roam.

Oh, stars, and dreams, and gentle night;
  Oh, night and stars return!
And hide me from the hostile light,
  That does not warm, but burn;

That drains the blood of suffering men;
  Drinks tears, instead of dew;
Let me sleep through his blinding reign,
  And only wake with you!

(1846)

173 *The Philosopher*

[*The entities in this dialogue appear to be Seer (lines 1–14), who quotes the Philosopher's words (lines 7–14); Philosopher (lines 15–26); Seer (lines 27–40); Philosopher (lines 41–56). Eds.*]

'ENOUGH of thought, philosopher!
  Too long hast thou been dreaming
Unlightened, in this chamber drear,
  While summer's sun is beaming!
Space-sweeping soul, what sad refrain
Concludes thy musings once again?

'Oh, for the time when I shall sleep
  Without identity,
  And never care how rain may steep,
  Or snow may cover me!
  No promised heaven, these wild desires,
  Could all, or half fulfil;
  No threatened hell, with quenchless fires,
  Subdue this quenchless will!'

'So said I, and still say the same;
  Still, to my death, will say—
Three gods, within this little frame,
  Are warring night and day;
Heaven could not hold them all, and yet
  They all are held in me;
And must be mine till I forget
  My present entity!
Oh, for the time, when in my breast
  Their struggles will be o'er!
Oh, for the day, when I shall rest,
  And never suffer more!'

'I saw a spirit, standing, man,
  Where thou dost stand—an hour ago,
And round his feet three rivers ran,

Of equal depth, and equal flow—
A golden stream—and one like blood;
And one like sapphire seemed to be;
But, where they joined their triple flood
It tumbled in an inky sea.
The spirit sent his dazzling gaze
Down through that ocean's gloomy night
Then, kindling all, with sudden blaze,
The glad deep sparkled wide and bright—
White as the sun, far, far more fair
Than its divided sources were!'

'And even for that spirit, seer,
I've watched and sought my life-time long;
Sought him in heaven, hell, earth, and air—
An endless search, and always wrong!
Had I but seen his glorious eye
Once light the clouds that wilder me,
I ne'er had raised this coward cry
To cease to think, and cease to be;
I ne'er had called oblivion blest,
Nor, stretching eager hands to death,
Implored to change for senseless rest
This sentient soul, this living breath—
Oh, let me die—that power and will
Their cruel strife may close;
And conquered good, and conquering ill
Be lost in one repose!'

(1846)

174 *Remembrance*

COLD in the earth—and the deep snow piled above thee,
Far, far, removed, cold in the dreary grave!
Have I forgot, my only Love, to love thee,
Severed at last by Time's all-severing wave?

Now, when alone, do my thoughts no longer hover
Over the mountains, on that northern shore,
Resting their wings where heath and fern-leaves cover
Thy noble heart for ever, ever more?

Cold in the earth—and fifteen wild Decembers,
From those brown hills, have melted into spring:
Faithful, indeed, is the spirit that remembers
After such years of change and suffering!

Sweet Love of youth, forgive, if I forget thee,
While the world's tide is bearing me along;
Other desires and other hopes beset me,
Hopes which obscure, but cannot do thee wrong!

No later light has lightened up my heaven,
No second morn has ever shone for me;
All my life's bliss from thy dear life was given,
All my life's bliss is in the grave with thee.

But, when the days of golden dreams had perished,
And even Despair was powerless to destroy;
Then did I learn how existence could be cherished,
Strengthened, and fed without the aid of joy.

Then did I check the tears of useless passion—
Weaned my young soul from yearning after thine;
Sternly denied its burning wish to hasten
Down to that tomb already more than mine.

And, even yet, I dare not let it languish,
Dare not indulge in memory's rapturous pain;
Once drinking deep of that divinest anguish,
How could I seek the empty world again?

(1846)

175 *Song*

THE linnet in the rocky dells,
 The moor-lark in the air,
The bee among the heather bells,
 That hide my lady fair:

The wild deer browse above her breast;
 The wild birds raise their brood;
And they, her smiles of love caressed,
 Have left her solitude!

I ween, that when the grave's dark wall
 Did first her form retain;
They thought their hearts could ne'er recall
 The light of joy again.

They thought the tide of grief would flow
 Unchecked through future years;
But where is all their anguish now,
 And where are all their tears?

Well, let them fight for honour's breath,
  Or pleasure's shade pursue—
The dweller in the land of death
  Is changed and careless too.

And, if their eyes should watch and weep
  Till sorrow's source were dry,
She would not, in her tranquil sleep,
  Return a single sigh!

Blow, west-wind, by the lonely mound,
  And murmur, summer-streams—
There is no need of other sound
  To soothe my lady's dreams.

(1846)

176 *The Prisoner. A Fragment*

In the dungeon-crypts, idly did I stray,
Reckless of the lives wasting there away;
'Draw the ponderous bars! open, Warder stern!'
He dared not say me nay—the hinges harshly turn.

'Our guests are darkly lodged,' I whisper'd, gazing through
The vault, whose grated eye showed heaven more grey than blue;
(This was when glad spring laughed in awaking pride;)
'Aye, darkly lodged enough!' returned my sullen guide.

Then, God forgive my youth; forgive my careless tongue;
I scoffed, as the chill chains on the damp flag-stones rung:
'Confined in triple walls, art thou so much to fear,
That we must bind thee down and clench thy fetters here?'

The captive raised her face, it was as soft and mild
As sculptured marble saint, or slumbering unwean'd child;
It was so soft and mild, it was so sweet and fair,
Pain could not trace a line, nor grief a shadow there!

The captive raised her hand and pressed it to her brow;
'I have been struck,' she said, 'and I am suffering now;
Yet these are little worth, your bolts and irons strong,
And, were they forged in steel, they could not hold me long.'

Hoarse laughed the jailor grim: 'Shall I be won to hear;
Dost think, fond, dreaming wretch, that *I* shall grant thy prayer?
Or, better still, wilt melt my master's heart with groans?
Ah! sooner might the sun thaw down these granite stones.

'My master's voice is low, his aspect bland and kind,
But hard as hardest flint, the soul that lurks behind;
And I am rough and rude, yet not more rough to see
Than is the hidden ghost that has its home in me.'

About her lips there played a smile of almost scorn,
'My friend,' she gently said, 'you have not heard me mourn;
When you my kindred's lives, *my* lost life, can restore,
Then may I weep and sue,—but never, friend, before!

Still, let my tyrants know, I am not doomed to wear
Year after year in gloom, and desolate despair;
A messenger of Hope, comes every night to me,
And offers for short life, eternal liberty.

He comes with western winds, with evening's wandering airs,
With that clear dusk of heaven that brings the thickest stars.
Winds take a pensive tone, and stars a tender fire,
And visions rise, and change, that kill me with desire.

Desire for nothing known in my maturer years,
When Joy grew mad with awe, at counting future tears.
When, if my spirit's sky was full of flashes warm,
I knew not whence they came, from sun, or thunder storm.

But, first, a hush of peace—a soundless calm descends;
The struggle of distress, and fierce impatience ends.
Mute music soothes my breast, unuttered harmony,
That I could never dream, till Earth was lost to me.

Then dawns the Invisible; the Unseen its truth reveals;
My outward sense is gone, my inward essence feels:
Its wings are almost free—its home, its harbour found,
Measuring the gulph, it stoops, and dares the final bound.

Oh, dreadful is the check—intense the agony—
When the ear begins to hear, and the eye begins to see;
When the pulse begins to throb, the brain to think again,
The soul to feel the flesh, and the flesh to feel the chain.

Yet I would lose no sting, would wish no torture less,
The more that anguish racks, the earlier it will bless;
And robed in fires of hell, or bright with heavenly shine,
If it but herald death, the vision is divine!'

She ceased to speak, and we, unanswering, turned to go—
We had no further power to work the captive woe:
Her cheek, her gleaming eye, declared that man had given
A sentence, unapproved, and overruled by Heaven.

(1846)

177 *To Imagination*

WHEN weary with the long day's care,
  And earthly change from pain to pain,
And lost and ready to despair,
  Thy kind voice calls me back again:
Oh, my true friend! I am not lone,
While thou canst speak with such a tone!

So hopeless is the world without;
  The world within I doubly prize;
Thy world, where guile, and hate, and doubt,
  And cold suspicion never rise;
Where thou, and I, and Liberty,
Have undisputed sovereignty.

What matters it, that, all around,
  Danger, and guilt, and darkness lie,
If but within our bosom's bound
  We hold a bright, untroubled sky,
Warm with ten thousand mingled rays
Of suns that know no winter days?

Reason, indeed, may oft complain
  For Nature's sad reality,
And tell the suffering heart, how vain
  Its cherished dreams must always be;
And Truth may rudely trample down
The flowers of Fancy, newly-blown:

But, thou art ever there, to bring
  The hovering vision back, and breathe
New glories o'er the blighted spring,
  And call a lovelier Life from Death,
And whisper, with a voice divine,
Of real worlds, as bright as thine.

I trust not to thy phantom bliss,
  Yet, still, in evening's quiet hour,
With never-failing thankfulness,
  I welcome thee, Benignant Power;
Sure solacer of human cares,
And sweeter hope, when hope despairs!

(1846)

178 *Sympathy*

THERE should be no despair for you
While nightly stars are burning;
While evening pours its silent dew
And sunshine gilds the morning.
There should be no despair—though tears
May flow down like a river:
Are not the best beloved of years
Around your heart for ever?

They weep, you weep, it must be so;
Winds sigh as you are sighing,
And Winter sheds his grief in snow
Where Autumn's leaves are lying:
Yet, these revive, and from their fate
Your fate cannot be parted:
Then, journey on, if not elate,
Still, *never* broken-hearted!

(1846)

179 *Death*

DEATH! that struck when I was most confiding
In my certain faith of joy to be—
Strike again, Time's withered branch dividing
From the fresh root of Eternity!

Leaves, upon Time's branch, were growing brightly,
Full of sap, and full of silver dew;
Birds beneath its shelter gathered nightly;
Daily round its flowers the wild bees flew.

Sorrow passed, and plucked the golden blossom;
Guilt stripped off the foliage in its pride;
But, within its parent's kindly bosom,
Flowed for ever Life's restoring tide.

Little mourned I for the parted gladness,
For the vacant nest and silent song—
Hope was there, and laughed me out of sadness;
Whispering, 'Winter will not linger long!

And, behold! with tenfold increase blessing,
Spring adorned the beauty-burdened spray;
Wind and rain and fervent heat, caressing,
Lavished glory on that second May!

High it rose—no winged grief could sweep it;
Sin was scared to distance with its shine;
Love, and its own life, had power to keep it
From all wrong—from every blight but thine!

Cruel Death! The young leaves droop and languish;
Evening's gentle air may still restore—
No! the morning sunshine mocks my anguish—
Time, for me, must never blossom more!

Strike it down, that other boughs may flourish
Where that perished sapling used to be;
Thus, at least, its mouldering corpse will nourish
That from which it sprung—Eternity.

(1846)

180 *Stanzas to—*

WELL, some may hate, and some may scorn,
And some may quite forget thy name;
But my sad heart must ever mourn
Thy ruined hopes, thy blighted fame!
'Twas thus I thought, an hour ago,
Even weeping o'er that wretch's woe;
One word turned back my gushing tears,
And lit my altered eye with sneers.
Then 'Bless the friendly dust,' I said,
'That hides thy unlamented head!
Vain as thou wert, and weak as vain,
The slave of Falsehood, Pride, and Pain,—
My heart has nought akin to thine;
Thy soul is powerless over mine.'

But these were thoughts that vanished too;
Unwise, unholy, and untrue:
Do I despise the timid deer,
Because his limbs are fleet with fear?
Or, would I mock the wolf's death-howl,
Because his form is gaunt and foul?
Or, hear with joy the leveret's cry,
Because it cannot bravely die?
No! Then above his memory
Let Pity's heart as tender be;
Say, 'Earth, lie lightly on that breast,
And, kind Heaven, grant that spirit rest!'

(1846)

181 *My Comforter*

WELL hast thou spoken, and yet, not taught
  A feeling strange or new;
Thou hast but roused a latent thought,
A cloud-closed beam of sunshine, brought
  To gleam in open view.

Deep down, concealed within my soul,
  That light lies hid from men;
Yet, glows unquenched—though shadows roll,
Its gentle ray cannot control,
  About the sullen den.

Was I not vexed, in these gloomy ways
  To walk alone so long?
Around me, wretches uttering praise,
Or howling o'er their hopeless days,
  And each with Frenzy's tongue;—

A brotherhood of misery,
  Their smiles as sad as sighs;
Whose madness daily maddened me,
Distorting into agony
  The bliss before my eyes!

So stood I, in Heaven's glorious sun,
  And in the glare of Hell;
My spirit drank a mingled tone,
Of seraph's song, and demon's moan;
What my soul bore, my soul alone
  Within itself may tell!

Like a soft air, above a sea,
  Tossed by the tempest's stir;
A thaw-wind, melting quietly
The snow-drift, on some wintry lea;
No: what sweet thing resembles thee,
  My thoughtful Comforter?

And yet a little longer speak,
  Calm this resentful mood;
And while the savage heart grows meek,
For other token do not seek,
But let the tear upon my cheek
  Evince my gratitude!

(1846)

182 *The Old Stoic*

RICHES I hold in light esteem;
And Love I laugh to scorn;
And lust of fame was but a dream
That vanished with the morn:

And if I pray, the only prayer
That moves my lips for me
Is, 'Leave the heart that now I bear,
And give me liberty!'

Yes, as my swift days near their goal,
'Tis all that I implore;
In life and death, a chainless soul,
With courage to endure.

(1846)

GEORGE ELIOT (MARY ANN EVANS) (1819–1880)

GEORGE ELIOT was the pen name of Mary Ann Evans, undoubtedly one of the most distinguished novelists, essayists, and poets of the Victorian period. Born at Chilvers Coten in Warwickshire, she was the the gifted third child of Robert Evans, who served as an agent for two large estates in the Midlands. Between 1825 and 1835, she attended a number of schools: Miss Lathom's at Attleborough, Mrs Wallington's at Nuneaton, and the Misses Franklins' at Coventry. Particularly significant during her schooling was the influence of Maria Lewis, a teacher at Mrs Wallington's school, whose evangelical principles would hold sway over Eliot's remarkable intellectual development for some years to come. On her mother's death in 1836, Eliot returned home to live with her father. It was during this period that she decided to strengthen her education by reading widely in philosophy, theology, and literature. Special energy was devoted to learning German, a feat that would prepare her for her future translations of works that challenged orthodox Christian belief. It was in 1841 that she moved to Foleshill, Coventry, with her father, and soon came into contact with a circle of radical philanthropists and intellectuals. Through her friendships with the ribbon manufacturer, Charles Bray, and his spouse, Caroline Bray, she came to know Caroline's freethinking brother, Charles Hennell. By early 1842, much to the distress of her father, Eliot decided not to attend church any longer. Thereafter, her personal life would involve remarkably unorthodox behaviour for which she would to some degree suffer in coming years.

Hennell encouraged Eliot to translate David Friedrich Strauss's considerable challenge to the truth claimed by the Gospels, *The Life of Jesus*. This demanding three-volume study was published in 1846. Thereafter, she frequently reviewed polemical works, such as J. A. Froude's *The Nemesis of Faith* (1849). Granted a small annuity from her father's will, Eliot seized on the opportunity to move to London, where she established herself as the assistant to John Chapman, editor of the progressive *Westminster Review*, a married man with whom she became intimate. Throughout the 1850s, she made a great many contributions to the *Westminster*, notably 'The Natural History of German Life' and 'Silly Novels by Lady Novelists' (both 1856). At the same time, she completed a translation of Ludwig Feuerbach's *Essence of Christianity* (1854), a work that, in the original German, had had a significant influence on the materialist thinking of Karl Marx. Having completed this substantial body of reviews, essays, and translations, Eliot would gradually turn her attention more and more to writing fiction. Encouragement in this direction came from George Henry Lewes, whom she had first met in 1851, and with whom she resided as his common-law wife from 1854 until the time of his death in 1878. The nature of this relationship cut her off from the members of her immediate family, especially her brother Isaac, who had taken over their father's work. Eliot survived Lewes only by two years, and in that period she married John Walter Cross, her junior by some two decades. The legitimacy of her marriage to Cross meant that her brother was willing to renew contact with her after a period of some twenty-five years. Cross published the first of the many biographies that were to follow in 1885. Her reputation as a writer declined somewhat after her death. But during the mid-twentieth century, largely through the offices of F. R. Leavis, who located her work at the heart of the 'Great Tradition', her reputation was restored.

Eliot's earliest stories appeared in *Blackwood's Edinburgh Magazine*, and these were collected in *Scenes from Clerical Life*, published in two volumes in 1858. Thereafter, Eliot produced a steady stream of imposing novels, notably *Adam Bede* (1859), *The Mill on the Floss* (1860), *Romola* (1863), *Felix Holt the Radical* (1866), and *Middlemarch* (1871–72). Her final novel, and arguably her best, was *Daniel Deronda* (1876). By the time she was writing *Romola*, Eliot could command staggeringly high advances for her fiction.

Eliot's two volumes of poetry, *The Spanish Gypsy* (1868), which casts light on Victorian theories of race, and *The Legend of Jubal and Other Poems* (1874), count among her most neglected works. Both received favourable notices in the press, with reviewers often comparing her rhetorical power equal, if not superior, to that Elizabeth Barrett Browning. In 1874, even the *Saturday Review*—a journal with a longstanding history of making demeaning remarks about 'authoresses' and 'poetesses'—was moved to declare: 'in her poems, few as they have been she has shown a choice and command of various moods such as few of our living poets can claim.' Readers well acquainted with Eliot's fiction will quickly see how similar subject-matter appears in her poetry: the sonnet sequence, 'Brother and Sister', evokes the mood of *The Mill on the Floss*, while the closet-drama, *Armgart*, in telling the story of a woman artist, recalls the presence of another of Eliot's female singers, the Alcharisi in *Daniel Deronda*. There has been a limited amount of criticism on Eliot's poems, a notable exception being Gillian Beer, *George Eliot* (1986).

183 *'O May I Join the Choir Invisible'*

Longum illud tempus, quum non ero, magis me movet, quam hoc exiguum.

Cicero, *Ad Atticum*, xii. 18

O MAY I join the choir invisible
Of those immortal dead who live again
In minds made better by their presence: live
In pulses stirred to generosity,
In deeds of daring rectitude, in scorn
For miserable aims that end with self,
In thoughts sublime that pierce the night like stars,
And with their mild persistence urge man's search
To vaster issues.
So to live is heaven:
To make undying music in the world,
Breathing as beauteous order that controls
With growing sway the growing life of man.
So we inherit that sweet purity
For which we struggled, failed, and agonised
With widening retrospect that bred despair.
Rebellious flesh that would not be subdued,
A vicious parent shaming still its child
Poor anxious penitence, is quick dissolved;
Its discords, quenched by meeting harmonies,
Die in the large and charitable air.
And all our rarer, better, truer self,
That sobbed religiously in yearning song,
That watched to ease the burthen of the world,
Laboriously tracing what must be,
And what may yet be better—saw within
A worthier image for the sanctuary,
And shaped it forth before the multitude
Divinely human, raising worship so
To higher reverence more mixed with love—
That better self shall live till human Time
Shall fold its eyelids, and the human sky
Be gathered like a scroll within the tomb
Unread for ever.
This is life to come,
Which martyred men have made more glorious
For us who strive to follow. May I reach
That purest heaven, be to other souls
The cup of strength in some great agony,
Enkindle generous ardour, feed pure love,
Beget the smiles that have no cruelty—

Be the sweet presence of a good diffused,
And in diffusion ever more intense.
So shall I join the choir invisible
Whose music is the gladness of the world.

(1874)

184 *A Minor Prophet*

I HAVE a friend, a vegetarian seer,
By name Elias Baptist Butterworth,
A harmless, bland, disinterested man,
Whose ancestors in Cromwell's day believed
The Second Advent certain in five years,
But when King Charles the Second came instead,
Revised their date and sought another world:
I mean—not heaven but—America.
A fervid stock, whose generous hope embraced
The fortunes of mankind, not stopping short
At rise of leather, or the fall of gold,
Nor listening to the voices of the time
As housewives listen to a cackling hen,
With wonder whether she has laid her egg
On their own nest-egg. Still they did insist
Somewhat too wearisomely on the joys
Of their Millennium, when coats and hats
Would all be of one pattern, books and songs
All fit for Sundays, and the casual talk
As good as sermons preached extempore.

And in Elias the ancestral zeal
Breathes strong as ever, only modified
By Transatlantic air and modern thought.
You could not pass him in the street and fail
To note his shoulders' long declivity,
Beard to the waist, swan-neck, and large pale eyes;
Or, when he lifts his hat, to mark his hair
Brushed back to show his great capacity—
A full grain's length at the angle of the brow
Proving him witty, while the shallower men
Only seem witty in their repartees.
Not that he's vain, but that his doctrine needs
The testimony of his frontal lobe.
On all points he adopts the latest views;
Takes for the key of universal Mind
The 'levitation' of stout gentlemen;
Believes the Rappings are not spirits' work,

But the Thought-atmosphere's, a steam of brains
In correlated force of raps, as proved
By motion, heat, and science generally;
The spectrum, for example, which has shown
The self-same metals in the sun as here;
So the Thought-atmosphere is everywhere:
High truths that glimmered under other names
To ancient sages, whence good scholarship
Applied to Eleusinian mysteries—
The Vedas—Tripitaka—Vendidad—
Might furnish weaker proof for weaker minds
That Thought was rapping in the hoary past,
And might have edified the Greeks by raps
At the greater Dionysia, if their ears
Had not been filled with Sophoclean verse.
And when all Earth is vegetarian—
When, lacking butchers, quadrupeds die out,
And less Thought-atmosphere is reabsorbed
By nerves of insects parasitical,
Those higher truths, seized now by higher minds
But not expressed (the insects hindering)
Will either flash out into eloquence,
Or better still, be comprehensible
By rappings simply, without need of roots.

'Tis on this theme—the vegetarian world—
That good Elias willingly expands:
He loves to tell in mildly nasal tones
And vowels stretched to suit the widest views,
The future fortunes of our infant Earth—
When it will be too full of human kind
To have the room for wilder animals.
Saith he, Sahara will be populous
With families of gentlemen retired
From commerce in more Central Africa,
Who order coolness as we order coal,
And have a lobe anterior strong enough
To think away the sand-storms. Science thus
Will leave no spot on this terraqueous globe
Unfit to be inhabited by man,
The chief of animals: all meaner brutes
Will have been smoked and elbowed out of life.
No lions then shall lap Caffrarian pools,
Or shake the Atlas with their midnight roar:
Even the slow, slime-loving crocodile,
The last of animals to take a hint,
Will then retire for ever from a scene

Where public feeling strongly sets against him.
Fishes may lead carnivorous lives obscure,
But must not dream of culinary rank
Or being dished in good society.
Imagination in that distant age,
Aiming at fiction called historical,
Will vainly try to reconstruct the times
When it was men's preposterous delight
To sit astride live horses, which consumed
Materials for incalculable cakes;
When there were milkmaids who drew milk from cows
With udders kept abnormal for that end
Since the rude mythopoeic period
Of Aryan dairymen, who did not blush
To call their milkmaid and their daughter one—
Helplessly gazing at the Milky Way,
Nor dreaming of the astral cocoa-nuts
Quite at the service of posterity.
'Tis to be feared, though, that the duller boys,
Much given to anachronisms and nuts,
(Elias has confessed boys will be boys)
May write a jockey for a centaur, think
Europa's suitor was an Irish bull,
Æsop a journalist who wrote up Fox,
And Bruin a chief swindler upon 'Change.
Boys will be boys, but dogs will all be moral,
With longer alimentary canals
Suited to diet vegetarian.
The uglier breeds will fade from memory,
Or, being palaeontological,
Live but as portraits in large learned books,
Distasteful to the feelings of an age
Nourished on purest beauty. Earth will hold
No stupid brutes, no cheerful queernesses,
No naïve cunning, grave absurdity.
Wart-pigs with tender and parental grunts,
Wombats much flattened as to their contour,
Perhaps from too much crushing in the ark,
But taking meekly that fatality;
The serious cranes, unstung by ridicule;
Long-headed, short-legged, solemn-looking curs,
(Wise, silent critics of a flippant age);
The silly straddling foals, the weak-brained geese
Hissing fallaciously at sound of wheels—
All these rude products will have disappeared
Along with every faulty human type.
By dint of diet vegetarian

All will be harmony of hue and line,
Bodies and minds all perfect, limbs well-turned,
And talk quite free from aught erroneous.

Thus far Elias in his seer's mantle:
But at this climax in his prophecy
My sinking spirits, fearing to be swamped,
Urge me to speak. 'High prospects these, my friend,
Setting the weak carnivorous brain astretch;
We will resume the thread another day.'
'To-morrow,' cries Elias, 'at this hour?'
'No, not to-morrow—I shall have a cold—
At least I feel some soreness—this endemic—
Good-bye.'
No tears are sadder than the smile
With which I quit Elias. Bitterly
I feel that every change upon this earth
Is bought with sacrifice. My yearnings fail
To reach that high apocalyptic mount
Which shows in bird's-eye view a perfect world,
Or enter warmly into other joys
Than those of faulty, struggling human kind.
That strain upon my soul's too feeble wing
Ends in ignoble floundering: I fall
Into short-sighted pity for the men
Who living in those perfect future times
Will not know half the dear imperfect things
That move my smiles and tears—will never know
The fine old incongruities that raise
My friendly laugh; the innocent conceits
That like a needless eyeglass or black patch
Give those who wear them harmless happiness;
The twists and cracks in our poor earthenware,
That touch me to more conscious fellowship
(I am not myself the finest Parian)
With my coevals. So poor Colin Clout,
To whom raw onion gives prospective zest,
Consoling hours of dampest wintry work,
Could hardly fancy any regal joys
Quite unimpregnate with the onion's scent:
Perhaps his highest hopes are not all clear
Of waftings from that energetic bulb:
'Tis well that onion is not heresy.
Speaking in parable, I am Colin Clout.
A clinging flavour penetrates my life—
My onion is imperfectness: I cleave
To nature's blunders, evanescent types

Which sages banish from Utopia.
'Not worship beauty?' say yoù. Patience, friend!
I worship in the temple with the rest;
But by my hearth I keep a sacred nook
For gnomes and dwarfs, duck-footed waddling elves
Who stitched and hammered for the weary man
In days of old. And in that piety
I clothe ungainly forms inherited
From toiling generations, daily bent
At desk, or plough, or loom, or in the mine,
In pioneering labours for the world.
Nay, I am apt when floundering confused
From too rash flight, to grasp at paradox,
And pity future men who will not know
A keen experience with pity blent,
The pathos exquisite of lovely minds
Hid in harsh forms—not penetrating them
Like fire divine within a common bush
Which glows transfigured by the heavenly guest,
So that men put their shoes off; but encaged
Like a sweet child within some thick-walled cell,
Who leaps and fails to hold the window-bars,
But having shown a little dimpled hand
Is visited thenceforth by tender hearts
Whose eyes keep watch about the prison walls.
A foolish, nay, a wicked paradox!
For purest pity is the eye of love
Melting at sight of sorrow; and to grieve
Because it sees no sorrow, shows a love
Warped from its truer nature, turned to love
Of merest habit, like the miser's greed.
But I am Colin still: my prejudice
Is for the flavour of my daily food.
Not that I doubt the world is growing still
As once it grew from Chaos and from Night;
Or have a soul too shrunken for the hope
Which dawned in human breasts, a double morn,
With earliest watchings of the rising light
Chasing the darkness; and through many an age
Has raised the vision of a future time
That stands an Angel with a face all mild
Spearing the demon. I too rest in faith
That man's perfection is the crowning flower,
Toward which the urgent sap in life's great tree
Is pressing,—seen in puny blossoms now,
But in the world's great morrows to expand
With broadest petal and with deepest glow.

Yet, see the patched and plodding citizen
Waiting upon the pavement with the throng
While some victorious world-hero makes
Triumphal entry, and the peal of shouts
And flash of faces 'neath uplifted hats
Run like a storm of joy along the streets!
He says, 'God bless him!' almost with a sob,
As the great hero passes; he is glad
The world holds mighty men and mighty deeds;
The music stirs his pulses like strong wine,
The moving splendour touches him with awe—
'Tis glory shed around the common weal,
And he will pay his tribute willingly,
Though with the pennies earned by sordid toil.
Perhaps the hero's deeds have helped to bring
A time when every honest citizen
Shall wear a coat unpatched. And yet he feels
More easy fellowship with neighbours there
Who look on too; and he will soon relapse
From noticing the banners and the steeds
To think with pleasure there is just one bun
Left in his pocket, that may serve to tempt
The wide-eyed lad, whose weight is all too much
For that young mother's arms: and then he falls
To dreamy picturing of sunny days
When he himself was a small big-cheeked lad
In some far village where no heroes came,
And stood a listener 'twixt his father's legs
In the warm fire-light, while the old folk talked
And shook their heads and looked upon the floor;
And he was puzzled, thinking life was fine—
The bread and cheese so nice all through the year
And Christmas sure to come. O that good time!
He, could he choose, would have those days again
And see the dear old-fashioned things once more.
But soon the wheels and drums have all passed by
And tramping feet are heard like sudden rain:
The quiet startles our good citizen;
He feels the child upon his arms, and knows
He is with the people making holiday
Because of hopes for better days to come.
But Hope to him was like the brilliant west
Telling of sunrise in a world unknown,
And from that dazzling curtain of bright hues
He turned to the familiar face of fields
Lying all clear in the calm morning land.

Maybe 'tis wiser not to fix a lens
Too scrutinising on the glorious times
When Barbarossa shall arise and shake
His mountain, good King Arthur come again,
And all the heroes of such giant soul
That, living once to cheer mankind with hope,
They had to sleep until the time was ripe
For greater deeds to match their greater thought.
Yet no! the earth yields nothing more Divine
Than high prophetic vision—than the Seer
Who fasting from man's meaner joy beholds
The paths of beauteous order, and constructs
A fairer type, to shame our low content.
But prophecy is like potential sound
Which turned to music seems a voice sublime
From out the soul of light; but turns to noise
In scrannel pipes, and makes all ears averse.

The faith that life on earth is being shaped
To glorious ends, that order, justice, love
Mean man's completeness, mean effect as sure
As roundness in the dew-drop—that great faith
Is but the rushing and expanding stream
Of thought, of feeling, fed by all the past.
Our finest hope is finest memory,
As they who love in age think youth is blest
Because it has a life to fill with love.
Full souls are double mirrors, making still
An endless vista of fair things before
Repeating things behind: so faith is strong
Only when we are strong, shrinks when we shrink.
It comes when music stirs us, and the chords
Moving on some grand climax shake our souls
With influx new that makes new energies.
It comes in swellings of the heart and tears
That rise at noble and at gentle deeds—
At labours of the master-artist's hand
Which, trembling, touches to a finer end,
Trembling before an image seen within.
It comes in moments of heroic love,
Unjealous joy in joy not made for us—
In conscious triumph of the good within
Making us worship goodness that rebukes.
Even our failures are a prophecy,
Even our yearnings and our bitter tears

After that fair and true we cannot grasp;
As patriots who seem to die in vain
Make liberty more sacred by their pangs.

Presentiment of better things on earth
Sweeps in with every force that stirs our souls
To admiration, self-renouncing love,
Or thoughts, like light, that bind the world in one:
Sweeps like the sense of vastness, when at night
We hear the roll and dash of waves that break
Nearer and nearer with the rushing tide,
Which rises to the level of the cliff
Because the wide Atlantic rolls behind
Throbbing respondent to the far-off orbs.

(1874)

185 *Brother and Sister*

I

I CANNOT choose but think upon the time
When our two lives grew like two buds that kiss
At lightest thrill from the bee's swinging chime,
Because the one so near the other is.

He was the elder and a little man
Of forty inches, bound to show no dread,
And I the girl that puppy-like now ran,
Now lagged behind my brother's larger tread.

I held him wise, and when he talked to me
Of snakes and birds, and which God loved the best,
I thought his knowledge marked the boundary
Where men grew blind, though angels knew the rest.

If he said 'Hush!' I tried to hold my breath;
Wherever he said 'Come!' I stepped in faith.

II

Long years have left their writing on my brow,
But yet the freshness and the dew-fed beam
Of those young mornings are about me now,
When we two wandered toward the far-off stream

With rod and line. Our basket held a store
Baked for us only, and I thought with joy
That I should have my share, though he had more,
Because he was the elder and a boy.

The firmaments of daisies since to me
Have had those mornings in their opening eyes,
The bunchèd cowslip's pale transparency
Carries that sunshine of sweet memories,

  And wild-rose branches take their finest scent
  From those blest hours of infantine content.

III

Our mother bade us keep the trodden ways,
Stroked down my tippet, set my brother's frill,
Then with the benediction of her gaze
Clung to us lessening, and pursued us still

Across the homestead to the rookery elms,
Whose tall old trunks had each a grassy mound,
So rich for us, we counted them as realms
With varied products: here were earth-nuts found,

And here the Lady-fingers in deep shade;
Here sloping toward the Moat the rushes grew,
The large to split for pith, the small to braid;
While over all the dark rooks cawing flew,

  And made a happy strange solemnity,
  A deep-toned chant from life unknown to me.

IV

Our meadow-path had memorable spots:
One where it bridged a tiny rivulet,
Deep hid by tangled blue Forget-me-nots;
And all along the waving grasses met

My little palm, or nodded to my cheek,
When flowers with upturned faces gazing drew
My wonder downward, seeming all to speak
With eyes of souls that dumbly heard and knew.

Then came the copse, where wild things rushed unseen,
And black-scathed grass betrayed the past abode
Of mystic gypsies, who still lurked between
Me and each hidden distance of the road.

  A gypsy once had startled me at play,
  Blotting with her dark smile my sunny day.

V

Thus rambling we were schooled in deepest lore,
And learned the meanings that give words a soul,
The fear, the love, the primal passionate store,
Whose shaping impulses make manhood whole.

Those hours were seed to all my after good;
My infant gladness, through eye, ear, and touch,
Took easily as warmth a various food
To nourish the sweet skill of loving much.

For who in age shall roam the earth and find
Reasons for loving that will strike out love
With sudden rod from the hard year-pressed mind?
Were reasons sown as thick as stars above,

'Tis love must see them, as the eye sees light:
Day is but Number to the darkened sight.

VI

Our brown canal was endless to my thought;
And on its banks I sat in dreamy peace,
Unknowing how the good I loved was wrought,
Untroubled by the fear that it would cease.

Slowly the barges floated into view
Rounding a grassy hill to me sublime
With some Unknown beyond it, whither flew
The parting cuckoo toward a fresh spring time.

The wide-arched bridge, the scented elder-flōwers,
The wondrous watery rings that died too soon,
The echoes of the quarry, the still hours
With white robe sweeping-on the shadeless noon,

Were but my growing self, are part of me,
My present Past, my root of piety.

VII

Those long days measured by my little feet
Had chronicles which yield me many a text;
Where irony still finds an image meet
Of full-grown judgments in this world perplext.

One day my brother left me in high charge,
To mind the rod, while he went seeking bait,
And bade me, when I saw a nearing barge,
Snatch out the line, lest he should come too late.

Proud of the task, I watched with all my might
For one whole minute, till my eyes grew wide,
Till sky and earth took on a strange new light
And seemed a dream-world floating on some tide—

  A fair pavilioned boat for me alone
  Bearing me onward through the vast unknown.

VIII

But sudden came the barge's pitch-black prow,
Nearer and angrier came my brother's cry,
And all my soul was quivering fear, when lo!
Upon the imperilled line, suspended high,

A silver perch! My guilt that won the prey,
Now turned to merit, had a guerdon rich
Of songs and praises, and made merry play,
Until my triumph reached its highest pitch

When all at home were told the wondrous feat,
And how the little sister had fished well.
In secret, though my fortune tasted sweet,
I wondered why this happiness befell.

  'The little lass had luck,' the gardener said:
  And so I learned, luck was with glory wed.

IX

We had the self-same world enlarged for each
By loving difference of girl and boy:
The fruit that hung on high beyond my reach
He plucked for me, and oft he must employ

A measuring glance to guide my tiny shoe
Where lay firm stepping-stones, or call to mind
'This thing I like my sister may not do,
For she is little, and I must be kind.'

Thus boyish Will the nobler mastery learned
Where inward vision over impulse reigns,
Widening its life with separate life discerned,
A Like unlike, a Self that self restrains.

  His years with others must the sweeter be
  For those brief days he spent in loving me.

X

His sorrow was my sorrow, and his joy
Sent little leaps and laughs through all my frame;
My doll seemed lifeless and no girlish toy
Had any reason when my brother came.

I knelt with him at marbles, marked his fling
Cut the ringed stem and make the apple drop,
Or watched him winding close the spiral string
That looped the orbits of the humming top.

Grasped by such fellowship my vagrant thought
Ceased with dream-fruit dream-wishes to fulfil;
My aëry-picturing fantasy was taught
Subjection to the harder, truer skill

That seeks with deeds to grave a thought-tracked line,
And by 'What is,' 'What will be' to define.

XI

School parted us; we never found again
That childish world where our two spirits mingled
Like scents from varying roses that remain
One sweetness, nor can evermore be singled.

Yet the twin habit of that early time
Lingered for long about the heart and tongue:
We had been natives of one happy clime
And its dear accent to our utterance clung.

Till the dire years whose awful name is Change
Had grasped our souls still yearning in divorce,
And pitiless shaped them in two forms that range
Two elements which sever their life's course.

But were another childhood-world my share,
I would be born a little sister there.

(1874)

ANNE BRONTË
(1820–1849)

ANNE BRONTË'S reputation has suffered alongside the greater fame of her literary sisters, Charlotte and Emily. She outlived her brother, Branwell, by one year, whose death in 1848 was induced by his addiction to alcohol and opium, and also her sisters, Maria and Elizabeth, who died while still at school. The youngest daughter of Patrick Brontë, a curate, and Maria (née Branwell), she was born at Thornton Parsonage in the parish of Bradford. In the same year, the family moved to her father's new curacy at Haworth. After the death of the mother in 1821, her sister supervised the household. Anne Brontë was formally educated for only two years (1835–37) at a boarding-school in Roe Head, which was relocated to Dewsbury Moor, near Leeds, while she was a pupil. The family's financial difficulties led to her becoming a governess during 1839 and then again between 1840 and 1845, this time at the home of the Robinsons of Thorp Green Hall, near York, where she was joined by Branwell Brontë, as tutor, in 1843. She then spent her few remaining years at Howarth Parsonage.

Following the fashion of Branwell and Charlotte Brontë, she and her sister, Emily, had begun to write about a fictitious island, Gondal, from about 1831. This was expressed in verse and prose, and twenty-one of Anne Brontë's early poems were to be published in a volume with her two sisters' verses and presented under pseudonyms: *Poems by Currer, Ellis and Acton Bell* (1846). Only two copies of the book were sold and it received little critical reception. Of the few reviews that were published, that by Sydney Dobell was not encouraging. He wrote of Acton Bell's (Anne Brontë's) poems that they required 'the indulgencies of affection' to be palatable (*Athenaeum*, July 1846). A year later, however, her first novel, *Agnes Grey* (1847), was published with Emily Brontë's *Wuthering Heights*, and Anne Brontë's work was the more favourably reviewed of the two. These novels were republished in 1850 (again in one volume), with Charlotte Brontë as editor, and the book also included nine poems by Anne Brontë, seven of which were previously unpublished. Her remaining twenty-three unpublished verses were to appear in *The Complete Poems of Anne Brontë* (1921). The second, and last, of her novels, *The Tenant of Wildfell Hall*, came out in 1848. She retained her pseudonym throughout her life as a writer.

186 *The Arbour*

I'LL rest me in this sheltered bower,
And look upon the clear blue sky
That smiles upon me through the trees,
Which stand so thickly clustering by;

And view their green and glossy leaves,
All glistening in the sunshine fair;
And list the rustling of their boughs,
So softly whispering through the air.

And while my ear drinks in the sound,
My winged soul shall fly away;
Reviewing long departed years
As one mild, beaming, autumn day;

And soaring on to future scenes,
Like hills and woods, and valleys green,
All basking in the summer's sun,
But distant still, and dimly seen.

Oh, list! 'tis summer's very breath
That gently shakes the rustling trees—
But look! the snow is on the ground—
How can I think of scenes like these?

'Tis but the *frost* that clears the air,
And gives the sky that lovely blue;
They're smiling in a *winter's* sun,
Those evergreens of sombre hue.

And winter's chill is on my heart—
How can I dream of future bliss?
How can my spirit soar away,
Confined by such a chain as this?

(1846)

187 *If This Be All*

O GOD! if this indeed be all
  That Life can show to me;
If on my aching brow may fall
  No freshening dew from Thee,—

If with no brighter light than this
  The lamp of hope may glow,
And I may only *dream* of bliss,
  And wake to weary woe;

If friendship's solace must decay,
  When other joys are gone,
And love must keep so far away,
  While I go wandering on,—

Wandering and toiling without gain,
  The slave of others' will,
With constant care, and frequent pain,
  Despised, forgotten still;

Grieving to look on vice and sin,
  Yet powerless to quell
The silent current from within,
  The outward torrent's swell:

While all the good I would impart,
  The feelings I would share,
Are driven backward to my heart,
  And turned to wormwood, there;

If clouds must *ever* keep from sight
  The glories of the Sun,
And I must suffer Winter's blight,
  Ere Summer is begun;

If Life must be so full of care,
  Then call me soon to Thee;
Or give me strength enough to bear
  My load of misery.

(1846)

188 *A Word to the 'Elect'*

YOU may rejoice to think *yourselves* secure;
You may be grateful for the gift divine—
That grace unsought, which made your black hearts pure,
And fits your earth-born souls in Heaven to shine.

But, is it sweet to look around, and view
Thousands excluded from that happiness
Which they deserved, at least, as much as you,—
Their faults not greater, nor their virtues less?

And, wherefore should you love your God the more,
Because to you alone his smiles are given;
Because he chose to pass the *many* o'er,
And only bring the favoured *few* to Heaven?

And, wherefore should your hearts more grateful prove,
Because for ALL the Saviour did not die?
Is yours the God of justice and of love?
And are your bosoms warm with charity?

Say, does your heart expand to all mankind?
And, would you ever to your neighbour do—
The weak, the strong, the enlightened, and the blind—
As you would have your neighbour do to you?

And, when you, looking on your fellow-men,
Behold them doomed to endless misery,
How can you talk of joy and rapture then?—
May God withhold such cruel joy from me!

That none deserve eternal bliss I know;
Unmerited the grace in mercy given:
But, none shall sink to everlasting woe,
That have not well deserved the wrath of Heaven.

And, oh! there lives within my heart
  A hope, long nursed by me;
(And, should its cheering ray depart,
  How dark my soul would be!)

That as in Adam all have died,
 In Christ shall all men live;
And ever round his throne abide,
 Eternal praise to give.

That even the wicked shall at last
 Be fitted for the skies;
And, when their dreadful doom is past,
 To life and light arise.

I ask not, how remote the day,
 Nor what the sinners' woe,
Before their dross is purged away;
 Enough for me, to know

That when the cup of wrath is drained,
 The metal purified,
They'll cling to what they once disdained,
 And live by Him that died.

(1846)

ANNE EVANS
(1820–1870)

BORN in Britwell Court, near Burnham in Buckinghamshire, Anne Evans was one of six children. When she was 8 or 9 years old, the family moved to Bosworth, where her father, Dr Arthur Evans, became headmaster of Market Bosworth Grammar School. After his death in 1855, some of the remaining family transferred to Kensington Square in London. Anne Evans and her mother were to remain there together.

The first known piece of writing by Anne Evans is a manuscript short story, 'The Rose and the Ring', which she showed to the novelist, William Makepeace Thackeray. It is not known how he responded to this work, but the story seems not to have been published. She had met the novelist through his daughter, Anne Thackeray Ritchie, who was to write the memorial preface to and edit Anne Evans's only collection of poems in 1880: *Poems and Music*. The volume demonstrates an impressive variety of form, from sonnets to witty dramatic monologues. A brother, Sebastian Evans, also wrote poetry and he may also have known the Thackerays: his 'To the Memory of William Makepeace Thackeray. A Poem' was published in 1899.

189

Over!

A KNIGHT came prancing on his way,
And across the path a lady lay:
'Stoop a little and hear me speak!'
Then, 'You are strong, and I am weak:
Ride over me now, and kill me.'

He opened wide his gay blue eyes,
Like one o'ermastered by surprise;
His cheek and brow grew burning red,
'Long looked-for, come at last,' she said,
'Ride over me now, and kill me.'

Then softly spoke the knight, and smiled:
'Fair maiden, whence this mood so wild?'
'Smile on,' said she, 'my reign is o'er,
But do my bidding yet once more:
Ride over me now, and kill me.'

He smote his steed of dapple-gray,
And lightly cleared her where she lay;
But still, as he sped on amain,
She murmured ever, 'Turn again:
Ride over me now, and kill me.'

(1880)

190

Fragments

I

UP sprang the merry grasshoppers
Around her very feet;
A charm of many little wings
O'erspread the herbage sweet.

And from their city in the earth
To sunny thyme and heather.
The little conies in their mirth
Were come to play together.

The cuckoo's note came floating by,
To greet the sad new-comer;
But she stood frozen through and through,
Against the glee of summer.

'I have not happiness enow
To keep me warm,' said she;
'What should I do with all the days
That may remain to me?'

(1880)

191 *Outcry*

AWAY with loving! Let it all go by;
For losing is too grievous,
And our beloved successively
Turn cold and leave us!
What matter whence the cold may come
Which makes them deaf to us, and blind, and dumb—
Whether from dark thoughts clouding old regard,
Or from their lodging out in the churchyard?
Friends? We may lose our best
Through some poor jest,
And all our after-days lament the losing!
Besides, there is no choosing
One of them all on whom to reckon
If death should beckon.
O miserable men!
O dreary doom!
Our love's delight is hollow—
Hollow as treachery, hollow as the tomb!
Away, away with loving then,
With hoping and believing;
For what should follow,
But grieving, grieving?

(1880)

192 *from Orinda: A Ballad*

[*Orinda moves somnambulistically through a symbolic dream landscape. Although this extract ends with her dedication to religion, she finally escapes from the cloister to a life dedicated to joy. Eds.*]

ACROSS the shadow of the tree
   There flowed a glittering brook:
Orinda turned and followed it,
   With never a backwood look.

The brook flowed on from East to West,
   Flowed on from North to South;
Flowed on below a rugged rock,
   And past a cavern's mouth.

And when she saw that same cavern
   She balanced never a whit,
But waded through the chill water
   And entered into it.

All in the low and black cavern
   She reckoned slowly o'er

Twenty paces at the side;
  Twenty, and no more.

Thereby a hidden opening was,
  The trick whereof she knew,
Which groping in the damp darkness
  She found, and so passed through.

Thence mounted she a winding stair
  Up to a narrow door:
The key which should that door undo
  On a silken string she wore.

She kissed the faded silken string,
  She kissed the little key:
'O mother dear! O mother dead!
  Thy lost love rescues me!'

So entered she a dim chapel,
  By veinéd vaulting spanned,
On many clustered marble shafts
  Upreared on either hand;

Wherein, through mazy masonry,
  Deep-set in arches old,
Fell window-slants of stained moonshine
  Across the pavement cold.

And as Orinda lightly trod
  Adown that chapel fair,
The lustres rose up one by one,
  And glided over her hair.

Into an ancient rich cloister
  She from the chapel passed,
And where the shadow shrouded her,
  Made she her halt at last.

All black and white, in the clear moonlight,
  Stood up the chapel wall:
Right to the tip of the pinnacles
  You might scan the tracery small;

And eke the grim and starkthroat crew
  Of gurgoyles gaping wide,
Which, weather-scarred, with eyeballs hard,
  Into the cloister pried.

So quiet was all, that high on the wall,
  In a little whiff of wind,
You might hear the edge of an ivy-leaf
  Grate on the stone behind.

Also the beat of the old clock
  At work within his tower:
Orinda hearkened wistfully
  What time he told the hour.

And 'Dost thou count to me,' she said,
  'These hours which come and go;
Or count them to the waiting Dead,
  Whose bodies lie below?'

But when the last of the midnight strokes
  Came shivered in its fall,
A sound of rustling raiment rose,
  And pattering feet withal.

And straight there swept a darksome train
  The lofty cloister through,
Of nuns who toward the chapel went
  In silence, two and two.

And last of all walked slowly by
  The abbess old and frail,
Who led a little blooming maid
  With never a hood nor veil.

So passed they into chapel all,
  And soon upon the air
Came echoes of low orisons
  Across the cloister-square.

Then suddenly there burst abroad
  Strong harmony of praise:—
Orinda stood and wept aloud:
  So would she end her days!

(1880)

JEAN INGELOW
(1820–1897)

BORN in Boston, Lincolnshire, Jean Ingelow is probably best remembered as a poet for the dazzling stanzas that record the high tide on the coast of her home county in 1571. She was the oldest child of a large family of four sisters and five brothers. Educated at home first in Lincolnshire, she then moved to Ipswich where her father took a position as a bank manager. When the bank failed in 1845, the family was forced to move, probably to lodgings in Tamworth. In 1850, the family eventually settled in London, where she lived as a single woman with members of her large family for the rest of her life. It is likely that she started writing poetry in her teenage years. Her first collection, issued by an established London publisher, was *A Rhyming Chronicle of Incidents and Feelings* (1850), edited by Reverend Edward Harlston, curate of Tamworth. Her first novel, *Allerton and Dreux*, appeared the following year. Neither work made much impression.

It was well over a decade before Ingelow caught the attention of a large readership. Success came with her immensely popular *Poems* (1863), which contained some of her best-loved works, including 'Divided'. This volume, which passed into numerous editions in her lifetime, reputedly sold 200,000 copies in the United States. It was followed by *Home Thoughts and Home Scenes* (1867), a collection of poetry for children that she edited with Dora Greenwell, among others. In the same year, she published *A Story of Doom and Other Poems*. *Poems: Second Series* appeared in 1874, with a third series, which included 'Echo and the Ferry' (1885), on sale just over ten years later.

Ingelow was an active member of the Portfolio Society, which she joined in 1860. This group of talented writers brought together established and aspiring poets who agreed to compose poems on set themes. Its members included the leading lights of Langham Place—Isa Craig, Emily Faithfull, Bessie Rayner Parkes, Adelaide Anne Procter, and Barbara Leigh Smith (later Bodichon)—all known for their feminist campaigning in the 1850s. The Portfolio Society also included within its ranks the celebrated parodist, Charles Stuart Calverley, whose humorous skit of 'Divided' (1863) appears in his *Fly Leaves* (1872). In addition, the poet Dora Greenwell contributed to the Society. Christina Rossetti in all probability only exchanged letters and manuscripts with this circle of friends who circulated drafts of one another's poems. But it was clear from Rossetti's correspondence that Ingelow was by that time held in high regard by her contemporaries. Rossetti informed her publisher, Macmillan, in 1863: 'Miss Procter I am not afraid of; but Miss Ingelow (judging by extracts; I have not yet seen the actual volume) would be a formidable rival to most men, and to any woman. Indeed I have been bewailing that she did not publish with you.' A year later, Rossetti remarked to her friend, Anne Gilchrist, that she had now met this professional competitor, finding her 'as unaffected as her verses'. Rossetti was undoubtedly right in predicting Ingelow's commercial prosperity; in 1865, she exclaimed to the same correspondent: 'I have just received a present of Jean Ingelow's 8th edition; imagine my feelings of envy and humiliation.' To be sure, Ingelow won a great many admirers, including the poet and translator, Edward FitzGerald. In 1870, she visited Alfred Tennyson; this resulted in a significant friendship. There is no doubt that Ingelow was very much a part of London literary life.

But it was not only for poetry that Ingelow established her formidable reputation. She published a substantial amount of prose fiction both for adults and for children. *Stories Told to a Child* (1865), an abridged edition of *Tales of Orris* (1860), was illustrated by John Millais. More popular was *Mopsa the Fairy*, now a recognized children's classic, which appeared in 1869. In the same year, she published *Off the Skelligs*, which draws on her Lincolnshire background. Her second work of adult fiction, *Sarah de Berenger* was published in 1872, and *Fated to be Free* appeared in 1876. *Don Juan*, her last work of prose fiction, went out on sale in 1879.

Ingelow's poetry often received encouraging notices in the press. In 1863, the *Saturday Review* found *Poems* to be full of 'very great promise indeed'. Strong support, not unsuprisingly, came from the *English Woman's Journal*, published from Langham Place, which in 1864 saw fit to quote the 'High Tide' in full.

Many reviewers praised her attention to natural detail, as well as the musicality of her writing. 'There is', the *Englishwoman's Review* noted in an obituary, 'a musical ring about her poems which has been recognised by some of our leading composers, who have set many of them to music, and they are marked by love of nature and close observation of the sights and sounds of country life.' Four years after her death, *Some Recollections of Jean Ingelow and Her Early Friends*, was published anonymously. Although celebrated for her poems focusing on broken love affairs, about which there has been some biographical speculation, Ingelow's strengths also lie in her polemical defence of single women, as is made clear in her most ambitious and arguably most accomplished poem, 'Gladys and Her Island' (1874).

193 *Divided*

I

AN empty sky, a world of heather,
  Purple of foxglove, yellow of broom;
We two among them wading together,
  Shaking out honey, treading perfume.

Crowds of bees are giddy with clover,
  Crowds of grasshoppers skip at our feet,
Crowds of larks at their matins hang over,
  Thanking the Lord for a life so sweet.

Flusheth the rise with her purple favour,
  Gloweth the cleft with her golden ring,
'Twixt the two brown butterflies waver,
  Lightly settle, and sleepily swing.

We two walk till the purple dieth
  And short dry grass under foot is brown;
But one little streak at a distance lieth
  Green like a ribbon to prank the down.

II

Over the grass we stepped unto it,
  And God He knoweth how blithe we were!
Never a voice to bid us eschew it:
  Hey the green ribbon that showed so fair!

Hey the green ribbon! we kneeled beside it,
  We parted the grasses dewy and sheen;
Drop over drop there filtered and slided
  A tiny bright beck that trickled between.

Tinkle, tinkle, sweetly it sang to us,
  Light was our talk as of faëry bells—
Faëry wedding-bells faintly rung to us
  Down in their fortunate parallels.

Hand in hand, while the sun peered over,
  We lapped the grass on that youngling spring;
Swept back its rushes, smoothed its clover,
  And said, 'Let us follow it westering.'

III

A dappled sky, a world of meadows,
  Circling above us the black rooks fly
Forward, backward; lo, their dark shadows
  Flit on the blossoming tapestry—

Flit on the beck, for her long grass parteth
  As hair from a maid's bright eyes blown back;
And, lo, the sun like a lover darteth
  His flattering smile on her wayward track.

Sing on! we sing in the glorious weather
  Till one steps over the tiny strand,
So narrow, in sooth, that still together
  On either brink we go hand in hand.

The beck grows wider, the hands must sever.
  On either margin, our songs all done,
We move apart, while she singeth ever,
  Taking the course of the stooping sun.

He prays, 'Come over'—I may not follow;
  I cry, 'Return'—but he cannot come:
We speak, we laugh, but with voices hollow;
  Our hands are hanging, our hearts are numb.

IV

A breathing sigh, a sigh for answer,
  A little talking of outward things:
The careless beck is a merry dancer,
  Keeping sweet time to the air she sings.

A little pain when the beck grows wider;
  'Cross to me now—for her wavelets swell':
'I may not cross'—and the voice beside her
  Faintly reacheth, though heeded well.

No backward path; ah! no returning;
  No second crossing that ripple's flow:
'Come to me now, for the west is burning;
  Come ere it darkens;'—'Ah, no! ah, no!'

Then cries of pain, and arms outreaching—
  The beck grows wider and swift and deep:
Passionate words as of one beseeching—
  The loud beck drowns them; we walk, and weep.

V

A yellow moon in splendour drooping,
  A tired queen with her state oppressed,
Low by rushes and swordgrass stooping,
  Lies she soft on the waves at rest.

The desert heavens have felt her sadness;
  Her earth will weep her some dewy tears;
The wild beck ends her tune of gladness,
  And goeth stilly as soul that fears.

We two walk on in our grassy places
  On either marge of the moonlit flood,
With the moon's own sadness in our faces,
  Where joy is withered, blossom and bud.

VI

A shady freshness, chafers whirring,
  A little piping of leaf-hid birds;
A flutter of wings, a fitful stirring,
  A cloud to the eastward snowy as curds.

Bare grassy slopes, where kids are tethered;
  Round valleys like nests all fern-y-lined;
Round hills, with fluttering tree-tops feathered,
  Swell high in their freckled robes behind.

A rose-flush tender, a thrill, a quiver,
  When golden gleams to the tree-tops glide;
A flashing edge for the milk-white river,
  The beck, a river—with still sleek tide.

Broad and white, and polished as silver,
  On she goes under fruit-laden trees;
Sunk in leafage cooeth the culver,
  And 'plaineth of love's disloyalties.

Glitters the dew and shines the river,
Up comes the lily and dries her bell;
But two are walking apart for ever,
And wave their hands for a mute farewell.

VII

A braver swell, a swifter sliding;
The river hasteth, her banks recede:
Wing-like sails on her bosom gliding
Bear down the lily and drown the reed.

Stately prows are rising and bowing
(Shouts of mariners winnow the air),
And level sands for banks endowing
The tiny green ribbon that showed so fair.

While, O my heart! as white sails shiver,
And crowds are passing, and banks stretch wide,
How hard to follow, with lips that quiver,
That moving speck on the far-off side!

Farther, farther—I see it—know it—
My eyes brim over, it melts away:
Only my heart to my heart shall show it
As I walk desolate day by day.

VIII

And yet I know past all doubting, truly
A knowledge greater than grief can dim—
I know, as he loved, he will love me duly—
Yea, better—e'en better than I love him.

And as I walk by the vast calm river,
The awful river so dread to see,
I say, 'Thy breadth and thy depth for ever
Are bridged by his thoughts that cross to me.'

(1863)

194 *The High Tide on the Coast of Lincolnshire (1571)*

THE old mayor climbed the belfry tower,
  The ringers ran by two, by three;
'Pull, if ye never pulled before;
  Good ringers, pull your best,' quoth he.
'Play uppe, play uppe, O Boston bells!
Ply all your changes, all your swells,
  Play uppe "The Brides of Enderby."'

Men say it was a stolen tyde—
  The Lord that sent it, He knows all;
But in myne ears doth still abide
  The message that the bells let fall:
And there was nought of strange, beside
The flights of mews and peewits pied
  By millions crouched on the old sea wall.

I sat and spun within the doore,
  My thread brake off, I raised myne eyes;
The level sun, like ruddy ore,
  Lay sinking in the barren skies,
And dark against day's golden death
She moved where Lindis wandereth,
My sonne's faire wife, Elizabeth.

'Cusha! Cusha! Cusha!' calling,
Ere the early dews were falling,
Farre away I heard her song.
'Cusha! Cusha!' all along
Where the reedy Lindis floweth,
    Floweth, floweth;
From the meads where melick groweth
Faintly came her milking song—

'Cusha! Cusha! Cusha!' calling,
'For the dews will soone be falling;
Leave your meadow grasses mellow,
    Mellow, mellow;
Quit your cowslips, cowslips yellow;
Come uppe Whitefoot, come uppe Lightfoot,
Quit the stalks of parsley hollow,
    Hollow, hollow;
Come uppe Jetty, rise and follow,
From the clovers lift your head;

Come uppe Whitefoot, come uppe Lightfoot,
Come uppe Jetty, rise and follow,
Jetty, to the milking shed.'

If it be long, ay, long ago,
  When I beginne to think howe long,
Againe I hear the Lindis flow,
  Swift as an arrowe, sharpe and strong;
And all the aire, it seemeth mee,
Bin full of floating bells (sayth shee),
That ring the tune of Enderby.

Alle fresh the level pasture lay,
  And not a shadowe mote be seene,
Save where full fyve good miles away
  The steeple towered from out the greene;
And lo! the great bell farre and wide
Was heard in all the country side
That Saturday at eventide.

The swanherds where their sedges are
  Moved on in sunset's golden breath,
The shepherde lads I heard afarre,
  And my sonne's wife, Elizabeth;
Till floating o'er the grassy sea
Came downe that kindly message free,
The 'Brides of Mavis Enderby'.

Then some looked uppe into the sky,
  And all along where Lindis flows
To where the goodly vessels lie,
  And where the lordly steeple shows.
They sayde, 'And why should this thing be?
What danger lowers by land or sea?
They ring the tune of Enderby!

'For evil news from Mablethorpe,
  Of pyrate galleys warping down;
For shippes ashore beyond the scorpe,
  They have not spared to wake the towne:
But while the west bin red to see,
And storms be none, and pyrates flee,
Why ring "The Brides of Enderby"?'

I looked without, and lo! my sonne
  Came riding downe with might and main:
He raised a shout as he drew on,
  Till all the welkin rang again,
'Elizabeth! Elizabeth!'

(A sweeter woman ne'er drew breath
Than my sonne's wife, Elizabeth.)

'The olde sea wall (he cried) is downe,
The rising tide comes on apace,
And boats adrift in yonder towne
Go sailing uppe the market-place.'
He shook as one that looks on death:
'God save you, mother!' straight he saith;
'Where is my wife, Elizabeth?'

'Good sonne, where Lindis winds away,
With her two bairns I marked her long;
And ere yon bells beganne to play
Afar I heard her milking song.'
He looked across the grassy lea,
To right, to left, 'Ho Enderby!'
They rang 'The Brides of Enderby'!

With that he cried and beat his breast;
For, lo! along the river's bed
A mighty eygre reared his crest,
And uppe the Lindis raging sped.
It swept with thunderous noises loud;
Shaped like a curling snow-white cloud,
Or like a demon in a shroud.

And rearing Lindis backward pressed
Shook all her trembling bankes amaine;
Then madly at the eygre's breast
Flung uppe her weltering walls again.
Then bankes came downe with ruin and rout—
Then beaten foam flew round about—
Then all the mighty floods were out.

So farre, so fast the eygre drave,
The heart had hardly time to beat,
Before a shallow seething wave
Sobbed in the grasses at oure feet:
The feet had hardly time to flee
Before it brake against the knee,
And all the world was in the sea.

Upon the roofe we sate that night,
The noise of bells went sweeping by;
I marked the lofty beacon light
Stream from the church tower, red and high—
A lurid mark and dread to see;
And awsome bells they were to mee,
That in the dark rang 'Enderby'.

They rang the sailor lads to guide
  From roofe to roofe who fearless rowed;
And I—my sonne was at my side,
  And yet the ruddy beacon glowed;
And yet he moaned beneath his breath,
'O come in life, or come in death!
O lost! my love, Elizabeth.'

And didst thou visit him no more?
  Thou didst, thou didst, my daughter deare;
The waters laid thee at his doore,
  Ere yet the early dawn was clear.
Thy pretty bairns in fast embrace,
The lifted sun shone on thy face,
Downe drifted to thy dwelling-place.

That flow strewed wrecks about the grass,
  That ebbe swept out the flocks to sea;
A fatal ebbe and flow, alas!
  To manye more than myne and mee:
But each will mourn his own (she saith),
And sweeter woman ne'er drew breath
Than my sonne's wife, Elizabeth.

  I shall never hear her more
  By the reedy Lindis shore,
  'Cusha! Cusha! Cusha!' calling,
  Ere the early dews be falling;
  I shall never hear her song,
  'Cusha! Cusha!' all along
  Where the sunny Lindis floweth,
        Goeth, floweth;
  From the meads where melick groweth,
  When the water winding down,
  Onward floweth to the town.

  I shall never see her more
  Where the reeds and rushes quiver,
        Shiver, quiver;
  Stand beside the sobbing river,
  Sobbing, throbbing, in its falling
  To the sandy lonesome shore;
  I shall never hear her calling,
  Leave your meadow grasses mellow,
        Mellow, mellow;
  Quit your cowslips, cowslips yellow;
  Come uppe Whitefoot, come uppe Lightfoot;
  Quit your pipes of parsley hollow,
        Hollow, hollow;

Come uppe Lightfoot, rise and follow;
Lightfoot, Whitefoot,
From your clovers lift the head;
Come uppe Jetty, follow, follow,
Jetty, to the milking shed.

(1863)

195 *Gladys and Her Island (On the Advantages of the Poetical Temperament)*

AN IMPERFECT FABLE WITH A DOUBTFUL MORAL

O HAPPY Gladys! I rejoice with her,
For Gladys saw the island.
It was thus:
They gave a day for pleasure in the school
Where Gladys taught; and all the other girls
Were taken out, to picnic in a wood.
But it was said, 'We think it were not well
That little Gladys should acquire a taste
For pleasure, going about, and needless change.
It would not suit her station: discontent
Might come of it; and all her duties now
She does so pleasantly, that we were best
To keep her humble.' So they said to her,
'Gladys, we shall not want you all to-day.
Look, you are free; you need not sit at work:
No, you may take a long and pleasant walk
Over the sea-cliff, or upon the beach
Among the visitors.'
Then Gladys blushed
For joy, and thanked them. What! a holiday,
A whole one, for herself! How good, how kind!
With that, the marshalled carriages drove off;
And Gladys, sobered with her weight of joy,
Stole out beyond the groups upon the beach—
The children with their wooden spades, the band
That played for lovers, and the sunny stir
Of cheerful life and leisure—to the rocks,
For these she wanted most, and there was time
To mark them; how like ruined organs prone
They lay, or leaned their giant fluted pipes,
And let the great white-crested reckless wave
Beat out their booming melody.
The sea

Was filled with light; in clear blue caverns curled
The breakers, and they ran, and seemed to romp,
As playing at some rough and dangerous game,
While all the nearer waves rushed in to help,
And all the farther heaved their heads to peep,
And tossed the fishing boats. Then Gladys laughed,
And said, 'O, happy tide, to be so lost
In sunshine, that one dare not look at it;
And lucky cliffs, to be so brown and warm;
And yet how lucky are the shadows, too,
That lurk beneath their ledges. It is strange,
That in remembrance though I lay them up,
They are for ever, when I come to them,
Better than I had thought. O, something yet
I had forgotten. Oft I say, "At least
This picture is imprinted; thus and thus,
The sharpened serried jags run up, run out,
Layer on layer." And I look—up—up—
High, higher up again, till far aloft
They cut into their aether—brown, and clear,
And perfect. And I, saying, "This is mine,
To keep," retire; but shortly come again,
And they confound me with a glorious change.
The low sun out of rain-clouds stares at them;
They redden, and their edges drip with—what?
I know not, but 't is red. It leaves no stain,
For the next morning they stand up like ghosts
In a sea-shroud, and fifty thousand mews
Sit there, in long white files, and chatter on,
Like silly school-girls in their silliest mood.

'There is the boulder where we always turn.
O! I have longed to pass it; now I will.
What would THEY say? for one must slip and spring;
"Young ladies! Gladys! I am shocked. My dears,
Decorum, if you please: turn back at once.
Gladys, we blame you most; you should have looked
Before you." Then they sigh—how kind they are!—
"What will become of you, if all your life
You look a long way off?—look anywhere,
And everywhere, instead of at your feet,
And where they carry you!" Ah, well, I know
It is a pity,' Gladys said; 'but then
We cannot all be wise: happy for me,
That other people are.
                    And yet I wish—
For sometimes very right and serious thoughts

Come to me—I do wish that they would come
When they are wanted!—when I teach the sums
On rainy days, and when the practising
I count to, and the din goes on and on,
Still the same tune and still the same mistake,
Then I am wise enough: sometimes I feel
Quite old. I think that it will last, and say,
"Now my reflections do me credit! now
I am a woman!" and I wish they knew
How serious all my duties look to me.
And how, my heart hushed down and shaded lies,
Just like the sea when low, convenient clouds,
Come over, and drink all its sparkles up.
But does it last? Perhaps, that very day,
The front door opens: out we walk in pairs;
And I am so delighted with this world,
That suddenly has grown, being new washed,
To such a smiling, clean, and thankful world,
And with a tender face shining through tears,
Looks up into the sometime lowering sky,
That has been angry, but is reconciled,
And just forgiving her, that I—that I—
O, I forget myself: what matters how!
And then I hear (but always kindly said)
Some words that pain me so—but just, but true:
"For if your place in this establishment
Be but subordinate, and if your birth
Be lowly, it the more behoves—well, well,
No more. We see that you are sorry." Yes!
I am always sorry THEN; but now—O, now,
Here is a bight more beautiful than all.'

'And did they scold her, then, my pretty one?
And did she want to be as wise as they,
To bear a bucklered heart and priggish mind?
Ay, you may crow; she did! but no, no, no,
The night-time will not let her, all the stars
Say nay to that—the old sea laughs at her.
Why, Gladys is a child; she has not skill
To shut herself within her own small cell,
And build the door up, and to say, "Poor me!
I am a prisoner"; then to take hewn stones,
And, having built the windows up, to say,
"O, it is dark! there is no sunshine here;
There never has been." '
Strange! how very strange!
A woman passing Gladys with a babe,

To whom she spoke these words, and only looked
Upon the babe, who crowed and pulled her curls,
And never looked at Gladys, never once.
'A simple child,' she added, and went by,
'To want to change her greater for their less;
But Gladys shall not do it, no, not she;
We love her—don't we?—far too well for that.'

Then Gladys, flushed with shame and keen surprise,
'How could she be so near, and I not know?
And have I spoken out my thought aloud?
I must have done, forgetting. It is well
She walks so fast, for I am hungry now,
And here is water cantering down the cliff,
And here a shell to catch it with, and here
The round plump buns they gave me, and the fruit.
Now she is gone behind the rock. O, rare
To be alone!' So Gladys sat her down,
Unpacked her little basket, ate and drank,
Then pushed her hands into the warm dry sand,
And thought the earth was happy, and she too
Was going round with it in happiness,
That holiday. 'What was it that she said?'
Quoth Gladys, cogitating; 'they were kind,
The words that woman spoke. She does not know!
"Her greater for their less"—it makes me laugh—
But yet,' sighed Gladys, 'though it must be good
To look and to admire, one should not wish
To steal THEIR virtues, and to put them on,
Like feathers from another wing; beside,
That calm, and that grave consciousness of worth,
When all is said, would little suit with me,
Who am not worthy. When our thoughts are born,
Though they be good and humble, one should mind
How they are reared, or some will go astray
And shame their mother. Cain and Abel both
Were only once removed from innocence.
Why did I envy them? That was not good;
Yet it began with my humility.'

But as she spake, lo, Gladys raised her eyes,
And right before her, on the horizon's edge,
Behold, an island! First, she looked away
Along the solid rocks and steadfast shore,
For she was all amazed, believing not,
And then she looked again, and there again
Behold, an island! And the tide had turned,
The milky sea had got a purple rim,

And from the rim that mountain island rose,
Purple, with two high peaks, the northern peak
The higher, and with fell and precipice,
It ran down steeply to the water's brink;
But all the southern line was long and soft,
Broken with tender curves, and, as she thought,
Covered with forest or with sward. But, look!
The sun was on the island; and he showed
On either peak a dazzling cap of snow.
Then Gladys held her breath; she said, 'Indeed,
Indeed it is an island: how is this,
I never saw it till this fortunate
Rare holiday?' And while she strained her eyes,
She thought that it began to fade; but not
To change as clouds do, only to withdraw
And melt into its azure; and at last,
Little by little, from her hungry heart,
That longed to draw things marvellous to itself,
And yearned towards the riches and the great
Abundance of the beauty God hath made,
It passed away. Tears started in her eyes,
And when they dropped, the mountain isle was gone;
The careless sea had quite forgotten it,
And all was even as it had been before.

And Gladys wept, but there was luxury
In her self-pity, while she softly sobbed,
'O, what a little while! I am afraid
I shall forget that purple mountain isle,
The lovely hollows atween her snow-clad peaks,
The grace of her upheaval where she lay
Well up against the open. O, my heart,
Now I remember how this holiday
Will soon be done, and now my life goes on
Not fed; and only in the noonday walk
Let to look silently at what it wants,
Without the power to wait or pause awhile,
And understand and draw within itself
The richness of the earth. A holiday!
How few I have! I spend the silent time
At work, while all THEIR pupils are gone home,
And feel myself remote. They shine apart;
They are great planets, I a little orb;
My little orbit far within their own
Turns, and approaches not. But yet, the more
I am alone when those I teach return;
For they, as planets of some other sun,

Not mine, have paths that can but meet my ring
Once in a cycle. O, how poor I am!
I have not got laid up in this blank heart
Any indulgent kisses given me
Because I had been good, or, yet more sweet,
Because my childhood was itself a good
Attractive thing for kisses, tender praise,
And comforting. An orphan-school at best
Is a cold mother in the winter time,
('Twas mostly winter when new orphans came)
An unregardful mother in the spring.

'Yet once a year (I did mine wrong) we went
To gather cowslips. How we thought on it
Beforehand, pacing, pacing the dull street,
To that one tree, the only one we saw
From April,—if the cowslips were in bloom
So early; or if not, from opening May
Even to September. Then there came the feast
At Epping. If it rained that day, it rained
For a whole year to us; we could not think
Of fields and hawthorn hedges, and the leaves
Fluttering, but still it rained, and ever rained.

'Ah, well, but I am here; but I have seen
The gay gorse bushes in their flowering time;
I know the scent of bean-fields; I have heard
The satisfying murmur of the main.'

The woman! She came round the rock again
With her fair baby, and she sat her down
By Gladys, murmuring, 'Who forbad the grass
To grow by visitations of the dew?
Who said in ancient time to the desert pool,
"Thou shalt not wait for angel visitors
To trouble thy still water"? Must we bide
At home? The lore, beloved, shall fly to us
On a pair of sumptuous wings. Or may we breathe
Without? O, we shall draw to us the air
That times and mystery feed on. This shall lay
Unchidden hands upon the heart o' the world,
And feel it beating. Rivers shall run on,
Full of sweet language as a lover's mouth,
Delivering of a tune to make her youth
More beautiful than wheat when it is green.

'What else?—(O, none shall envy her!) The rain
And the wild weather will be most her own,
And talk with her o'nights; and if the winds

Have seen aught wondrous, they will tell it her
In a mouthful of strange moans—will bring from far,
Her ears being keen, the lowing and the mad
Masterful tramping of the bison herds,
Tearing down headlong with their bloodshot eyes,
In savage rifts of hair; the crack and creak
Of ice-floes in the frozen sea, the cry
Of the white bears, all in a dim blue world
Mumbling their meals by twilight; or the rock
And majesty of motion, when their heads
Primeval trees toss in a sunny storm,
And hail their nuts down on unweeded fields.
No holidays,' quoth she; 'drop, drop, O, drop,
Thou tirèd skylark, and go up no more;
You lime trees, cover not your heads with bees,
Nor give out your good smell. She will not look
No, Gladys cannot draw your sweetness in,
For lack of holidays.' So Gladys thought,
'A most strange woman, and she talks of me.'
With that a girl ran up; 'Mother,' she said,
'Come out of this brown bight, I pray you now
It smells of fairies.' Gladys thereon thought,
'The mother will not speak to me, perhaps
The daughter may,' and asked her courteously,
'What do the fairies smell of?' But the girl
With peevish pout replied, 'You know, you know.'
'Not I,' said Gladys; then she answered her,
'Something like buttercups. But, mother, come,
And whisper up a porpoise from the foam,
Because I want to ride.'
Full slowly, then,
The mother rose, and ever kept her eyes
Upon her little child. 'You freakish maid,'
Said she, 'now mark me, if I call you one,
You shall not scold nor make him take you far.'

'I only want—you know I only want,'
The girl replied, 'to go and play awhile
Upon the sand by Lagos.' Then she turned
And muttered low, 'Mother, is this the girl
Who saw the island?' But the mother frowned.
'When may she go to it?' the daughter asked.
And Gladys, following them, gave all her mind
To hear the answer. 'When she wills to go;
For yonder comes to shore the ferry boat.'
Then Gladys turned to look, and even so
It was; a ferry boat, and far away

Reared in the offing, lo, the purple peaks
Of her loved island.
                Then she raised her arms,
And ran toward the boat, crying out, 'O rare,
The island! fair befall the island; let
Me reach the island.' And she sprang on board.
And after her stepped in the freakish maid
And the fair mother, brooding o'er her child;
And this one took the helm, and that let go
The sail, and off they flew, and furrowed up
A flaky hill before, and left behind
A sobbing snake-like tail of creamy foam;
And dancing hither, thither, sometimes shot
Toward the island; then, when Gladys looked,
Were leaving it to leeward. And the maid
Whistled a wind to come and rock the craft,
And would be leaning down her head to mew
At cat-fish, then lift out into her lap
And dandle baby-seals, which, having kissed,
She flung to their sleek mothers, till her own
Rebuked her in good English; after cried,
'Luff, luff, we shall be swamped.' 'I will not luff,'
Sobbed the fair mischief; 'you are cross to me.'
'For shame!' the mother shrieked! 'luff, luff, my dear;
Kiss and be friends, and thou shalt have the fish
With the curly tail to ride on.' So she did,
And presently a dolphin bouncing up,
She sprang upon his slippery back—'Farewell,'
She laughed, was off, and all the sea grew calm.

Then Gladys was much happier, and was 'ware
In the smooth weather that this woman talked
Like one in sleep, and murmured certain thoughts
Which seemed to be like echoes of her own.
She nodded, 'Yes, the girl is going now
To her own island. Gladys poor? Not she!
Who thinks so? Once I met a man in white,
Who said to me, "The thing that might have been
Is called, and questioned why it hath not been;
And can it give good reason, it is set
Beside the actual, and reckoned in
To fill the empty gaps of life." Ah, so
The possible stands by us ever fresh,
Fairer than aught which any life hath owned,
And makes divine amends. Now this was set
Apart from kin, and not ordained a home;
An equal;—and not suffered to fence in

A little plot of earthly good, and say,
''Tis mine'; but in bereavement of the part,
O, yet to taste the whole,—to understand
The grandeur of the story, not to feel
Satiate with good possessed, but evermore
A healthful hunger for the great idea,
The beauty and the blessedness of life.

'Lo, now, the shadow!' quoth she, breaking off,
'We are in the shadow.' Then did Gladys turn,
And, O, the mountain with the purple peaks
Was close at hand. It cast a shadow out,
And they were in it: and she saw the snow,
And under that the rocks, and under that
The pines, and then the pasturage; and saw
Numerous dips, and undulations rare,
Running down seaward, all astir with lithe
Long canes, and lofty feathers; for the palms
And spice trees of the south, nay, every growth,
Meets in that island.
So that woman ran
The boat ashore, and Gladys set her foot
Thereon. Then all at once much laughter rose;
Invisible folk set up exultant shouts,
'It all belongs to Gladys'; and she ran
And hid herself among the nearest trees
And panted, shedding tears.
So she looked round,
And saw that she was in a banyan grove,
Full of wild peacocks,—pecking on the grass,
A flickering mass of eyes, blue, green, and gold,
Or reaching out their jewelled necks, where high
They sat in rows along the boughs. No tree
Cumbered with creepers let the sunshine through,
But it was caught in scarlet cups, and poured
From these on amber tufts of bloom, and dropped
Lower on azure stars. The air was still,
As if awaiting somewhat, or asleep,
And Gladys was the only thing that moved,
Excepting—no, they were not birds—what then?
Glorified rainbows with a living soul?
While they passed through a sunbeam they were seen,
Not otherwhere, but they were present yet
In shade. They were at work, pomegranate fruit
That lay about removing—purple grapes,
That clustered in the path, clearing aside.
Through a small spot of light would pass and go,

The glorious happy mouth and two fair eyes
Of somewhat that made rustlings where it went;
But when a beam would strike the ground sheer down,
Behold them! they had wings, and they would pass
One after other with the sheeny fans,
Bearing them slowly, that their hues were seen,
Tender as russet crimson dropt on snows,
Or where they turned flashing with gold and dashed
With purple glooms. And they had feet, but these
Did barely touch the ground. And they took heed
Not to disturb the waiting quietness;
Nor rouse up fawns, that slept beside their dams;
Nor the fair leopard, with her sleek paws laid
Across her little drowsy cubs; nor swans,
That, floating, slept upon a glassy pool;
Nor rosy cranes, all slumbering in the reeds,
With heads beneath their wings. For this, you know,
Was Eden. She was passing through the trees
That made a ring about it, and she caught
A glimpse of glades beyond. All she had seen
Was nothing to them; but words are not made
To tell that tale. No wind was let to blow,
And all the doves were bidden to hold their peace.
Why? One was working in a valley near,
And none might look that way. It was understood
That He had nearly ended that His work;
For two shapes met, and one to other spake,
Accosting him with, 'Prince, what worketh He?'
Who whispered, 'Lo! He fashioneth red clay.'
And all at once a little trembling stir
Was felt in the earth, and every creature woke,
And laid its head down, listening. It was known
Then that the work was done; the new-made king
Had risen, and set his feet upon his realm,
And it acknowledged him.
But in her path
Came some one that withstood her, and he said,
'What dost thou here?' Then she did turn and flee,
Among those coloured spirits, through the grove,
Trembling for haste; it was not well with her
Till she came forth of those thick banyan trees,
And set her feet upon the common grass,
And felt the common wind.
Yet once beyond,
She could not choose but cast a backward glance.
The lovely matted growth stood like a wall,
And means of entering were not evident—

The gap had closed. But Gladys laughed for joy;
She said, 'Remoteness and a multitude
Of years are counted nothing here. Behold,
To-day I have been in Eden. O, it blooms
In my own island.'
And she wandered on,
Thinking, until she reached a place of palms,
And all the earth was sandy where she walked—
Sandy and dry—strewn with papyrus leaves,
Old idols, rings and pottery, painted lids
Of mummies (for perhaps it was the way
That leads to dead old Egypt), and withal
Excellent sunshine cut out sharp and clear
The hot prone pillars, and the carven plinths—
Stone lotus cups, with petals dipped in sand,
And wicked gods, and sphinxes bland, who sat,
And smiled upon the ruin. O how still!
Hot, blank, illuminated with the clear
Stare of an unveiled sky. The dry stiff leaves
Of palm trees never rustled, and the soul
Of that dead ancientry was itself dead.
She was above her ankles in the sand,
When she beheld a rocky road, and, lo!
It bare in it the ruts of chariot wheels,
Which erst had carried to their pagan prayers
The brown old Pharaohs; for the ruts led on
To a great cliff, that either was a cliff
Or some dread shrine in ruins—partly reared
In front of that same cliff, and partly hewn
Or excavate within its heart. Great heaps
Of sand and stones on either side there lay;
And, as the girl drew on, rose out from each,
As from a ghostly kennel, gods unblest,
Dog-headed, and behind them wingèd things
Like angels; and this carven multitude
Hedged in, to right and left, the rocky road.
At last, the cliff—and in the cliff a door
Yawning: and she looked in, as down the throat
Of some stupendous giant, and beheld
No floor, but wide, worn, flights of steps, that led
Into a dimness. When the eyes could bear
That change to gloom, she saw flight after flight,
Flight after flight, the worn long stair go down,
Smooth with the feet of nations dead and gone.
So she did enter; also she went down
Till it was dark, and yet again went down,
Till, gazing upward at that yawning door,

It seemed no larger, in its height remote,
Than a pin's head. But while, irresolute,
She doubted of the end, yet farther down
A slender ray of lamplight fell away
Along the stair, as from a door ajar:
To this again she felt her way, and stepped
Adown the hollow stair, and reached the light;
But fear fell on her, fear; and she forbore
Entrance, and listened. Ay! 't was even so—
A sigh; the breathing as of one who slept
And was disturbed. So she drew back awhile,
And trembled; then her doubting hand she laid
Against the door, and pushed it; but the light
Waned, faded, sank; and as she came within—
Hark, hark! A spirit was it, and asleep?
A spirit doth not breathe like clay. There hung
A cresset from the roof, and thence appeared
A flickering speck of light, and disappeared;
Then dropped along the floor its elfish flakes,
That fell on some one resting, in the gloom—
Somewhat, a spectral shadow, then a shape
That loomed. It was a heifer, ay, and white,
Breathing and languid through prolonged repose.

Was it a heifer? all the marble floor
Was milk-white also, and the cresset paled,
And straight their whiteness grew confused and mixed.

But when the cresset, taking heart, bloomed out—
The whiteness—and asleep again! but now
It was a woman, robed, and with a face
Lovely and dim. And Gladys while she gazed
Murmured, 'O terrible! I am afraid
To breathe among these intermittent lives,
That fluctuate in mystic solitude,
And change and fade. Lo! where the goddess sits
Dreaming on her dim throne; a crescent moon
She wears upon her forehead. Ah! her frown
Is mournful, and her slumber is not sweet.
What dost thou hold, Isis, to thy cold breast?
A baby god with finger on his lips,
Asleep, and dreaming of departed sway?
Thy son. Hush, hush; he knoweth all the lore
And sorcery of old Egypt; but his mouth
He shuts; the secret shall be lost with him,
He will not tell.'
The woman coming down!
'Child, what art doing here?' the woman said:

'What wilt thou of Dame Isis and her bairn?
(*Ay, ay, we see thee breathing in thy shroud—*
Thy pretty shroud, all frilled and furbelowed.)
The air is dim with dust of spicèd bones.
I mark a crypt down there. Tier upon tier
Of painted coffers fills it. What if we,
Passing, should slip, and crash into their midst—
Break the frail ancientry, and smothered lie,
Tumbled among the ribs of queens and kings,
And all the gear they took to bed with them!
Horrible! let us hence.'
                                        And Gladys said,
'O, they are rough to mount, those stairs'; but she
Took her and laughed, and up the mighty flight
Shot like a meteor with her. 'There,' said she;
'The light is sweet when one has smelled of graves,
Down in unholy heathen gloom; farewell.'
She pointed to a gateway, strong and high,
Reared of hewn stones; but, look! in lieu of gate,
There was a glittering cobweb drawn across,
And on the lintel there were writ these words:
'Ho, every one that cometh, I divide
What hath been from what might be, and the line
Hangeth before thee as a spider's web;
Yet, wouldst thou enter thou must break the line,
Or else forbear the hill.'
                                        The maiden said,
'So, cobweb, I will break thee.' And she passed
Among some oak trees on the farther side,
And waded through the bracken round their bolls,
Until she saw the open, and drew on
Toward the edge o' the wood, where it was mixed
With pines and heathery places wild and fresh.
Here she put up a creature, that ran on
Before her, crying, 'Tint, tint, tint,' and turned,
Sat up, and stared at her with elfish eyes,
Jabbering of gramarye, one Michael Scott.
The wizard that wonned somewhere underground,
With other talk enough to make one fear
To walk in lonely places. After passed
A man-at-arms, William of Deloraine;
He shook his head, 'An' if I list to tell,'
Quoth he, 'I know, but how it matters not';
Then crossed himself, and muttered of a clap
Of thunder, and a shape in amice grey,
But still it mouthed at him, and whimpered, 'Tint,
Tint, tint.' 'There shall be wild work some day soon,'

Quoth he, 'thou limb of darkness: he will come,
Thy master, push a hand up, catch thee, imp,
And so good Christians shall have peace, perdie.'

Then Gladys was so frightened, that she ran,
And got away, towards a grassy down,
Where sheep and lambs were feeding, with a boy
To tend them. 'T was the boy who wears that herb
Called heartsease in his bosom, and he sang
So sweetly to his flock, that she stole on
Nearer to listen. 'O, Content, Content,
Give me,' sang he, 'thy tender company.
I feed my flock among the myrtles; all
My lambs are twins, and they have laid them down
Along the slopes of Beulah. Come, fair love,
From the other side the river, where their harps
Thou hast been helping them to tune. O come,
And pitch thy tent by mine; let me behold
Thy mouth—that even in slumber talks of peace—
Thy well-set locks, and dove-like countenance.'

And Gladys hearkened, couched upon the grass,
Till she had rested; then did ask the boy,
For it was afternoon, and she was fain
To reach the shore, 'Which is the path, I pray,
That leads one to the water?' But he said,
'Dear lass, I only know the narrow way,
The path that leads one to the golden gate
Across the river.' So she wandered on;
And presently her feet grew cool, the grass
Standing so high, and thyme being thick and soft.
The air was full of voices, and the scent
Of mountain blossom loaded all its wafts;
For she was on the slopes of a goodly mount,
And reared in such a sort that it looked down
Into the deepest valleys, darkest glades,
And richest plains o' the island. It was set
Midway between the snows majestical
And a wide level, such as men would choose
For growing wheat; and some one said to her,
'It is the hill Parnassus.' So she walked
Yet on its lower slope, and she could hear
The calling of an unseen multitude
To some upon the mountain, 'Give us more';
And others said, 'We are tired of this old world:
Make it look new again.' Then there were some
Who answered lovingly—(the dead yet speak
From that high mountain, as the living do);

But others sang desponding, 'We have kept
The vision for a chosen few: we love
Fit audience better than a rough huzza
From the unreasoning crowd.'
Then words came up:
'There was a time, you poets, was a time
When all the poetry was ours, and made
By some who climbed the mountain from our midst.
We loved it then, we sang it in our streets.
O, it grows obsolete! Be you as they:
Our heroes die and drop away from us;
Oblivion folds them 'neath her dusky wing,
Fair copies wasted to the hungering world.
Save them. We fall so low for lack of them,
That many of us think scorn of honest trade,
And take no pride in our own shops; who care
Only to quit a calling, will not make
The calling what it might be: who despise
Their work, fate laughs at, and doth let the work
Dull, and degrade them.'
Then did Gladys smile:
'Heroes!' quoth she; 'yet, now I think on it,
There was the jolly goldsmith, brave Sir Hugh,
Certes, a hero ready made. Methinks
I see him burnishing of golden gear,
Tankard and charger, and a-muttering low,
"London is thirsty"—(then he weighs a chain):
"'T is an ill thing, my masters. I would give
The worth of this, and many such as this,
To bring it water."
Ay, and after him
There came up Guy of London, lettered son
O' the honest lighterman. I'll think on him,
Leaning upon the bridge on summer eves,
After his shop was closed: a still, grave man,
With melancholy eyes. "While these are hale,"
He saith, when he looks down and marks the crowd
Cheerily working; where the river marge
Is blocked with ships and boats; and all the wharves
Swarm, and the cranes swing in with merchandise—
"While these are hale, 't is well, 't is very well.
But, O good Lord," saith he, "when these are sick—
I fear me, Lord, this excellent workmanship
Of Thine is counted for a cumbrance then.
Ay, ay, my hearties! many a man of you,
Struck down, or maimed, or fevered, shrinks away,
And, mastered in that fight for lack of aid,

Creeps shivering to a corner, and there dies."
Well, we have heard the rest.
Ah, next I think
Upon the merchant captain, stout of heart
To dare and to endure. "Robert," saith he,
(The navigator Knox to his manful son,)
"I sit a captive from the ship detained;
This heathenry doth let thee visit her.
Remember, son, if thou, alas! shouldst fail
To ransom thy poor father, they are free
As yet, the mariners; have wives at home,
As I have; ay, and liberty is sweet
To all men. For the ship, she is not ours,
Therefore, 'beseech thee, son, lay on the mate
This my command, to leave me, and set sail.
As for thyself—" "Good father," saith the son,
"I will not, father, ask your blessing now,
Because, for fair, or else for evil, fate
We two shall meet again." And so they did.
The dusky men, peeling off cinnamon,
And beating nutmeg clusters from the tree,
Ransom and bribe contemned. The good ship sailed,—
The son returned to share his father's cell.

'O, there are many such. Would I had wit
Their worth to sing!' With that, she turned her feet.
'I am tired now', said Gladys, 'of their talk
Around this hill Parnassus.' And, behold,
A piteous sight—an old, blind, greybeard king
Led by a fool with bells. Now this was loved
Of the crowd below the hill; and when he called
For his lost kingdom, and bewailed his age,
And plained on his unkind daughters, they were known
To say, that if the best of gold and gear
Could have bought him back his kingdom, and made kind
The hard hearts which had broken his erewhile,
They would have gladly paid it from their store
Many times over. What is done is done,
No help. The ruined majesty passed on.
And look you! one who met her as she walked
Showed her a mountain nymph lovely as light.
Her name Œnone; and she mourned and mourned
'O Mother Ida,' and she could not cease,
No, nor be comforted.
And after this,
Soon there came by, arrayed in Norman cap
And kirtle, an Arcadian villager,

Who said, 'I pray you, have you chanced to meet
One Gabriel?' and she sighed; but Gladys took
And kissed her hand: she could not answer her,
Because she guessed the end.
With that it drew
To evening; and as Gladys wandered on
In the calm weather, she beheld the wave,
And she ran down to set her feet again
On the sea margin, which was covered thick
With white shell-skeletons. The sky was red
As wine. The water played among bare ribs
Of many wrecks, that lay half-buried there
In the sand. She saw a cave, and moved thereto
To ask her way, and one so innocent
Came out to meet her, that with marvelling mute
She gazed and gazed into her sea-blue eyes,
For in them beamed the untaught ecstasy
Of childhood, that lives on though youth be come,
And love just born.

She could not choose but name her shipwrecked prince,
All blushing. She told Gladys many things
That are not in the story—things, in sooth,
That Prospero her father knew. But now
'T was evening, and the sun dropped; purple stripes
In the sea were copied from some clouds that lay
Out in the west. And lo! the boat, and more,
The freakish thing to take fair Gladys home.
She mowed at her, but Gladys took the helm:
'Peace, peace!' she said; 'be good: you shall not steer,
For I am your liege lady.' Then she sang
The sweetest songs she knew all the way home.

So Gladys set her feet upon the sand;
While in the sunset glory died away
The peaks of that blest island.
'Fare you well,
My country, my own kingdom,' then she said,
'Till I go visit you again, farewell.'

She looked toward their house with whom she dwelt,
The carriages were coming. Hastening up,
She was in time to meet them at the door,
And lead the sleepy little ones within;
And some were cross and shivered, and her dames
Were weary and right hard to please; but she
Felt like a beggar suddenly endowed
With a warm cloak to 'fend her from the cold.

'For, come what will,' she said, 'I had *to-day*.
There is an island.'

THE MORAL.

WHAT is the moral? Let us think awhile,
Taking the editorial WE to help,
It sounds respectable.
The moral; yes,
We always read, when any fable ends,
'Hence we may learn'. A moral must be found.
What do you think of this: 'Hence we may learn
That dolphins swim about the coast of Wales,
And Admiralty maps should now be drawn
By teacher-girls, because their sight is keen,
And they can spy out islands.' Will that do?
No, that is far too plain—too evident.

Perhaps a general moralising vein—
(We know we have a happy knack that way.
We have observed, moreover, that young men
Are fond of good advice, and so are girls;
Especially of that meandering kind,
Which winding on so sweetly, treats of all
They ought to be and do and think and wear,
As one may say, from creeds to comforters.
Indeed, we much prefer that sort ourselves,
So soothing). Good, a moralising vein:
That is the thing; but how to manage it?
'*Hence we may learn*', if we be so inclined,
That life goes best with those who take it best;
That wit can spin from work a golden robe
To queen it in; that who can paint at will
A private picture gallery, should not cry
For shillings that will let him in to look
At some by others painted. Furthermore,
Hence we may learn, you poets—(*and we count*
For poets all who ever felt that such
They were, and all who secretly have known
That such they could be; ay, moreover, all
Who wind the robes of ideality
About the bareness of their lives, and hang
Comforting curtains, knit of fancy's yarn,
Nightly betwixt them and the frosty world)—
Hence we may learn, you poets, that of all
We should be most content. The earth is given
To us: we reign by virtue of a sense
Which lets us hear the rhythm of that old verse,

The ring of that old tune whereto she spins.
Humanity is given to us: we reign
By virtue of a sense, which lets us in
To know its troubles ere they have been told,
And take them home and lull them into rest
With mournfullest music. Time is given to us—
Time past, time future. Who, good sooth, beside
Have seen it well, have walked this empty world
When she went steaming, and from pulpy hills
Have marked the spurting of their flamy crowns?

Have not we seen the tabernacle pitched,
And peered between the linen curtains, blue,
Purple, and scarlet, at the dimness there,
And, frighted, have not dared to look again?
But, quaint antiquity! beheld, we thought,
A chest that might have held the manna pot
And Aaron's rod that budded. Ay, we leaned
Over the edge of Britain, while the fleet
Of Caesar loomed and neared; then, afterwards,
We saw fair Venice looking at herself
In the glass below her, while her Doge went forth
In all his bravery to the wedding.
This,
However, counts for nothing to the grace
We wot of in time future:—therefore add,
And afterwards have done: '*Hence we may learn*,'
That though it be a grand and comely thing
To be unhappy—(and we think it is,
Because so many grand and clever folk
Have found out reasons for unhappiness,
And talked about uncomfortable things—
Low motives, bores, and shams, and hollowness,
The hollowness o' the world, till we at last
Have scarcely dared to jump or stamp, for fear,
Being so hollow, it should break some day,
And let us in)—yet, since we are not grand,
O, not at all, and as for cleverness,
That may be or may not be—it is well
For us to be as happy as we can!

Agreed: and with a word to the noble sex,
As thus: we pray you carry not your guns
On the full-cock; we pray you set your pride
In its proper place, and never be ashamed
Of any honest calling—let us add,
And end; for all the rest, hold up your heads
And mind your English.

(1874)

196 *Echo and the Ferry*

Ay Oliver! I was but seven, and he was eleven;
He looked at me pouting and rosy. I blushed where I stood.
They had told us to play in the orchard (and I only seven!
A small guest at the farm); but he said, 'Oh, a girl was no good!'
So he whistled and went, he went over the stile to the wood.
It was sad, it was sorrowful! Only a girl—only seven!
At home in the dark London smoke I had not found it out.
The pear-trees looked on in their white, and blue birds flash'd about,
And they too were angry as Oliver. Were they eleven?
I thought so. Yes, everyone else was eleven—eleven!

So Oliver went, but the cowslips were tall at my feet,
And all the white orchard with fast-falling blossom was litter'd;
And under and over the branches those little birds twitter'd,
While hanging head downwards they scolded because I was seven.
A pity. A very great pity. One should be eleven.
But soon I was happy, the smell of the world was so sweet,
And I saw a round hole in an apple-tree rosy and old.
Then I knew! for I peeped, and I felt it was right they should scold!
Eggs small and eggs many. For gladness I broke into laughter;
And then some one else—oh, how softly!—came after, came after
With laughter—with laughter came after.

And no one was near us to utter that sweet mocking call,
That soon very tired sank low with a mystical fall.
But this was the country—perhaps it was close under heaven;
Oh, nothing so likely; the voice might have come from it even.
I knew about heaven. But this was the country, of this
Light, blossom, and piping, and flashing of wings not at all.
Not at all. No. But one little bird was an easy forgiver:
She peeped, she drew near as I moved from her domicile small,
Then flashed down her hole like a dart—like a dart from the quiver.
And I waded atween the long grasses and felt it was bliss.

—So this was the country; clear dazzle of azure and shiver
And whisper of leaves, and a humming all over the tall
White branches, a humming of bees. And I came to the wall—
A little low wall—and looked over, and there was the river,
The lane that led on to the village, and then the sweet river
Clear shining and slow, she had far far to go from her snow;
But each rush gleamed a sword in the sunlight to guard her long flow,
And she murmur'd, methought, with a speech very soft—very low.
'The ways will be long, but the days will be long,' quoth the river,
'To me a long liver, long, long!' quoth the river—the river.

I dreamed of the country that night, of the orchard, the sky,
The voice that had mocked coming after and over and under.
But at last—in a day or two namely—Eleven and I
Were very fast friends, and to him I confided the wonder.
He said that was Echo. 'Was Echo a wise kind of bee
That had learned how to laugh: could it laugh in one's ear and then
fly
And laugh again yonder?' 'No; Echo'—he whispered it low—
'Was a woman, they said, but a woman whom no one could see
And no one could find; and he did not believe it, not he,
But he could not get near for the river that held us asunder.
Yet I that had money—a shilling, a whole silver shilling—
We might cross if I thought I would spend it.' 'Oh yes, I was willing'—
And we ran hand in hand, we ran down to the ferry, the ferry,
And we heard how she mocked at the folk with a voice clear and merry
When they called for the ferry; but oh! she was very—was very
Swift-footed. She spoke and was gone; and when Oliver cried,
'Hie over! hie over! you man of the ferry—the ferry!'
By the still water's side she was heard far and wide—she replied
And she mocked in her voice sweet and merry, 'You man of the ferry,
You man of—you man of the ferry!'

'Hie over!' he shouted. The ferryman came at his calling,
Across the clear reed-border'd river he ferried us fast;—
Such a chase! Hand in hand, foot to foot, we ran on; it surpass'd
All measure her doubling—so close, then so far away falling,
Then gone, and no more. Oh! to see her but once unaware,
And the mouth that had mocked, but we might not (yet sure she was
there!),
Nor behold her wild eyes and her mystical countenance fair.

We sought in the wood, and we found the wood-wren in her stead;
In the field, and we found but the cuckoo that talked overhead;
By the brook, and we found the reed-sparrow deep-nested, in
brown—
Not Echo, fair Echo! for Echo, sweet Echo! was flown.

So we came to the place where the dead people wait till God call.
The church was among them, grey moss over roof, over wall.
Very silent, so low. And we stood on a green grassy mound
And looked in at a window, for Echo, perhaps, in her round
Might have come in to hide there. But no; every oak-carven seat
Was empty. We saw the great Bible—old, old, very old,
And the parson's great Prayer-book beside it; we heard the slow beat
Of the pendulum swing in the tower; we saw the clear gold
Of a sunbeam float down to the aisle and then waver and play
On the low chancel step and the railing, and Oliver said,
'Look, Katie! look, Katie! when Lettice came here to be wed

She stood where that sunbeam drops down, and all white was her
gown;
And she stepped upon flowers they strew'd for her.' Then quoth small
Seven:
'Shall I wear a white gown and have flowers to walk upon ever?'
All doubtful: 'It takes a long time to grow up,' quoth Eleven;
'You're so little, you know, and the church is so old, it can never
Last on till you 're tall.' And in whispers—because it was old
And holy, and fraught with strange meaning, half felt, but not told,
Full of old parsons' prayers, who were dead, of old days, of old folk,
Neither heard nor beheld, but about us, in whispers we spoke.
Then we went from it softly and ran hand in hand to the strand,
While bleating of flocks and birds' piping made sweeter the land.
And Echo came back e'en as Oliver drew to the ferry
'O Katie!' 'O Katie!' 'Come on, then!' 'Come on, then!' 'For, see,
The round sun, all red, lying low by the tree'—'by the tree.'
'By the tree.' Ay, she mocked him again, with her voice sweet and
merry:
'Hie over!' 'Hie over!' 'You man of the ferry'—'the ferry.'
'You man of the ferry—
You man of—you man of—the ferry.'

Ay, here—it was here that we woke her, the Echo of old;
All life of that day seems an echo, and many times told.
Shall I cross by the ferry to-morrow, and come in my white
To that little low church? and will Oliver meet me anon?
Will it all seem an echo from childhood pass'd over—pass'd on?
Will the grave parson bless us? Hark, hark! in the dim failing light
I hear her! As then the child's voice clear and high, sweet and merry
Now she mocks the man's tone with 'Hie over! Hie over the ferry!'
'And Katie.' 'And Katie.' 'Art out with the glow-worms to-night,
My Katie?' 'My Katie!' For gladness I break into laughter
And tears. Then it all comes again as from far-away years;
Again, some one else—oh, how softly!—with laughter comes after,
Comes after—with laughter comes after.

(1885)

197 *Perdita*

'I GO *beyond the commandment.*' So be it. Then mine be the blame,
The loss, the lack, the yearning, till life's last sand be run,—
I go beyond the commandment, yet Honour stands fast with her claim,
And what I have rued I shall rue; for what I have done—I have done.

Hush, hush! for what of the future; you cannot the base exalt,
There is no bridging a chasm over, that yawns with so sheer incline;
I will not any sweet daughter's cheek should pale for this mother's fault,
Nor son take leave to lower his life a-thinking on mine.

'*Will I tell you all?*' So! this, e'en this, will I do for your great love's sake;
Think what it costs. '*Then let there be silence—silence you'll count consent.*'
No, and no, and for ever no: rather to cross and to break,
And to lower your passion I speak—that other it was I meant.

That other I meant (but I know not how) to speak of, nor April days,
Nor a man's sweet voice that pleaded—O (but I promised this)—
He never talked of marriage, never; I grant him that praise;
And he bent his stately head, and I lost, and he won with a kiss.

He led me away—O, how poignant sweet the nightingale's note that noon—
I beheld, and each crispèd spire of grass to him for my sake was fair,
And warm winds flattered my soul, blowing straight from the soul of June,
And a lovely lie was spread on the fields, but the blue was bare.

When I looked up, he said: 'Love, fair love! O rather look in these eyes
With thine far sweeter than eyes of Eve when she stepped the valley unshod'—
For ONE might be looking through it, he thought, and he would not in any wise
I should mark it open, limitless, empty, bare 'neath the gaze of God.

Ah me! I was happy—yes, I was; 't is fit you should know it all,
While love was warm and tender and yearning, the rough winds troubled me not;
I heard them moan without in the forest; heard the chill rains fall—
But I thought my place was sheltered with him—I forgot, I forgot.

After came news of a wife; I think he was glad I should know,
To stay my pleading, 'take me to church and give me my ring';
'You should have spoken before,' he had sighed, when I prayed him so,
For his heart was sick for himself and me, and this bitter thing.

But my dream was over me still,—I was half beguiled,
And he in his kindness left me seldom, O seldom, alone,
And yet love waxed cold, and I saw the face of my little child,
And then at the last I knew what I was, and what I had done.

'You *will give me the name of wife*. You *will give me a ring*.'—O peace!
You are not let to ruin your life because I ruined mine;
You will go to your people at home. There will be rest and release;
The bitter now will be sweet full soon—ay, and denial divine.

But spare me the ending. I did not wait to be quite cast away;
I left him asleep, and the bare sun rising shone red on my gown.
There was dust in the lane, I remember; prints of feet in it lay,
And honeysuckle trailed in the path that led on to the down.

I was going nowhere—I wandered up, then turned and dared to
look back,
Where low in the valley he careless and quiet—quiet and careless
slept.
'*Did I love him yet?*' I loved him. Ay, my heart on the upland track
Cried to him, sighed to him out by the wheat, as I walked, and I wept.

I knew of another alas, one that had been in my place,
Her little ones, she forsaken, were almost in need;
I went to her, and carried my babe, then all in my satins and lace
I sank at the step of her desolate door, a mourner indeed.

I cried, ''Tis the way of the world, would I had never been born!'
'Ay, 'tis the way of the world, but have you no sense to see
For all the way of the world,' she answers and laughs me to scorn,
'The world is made the world that it is by fools like you, like me?'

Right hard upon me, hard on herself, and cold as the cold stone,
But she took me in; and while I lay sick I knew I was lost,
Lost with the man I loved, or lost without him, making my moan
Blighted and rent of the bitter frost, wrecked, tempest tossed, lost,
lost!

How am I fallen:—we that might make of the world what we would,
Some of us sink in deep waters. Ah! '*you would raise me again?*'
No, true heart,—you cannot, you cannot, and all in my soul that is
good
Cries out against such a wrong. Let be, your quest is for ever in vain.

For I feel with another heart, I think with another mind,
I have worsened life, I have wronged the world, I have lowered the
light;
But as for him, his words and his ways were after his kind,
He did but spoil where he could, and waste where he might.

For he was let to do it; I let him and left his soul
To walk mid the ruins he made of home in remembrance of love's
despairs,
Despairs that harden the hearts of men and shadow their heads with
dole,
And woman's fault, though never on earth, may be healed,—but
what of theirs?

'T was fit you should hear it all—What, tears? they comfort me;
now you will go,
Nor wrong your life for the nought you call 'a pair of beautiful eyes,'
'*I will not say I love you.*' Truly I will not, no.
'*Will I pity you?*' Ay, but the pang will be short, you shall wake and
be wise.

'*Shall we meet?*' We shall meet on the other side, but not before.
I shall be pure and fair, I shall hear the sound of The Name,
And see the form of His face. You too will walk on that shore,
In the garden of the Lord God, where neither is sorrow nor shame.

Farewell, I shall bide alone, for God took my one white lamb,
I work for such as she was, and I will the while I last,
But there's no beginning again, ever I am what I am,
And nothing, nothing, nothing, can do away with the past.

(1885)

MENELLA BUTE SMEDLEY
(1820–1877)

MENELLA BUTE SMEDLEY was the daughter of Mary (née Hume) and of the Revd Edward Smedley, who was also an encyclopaedia editor and occasional poet. She was educated by her father. Ill-health later moved her away from London to the seaside town of Tenby. Her philanthropic concerns included the education of 'pauper' children and she produced a report on *Boarding-Out and Pauper Schools* in 1875 and two articles on girls' education (*Contemporary Review*, April 1870; *Macmillan's Magazine*, November 1874).

Smedley and her sister, Mrs. E. A. Hart, were to produce books of children's poetry together in the 1860s, but she began by writing tales from 1849. These were to be followed by three novels published between 1863 and 1871. Her primary focus, however, was to be poetry, and the first of her four books of poetry, *Lays and Ballads from English Poetry*, came out in 1856. She seems to have been reluctant to disclose her identity, as this volume appeared under the signature, 'S.M.' (to be reversed for her next collection in 1863), and her only known contribution of a poem to a journal, 'Lines Suggested by the Greek Massacre' (*Macmillan's Magazine*, June 1870) appeared anonymously. It was not until her *Poems* (1868) that she put her full name alongside her own poetry.

198 *Garibaldi at Varignano*

NEVER subdued till now,
  Wounded perhaps to death,
Did Italy strike the blow?
  Say it under your breath!
She struck him; we strive in vain
  To cover the pain, the shame,—
She struck him who struck not again,
  But fell while shouting her name.

See he is sleeping at last,
  How can you wish him to wake?
Can you give him back to his Past,
  Crush'd by your hand, for your sake?
True to the king he has braved,
  And who mourns him, misled, undone,
Chain'd on the soil he saved,
  And conquer'd at last, by his own!

Write this conquest in tears,
  And let its record be dim;
Hide this year from the stainless years
  Which had each a wreath for him,—
And tell him, there as he lies,
  He is still our darling chief,
And never shame shall touch his name,
  But only love and grief.

Blame his error, and then
  Blush while his deeds you tell;
Guard his prison, Italian men,
  For whom his name is a spell;
Breathe his sentence, thou land!
  Of which he is still the pride,
Sign it, oh! brother-hand,
  Which fought so long by his side!

Italy, royal and free,
  Forget not the means in the end!
And, King, if this thy rebel be,
  Tell us, who is thy friend?
Hide him a little time
  And bear it! The day shall come
For counting his generous crime
  Among the steps to Rome.

Italy, blood like this
  Should make thee pure as strong;
Italy, hearts like his
  Are precious even in wrong.
The heroes of Europe scan,
  And lift up thy head, and boast
Thy TRAITOR is the truest man
  Of all the glorious host.

(1863)

199 *Lines on the Greek Massacre*

WHITE Angels, listening all around
  The terror, wrath, and strife of men,
For faint heroic notes that sound
  Through the mean tumult now and then,
What heard ye, that your watching eyes
  Received such rapture in their calm
As if through common agonies
  They saw the halo and the palm?
We only heard the bitter wail
Of hearts that break, and prayers that fail;
We only saw the shame, the pain,
Of England on her knees in vain,
Pleading for sons ignobly slain;
That fruitless death, these helpless tears,
Shall scar and stain the coming years
With savage infamy of crime
Thrust through our tender modern Time.
On this grand soil which year by year
  Renews the unforgotten bloom
Of deeds which Time but makes more clear
  And Deaths which nothing can entomb,
They fell, but did not add a name
  To Earth's broad characters of gold;
There, in the citadel of Fame
  They died, with nothing to be told,
While schoolboy memories thronged their ears
With echoes from the calling years,
And brought the happy Morning back
As closed the darkness cold and black;
How fair was Life when first they read
  Of these familiar glorious themes!
The classic ground which holds them dead
  Was longed for in their college dreams,

When links of light bound land to land
Like comrades clasping hand in hand,
As English youth, athirst for fame,
Caught up the old Athenian flame;

Yet, mourners, on these nameless pangs
Henceforth a new tradition hangs,
For here, by loftier hopes consoled
Than soothed the Demigods of old,
By angel ministries upheld,
By saints awaited and beheld,
These perished not, but passed from sight
Into the Bosom of the Light.
For us, one tremulous sigh of prayer
Hallows the conquest-breathing air
More than all shouts for heroes spent
Who died not knowing where they went.
Here shall be told, when pilgrims come,
  How each his brother strove to cheer;
How tenderly they talked of home,
  How they seemed ignorant of fear,
Patient and yet prepared for strife;
While one, the gentlest, turned from life
So sweetly, that no tongue can say
If it was rent or given away.
And as, where loyal warriors sink,
  We, passing by the place, may pause,
To think, not of their names, but think
  Of their great Leader and their Cause;
So, by this grave and gate of death
Abides the murmur of a breath
Recalling to the passers-by
Not Marathon, but Calvary!

(1870 *1874*)

DORA GREENWELL
(1821–1882)

DORA GREENWELL's early life was mainly spent at the family home, Greenwell Ford, in County Durham. Her father was a squire, a magistrate, and a Deputy Lieutenant of the county. She was the only daughter of a large family of four brothers, one of whom, William Greenwell, later became Canon of Durham Cathedral, and was later known for his study, *British Barrows* (1877). After family debts forced the sale of the estate in 1847, Greenwell moved to Ovingham in Northumberland, and thence to Lancashire. Thereafter, she settled with her mother in Durham City, residing there for eighteen years. It was in Durham City that Greenwell, between the ages of 33 and 51, composed most of her extensive body of writing.

In the late 1840s, Greenwell began to establish herself as a poet, becoming chiefly known for lyrical and religious verse. *Poems* (1848) was followed by a further seven volumes of poetry, including two largely devotional works, *Carmina Crucis* (1869) and *Camera Obscura* (1876). She collaborated with Jean Ingelow and others on a book of poetry for children, *Home Thoughts and Home Scenes* (1865). In her day, Greenwell was thought to belong to a 'trio' of eminent 'poetesses', including Ingelow and Christina Rossetti. An article in the *Athenaeum* for 1897 gives details of a supposed needlework competition between them, suggesting that all three writers met together for the first time in 1864. The work of each poet reveals many shared interests. There is the possibility that Greenwell's poem, 'Christina' (composed 1851), may have had some influence on the poems about women and sexual temptation that Rossetti included in the first two volumes of poetry she published in the 1860s. Elizabeth Barrett Browning is a repeatedly acknowledged source of inspiration in Greenwell's work, and two sonnets are dedicated to this eminent precursor.

At its best, Greenwell's poetry is strongly impassioned, whether in the vigorous movement of 'A Scherzo' or the rapid couplets of 'Madana' (on the Hindu cupid). But, driven by religious conviction, her writing could be as solemn as it is exuberant. Her most explicitly devotional writings lay a firm emphasis on the need to commune with other souls. Much of her meditative Christian prose, including *The Patience of Hope* (1860) and *Colloquia Crucis* (1877), takes the form of dialogues with an imaginary friend called Philip. It is significant that *The Patience of Hope* is dedicated to Josephine Butler, the inveterate feminist campaigner against the pernicious Contagious Diseases Acts of the 1860s. Greenwell met Butler at the rectory at Ovingham in 1850, and they enjoyed a long and rewarding friendship. Two other volumes were published: *A Present Heaven* (1855) and *Two Friends* (1862). Here, too, Greenwell stresses the importance of spiritual revelation.

In addition, Greenwell earned a distinguished reputation for her non-devotional prose. A biography of Lacordaire was published in 1867, and a study of the Quaker, John Woolman, appeared in 1871. Her collected *Essays* of 1866 brought together a number of articles that had already been contributed to the *North British Review*. Among these are 'Popular Religious Education' (1865) and 'On the Education of the Imbecile' (1868). Perhaps her most influential polemic was 'Our Single Women' (1862). In this essay, she writes passionately of the role of literary writing in women's lives:

> It is surely that woman, bound, as she is, no less by the laws of society than by the immutable instincts of her nature, to a certain suppression in all that relates to personal feeling, should attain, in print, to the fearless, uncompromising sincerity she misses in real life: so that in the poem,—above all, in the novel, that epic, as it has been truly called, of our modern day, a living soul, a living voice, should greet us; a voice that is so truthful, so earnest, that we have felt as if some intimate secret were at once communicated and withheld,—an Open Secret free to all who could find its key—the secret of a woman's soul with all its needs, its struggles, and its aspirations.

Keenly aware of political injustice, Greenwell tackled issues such as slavery (in 'The East Africa Slave Trade', *Contemporary Review*, 1873), the mentally ill, and the social prejudice against spinsters: all objects of social injustice. Less well-known essays were published in *Liber Humanitatis* (1875) and *A Basket of Summer Fruit* (1876).

Greenwell was a respected writer whose work received several favourable notices in periodicals, and a substantial selection of her poems was published by Walter Scott in 1889. Her poetry regularly appeared in journals with a strong religious bias, such as *Good Words* and the *Sunday Magazine*. Her devotional prose gained some distinction among what was still a large readership for contemplative religious writings. It was probably successful because of its generally ecumenical attitude to Christianity, open-mindedly debating aspects of Evangelicalism, Methodism, and Roman Catholicism. Given her interest in John Woolman, there is the possibility that she joined the Society of Friends in the 1870s. Her approach to religious and philosophical questions is recorded in her long correspondence with the Reverend William Knight, Professor of Moral Philosophy at the University of St Andrew's, whom she met during the 1860s. Many of her letters to him are to be found in William Dorling's edition of her *Memoirs* (1885).

An obituary in the *Athenaeum* observed that 'poetry was to her second to the pious motive that inspired it'. In *Two Friends*, she expresses her unwavering belief in the noble spiritual power of poetry:

> I have long loved art and poetry, because I saw that they had a power to raise and soften Humanity; more lately I have seen that *they are good in themselves*—or whence, but from their native affinity with the things that are more excellent, should come this acknowledged power? Why, when the heart would reveal its truest, deepest instincts, does it seek to express itself in music? Why, when the mind would utter forth words of nobleness—when it would be truer and sweeter than it can be under ordinary conditions, does it speak in poetry?

A note on Greenwell, printed in the *Academy* in 1885, states that her 'life was entirely uneventful'. Her last years were spent in the company her brothers, first at London, and finally at Bristol, where she is buried in Arno's Vale Cemetery. Her tombstone bears the engraving 'Et Teneo et Teneor' ('I hold and I am held'), placed next to a hand grasping a cross. This memorable image was printed on the frontispiece of several of her books, and became her hallmark.

200 *Christina*

FATHER, when I am in my grave, kind Father,
Take thou this cross,—I had it from a girl,—
Take it to one that I will tell thee of,
Unto Christina.

I may not part with it while I have life;
I kept it by me, treasured it through years
Of evil, when I dared not look upon it;
But of the love and reconciling mercy
Whereof it is a token, now it speaks.
Sore bitten by the fiery flying serpent,
Yet have I strength to raise my languid eyes,
And fix them on that Sign, for sin uplift

Within the wilderness, and there my gaze—
My straining gaze—will fasten to the last,
Death-glazed upon it. Oh! may then my soul
Be drawn up after it unperishing!

Thou knowest of my life, that I have been
Saved as by fire,—a brand plucked from the burning;
But not before the breath of flame had passed
On all my garments, not before my spirit
Shrunk up within it as a shrivelled scroll
Falls from the embers, black,—yet unconsumed,
For One in Heaven still loved me, one on earth!
O Father, I would speak to thee of Love;
We learn the price of goodliest things through losing.
They who have sat in darkness bless the light,
And sweetest songs have risen to Liberty
From souls once bound in misery and iron;
So, Father, I would speak to thee of Love.
Fain are my lips, and fain my heart to sing
The glad new song that both have learned so late.
Once, ere my soul had burst the fowler's snare,
I heard a wild stern man, that stood and cried
Within the market-place; a man by love
Of souls sent forth among the lanes and highways,
To seek, and haply save, some wandering one
Long strayed, like mine, from flock, and fold, and pastor.
His words were bold and vehement; as one
Set among flints, that strove to strike a spark
From out dull, hardened natures, then he used
The terrors of the Lord in his persuading;
Death, Judgment, and their fearful after-looking,
Grew darker at his words: 'How long,' he said,
'O simple ones, will ye be fain to follow
Hard service and hard wages, Sin and Death?
Now, the world comes betwixt your souls and God;
Here, you can do without Him and be happy;
He speaks to you by love, ye put Him by;
But He will speak to you by wrath, and then
Vain will it be to shun Him, to forget,—
In the next world ye may not do without Him:
Seek God, run after Him, for ye must *die!*'
Oh! then, I thought, if one like me might speak,
If I might find a voice, now would I raise
A yet more bitter and exceeding cry,
'Seek God, run after Him, for ye must LIVE!
I know not what it may be in that world,
The future world, the wide unknown hereafter,

That waits for us, to be afar from God;
Yet can I witness of a desolation
That I have known; can witness of a place
Where spirits wander up and down in torment,
And tell you what it is to want Him *here*.'

I had no friends, no parents; I was poor
In all but beauty, and an innocence
That was not virtue—failing in the trial.
Mine is a common tale, and all the sadder
Because it is so common; I was sought
By one that wore me for a time, then flung
Me off, a rose with all its sweetness gone,
Yet with enough of bloom to flaunt awhile,
Although the worm was busy at its core.
So I lived on in splendour, lived through years
Of scorning, till my brow grew hard to meet it;
Though all the while, behind that brazen shield,
My spirit shrank before each hurtling arrow
That sang and whistled past me in the air.
On every wall methought I saw a Hand
Write evil things and bitter; yea, the stones
Took up a taunting parable against me.
I looked unto the right hand and the left,
But not for help, for there was none would know me.
I knew that no man carèd for my soul;
Yet One in heaven still loved me, one on earth!
But being then unto myself so hateful,
I deemed that all did hate me, hating all;
Yet one there was I hated not, but envied,
A sad, despairing envy, having this
Of virtue, that it did not seek to soil
The whiteness that it gazed upon, and pined.
For I had loved Christina! we had been
Playmates in innocent childhood; girlish friends,
With hearts that, like the summer's half-oped buds,
Grew close, and hived their sweetness for each other.
She was not fair like me unto the eye,
But to the heart, that showed her by its light
Most lovely in the loveliness of love.
I parted from her on Life's cross-road, where
I parted from all good; yet even then,
Had prayers and tears prevailed, we had not parted.
Long after me I heard her kind voice calling,
'Return!' yet I went on; our paths struck wide,
As were the issues that they led to; then
She lost me, but I never lost her: still

Across the world-wide gulf betwixt us set
My soul stretched out a bridge, a slender hair,
Whereon repassing swiftly to and fro,
It linked itself unseen with all her lot,
Oft seeking for a moment but to lose
The bitter consciousness of self, to be
Aught other e'en in thought than that I was.
I took a portion of her innocent life
Within myself; I watched her in her ways,
Unseen I looked upon her in her home,
Her humble home. Yes; I that once had scorned
At lowly poverty and honest love,—
I know not if it were its joys or sorrows
I envied most! *Her* tears were like the dew
That lies all night upon the fruitful field
That Heaven hath blessed, and rises there again.
I was like blasted corn shrunk up and mildewed,
Like sere, dry grass upon the housetops growing,
Whereof the mower filleth not his arms,
Nor he that bindeth up his sheaves his bosom.
Earth, earth methought and Heaven alike refused me:
None gave me the kind wish, the holy word.
I had no joys, no griefs; yet had I joyed,
Then none had said, 'God bless thee!' had I grieved,
Then none that passed had said, 'God pity thee!'

I said, Christina wept. Within her home
There was one only little one, a girl:
Oft had I marked her playing in the sunshine,
Oft by the hearth-light on her father's knee
I watched her (little did Christina think
Who stood without); but she was taken from her,
This child of many prayers and hopes: I saw
The little bier borne forth; this tender flower
That Love had nursed so warm, yet could not keep,
Did seem to leave a blank where it had been.
Christina wept, but yet as one whose tears
Rained inward on her heart, whence rising oft
They filled her eyes, but did not overflow them:
For still she moved about the house, serene,
And when her husband sought his home at eve
She met him now, as ever, with a smile,
So sweet, I know not if he missed its joy.
But oft I tracked her thoughts unto a field,
Quiet, yet populous as the city round it,
Thick sown with graves; yet there the mother's heart
Had marked a place, and there her constant feet

Had worn a path. At early morn, I knew
Oft went she by the grave to weep unseen,
So oft at nightfall there I scattered flowers,
The fairest and the sweetest I could find.
I thought—She will not know whose hand hath strewed them,
So wonder and a loving guess may cheat
Her mind, a moment taking it from grief.

I stood beside that grave one summer night;
The skies were moonless, yet their dusk serene
Was grateful to my spirit, for it seemed
To wrap me from the world, myself, and heaven;
And all the air was soft and cool, methought
It kissed my cheek as if it were a child
That loved me,—sinless, shrinking not from sin.
Old legends say, that when the faithful join
On holy Sabbaths with one fervent voice,
Then doth prevailing prayer hold back awhile
The edge of torment, and the lost have rest.
So then, perchance, some gracious spirit wept,
And prayed for sinners, for the voices died,
The wailing ones, the mocking, at my heart;
And through the hush came up a wish, a yearning—
I know not where it took me—not to heaven,—
Yet, had I ever prayed, it had been then;
I sought not death, for that were but a change
Of being, and a passage to a world
Where thought would after me to hunt and vex;
But to cease utterly to be, to find
A place among the rocks, among the stones,
With things that live not, that would never live,
To pass absorbed, and be at rest for ever.
So stood I, holding in that trance the flowers,
A wreath of white Immortelles, that as yet
I hung not on the gravestone, when I heard
A sudden step, and was aware that one
Had come upon me in the gloom; I felt
A grasp upon my arm, detaining kindly,
A hand that sought to fold itself in mine:
Before she spoke, I knew it was Christina.
'And who art thou, with charitable hand
Such kindness showing to the dead, the living?
Now let me look upon thy face, for long
My soul hath deemed of thee as of the angels
That come and go unseen, and only traced
By deeds that show some gracious Presence near;
Yet, surely thou art one whom earth had taught,

Through sorrow and through love, this gentleness
With grieving hearts, with stricken ones; from mine
The blessing of the sorrowful be on thee!'
But at her words a madness took my soul;
They seemed to mock me; falling one by one
Like gracious drops upon my heart, they smote
Its stagnant waters, stirring there no spring
Of life or wholesomeness: yet were they stirred.
Now would I speak with her, the fire was kindled;
Long had it smouldered, long enough consumed me.
Now by its flashes she shall read my soul,
Methought, and look upon me as I am;
So, with a gesture of the hand, I led
Christina, following on my rapid steps
Like an unquestioning child, as if my will
Had power to draw her, till within the door
Of the great Minster passing, in the aisle's
Dim light we stood, together and alone.

Oft had I shunned Christina; now beneath
A steadfast lamp that burned before a shrine,
Confronting her, I said, 'Now look on me;
Where is the blessing that thou spakest of?'
But to my words she answered not; methought
She did not catch their import—so her gaze
Was fastened on me—then her very soul
Gave way in tears; she took me in her arms,—
Me, wretched one, that never thought to feel,
In this, or in the after world, again
Such pure embrace around me; to her heart,
That heaved as if it could not hold a joy
Made out of such an anguish, close she pressed me,
And, sobbing, murm'ring to herself or heaven,
In language half articulate, the words
Came broken: 'I have found thee! I have found thee!'

'What hast thou found, Christina?' then I said,
And with the words unto my lips arose
A laugh of bitterness, whose mocking tones
Through all the dreary hollow of my heart
Woke up the echoes of its desolation;
'What hast thou found? Speak not to me of her
Whose name perchance thy lips are framing now,
The Magdalene; my life hath been as hers
But not my heart, for she loved much—for this
The more forgiveness meeting; I love none!'
But then Christina pointed to the flowers
Still hanging on my arm; '*Thou* lovest none!'

And gently laid upon my mouth her hand,
A soft restraining curb that now my speech,
Like an ungovernable steed sore stung
And goaded into frenzy, spurned aside,
And sprang the wilder; 'None, not even thee!'
I cried; but then the whiteness of her face
Smote on my spirit, taming scorn to sadness.
'Why should I vex thee with my words? of love
I know but as I know of God, of good,
Of hope, of heaven, of all things counted holy,
Know only by their names, for nought in me
Gives witness to their natures; so, to speak
Of them is but to take their names in vain.
Oft hast thou told me how souls hang on God
Like leaves upon a gracious bough, that draw
Their juices from its fulness; long ago
Mine fell from off that Tree of Life, thereon
Retaining not its hold; a withered leaf
It lies, and bears the lightning's brand upon it.'
'Yea, truly,' said Christina, 'it may bear
The spoiler's mark upon it, yet, like his[1]
Of whom the Scriptures tell us, may thy soul
(A watcher and an Holy One befriending)
Have yet a root within the earth; though bound
About with brass and iron, still the dews
Lie on it, and the tender grass around
Is wet with tears from heaven; so may it spring
Once more to greenness and to life, for all
The years it felt the pressure of the band
So close and grievous round it.' But I cried,
'There is no root! a leaf, a withered leaf,
Long tossed upon the wind, and under foot
Of men long trodden in the streets and trampled,—
God will not gather it within His bosom!'
'And who art thou that answerest for God?
Now from this mouth of thine will I condemn thee;
For, saying that thou knowest nought of love,
How canst thou judge of Him whose name it is?'
But here she clasped her fervent hands, and all
The sternness melted from her: 'Look on me,
A sinner such as thou,—yet I have loved thee;
Remembering thee above my mirth, how oft
Beside the cheerful board that Heaven had blessed,
I ate my bread in heaviness; and then,
Had I known where to seek thee, had risen up

[1] Daniel 4.

And left my food untasted, till I brought
Thee in to share it; to my lips thy name
Rose never, so I feared some bitter word
Might chide it back within my wounded heart,
That shut it in from blame; but then my prayers
Grew dearer to me, for the thought that *here*,
In this pure Presence only, could I meet thee;
Here only to the Merciful could name thee,
Could love thee, plead for thee without rebuke.
Yes! even in my sleep my quest went on;
Through dreams I ever tracked thee, following hard
Upon thy steps, pursuing thee, and still
Before I reached thee (thus it is in dreams)
Came somewhat sundering us, and I awoke
With tearful eyes, and on my lips half-framed
Some loving word, recalling so the past,
I thought thou couldst not turn from it away.
Yes! I have loved thee, I, a poor weak woman,
One like to thee, yet holding in my heart,
That else were dry and barren to all good,
One drop of love from out of God's great ocean.
And thinkest thou that we can love each other
As He loves us,—as He that made us loves us?
And sayest thou, "I am cast out from God"?
No! He hath loved thee from everlasting,
Therefore with loving-kindness will He draw thee.
Oft doth He chide, yet earnestly remember,
Long waiting to be gracious: come, poor child,
Thy brethren scorn thee, come unto thy Father!
Away from Him, in that far country dwelling,
Long hast thou fed upon the husks, too long
Hast hungered sore, while no man gave unto thee;
But there, within thy Father's house, is Bread
Enough and still to spare, and no upbraiding.
My little Child, my Innocent, that scarce
Had left His arms, nor angered Him, nor grieved,
Was not so welcome back to them as thou:
Even now, a great way off, even now. He sees thee;
And comes to meet thee—rise and go to Him!
The home is distant, but the way is nigh.
Oh, Thou who, dying, madest us a way,
Who, living, for us keepest ever open
That access to the Father, look on us!'
So speaking solemn, looking up to heaven,
She knelt down where we stood; upon my knees
Beside her drew me; holding both my hands
Firm folded 'twixt her own, she lifted them

Towards the Mercy-seat; within her arms
She held me, still supporting me; it seemed
As then the very fountains of her soul
Were broken up within her; so she wept,
So pleaded: 'Jesu, Lamb of God, O Thou,
The Father's righteous Son, that takest all
The sin of earth away, have mercy on us!'
But I was passive in her arms, I knew
She wrestled sorely for me; yet as one
That feels in heavy dreams a strife go on,
And may not stir a finger, by the chain
Of slumber compassed; so my torpid soul
Slept numb, yet conscious, till within my heart,
That had no movement of its own, but rose
Upon Christina's heart that heaved beneath it,
At length this miracle of love was wrought:
Her spirit lay on mine, as once of old
The Prophet on the little clay-cold child
Outstretched, through warmth compelling warmth again,
And o'er the chaos of the void within
A breath moved lightly, and my soul stretched out
Its feelers darkly, as a broken vine
Puts forth its bruisèd tendrils to the sun:
A mighty yearning took me, and a sigh
Burst from my bosom, cleaving for my soul
A way to follow it, and in that hour
Methought I could have died, and known no pain
In parting from the body; then I cried,
'Oh, turn Thou me, and so I shall be turned!'

* * *

When we arose up from our knees, her face
Was calm and happy, then she kissed me, saying,
'I call thee not my Sister, as of old,
But come with me unto my home, and there
Be thou unto me even as a Daughter,
In place of her God gave and took again,—
So hath He given thee to me.' Thus she spoke,
And drew me on constraining; but my soul
Held other counsel, minded in itself
That I would look upon her face no more,
Though all my soul clave unto her; as he
From whom our Lord drave out the vexing demon,
Had followed fain upon His steps for ever,
So had I tarried by her well content;
And yet I answered her, 'Entreat me not;
This may not be: yet fear not thou for me;

I go upon my way, that crosses thine
Perchance no more; so give me counsel now
Upon my journey, for, as thou hast said,
The home I seek is far away, the road
Is strait and narrow, hard for erring feet
Like mine to walk in.' Then Christina said,
'I can but give thee counsel in the words
Of Him our Master, "Go and sin no more!"
Keep in the Way, and as thou goest, there
A Blessing will o'ertake thee; thou shalt meet
With One to pour within thy wounds the wine
And oil of consolation; He will set thee
On His own steed, and bring thee to an inn
Where thou mayst tarry till He comes again;
Yea! all thou spendest more He will account for,
For thou wert purchased and redeemed of old:
Now must I leave thee, for the night wears on.'
But still I held her closer, 'Not before
I too have blessed thee, even I, Christina;
May now the blessing of a soul well-nigh
To perishing be on thee! may thy love
Be poured, a thousandfold by God requited,
Within thy bosom.' Then Christina turned
Once more beneath the lamp, and smiled farewell,
Smiled as if then the sweetness of her soul
Rose to her very lips and overflowed them,
But spoke not: passing swiftly through the porch,
The darkness took her from me.

That same night
I left the guilty city far behind me;
Thou knowest, Father, of my life since then.
Here have I found the place Christina spoke of,
A goodly inn, where they have cared for me,
These gracious souls, who loving so their Lord,
And covetous for Him, upon the coin
Long-lost, defaced, and soiled, could trace His image
And read His superscription, half outworn.
Soon must I leave it for a surer refuge.
I sent Christina long ago a token,
To tell her it was well with me, and now
Fain would I send this other one, a sign
From Him that loved me in the heavens, to her
That loved so true on earth. When I am gone,
Kind Father, to my rest, take thou this cross,
Take it to her that I have told thee of—
Unto Christina.

(1867)

201 *Madana*

THE invisible Madana (or Kama), the Hindu Cupid, is armed with a bow of Sugar-cane, strung with bees, and five arrows, each tipped with a flower exercising a peculiar and distinct influence on the heart; among these, *one* alone of fatal and unerring flight is headed, and the head covered with honeycomb.

SUMMER! Summer! soft around,
With a hushed and dream-like sound,
From a beating heart that knows
Too much rapture for repose,
Breathless, tremulous, arise
Murmurs; thick mysterious sighs;
Whispers, faintly wandering by,
Breathe a warning out and die;
Lightly o'er the bending grass,
Changeful gleams and shadows pass;
Through the leaves a conscious thrill
Lightly runs, and all is still;
Like the tree[1] whose branch and stem
Flame with many a sudden gem,
Blushing in its haste to greet
Touch of Beauty's slender feet;
Earth with inner joy opprest,
Shaken from her central rest,
Through her bursting bloom reveals
Hidden ecstasy she feels:
Now the rich, unfolding Rose
Through its crimson splendour glows;
Jasmine blossoms manifold
Shed their stars of paly gold;
On the lake's broad bosom borne,
Reddening to the reddening dawn,
Flashes many a floating cup
Raised to drink the sunbeams up;
Drooping on the heavy air
Faint with sweetness that they bear,
Now the Mango buds grow pale
O'er their passion-breathing tale;
And the Champak's leaves disclose
Where, amid their vestal snows,
Kindling at deep gleaming eyes
Fiery-hearted fragrance lies;

[1] The red Asoka, supposed to blossom when its stem comes in contact with the foot of a beautiful woman.

Summer! Summer! now the air
Trembles—Madana is there!
Watch not for his flitting wing,
List not for the bounding string,
Floating 'mid the groves to choose
Gorgeous blossoms, mingled hues,
Viewless as the viewless wind,
Weaving spells for heart and mind,
Flower-armed, flower-crowned Deity,
Light his unseen arrows fly!
Tremble not! the archer's smile
Plays but carelessly the while
Summer lightning o'er the sky
Flashing, flickering restlessly;
Sporting with the passing hours,
He hath winged their flight with flowers;
Gentle witchery and brief,
He hath breathed o'er bud and leaf,
That hath lent to glance and tone
Light and sweetness not their own;
And as these shall fade away,
Will the pleasant charm decay,
Droop, and leave no trace behind
Where its clasping tendrils twined,
Fading, fleeting, like the sigh
Of some wandering melody;
Like a blissful dream that flings
Light upon the coming day,
Like a bird whose gorgeous wings
Glitter as it flits away;
So they vanish! yet the heart,
Ere its gentle guests depart,
Links a thought for after hours,
Summer! to thy songs and flowers!

Yet beware the hidden power,
Madana hath yet his hour:
These were but the chords that thrill
Lightly to a master's will,
Tones, his wandering fingers fling
Breeze-like from the trembling string,
Ere he call forth all the fire,
All the passion of the Lyre,
Ere he stir through one deep strain
All the founts of joy and pain;
One full chord is yet unshaken,
One wild note hath yet to waken,

One keen arrow yet to fly,
Tremble! Madana is nigh!
O'er the fatal shaft is thrown
Sweetness all the archer's own;
For his strength in sweetness lies—
Sweetness, that through gentle eyes
(E'en in gazing half withdrawn)
Sheds upon the soul a dawn;
Sweetness lingering in a word,
Softly uttered, faintly heard,
Yet within the heart to dwell,
Treasured deep in many a cell,
Long with haunting echoes rife,
When the sounds have died to life;
From that subtle arrow's might,
Vain is wisdom, vain is flight!
Vain the charmer's boasted spell
Mightier charms than his to quell;
Groves of sandal and of balm
Yield no soothing, yield no calm,
Though their odorous branches shed
Fragrant tears upon thy head,
Vainly o'er thine aching brow
Droops the incense-breathing bough,
Not the cooling[1] Lotus leaf
Gives to hurt like thine relief;
To thy throbbing temples prest,
Bound upon thy burning breast;
Vainly! still through pulse and vein
Glows the dull unceasing pain;
Vainly, vainly! still the smart
Rankles in thy stricken heart.
Therefore from the earth a sound,
Hushed, and dreamlike, and profound,
Gathers—warning whispers rise,
Murmurs thick, mysterious sighs!
Therefore all the haunted air
Trembles—Madana is there!

(1867)

[1] The flower and leaf of the lotus are used by Hindu writers as the type of all grace and beauty, and they suppose the latter to possess a peculiar efficacy in allaying mental disquietude.

202 *To Elizabeth Barrett Browning in 1851*

I LOSE myself within thy mind—from room
To goodly room thou leadest me, and still
Dost show me of thy glory more, until
My soul like Sheba's Queen faints, overcome,
And all my spirit dies within me, numb,
Sucked in by thine, a larger star, at will;
And hasting like thy bee, my hive to fill,
I 'swoon for very joy' amid thy bloom;
Till—not like that poor bird (as poets feign)
That tried against the Lutanist's her skill,
Crowding her thick precipitate notes, until
Her weak heart brake above the contest vain—
Did not thy strength a nobler thought instil,
I feel as if I ne'er could sing again!

(1867)

203 *To Elizabeth Barrett Browning in 1861*

I PRAISED thee not while living; what to thee
Was praise of mine? I mourned thee not when dead;
I only loved thee,—love thee! oh thou fled
Fair spirit, free at last where all are free,
I only love thee, bless thee, that to me
For ever thou hast made the rose more red,
More sweet each word by olden singers said
In sadness, or by children in their glee;
Once, only once in life I heard thee speak,
Once, only once I kissed thee on the cheek,
And met thy kiss and blessing; scarce I knew
Thy smile, I only loved thee, only grew
Through wealth, through strength of thine, less poor, less weak;
Oh what hath death with souls like thine to do?

(1867)

204 *A Scherzo (A Shy Person's Wishes)*

WITH the wasp at the innermost heart of a peach,
On a sunny wall out of tip-toe reach,
With the trout in the darkest summer pool,
With the fern-seed clinging behind its cool
Smooth frond, in the chink of an aged tree,
In the woodbine's horn with the drunken bee,

With the mouse in its nest in a furrow old,
With the chrysalis wrapt in its gauzy fold;
With things that are hidden, and safe, and bold,
With things that are timid, and shy, and free,
Wishing to be;
With the nut in its shell, with the seed in its pod,
With the corn as it sprouts in the kindly clod,
Far down where the secret of beauty shows
In the bulb of the tulip, before it blows;
With things that are rooted, and firm, and deep,
Quiet to lie, and dreamless to sleep;
With things that are chainless, and tameless, and proud,
With the fire in the jagged thunder-cloud,
With the wind in its sleep, with the wind in its waking,
With the drops that go to the rainbow's making,
Wishing to be with the light leaves shaking,
Or stones on some desolate highway breaking;
Far up on the hills, where no foot surprises
The dew as it falls, or the dust as it rises;
To be couched with the beast in its torrid lair,
Or drifting on ice with the polar bear,
With the weaver at work at his quiet loom;
Anywhere, anywhere, out of this room!

(1867)

'SPERANZA' (JANE FRANCESCA WILDE) (1821–1896)

THE daughter of Sarah (née Kingsbury) and Charles Elgee, a lawyer, Jane Francesca Wilde was was educated at home in Dublin. There she was to meet her future husband, Sir William Robert Wills Wilde, in 1851. With him she had two sons, William, a journalist, and Oscar, the writer. Active in the feminist movement, she also set up literary salons in Dublin and later in London. She moved to London after the death of her husband in 1876.

She was to become famous for her nationalist verse. Converted to nationalism, she began contributing poetry (often translations) and articles to the *Nation*, as 'Speranza', from 1847. Her article, 'Jacta Alea Est' ('The Die is Cast'), which exhorted Irishmen to take up arms, led to the suppression of the journal and the arrest of its editor, Charles Gavan Duffy. From the next year her poetry was published in the more conservative *Dublin University Magazine*. Her *Poems* (1864), again signed 'Speranza', were dedicated to her sons. Her *Ugo Bassi: A Tale of the Italian Revolution* (1857) was dedicated to the Italian exiles. Other publications include books of Irish folklore (1887; 1890) and of essays (1891; 1893).

Although she received a grant from the Royal Literary Fund in 1888 and a civil list pension in 1890, 'in recognition of her services to literature', she died in poverty, while Oscar Wilde was still in prison.

205 *A Supplication*

'De profundis clamavi ad te domine.'

By our looks of mute despair,
By the sighs that rend the air,
From lips too faint to utter prayer,
Kyrie Eleison.

By the last groans of our dying,
Echoed by the cold wind's sighing,
On the wayside as they're lying,
Kyrie Eleison.

By our fever-stricken bands,
Lifting up their wasted hands,
For bread throughout the far-off lands,
Kyrie Eleison.

Miserable outcasts we,
Pariahs of humanity,
Shunned by all where'er we flee,
Kyrie Eleison.

For our dead no bell is ringing,
Round their forms no shroud is clinging,
Save the rank grass newly springing,
Kyrie Eleison.

Golden harvests we are reaping,
With golden grain our barns heaping,
But for us our bread is weeping,
Kyrie Eleison.

Death-devoted in our home,
Sad we cross the salt sea's foam,
But death we bring where'er we roam,
Kyrie Eleison.

Whereso'er our steps are led,
They can track us by our dead,
Lying on their cold earth bed,
Kyrie Eleison.

We have sinned—in vain each warning—
Brother lived his brother scorning,
Now in ashes see us mourning,
Kyrie Eleison.

Heeding not our country's state,
Trodden down and desolate,
While we strove in senseless hate,
Kyrie Eleison.

We have sinned, but holier zeal
May we Christian patriots feel,
Oh! for our dear country's weal,
Kyrie Eleison.

Let us lift our streaming eyes
To God's throne above the skies,
He will hear our anguish cries,
Kyrie Eleison.

Kneel beside me, oh! my brother,
Let us pray each with the other,
For Ireland, our mourning mother,
Kyrie Eleison.

(1864)

206 *The Exodus*

I

'A MILLION a decade!' Calmly and cold
The units are read by our statesmen sage;
Little they think of a Nation old,
Fading away from History's page;
Outcast weeds by a desolate sea—
Fallen leaves of Humanity.

II

'A million a decade!'—of human wrecks,
Corpses lying in fever sheds—
Corpses huddled on foundering decks,
And shroudless dead on their rocky beds;
Nerve and muscle, and heart and brain,
Lost to Ireland—lost in vain.

III

'A million a decade!' Count ten by ten,
Column and line of the record fair;
Each unit stands for ten thousand men,
Staring with blank, dead eye-balls there;
Strewn like blasted trees on the sod,
Men that were made in the image of God.

IV

'A million a decade!'—and nothing done;
The Cæsars had less to conquer a world;
The war for the Right not yet begun,
The banner of Freedom not yet unfurled:
The soil is fed by the weed that dies;
If forest leaves fall, yet they fertilise.

V

But ye—dead, dead, not climbing the height,
Not clearing a path for the future to tread;
Not opening the golden portals of light,
Ere the gate was choked by your piled-up dead:
Martyrs ye, yet never a name
Shines on the golden roll of Fame.

VI

Had ye rent one gyve of the festering chain,
Strangling the life of the Nation's soul;
Poured your life-blood by river and plain,
Yet touched with your dead hand Freedom's goal;
Left of heroes one footprint more
On our soil, tho' stamped in your gore—

VII

We could triumph while mourning the brave,
Dead for all that was holy and just,
And write, through our tears, on the grave,
As we flung down the dust to dust—
'They died for their country, but led
Her up from the sleep of the dead.'

VIII

'A million a decade!' What does it mean?
A Nation dying of inner decay—
A churchyard silence where life has been—
The base of the pyramid crumbling away:
A drift of men gone over the sea,
A drift of the dead where men should be.

IX

Was it for this ye plighted your word,
Crowned and crownless rulers of men?
Have ye kept faith with your crucified Lord,
And fed His sheep till He comes again?
Or fled like hireling shepherds away,
Leaving the fold the gaunt wolf's prey?

X

Have ye given of your purple to cover,
Have ye given of your gold to cheer,
Have ye given of your love, as a lover
Might cherish the bride he held dear,
Broken the Sacrament-bread to feed
Souls and bodies in uttermost need?

XI

Ye stand at the Judgment-bar to-day—
The Angels are counting the dead-roll, too;
Have ye trod in the pure and perfect way,
And ruled for God as the crowned should do?
Count our dead—before angels and men,
Ye're judged and doomed by the Statist's pen.

(1864)

207 *The Fisherman*

I

THE water rushes—the water foams—
A fisherman sat on the bank,
And calmly gazed on his flowing line,
As it down in the deep wave sank.
The water rushes—the water foams—
The bright waves part asunder,
And with wondering eyes he sees arise
A nymph from the caverns under.

II

She sprang to him—she sang to him—
Ah! wherefore dost thou tempt
With thy deadly food, my bright-scaled brood
From out their crystal element?

Could'st thou but know our joy below,
  Thou would'st leave the harsh, cold land,
And dwell in our caves 'neath the glittering waves,
  As lord of our sparkling band.

III

See you not now the bright sun bow
  To gaze on his form here;
And the pale moon's face wears a softer grace
  In the depths of our silver sphere.
See the fleecy shroud of the azure cloud
  In the heaven beneath the sea;
And look at thine eyes, what a glory lies
  In their lustre. Come, look with me.

IV

The water rushes—the water foams—
  The cool wave kiss'd his feet.
The maiden's eyes were like azure skies,
  And her voice was low and sweet.
She sung to him—she clung to him—
  O'er the glittering stream they lean;
Half drew she him, half sunk he in,
  And never more was seen.

(1864)

ELIZA KEARY
(*c.*1822–*c.*1889)

Eliza Keary may be thought of as either an English or a second generation Irish poet. Although she was probably born in England and is known to have lived in Nunnington, North Riding, and Hull as a child, she could claim Irish descent through her father, William Keary, who came from Galway and moved to England only after the loss of his property forced him to sell out to the army. There he was to become a preacher. Her mother was Lucy (née Plumer) of Bilton Hall, near Wetherby in Yorkshire.

Eliza Keary's brother, Charles F. Keary, was an author and her younger sister, Annie, a novelist and children's poet. Her collaborations with her sister include children's poetry and their *Early Egyptian History for the Young* (1861) (Annie Keary having travelled in Egypt during the winter of 1858). She was to write a *Memoir of Annie Keary* (1882) and edit her letters (1883). Eliza Keary also published children's poetry on her own in 1886 and 1888. Her main work, which was addressed to an adult readership, is *Little Seal-Skin and Other Poems* (1874) and this includes her religious poem, 'Christine and Mary:

A Correspondence'. Most unusually for a woman writer of this period, many of the poems in *Little Seal-Skin* approach free verse. Both rhyme and metrical schemes are unorthodox.

208 *Disenchanted*

I TOOK my heart up in my hand,
I climbed the hill;
That superb height on which you stand;
And my strung will
Found only sweet
The labour that it was to reach your feet.

I poured my life out at your feet;
I almost ceased
To breathe or be; my heart scarce beat;
No flutter teased
My calm; strength fast
Struck through my soul, that worshipped, loved, at last.

But then I looked up at your face,
And your self spoke;
My stung soul shuddered from its place
As my love broke
Wild from its chain,
And rebegotten in the womb of pain.

I dragged my life up from the ground,
And went forth bare,
(I had not found, I had not found)
Through sharp, stern air
Alone I went,
Alone I go, through vast abandonment.

(1874)

209 *Through the Wood*

OUTSIDE,
A world in sunshine;
Upon an afternoon
Once in June.
Such a wide,
Deep light-flooding, we were almost
Drowned in it where we stood,
Nellie and I; but inside the Wood
Clean stems grew close to each other; overhead
The intertwined light branches threw

Sweet shade on the rough ground.
I said, 'Nellie,
Let us walk into the tall Wood.'
She, putting her hand in mine,
Led me on softly, and so replied.
We made the only sound that there was,
With our footsteps crushing
The light tumble of leaves on scant grass;
Not the ghost of a bird's song under
Any cover of bush.
So along and along
We went, pushing
Our way where the tangled wood came,
Neither inclined for talking. As for me,
It was all I wanted, to walk by Nellie;
And she—. O! no blame
To the rapt wonder in her face.
This was Nellie—
The great silent glory
Of the beautiful day
Had found a place that he could stay
In—Nellie—
And wrote her through with his story.
So she passed on silently,
Walking by me,
Heaven's temple by me.
Heaven is full of love,
I thought, over and over,
And said to my heart, 'Hush!
You are happy, certainly.'
Just then, from above,
Came three notes of a thrush,
Satisfied, low, out of a full breast;
Then Nellie broke silence, and said,
'You know we shall part presently, you and I,
At the end of the Wood. Friend,
I've a favour to ask of you;—
I may call you friend, and won't tell
A long tale; one word's best.
This little packet—well,
Give it to Robert,
Into his own hand.
Thank you. He will understand.
I knew you wouldn't mind it for me.
You're not hurt?'
'I—Oh, no!' I understood.
After that, silently,

We walked on to the end of the Wood.

* * *

Outside,
A world in sunshine;
She with her hand in mine:
Such a wide, dark flood;
I died in it, where I stood—
By the side of Nellie.

(1874)

210 *A Mother's Call*

COME back, sons, over the sea!
Strong limbs I bore,
Ye are mine still!
Do you rise, do you move to me?
Do you hear there, across the tossing brine,
Sons?—for the great seas swell;
I smell the breath of them, I hear the roar of them,
Leaping, tossing, toppling over one another,
Lapping up to the shore,
Lashing the rock—furies,
What do they come for?
Sires of yours, yearsfull agonies—
Home with a wild lament?
Seas, is it this you bear?
No. But the times that come,
And the thunders I hear,
And the rent wide apart in her garment
That covered us, blinded us, wound us—
Chains ground that bound us,
That gyved us, sword that drank at our heart!
Leap to the rock, waves!
Leap to the land, sons, O braves!
Over graves, upon blood-trodden graves
Plant your feet!
Come, times, God-revenge,
Slow, sure, complete!

(1874)

211 *A Flower to the Moon*

O MOON! O moon!
Sailing light of the night,
O beautiful moon;
You glide by so quickly,
Linger awhile, one little while,
Moon, spare just a smile
Out of your white light,
Out of your broad, soft eye;
To beguile this little, low life, me.
There you go, on and on,
Tenderly, widely, over the earth and the sky;
Have pity, sweet pity, upon
Only a lilybud, queen, a white lily;
Yesternight I could peep
At you fair—that was all; half asleep
In my bud life, with scarcely an outlook even;
But to-day I have riven
My prison, and grown,
All the hot afternoon,
So large that I see you, moon—
Beautiful, brave, ay, and pant
For the free air above,
And faint at the scant
Life below.
Is it love that I feel, do I grow
Up to loving and sorrow?

(1874)

212 *Doctor Emily*

HER room, bare of all beauty.
She in the gloom of the dull hour,
Midwinter's afternoon,
By the fire, grey and low,
Left of her hours ago,
Now with a little glow
And new stir in it just made by her,
Weary, come in alone,
Musing, 'Did I ever wince
At sorrow, or pain of my profession, the parish doctor,
Chosen eleven years since,
As now? Though there has been torture enough, I trow,
Only a word or two just heard

Have set my heart throbbing so—
Can it rest again?
Matched with this, it was scarcely pain
That I felt by the dying man yonder,
All agony of sympathy,
As I watched the cruel death-blow
Dealt, long gathered up of want, sin, and woe.

It was thus I heard—walking
From the blank house with friends, talking
Of this sorrow and of some
Hope, might we cherish, in the long years to come,
When sin and pain,
Bound with health's chain,
Not even one should lie
Shut up in misery:
I still continually
Shadowed by *his* last sigh,
As we spoke;
One, silent till then alone, broke
On our converse: 'Friend,
You are over sad, we must embrace the whole, the end
Each serves, *must* serve, purpose
Better or worse. Are not all
Fitted in due places they cannot fall
From, glory or shame,
Fulness of pleasure, inextinguishable flame?
All cannot win,
Or the *same* goal reach,
Since some by virtue, some by vice teach,
But why quail at each miserable wail,
And yet forget the praise
That from endless days
Swells through the universe?
Let the curse lie
In its own place—needed, verily.'
Whereat we,
Chilled through our very pain as to death,
'Not that *He* wills it,' cry,
'Say 'tis not that you mean.'
And gasped for his reply,
This that came pityingly, 'He!
Him I know not, but the things that be.'

Chilled as to death whilst here alone
I ponder, ah! and he is not one

Saying thus we know, nor are they few;
And these are they we love,
Towards whom our hopes move,
With whom we would prove
That we can friendly seek, and sympathize, and do;
These, who, whate'er betide,
We find, all tested, still on the generous side,
Who reach strong hands
Of help and kindliness to brother lands,
Would shatter lawless might,
Who claim us, all, for right in the name of right.
What small cloud in their fair, deep sky do we see?
'Him, one I know not, but the things that be.'
One in the hidden, in the finite
Lost, loss infinite.
Seek we the True that we dare,
They say, we dare face, be it foul, be it fair?
It, not *He*, then. Has it a heart, this, the True?
Faithless and hopeless; must we be loveless too?

But 'tis the age of woman, they say,
All say it, of her full message,
Presage of good, do we deem? Ah! blind,
Weak, awe-stricken, what do we strive
For? All that we *are* to *give*.
Are we a message to this scorching age
Whilst our tears rain upon it?
Want and woe and sin,
Searching that cannot find—
Would that we could win
Some influence from the skies!
Was not Christ born of Mary for mankind?
Alas! our eyes are dim,
Pining for Him.
Lo! we are broken with fears
Lest *One* belied,
Love should be crucified
Through countless years.

Must they not see that seek
Then? Can there be aught
Empty of Him, forgot,
Or does His promise break?
Some approach there must be.
And we, shall we
Who, fearfully, think
That we feel Him, tremble on His brink,
Have such fear of a deep

As to be prisoned in pain lest loved feet graze the steep?
Can light quench light?
May not the near the far?
Obscure our vision of it—
Nay, He is far and near,
Yea, who is more than light.
Can He fail? we will not fear.

Seek on, then, spurn
Giants of thought, old thoughts, turn
Still to new days. Hew
The immense tree with the strong axes two,
Even as visions of old
Tell how the giants hewed:
And lo! it fell, and lo! it stood, and lo! it grew.
Watching the while, we
Smile of sorrow and hope,
Saying God speed,
As loved faiths stricken from life
Thicken around us, darkening our skies,
Praying God speed,
Till the new dawn arise.
Yet we are home-birds, we must sing from home, place
Of sure refuge for our faltering race,
Low from the yearning of the Father's breast,
Wooing you hitherward,
Where love is Lord.
Children, come home, we seek His face;
When will ye come?
Home—not for rest—
Measureless labour, 'tensest sacrifice,
Price of the very life—'

So, musing this wise
With tears and sighs,
Into the night, till night had set,
Watching her, musing yet,
When 'Doctor' a voice cries
From without, a weak child's voice, 'come quick,
Come to us, sister. Mother fell sick
At noon, and she dies in the dawn alone.'
She, 'Ready, I am ready,
I am coming, little one.'

(1874)

213 *from Christine and Mary: A Correspondence*

[*This long epistolary poem is the correspondence between two women who love each other, but each feels betrayed. Mary has changed her name and converted to Roman Catholicism. Christine is appalled by Mary's intellectual capitulation and spiritual self-indulgence, as well as by her tolerance of the reactionary politics of the Catholic church. The passionate argument between the two is never resolved. Eds.*]

Christine to Mary

WHAT! for Him, Mary,
All your pity, all your worship, all your love!
So fallen out of pity's height
To the slave's ignominy,
Base, with adoring face
Turned heavenwards to the smiter,
From crushed humanity to might,
In extravagant blasphemy of worship!
Calling that love that made for its glory all,
Angel and devil lives!
Calling that love that craves for itself whilst it gives!
Calling that God—phantasm that a weary brain,
Surfeited with th' inexhaustible life pain,
Flings upon nothingness,
Drawn out of its best or its worst
Verily I know not!
To cling to, or cringe to, or what—
But thrice accurst let every lie be,
If it torture, or comfort us equally.
You're athirst? Is humanity?
So you try, has *it* not ever tried,
Filling the great void with lies;
Ignorant, so very wise
In the darkness, naked, blind,
Piling up for a covering amidst the emptiness,
Battlements that are naught.
Mary, not any height
Of passion for that which you call Him and Infinite,
Nor interchange of love, if it were possible even,
Between that and the soul—
Seems to me great, sublime, beside
The story of how one atheist died.
Listen, in the pitiless time
When you swooned with love,
When the blood of men cried
From the ground to the wide reach of being,
If haply there might be found

One pitiful to bless, not to save—
Out of the hunted brood
Driven to the slaughter, e'en in the battle's stay,
Three by an open grave stood
Together upon a day.
Who maketh His sun to shine, verily
Upon the evil and the good doth He?
In the delicious wood,
Spring-blossoming that day—
Maketh His sun to shine
Through delicate atmosphere,
To rise and shine and smile upon the day of death,
Warm with May's breath,
Sweet with new life in the bud—
Sweet day, dear life!
Listen; they stood
One with eyes blinded, shrinking with natural fear,
Two with clear outlook on their murderers.
And of these two, one calling on God
Looked Heavenward as he fell;
The fearful gave no sign, but fell
As the tree falls or flower cut down,
Or beast before the knife,
Yielding his life
A martyr to men's uses helplessly.
And one, neither with faith, nor fear,
Nor hope, nor penitence fell.
Did I say faithless? O, but he had a creed
Most precious to him, and flung it forth defiantly,
'Liberty' the last word on his lip,
Purer than any worship
Chanted round blood-stained altars of the city,
Even though he too was pitiless,
Made pitiless by pity.
Think of him, Mary, who fell thus—
Nay, is it possible for us,
You and me, Mary,
Inheritors of that fair lie,
Taught to us also through gentle infancy,
Of the inextinguishable life in us,
(Sweet words delirious, delicious cheat,)
Saying 'death,' to reach even the verge of this intense thought,
That life for ever changing thro' multitudinous form
Of earth, worm of earth up to highest developed man,
Is and is and is—whilst *I*, this
That is conscious here now, thinks and feels,
Shall cease utterly.

(1874)

ANNA LETITIA WARING
(1823–1910)

ANNA LETITIA WARING was born at Plas-y-velin, Neath, to a large family of seven children. Her parents, Deborah and Elijah, were attached members of the Society of Friends. It appears that much of her childhood was spent in Neath, as well as in Hampshire at her grandfather's home. In her brief biographical appreciation, Mary S. Talbot notes that Elijah Waring was a man of literary tastes who had deep sympathies with those in distress or need. No one can underestimate the profound influence of the poet's religious upbringing. Soon, however, it became clear to Waring that the Society of Friends did not entirely meet her spiritual needs. She recalls that while attending the Meeting House she felt that the church bells were calling her away. By her late teens, she was sure that her commitment lay with the Church of England, which for her enabled a more expressive form of faith. Consequently, she was baptized at Winchester in May 1842. Much of her life was given over to philanthropic work, such as visiting prisons.

During the 1840s, she set to work on a great number of hymns, which would be collected in countless editions until the end of the nineteenth century. These works repeatedly insist on the power of salvation. Nowhere does one encounter a trace of doubt in her writings. She died at her home in Clifton, Bristol, at the age of 87.

214 *'Father, I Know that All My Life'*

'My times are in Thy hand.'
Psalms 31: 15

FATHER, I know that all my life
   Is portioned out for me,
And the changes that are sure to come,
   I do not fear to see;
But I ask Thee for a present mind
   Intent on pleasing Thee.

I ask Thee for a thoughtful love,
   Through constant watching wise,
To meet the glad with joyful smiles,
   And to wipe the weeping eyes;
And a heart at leisure from itself
   To soothe and sympathise.

I would not have the restless will
   That hurries to and fro,
Seeking for some great thing to do
   Or secret thing to know;
I would be treated as a child,
   And guided where I go.

Wherever in the world I am,
 In whatsoe'er estate,
I have a fellowship with hearts
 To keep and cultivate;
And a work of lowly love to do
 For the Lord on whom I wait.

So I ask Thee for the daily strength,
 To none that ask denied,
And a mind to blend with outward life
 While keeping at Thy side;
Content to fill a little space,
 If Thou be glorified.

And if some things I do not ask,
 In my cup of blessing be,
I would have my spirit filled the more
 With grateful love to Thee—
More careful—not to serve Thee much,
 But to please Thee perfectly.

There are briers besetting every path,
 That call for patient care;
There is a cross in every lot,
 And an earnest need for prayer;
But a lowly heart that leans on Thee
 Is happy anywhere.

In a service which Thy will appoints,
 There are no bonds for me,
For my inmost heart is taught 'the truth'
 That makes Thy children 'free;'
And a life of self-renouncing love
 Is a life of liberty.

(1852)

LOUISA SHORE
(1824–1895)

LOUISA CATHERINE SHORE was the youngest daughter of Margaret Anne (née Twopeny) and Thomas Shore, the latter a teacher and curate, whose expressed sympathies with Free-thinking rendered his position within the Church of England rather controversial. The three daughters were educated by their father. Louisa Shore was born in Potton, Bedfordshire, and, after a move to Woodbury, she and her family were to live for brief periods in Madeira and Paris.

All three sisters were literary. The eldest, Margaret Emily Shore, wrote poetry and fiction, but was to die from consumption when in her twentieth year. Arabella and Louisa Shore worked collaboratively to produce four books of poetry between 1855 and 1890, the principal poems in these volumes being written by Louisa. Her first poem, 'War Music', was published in the *Spectator* (1854) and then reprinted in the first joint volume with her sister, *War Lyrics* (1855). This collection, written in response to the Crimean War, was dedicated to the friends of the dead soldiers. Louisa Shore's advocacy of women's rights is most noticeable in her poems, 'Lamentations' and 'Story of Woman' (published in a volume with her sister, *Elegies and Memorials*, 1890), and an article, which was to be reprinted as a pamphlet, 'Citizenship of Women Socially Considered' (*Westminster Review*, July 1874). From the 1860s onwards, her interest in social and political issues was to become increasingly pronounced and her liberal views were articulated in numerous articles.

A posthumous collection of her poems was published in 1897 with a memoir by her sister, Arabella Shore, and *Poems by Arabella and Louisa Shore* came out in the same year.

215 *War Music*

THE merest soldier is to-day
  The poet of his art,
Though he can neither sing nor say
  The transports of his heart.

His genius writes in words of steel,
  And utters them in thunder,
Whilst we want breath for what we feel,
  Who sit at home and wonder.

Yes, these whom England with a cry
  Saw dashed into the strife,
These men of ours who rode to die,
  Like men who ride for life;

Whose souls, ere well the word was gone,
  Into the smoke was hurled,
Who, bound on bound, went charging on
  Into another world.

(No lover nobler frenzy knew,
  Nor 'sighed a truer breath'
Than theirs who with loose bridles flew
  Into the arms of death,)

Doubt not, I say, the hearts of all
  A grander music played
When dancing to that funeral
  Than ever clarion made.

And she no less who, three times blest,
  No longer reads and hears,
But, laying down the dumb death list,
  Gives help instead of tears;

She, champion of her country's cause,
  As faithful and as brave
As he who sword in battle draws
  Before an open grave;
E'en she, who bleeding at her feet
  Sees many a hero laid,
Whose task, though terrible as sweet,
  Has found her not afraid,
Deep in her heart of holy fire,
  Be sure, such music rings
As never yet Apollo's lyre
  Felt trembling in its strings

(1854 *1897*)

ADELAIDE ANNE PROCTER
(1825–1864)

ONE of the most popular poets of the mid-century, Adelaide Anne Procter came from a highly distinguished literary background. Her mother, Anne Procter (née Skepper), was celebrated for her great skills in conversation, and ran a lively salon that attracted Charles Dickens, William Makepeace Thackeray, and William Charles Macready into its circle. Bryan Waller Procter, her father, was a solicitor, who had also become an established poet with the volumes he published under the pseudonym 'Barry Cornwall'. Although Procter was immersed in the busy cultural life of literary London, she did not exploit her contacts when seeking to secure the publication of her earliest works. Eight lyrics were sent under the name of Mary Berwick to Dickens' *Household Words* in 1853. The influential editor and novelist was immediately impressed by the 'sentiment and grace' of her carefully measured poems. Only eighteen months later did Dickens discover that he in fact knew the author, and for a period of ten years Procter became a regular contributor to his journal. In fact, her work accounts for almost one-sixth of the poetry published in *Household Words*. Practically all the fifty-seven poems Dickens printed in his journal appear in her substantial first volume, *Legends and Lyrics* (1858). So successful were these poems that rumours abounded which told of how young people were copying out these verses and then sending them to the objects of their adoration as if the lines were their own.

Legends and Lyrics was warmly received, and twelve editions rapidly followed. In the columns of the *North British Review*, Coventry Patmore praised the lyrical sweetness of Procter's writing in preference to the remonstrations on the 'woman question' that he deplored in Elizabeth Barrett Browning's *Aurora Leigh* (1856). But this is very much the preferred image of Procter as the graceful feminine lyricist, whose most memorable poem, 'A Lost Chord', was set to music by Arthur Sullivan. It should not be forgotten that Procter was centrally involved in the debates about women's rights generated by the Langham Place group, whose membership included several aspiring poets, including Isa Craig and Bessie Rayner Parkes. Her poetry had a strong emotional appeal not only to

Dickens' readers, but also to the politicized audience of the *English Woman's Journal*, edited from Langham Place between 1858 and 1862. Like *Household Words*, the *Journal* made Procter one of its principal poets, printing some of her most moving lyrics, among them 'A Comforter' in 1860. Reviewing her work, this periodical noted how Procter presented 'the genuine utterance of a warm, loving heart; full of sympathy, full of comprehension of things good and evil; strong to suffer and to hope;—a heart linked in every fibre to the common heart of humanity'. The *Journal* was only too aware of the political commitment informing the kind of sentiment voiced in these poems. In 1859, Procter was appointed secretary to the Society for Promoting the Employment of Women, and two years later she edited *Victoria Regia*, an impressive collection of poetry and prose, including contributions from distinguished contemporaries such as Matthew Arnold, Harriet Martineau, and William Makepeace Thackeray. This beautifully produced volume was typeset, printed, and bound by the women of the Victoria Press, established by Emily Faithfull.

Dickens notes that in 1851 Procter converted to Roman Catholicism. Her conversion was probably influenced by her aunt, Madame de Viry. Procter's sister, Agnes, also converted, joining to the Irish Sisters of Mercy. The proceeds of the poet's second collection, *A Chaplet of Verses* (1862), went to a night shelter for women run by the church. Her confessor, Monsignor Gilbert, requested the poem entitled 'Homeless', and he founded a bed at the Catholic Night Refuge in Procter's honour. Her death from consumption in 1864 was hardly unexpected. For many years she had been seriously incapacitated by illness, and her letters to Bessie Rayner Parkes indicate the level of her infirmity. 'Now' was selected to accompany the obituary of the poet in the *English Woman's Journal*, which remarked:

> Miss Procter at all times repudiated the idea that poets ought to be excused the usual duties of life, or were less responsible than others for the use they made of the talents entrusted to them. She would argue that if poetic genius really did unfit its owners for the practical business of life, then its possession was a misfortune, and poets ought to be classed with cripples and other helpless or deficient beings.

In 1866, Dickens furnished an admiring introduction to an imposing edition of her poetry, which was graced with illustrations by John Tenniel and George du Maurier. Friends always remembered her warmly, never failing to stress Procter's modesty. 'Papa is a poet,' she is reputed to have said. 'I only write verses.' Such understatement can perhaps distract from the complex emotions articulated in her work.

216 *Now*

RISE! for the day is passing,
    And you lie dreaming on;
The others have buckled their armour,
    And forth to the fight are gone:
A place in the ranks awaits you,
    Each man has some part to play;
The Past and the Future are nothing,
    In the face of the stern To-day.

Rise from your dreams of the Future—
  Of gaining some hard-fought field;
Of storming some airy fortress,
  Or bidding some giant yield;
Your future has deeds of glory,
  Of honour (God grant it may!)
But your arm will never be stronger,
  Or the need so great as To-day.

Rise! if the Past detains you,
  Her sunshine and storms forget;
No chains so unworthy to hold you
  As those of a vain regret:
Sad or bright, she is lifeless ever,
  Cast her phantom arms away,
Nor look back, save to learn the lesson
  Of a nobler strife To-day.

Rise! for the day is passing:
  The sound that you scarcely hear
Is the enemy marching to battle—
  Arise! for the foe is here!
Stay not to sharpen your weapons,
  Or the hour will strike at last,
When, from dreams of a coming battle,
  You may wake to find it past!

(1853 *1858*)

217 *The Lesson of the War (1855)*

THE feast is spread through England
  For rich and poor to-day;
Greetings and laughter may be there,
  But thoughts are far away;
Over the stormy ocean,
  Over the dreary track,
Where some are gone, whom England
  Will never welcome back.

Breathless she waits, and listens
  For every eastern breeze
That bears upon its bloody wings
  News from beyond the seas.
The leafless branches stirring
  Make many a watcher start;
The distant tramp of steed may send
  A throb from heart to heart.

The rulers of the nation,
  The poor ones at their gate,
With the same eager wonder
  The same great news await.
The poor man's stay and comfort,
  The rich man's joy and pride,
Upon the bleak Crimean shore
  Are fighting side by side.

The bullet comes—and either
  A desolate hearth may see;
And God alone to-night knows where
  The vacant place may be!
The dread that stirs the peasant
  Thrills nobles' hearts with fear—
Yet above selfish sorrow
  Both hold their country dear.

The rich man who reposes
  In his ancestral shade,
The peasant at his ploughshare,
  The worker at his trade,
Each one his all has perilled,
  Each has the same great stake,
Each soul can but have patience,
  Each heart can only break!

Hushed is all party clamour;
  One thought in every heart,
One dread in every household,
  Has bid such strife depart.
England has called her children;
  Long silent—the word came
That lit the smouldering ashes
  Through all the land to flame.

Oh you who toil and suffer,
  You gladly heard the call;
But those you sometimes envy
  Have they not given their all?
Oh you who rule the nation,
  Take now the toil-worn hand—
Brothers you are in sorrow,
  In duty to your land.
Learn but this noble lesson
  Ere Peace returns again,
And the life-blood of Old England
  Will not be shed in vain.

(1855 *1858*)

218 *A Tomb in Ghent*

A SMILING look she had, a figure slight,
With cheerful air, and step both quick and light;
A strange and foreign look the maiden bore,
That suited the quaint Belgian dress she wore;
Yet the blue fearless eyes in her fair face,
And her soft voice told her of English race;
And ever, as she flitted to and fro,
She sang, (or murmured, rather,) soft and low,
Snatches of song, as if she did not know
That she was singing, but the happy load
Of dream and thought thus from her heart o'erflowed:
And while on household cares she passed along,
The air would bear me fragments of her song;
Not such as village maidens sing, and few
The framers of her changing music knew;
Chants such as heaven and earth first heard of when
The master Palestrina held the pen.
But I with awe had often turned the page,
Yellow with time, and half defaced by age,
And listened, with an ear not quite unskilled,
While heart and soul to the grand echo thrilled;
And much I marvelled, as her cadence fell
From the Laudate, that I knew so well,
Into Scarlatti's minor fugue, how she
Had learned such deep and solemn harmony.
But what she told I set in rhyme, as meet
To chronicle the influence, dim and sweet,
'Neath which her young and innocent life had grown:
Would that my words were simple as her own.

Many years since, an English workman went
Over the seas, to seek a home in Ghent,
Where English skill was prized; nor toiled in vain;
Small, yet enough, his hard-earned daily gain.
He dwelt alone—in sorrow, or in pride,
He mixed not with the workers by his side;
He seemed to care but for one present joy—
To tend, to watch, to teach his sickly boy.
Severe to all beside, yet for the child
He softened his rough speech to soothings mild;
For him he smiled, with him each day he walked
Through the dark gloomy streets; to him he talked
Of home, of England, and strange stories told
Of English heroes in the days of old;
And, (when the sunset gilded roof and spire,)

The marvellous tale which never seemed to tire:
How the gilt dragon, glaring fiercely down
From the great belfry, watching all the town,
Was brought, a trophy of the wars divine,
By a Crusader from far Palestine,
And given to Bruges; and how Ghent arose,
And how they struggled long as deadly foes,
Till Ghent, one night, by a brave soldier's skill,
Stole the great dragon; and she keeps it still.
One day the dragon—so 'tis said—will rise,
Spread his bright wings, and glitter in the skies,
And over desert lands and azure seas,
Will seek his home 'mid palm and cedar trees.
So, as he passed the belfry every day,
The boy would look if it were flown away;
Each day surprised to find it watching there,
Above him, as he crossed the ancient square,
To seek the great cathedral, that had grown
A home for him—mysterious and his own.

Dim with dark shadows of the ages past,
St Bavon stands, solemn and rich and vast;
The slender pillars, in long vistas spread,
Like forest arches meet and close o'erhead;
So high that, like a weak and doubting prayer,
Ere it can float to the carved angels there,
The silver clouded incense faints in air:
Only the organ's voice, with peal on peal,
Can mount to where those far-off angels kneel.
Here the pale boy, beneath a low side-arch,
Would listen to its solemn chant or march;
Folding his little hands, his simple prayer
Melted in childish dreams, and both in air:
While the great organ over all would roll,
Speaking strange secrets to his innocent soul,
Bearing on eagle-wings the great desire
Of all the kneeling throng, and piercing higher
Than aught but love and prayer can reach, until
Only the silence seemed to listen still;
Or gathering like a sea still more and more,
Break in melodious waves at heaven's door,
And then fall, slow and soft, in tender rain,
Upon the pleading longing hearts again.

Then he would watch the rosy sunlight glow,
That crept along the marble floor below,
Passing, as life does, with the passing hours,
Now by a shrine all rich with gems and flowers,

Now on the brazen letters of a tomb,
Then, leaving it again to shade and gloom,
And creeping on, to show, distinct and quaint,
The kneeling figure of some marble saint:
Or lighting up the carvings strange and rare,
That told of patient toil, and reverent care;
Ivy that trembled on the spray, and ears
Of heavy corn, and slender bulrush spears,
And all the thousand tangled weeds that grow
In summer, where the silver rivers flow;
And demon-heads grotesque, that seemed to glare
In impotent wrath on all the beauty there:
Then the gold rays up pillared shaft would climb
And so be drawn to heaven, at evening time.
And deeper silence, darker shadows flowed
On all around, only the windows glowed
With blazoned glory, like the shields of light
Archangels bear, who, armed with love and might,
Watch upon heaven's battlements at night.
Then all was shade; the silver lamps that gleamed,
Lost in the daylight, in the darkness seemed
Like sparks of fire in the dim aisles to shine,
Or trembling stars before each separate shrine.
Grown half afraid, the child would leave them there,
And come out, blinded by the noisy glare
That burst upon him from the busy square.

The church was thus his home for rest or play;
And as he came and went again each day,
The pictured faces that he knew so well,
Seemed to smile on him welcome and farewell.
But holier, and dearer far than all,
One sacred spot his own he loved to call;
Save at mid-day, half-hidden by the gloom;
The people call it The White Maiden's Tomb:
For there she stands; her folded hands are pressed
Together, and laid softly on her breast,
As if she waited but a word to rise
From the dull earth, and pass to the blue skies;
Her lips expectant part, she holds her breath,
As listening for the angel voice of death.
None know how many years have seen her so,
Or what the name of her who sleeps below.
And here the child would come, and strive to trace,
Through the dim twilight, the pure gentle face
He loved so well, and here he oft would bring
Some violet blossom of the early spring;

And climbing softly by the fretted stand,
Not to disturb her, lay it in her hand:
Or, whispering a soft loving message sweet,
Would stoop and kiss the little marble feet.
So, when the organ's pealing music rang,
He thought amid the gloom the Maiden sang;
With reverent simple faith by her he knelt,
And fancied what she thought, and what she felt.
'Glory to God,' re-echoed from her voice,
And then his little spirit would rejoice;
Or when the Requiem sobbed upon the air,
His baby tears dropped with her mournful prayer.

So years fled on, while childish fancies past,
The childish love and simple faith could last.
The artist-soul awoke in him, the flame
Of genius, like the light of Heaven, came
Upon his brain, and (as it will, if true)
It touched his heart and lit his spirit, too.
His father saw, and with a proud content
Let him forsake the toil where he had spent
His youth's first years, and on one happy day
Of pride, before the old man passed away,
He stood with quivering lips, and the big tears
Upon his cheek, and heard the dream of years
Living and speaking to his very heart—
The low hushed murmur at the wondrous art
Of him, who with young trembling fingers made
The great church-organ answer as he played;
And, as the uncertain sound grew full and strong,
Rush with harmonious spirit-wings along,
And thrill with master-power the breathless throng.

The old man died, and years passed on, and still
The young musician bent his heart and will
To his dear toil. St Bavon now had grown
More dear to him, and even more his own;
And as he left it every night he prayed
A moment by the archway in the shade,
Kneeling once more within the sacred gloom
Where the White Maiden watched upon her tomb.
His hopes of travel and a world-wide fame,
Cold Time had sobered, and his fragile frame;
Content at last only in dreams to roam,
Away from the tranquillity of home;
Content that the poor dwellers by his side
Saw in him but the gentle friend and guide,
The patient counsellor in the poor strife

And petty details of their common life,
Who comforted where woe and grief might fall,
Nor slighted any pain or want as small,
But whose great heart took in and felt for all.

Still he grew famous—many came to be
His pupils in the art of harmony.
One day a voice floated so pure and free
Above his music, that he turned to see
What angel sang, and saw before his eyes,
What made his heart leap with a strange surprise,
His own White Maiden, calm, and pure, and mild.
As in his childish dreams she sang and smiled;
Her eyes raised up to Heaven, her lips apart,
And music overflowing from her heart.
But the faint blush that tinged her cheek betrayed
No marble statue, but a living maid;
Perplexed and startled at his wondering look,
Her rustling score of Mozart's Sanctus shook;
The uncertain notes, like birds within a snare,
Fluttered and died upon the trembling air.

Days passed; each morning saw the maiden stand,
Her eyes cast down, her lesson in her hand,
Eager to study, never weary, while
Repaid by the approving word or smile
Of her kind master; days and months fled on;
One day the pupil from the choir was gone;
Gone to take light, and joy, and youth once more
Within the poor musician's humble door;
And to repay, with gentle happy art,
The debt so many owed his generous heart.
And now, indeed, was one who knew and felt
That a great gift of God within him dwelt;
One who could listen, who could understand,
Whose idle work dropped from her slackened hand,
While with wet eyes entranced she stood, nor knew
How the melodious wingèd hours flew;
Who loved his art as none had loved before,
Yet prized the noble tender spirit more.
While the great organ brought from far and near
Lovers of harmony to praise and hear,
Unmarked by aught save what filled every day,
Duty; and toil, and rest, years passed away:
And now by the low archway in the shade
Beside her mother knelt a little maid,
Who, through the great cathedral learned to roam,
Climb to the choir, and bring her father home;

And stand, demure and solemn by his side,
Patient till the last echo softly died;
Then place her little hand in his, and go
Down the dark winding stair to where below
The mother knelt, within the gathering gloom
Waiting and praying by the Maiden's Tomb.

So their life went, until, one winter's day,
Father and child came there alone to pray—
The mother, gentle soul, had fled away!
Their life was altered now, and yet the child
Forgot her passionate grief in time, and smiled,
Half wondering why, when spring's fresh breezes came,
To see her father was no more the same.
Half guessing at the shadow of his pain,
And then contented if he smiled again,
A sad cold smile, that passed in tears away,
As re-assured she ran once more to play.
And now each year that added grace to grace,
Fresh bloom and sunshine to the young girl's face,
Brought a strange light in the musician's eyes,
As if he saw some starry hope arise,
Breaking upon the midnight of sad skies.
It might be so: more feeble year by year,
The wanderer to his resting-place drew near.
One day the Gloria he could play no more,
Echoed its grand rejoicing as of yore;
His hands were clasped, his weary head was laid,
Upon the tomb where the White Maiden prayed:
Where the child's love first dawned, his soul first spoke,
The old man's heart there throbbed its last and broke.
The grave cathedral that had nursed his youth,
Had helped his dreaming, and had taught him truth,
Had seen his boyish grief and baby tears,
And watched the sorrows and the joys of years,
Had lit his fame and hope with sacred rays,
And consecrated sad and happy days—
Had blessed his happiness, and soothed his pain,
Now took her faithful servant home again.

He rests in peace: some travellers mention yet
An organist whose name they all forget.
He has a holier and a nobler fame
By poor men's hearths, who love and bless the name
Of a kind friend; and in low tones to-day,
Speak tenderly of him who passed away.
Too poor to help the daughter of their friend,
They grieved to see the little pittance end;

To see her toil and strive with cheerful heart,
To bear the lonely orphan's struggling part;
They grieved to see her go at last alone
To English kinsmen she had never known:
And here she came; the foreign girl soon found
Welcome, and love, and plenty all around,
And here she pays it back with earnest will,
By well-taught housewife watchfulness and skill;
Deep in her heart she holds her father's name,
And tenderly and proudly keeps his fame;
And while she works with thrifty Belgian care,
Past dreams of childhood float upon the air;
Some strange old chant, or solemn Latin hymn,
That echoed through the old cathedral dim,
When as a little child each day she went
To kneel and pray by an old tomb in Ghent.

(1855 *1858*)

219 *A Woman's Question*

BEFORE I trust my Fate to thee,
  Or place my hand in thine,
Before I let thy Future give
  Colour and form to mine,
Before I peril all for thee, question thy soul to-night for me.

I break all slighter bonds, nor feel
  A shadow of regret:
Is there one link within the Past,
  That holds thy spirit yet?
Or is thy Faith as clear and free as that which I can pledge to thee?

Does there within thy dimmest dreams
  A possible future shine,
Wherein thy life could henceforth breathe,
  Untouched, unshared by mine?
If so, at any pain or cost, oh, tell me before all is lost.

Look deeper still. If thou canst feel
  Within thy inmost soul,
That thou hast kept a portion back,
  While I have staked the whole;
Let no false pity spare the blow, but in true mercy tell me so.

Is there within thy heart a need
  That mine cannot fulfil?
One chord that any other hand
  Could better wake or still?
Speak now—lest at some future day my whole life wither and decay.

Lives there within thy nature hid
  The demon-spirit Change,
Shedding a passing glory still
  On all things new and strange?—
It may not be thy fault alone—but shield my heart against thy own.

Couldst thou withdraw thy hand one day
  And answer to my claim,
That Fate, and that to-day's mistake,
  Not thou—had been to blame?
Some soothe their conscience thus: but thou, wilt surely warn and save me now.

Nay, answer *not*—I dare not hear,
  The words would come too late;
Yet I would spare thee all remorse,
  So, comfort thee, my Fate—
Whatever on my heart may fall—remember, I *would* risk it all!

(1858 *1858*)

220 *Envy*

He was the first always: Fortune
  Shone bright in his face.
I fought for years; with no effort
  He conquered the place:
We ran; my feet were all bleeding,
  But he won the race.

Spite of his many successes
  Men loved him the same;
My one pale ray of good fortune
  Met scoffing and blame.
When we erred, they gave him pity,
  But me—only shame.

My home was still in the shadow,
  His lay in the sun:
I longed in vain: what he asked for
  It straightway was done.
Once I staked all my heart's treasure,
  We played—and he won.

Yes; and just now I have seen him,
  Cold, smiling, and blest,
Laid in his coffin. God help me!
  While he is at rest,
I am cursed still to live:—even
  Death loved him the best.

(1859 *1861*)

221

A Lost Chord

SEATED one day at the Organ,
  I was weary and ill at ease,
And my fingers wandered idly
  Over the noisy keys.

I do not know what I was playing,
  Or what I was dreaming then;
But I struck one chord of music,
  Like the sound of a great Amen.

It flooded the crimson twilight
  Like the close of an Angel's Psalm,
And it lay on my fevered spirit
  With a touch of infinite calm.

It quieted pain and sorrow,
  Like love overcoming strife;
It seemed the harmonious echo
  From our discordant life.

It linked all perplexèd meanings
  Into one perfect peace,
And trembled away into silence
  As if it were loth to cease.

I have sought, but I seek it vainly,
  That one lost chord divine,
Which came from the soul of the Organ,
  And entered into mine.

It may be that Death's bright angel
  Will speak in that chord again,—
It may be that only in Heaven
  I shall hear that grand Amen.

(1860 *1861*)

222 *The Requital*

LOUD roared the Tempest,
  Fast fell the sleet;
A little Child Angel
  Passed down the street,
With trailing pinions,
  And weary feet.

The moon was hidden;
  No stars were bright;
So she could not shelter
  In heaven that night,
For the Angel's ladders
  Are rays of light.

She beat her wings
  At each window pane,
And pleaded for shelter,
  But all in vain:—
'Listen,' they said,
  'To the pelting rain!'

She sobbed, as the laughter
  And mirth grew higher,
'Give me rest and shelter
  Beside your fire,
And I will give you
  Your heart's desire.'

The dreamer sat watching
  His embers gleam,
While his heart was floating
  Down hope's bright stream;
. . . So he wove her wailing
  Into his dream.

The worker toiled on,
  For his time was brief;
The mourner was nursing
  Her own pale grief:
They heard not the promise
  That brought relief.

But fiercer the Tempest
  Rose than before,
When the Angel paused
  At a humble door,
And asked for shelter
  And help once more.

A weary woman,
  Pale, worn, and thin,
With the brand upon her
  Of want and sin,
Heard the Child Angel
  And took her in.

Took her in gently,
  And did her best
To dry her pinions;
  And made her rest
With tender pity
  Upon her breast.

With the eastern morning
  Grew bright and red,
Up the first sunbeam
  The Angel fled;
Having kissed the woman
  And left her—dead.

(1860 *1861*)

223 *A Comforter*

I

WILL she come to me, little Effie,
  Will she come in my arms to rest,
And nestle her head on my shoulder,
  While the sun goes down in the west?

II

'I and Effie will sit together,
  All alone, in this great arm-chair:—
Is it silly to mind it, darling,
  When life is so hard to bear?

III

'No one comforts me like my Effie,
  Just I think that she does not try,—
Only looks with a wistful wonder
  Why grown people should ever cry;

IV

'While her little soft arms close tighter
Round my neck in their clinging hold:—
Well, I must not cry on your hair, dear,
For my tears might tarnish the gold.

V

'I am tired of trying to read, dear;
It is worse to talk and seem gay:
There are some kinds of sorrow, Effie,
It is useless to thrust away.

VI

'Ah, advice may be wise, my darling,
But one always knows it before;
And the reasoning down one's sorrow
Seems to make one suffer the more.

VII

'But my Effie won't reason, will she?
Or endeavour to understand;
Only holds up her mouth to kiss me,
As she strokes my face with her hand.

VIII

'If you break your plaything yourself, dear,
Don't you cry for it all the same?
I don't think it is such a comfort,
One has only oneself to blame.

IX

'People say things cannot be helped, dear,
But then that is the reason why;
For if things could be helped or altered,
One would never sit down to cry:

X

'They say, too, that tears are quite useless
To undo, amend, or restore,—
When I think *how* useless, my Effie,
Then my tears only fall the more.

XI

'All to-day I struggled against it;
  But that does not make sorrow cease;
And now, dear, it is such a comfort
  To be able to cry in peace.

XII

'Though wise people would call that folly,
  And remonstrate with grave surprise;
We won't mind what they say, my Effie;—
  We never professed to be wise.

XIII

'But my comforter knows a lesson
  Wiser, truer than all the rest:—
That to help and to heal a sorrow,
  Love and silence are always best.

XIV

'Well, who is my comforter—tell me?
  Effie smiles, but she will not speak;
Or look up through the long curled lashes
  That are shading her rosy cheek.

XV

'Is she thinking of talking fishes,
  The blue bird, or magical tree?
Perhaps I am thinking, my darling,
  Of something that never can be.

XVI

'You long—don't you, dear?—for the Genii,
  Who were slaves of lamps and of rings;
And I—I am sometimes afraid, dear,—
  I want as impossible things.

XVII

'But hark! there is Nurse calling Effie!
  It is bedtime, so run away,
And I must go back, or the others
  Will be wondering why I stay.

XVIII

'So good-night to my darling Effie;
  Keep happy, sweetheart, and grow wise:—
There's one kiss for her golden tresses,
  And two for her sleepy eyes.'

(1860 *1861*)

224 *A Woman's Last Word*

WELL—the links are broken,
    All is past;
This farewell, when spoken,
    Is the last.
I have tried and striven
    All in vain;
Such bonds must be riven,
    Spite of pain,
And never, never, never
    Knit again.

So I tell you plainly
    It must be:
I shall try, not vainly,
    To be free;
Truer, happier chances
    Wait me yet,
While you, through fresh fancies
    Can forget;—
And life has nobler uses
    Than Regret.

All past words retracing,
    One by one,
Does not help effacing
    What is done.
Let it be. Oh, stronger
    Links can break!
Had we dreamed still longer
    We could wake,—
Yet let us part in kindness
    For Love's sake.

Bitterness and sorrow
    Will at last,
In some bright to-morrow,
    Heal their past;

But future hearts will never
Be as true
As mine was—is ever,
Dear, for you . . .
Then must we part, when loving
As we do?

(1861)

225

Homeless

IT is cold dark midnight, yet listen
To that patter of tiny feet!
Is it one of your dogs, fair lady,
Who whines in the bleak cold street?
Is it one of your silken spaniels
Shut out in the snow and the sleet?

My dogs sleep warm in their baskets,
Safe from the darkness and snow;
All the beasts in our Christian England,
Find pity wherever they go—
(Those are only the homeless children
Who are wandering to and fro.)

Look out in the gusty darkness—
I have seen it again and again,
That shadow, that flits so slowly
Up and down past the window pane:—
It is surely some criminal lurking
Out there in the frozen rain?

Nay, our Criminals all are sheltered,
They are pitied and taught and fed:
That is only a sister-woman
Who has got neither food nor bed—
And the Night cries 'sin to be living',
And the River cries 'sin to be dead'.

Look out at that farthest corner
Where the wall stands blank and bare:—
Can that be a pack which a Pedlar
Has left and forgotten there?
His goods lying out unsheltered
Will be spoilt by the damp night air.

Nay;—goods in our thrifty England
   Are not left to lie and grow rotten,
For each man knows the market value
   Of silk or woollen or cotton...
But in counting the riches of England
   I think our Poor are forgotten.

Our Beasts and our Thieves and our Chattels
   Have weight for good or for ill;
But the Poor are only His image,
   His presence, His word, His will—
And so Lazarus lies at our doorstep
   And Dives neglects him still.

(1862)

DINAH MARIA MULOCK CRAIK (1826–1887)

BORN in Stoke-on-Trent, Dinah Mulock Craik was the oldest of three children. Her father, Thomas Mulock, was a Nonconforminist minister whose eventual neglect of his family would have a profound influence on the course taken by her literary career. It is clear that Mulock's instability forced him to resign from his chapel. Meanwhile, her mother, Dinah (née Mellard), kept a small school, which presumably assisted with much-needed family income. Such an environment fostered Craik's commitment to the Baptist way of life, her passion for learning, and her interest in literary composition. Both scholarly and creative in inclination, Craik was sufficiently skilled in Latin at the age of 13 to teach it to her mother's pupils. Within a matter of years, she was sending out her work to editors, and her first published poem, on the birth of the Princess Royal, was printed in the *Staffordshire Advertiser* when she was only 16. Assured that she would succeed as a professional writer, Craik took a dramatic decision at the age of 20. In the face of her father's behaviour, she led her invalid mother and small brothers to London, proposing that she could support them by her pen. Although circumstances were at first difficult, Craik soon managed to make the contacts she needed, and encouragement came from two influential sources: Charles Mudie, the proprietor of the famous circulating library, and Alexander Macmillan of the publishing house. To make her name, she began placing poems and stories in popular magazines, such as *Good Words* and *Once a Week*. Her first books appeared in 1849. *Cola Monti; or The Story of Genius* was written for children, while *The Ogilvies* was an adult novel focusing on marriage, a topic that would frequently preoccupy her later writings. By this time, she had enough income to maintain her mother and brothers in a cottage at Hampstead. Fame arrived with the publication of her finest and perhaps most ambitious novel, *John Halifax, Gentleman* (1856), which tells an affecting tale of rags to riches. This novel, in many ways, stands as the paradigmatic story of the Victorian self-made man. The ideal upheld by the novel had a moral of its own for Craik, since the considerable proceeds from its sale would enable her, in

1869, to build Corner House at Shortlands, Kent. This imposing property was designed by William Morris, and she resided there until her death in 1887.

Craik was sufficiently established in 1864 to be awarded a civil list pension of £60 annually. A year later, she married George Lillie Craik, a partner in Macmillan, the publishing company with which she brought out several of her later works. Although known mainly by her contemporaries for her novels, Dinah Mulock was a poet of considerable distinction. Among the forty-five volumes she published during her lifetime are several books of poetry for adults, and one for children. Her first collection, simply entitled *Poems*, appeared in 1859. *Songs of Our Youth* followed much later in 1875. *Thirty Years: Being Poems Old and New* was published in 1881, being reissued as *Poems* in 1888. Her substantial body of work extends to other areas of concern, such as women's role in society. *A Woman's Thoughts about Women* (1858) reveals her as a quite conservative thinker, who wished women to succeed in traditional areas of endeavour, such as the arts—the sphere in which she herself had made her mark.

226 *Only a Woman*

She loves with love that cannot tire:
And if, ah, woe! she loves alone,
Through passionate duty love flames higher,
As grass grows taller round a stone.
Coventry Patmore

So, the truth's out. I'll grasp it like a snake,—
It will not slay me. My heart shall not break
Awhile, if only for the children's sake.

For his too, somewhat. Let him stand unblamed;
None say, he gave me less than honor claimed,
Except—one trifle scarcely worth being named—

The *heart*. That's gone. The corrupt dead might be
As easily raised up, breathing—fair to see,
As he could bring his whole heart back to me.

I never sought him in coquettish sport,
Or courted him as silly maidens court,
And wonder when the longed-for prize falls short.

I only loved him—any woman would:
But shut my love up till he came and sued,
Then poured it o'er his dry life like a flood.

I was so happy I could make him blest!
So happy that I was his first and best,
As he mine—when he took me to his breast.

Ah me! if only then he had been true!
If for one little year, a month or two,
He had given me love for love, as was my due!

Or had he told me, ere the deed was done,
He only raised me to his heart's dear throne—
Poor substitute—because the queen was gone!

O, had he whispered, when his sweetest kiss
Was warm upon my mouth in fancied bliss,
He had kissed another woman even as this,—

It were less bitter! Sometimes I could weep
To be thus cheated, like a child asleep:—
Were not my anguish far too dry and deep.

So I built my house upon another's ground;
Mocked with a heart just caught at the rebound—
A cankered thing that looked so firm and sound.

And when that heart grew colder—colder still,
I, ignorant, tried all duties to fulfil,
Blaming my foolish pain, exacting will,

All—anything but him. It was to be:
The full draught others drink up carelessly
Was made this bitter Tantalus-cup for me.

I say again—he gives me all I claimed,
I and my children never shall be shamed:
He is a just man—he will live unblamed.

Only—O God, O God, to cry for bread,
And get a stone! Daily to lay my head
Upon a bosom where the old love's dead!

Dead?—Fool! It never lived. It only stirred
Galvanic, like an hour-cold corpse. None heard:
So let me bury it without a word.

He'll keep that other woman from my sight.
I know not if her face be foul or bright;
I only know that it was his delight—

As his was mine: I only know he stands
Pale, at the touch of their long-severed hands,
Then to a flickering smile his lips commands,

Lest I should grieve, or jealous anger show.
He need not. When the ship's gone down, I trow,
We little reck whatever wind may blow.

And so my silent moan begins and ends.
No world's laugh or world's taunt, no pity of friends
Or sneer of foes with this my torment blends.

None knows—none heeds. I have a little pride;
Enough to stand up, wife-like, by his side,
With the same smile as when I was a bride.

And I shall take his children to my arms;
They will not miss these fading, worthless charms;
Their kiss—ah, unlike his—all pain disarms.

And haply, as the solemn years go by,
He will think sometimes with regretful sigh,
The other woman was less true than I.

(1872)

227 *To Elizabeth Barrett Browning on Her Later Sonnets. 1856*

I KNOW not if the cycle of strange years
Will ever bring thy human face to me,
Sister!—I say this, not as of thy peers,
But like as those who their own grief can see
In the large mirror of another's tears.

Comforter! many a time thy soul's white feet
Stole on the silent darkness where I lay
With voice of distant singing—solemn sweet—
'Be of good cheer, I too have trod that way;'
And I rose up and walked in strength complete.

Oft, as amidst the furnace of fierce woe
My own will lit, I writhing stood, yet calm,
I saw thee moving near me, meek and low,
Not speaking,—only chaunting the one psalm,
'God's love suffices when all world-loves go.'

Year after year have I, in passion strong,
Clung to thy garments when my soul was faint,—
Touching thee, all unseen amid the throng;
But now, thou risest to joy's heaven—my saint!
And I look up—and cannot hear thy song.

Or hearing, understand not; save as those
Who from without list to the bridegroom-strain
They might have sung—but that the dull gates close—
And so they smile a blessing through their pain,
Then, turning, lie and sleep among the snows.

So, go thou in, saint—sister—comforter!
Of this, thy house of joy, heaven keep the doors!
And sometimes through the music and the stir
Set thy lamp shining from the upper floors,
That we without may say—'Bless God—and her!'

(1872)

EMILY PFEIFFER
(1827–1890)

BORN in London, Emily Jane Davis was brought up in a respectable family that suffered financial hardship. Her mother, from the ancient Tyldesley family of Lancashire, was the daughter of a Montgomeryshire banker. Her father was an army officer with extensive property in Oxfordshire. Events conspired against her parents' fortunes with the failure of the family bank. Lack of funds prevented the poet from receiving any formal education. In 1853, she married Jürgen Edward Pfeiffer, a German banker based in London. During the next ten years, she published two volumes of poetry, *Valisneria; or A Midsummer Night's Dream* (1857) and *Margaret; or The Motherless* (1861). It was, however, for the volumes she produced in the 1870s that Emily Pfeiffer earned her considerable poetic reputation. In rapid succession, *Gerard's Monument and Other Poems* (1873), *Poems* (1873), *Glen-Alarch: His Silence and His Song* (1877), *Quarterman's Grace and Other Poems* (1879), and *Under the Aspens* (1882) frequently gained favourable notices in the press, although like many of her female contemporaries she was not uncommonly subjected to the arrogance of the literary establishment. *The Times*, for example, took the opportunity to make the following observations when reviewing *Gerard's Monument*

> Whatever is said, the fact remains that that the female mind has seldom or never produced poetry of the first order, but it must be remembered that women have not been prevented from becoming poets as they have been prevented from becoming soliders or members of Parliament. They have tried and they have failed— because it was not in them. No disabilities of education have intervened. *Poeta nascitur, non fit*. Ploughmen and apothecaries' boys may thrill mankind, but it is a thousand to one that the most cultivated woman in the world will set us yawning if she takes to writing verse. It is women who inspire the best poetry in the world; how, then, can it be expected that they should write it? Mythology taught that the Muses of poetry were women, but that Apollo was its god; and facts teach the same.

The Times condescends to add that Pfeiffer is an 'accomplished authoress', one who is 'never at a loss for graceful and apposite fancies'. Although the reviewer concludes that by virtue of being a woman Emily Pfeiffer simply cannot rank as a poet, he concedes that her work 'shows us that it is quite possible for a woman to write verse that shall be agreeable even to palates which scarcely care to quench their thirst with anything less than the nectar of the gods'.

Faced with such criticisms, Pfeiffer promply made a vigorous response. Rather than defend the merit of her poetry, she demanded 'a moment's hearing' on 'a subject of far wider interest', and her comments on this topic are worth quoting at some length:

> [A]s a woman I cannot but lift up a protesting voice against any attempt to close 'our case', while every day is bringing fresh witnesses into the action. It may or may not be true that—(to specialise the words of Rasselas)—'no *woman* can be a poet'; but the matter is I believe one of the many which it would be well to put aside pending further proof.
>
> That we can be speculated about now in this advanced stage of the world's history more as if we were some extinct species than beings who have stood side by side with man from the beginning, is in itself a striking result of that tyranny of circumstances which has retarded female development. So much has the present generation had to learn of the latent abilities of women, that not a few of the more distinguished of the sex who are now regarded as natural (if curious) products of the time, would have a century ago been looked upon less as miracles, than as monsters... Every authoritative announcement of woman's inherent disqualification for the highest labours of the mind retards the issue which time has still to resolve.

Like several other women poets who came to prominence in the 1870s, Pfeiffer's poetry was celebrated for its interest in women's rights, particularly in gaining access to professional employment. Among her essays on such topics are 'Woman's Claim' (*Contemporary Review*, 1881) and 'The Suffrage for Woman' (*Contemporary Review*, 1885). Her prose writings on these pressing issues are collected in *Women and Work* (1887).

Pfeiffer's final book of poems, *Flowers of the Night*, appeared one year before her death in London. In the course of her long and distinguished career, she published three other volumes: a verse-drama, *The Wynnes of Wynhavod* (1881); a medley of poetry and prose on women and art, *The Rhyme of the Lady and the Rock and How It Grew* (1881); and a travel book, *Flying Leaves from East to West* (1885). Part of her estate went to a number of educational causes, including the building of a hall of residence for women students at University College, Cardiff.

228 *A Rhyme for the Time*

WHAT is to say, had best be said,
    So, Lilian, look another way;
Just droop your eyes or turn your head,—
    Let reason have due course to-day.
Well, well, this giddy time just past,
    It has been, yes, it has been worth
The life we've spent on it so fast
    That we seem beggars now on earth.
But let me argue out our case,—
    My case,—since yours is all too plain,
So many press to fill my place
    That, faith! my loss may be your gain.
Nay, do not look or speak just now,—
    Man's reason is a thing so fine
That the least touch may overthrow
    The strongest chain he can combine;
And eyes there are, which meeting mine,
    Mislead me like a marsh-fire light;—

Eyes with the glow and hue of wine
    Like yours, can daze a man outright.
And deadlier peril when you speak
    Awaits my boasted self-control,
For then there comes upon your cheek
    An eddy which sucks in my soul!
How is it that I could behold
    Your image better made in wax,
And—do not judge me overbold—
    Could coldly gaze on it, and tax
The maker that he had not given
    Some easy grace which should fulfil
My whole ideal? while now, oh heaven!
    I see you perfect at your will.

But this is scarce the way to come
    At any reasonable end;
Before I take you in the sum
    I will resolve you, and so mend
My notion of you by a stern
    Analysis of your pretensions;
By isolating facts we learn
    To see them in their true dimensions.

A little woman, five feet two;
    (Nay, love, I mark'd it on the wall,
And what the wall says must be true,
    Tho'truly I had call'd you tall);
A maze of tawny hair, with eyes
    That lurk beneath at whiles to daunt
With wicked brightness, but for size
    And form, what are they? Eyes, avaunt!
Of dimples, would they keep but still,
    One soon would weary, and then time
Turns them to wrinkles; he does ill,
    I count it for his heaviest crime;
Still they are worse than nought, you see;
    And for your waist,—band or no bands,—
No waist so slender ought to be,
    It can be crush'd between two hands.
Thus I withstand you when I dole
    You out in parts, but—heart of youth,
Fire, folly, madness, on the whole
    Are ye more far from sober truth
Than these and such-like ways men have
    To put in doubt the thing they know,
And make their pathway to the grave
    Decently dull with hollow show?

Pardon my earnestness; I smile,
    Now seeing you so slight and small,
To think that it should take a mile
    Of silk to cover you withal!
I would it were not so, and I
    Might hope to win with honest toil
The vestments which should over-lie
    Your beauty as its humble foil.
See, love, I smile again, I think
    How in the happy days just pass'd
Your dainty share of meat and drink
    Had made a hermit's lenten fast.
I would that I might take you home
    And keep you as we keep a bird;
But there are laws that where you come—
    You women—there must come a herd
That we must feast at periods,
    That we must dress for, live for, die for;—
I dare not hope against such odds
    To win the modest ends I sigh for.

Now, sweet, I listen. What? You say
    You do not care for all this throng?
That you and I might take our way,
    Nor think we did our neighbour wrong
If we should only strive to feed,
    To house, and clothe our happy selves,
With, now and then, for some great need,
    A morsel from our frugal shelves?
You social Titan! would you dare
    The world's exactions thus to flout?
But what if silk fail everywhere,
    And cotton may not eke it out?
Ah! how is this? I hear you laugh,—
    I will not see;—how say you then,—
That women never yet were half
    So eager for their toys as men?
That in your wildest fancy-flights
    There is more measure than in ours;
That you would lie on thorns for nights
    About an unpaid bill for flowers;
That all that marks the maddest she,
    Who wanders thriftless out of bounds
In matters of finance, will be
    A difference of some few poor pounds,—
Tens to our hundreds. Then you joke
    About our love of bygone things:

Old pictures, grim with priceless smoke,
    Old wines, their cob-webs and bees-wings;
Till pressing harder, you declare
    That, like the gondolas of Venice,
The dusky garb which now we wear,
    Saves us from dangers that would menace
Our sightlier persons through the clashing
    Of rival suits; that in our case
'Tis well, for swords were always flashing
    When men wore silks and Flanders lace!
Then, almost breathless, you sum up;
    Antiques, plates, clubs, the opera stall,
The horse that is to win the cup,
    The *coup* that is to pay for all;
Cigars and yachting, needy friends,
    And building manias;—he who searches,
You say, will find 'tis man who spends—
    Save in the luxury of churches!

No more? You've done? Why, child, so pale?
    Nay, not 'with counting up men's crimes';
Lilian, throw down this idle veil,
    Jesting is bitter work at times.
Do I but dream I can discern
    A secret hid with female art?
Speak, and God's truth! By heaven, I burn
    To strain you with it to my heart.
'No more than this,' you say, 'the hold
    Your feeble woman's will can take
On such things is so slight, so cold,
    You could release them for love's sake.'

Now let me pause upon that word,
    I feel as one before whose eyes
A mist, whereby his life seem'd blurr'd,
    Had parted and reveal'd the skies.
Nay, turn not now away, I must,
    Yes, must, will, read your face, and know
Whether this wild new hope and trust
    Will bear the light; one moment, so;
Now veil your eyes, as best you may,
    I've seen the thing I wished to see,
My soul retires within, I pray
    That what your love divines in me,
Mine may accomplish; I shall prize
    Myself less meanly, having found
My humble image thron'd in eyes
    That frame it with a glory round;

For there I show, so brave, so strong,
    A true man conquering the place
Which shall be ours amid the throng,
    The hurtling crowd of fortune's race;
And there I show as wise and pure
    As I shall be when we have trod
That path which some way hence is sure
    To land us at the feet of God.
I take it that the only seer
    Possess'd of true divining powers,
Is this same love, who, trumpet-clear,
    Now speaks in these two hearts of ours.
He tells me you are brave and true,
    And fond, yes,—spite your fierce denial!—
And if he say as much to you
    Of me—Oh, put me on my trial!
I would not be the fool to shrink
    From danger to your outward fate,
While hurling back your love to sink
    Your life beneath its costly freight.

I see, I see, that panther gaze,
    It could deceive me once, but now
I know your little winsome ways,
    They shall not fright me more, I vow.
The hand that would not feel its sting,
    'Tis said, should boldly grasp the nettle.
Lie still, you little prickly thing,
    You only put me on my mettle.
But, child, I fain would serve alone,
    And keep you queen-like at my side;
I feel your burthen, not my own;
    It presses on my love, and pride.
Still, God be prais'd! the woman's fate,
    Who serves her turn for love, is finer,
More noble than the idle state
    To which we blindly would consign her.
And so again, again I seal
    Our contract, and thus nerv'd, thus blest,
I'll labour stoutly for your weal,
    And trust your Maker for the rest.

(1873)

229 *Longing and Asking*

MOTHER, when we meet upon that shore,
Where I too may hope to be at rest,
Shall mine eyes behold thee evermore,
As my heart must ever love thee best?
Wilt thou claim me as I stand amaz'd
While the veil still clogs my spirit-feet—
Claim me with the mother-love that gaz'd
From thy mortal eyes with such mild heat?
Shall I owe thee sweet obedience then?
Shall I pay thee back each foregone due?
Shall I grow a child beneath thy ken?
Or appear such haply in thy view?

There are bonds which we call bonds of flesh,
That do enter deep into the soul;
Or surround it closely, as a mesh
That must leave its impress on the whole.
So our human loves, which at their birth
Lowliest human faculties enfold,
Grow beyond the limits of this earth,
In the spirits they have help'd to mould.
Spirit that has deeply sounded spirit
Here, must meet hereafter, we should know;
But I would our future might inherit
All that keeps our present life a-glow:
Not the substance only, but the form
Of the dear affections that now bind us,
That our bright eternal home be warm
As the mouldering hearths we leave behind us.

So I pray that when upon that shore
I may land and enter into rest,
I shall see thee, mother, evermore,
As my heart must ever love thee best.
All thy being, bore it not the sign
Shadow'd in the woman's name—Eve, Life?
Life that she in sharing dares resign,—
Mortal weakness conquering in the strife.
Mother, shall thy children dare to doubt
That the end of perfect womanhood
Endlessly shall compass thee about,
In the reign of all things true and good?

When we stood on that white winter day,
And the sunlight, filtering through the snow,
Lighted on that white and frozen clay,

With the crown of peace upon its brow;
Who had deem'd the woman pale and worn,
Gazing as they will who look their last,
Could have been a child left there to mourn,
One who seem'd so early to have past.
Finely moulded, with the hair's dark sweep,
Straightly parted from the fair, still face;
Calm and grand as some diviner sleep
Held the wearied one in close embrace;
Smooth and firm, and all untouch'd with care,
Men had deem'd that little children's cries
Should bewail thee, not the long despair
Looking from a full-grown woman's eyes.

Yet I think not that to outward ken,
In thy day of youth thou could'st have been
All complete as that I look'd on then—
Awful, tender, beautiful, serene!
Fades the blossom here before the fruit
Forms upon the bough; our wither'd leaves—
Strength and beauty—go to feed our root;
In the dusk we gather in our sheaves.
Souls that into fuller beauty break,
Ripen on the body's slow decay;
Thus in perfect likeness none can wake,
But to look upon the perfect day.

But as such may we on high behold
Thee, the mother of our thoughts, hopes, lives;
Not as one whose clinging arms should fold
Infant forms, but when as women, wives,
Happy in ourselves and in one other,
From thyself thou badest us go free;
Then in angels' eyes thou wert a MOTHER,
In the highest, last, supreme degree!
Oh, how short a time he thus possess'd thee—
He, the widow'd! Growing great beneath
All the sore temptations that oppress'd thee,
With the last thy spirit broke its sheath.
Gone the little one as went the rest,
Scatter'd wide, and wider over space;
Could the heart within the mother's breast
Keep on beating still in one fix'd place?
All day long she hears her children's voices,—
Day or night they will not let her sleep;
Far away with this one she rejoices,—
Farther still with that one she must weep.
Surely it were better she should go,

Than live on with such divided life;
Ah, we too much wrong'd thee with our woe,
Standing by, sweet mother, and true wife,
When the struggle which so rent thy frame,
God, in pity, made at last to cease;
And the angel of his mercy came
With the order for thy soul's release!

Thus I wander on,—my thoughts are drawn
Blindly by the current which will set
Ever to that past which is not gone—
But alive with hope, not vain regret.
Here I pause, still praying as before,
That when I shall enter into rest,
I may see thee, mother, evermore,
At thy noblest, fullest, latest, best.

(1873)

230 *'Peace to the Odalisque', I*

PEACE to the odalisque, the facile slave,
Whose uninvidious love rewards the brave,
Or cherishes the coward; she who yields
Her lord the fief of waste, uncultur'd fields
To perish in non-using; she whose hour
Is measur'd by her beauties' transient flower;
Who lives in him, as he in God, and dies
The death of parasites, no more to rise.
Graceful ephemera! Fair morning dream
Of the young world! In vain would women's hearts
In love with sacrifice, withstand the stream
Of human progress; other spheres, new parts
Await them. God be with them in their quest—
Our brave, sad working-women of the west!

(1873)

231 *'Peace to the Odalisque', II*

PEACE to the odalisque, whose morning glory
Is vanishing, to live alone in story.
Firm in her place, a dull-rob'd figure stands,
With wistful eyes, and earnest, grappling hands:
The working-woman, she whose soul and brain—
Her tardy right—is bought with honest pain.

Oh woman! sacrifice may still be thine—
More fruitful than the souls ye did resign
To sated masters; from your lives, so real,
Shall shape itself a pure and high ideal,
That ye shall seek with sad, wide-open eyes,
Till, finding nowhere, baffled love shall rise
To higher planes, where passion may look pale,
But charity's white light shall never fail.

(1873)

232 *Ode to the Teuton Women*

FAIR Teuton woman, sister with blond hair,
And patient cheek, untimely worn with care,
How is it that the vision of thine eyes
Is dim with tears, and tremulous with sighs?

Oh woman! what the labour which assails
Thy spirit's temple thus, and fretting, fails
To lift thee—brave co-worker with thy mate—
To work's true reverence, and high estate?

Meek Teuton woman! thou hast borne too long
The chain to know its weight, or own its wrong,
And lovest it for those reliquary flowers
Which dropt from off it in the early hours.

I see a beauty in thy faded cheek,
I see a glory in thine aspect meek,
I see a state in thy humility,
I see—I veil mine eyes at what I see!

I see the Bridegroom, Him, the Lord, the Son,
Step forth and lead ye forward one by one,
I see Him take each weary, toil-worn hand,
And guide ye shrinking to the higher stand.

Ay, one by one; so may each separate soul
Weave its own garment, reach its lonely goal,
Accept the lowliest, bow before the worst,
Until the 'first be last, the last be first!'

But not in isolation chill and drear
May heart of woman fill its human sphere;
Content to wear a single crown of life,
And heedless of the call to generous strife.

Yield one and all what each may yield alone,
Give one and all what each may call her own,
But, trampling pride, and scorning earthly good,
Still guard the pact of sacred womanhood!

For ever borne upon the foremost wave
Of human progress, as it brake, and drave
Error and sloth before it, have been seen
A woman's faithful eyes and hopeful mien.

And where the woman's shape appears no more,
It is upon some barren, rock-bound shore,
Or else where Custom builds his blank sea-wall,
And back upon themselves the breakers fall.

Sweet Abnegation, mother Love's own child!
Who love of all her secrets hast beguiled,
Can it be so that Love thou wouldst betray,
Rob of her crown, and circumscribe her sway?

Say it be well that Gretchen lonely sit,
Weaving dumb thoughts, the while her fingers knit,
And Hans—whose youth her love renew'd one day—
Clash words with wit the other side the way!

Say it be well one wife shall quit her post,
Descend, and leave her lord a lonely host,
Take from the steam of seething meats, her share,
And make of grossest sense her chiefest care.

Say it be well that beauty have no pride,
And youth no conscience of its claims denied,
That fifty—all the gulf of life between—
Kneel at the altar steps with seventeen;

Grant it as seemly that the folded rose
Of maiden thought and fancy first unclose
To meet the fading light and chilly breath
Of love thrice widow'd, fresh escap'd from death!

Concede that beauty at its best is shown
Ere yet the soul has claim'd it for its own,
While still the pulpy lip, and rounded cheek
Is—anybody's beauty, so to speak;

Grant this, and more: say it be well indeed
That saints should of the flesh be timely freed,
And best that Teuton woman's life should span
A circle less than that of Teuton man;

Take no exception e'en that Teuton thrift
Should fail to gauge the cause, or seek the drift
Of such a fact as this: that Teuton wife
So oft drops midway on the road of life;

Accept the whole for each meek wife or maid,
With wage celestial will her cross be paid;
But, Womanhood, your work is in the world,
And back upon man's head your wrongs are hurl'd!

You stand aside, you droop with grief and shame,
While humbled girlhood suffers in your name,
And blur with tears the vision of those eyes
Which else had help'd to make the world more wise.

Oh deep, strong mountain stream of Teuton mind,
Fate-frought with pregnant germs for humankind!
You flood the plains of stony fact, and bring,
Where'er you flow, the breathings of the spring.

So strong with only half your life, so grand
With only half your strength, what nobler stand
And gentler service for the world had wrought
The fair, completed whole of German thought!

It is not that your women voices fail.
From out the chorus that the nation's hail,
Or that the wavering notes they dare to raise
Are sometimes false for lack of heartening praise;

It is that by the hearth the woman's share
In man is but a partnership of care,
Which leaves her standing, with her pinions furl'd,
Upon the threshold of his higher world;

It is that by her lord she still is thrust,
A pining Cinderella, in the dust
Of household toil, while on his spirits fall
The magic and the music of the ball.

But sisters, mates, and mothers, all the same
Ye own the dauntless mind and hardy frame
Of those who bear the burthens of their age
So bravely, and its noblest battles wage.

And doubtless on your bow'd blond heads has come
The blessing in a duly portion'd sum—
The sad cross-handed blessing of high gifts,
Which weights and bends the spirits it uplifts.

Where now the fires of thought burn dead, a spark
Will kindle flame anew, and cleave the dark
Which folds the world, when no more strange and single;
The Teuton man and woman souls commingle.

On German soil, in lonely kingship trod
A man—my pen had almost writ—a god!
His radiant soul so form'd to rule the day,
Of lesser lights, to kindle, and to sway.

All worshipp'd him; and he—he worshipp'd, too,
The Moloch of his god-like brain, and threw
His manhood's sacred instincts and desires
As human sacrifice to feed its fires.

A poet's, as an 'angel's', measure can
Be but at last 'the measure of a man'.[1]
How are those wailing women overthrown
On Goethe's path avenged, when all is known!

That front Olympian, which had fill'd the round
Of vastest crown of genius, is not crown'd
With Dante, and with Shakespeare, as were meet
To make the trinity of song complete;

The holy flame of sacrificial love,
Quench'd, trampled, spurn'd at by your Teuton Jove,
No Beatrice has left her shining cars
To flash upon his brow her crown of stars.

He had not fed on earth that inner glow,
Which, all in loving, teaches men to know;
So no bright band of women, loved or dream'd,
Hail'd him their king, and throned him as beseem'd.

Rise, Teuton woman! claim your right denied
To nobler labour; show your strength defied,
And on Germania's mighty forehead place -
The absent touch of glory and of grace!

Not *Mädchen*, and not *Mütterchen*, who stand
For womanhood throughout the Fatherland,—
Not they, but Woman in her thoughtful prime,
The last achievement of evolving time;

The womanhood that through the low estate
Of thrall and odalisque has joined her mate,
And brings, to meet new problems which unroll,
The full-orb'd radiance of the human soul.

[1] Rev. 21:17

Rise, Teuton woman, rise, and rise above
Your loving weakness, with a higher love!
Let not Germania's sons, so proudly banded,
Alone in all the world, strive single-handed.

(1876)

233 *Kassandra, I*

VIRGIN of Troy, the days were well with thee
  When wandering singing by the singing streams
  Of Ilion, thou beheld'st the golden gleams
Of the bold sun that might not facëd be,
Come murmuring to thy feet caressingly;
  But best that day when, steeped in noontide dreams,
  The young Apollo wrapped thee in his beams,
And quenched his love in thine as in a sea!
And later, in thy tower 'twas sweet to teach
  The loveless night the joys high day had known;
To dream, to wake,—and find thy love impeach
  Late sleep with kisses, and thy spirit flown
To his, and at the ivory gates of speech
  Breaking in words as burning as his own.

(1879)

234 *Kassandra, II*

HOW far from Ilion, and how far from joy,
  Captive Kassandra, wert thou, when in sight
  Of conquering Greece thou satest on thy height
Of shame,—a waif from out the wreck of Troy!
Thine still the burning word, but slave's employ
  Had from thy trembling lip effacëd quite
  The kisses of the god, and heaven's light
Now shone upon thee only to destroy.
For thee, sun-stricken one, th' abysmal sties
  Of sin lay open as the secret grave,—
Things of which speech seemed madness,—while thy cries
  On wronged Apollo lost the way to save;
Till at the last, the faith of upturned eyes
  Brought him to right, as death to free the slave.

(1879)

235 *Klytemnestra, I*

DAUGHTER of gods and men, great ruling will,
Seething in oily rage within the sphere
Which gods and men assign the woman here,
Till, stricken where the wound approved thee still
Mother and mortal, all the tide of ill
Rushed through the gap, and nothing more seemed dear
But power to wreak high ruin, nothing clear
But the long dream you waited to fulfil.
Mother and spouse,—queen of the king of men,—
What fury brought Ægysthus to thy side?—
That bearded semblant, man to outward ken,
But else mere mawworm, made to fret man's pride;
Woman, thy foot was on thy tyrant then,—
Mother, thou wert avenged for love defied!

(1879)

236 *Klytemnestra, II*

WOMAN and Greek,—so doubly trained in art!—
Spreading the purple for the conqueror's tread,
Bowing with feline grace thy royal head,—
How perfect whelp-robbed lioness thy part!
One wrong the more to wring the ancient smart,
Then three swift strokes, and the slow hope blooms red,
Who shamed the hero lays him with the dead,
Where nevermore his word may vex her heart.
Bold queen, what were to thee the gods of Greece?
What had been any god of any name,
More than the lion-heart you made to cease,
Or the live dog to all your humours tame?—
The very furies left your soul in peace
Until Orestes' sword drave home their claim.

(1879)

'CLARIBEL' (CHARLOTTE ALINGTON, LATER BARNARD) (1829–1869)

CLARIBEL was one of the most highly admired songwriters of her day. Born near Boston, Lincolnshire, she was the only daughter of Henry Alington, a solicitor in Lough, and Charlotte Mary (née Yerburgh). Her family were acquainted with the two most prominent literary Lincolnshire families, the Tennysons and the Ingelows. In 1854, she married a curate, Charles Cary Barnard, of Ashby-de-la-Zouch. They settled at The Firs, in Westgate, Lincolnshire, where he held responsibility for two parishes. By this time, she was circulating her lyrics and music for publication, and 'I Remember It' was brought out by Boosey in 1854. As her fame grew, she was increasingly keen to participate in the literary life of London. In 1857, the opportunity rose to move there, and she and her husband settled in Eccleston Square. Claribel's most important contact there was the poet Jean Ingelow, who in 1858 was editing the *Youth's Magazine*. Ingelow introduced her to the Portfolio Society, which provided a focus for several well-known Victorian poets to discuss drafts of their work. Notable members included Adelaide Anne Procter and Charles Stuart Calverley. Further success came with her musical adaptation of Tennyson's 'The Brook', and a music publisher, Emery, suggested that the title of one Tennyson's poems, 'Claribel', could be become her pen name, since it included her initials, C.A.B. Her songs were performed by a number of notable contemporary performers, including Charlotte Dolby and Euphrosyne Parepa (who had made her startling debut at the Italian Opera in London in 1857). Among the most celebrated of these compositions was 'Five O'Clock in the Morning', which Parepa sang to great acclaim in the United States. Claribel took several singing lessons with Parepa. In addition, she placed poems in a number of magazines, among them the popular *Family Friend*, in 1860. By 1863, her fame had grown so much that she was held on a retainer by Boosey. Her career continued to flourish in the 1860s when she adapted, possibly with his permission, Tennyson's 'All Along the Valley', from *Enoch Arden* (1864). Many of her most cherished pieces were brought together in *Fireside Thoughts* (1865). She also set to music the works of a number of other poets, including Procter, notably the poem 'Threefold' (from *A Chaplet of Verses*, 1862). Amid this success, she and her husband returned to Lincolnshire, this time to the vicarage at Kirmington. It was there that she performed a selection of her songs with Mme Dolby to raise funds for a peal of bells and a clock for her husband's church.

Matters took a turn for the worse in 1868 when her father was declared bankrupt on the basis of committing fraud. Remaining loyal to her father, she settled in Ostend, after the family had been publicly humiliated. Claribel earned enough from the proceeds of her songwriting to conduct what was left of her father's business while they lived together in Belgium. In 1869, she was taken seriously ill while on a visit to England. She was buried at Dover.

237 *I Remember It*

'TWAS a still soft eve in summer,
And the west wind sigh'd o'er the lea,
And the linnet shook the dew
From the ivy as he flew
To his nest in the old thorn tree;
The white rose clung to the lattice,
So heavy at the heart with dew,
And stars were alight
In the heaven all that night,
Brightening the far pale blue.
I remember it,
    I remember it.

The bold gray spire look'd taller
In the shadowy evening light,
And I thought it seem'd to be
Pointing heavenward to me,
As I watch'd all alone that night;
The white rose wept to the west wind,
So heavy at the heart with dew,
And o'er the moonlit trees
Murmur'd now the willing breeze,
Wandering the woodland through.
I remember it,
    I remember it.

(1865)

BESSIE RAYNER PARKES (MADAME BELLOC) (1829–1925)

REMEMBERED for her active involvement in the feminist work of Langham Place, Bessie Rayner Parkes was born into an established Unitarian family; in fact, her maternal grandfather was Joseph Priestley, the scientist, and one of the prominent Unitarians of the Revolutionary period. (See headnote on Anna Laetitia Barbauld, p. 1.) Her father, Joseph Parkes, was closely associated with Whig and Liberal politics influenced by Benthamite thought. This background undoubtedly heightened her awareness of the need for political reform. Educated at a Unitarian school for girls in Warwickshire, Parkes had early ambitions to succeed as a poet. Her most important friendship was with the slightly older Barbara Leigh Smith (later Bodichon), whom she met, while on holiday in Hastings, at the age of eighteen. In their early twenties, Parkes and Smith braved the world by acting as chaperones for each other when travelling widely through Europe. During the 1850s, Parkes focused her attention on women's issues, particularly those connected with education, professional employment, and property. Her *Remarks upon the Education of Girls* appeared in 1854. In 1855, she became a member of the Married Women's Property Committee, which is generally regarded as one of the first organizations of modern feminism. With Smith, she founded the pioneering *English Woman's Journal* (1858–62). Having travelled to Nottingham and Leicester in 1861 to observe the conditions of women mill-workers, she developed her *Essays on Women's Work* (1865); in the Introductory, she writes: 'I believe that now, as in all ages of the world, the substantial equality of nature renders the two sexes equal weight and value in the moral world, and that their action upon each other in every relation of life is far too complex to admit any great difference between them in any given rank.'

Parkes's political work intertwined with her literary and cultural interests. Through Langham Place, she came to know the poets Isa Craig and Adelaide Anne Procter. Her fond memories of Procter are recalled in *In a Walled Garden* (1895). These poets were also involved with the Portfolio Society, which circulated drafts of manuscripts among its members. Dora Greenwell, Jean Ingelow, and Christina Rossetti contributed to the Portfolio. She published several volumes of poetry, including *Poems* (1852), *Summer Sketches* (1854), and an experimental religious sequence entitled *Gabriel* (1856).

Friends and family opposed her marriage to Louis Belloc in 1867, which lasted happily for five years until his death. Although Parkes remained friends with Barbara Bodichon, she never returned to campaigning for women's rights. In fact, one of her two children, the writer Hilaire Belloc, became a well-known anti-feminist. It is possible that Parkes's attitudes to sexual politics altered because of her conversion to Roman Catholicism in the early 1860s. Her extensive papers are held at Girton College, Cambridge.

238 *To Elizabeth Barrett Browning*

I WAS a child when first I read your books,
And loved you dearly, so far as I could see
Your obvious meanings, your more subtle depths
Being then (as still, perhaps,) a mystery.
I had no awe of you, so much does love,
In simple daring, all shy fears transcend;
And when they told me, 'You shall travel south',
I chiefly thought, 'In Florence dwells my friend!'
In those first days I seldom heard your name,
You seem'd in my strange fancy all my own,
Or else as if you were some saint in Heaven
Whose image took my bookcase for a throne.
As time went on, your words flew far and wide,
I heard them quoted, critically scann'd
With grave intentness, learnt, half mournfully,
That you were *a great Poet in the land*,
So far, so far from me, who loved you so,
And never might one human blessing claim;
Yet oh! how I rejoiced that you were great,

And all my heart exulted in your fame;
A woman's fame, and *yours!* I use no words
Of any careful beauty, being plain
As earnestness, and quiet as that truth
Which shrinks from any flattering speech with pain.
Indeed, I should not dare—but that this love,
Long nursed, demands expression, and alone
Seeks by love's dear strength—to approach near you
In words so weak and poor beside your own.

(1852 *1855*)

239 *For Adelaide*

WHO is the Poet? He who sings
Of high, abstruse, and hidden things,
Or rather he who with a liberal voice
Does with the glad hearts of all earth rejoice?
O sweetest Singer! rather would I be
Gifted with thy kind melody
Than weave mysterious rhymes and such as seem
Born in the dim depths of some sage's dream:
But I have no such art; they will not choose
The utterance of my harsh ungenial muse
For any cradle chant; I shall not aid
The mournful mother or the loving maid
To find relief in song. I shall not be
Placed side by side, O Poet dear, with thee
In any grateful thoughts, yet if it be known
By all who read how much thou hast mine own!
When, with bent brow and all too anxious heart,
I walk with hurrying step the crowded mart,
And look abroad on men with faithless eyes,
Then do sweet snatches of thy song arise,
And float into my heart like melodies
Down dropping from the far blue deeps of heaven,
Or sweet bells wafted over fields at even.
Therefore, if thanks for any gifts be due,
If any service be esteemed true,
If any virtues do to verse belong,
Take thou the Poet's name, by right of song!
Suffer that I, who never yet did give
False words to that dear art by which I live,
Pluck down bright bay-leaves from the eternal tree,
And place them where they have true right to be!

(1855)

ELIZABETH SIDDAL
(1829–1862)

ELIZABETH ELEANOR SIDDAL was the third of seven children of Charles Siddall, a Sheffield-born cutler who ran a wholesale and retail business off the Old Kent Road in London, and Elizabeth Eleanor Evans. Little is known about her childhood. But it would seem that she received a basic education at home. Like her three sisters, she learned dressmaking, and it appears that she first came into contact with members of the Pre-Raphelite Brotherhood as a dressmaker to the Deverell family. She was 20 years old when the painter Walter Howell Deverell came across her in a milliner's shop off Leicester Square. Given her distinctive red hair, she became one of the most noted models for Pre-Raphaelite painters. In 1850, she sat for the figure of the girl looking after the fugitive priest in William Holman Hunt's *A Converted British Family Rescuing a Christian Priest from Persecution by the Druids*. She also modelled as Sylvia in Hunt's *The Two Gentlemen of Verona* (1851). Early in 1852, John Everett Millais infamously employed her when painting *Ophelia*; since Millais had kept her afloat in a bath of cold water, she contracted a severe cold, and her father threatened to sue for damages. It was not until 1852, when she sat for several studies of Beatrice and the Virgin Mary by Dante Gabriel Rossetti, that her own drawings received attention. It would seem that she began to receive tuition in drawing from Rossetti at this time. By 1854, Siddal had been introduced to several of Rossetti's female friends, including the feminist campaigners, Barbara Leigh Smith (later Bodichon) and Bessie Rayner Parkes. Smith felt that Siddal had the potential to become a great artist. Her relationship with Rossetti grew very close, and they holidayed together at Hastings in 1854. John Ruskin, who came to know Siddal in 1855, inquired whether there were financial difficulties preventing Rossetti from marrying her. Throughout this period, Siddal was considered to be suffering from an unspecified form of mental illness, and it is reasonable to speculate that Rossetti's unwillingness to wed her was the cause of her complaint. Yet she proved resistant to the forms of treatment suggested by the eminent physician, Henry Acland. Close personal support came from other sources, including the painter Ford Madox Brown, and his spouse, Emma. A tour to the Continent in 1856 did not reduce the emotional problems she had been experiencing, and on her return to London, her impatience and irritation with Rossetti were all too evident to their friends. After the small Pre-Raphaelite exhibition mounted at Russell Place in 1857, Siddal used the money from the sale of one her paintings to move away from London. It is possible that she spent the next two years in Sheffield. Her heavy addiction to laudanum may have led her in 1860 to contact Ruskin for support, thus alerting Rossetti, her ertswhile lover, to her predicament. Rossetti responded by taking her on holiday to Hastings once again, where they were married in St Clement's Church in 1860. During this period, she was frequently in the company of other women noted for their association with the Pre-Raphaelites, Georgiana Burne-Jones and Janey Morris, and she developed a significant friendship with Algernon Charles Swinburne. Her health, however, did not improve. In May 1861, she was delivered of a stillborn daughter, and the effect of this tragedy was devastating. Some ten months later, on returning to their home after teaching a class at the Working Men's College, Rossetti found Siddal dead from an overdose of laudanum. The inquest returned a verdict of accidental death. But there were many rumours of suicide. She was buried in Highgate Cemetery. In a sentimental gesture, Rossetti committed his manuscript notebook of poems to her coffin. Seven years later, however, he decided to retrieve this document, and various lurid tales about the state of her exhumed body circulated thereafter.

Siddal's poetry remained a private affair, unlike her pictorial work. No one in her immediate circle seemed to know of these writings during her lifetime. Four years after her death, Rossetti copied out and gave titles to six of her finished poems. But it was not until the end of the century that William Michael Rossetti published fifteen of them in some of the collections of letters and reminiscences connected with the Pre-Raphaelites that he completed between 1895 and 1906, including his essay on Siddal in the *Burlington Magazine* (May 1903). The first edition of her poetical works was brought out by a small Canadian press in 1978. Manuscripts of her poems are held by the Ashmolean Museum, Oxford. Jan Marsh notes that it is difficult to date these works, although 'True Love' was clearly copied out after Siddal's marriage in 1860.

240 *True Love*

FAREWELL, Earl Richard,
  Tender and brave;
Kneeling I kiss
  The dust from thy grave.

Pray for me, Richard,
  Lying alone
With hands pleading earnestly
  All in white stone.

Soon must I leave thee
  This sweet summer tide;
That other is waiting
  To claim his pale bride.

Soon I'll return to thee
  Hopeful and brave,
When the dead leaves
  Blow over thy grave.

Then shall they find me
  Close at thy head
Watching or fainting,
  Sleeping or dead.

(Composed *c.*1860 *1991*)

241 *Dead Love*

OH never weep for love that's dead
  Since love is seldom true
But changes his fashion from blue to red,
  From brightest red to blue,
And love was born to an early death
  And is so seldom true.

Then harbour no smile on your bonny face
  To win the deepest sigh.
The fairest words on truest lips
  Pass on and surely die,
And you will stand alone, my dear,
  When wintry winds draw nigh.

Sweet, never weep for what cannot be,
  For this God has not given.
If the merest dream of love were true
  Then, sweet, we should be in heaven,
And this is only earth, my dear,
  Where true love is not given.

(Composed *c.*1860? *1991*)

242 *He and She and Angels Three*

RUTHLESS hands have torn her
  From one that loved her well;
Angels have upborn her,
  Christ her grief to tell.

She shall stand to listen,
  She shall stand and sing,
Till three winged angels
  Her lover's soul shall bring.

He and she and the angels three
  Before God's face shall stand;
There they shall pray among themselves
  And sing at His right hand.

(Composed *c.*1860? *1991*)

243 *Love and Hate*

OPE not thy lips, thou foolish one,
  Nor turn to me thy face;
The blasts of heaven shall strike thee down
  Ere I will give thee grace.

Take thou thy shadow from my path,
  Nor turn to me and pray;
The wild wild winds thy dirge may sing
  Ere I will bid thee stay.

Lift thy false brow from out the dust
  Nor wild thine hands entwine
Among the golden summer leaves
  To mock this gay sunshine.

And turn away thy false dark eyes,
  Nor gaze upon my face;
Great love I bore thee: now great hate
  Sits grimly in its place.

All changes pass me like a dream,
  I neither sing nor pray;
And thou art like the poisonous tree
  That stole my life away.

(Composed *c.*1860? *1991*)

LOUISA A. HORSFIELD
(1830–?1865)

Louisa Adelaide Horsfield (whose maiden name is not known) was born in Rothwell, near Leeds, and received a minimal education at Sabbath-Schools. After the death of her father when she was very young, her mother remarried and they moved to Blacker Hill, near Barnsley. At about 25 years old, she met Edwin Horsfield, whom she was to marry.

Her parents are said to have been very pious, and it is most likely that the family were Primitive Methodists. She had written poetry since childhood and was to have her first poems published in the *Primitive Methodist Magazine* when she was about eighteen years old, and these attracted some attention. A gift of a few of her manuscript poems to an acquaintance led to his printing and privately circulating them. The interest aroused in these verses encouraged her to publish, and her one book of poetry, *The Cottage Lyre: Being Miscellaneous Poetry* was probably produced in 1861. An enlarged, second edition followed in 1862.

244 *To My Departed Baby*

THE flowers will bud and bloom again,
The leaves bedeck the forest-tree,
The grass enrobe the wither'd plain;—
But thou wilt not return to me!

The black-bird and the thrush will sing
Their songs of gushing melody,
To greet again the blushing Spring;—
But thou wilt not return to me!

Ah no! thy blighted buds no more
Shall blossom with returning Spring;
They bloom on yon celestial shore,
To grace the palace of their King.

One fetter less hath earth for me,
But heaven one bright attraction more;
My gather'd flower, I'll follow thee
To Canaan's ever-blooming shore.

(1861? *1862*)

245 *Lines to a Friend in Australia*

WE think of thee, when smiling Spring
Adorns the earth with flowers:
And when the Summer-days forth fling
Bright sunshine o'er the bowers.

We think of thee, when Autumn weaves
Her robe of golden hues,
And ripen'd fruits and wither'd leaves
Around our pathway strews.

We think of thee, when Winter reigns
With desolating sway,
And holds the dreary earth in chains,
And daylight fades away.

Though thou a wanderer dost roam
'Neath Austral skies so fair;
Yet thou hast still an English home,
And those that love thee there.

Warm hearts throb faster at thy name,
And tears unbidden start;
And looks, far more than words, proclaim
How very dear thou art.

With yearning hearts they long for thee
To bless thy home again;
And from that home no more to be
A wanderer o'er the main.

May He, who heard and answer'd thee,
And on thy pathway smiled,
When thou, a lost one, bent'st thy knee
On that Australian wild—

With tender care o'ershadow thee
Beneath his mighty wing,
And safely o'er the roaring sea
The bark that bears thee bring.

May prosperous breezes fill the sail,
That o'er the ocean's foam
Shall waft thee to the lovely vale,
Where smiles thine English home.

(1861? *1862*)

CHRISTINA ROSSETTI
(1830–1894)

CHRISTINA GEORGINA ROSSETTI was the youngest daughter of Gabriele Rossetti, Professor of Italian at King's College London, and Frances Polidori, sister of John Polidori (one-time physician and secretary to Byron, and author of the Gothic novel, *The Vampyre* (1819)). Both Italian and English were spoken at home, and Rossetti subsequently wrote poetry in both languages. Creative endeavour was clearly encouraged in the Rossetti household. From an early age, she enjoyed making *bouts rimés* with her brothers, William and Gabriel, and her sister, Maria, the oldest of the four children. All would in later life gain distinction in related areas of the arts—Maria in Dante scholarship, William in literary and art criticism, and Gabriel in poetry and painting. Tutored mainly by her mother, Rossetti started writing poetry in her early teens, and a volume of her work was privately published by her maternal grandfather, Gaetano Polidori, in 1847. Although in 1850 she published poems under the pseudonym Ellen Alleyne in the Pre-Raphaelite journal, the *Germ*, it was not until 1862 that Macmillan produced her first collection, *Goblin Market and Other Poems*, which firmly established her reputation. This volume contains many of the poems she had drafted in the 1840s. Many other books would follow. *The Prince's Progress and Other Poems* appeared in 1866, and it contained, like the previous collection, a frontispiece designed by her brother, Gabriel. In 1879, she published a collection of nursery rhymes entitled *Sing-Song*, which was augmented in 1893. By 1875 her success encouraged Macmillan to bring out her collected poems, including a great many that had since the early 1860s appeared in periodicals, including the *English Woman's Journal*. Her final book of largely secular verse was *A Pageant and Other Poems* (1881). This collection includes her impressive sonnet sequence, 'Monna Innominata', which revises Dante's and Petrarch's celebrated love poetry. *Verses* (1893) is an exclusively religious collection that brings together poems included in her extensive devotional prose produced for the Society for the Promotion of Christian Knowledge.

Committed to the High Anglican church, Rossetti was not, as her religious writings might suggest, narrowly sectarian in her doctrinal outlook nor necessarily orthodox in her interpretation of Scripture. *Annus Domini* (1874), *Seek and Find: A Double Series of Short Studies of the Benedicte* (1879), *Called to Be Saints* (1881), *Letter and Spirit* (1883), *Time Flies: A Reading Diary* (1885), and *The Face of the Deep* (1893) comprise her substantial body of devotional prose. It is possible that acquaintance with the poet, Dora Greenwell, who had written extensively on the Christian soul, may have encouraged Rossetti to concentrate much of her attention on this area of work. (Rossetti's sonnet, 'Autumn Violets', was written for Greenwell.) In addition, Rossetti wrote a modest amount of prose fiction both for adults and for children. The themes of her book of short stories entitled *Commonplace* (1870) have a significant bearing on the preoccupations to be found in her earliest poetry, especially on the special religious and familial values attributed to the idea of sisterhood. *Speaking Likenesses* (1874) reads like a biting satire upon the 'Alice' stories by Charles Lutwidge Dodgson ('Lewis Carroll'), who photographed members of her family, and it includes some startling illustrations by Arthur Hughes. Rossetti had a strong and informed interest in the poet Dante, and the first of her two published essays on his work appeared in the *Churchman's Shilling Magazine* in 1867, five years before Maria Rossetti's influential *A Shadow of Dante*. 'Dante: The Poet Illustrated out of the Poem' was contributed to the *Century* in 1884. Some time after her death, one of her earliest short fictions was printed in a special edition. *Maude*, like the title story in *Commonplace*, examines conflicts between religious duties and family loyalties, and it has been tempting to read this revealing work as semi-autobiographical.

For many years, Rossetti's biographers were swayed by the unintentionally demeaning memoir that her brother William furnished for the *Poetical Works* of 1904. 'Upon her reputation as a poetess', he remarked, 'she never presumed, nor did she ever volunteer an allusion to any of her performances: in a roomful of mediocrities she consented to seem the most mediocre as the most unobtrusive of all.' The power of this image of a woman who drew attention to herself through her reticence impressed many subsequent writers, including Virginia Woolf in her essay, 'I Am Christina Rossetti' (1932). Subsequent inquiries into her outwardly uneventful life have sometimes been confounded by Rossetti's undemonstrative and pious manner. It is true that as a child Rossetti had an uncontrollable temper, and it has proved difficult to understand exactly why she displayed such a reserved attitude in her teens. It has often been suggested that she was profoundly affected by two unsuccessful romances, first with the painter James Collinson, whose reversion to Roman Catholicism in 1850 may well have made him an unsuitable partner. Similar difficulties arose with the poet and translator, Charles Bagot Cayley, who appears to have proved unacceptable because of his lack of belief. Cayley, however, remained in touch with Rossetti for the rest of his life, bequeathing his 'best writing desk' to her in his will. Both of the most substantial biographies to date have put forward unlikely hypotheses about Rossetti's behaviour. Although lacking any supporting evidence, Lona Mosk Packer insisted in 1963 that Rossetti's poems charted a jilted love affair with the painter and poet, William Bell Scott. More recently, Jan Marsh has speculated that sexual abuse by the poet's father may have caused Rossetti's decisive change in temperament. It is clear that Rossetti's Anglican convictions, shaped by the Puseyite sermons of William Dodsworth of Christ Church, London, deeply influenced her. For several years, she worked with fallen women at the Highgate Penitentiary. She also travelled quite widely, making a visit with her mother and William to Italy in 1864. But after contracting Graves's disease in 1871, which adversely altered her facial appearance, she more or less completely withdrew from any public activities.

Rossetti, however, was not entirely isolated from her contemporaries. It seems that she was a corresponding member of the Portfolio Society, which circulated drafts of poems among its members. Among her acquaintances were two prominent figures in this group, Jean Ingelow and Adelaide Anne Procter. Her correspondence also includes letters to the poet Augusta Webster. Through her brother Gabriel, she came to know—if only slightly—the poet and painter, Elizabeth Siddal, whom it seems she did not admire. In old age, she was regularly visited by Lisa Wilson, whose own poems are styled on Rossetti's. Many Victorian reviewers, if admiring Rossetti's work, often paid tributes to her talents in condescending terms, drawing special attention to her lightness of touch and lyric sweetness. This trend persisted well into the twentieth century. Since the 1970s, however, Rossetti's poetry has attracted an immense amount of critical attention, particularly from feminist critics. These recent approaches have occasioned the complete reappraisal of this poet's remarkable creative and intellectual life.

246 *Song*

When I am dead, my dearest,
   Sing no sad songs for me;
Plant thou no roses at my head,
   Nor shady cypress tree:
Be the green grass above me
   With showers and dewdrops wet;
And if thou wilt, remember,
   And if thou wilt, forget.

I shall not see the shadows,
   I shall not feel the rain;
I shall not hear the nightingale
   Sing on, as if in pain:
And dreaming through the twilight
   That doth not rise nor set,
Haply I may remember,
   And haply may forget.

(1862)

247 *My Dream*

HEAR now a curious dream I dreamed last night,
Each word whereof is weighed and sifted truth.

I stood beside Euphrates while it swelled
Like overflowing Jordan in its youth:
It waxed and coloured sensibly to sight,
Till out of myriad pregnant waves there welled
Young crocodiles, a gaunt blunt-featured crew,
Fresh-hatched perhaps and daubed with birthday dew.
The rest if I should tell, I fear my friend,
My closest friend would deem the facts untrue;
And therefore it were wisely left untold;
Yet if you will, why, hear it to the end.

Each crocodile was girt with massive gold
And polished stones that with their wearers grew:
But one there was who waxed beyond the rest,
Wore kinglier girdle and a kingly crown,
Whilst crowns and orbs and sceptres starred his breast.
All gleamed compact and green with scale on scale,
But special burnishment adorned his mail
And special terror weighed upon his frown;
His punier brethren quaked before his tail,
Broad as a rafter, potent as a flail.
So he grew lord and master of his kin:
But who shall tell the tale of all their woes?
An execrable appetite arose,
He battened on them, crunched, and sucked them in.
He knew no law, he feared no binding law,
But ground them with inexorable jaw:
The luscious fat distilled upon his chin,
Exuded from his nostrils and his eyes,
While still like hungry death he fed his maw;
Till every minor crocodile being dead
And buried too, himself gorged to the full,
He slept with breath oppressed and unstrung claw.
Oh marvel passing strange which next I saw:
In sleep he dwindled to the common size,
And all the empire faded from his coat.
Then from far off a wingèd vessel came,
Swift as a swallow, subtle as a flame:
I know not what it bore of freight or host,
But white it was as an avenging ghost.
It levelled strong Euphrates in its course;
Supreme yet weightless as an idle mote

It seemed to tame the waters without force
Till not a murmur swelled or billow beat:
Lo, as the purple shadow swept the sands,
The prudent crocodile rose on his feet
And shed appropriate tears and wrung his hands.

What can it mean? you ask. I answer not
For meaning, but myself must echo, What?
And tell it as I saw it on the spot.

(1862)

248 *My Secret*

I TELL my secret? No indeed, not I:
Perhaps some day, who knows?
But not today; it froze, and blows, and snows,
And you're too curious: fie!
You want to hear it? well:
Only, my secret's mine, and I won't tell.

Or, after all, perhaps there's none:
Suppose there is no secret after all,
But only just my fun.
Today's a nipping day, a biting day;
In which one wants a shawl,
A veil, a cloak, and other wraps:
I cannot ope to every one who taps,
And let the draughts come whistling thro' my hall;
Come bounding and surrounding me,
Come buffeting, astounding me,
Nipping and clipping thro' my wraps and all.
I wear my mask for warmth: who ever shows
His nose to Russian snows
To be pecked at by every wind that blows?
You would not peck? I thank you for good will,
Believe, but leave that truth untested still.

Spring's an expansive time: yet I don't trust
March with its peck of dust,
Nor April with its rainbow-crowned brief showers,
Nor even May, whose flowers
One frost may wither thro' the sunless hours.

Perhaps some languid summer day,
When drowsy birds sing less and less,
And golden fruit is ripening to excess,

If there's not too much sun nor too much cloud,
And the warm wind is neither still nor loud,
Perhaps my secret I may say,
Or you may guess.

(1862)

249 *Winter Rain*

EVERY valley drinks,
  Every dell and hollow:
Where the kind rain sinks and sinks,
  Green of Spring will follow.

Yet a lapse of weeks
  Buds will burst their edges,
Strip their wool-coats, glue-coats, streaks,
  In the woods and hedges;

Weave a bower of love
  For birds to meet each other,
Weave a canopy above
  Nest and egg and mother.

But for fattening rain
  We should have no flowers,
Never a bud or leaf again
  But for soaking showers;

Never a mated bird
  In the rocking tree-tops,
Never indeed a flock or herd
  To graze upon the lea-crops.

Lambs so woolly white,
  Sheep the sun-bright leas on,
They could have no grass to bite
  But for rain in season.

We should find no moss
  In the shadiest places,
Find no waving meadow grass
  Pied with broad-eyed daisies:

But miles of barren sand,
  With never a son or daughter,
Not a lily on the land,
  Or lily on the water.

(1862)

250 *Goblin Market*

MORNING and evening
Maids heard the goblins cry:
'Come buy our orchard fruits,
Come buy, come buy:
Apples and quinces,
Lemons and oranges,
Plump unpecked cherries,
Melons and raspberries,
Bloom-down-cheeked peaches,
Swart-headed mulberries,
Wild free-born cranberries,
Crab-apples, dewberries,
Pine-apples, blackberries,
Apricots, strawberries;—
All ripe together
In summer weather,—
Morns that pass by,
Fair eves that fly;
Come buy, come buy:
Our grapes fresh from the vine,
Pomegranates full and fine,
Dates and sharp bullaces,
Rare pears and greengages,
Damsons and bilberries,
Taste them and try:
Currants and gooseberries,
Bright-fire-like barberries,
Figs to fill your mouth,
Citrons from the South,
Sweet to tongue and sound to eye;
Come buy, come buy.'

Evening by evening
Among the brookside rushes,
Laura bowed her head to hear,
Lizzie veiled her blushes:
Crouching close together
In the cooling weather,
With clasping arms and cautioning lips,
With tingling cheeks and finger tips.
'Lie close,' Laura said,
Pricking up her golden head:
'We must not look at goblin men,
We must not buy their fruits:
Who knows upon what soil they fed

Their hungry thirsty roots?'
'Come buy,' call the goblins
Hobbling down the glen.
'Oh,' cried Lizzie, 'Laura, Laura,
You should not peep at goblin men.'
Lizzie covered up her eyes,
Covered close lest they should look;
Laura reared her glossy head,
And whispered like the restless brook:
'Look, Lizzie, look, Lizzie,
Down the glen tramp little men.
One hauls a basket,
One bears a plate,
One lugs a golden dish
Of many pounds weight.
How fair the vine must grow
Whose grapes are so luscious;
How warm the wind must blow
Thro' those fruit bushes.'
'No,' said Lizzie: 'No, no, no;
Their offers should not charm us,
Their evil gifts would harm us.'
She thrust a dimpled finger
In each ear, shut eyes and ran:
Curious Laura chose to linger
Wondering at each merchant man.
One had a cat's face,
One whisked a tail,
One tramped at a rat's pace,
One crawled like a snail,
One like a wombat prowled obtuse and furry,
One like a ratel tumbled hurry skurry.
She heard a voice like voice of doves
Cooing all together:
They sounded kind and full of loves
In the pleasant weather.

Laura stretched her gleaming neck
Like a rush-imbedded swan,
Like a lily from the beck,
Like a moonlit poplar branch,
Like a vessel at the launch
When its last restraint is gone.

Backwards up the mossy glen
Turned and trooped the goblin men,
With their shrill repeated cry,
'Come buy, come buy.'

When they reached where Laura was
They stood stock still upon the moss,
Leering at each other,
Brother with queer brother;
Signalling each other,
Brother with sly brother.
One set his basket down,
One reared his plate;
One began to weave a crown
Of tendrils, leaves and rough nuts brown
(Men sell not such in any town);
One heaved the golden weight
Of dish and fruit to offer her:
'Come buy, come buy,' was still their cry.
Laura stared but did not stir,
Longed but had no money:
The whisk-tailed merchant bade her taste
In tones as smooth as honey,
The cat-faced purr'd,
The rat-paced spoke a word
Of welcome, and the snail-paced even was heard;
One parrot-voiced and jolly
Cried 'Pretty Goblin' still for 'Pretty Polly';—
One whistled like a bird.

But sweet-tooth Laura spoke in haste:
'Good folk, I have no coin;
To take were to purloin:
I have no copper in my purse,
I have no silver either,
And all my gold is on the furze
That shakes in windy weather
Above the rusty heather.'
'You have much gold upon your head,'
They answered all together:
'Buy from us with a golden curl.'
She clipped a precious golden lock,
She dropped a tear more rare than pearl,
Then sucked their fruit globes fair or red:
Sweeter than honey from the rock,
Stronger than man-rejoicing wine,
Clearer than water flowed that juice;
She never tasted such before,
How should it cloy with length of use?
She sucked and sucked and sucked the more
Fruits which that unknown orchard bore;
She sucked until her lips were sore;

Then flung the emptied rinds away
But gathered up one kernel-stone,
And knew not was it night or day
As she turned home alone.

Lizzie met her at the gate
Full of wise upbraidings:
'Dear, you should not stay so late,
Twilight is not good for maidens;
Should not loiter in the glen
In the haunts of goblin men.
Do you not remember Jeanie,
How she met them in the moonlight,
Took their gifts both choice and many,
Ate their fruits and wore their flowers
Plucked from bowers
Where summer ripens at all hours?
But ever in the noonlight
She pined and pined away;
Sought them by night and day,
Found them no more but dwindled and grew grey;
Then fell with the first snow,
While to this day no grass will grow
Where she lies low:
I planted daisies there a year ago
That never blow.
You should not loiter so.'
'Nay, hush,' said Laura;
'Nay, hush, my sister:
I ate and ate my fill,
Yet my mouth waters still;
Tomorrow night I will
Buy more': and kissed her:
'Have done with sorrow;
I'll bring you plums tomorrow
Fresh on their mother twigs,
Cherries worth getting;
You cannot think what figs
My teeth have met in,
What melons icy-cold
Piled on a dish of gold
Too huge for me to hold,
What peaches with a velvet nap,
Pellucid grapes without one seed:
Odorous indeed must be the mead
Whereon they grow, and pure the wave they drink
With lilies at the brink,
And sugar-sweet their sap.'

Golden head by golden head,
Like two pigeons in one nest
Folded in each other's wings,
They lay down in their curtained bed:
Like two blossoms on one stem,
Like two flakes of new-fall'n snow,
Like two wands of ivory
Tipped with gold for awful kings.
Moon and stars gazed in at them,
Wind sang to them lullaby,
Lumbering owls forbore to fly,
Not a bat flapped to and fro
Round their rest:
Cheek to cheek and breast to breast
Locked together in one nest.

Early in the morning
When the first cock crowed his warning,
Neat like bees, as sweet and busy,
Laura rose with Lizzie:
Fetched in honey, milked the cows,
Aired and set to rights the house,
Kneaded cakes of whitest wheat,
Cakes for dainty mouths to eat,
Next churned butter, whipped up cream,
Fed their poultry, sat and sewed;
Talked as modest maidens should:
Lizzie with an open heart,
Laura in an absent dream,
One content, one sick in part;
One warbling for the mere bright day's delight,
One longing for the night.

At length slow evening came:
They went with pitchers to the reedy brook;
Lizzie most placid in her look,
Laura most like a leaping flame.
They drew the gurgling water from its deep;
Lizzie plucked purple and rich golden flags,
Then turning homewards said: 'The sunset flushes
Those furthest loftiest crags;
Come, Laura, not another maiden lags,
No wilful squirrel wags,
The beasts and birds are fast asleep.'
But Laura loitered still among the rushes
And said the bank was steep.

And said the hour was early still,
The dew not fall'n, the wind not chill:
Listening ever, but not catching
The customary cry,
'Come buy, come buy,'
With its iterated jingle
Of sugar-baited words:
Not for all her watching
Once discerning even one goblin
Racing, whisking, tumbling, hobbling;
Let alone the herds
That used to tramp along the glen,
In groups or single,
Of brisk fruit-merchant men.

Till Lizzie urged, 'O Laura, come;
I hear the fruit-call but I dare not look:
You should not loiter longer at this brook:
Come with me home.
The stars rise, the moon bends her arc,
Each glowworm winks her spark,
Let us get home before the night grows dark:
For clouds may gather
Tho' this is summer weather,
Put out the lights and drench us thro';
Then if we lost our way what should we do?'

Laura turned cold as stone
To find her sister heard that cry alone,
That goblin cry,
'Come buy our fruits, come buy.'
Must she then buy no more such dainty fruit?
Must she no more such succous pasture find,
Gone deaf and blind?
Her tree of life drooped from the root:
She said not one word in her heart's sore ache;
But peering thro' the dimness, nought discerning,
Trudged home, her pitcher dripping all the way;
So crept to bed, and lay
Silent till Lizzie slept;
Then sat up in a passionate yearning,
And gnashed her teeth for baulked desire, and wept
As if her heart would break.

Day after day, night after night,
Laura kept watch in vain
In sullen silence of exceeding pain.
She never caught again the goblin cry:
'Come buy, come buy';—

She never spied the goblin men
Hawking their fruits along the glen:
But when the noon waxed bright
Her hair grew thin and gray;
She dwindled, as the fair full moon doth turn
To swift decay and burn
Her fire away.

One day remembering her kernel-stone
She set it by a wall that faced the south;
Dewed it with tears, hoped for a root,
Watched for a waxing shoot,
But there came none;
It never saw the sun,
It never felt the trickling moisture run:
While with sunk eyes and faded mouth
She dreamed of melons, as a traveller sees
False waves in desert drouth
With shade of leaf-crowned trees,
And burns the thirstier in the sandful breeze.

She no more swept the house,
Tended the fowls or cows,
Fetched honey, kneaded cakes of wheat,
Brought water from the brook:
But sat down listless in the chimney-nook
And would not eat.

Tender Lizzie could not bear
To watch her sister's cankerous care
Yet not to share.
She night and morning
Caught the goblins' cry:
'Come buy our orchard fruits,
Come buy, come buy':—
Beside the brook, along the glen,
She heard the tramp of goblin men,
The voice and stir
Poor Laura could not hear;
Longed to buy fruit to comfort her,
But feared to pay too dear.
She thought of Jeanie in her grave,
Who should have been a bride;
But who for joys brides hope to have
Fell sick and died
In her gay prime,
In earliest Winter time,
With the first glazing rime,
With the first snow-fall of crisp Winter time.

Till Laura dwindling
Seemed knocking at Death's door:
Then Lizzie weighed no more
Better and worse;
But put a silver penny in her purse,
Kissed Laura, crossed the heath with clumps of furze
At twilight, halted by the brook:
And for the first time in her life
Began to listen and look.

Laughed every goblin
When they spied her peeping:
Came towards her hobbling,
Flying, running, leaping,
Puffing and blowing,
Chuckling, clapping, crowing,
Clucking and gobbling,
Mopping and mowing,
Full of airs and graces,
Pulling wry faces,
Demure grimaces,
Cat-like and rat-like,
Ratel-and wombat-like,
Snail-paced in a hurry,
Parrot-voiced and whistler,
Helter skelter, hurry skurry,
Chattering like magpies,
Fluttering like pigeons,
Gliding like fishes,—
Hugged her and kissed her,
Squeezed and caressed her:
Stretched up their dishes,
Panniers, and plates:
'Look at our apples
Russet and dun,
Bob at our cherries,
Bite at our peaches,
Citrons and dates,
Grapes for the asking,
Pears red with basking
Out in the sun,
Plums on their twigs;
Pluck them and suck them,
Pomegranates, figs.'—

'Good folk,' said Lizzie,
Mindful of Jeanie:
'Give me much and many':—

Held out her apron,
Tossed them her penny.
'Nay, take a seat with us,
Honour and eat with us,'
They answered grinning:
'Our feast is but beginning.
Night yet is early,
Warm and dew-pearly,
Wakeful and starry:
Such fruits as these
No man can carry;
Half their bloom would fly,
Half their dew would dry,
Half their flavour would pass by.
Sit down and feast with us,
Be welcome guest with us,
Cheer you and rest with us.'—
'Thank you,' said Lizzie: 'But one waits
At home alone for me:
So without further parleying,
If you will not sell me any
Of your fruits tho' much and many,
Give me back my silver penny
I tossed you for a fee.'—
They began to scratch their pates,
No longer wagging, purring,
But visibly demurring,
Grunting and snarling.
One called her proud,
Cross-grained, uncivil;
Their tones waxed loud,
Their looks were evil.
Lashing their tails
They trod and hustled her,
Elbowed and jostled her,
Clawed with their nails,
Barking, mewing, hissing, mocking,
Tore her gown and soiled her stocking,
Twitched her hair out by the roots,
Stamped upon her tender feet,
Held her hands and squeezed their fruits
Against her mouth to make her eat.

White and golden Lizzie stood,
Like a lily in a flood,—
Like a rock of blue-veined stone
Lashed by tides obstreperously,—
Like a beacon left alone

In a hoary roaring sea,
Sending up a golden fire,—
Like a fruit-crowned orange-tree
White with blossoms honey-sweet
Sore beset by wasp and bee,—
Like a royal virgin town
Topped with gilded dome and spire
Close beleaguered by a fleet
Mad to tug her standard down.

One may lead a horse to water,
Twenty cannot make him drink.
Tho' the goblins cuffed and caught her,
Coaxed and fought her,
Bullied and besought her,
Scratched her, pinched her black as ink,
Kicked and knocked her,
Mauled and mocked her,
Lizzie uttered not a word;
Would not open lip from lip
Lest they should cram a mouthful in:
But laughed in heart to feel the drip
Of juice that syrupped all her face,
And lodged in dimples of her chin,
And streaked her neck which quaked like curd.
At last the evil people
Worn out by her resistance
Flung back her penny, kicked their fruit
Along whichever road they took,
Not leaving root or stone or shoot;
Some writhed into the ground,
Some dived into the brook
With ring and ripple,
Some scudded on the gale without a sound,
Some vanished in the distance.

In a smart, ache, tingle,
Lizzie went her way;
Knew not was it night or day;
Sprang up the bank, tore thro' the furze,
Threaded copse and dingle,
And heard her penny jingle
Bouncing in her purse,
Its bounce was music to her ear.
She ran and ran
As if she feared some goblin man
Dogged her with gibe or curse
Or something worse:

But not one goblin skurried after,
Nor was she pricked by fear;
The kind heart made her windy-paced
That urged her home quite out of breath with haste
And inward laughter.

She cried 'Laura,' up the garden,
'Did you miss me?
Come and kiss me.
Never mind my bruises,
Hug me, kiss me, suck my juices
Squeezed from goblin fruits for you,
Goblin pulp and goblin dew.
Eat me, drink me, love me;
Laura, make much of me:
For your sake I have braved the glen
And had to do with goblin merchant men.'

Laura started from her chair,
Flung her arms up in the air,
Clutched her hair:
'Lizzie, Lizzie, have you tasted
For my sake the fruit forbidden?
Must your light like mine be hidden,
Your young life like mine be wasted,
Undone in mine undoing
And ruined in my ruin,
Thirsty, cankered, goblin-ridden?'—
She clung about her sister,
Kissed and kissed and kissed her:
Tears once again
Refreshed her shrunken eyes,
Dropping like rain
After long sultry drouth;
Shaking with aguish fear, and pain,
She kissed and kissed her with a hungry mouth.

Her lips began to scorch,
That juice was wormwood to her tongue,
She loathed the feast:
Writhing as one possessed she leaped and sung,
Rent all her robe, and wrung
Her hands in lamentable haste,
And beat her breast.
Her locks streamed like the torch
Borne by a racer at full speed,
Or like the mane of horses in their flight,
Or like an eagle when she stems the light

Straight toward the sun,
Or like a caged thing freed,
Or like a flying flag when armies run.

Swift fire spread through her veins, knocked at her heart,
Met the fire smouldering there
And overbore its lesser flame;
She gorged on bitterness without a name:
Ah! fool, to choose such part
Of soul-consuming care!
Sense failed in the mortal strife:
Like the watch-tower of a town
Which an earthquake shatters down,
Like a lightning-stricken mast,
Like a wind-uprooted tree
Spun about,
Like a foam-topped waterspout
Cast down headlong in the sea,
She fell at last;
Pleasure past and anguish past,
Is it death or is it life?

Life out of death.
That night long Lizzie watched by her,
Counted her pulse's flagging stir,
Felt for her breath,
Held water to her lips, and cooled her face
With tears and fanning leaves:
But when the first birds chirped about their eaves,
And early reapers plodded to the place
Of golden sheaves,
And dew-wet grass
Bowed in the morning winds so brisk to pass,
And new buds with new day
Opened of cup-like lilies on the stream,
Laura awoke as from a dream,
Laughed in the innocent old way,
Hugged Lizzie but not twice or thrice;
Her gleaming locks showed not one thread of grey,
Her breath was sweet as May
And light danced in her eyes.

Days, weeks, months, years
Afterwards, when both were wives
With children of their own;
Their mother-hearts beset with fears,
Their lives bound up in tender lives;
Laura would call the little ones

And tell them of her early prime,
Those pleasant days long gone
Of not-returning time:
Would talk about the haunted glen,
The wicked, quaint fruit-merchant men,
Their fruits like honey to the throat
But poison in the blood;
(Men sell not such in any town:)
Would tell them how her sister stood
In deadly peril to do her good,
And win the fiery antidote:
Then joining hands to little hands
Would bid them cling together,
'For there is no friend like a sister
In calm or stormy weather;
To cheer one on the tedious way,
To fetch one if one goes astray,
To lift one if one totters down,
To strengthen whilst one stands.'

(1862)

251 *Up-Hill*

DOES the road wind up-hill all the way?
  Yes, to the very end.
Will the day's journey take the whole long day?
  From morn to night, my friend.

But is there for the night a resting-place?
  A roof for when the slow dark hours begin.
May not the darkness hide it from my face?
  You cannot miss that inn.

Shall I meet other wayfarers at night?
  Those who have gone before.
Then must I knock, or call when just in sight?
  They will not keep you standing at that door.

Shall I find comfort, travel-sore and weak?
  Of labour you shall find the sum.
Will there be beds for me and all who seek?
  Yea, beds for all who come.

(1862)

252 *A Royal Princess*

I, A PRINCESS, king-descended, decked with jewels, gilded, drest,
Would rather be a peasant with her baby at her breast,
For all I shine so like the sun, and am purple like the west.

Two and two my guards behind, two and two before,
Two and two on either hand, they guard me evermore;
Me, poor dove that must not coo—eagle that must not soar.

All my fountains cast up perfumes, all my gardens grow
Scented woods and foreign spices, with all flowers in blow
That are costly, out of season as the seasons go.

All my walls are lost in mirrors, whereupon I trace
Self to right hand, self to left hand, self in every place,
Self-same solitary figure, self-same seeking face.

Then I have an ivory chair high to sit upon,
Almost like my father's chair, which is an ivory throne;
There I sit uplift and upright, there I sit alone.

Alone by day, alone by night, alone days without end;
My father and my mother give me treasures, search and spend—
O my father! O my mother! have you ne'er a friend?

As I am a lofty princess, so my father is
A lofty king, accomplished in all kingly subtilties,
Holding in his strong right hand world-kingdoms' balances.

He has quarrelled with his neighbours, he has scourged his foes;
Vassal counts and princes follow where his pennon goes,
Long-descended valiant lords whom the vulture knows,

On whose track the vulture swoops, when they ride in state
To break the strength of armies and topple down the great:
Each of these my courteous servant, none of these my mate.

My father counting up his strength sets down with equal pen
So many head of cattle, head of horses, head of men;
These for slaughter, these for labour, with the how and when.

Some to work on roads, canals; some to man his ships;
Some to smart in mines beneath sharp overseers' whips;
Some to trap fur-beasts in lands where utmost winter nips.

Once it came into my heart and whelmed me like a flood,
That these too are men and women, human flesh and blood;
Men with hearts and men with souls, tho' trodden down like mud.

Our feasting was not glad that night, our music was not gay;
On my mother's graceful head I marked a thread of grey,
My father frowning at the fare seemed every dish to weigh.

I sat beside them sole princess in my exalted place,
My ladies and my gentlemen stood by me on the dais:
A mirror showed me I look old and haggard in the face;

It showed me that my ladies all are fair to gaze upon,
Plump, plenteous-haired, to every one love's secret lore is known,
They laugh by day, they sleep by night; ah, me, what is a throne?

The singing men and women sang that night as usual,
The dancers danced in pairs and sets, but music had a fall,
A melancholy windy fall as at a funeral.

Amid the toss of torches to my chamber back we swept;
My ladies loosed my golden chain; meantime I could have wept
To think of some in galling chains whether they waked or slept.

I took my bath of scented milk, delicately waited on,
They burned sweet things for my delight, cedar and cinnamon,
They lit my shaded silver lamp, and left me there alone.

A day went by, a week went by. One day I heard it said:
'Men are clamouring, women, children, clamouring to be fed;
Men like famished dogs are howling in the streets for bread.'

So two whispered by my door, not thinking I could hear,
Vulgar naked truth, ungarnished for a royal ear;
Fit for cooping in the background, not to stalk so near.

But I strained my utmost sense to catch this truth, and mark:
'There are families out grazing like cattle in the park.'
'A pair of peasants must be saved, even if we build an ark.'

A merry jest, a merry laugh, each strolled upon his way;
One was my page, a lad I reared and bore with day by day;
One was my youngest maid, as sweet and white as cream in May.

Other footsteps followed softly with a weightier tramp;
Voices said: 'Picked soldiers have been summoned from the camp,
To quell these base-born ruffians who make free to howl and stamp.'

'Howl and stamp?' one answered: 'They made free to hurl a stone
At the minister's state coach, well aimed and stoutly thrown.'
'There's work then for the soldiers, for this rank crop must be mown.'

'One I saw, a poor old fool with ashes on his head,
Whimpering because a girl had snatched his crust of bread:
Then he dropped; when some one raised him, it turned out he was dead.'

'After us the deluge,' was retorted with a laugh:
'If bread's the staff of life, they must walk without a staff.'
'While I've a loaf they're welcome to my blessing and the chaff.'

These passed. 'The king': stand up. Said my father with a smile:
'Daughter mine, your mother comes to sit with you awhile,
She's sad today, and who but you her sadness can beguile?'

He too left me. Shall I touch my harp now while I wait,—
(I hear them doubling guard below before our palace gate)—
Or shall I work the last gold stitch into my veil of state;

Or shall my woman stand and read some unimpassioned scene,
There's music of a lulling sort in words that pause between;
Or shall she merely fan me while I wait here for the queen?

Again I caught my father's voice in sharp word of command:
'Charge!' a clash of steel: 'Charge again, the rebels stand.
Smite and spare not, hand to hand; smite and spare not, hand to
hand.'

There swelled a tumult at the gate, high voices waxing higher;
A flash of red reflected light lit the cathedral spire;
I heard a cry for faggots, then I heard a yell for fire.

'Sit and roast there with your meat, sit and bake there with your
bread,
You who sat to see us starve,' one shrieking woman said:
'Sit on your throne and roast with your crown upon your head.'

Nay, this thing will I do, while my mother tarrieth,
I will take my fine spun gold, but not to sew therewith,
I will take my gold and gems, and rainbow fan and wreath;

With a ransom in my lap, a king's ransom in my hand,
I will go down to this people, will stand face to face, will stand
Where they curse king, queen, and princess of this cursed land.

They shall take all to buy them bread, take all I have to give;
I, if I perish, perish; they today shall eat and live;
I, if I perish, perish; that's the goal I half conceive:

Once to speak before the world, rend bare my heart and show
The lesson I have learned, which is death, is life, to know.
I, if I perish, perish; in the name of God I go.

(1863 *1866*)

253 *The Lowest Room*

LIKE flowers sequestered from the sun
And wind of summer, day by day
I dwindled paler, whilst my hair
Showed the first tinge of grey.

'Oh what is life, that we should live?
  Or what is death, that we must die?
A bursting bubble is our life:
    I also, what am I?'

'What is your grief? now tell me, sweet,
  That I may grieve,' my sister said;
And stayed a white embroidering hand
    And raised a golden head:

Her tresses showed a richer mass,
  Her eyes looked softer than my own,
Her figure had a statelier height,
    Her voice a tenderer tone.

'Some must be second and not first;
  All cannot be the first of all:
Is not this, too, but vanity?
    I stumble like to fall.

'So yesterday I read the acts
  Of Hector and each clangorous king
With wrathful great Aeacides:—
    Old Homer leaves a sting.'

The comely face looked up again,
  The deft hand lingered on the thread:
'Sweet, tell me what is Homer's sting,
    Old Homer's sting?' she said.

'He stirs my sluggish pulse like wine,
  He melts me like the wind of spice,
Strong as strong Ajax' red right hand,
    And grand like Juno's eyes.

'I cannot melt the sons of men,
  I cannot fire and tempest-toss:—
Besides, those days were golden days,
    Whilst these are days of dross.'

She laughed a feminine low laugh,
  Yet did not stay her dexterous hand:
'Now tell me of those days,' she said,
    'When time ran golden sand.'

'Then men were men of might and right,
  Sheer might, at least, and weighty swords;
Then men in open blood and fire
    Bore witness to their words,

'Crest-rearing kings with whistling spears;
  But if these shivered in the shock
They wrenched up hundred-rooted trees,
    Or hurled the effacing rock.

'Then hand to hand, then foot to foot,
  Stern to the death-grip grappling then,
Who ever thought of gunpowder
    Amongst these men of men?

'They knew whose hand struck home the death,
  They knew who broke but would not bend,
Could venerate an equal foe
    And scorn a laggard friend.

'Calm in the utmost stress of doom,
  Devout toward adverse powers above,
They hated with intenser hate
    And loved with fuller love.

'Then heavenly beauty could allay
  As heavenly beauty stirred the strife:
By them a slave was worshipped more
    Than is by us a wife.'

She laughed again, my sister laughed;
  Made answer o'er the laboured cloth:
'I rather would be one of us
    Than wife, or slave, or both.'

'Oh better then be slave or wife
  Than fritter now blank life away:
Then night had holiness of night,
    And day was sacred day.

'The princess laboured at her loom,
  Mistress and handmaiden alike;
Beneath their needles grew the field
    With warriors armed to strike.

'Or, look again, dim Dian's face
  Gleamed perfect thro' the attendant night;
Were such not better than those holes
    Amid that waste of white?

'A shame it is, our aimless life:
  I rather from my heart would feed
From silver dish in gilded stall
    With wheat and wine the steed—

'The faithful steed that bore my lord
In safety thro' the hostile land,
The faithful steed that arched his neck
To fondle with my hand.'

Her needle erred; a moment's pause,
A moment's patience, all was well.
Then she: 'But just suppose the horse,
Suppose the rider fell?

'Then captive in an alien house,
Hungering on exile's bitter bread,—
They happy, they who won the lot
Of sacrifice,' she said.

Speaking she faltered, while her look
Showed forth her passion like a glass:
With hand suspended, kindling eye,
Flushed cheek, how fair she was!

'Ah well, be those the days of dross;
This, if you will, the age of gold:
Yet had those days a spark of warmth,
While these are somewhat cold—

'Are somewhat mean and cold and slow,
Are stunted from heroic growth:
We gain but little when we prove
The worthlessness of both.'

'But life is in our hands,' she said:
'In our own hands for gain or loss:
Shall not the Sevenfold Sacred Fire
Suffice to purge our dross?

'Too short a century of dreams,
One day of work sufficient length:
Why should not you, why should not I
Attain heroic strength?

'Our life is given us as a blank;
Ourselves must make it blest or curst:
Who dooms me I shall only be
The second, not the first?

'Learn from old Homer, if you will,
Such wisdom as his books have said:
In one the acts of Ajax shine,
In one of Diomed.

'Honoured all heroes whose high deeds
  Thro' life, thro' death, enlarge their span:
Only Achilles in his rage
    And sloth is less than man.'

'Achilles only less than man?
  He less than man who, half a god,
Discomfited all Greece with rest,
    Cowed Ilion with a nod?

'He offered vengeance, lifelong grief
  To one dear ghost, uncounted price:
Beasts, Trojans, adverse gods, himself,
    Heaped up the sacrifice.

'Self-immolated to his friend,
  Shrined in world's wonder, Homer's page,
Is this the man, the less than men
    Of this degenerate age?'

'Gross from his acorns, tusky boar
  Does memorable acts like his;
So for her snared offended young
    Bleeds the swart lioness.'

But here she paused; our eyes had met,
  And I was whitening with the jeer;
She rose: 'I went too far,' she said;
    Spoke low: 'Forgive me, dear.

'To me our days seem pleasant days,
  Our home a haven of pure content;
Forgive me if I said too much,
    So much more than I meant.

'Homer, tho' greater than his gods,
  With rough-hewn virtues was sufficed
And rough-hewn men: but what are such
    To us who learn of Christ?'

The much-moved pathos of her voice,
  Her almost tearful eyes, her cheek
Grown pale, confessed the strength of love
    Which only made her speak:

For mild she was, of few soft words,
  Most gentle, easy to be led,
Content to listen when I spoke
    And reverence what I said;

I elder sister by six years;
Not half so glad, or wise, or good:
Her words rebuked my secret self
And shamed me where I stood.

She never guessed her words reproved
A silent envy nursed within,
A selfish, souring discontent
Pride-born, the devil's sin.

I smiled, half bitter, half in jest:
'The wisest man of all the wise
Left for his summary of life
"Vanity of vanities."

'Beneath the sun there's nothing new:
Men flow, men ebb, mankind flows on:
If I am wearied of my life,
Why so was Solomon.

'Vanity of vanities he preached
Of all he found, of all he sought:
Vanity of vanities, the gist
Of all the words he taught.

'This in the wisdom of the world,
In Homer's page, in all, we find:
As the sea is not filled, so yearns
Man's universal mind.

'This Homer felt, who gave his men
With glory but a transient state:
His very Jove could not reverse
Irrevocable fate.

'Uncertain all their lot save this—
Who wins must lose, who lives must die:
All trodden out into the dark
Alike, all vanity.'

She scarcely answered when I paused,
But rather to herself said: 'One
Is here,' low-voiced and loving, 'Yea,
Greater than Solomon.'

So both were silent, she and I:
She laid her work aside, and went
Into the garden-walks, like spring,
All gracious with content;

A little graver than her wont,
  Because her words had fretted me;
Not warbling quite her merriest tune
    Bird-like from tree to tree.

I chose a book to read and dream:
  Yet half the while with furtive eyes
Marked how she made her choice of flowers
    Intuitively wise,

And ranged them with instinctive taste
  Which all my books had failed to teach;
Fresh rose herself, and daintier
    Than blossom of the peach.

By birthright higher than myself,
  Tho' nestling of the selfsame nest:
No fault of hers, no fault of mine,
    But stubborn to digest.

I watched her, till my book unmarked
  Slid noiseless to the velvet floor;
Till all the opulent summer-world
    Looked poorer than before.

Just then her busy fingers ceased,
  Her fluttered colour went and came;
I knew whose step was on the walk,
    Whose voice would name her name.

* * *

Well, twenty years have passed since then:
  My sister now, a stately wife
Still fair, looks back in peace and sees
    The longer half of life—

The longer half of prosperous life,
  With little grief, or fear, or fret:
She, loved and loving long ago,
    Is loved and loving yet.

A husband honourable, brave,
  Is her main wealth in all the world:
And next to him one like herself,
    One daughter golden-curled;

Fair image of her own fair youth,
  As beautiful and as serene,
With almost such another love
    As her own love has been.

Yet, tho' of world-wide charity,
And in her home most tender dove,
Her treasure and her heart are stored
In the home-land of love:

She thrives, God's blessed husbandry;
Most like a vine which full of fruit
Doth cling and lean and climb toward heaven
While earth still binds its root.

I sit and watch my sister's face:
How little altered since the hours
When she, a kind, light-hearted girl,
Gathered her garden flowers;

Her song just mellowed by regret
For having teased me with her talk;
Then all-forgetful as she heard
One step upon the walk.

While I? I sat alone and watched;
My lot in life, to live alone
In mine own world of interests,
Much felt but little shown.

Not to be first: how hard to learn
That lifelong lesson of the past;
Line graven on line and stroke on stroke;
But, thank God, learned at last.

So now in patience I possess
My soul year after tedious year,
Content to take the lowest place,
The place assigned me here.

Yet sometimes, when I feel my strength
Most weak, and life most burdensome,
I lift mine eyes up to the hills
From whence my help shall come:

Yea, sometimes still I lift my heart
To the Archangelic trumpet-burst,
When all deep secrets shall be shown,
And many last be first.

(1864 *1875*)

254

L.E.L.

'Whose heart was breaking for a little love.'
E.B. Browning

Downstairs I laugh, I sport and jest with all:
But in my solitary room above
I turn my face in silence to the wall;
My heart is breaking for a little love.
Tho' winter frosts are done,
And birds pair every one,
And leaves peep out, for springtide is begun.

I feel no spring, while spring is wellnigh blown,
I find no nest, while nests are in the grove:
Woe's me for mine own heart that dwells alone,
My heart that breaketh for a little love.
While golden in the sun
Rivulets rise and run,
While lilies bud, for springtide is begun.

All love, are loved, save only I; their hearts
Beat warm with love and joy, beat full thereof:
They cannot guess, who play the pleasant parts,
My heart is breaking for a little love.
While beehives wake and whirr,
And rabbit thins his fur,
In living spring that sets the world astir.

I deck myself with silks and jewelry,
I plume myself like any mated dove:
They praise my rustling show, and never see
My heart is breaking for a little love.
While sprouts green lavender
With rosemary and myrrh,
For in quick spring the sap is all astir.

Perhaps some saints in glory guess the truth,
Perhaps some angels read it as they move,
And cry one to another full of ruth,
'Her heart is breaking for a little love.'
Tho' other things have birth,
And leap and sing for mirth,
When springtime wakes and clothes and feeds the earth.

Yet saith a saint: 'Take patience for thy scathe';
Yet saith an angel: 'Wait, for thou shalt prove
True best is last, true life is born of death,
O thou, heart-broken for a little love

Then love shall fill thy girth,
And love make fat thy dearth,
When new spring builds new heaven and clean new earth.'

(1863 *1866*)

255 *Under the Rose*

'THE INIQUITY OF THE FATHERS UPON THE CHILDREN'

Oh the rose of keenest thorn!
One hidden summer morn
Under the rose I was born.

I do not guess his name
Who wrought my Mother's shame,
And gave me life forlorn,
But my Mother, Mother, Mother,
I know her from all other.
My Mother pale and mild,
Fair as ever was seen,
She was but scarce sixteen,
Little more than a child,
When I was born
To work her scorn.
With secret bitter throes,
In a passion of secret woes,
She bore me under the rose.

One who my Mother nursed
Took me from the first:—
'O nurse, let me look upon
This babe that costs so dear;
Tomorrow she will be gone:
Other mothers may keep
Their babes awake and asleep,
But I must not keep her here.'—
Whether I know or guess,
I know this not the less.

So I was sent away
That none might spy the truth:
And my childhood waxed to youth
And I left off childish play.
I never cared to play
With the village boys and girls;
And I think they thought me proud,
I found so little to say
And kept so from the crowd:
But I had the longest curls

And I had the largest eyes,
And my teeth were small like pearls;
The girls might flout and scout me,
But the boys would hang about me
In sheepish mooning wise.

Our one-street village stood
A long mile from the town,
A mile of windy down
And bleak one-sided wood,
With not a single house.
Our town itself was small,
With just the common shops,
And throve in its small way.
Our neighbouring gentry reared
The good old-fashioned crops,
And made old-fashioned boasts
Of what John Bull would do
If Frenchman Frog appeared,
And drank old-fashioned toasts,
And made old-fashioned bows
To my Lady at the Hall.

My Lady at the Hall
Is grander than they all:
Hers is the oldest name
In all the neighbourhood;
But the race must die with her
Tho' she's a lofty dame,
For she's unmarried still.
Poor people say she's good
And has an open hand
As any in the land,
And she's the comforter
Of many sick and sad;
My nurse once said to me
That everything she had
Came of my Lady's bounty:
'Tho' she's greatest in the county
She's humble to the poor,
No beggar seeks her door
But finds help presently.
I pray both night and day
For her, and you must pray:
But she'll never feel distress
If needy folk can bless.'

I was a little maid
When here we came to live
From somewhere by the sea.
Men spoke a foreign tongue
There where we used to be
When I was merry and young,
Too young to feel afraid;
The fisher-folk would give
A kind strange word to me,
There by the foreign sea:
I don't know where it was,
But I remember still
Our cottage on a hill,
And fields of flowering grass
On that fair foreign shore.

I liked my old home best,
But this was pleasant too:
So here we made our nest
And here I grew.
And now and then my Lady
In riding past our door
Would nod to Nurse and speak,
Or stoop and pat my cheek;
And I was always ready
To hold the field-gate wide
For my Lady to go thro';
My Lady in her veil
So seldom put aside,
My Lady grave and pale.

I often sat to wonder
Who might my parents be,
For I knew of something under
My simple-seeming state.
Nurse never talked to me
Of mother or of father,
But watched me early and late
With kind suspicious cares:
Or not suspicious, rather
Anxious, as if she knew
Some secret I might gather
And smart for unawares.
Thus I grew.

But Nurse waxed old and grey,
Bent and weak with years.
There came a certain day

That she lay upon her bed
Shaking her palsied head,
With words she gasped to say
Which had to stay unsaid.
Then with a jerking hand
Held out so piteously
She gave a ring to me
Of gold wrought curiously,
A ring which she had worn
Since the day that I was born,
She once had said to me:
I slipped it on my finger;
Her eyes were keen to linger
On my hand that slipped it on;
Then she sighed one rattling sigh
And stared on with sightless eyes:—
The one who loved me was gone.

How long I stayed alone
With the corpse, I never knew,
For I fainted dead as stone:
When I came to life once more
I was down upon the floor,
With neighbours making ado
To bring me back to life.
I heard the sexton's wife
Say: 'Up, my lad, and run
To tell it at thc Hall;
She was my Lady's nurse,
And done can't be undone.
I'll watch by this poor lamb.
I guess my Lady's purse
Is always open to such:
I'd run up on my crutch
A cripple as I am,'
(For cramps had vexed her much)
'Rather than this dear heart
Lack one to take her part.'

For days day after day
On my weary bed I lay
Wishing the time would pass;
Oh, so wishing that I was
Likely to pass away:
For the one friend whom I knew
Was dead, I knew no other,
Neither father nor mother;
And I, what should I do?

One day the sexton's wife
Said: 'Rouse yourself, my dear:
My Lady has driven down
From the Hall into the town,
And we think she's coming here.
Cheer up, for life is life.'

But I would not look or speak,
Would not cheer up at all.
My tears were like to fall,
So I turned round to the wall
And hid my hollow cheek
Making as if I slept,
As silent as a stone,
And no one knew I wept.
What was my Lady to me,
The grand lady from the Hall?
She might come, or stay away,
I was sick at heart that day:
The whole world seemed to be
Nothing, just nothing to me,
For aught that I could see.

Yet I listened where I lay:
A bustle came below,
A clear voice said: 'I know;
I will see her first alone,
It may be less of a shock
If she's so weak today':—
A light hand turned the lock,
A light step crossed the floor,
One sat beside my bed:
But never a word she said.

For me, my shyness grew
Each moment more and more:
So I said never a word
And neither looked nor stirred;
I think she must have heard
My heart go pit-a-pat:
Thus I lay, my Lady sat,
More than a mortal hour—
(I counted one and two
By the house-clock while I lay):
I seemed to have no power
To think of a thing to say,
Or do what I ought to do,
Or rouse myself to a choice.

At last she said: 'Margaret,
Won't you even look at me?'
A something in her voice
Forced my tears to fall at last,
Forced sobs from me thick and fast;
Something not of the past,
Yet stirring memory;
A something new, and yet
Not new, too sweet to last,
Which I never can forget.

I turned and stared at her:
Her cheek showed hollow-pale;
Her hair like mine was fair,
A wonderful fall of hair
That screened her like a veil;
But her height was statelier,
Her eyes had depth more deep;
I think they must have had
Always a something sad,
Unless they were asleep.

While I stared, my Lady took
My hand in her spare hand
Jewelled and soft and grand,
And looked with a long long look
Of hunger in my face;
As if she tried to trace
Features she ought to know,
And half hoped, half feared, to find.
Whatever was in her mind
She heaved a sigh at last,
And began to talk to me.

'Your nurse was my dear nurse,
And her nursling's dear,' said she:
'No one told me a word
Of her getting worse and worse,
Till her poor life was past'
(Here my Lady's tears dropped fast):
'I might have been with her,
I might have promised and heard,
But she had no comforter.
She might have told me much
Which now I shall never know,
Never never shall know.'
She sat by me sobbing so,
And seemed so woe-begone,

That I laid one hand upon
Hers with a timid touch,
Scarce thinking what I did,
Not knowing what to say:
That moment her face was hid
In the pillow close by mine,
Her arm was flung over me,
She hugged me, sobbing so
As if her heart would break,
And kissed me where I lay.

After this she often came
To bring me fruit or wine,
Or sometimes hothouse flowers.
And at nights I lay awake
Often and often thinking
What to do for her sake.
Wet or dry it was the same:
She would come in at all hours,
Set me eating and drinking
And say I must grow strong;
At last the day seemed long
And home seemed scarcely home
If she did not come.

Well, I grew strong again:
In time of primroses,
I went to pluck them in the lane;
In time of nestling birds,
I heard them chirping round the house;
And all the herds
Were out at grass when I grew strong,
And days were waxen long,
And there was work for bees
Among the May-bush boughs,
And I had shot up tall,
And life felt after all
Pleasant, and not so long
When I grew strong.

I was going to the Hall
To be my Lady's maid:
'Her little friend,' she said to me,
'Almost her child,'
She said and smiled
Sighing painfully;
Blushing, with a second flush
As if she blushed to blush.

Friend, servant, child: just this
My standing at the Hall;
The other servants call me 'Miss,'
My Lady calls me 'Margaret,'
With her clear voice musical.
She never chides when I forget
This or that; she never chides.
Except when people come to stay,
(And that's not often) at the Hall,
I sit with her all day
And ride out when she rides.
She sings to me and makes me sing;
Sometimes I read to her,
Sometimes we merely sit and talk.
She noticed once my ring
And made me tell its history:
That evening in our garden walk
She said she should infer
The ring had been my father's first,
Then my mother's, given for me
To the nurse who nursed
My mother in her misery,
That so quite certainly
Some one might know me, who...
Then she was silent, and I too.

I hate when people come:
The women speak and stare
And mean to be so civil.
This one will stroke my hair,
That one will pat my cheek
And praise my Lady's kindness,
Expecting me to speak;
I like the proud ones best
Who sit as struck with blindness,
As if I wasn't there.
But if any gentleman
Is staying at the Hall
(Tho' few come prying here),
My Lady seems to fear
Some downright dreadful evil,
And makes me keep my room
As closely as she can:
So I hate when people come,
It is so troublesome.
In spite of all her care,
Sometimes to keep alive

I sometimes do contrive
To get out in the grounds
For a whiff of wholesome air,
Under the rose you know:
It's charming to break bounds,
Stolen waters are sweet,
And what's the good of feet
If for days they mustn't go?
Give me a longer tether,
Or I may break from it.

Now I have eyes and ears
And just some little wit:
'Almost my Lady's child';
I recollect she smiled,
Sighed and blushed together;
Then her story of the ring
Sounds not improbable,
She told it me so well
It seemed the actual thing:—
Oh, keep your counsel close,
But I guess under the rose,
In long past summer weather
When the world was blossoming,
And the rose upon its thorn:
I guess not who he was
Flawed honour like a glass
And made my life forlorn,
But my Mother, Mother, Mother,
Oh, I know her from all other.

My Lady, you might trust
Your daughter with your fame.
Trust me, I would not shame
Our honourable name,
For I have noble blood
Tho' I was bred in dust
And brought up in the mud.
I will not press my claim,
Just leave me where you will:
But you might trust your daughter,
For blood is thicker than water
And you're my mother still.

So my Lady holds her own
With condescending grace,
And fills her lofty place
With an untroubled face

As a queen may fill a throne.
While I could hint a tale—
(But then I am her child)—
Would make her quail;
Would set her in the dust,
Lorn with no comforter,
Her glorious hair defiled
And ashes on her cheek:
The decent world would thrust
Its finger out at her,
Not much displeased I think
To make a nine days' stir;
The decent world would sink
Its voice to speak of her.

Now this is what I mean
To do, no more, no less:
Never to speak, or show
Bare sign of what I know.
Let the blot pass unseen;
Yea, let her never guess
I hold the tangled clue
She huddles out of view.
Friend, servant, almost child,
So be it and nothing more
On this side of the grave.
Mother, in Paradise,
You'll see with clearer eyes;
Perhaps in this world even
When you are like to die
And face to face with Heaven
You'll drop for once the lie:
But you must drop the mask, not I.

My Lady promises
Two hundred pounds with me
Whenever I may wed
A man she can approve:
And since besides her bounty
I'm fairest in the county
(For so I've heard it said,
Tho' I don't vouch for this),
Her promised pounds may move
Some honest man to see
My virtues and my beauties;
Perhaps the rising grazier,
Or temperance publican,
May claim my wifely duties.

Meanwhile I wait their leisure
And grace-bestowing pleasure,
I wait the happy man;
But if I hold my head
And pitch my expectations
Just higher than their level,
They must fall back on patience:
I may not mean to wed,
Yet I'll be civil.

Now sometimes in a dream
My heart goes out of me
To build and scheme,
Till I sob after things that seem
So pleasant in a dream:
A home such as I see
My blessed neighbours live in
With father and with mother,
All proud of one another,
Named by one common name
From baby in the bud
To full-blown workman father;
It's little short of Heaven.
I'd give my gentle blood
To wash my special shame
And drown my private grudge;
I'd toil and moil much rather
The dingiest cottage drudge
Whose mother need not blush,
Than live here like a lady
And see my Mother flush
And hear her voice unsteady
Sometimes, yet never dare
Ask to share her care.

Of course the servants sneer
Behind my back at me;
Of course the village girls,
Who envy me my curls
And gowns and idleness,
Take comfort in a jeer;
Of course the ladies guess
Just so much of my history
As points the emphatic stress
With which they laud my Lady;
The gentlemen who catch
A casual glimpse of me
And turn again to see,

Their valets on the watch
To speak a word with me,
All know and sting me wild;
Till I am almost ready
To wish that I were dead,
No faces more to see,
No more words to be said,
My Mother safe at last
Disburdened of her child,
And the past past.

'All equal before God'—
Our Rector has it so,
And sundry sleepers nod:
It may be so; I know
All are not equal here,
And when the sleepers wake
They make a difference.
'All equal in the grave'—
That shows an obvious sense:
Yet something which I crave
Not death itself brings near;
How should death half atone
For all my past; or make
The name I bear my own?

I love my dear old Nurse
Who loved me without gains;
I love my mistress even,
Friend, Mother, what you will:
But I could almost curse
My Father for his pains;
And sometimes at my prayer
Kneeling in sight of Heaven
I almost curse him still:
Why did he set his snare
To catch at unaware
My Mother's foolish youth;
Load me with shame that's hers,
And her with something worse,
A lifelong lie for truth?

I think my mind is fixed
On one point and made up:
To accept my lot unmixed;
Never to drug the cup
But drink it by myself.
I'll not be wooed for pelf;

I'll not blot out my shame
With any man's good name;
But nameless as I stand,
My hand is my own hand,
And nameless as I came
I go to the dark land.

'All equal in the grave'—
I bide my time till then:
'All equal before God'—
Today I feel His rod,
Tomorrow He may save:
Amen.

(1866)

256 *Autumn Violets*

KEEP love for youth, and violets for the spring:
Or if these bloom when worn-out autumn grieves,
Let them lie hid in double shade of leaves,
Their own, and others dropped down withering;
For violets suit when home birds build and sing,
Not when the outbound bird a passage cleaves;
Not with dry stubble of mown harvest sheaves,
But when the green world buds to blossoming.
Keep violets for the spring, and love for youth,
Love that should dwell with beauty, mirth, and hope:
Or if a later sadder love be born,
Let this not look for grace beyond its scope,
But give itself, nor plead for answering truth—
A grateful Ruth tho' gleaning scanty corn.

(1868 *1875*)

257 *Monna Innominata*

A SONNET OF SONNETS

Beatrice, immortalized by 'altissimo poeta . . . cotanto amante'; Laura, celebrated by a great tho' an inferior bard,—have alike paid the exceptional penalty of exceptional honour, and have come down to us resplendent with charms, but (at least, to my apprehension) scant of attractiveness.

These heroines of world-wide fame were preceded by a bevy of unnamed ladies 'donne innominate' sung by a school of less conspicuous poets; and in that land and that period which gave simultaneous birth to Catholics, to Albigenses, and to Troubadours, one can imagine many a lady as sharing her lover's poetic aptitude, while the barrier between them might be one held sacred by both, yet not such as to render mutual love incompatible with mutual honour.

Had such a lady spoken for herself, the portrait left us might have appeared more tender, if less dignified, than any drawn even-by a devoted friend. Or had the Great Poetess of our own day and nation only been unhappy instead of happy, her circumstances would have invited her to bequeath to us, in lieu of the 'Portuguese Sonnets', an inimitable 'donna innominata' drawn not from fancy but from feeling, and worthy to occupy a niche beside Beatrice and Laura.

1

'Lo di che han detto a' dolci amici addio.'
Dante
'Amor, con quanto sforzo oggi mi vinci!'
Petrarca

COME back to me, who wait and watch for you:—
Or come not yet, for it is over then,
And long it is before you come again,
So far between my pleasures are and few.
While, when you come not, what I do I do
Thinking 'Now when he comes,' my sweetest 'when':
For one man is my world of all the men
This wide world holds; O love, my world is you.
Howbeit, to meet you grows almost a pang
Because the pang of parting comes so soon;
My hope hangs waning, waxing, like a moon
Between the heavenly days on which we meet:
Ah me, but where are now the songs I sang
When life was sweet because you called them sweet?

2

'Era già l'ora che volge il desio.'
Dante
'Ricorro al tempo ch'io vi vidi prima.'
Petrarca

I WISH I could remember, that first day,
First hour, first moment of your meeting me,
If bright or dim the season, it might be
Summer or Winter for aught I can say;
So unrecorded did it slip away,
So blind was I to see and to foresee,
So dull to mark the budding of my tree
That would not blossom yet for many a May.
If only I could recollect it, such
A day of days! I let it come and go
As traceless as a thaw of bygone snow;
It seemed to mean so little, meant so much;
If only now I could recall that touch,
First touch of hand in hand—Did one but know!

3

'O ombre vane, fuor che ne l'aspetto!'
Dante

'Immaginata guida la conduce.'
Petrarca

I DREAM of you to wake: would that I might
  Dream of you and not wake but slumber on;
  Nor find with dreams the dear companion gone,
As Summer ended Summer birds take flight.
In happy dreams I hold you full in sight,
  I blush again who waking look so wan;
  Brighter than sunniest day that ever shone,
In happy dreams your smile makes day of night.
Thus only in a dream we are at one,
  Thus only in a dream we give and take
    The faith that maketh rich who take or give;
  If thus to sleep is sweeter than to wake,
    To die were surely sweeter than to live,
Tho' there be nothing new beneath the sun.

4

'Poca favilla gran fiamma seconda.'
Dante

'Ogni altra cosa, ogni pensier va fore,
E sol ivi con voi rimansi amore.'
Petrarca

I LOVED you first: but afterwards your love
  Outsoaring mine, sang such a loftier song
As drowned the friendly cooings of my dove.
  Which owes the other most? my love was long,
  And yours one moment seemed to wax more strong;
I loved and guessed at you, you construed me
And loved me for what might or might not be—
  Nay, weights and measures do us both a wrong.
For verily love knows not 'mine' or 'thine';
  With separate 'I' and 'thou' free love has done,
    For one is both and both are one in love:
Rich love knows nought of 'thine that is not mine';
    Both have the strength and both the length thereof,
  Both of us, of the love which makes us one.

5

'Amor che a nulla amato amar perdona.'
Dante

'Amor m'addusse in si gioiosa spene.'
Petrarca

O MY heart's heart, and you who are to me
More than myself myself, God be with you,
Keep you in strong obedience leal and true
To Him whose noble service setteth free,
Give you all good we see or can foresee,
Make your joys many and your sorrows few,
Bless you in what you bear and what you do,
Yea, perfect you as He would have you be.
So much for you; but what for me, dear friend?
To love you without stint and all I can
Today, tomorrow, world without an end;
To love you much and yet to love you more,
As Jordan at his flood sweeps either shore;
Since woman is the helpmeet made for man.

6

'Or puoi la quantitate
Comprender de l'amor che a te mi scalda.'
Dante

'Non vo'che da tal nodo amor mi sciogli a.'
Petrarca

TRUST me, I have not earned your dear rebuke,
I love, as you would have me, God the most;
Would lose not Him, but you, must one be lost,
Nor with Lot's wife cast back a faithless look
Unready to forego what I forsook;
This say I, having counted up the cost,
This, tho' I be the feeblest of God's host,
The sorriest sheep Christ shepherds with His crook.
Yet while I love my God the most, I deem
That I can never love you overmuch;
I love Him more, so let me love you too;
Yea, as I apprehend it, love is such
I cannot love you if I love not Him,
I cannot love Him if I love not you.

7

'Qui primavera sempre ed ogni frutto.'
Dante

'Ragionando con meco ed io con lui.'
Petrarca

'LOVE me, for I love you'—and answer me,
  'Love me, for I love you'—so shall we stand
  As happy equals in the flowering land
Of love, that knows not a dividing sea.
Love builds the house on rock and not on sand,
  Love laughs what while the winds rave desperately;
And who hath found love's citadel unmanned?
  And who hath held in bonds love's liberty?
My heart's a coward tho' my words are brave—
  We meet so seldom, yet we surely part
So often; there's a problem for your art!
    Still I find comfort in his Book, who saith,
Tho' jealousy be cruel as the grave,
    And death be strong, yet love is strong as death.

8

'Come dicesse a Dio: D'altro non calme.'
Dante

'Spero trovar pietà non che perdono.'
Petrarca

'I, IF I perish, perish'—Esther spake:
  And bride of life or death she made her fair
  In all the lustre of her perfumed hair
And smiles that kindle longing but to slake.
She put on pomp of loveliness, to take
  Her husband thro' his eyes at unaware;
  She spread abroad her beauty for a snare,
Harmless as doves and subtle as a snake.
She trapped him with one mesh of silken hair,
  She vanquished him by wisdom of her wit,
    And built her people's house that it should stand:—
If I might take my life so in my hand,
And for my love to Love put up my prayer,
  And for love's sake by Love be granted it!

9

'O dignitosa coscienza e netta!'
Dante

'Spirto più acceso di virtuti ardenti.'
Petrarca

THINKING of you, and all that was, and all
That might have been and now can never be,
I feel your honoured excellence, and see
Myself unworthy of the happier call:
For woe is me who walk so apt to fall,
So apt to shrink afraid, so apt to flee,
Apt to lie down and die (ah, woe is me!)
Faithless and hopeless turning to the wall.
And yet not hopeless quite nor faithless quite,
Because not loveless; love may toil all night,
But take at morning; wrestle till the break
Of day, but then wield power with God and man:–
So take I heart of grace as best I can,
Ready to spend and be spent for your sake.

10

'Con miglior corso e con migliore stella.'
Dante

'La vita fugge e non s'arresta un' ora.'
Petrarca

TIME flies, hope flags, life plies a wearied wing;
Death following hard on life gains ground apace;
Faith runs with each and rears an eager face,
Outruns the rest, makes light of everything,
Spurns earth, and still finds breath to pray and sing;
While love ahead of all uplifts his praise,
Still asks for grace and still gives thanks for grace,
Content with all day brings and night will bring.
Life wanes; and when love folds his wings above
Tired hope, and less we feel his conscious pulse,
Let us go fall asleep, dear friend, in peace:
A little while, and age and sorrow cease;
A little while, and life reborn annuls
Loss and decay and death, and all is love.

11

'Vien dietro a me e lascia dir le genti.'
Dante

'Contando i casi della vita nostra.'
Petrarca

MANY in aftertimes will say of you
  'He loved her'—while of me what will they say?
  Not that I loved you more than just in play,
For fashion's sake as idle women do.
Even let them prate; who know not what we knew
  Of love and parting in exceeding pain,
  Of parting hopeless here to meet again,
Hopeless on earth, and heaven is out of view.
But by my heart of love laid bare to you,
  My love that you can make not void nor vain,
Love that foregoes you but to claim anew
    Beyond this passage of the gate of death,
  I charge you at the Judgment make it plain
    My love of you was life and not a breath.

12

'Amor, che ne la mente mi ragiona.'
Dante

'Amor vien nel bel viso di costei.'
Petrarca

IF there be any one can take my place
  And make you happy whom I grieve to grieve,
  Think not that I can grudge it, but believe
I do commend you to that nobler grace,
That readier wit than mine, that sweeter face;
  Yea, since your riches make me rich, conceive
  I too am crowned, while bridal crowns I weave,
And thread the bridal dance with jocund pace.
For if I did not love you, it might be
  That I should grudge you some one dear delight;
    But since the heart is yours that was mine own,
  Your pleasure is my pleasure, right my right,
Your honourable freedom makes me free,
    And you companioned I am not alone.

13

'E drizzeremo gli occhi al Primo Amore.'
Dante

'Ma trovo peso non da le mie braccia.'
Petrarca

IF I could trust mine own self with your fate,
Shall I not rather trust it in God's hand?
Without Whose Will one lily doth not stand,
Nor sparrow fall at his appointed date;
Who numbereth the innumerable sand,
Who weighs the wind and water with a weight,
To Whom the world is neither small nor great,
Whose knowledge foreknew every plan we planned.
Searching my heart for all that touches you,
I find there only love and love's goodwill
Helpless to help and impotent to do,
Of understanding dull, of sight most dim;
And therefore I commend you back to Him
Whose love your love's capacity can fill.

14

'E la Sua Volontade è nostra pace.'
Dante

'Sol con questi pensier, con altre chiome.'
Petrarca

YOUTH gone, and beauty gone if ever there
Dwelt beauty in so poor a face as this;
Youth gone and beauty, what remains of bliss?
I will not bind fresh roses in my hair,
To shame a cheek at best but little fair,—
Leave youth his roses, who can bear a thorn,—
I will not seek for blossoms anywhere,
Except such common flowers as blow with corn.
Youth gone and beauty gone, what doth remain?
The longing of a heart pent up forlorn,
A silent heart whose silence loves and longs;
The silence of a heart which sang its songs
While youth and beauty made a summer morn,
Silence of love that cannot sing again.

(1881)

258 *The Thread of Life*

I

THE irresponsive silence of the land,
The irresponsive sounding of the sea,
Speak both one message of one sense to me:—
Aloof, aloof, we stand aloof, so stand
Thou too aloof bound with the flawless band
Of inner solitude; we bind not thee;
But who from thy self-chain shall set thee free?
What heart shall touch thy heart? what hand thy hand?—
And I am sometimes proud and sometimes meek,
And sometimes I remember days of old
When fellowship seemed not so far to seek
And all the world and I seemed much less cold,
And at the rainbow's foot lay surely gold,
And hope felt strong and life itself not weak.

2

Thus am I mine own prison. Everything
Around me free and sunny and at ease:
Or if in shadow, in a shade of trees
Which the sun kisses, where the gay birds sing
And where all winds make various murmuring;
Where bees are found, with honey for the bees;
Where sounds are music, and where silences
Are music of an unlike fashioning.
Then gaze I at the merrymaking crew,
And smile a moment and a moment sigh
Thinking: Why can I not rejoice with you?
But soon I put the foolish fancy by:
I am not what I have nor what I do;
But what I was I am, I am even I.

3

Therefore myself is that one only thing
I hold to use or waste, to keep or give;
My sole possession every day I live,
And still mine own despite Time's winnowing.
Ever mine own, while moons and seasons bring
From crudeness ripeness mellow and sanative;
Ever mine own, till Death shall ply his sieve;
And still mine own, when saints break grave and sing.
And this myself as king unto my King
I give, to Him Who gave Himself for me;

Who gives Himself to me, and bids me sing
  A sweet new song of His redeemed set free;
He bids me sing: O death, where is thy sting?
  And sing: O grave, where is thy victory?

(1881)

ISA CRAIG-KNOX
(1831–1903)

TOGETHER with Adelaide Anne Procter, Isa Craig was the most eminent poet of the feminist Langham Place group, whose political campaigning came to prominence in the late 1850s. Born in Edinburgh, she was the daughter of a hosier and glover. Her formal education was short-lived, presumably because both of her parents died when she was young. Removed from school at the age of 9, she was subsequently educated at home by her grandmother. During her late teens, Craig started contributing poems to the *Scotsman*, and in 1853 she joined its staff. Her poetry rapidly gained attention. Her first volume, *Poems by Isa*, appeared in 1856. Two years later, she won the Burns Centenary Festival prize for her ode in honour of the Scottish 'Poet peasant-born'. This poem was recited to a crowd of thousands who had gathered in the Crystal Palace.

It was at this time that Craig became deeply involved in feminist and progressive politics. In 1857, she came to London to work for the National Association for the Promotion of Social Science, becoming the first woman assistant secretary. Her appointment to this post, which she held until 1866, caused some controversy. On a number of occasions, Craig contributed essays on issues such as the education of the working classes to the *English Woman's Journal*, edited by Bessie Rayner Parkes. Her poems and stories appeared in popular magazines, such as *Good Words* and the *Sunday Magazine*. For a short period of time, she acted as editor of the *Argosy*.

Craig's poetry was collected in a number of later volumes, including *Duchess Agnes* (1864) and *Songs of Consolation* (1874). More popular, however, were her works of fiction, notably *Esther West* (1870), which was frequently reprinted. Her *Little Folks History of England* (1872) and *Tales of the Parables* (1872) were well received. After her marriage to her cousin, John Knox, in 1866, she remained politically active for some years, although little is known of her later life. Craig died in Suffolk, aged 74.

259 *The Building of the City*

BEHOLD the city is building!—
Why do ye gazing stand?
It is not in the clouds: the city
Is in the midst of the land.

The little hills are round it,
And a river flows between;
And I say, 'Behold the vision,'
For the city ye have seen.

Ye know its chiefest places,
And its houses, street on street:
Ye know, I know, the faces
Of the men and women we meet.

Men groan within that city,
And sinful women snare;
Hell can have no uncleanness
Worse than is harboured there.

The river they have polluted
Till its waters foam with death,
And the foul stream bubbles daily
With the self-destroyer's breath.

And alas! in that cruel city
The children bear such woe,
That tender hearts are asking
If the earth be God's or no.

Yet here is the city building,
A labour of many days;
And her walls shall be salvation,
Her gates shall all be praise.

A river of life, her river,
Shall flow and shall not cease,
And they who dwell within her
Shall dwell in joy and peace.

I see the white walls rising
By the river, day by day,
They are building, building, building,
Everywhere and alway.

I see the builders going
On the white walls to and fro;
I am joined unto the builders,
With some I surely know.

One struck hands with another
With whom he had been at strife:
'Let us live, instead of striving
About the way of life.'

'How come you here?' said another,
'For you are not one of us.'
'Let him build,' said a master builder
'It will never be built but thus.'

Some said, 'We will build the city
With our gold and precious stones,'
And some 'We will build the city
With our flesh and with our bones.'

But when shall we behold it?
For death comes swiftly thus—
We shall walk unseen amidst it
And Christ in the midst of us.

(1874)

MARIANNE FARNINGHAM (MARY ANNE HEARN) (1834–1909)

MARY ANNE HEARN took the pen-name, Marianne Farningham, from her place of birth: Farningham, Kent. Born into a Baptist, working-class family, her mother, Rebecca (née Bowers), was the daughter of a paper-maker, and her father, Joseph Hearn, practised as a small tradesman. Between the ages of 9 and 10, Marianne Farningham attended a nonconformist school and was to become a teacher in Gravesend in 1852. In the same year, she began sending verses to *The Gospel Magazine* and other magazines. For over fifty years, she continued to write articles and poems for *The Christian World* and *The Sunday School Times*.

Her eight volumes of poetry also cover an expanse of years: they were published between 1860 and 1909, with her *Poems* appearing in 1866. Along with tales and numerous books on domestic and family affairs, she wrote about the education of young women in the provinces. Her autobiography was published in 1907. Having lived in Barmouth, Derbyshire, she eventually moved to Brongwynedd in Wales.

260 *It is Well*

IT is well, though the sky should be overcast,
And the joy of thy life be for ever past.
Though sorrow should darken the path below,
It is well, it is well, as thou soon shalt know.

It is well to labour, and well to wait;
It is well to knock at the golden gate;
To pray in the morn and the dewy eve;
To ask though we may not yet receive.

It is well that faith, with its strong bright eyes,
Should look up, still up, to the sunny skies,
It is well to trust in the Father's love
When sorrow and trial our courage prove.

It is well when sorrow has spread its pall,
Darkly and thickly, over all—
When the spoken word, and the prayer of pain,
And the earnest pleading are all in vain.

It is well, all well, that our Father sends;
For his loving-kindness never ends.
It is well, all well, while we linger here;
And well, all well, when death is near.

(1866)

M. E. BRADDON
(1835–1915)

THE author of eighty books, Mary Elizabeth Braddon shot to fame with her shocking 'sensation' fictions of the 1860s. Featuring glamorous heroines committing acts of bigamy and murder, novels such as *Lady Audley's Secret* (1862) and *Aurora Floyd* (1863) sold by the thousand. Born in London, she was the daughter of Henry Braddon, a solicitor. Her mother, Fanny White, left her husband when Braddon was only four years old. Educated at home, Braddon started to write for popular magazines at quite an early age, and for several years she supported herself and her mother as an actress on the stage. Her writing career quickly developed in the late 1850s and early 1860, when she succeeded in placing her fiction in journals such as *Robin Goodfellow. Lady Audley's Secret* was her bid for fame. Appearing in William Tinsley's *Sixpenny Magazine*, it made her editor a fortune. Not only was her writing the subject of heated debate, her personal life became the focus of scandal and gossip. In 1862, she went to live with her publisher, John Maxwell, whose wife was committed to an asylum for the mentally ill. She acted as stepmother to Maxwell's children, and in 1862 she had her first child with him. They had six more children. But it was not until 1874, after his wife's death, that Maxwell married Braddon. Many of her fictions passed into 'cheap' editions, and she was a frequent contributor to popular journals, such as *All the Year Round*. Many of her contemporaries, notably Margaret Oliphant, held Braddon in considerable contempt for representing impure heroines. Braddon's only book of poetry, *Garibaldi and Other Poems*, appeared in 1861.

261 *Queen Guinevere*

I WEAR a crown of gems upon my brow,
  Bright gems drop down upon my yellow hair,
And none can tell beneath their grandeur, how
    My brain is racked with care:

How wicked love my lost soul is enchaining,—
  As sinful men are chained to torture's wheel,
So I, the prisoner of my griefs remaining,
    My own dark doom do seal.

There is a figure that I should not fashion,
  Whose form I shape from every changing shade;
The shadow of my wild and wicked passion,
    I meet in grove and glade.

There is a voice, whose music ever changing,
  I hear in ev'ry murmur of the sea,
In ev'ry wind o'er moor and mountain ranging,
    In ev'ry rustling tree.

There is a face I see in mournful splendour,
  In each star-jewel of the crown of night,
Whose lineaments all nature's beauties render,
    In shadow and in light.

There is a dream that I should perish, dreaming,
  A dream that haunts me still by night and day;
But yet so subtle am I in fair seeming,
    None dare my fame gainsay.

And thus I murmur: Oh, my Lancelot!
  First of all warriors breathing heaven's breath,
I pray to die, that thou mayst be forgot;
    If we forget in death.
Oh, my lost foul! Oh, my loved Lancelot!
  My broken faith! Those deep and dreaming eyes!
I cannot hide me where thou comest not,
    To shut me from the skies.

Oh, weary earth without my Lancelot!
  Oh, dreary life bereft of end or aim!
Save to seek out some solitary spot,
    Wherein to hide my shame.

Oh, fatal passion, that absorbs my life!
  Oh, dreadful madness, that consumes my soul!
A queen, aye, worse; oh, misery, a wife!
    God give me self-control!

God give me strength to bear, and silence keep;
Angels, once women, pity woman's pain,
And hush me to that slumber, calm and deep,
From which none wake again!

(1861)

262 *To a Coquette*

LADY, in thy radiant eyes,
A depth of deadly falsehood lies;
Lady, from thy low replies
Bitter memories arise
That recall past agonies;
When I hung upon thy sighs,
When I deemed thee true as wise;
But Time's wings, as fast he flies,
Sweep youth's stars from manhood's skies;
And I know thy fairest guise
Only masks thy cruelties.

(1861)

ELLEN JOHNSTON
(1835–1873)

ELLEN JOHNSTON, a Scottish poet, was known as the 'Factory Girl' and was also, to use her own words, 'a self-taught scholar'. Born in Muir Wynd, Hamilton, she was the only child of James Johnston, a stonemason, and Mary (née Bilsland). Her father, who had aspirations to becoming a poet, emigrated to America when she was only seven months old, her mother deciding to remain behind with her child at the last minute. Later believing (mistakenly) her husband to have died, Ellen Johnston's mother remarried to a man whom the poet was to regard as her 'tormentor'. He forced her to take up work as a power-loom weaver in an Edinburgh factory when she was only about 8 years old. She was to continue working in factories (later to win a case against a Dundee employer for what we would now call false dismissal) while also beginning to have her poetry published in journals.

In 1852 and unmarried, she gave birth to a daughter and it was then, as she writes in her autobiography, that 'duty' pushed her to 'turn the poetic gift that nature had given [her] to a useful and profitable account' (1867). Beset by ill-health, she temporarily escaped factory life through the receipt of £10 from a dockyard owner to whom she had sent a poem. After two years in Belfast, she returned to Scotland and contributed poems to *Poet's Corner*. Their success encouraged her to have published, through subscription, her *Autobiography, Poems and Songs of Ellen Johnston, The 'Factory Girl'* in 1867.

263 *The Last Sark. Written in 1859*

GUDE guide me, are you hame again, an' ha'e ye got nae wark,
We've naething noo tae put awa' unless yer auld blue sark;
My head is rinnin' roon about far lichter than a flee—
What care some gentry if they're weel though a' the puir wad dee!

Our merchants an' mill masters they wad never want a meal,
Though a' the banks in Scotland wad for a twelvemonth fail;
For some o' them have far mair goud than ony ane can see—
What care some gentry if they're weel though a' the puir wad dee!

This is a funny warld, John, for it's no divided fair,
And whiles I think some o' the rich have got the puir folk's share,
Tae see us starving here the nicht wi' no ae bless'd bawbee—
What care some gentry if they're weel though a' the puir wad dee!

Oor hoose ance bean an' cosey, John; oor beds ance snug an warm
Feels unco cauld an' dismal noo, an' empty as a barn;
The weans sit greeting in oor face, and we ha'e noucht to gie—
What care some gentry if they're weel though a' the puir wad dee!

It is the puir man's hard-won toil that fills the rich man's purse;
I'm sure his gouden coffers they are het wi' mony a curse;
Were it no for the working men what wad the rich men be?
What care some gentry if they're weel though a' the puir wad dee!

My head is licht, my heart is weak, my een are growing blin';
The bairn is faen' aff my knee—oh! John, catch haud o' him,
You ken I binna tasted meat for days far mair than three,
Were it no for my helpless bairns I wadna care to dee.

(1867)

'A FACTORY GIRL'
(dates not known)

264 *from The Cotton Famine and the Lancashire Operatives*

[*Nothing is known about the author of this temperance poem, except that she appears to have lived in Preston and to have been educated in Sunday Schools. Although she deplores the events which led to a factory lockout in Preston, she is relatively sympathetic to the factory workers. Eds.*]

BRITONS with slavery should have no part;
And you, ye boasting friends of liberty,

If you love freedom, set the captives free;
Or else no more assume the sacred name
Of followers of the meek and lowly lamb;
For this is His command, that you should do
To others as you'd have them do to you.
You send your gospel messengers abroad
To tell the heathen that there is a God;
While to the heathen, at your very door,
You scorn His precepts and deny His power.
You send your sons across the trackless main
To preach on India's coasts a Saviour slain;
While in yon vessel bound for Cuba's isle
Groan Afric's wretched sons—the slaver's spoil.
Wipe from your nation's page the shameful stains;
Loose from the captive's hands the galling chains,
Else will they break them, and the clanking sound
Of broken fetters falling to the ground—
Which tells the freedom of this injured race—
Will shake your nation to its lowest base.
But while for others woes I may repine,
My native town! I must remember thine,
For dark vicissitude has frown'd on thee;
Thine are the woes of want and poverty.
But how much misery may yet be traced
To drunkenness, improvidence, and waste;
First drunkenness,—the greatest ill of all,
Compar'd with this the rest are only small,—
This wastes more lives, and works more ruin far
Than famine, pestilence, or even war.
In our poor town—poor in more ways than one—
'Tis said that in the year so lately gone
One hundred thousand pounds were spent in drink.
A hundred thousand pounds. Ah! only think,
A hundred thousand pounds all spent for what?
What has it purchased for the wretched sot?
His ruined health, his poverty and shame;
E'en his own children blush to own his name.
What has it purchased for the drunkard's wife?
Turning to bitterest gall her cup of life—
Her life, which once with hope was bright and fair,
Now chang'd to hopeless woe and dark despair.
And worst of all, for him, what has it bought,
Whose mis-spent life meets with an end unsought,
Who, with his sins unwept for, unforgiven,
'Reels staggering drunk up to the bar of heaven'.

(1862)

RUTH WILLS
(dates not known)

RUTH WILLS was a self-educated poet who published two editions of her *Lays of Lowly Life* in 1861 and 1868. Although it is has not been possible to establish her dates, a preface to one of her books states that she was the daughter of an infantryman, who died when she was seven. As a young child, she attended first a dame school, and then the Bond Street Sunday School, at Leicester. But this period of formal education was short-lived. Her labouring life began when she was 8 years old. Although she worked a twelve-hour day, she managed to spend one hour a week at a Sunday School writing class. At the age of 11, she was employed in a warehouse belonging to the firm of N. Corah & Sons, Leicester, where she was still working when her second book went out on sale. This second edition, published by James Nisbet, is dedicated to her employer 'by one to whom their kindness has made labour sweet, and a long service pleasant'. It is significant that many of the poems in this volume concern slavery and the oppression of women.

Wills obviously read widely. At the age of 14, she discovered *Paradise Lost*, a work that brought about her religious awakening. One of her earliest poems was contributed to the *Children's Magazine* when she was in her mid-teens. *Lays of Lowly Life* attracted some attention in the periodical press, notably in an article published in the *Englishwoman's Review* in 1864, where John Plummer remarked: 'We have plenty of histories of self-made *men*, who have scaled the rocky precipices of misfortune and raised themselves to heroic heights; but the histories of self-made *women* are comparatively few and far between.'

265 *Anne Boleyn*

LADY Anne of Hever,
  Who so blithe as she?
Rose of English maidens,
  Beautiful and free;
Welcoming the morning
  With a lark-like song,
Light and happy-hearted
  All the glad day long.

Foolish Anne of Hever
  She hath bid adieu
To her halls ancestral
  To her kindred true,
Left the joyous freedom
  Of her maiden-bower,
Sought for courtly splendours,
  Sighed for pleasure's dower.

Woe for Anne of Hever,
  From his throne of pride
Stoops imperious Henry,
  Wooes her for his bride.
Vain, voluptuous despot,
  Monarch though he be
Foul and fickle-hearted,
  Prince of perfidy.

All too ready yields she
  To his words of guile;
See, he smiles upon her,
  Oh that treacherous smile!
She hath sold her beauty,
  Laid her freedom down,
For a bauble splendour,
  For a gew-gaw crown.

Music on the river,
  Sound of harp and horn,
Pomp of gay procession,
  'Tis the bridal morn;
Barge with floating steamer
  Gaily glides along,
Oh the pageant glitter,
  Oh the shouting throng!

Noble, hapless lady,
  Now elate and proud,
Queen of grace and beauty,
  Idol of the crowd;
Could'st thou from the future
  Life the shrouding veil,
How thy joy would darken!
  How thy cheek grow pale!

For thy heart's devotion
  And thy plighted faith,
Thou wilt meet with anguish,
  Bonds, and direful death;
Not thy winsome beauty,
  Not thy bright wit's charm
Will avail to shield thee
  From the tyrant's arm.

He will grow aweary
 Of thy now-sought smile,
At this pleasure charge thee
 With the fondest guile;
And though courtly minions
 Know thee blameless, still
They will dare to thwart not
 His imperious will.

But while English bosoms
 Glow with honour's flame,
Scorn shall wreath with hatred
 Round that despot's name;
And for three, the victim,
 At thy tale of woe,
Streams of gentlest pity
 From each age shall flow.

(1861)

266 *A New Gospel*

'The ideas entertained at the formation of the Old Constitution were, that the enslavement of the African race was in violation of the laws of nature; that it was wrong in principle socially, morally, politically. Our new government is founded on exactly opposite ideas; its foundations are laid, its corner-stone rests upon the great truth that the negro is not equal to the white man, that slavery—subordination to the superior race—is his natural and moral condition. Thus our government is the first in the history of the world based upon the great physical, philosophical, and moral truth. It is upon this that our social fabric is firmly planted, and I cannot permit myself to doubt the ultimate success of the full recognition of this principle throughout the civilized enlightened world.'

Mr A. H. Stephens, Vice-President of the Confederacy

So the South has been blest with a new revelation,
 Which its zealous disciples are eager to tell,
As a bitter evangel, the hope of their nation,
 And the joy of all lands who will study it well.

And this is its substance, its sun, and its glory,
 O Englishmen, sons of the free, be attent,
And patiently hear, if ye can, this new story,
 And judge if such gospel from heaven be sent.

God, they say, in his wisdom, two races created,
The white man to govern, the black to obey;
This truth philosophic thus faithfully stated,
As the chief corner-stone of our empire we lay.

Our new Constitution shall rest on this basis,
And rise like a palace, proportioned and fair;
It shall be in the world as a charming oasis
In the midst of a wilderness blackened and bare.

Is it so, are ye right, have we thus been mistaken?
Have we cherished fair hopes, oh, so fondly, in vain?
Have we slumbered in darkness, and now but awaken
To the music that lies in the clank of the chain?

We thought that the shadow of slavery blighted,
Like that of the upas, the lands where it lay;
Ye proclaim it a life-tree, too long by us slighted,
Whose leaves are for saving and healing, ye say.

We deemed it a monster, whose blandest caressing,
Like that of a serpent, wrought mischief and death;
Ye say 'tis an angel of mercy and blessing,
With life on its pinions and balm in its breath.

We hoped that ere long the foul harpy should perish,
And the lands be self-freed from the curse of its stain,
Ye say that in brightness anew it shall flourish,
And the nations rejoice in the power of its reign;

O, lie self-condemning, oh, falsehood accurst,
We hold your new gospel in loathing and scorn;
We abide by the old, which hath hope for the worst,
And teaches that all men to freedom are born.

The God whom ye worship I could not adore,
And rather than swallow your creed as divine,
I would worship some Moloch believed in of yore,
And own the worst faith of the pagan as mine.

(1868)

FRANCES RIDLEY HAVERGAL
(1836–1878)

COUNTING among the best known and most popular religious poets of her day, Frances Havergal was born at Astley, Worcestershire, where her father served as Rector. The youngest of six children, she had a delicate constitution, and much of her childhood and adult life would be racked by serious illness. Although she started school at Belmont at the age of 13, most of her education was received at home, both from her mother and her elder sister, Jane. She did, however, travel with her father and his second wife to Düsseldorf in Germany during 1852–53. Very little of her life was spent apart from the members of her immediate family, although she took a number of holidays abroad with friends.

During her teens, she became proficient in modern languages and in Hebrew, and from 1846 until 1860 she worked as a Sunday School teacher. In 1861, she took responsibility for teaching one of her sister's children at Okehampton, Devon. But from her early twenties the main part of her working life was devoted to writing rousing poems on religious themes. This substantial body of poetry proved especially appealing to evangelical Christians. Many of these works appeared in the periodical press, such as *Good Words*, and her verses were frequently set to music. In 1869, she published her first collection, *The Ministry of Song*. This volume was followed by *Under the Surface* in 1874. Several other works that combined scriptural writings with accompanying lyrics were published in rapid succession during the 1870s, including *Morning Bells; or Waking Thoughts for Little Ones* (1875). Her collected works were frequently reprinted until the end of the nineteenth century.

After the death of her stepmother, the family home at Leamington Spa was broken up, and Havergal settled at Caswell Bay, Swansea. But it was not long before she caught a fatal chill, dying of peritonitis in 1878, at the age of 42. Immediately, her sister Maria set to work on her *Memorials*, which include the text of Havergal's autobiography, written in 1859. This work set something of a trend for the admiring biographies that were published right through to the 1920s.

267 *The Ministry of Song*

IN God's great field of labour
  All work is not the same;
He hath a service for each one
  Who loves His holy name.
And you to whom the secrets
  Of all sweet sounds are known,
Rise up! for He hath called you
  To a mission of your own.
And rightly to fulfil it,
  His grace can make you strong,
Who to your charge hath given
  The Ministry of Song.

Sing to the little children,
  And they will listen well;
Sing grand and holy music,
  For they can feel its spell.
Tell them the tale of Jephthah;
  Then sing them what he said,—
'Deeper and deeper still,' and watch
  How the little cheek grows red,
And the little breath comes quicker;
  They will ne'er forget the tale,
Which the song has fastened surely,
  As with a golden nail.

I remember, late one evening,
  How the music stopped, for, hark!
Charlie's nursery door was open,
  He was calling in the dark,—
'Oh no! I am not frightened,
  And I do not want a light;
But I cannot sleep for thinking
  Of the song you sang last night.
Something about a "valley,"
  And "make rough places plain,"
And "Comfort ye"; so beautiful!
  Oh, sing it me again!'

Sing at the cottage bedside;
  They have no music there,
And the voice of praise is silent
  After the voice of prayer.
Sing of the gentle Saviour
  In the simplest hymns you know,
And the pain-dimmed eye will brighten
  As the soothing verses flow.
Better than loudest plaudits
  The murmured thanks of such,
For the King will stoop to crown them
  With His gracious 'Inasmuch.'

Sing, where the full-toned organ
  Resounds through aisle and nave,
And the choral praise ascendeth
  In concord sweet and grave.
Sing, where the village voices
  Fall harshly on your ear,
And, while more earnestly you join,
  Less discord you will hear.
The noblest and the humblest

Alike are 'common praise',
And not for human ear alone
The psalm and hymn we raise.

Sing in the deepening twilight,
When the shadow of eve is nigh,
And her purple and golden pinions
Fold o'er the western sky.
Sing in the silver silence,
While the first moonbeams fall;
So shall your power be greater
Over the hearts of all.
Sing till you bear them with you
Into a holy calm,
And the sacred tones have scattered
Manna, and myrrh, and balm.

Sing! that your song may gladden;
Sing like the happy rills,
Leaping in sparkling blessing
Fresh from the breezy hills.
Sing! that your song may silence
The folly and the jest,
And the 'idle word' be banished
As an unwelcome guest.
Sing! that your song may echo
After the strain is past,
A link of the love-wrought cable
That holds some vessel fast.

Sing to the tired and anxious;
It is yours to fling a ray,
Passing indeed, but cheering,
Across the rugged way.
Sing to God's holy servants,
Weary with loving toil,
Spent with their faithful labour
On oft ungrateful soil.
The chalice of your music
All reverently bear,
For with the blessëd angels
Such ministry you share.

When you long to bear the Message
Home to so me troubled breast,
Then sing with loving fervour,
'Come unto Him, and rest.'
Or would you whisper comfort,
Where words bring no relief,

Sing how 'He was despised,
  Acquainted with our grief.'
And, aided by His blessing,
  The song may win its way
Where speech had no admittance,
  And change the night to day.

Sing, when His mighty mercies
  And marvellous love you feel,
And the deep joy of gratitude
  Springs freshly as you kneel;
When words, like morning starlight,
  Melt powerless,—rise and sing!
And bring your sweetest music
  To Him, your gracious King.
Pour out your song before Him
  To whom our best is due;
Remember, He who hears your prayer
  Will hear your praises too.

Sing on in grateful gladness!
  Rejoice in this good thing
Which the Lord thy God hath given thee,
  The happy power to sing.
But yield to Him, the Sovereign,
  To whom all gifts belong,
In fullest consecration,
  Your ministry of song.
Until His mercy grant you
  That resurrection voice,
Whose only ministry shall be
  To praise Him and rejoice.

(1869 *1871*)

268 *An Indian Flag*

THE golden gates were opening
  For another welcome guest;
For a ransomed heir of glory
  Was entering into rest.

The first in far Umritzur
  Who heard the joyful sound,
The first who came to Jesus
  Within its gloomy bound.

Dark children of the Punjaub
  Stood by his dying bed,
And saw Christ's fearless witness
  Safe through the valley led.

And they whose faithful sowing
  Had not been all in vain,
Watched, while the angels waited,
  Their sheaf of ripened grain.

He spoke:—'We have a custom,
  Honour and love to pay,
By setting up a banner
  For friends who are away.

'And now my heart's desire,
  While waiting for the end,
Is to raise a flag for Jesus,
  My best and greatest Friend.

'So take my house and sell it,
  And all the gold shall be
To raise a flag for Jesus,
  Instead of one for me.'

And now in far Umritzur,
  That flag is waving bright,
Amid the heathen darkness,
  A clear and shining light.

A house where all may gather
  The words of peace to hear,
And seek the only Saviour
  Without restraint or fear.

Where patient toil of teaching,
  And kindly deeds abound;
Where holy festivals are kept,
  And holy songs resound.

First convert of Umritzur,
  Well hast thou led the way;
Now, who will rise and follow?
  Who dares to answer, 'Nay!'

Oh, children of salvation,
  Oh, dwellers in the light!
Have ye no 'flag for Jesus,'
  Far-waving, fair and bright?

Will ye not band together,
  And, working hand in hand,
Set up a 'flag for Jesus,'
  In that wide heathen land?

In many an Indian city,
  Oh, let a standard wave,
Our gift of love and honour,
  To Him who came to save.

To Him beneath whose banner
  Of wondrous love we rest;
Our Friend, the Friend of sinners,
  The Greatest and the Best.

(1874)

ANNIE LOUISA WALKER
(1836–1907)

ANNIE LOUISA WALKER (later Coghill) was born in England, but grew up in Canada. She moved from Point Levy, Quebec, to Sarnia, Ontario, where she and her sisters ran a ladies' private school. Returning to England in the 1870s, she became housekeeper to her novelist cousin, Margaret Oliphant, whose autobiography and letters she was to edit in 1899. This was published under her married name 'Mrs. Harry Coghill'. She had married and settled in Staffordshire in 1884.

Her first printed poems were published in Canadian newspapers and magazines, and from there into American ones. They were then collected together in her *Leaves from the Backwood*, which was published in Montreal in 1861. Many of these poems were republished in London, with new pieces added, as *Oak and Maple. English and Canadian Verses* (1890). She also wrote four novels (1877–1881), *Plays for Children* (1894) and a short story (1894).

269 *The Night Cometh*

WORK! for the night is coming;
  Work! through the morning hours;
Work! while the dew is sparkling;
  Work! 'mid the springing flowers;
Work! while the day grows brighter,
  Under the glowing sun;
Work! for the night is coming,—
  Night, when man's work is done.

Work! for the night is coming;
  Work! through the sunny noon;
Fill the bright hours with labour,
  Rest cometh sure and soon.
Give to each flying minute
  Something to keep in store;
Work! for the night is coming,—
  Night, when man works no more.

Work! for the night is coming;
  Under the sunset skies,
While their bright tints are glowing,
  Work! for the daylight flies;
Work! till the last beam fadeth,
  Fadeth to shine no more;
Work! while the night is darkening,—
  Night, when man's work is o'er.

(1861 *1890*)

AGNES MAULE MACHAR
(1837–1927)

KNOWN for her sympathies with feminism, nationalism, and campaigns for social reform, Agnes Maule Machar was born at Kingston, Ontario, to Scottish Presbyterian parents. Her father, John Machar, was a minister of the church. From 1846 to 1854, he served as Principal of Queen's College, later becoming Queen's University, Kingston. Her earliest poems and fictions were didactic in tone. Fame came with several volumes of this kind, including *Katie Johnstone's Cross: A Canadian Tale* (1870). The two poems reprinted here, from *Lays of the 'True North' and Other Canadian Poems* (1902), make her patriotic zeal perfectly clear.

270 *Canada to the Laureate. In Response to Tennyson's Lines*

'AND that true North, whereof we lately heard
A strain to shame us,—"Keep you to yourselves;
So loyal is too costly. Friends, your love
Is but a burden; loose the bond and go."
Is this the tone of empire?'

We thank thee, Laureate, for thy kindly words
Spoken for us to her to whom we look
With loyal love across the misty sea—
Thy noble words, whose generous ring may shame
The cold and heartless tone that said, 'Begone!
We want your love no longer; all our aim
Is riches. *That* your love cannot increase.'
Fain would we tell them that we do not seek
To hang dependent, like a helpless brood
Who, selfish, drag a weary mother down;
For we have British hearts and British blood
That leap up eager when the danger calls!
Once and again our sons have sprung to arms
To fight in Britain's quarrel—not our own—
And drive the covetous invader back,
Who would have let us, peaceful, keep our own—
So we had cast the British name away!
Canadian blood has dyed Canadian soil
For Britain's honour that we deemed our own;
Nor do we ask but for the right to keep
Unbroken, still, the cherished filial tie
That binds us to the distant sea-girt isles
Our fathers loved, and taught their sons to love,
As the dear home of freemen, brave and true,
And loving honour more than ease or gold!

Well do we love our own Canadian land,
Its breezy lakes, its rivers sweeping wide
Past stately towns and peaceful villages,
And banks begirt with forests, to the sea;
Its tranquil homesteads and its lonely woods,
Where sighs the summer breeze through pine and fern.

But well we love, too, Britain's daisied meads,
Her primrose-bordered lanes, her hedgerows sweet,
Her purple mountains and her heathery braes,
Her towers and ruins, ivy-crowned and gray,
Glistening with song and story as with dew;
Dear to our childhood's dreaming fancy, since
We heard of them from those whose hearts were sore
For home and country left, and left for aye,
That they might found, in these our western wilds,
New Britains, not unworthy of the old!

We hope to live a history of our own,
One worthy of the lineage that we claim;
Yet, as our past is but of yesterday,
We claim as ours, too, that emblazoned roll

Of golden deeds that bind with golden links
The long dim centuries since King Arthur 'passed.'
Fain would we thence new inspiration draw
To make our country's future still uphold
The high traditions of a noble past,
That crowned our Britain queen on her white cliffs,
Stretching her sceptre o'er the gleaming waves
Ever beyond the sunset! There were some
Who helped to found our wide Canadian realm,
Who left their cherished homes, their earthly all,
In the fair borders that disowned her sway,
Rather than sever the dear filial tie
That stretched so strong through all the tossing waves,
And came to hew out, in the trackless wild
New homes, where still their ancient flag should wave.

We would be worthy them, and worthy thee,
Our old ideal Britain! generous, true,
The helper of the helpless;—and perchance,
Seeing thyself in our revering eyes,
Might keep thee worthier of thine ancient name
And place among the nations! Still we would
Believe in thee, and strive to make our land
A brighter gem to deck the royal crown
Whose lustre is thy children's—*is our own!*[1]

(1902)

271 *Our Lads to the Front! Embarkation of the Canadian Contingent for South Africa;— Quebec, October 31, 1899*

RING out the British cheer,
  Swell forth its loud acclaim,—
The 'true North' sends her children dear
  To fight in Britain's name!

They go, as went the knights of old,
  O'er seas and arid plains to fare;—
Not for the love of fame or gold,
  But for the British hearts they bear!
They hear the mother land, afar,
  Calling her children,—scattered wide;—
They haste,—as wakes the note of war,—
  To face the conflict at her side!

[1] The above lines, originally published in *Good Words*, were generously acknowledged by the late Laureate in a cordial note to the author.

We follow on, with thoughts and prayer
    In the rich-freighted vessel's wake,
Through northern chill and tropic air,—
    O winds, blow softly, for her sake!
She bears the hopes of hearts that bleed
    With parting pain,—with haunting fears;
Her devious course in safety speed,
    Thou Who must guide, where duty steers!

What years of peace essayed to do
    Sorrow and danger swift complete,—
Fuse our great Empire through and through
    Till, with one throb, its pulses beat.
One prayer is breathed o'er sea and land
    From Queen and peasant, cot and hall,
From snow-capped hills, to sunbaked strand,
    God guard our soldiers—one and all!

O God of Justice, Truth, and Right,
    Who seest as no mortal may,—
Whose hand can guide through passion's night—
    To dawning of a glorious day—
Grant victory as thou deemest best,
    Turn hate to love,—bid slaughter cease,
Lay sword in sheath and lance in rest,
    And bring our warriors home in peace!

Ring out the British cheer!
    Swell forth its loud acclaim!
The 'true North' sends her children dear
    To fight in Britain's name!

(1902)

AUGUSTA WEBSTER
(1837–1894)

GIVEN the impressive technical and imaginative strengths of her work, there can be no doubt that Augusta Webster ranks as one the great Victorian poets. Born in Poole, Dorset, Webster was the daughter of Vice-Admiral George Davies and Julia (née Hume). She enjoyed an unusual early childhood aboard the *Griper* in Chichester Harbour. Thereafter, she lived for some six years at Banff Castle in Scotland while her father served as Inspecting Commander there. Her father eventually became Chief Constable at Cambridge, and it was there that she attended classes at the School of Art. During brief periods in Paris and Geneva, the young Augusta Davies became fluent in French. She was self-taught in several other languages, including Greek. In 1867, she married Thomas Webster, a fellow of Trinity College, Cambridge. Later, she moved to London, where her husband worked as a solicitor. At this time, Webster became actively involved in local government politics, and was twice elected (in 1879 and 1885) to the London School Board. She was highly regarded as a public speaker, known for her fervent humanitarianism.

By her early twenties, Webster was publishing poetry. Her earliest volumes—*Blanche Lisle and Other Poems* (1860) and *Lilian Gray* (1864)—appeared under the male pseudonym, 'Cecil Home'. Neither collection displays the confidence of those poems on which her reputation mainly rests, and which were published under her own name: *Dramatic Studies* (1866), *A Woman Sold and Other Poems* (1867), and *Portraits* (1870). Each of these works reveals her skilful remodelling of the dramatic poetry that Felicia Hemans, Robert Browning, and Alfred Tennyson had been developing in the late 1820s and 1830s. With both vigour and candour, Webster exploited the dramatic monologue to empower female personae, whose voices had never before been rendered so highly articulate by a woman poet. To Webster, the monologue offered opportunities foreclosed by conventional lyric poetry. In her essay, 'Poets and Personal Pronouns', collected in *A Housewife's Opinions* (1879), Webster was strongly critical of the naïve manner in which the poet's voice was treated by many readers of the day:

> [The poet] is taken as offering his readers the presentment of himself, his hopes, his loves, his sorrows, his guilt and remorses, his history and psychology generally. Some people so thoroughly believe this to be a proper view of the poet's position towards the public that they will despise a man as a hypocrite because, after having written and printed, 'I am the bridegroom of Despair', or 'No wine but the wine of death for me', or some such unsociable sentiment, he goes out to dinners and behaves like anybody else.

Reviewers could not fail to miss the rhetorical directness of her writing. Although in 1893 a commentator in the *Edinburgh Review* remarked that her work was the product of a 'powerful intellect expressing itself in metrical form rather than that of an inborn poet', it proved impossible to ignore how *Portraits*, first published in 1870, showed 'an observation of life and a power of dramatic characterisation very unusual in the writing of a woman'. *Portraits*, her most successful volume, passed into three editions. Some of her greatest critical support came from the *Westminster Review*.

Apart from *A Book of Rhyme* (1881), Webster published little poetry after 1870. Most of her creative energy went into producing verse-dramas, including *Disguises* (1879) and *The Sentence* (1887). She contributed essays and reviews to the *Athenaeum* and the *Examiner*. From what little biographical information is currently available, it would seem that Webster moved in various established literary circles, including George Eliot and the Rossetti family. William Michael Rossetti wrote an admiring introduction to her final volume, *Mother and Daughter*, a sequence of sonnets published one year after her death at the age of 57.

272 *Circe*

THE sun drops luridly into the west;
Darkness has raised her arms to draw him down
Before the time, not waiting as of wont
Till he has come to her behind the sea;
And the smooth waves grow sullen in the gloom

And wear their threatening purple; more and more
The plain of waters sways and seems to rise
Convexly from its level of the shores;
And low dull thunder rolls along the beach:
There will be storm at last, storm, glorious storm!

Oh welcome, welcome, though it rend my bowers,
Scattering my blossomed roses like the dust,
Splitting the shrieking branches, tossing down
My riotous vines with their young half-tinged grapes
Like small round amethysts or beryls strung
Tumultuously in clusters; though it sate
Its ravenous spite among my goodliest pines
Standing there round and still against the sky
That makes blue lakes between their sombre tufts,
Or harry from my silvery olive slopes
Some hoary king whose gnarled fantastic limbs
Wear rugged armour of a thousand years;
Though it will hurl high on my flowery shores
The hostile wave that rives at the poor sward
And drags it down the slants, that swirls its foam
Over my terraces, shakes their firm blocks
Of great bright marbles into tumbled heaps,
And makes my pleached and mossy labyrinths,
Where the small odorous blossoms grow like stars
Strewn in the milky way, a briny marsh.
What matter? let it come and bring me change,
Breaking the sickly sweet monotony.

I am too weary of this long bright calm;
Always the same blue sky, always the sea
The same blue perfect likeness of the sky,
One rose to match the other that has waned,
To-morrow's dawn the twin of yesterday's;
And every night the ceaseless crickets chirp
The same long joy and the late strain of birds
Repeats their strain of all the even month;
And changelessly the petty plashing surfs
Bubble their chiming burden round the stones;
Dusk after dusk brings the same languid trance
Upon the shadowy hills, and in the fields
The waves of fireflies come and go the same,
Making the very flash of light and stir
Vex one like dronings of the shuttles at task.

Give me some change. Must life be only sweet,
All honey-pap as babes would have their food?
And, if my heart must always be adrowse

In a hush of stagnant sunshine, give me, then,
Something outside me stirring; let the storm
Break up the sluggish beauty, let it fall
Beaten below the feet of passionate winds,
And then to-morrow waken jubilant
In a new birth; let me see subtle joy
Of anguish and of hopes, of change and growth.

What fate is mine, who, far apart from pains
And fears and turmoils of the cross-grained world,
Dwell like a lonely god in a charmed isle
Where I am first and only, and, like one
Who should love poisonous savours more than mead,
Long for a tempest on me and grow sick
Of rest and of divine free carelessness!
Oh me, I am a woman, not a god;
Yea, those who tend me, even, are more than I,
My nymphs who have the souls of flowers and birds
Singing and blossoming immortally.

Ah me! these love a day and laugh again,
And loving, laughing, find a full content;
But I know nought of peace, and have not loved.

Where is my love? Does someone cry for me
Not knowing whom he calls? Does his soul cry
For mine to grow beside it, grow in it?
Does he beseech the gods to give him me,
The one unknown rare woman by whose side
No other woman thrice as beautiful
Could once seem fair to him; to whose voice heard
In any common tones no sweetest sound
Of love made melody on silver lutes,
Or singing like Apollo's when the gods
Grow pale with happy listening, might be peered
For making music to him; whom once found
There will be no more seeking anything?

Oh love, oh love, oh love, art not yet come
Out of the waiting shadows into life?
Art not yet come after so many years
That I have longed for thee? Come! I am here.

Not yet. For surely I should feel a sound
Of his far answer if now in the world
He sought me who will seek me—Oh, ye gods,
Will he not seek me? Is it all a dream?
Will there be only these, these bestial things
Who wallow in their styes, or mop and mow

Among the trees, or munch in pens and byres,
Or snarl and filch behind their wattled coops;
These things who had believed that they were men?

Nay, but he *will* come. Why am I so fair,
And marvellously minded, and with sight
Which flashes suddenly on hidden things,
As the gods see, who do not need to look?
Why wear I in my eyes that stronger power
Than basilisks, whose gaze can only kill,
To draw men's souls to me to live or die
As I would have them? Why am I given pride
Which yet longs to be broken, and this scorn,
Cruel and vengeful, for the lesser men
Who meet the smiles I waste for lack of him,
And grow too glad? Why am I who I am?
But for the sake of him whom fate will send
One day to be my master utterly,
That he should take me, the desire of all,
Whom only he in the world could bow to him.

Oh, sunlike glory of pale glittering hairs,
Bright as the filmy wires my weavers take
To make me golden gauzes—Oh, deep eyes,
Darker and softer than the bluest dusk
Of August violets, darker and deep
Like crystal fathomless lakes in summer noons—
Oh, sad sweet longing smile—Oh, lips that tempt
My very self to kisses—oh, round cheeks
Tenderly radiant with the even flush
Of pale smoothed coral—perfect lovely face
Answering my gaze from out this fleckless pool—
Wonder of glossy shoulders, chiselled limbs—
Should I be so your lover as I am,
Drinking an exquisite joy to watch you thus
In all a hundred changes through the day,
But that I love you for him till he comes,
But that my beauty means his loving it?

Oh, look! a speck on this side of the sun,
Coming—yes, coming with the rising wind
That frays the darkening cloud-wrack on the verge
And in a little while will leap abroad,
Spattering the sky with rushing blacknesses,
Dashing the hissing mountainous waves at the stars.
'Twill drive me that black speck a shuddering hulk
Caught in the buffeting waves, dashed impotent
From ridge to ridge, will drive it in the night

With that dull jarring crash upon the beach,
And the cries for help and the cries of fear and hope.

And then to-morrow they will thoughtfully,
With grave low voices, count their perils up,
And thank the gods for having let them live
And tell of wives and mothers in their homes,
And children, who would have such loss in them
That they must weep (and maybe I weep too)
With fancy of the weepings had they died.
And the next morrow they will feel their ease
And sigh with sleek content, or laugh elate,
Tasting delight of rest and revelling,
Music and perfumes, joyaunce for the eyes
Of rosy faces and luxurious pomps,
The savour of the banquet and the glow
And fragrance of the wine-cup; and they'll talk
How good it is to house in palaces
Out of the storms and struggles, and what luck
Strewed their good ship on our accessless coast.
Then the next day the beast in them will wake,
And one will strike and bicker, and one swell
With puffed-up greatness, and one gibe and strut
In apish pranks, and one will line his sleeve
With pilfered booties, and one snatch the gems
Out of the carven goblets as they pass,
One will grow mad with fever of the wine,
And one will sluggishly besot himself,
And one be lewd, and one be gluttonous;
And I shall sickly look and loathe them all.

Oh my rare cup! my pure and crystal cup,
With not one speck of colour to make false
The entering lights, or flaw to make them swerve!
My cup of Truth! How the lost fools will laugh
And thank me for my boon, as if I gave
Some momentary flash of the gods' joy,
To drink where *I* have drunk and touch the touch
Of *my* lips with their own! Aye, let them touch.

Too cruel, am I? And the silly beasts,
Crowding around me when I pass their way,
Glower on me and, although they love me still,
(With their poor sorts of love such as they could)
Call wrath and vengeance to their humid eyes
To scare me into mercy, or creep near
With piteous fawnings, supplicating bleats.
Too cruel? Did I choose them what they are?

Or change them from themselves by poisonous charms?
But any draught, pure water, natural wine,
Out of my cup, revealed them to themselves
And to each other. Change? there was no change;
Only disguise gone from them unawares:
And had there been one true right man of them
He would have drunk the draught as I had drunk,
And stood unharmed and looked me in the eyes,
Abashing me before him. But these things—
Why, which of them has even shown the kind
Of some one nobler beast? Pah! yapping wolves,
And pitiless stealthy wild-cats, curs, and apes,
And gorging swine, and slinking venomous snakes—
All false and ravenous and sensual brutes
That shame the Earth that bore them, these they are.

Lo, lo! the shivering blueness darting forth
On half the heavens, and the forked thin fire
Strikes to the sea: and hark, the sudden voice
That rushes through the trees before the storm,
And shuddering of the branches. Yet the sky
Is blue against them still, and early stars
Sparkle above the pine-tops; and the air
Clings faint and motionless around me here.

Another burst of flame—and the black speck
Shows in the glare, lashed onwards. It were well
I bade make ready for our guests to-night.

(1870)

273 *The Happiest Girl in the World*

A WEEK ago; only a little week:
It seems so much much longer, though that day
Is every morning still my yesterday;
As all my life 'twill be my yesterday,
For all my life is morrow to my love.
Oh fortunate morrow! Oh sweet happy love!

A week ago; and I am almost glad
To have him now gone for this little while,
That I may think of him and tell myself
What to be his means, now that I am his,
And know if mine is love enough for him,
And make myself believe it all is true.

A week ago; and it seems like a life,
And I have not yet learned to know myself:
I am so other than I was, so strange,
Grown younger and grown older all in one;
And I am not so sad and not so gay;
And I think nothing, only hear him think.

That morning, waking, I remembered him,
'Will he be here to-day? he often comes;—
And is it for my sake or to kill time?'
And, wondering 'Will he come?' I chose the dress
He seemed to like the best, and hoped for him;
And did not think I could quite love him yet.
And did I love him then with all my heart?
Or did I wait until he held my hands
And spoke 'Say, shall it be?' and kissed my brow,
And I looked at him and he knew it all?

And did I love him from the day we met?
But I more gladly danced with someone else
Who waltzed more smoothly and was merrier:
And did I love him when he first came here?
But I more gladly talked with someone else
Whose words were readier and who sought me more.
When did I love him? How did it begin?

The small green spikes of snowdrops in the spring
Are there one morning ere you think of them;
Still we may tell what morning they pierced up:
June rosebuds stir and open stealthily,
And every new-blown rose is a surprise;
Still we can date the day when one unclosed:
But how can I tell when my love began?

Oh, was it like the young pale twilight star
That quietly breaks on the vacant sky,
Is sudden there and perfect while you watch,
And though you watch you have not seen it dawn,
The star that only waited and awoke?

But he knows when he loved me; for he says
The first time we had met he told a friend
'The sweetest dewy daisy of a girl,
But not the solid stuff to make a wife;'
And afterwards, the first time he was here,
When I had slipped away into our field
To watch alone for sunset brightening on
And heard them calling me, he says he stood
And saw me come along the coppice walk

Beneath the green and sparkling arch of boughs,
And, while he watched the yellow lights that played
With the dim flickering shadows of the leaves
Over my yellow hair and soft pale dress,
Flitting across me as I flitted through,
He whispered inly, in so many words,
'I see my wife; this is my wife who comes,
And seems to bear the sunlight on with her:'
And that was when he loved me, so he says.

Yet is he quite sure? was it only then?
And had he had no thought which I could feel?
For why was it I knew that he would watch,
And all the while thought in my silly heart,
As I advanced demurely, it was well
I had on the pale dress with sweeping folds
Which took the light and shadow tenderly,
And that the sunlights touched my hair and cheek,
Because he'd note it all and care for it?

Oh vain and idle poor girl's heart of mine,
Content with that coquettish mean content!
He, with his man's straight purpose, thinking 'wife,'
And I but that 'twas pleasant to be fair
And that 'twas pleasant he should count me fair.
But oh to think he should be loving me
And I be no more moved out of myself!
The sunbeams told him, but they told me nought,
Except that maybe I was looking well.
And oh had I but known! Why did not bird,
Trilling its own sweet lovesong as I passed,
So musically marvellously glad,
Sing one for me too, sing me 'It is he,'
Sing 'Love him,' and 'You love him: it is he,'
That I might then have loved him when he loved,
That one dear moment might be date to both?

And must I not be glad he hid his thought
And did not tell me then, when it was soon
And I should have been startled and not known
How he is just the one man I can love,
And only with some pain lest he were pained,
And nothing doubting, should have answered 'No.'
How strange life is! I should have answered 'No.'
Oh can I ever be half glad enough
He is so wise and patient and could wait!

He waited as you wait the reddening fruit
Which helplessly is ripening on the tree,
And not because it tries or longs or wills,
Only because the sun will shine on it:
But he who waited was himself that sun.

Oh, was it worth the waiting? was it worth?
For I am half afraid love is not love,
This love which only makes me rest in him
And be so happy and so confident,
This love which makes me pray for longest days
That I may have them all to use for him,
This love which almost makes me yearn for pain
That I might have borne something for his sake,
This love which I call love, is less than love.
Where are the fires and fevers and the pangs?
Where is the anguish of too much delight,
And the delirious madness at a kiss,
The flushing and the paling at a look,
And passionate ecstasy of meeting hands?
Where is the eager weariness at time
That will not bate a single measured hour
To speed to us the far-off wedding-day?
I am so calm and wondering, like a child
Who, led by a firm hand it knows and trusts
Along a stranger country beautiful
With a bewildering beauty to new eyes
If they be wise to know what they behold,
Finds newness everywhere but no surprise,
And takes the beauty as an outward part
Of being led so kindly by the hand.
I am so cold: is mine but a child's heart,
And not a woman's fit for such a man?
Alas am I too cold, am I too dull,
Can I not love him as another could?
And oh, if love be fire, what love is mine
That is but like the pale subservient moon
Who only asks to be earth's minister?
And oh, if love be whirlwind, what is mine
That is but like a little even brook
Which has no aim but flowing to the sea,
And sings for happiness because it flows?

Ah well, I would that I could love him more
And not be only happy as I am;
I would that I could love him to his worth,
With that forgetting all myself in him,
That subtle pain of exquisite excess,

That momentary infinite sharp joy,
I know by books but cannot teach my heart:
And yet I think my love must needs be love,
Since he can read me through—oh happy strange,
My thoughts that were my secrets all for me
Grown instantly his open easy book!—
Since he can read me through and is content.

And yesterday, when they all went away,
Save little Amy with her daisy chains,
And left us in that shadow of tall ferns,
And the child, leaning on me, fell asleep,
And I, tired by the afternoon long walk,
Said 'I could almost gladly sleep like her,'
Did he not answer, drawing down my head,
'Sleep, darling, let me see you rest on me,'
And when the child awaking wakened me,
Did he not say 'Dear, you have made me glad,
For, seeing you so sleeping in your peace,
I feel that you do love me utterly;
No questionings, no regrettings, but at rest.'

Oh yes, my good true darling you said well
'No questionings, no regrettings, but at rest:'
What should I question, what should I regret,
Now I have you who are my hope and rest?

I am the feathery wind-wafted seed
That flickered idly half a merry morn,
Now thralled into the rich life-giving earth
To root and bud and waken into leaf
And make it such poor sweetness as I may;
The prisoned seed that never more shall float
The frolic playfellow of summer winds
And mimic the free changeful butterfly;
The prisoned seed that prisoned finds its life
And feels its pulses stir and grows and grows.
Oh love who gathered me into yourself,
Oh love, I am at rest in you, and live.

And shall I for so many coming days
Be flower and sweetness to him? Oh pale flower,
Grow, grow, and blossom out and fill the air,
Feed on his richness, grow, grow, blossom out
And fill the air, and be enough for him.

Oh crystal music of the air-borne lark,
So falling, nearer, nearer, from the sky,
Are you a message to me of dear hopes?

Oh trilling gladness flying down to earth,
Have you brought answer of sweet prophecy?
Have you brought answer to the thoughts in me?
Oh happy answer, and oh happy thoughts!
And which is the bird's carol, which my heart's?

My love, my love, my love! And I shall be
So much to him, so almost everything:
And I shall be the friend whom he will trust,
And I shall be the child whom he will teach,
And I shall be the servant he will praise,
And I shall be the mistress he will love,
And I shall be his wife. Oh days to come,
Will ye not pass like gentle rhythmic steps
That fall to sweetest music noiselessly?

But I have known the lark's song half sound sad,
And I have seen the lake which rippled sun
Toss dimmed and purple in a sudden wind;
And let me laugh a moment at my heart
That thinks the summer-time must all be fair,
That thinks the good days always must be good:
Yes, let me laugh a moment—maybe weep.

But no, but no, not laugh; for through my joy
I have been wise enough to know the while
Some tears and some long hours are in all lives,
In every promised land some thorn-plants grow,
Some tangling weeds as well as laden vines:
And no, not weep; for is not my land fair,
My land of promise flushed with fruit and bloom?
And who would weep for fear of scattered thorns?
And very thorns bear oftentimes sweet fruits.

Oh, the black storm that breaks across the lake
Ruffles the surface, leaves the deeps at rest—
Deep in our hearts there always will be rest;
Oh, summer storms fall sudden as they rose,
The peaceful lake forgets them while they die—
Our hearts will always have it summer-time.

All rest, all summer-time. My love, my love,
I know it will be so; you are so good,
And I near you shall grow at last like you;
And you are tender, patient—oh I know
You will bear with me, help me, smile to me,
And let me make you happy easily;
And I, what happiness could I have more
Than that dear labour of a happy wife?

I would not have another. Is it wrong
And is it selfish that I cannot wish,
That I who yet so love the clasping hand
And innocent fond eyes of little ones,
I cannot wish that which I sometimes read
Is women's dearest wish hid in their love,
To press a baby creature to my breast?
Oh is it wrong? I would be all for him,
Not even children coming 'twixt us two
To call me from his service to serve them;
And maybe they would steal too much of love,
For, since I cannot love him now enough,
What would my heart be halved? Or would it grow?
But he perhaps would love me something less,
Finding me not so always at his side.

Together always, that was what he said;
Together always. Oh dear coming days!
Oh dear dear present days that pass too fast,
Although they bring such rainbow morrows on!
That pass so fast, and yet, I know not why,
Seem always to encompass so much time.
And I should fear I were too happy now,
And making this poor world too much my Heaven,
But that I feel God nearer and it seems
As if I had learned His love better too.

So late already! The sun dropping down,
And under him the first long line of red—
My truant should be here again by now,
Is come maybe. I will not seek him, I;
He would be vain and think I cared too much;
I will wait here, and he shall seek for me,
And I will carelessly—Oh, his dear step—
He sees me, he is coming; my own love!

(1870)

274 *A Castaway*

POOR little diary, with its simple thoughts,
Its good resolves, its 'Studied French an hour,'
'Read Modern History,' 'Trimmed up my grey hat,'
'Darned stockings,' 'Tatted,' 'Practised my new song,'
'Went to the daily service,' 'Took Bess soup,'
'Went out to tea.' Poor simple diary!
And did *I* write it? Was I this good girl,

This budding colourless young rose of home?
Did I so live content in such a life,
Seeing no larger scope, nor asking it,
Than this small constant round—old clothes to mend,
New clothes to make, then go and say my prayers,
Or carry soup, or take a little walk
And pick the ragged-robins in the hedge?
Then, for ambition, (was there ever life
That could forego that?) to improve my mind
And know French better and sing harder songs;
For gaiety, to go, in my best white
Well washed and starched and freshened with new bows,
And take tea out to meet the clergyman.
No wishes and no cares, almost no hopes,
Only the young girl's hazed and golden dreams
That veil the Future from her.

So long since:
And now it seems a jest to talk of me
As if I could be one with her, of me
Who am . . . me.

And what is that? My looking-glass
Answers it passably; a woman sure,
No fiend, no slimy thing out of the pools,
A woman with a ripe and smiling lip
That has no venom in its touch I think,
With a white brow on which there is no brand;
A woman none dare call not beautiful,
Not womanly in every woman's grace.

Aye, let me feed upon my beauty thus,
Be glad in it like painters when they see
At last the face they dreamed but could not find
Look from their canvas on them, triumph in it,
The dearest thing I have. Why, 'tis my all,
Let me make much of it: is it not this,
This beauty, my own curse at once and tool
To snare men's souls, (I know what the good say
Of beauty in such creatures) is it not this
That makes me feel myself a woman still,
With still some little pride, some little—

Stop!
'Some little pride, some little'—Here's a jest!
What word will fit the sense but modesty?

A wanton I, but modest!
                    Modest, true;
I'm not drunk in the streets, ply not for hire
At infamous corners with my likenesses
Of the humbler kind; yes, modesty's my word—
'Twould shape my mouth well too, I think I'll try:
'Sir, Mr What-you-will, Lord Who-knows-what,
My present lover or my next to come,
Value me at my worth, fill your purse full,
For I am modest; yes, and honour me
As though your schoolgirl sister or your wife
Could let her skirts brush mine or talk of me;
For I am modest.'

                    Well, I flout myself:
But yet, but yet—
                    Fie, poor fantastic fool,
Why do I play the hypocrite alone,
Who am no hypocrite with others by?
Where should be my 'But yet'? I am that thing
Called half a dozen dainty names, and none
Dainty enough to serve the turn and hide
The one coarse English worst that lurks beneath:
Just that, no worse, no better.

                    And, for me,
I say let no one be above her trade;
I own my kindredship with any drab
Who sells herself as I, although she crouch
In fetid garrets and I have a home
All velvet and marqueterie and pastilles,
Although she hide her skeleton in rags
And I set fashions and wear cobweb lace:
The difference lies but in my choicer ware,
That I sell beauty and she ugliness;
Our traffic's one—I'm no sweet slaver-tongue
To gloze upon it and explain myself
A sort of fractious angel misconceived—
Our traffic's one: I own it. And what then?
I know of worse that are called honourable.
Our lawyers, who with noble eloquence
And virtuous outbursts lie to hang a man,
Or lie to save him, which way goes the fee:
Our preachers, gloating on your future hell
For not believing what they doubt themselves:
Our doctors, who sort poisons out by chance
And wonder how they'll answer, and grow rich:
Our journalists, whose business is to fib

And juggle truths and falsehoods to and fro:
Our tradesmen, who must keep unspotted names
And cheat the least like stealing that they can:
Our—all of them, the virtuous worthy men
Who feed on the world's follies, vices, wants,
And do their businesses of lies and shams
Honestly, reputably, while the world
Claps hands and cries 'good luck,' which of their trades,
Their honourable trades, barefaced like mine,
All secrets brazened out, would shew more white?

And whom do I hurt more than they? as much?
The wives? Poor fools, what do I take from them
Worth crying for or keeping? If they knew
What their fine husbands look like seen by eyes
That may perceive there are more men than one!
But, if they can, let them just take the pains
To keep them: 'tis not such a mighty task
To pin an idiot to your apron-string;
And wives have an advantage over us,
(The good and blind ones have) the smile or pout
Leaves them no secret nausea at odd times.
Oh, they could keep their husbands if they cared,
But 'tis an easier life to let them go,
And whimper at it for morality.

Oh! those shrill carping virtues, safely housed
From reach of even a smile that should put red
On a decorous cheek, who rail at us
With such a spiteful scorn and rancorousness,
(Which maybe is half envy at the heart)
And boast themselves so measurelessly good
And us so measurelessly unlike them,
What is their wondrous merit that they stay
In comfortable homes whence not a soul
Has ever thought of tempting them, and wear
No kisses but a husband's upon lips
There is no other man desires to kiss—
Refrain in fact from sin impossible?
How dare they hate us so? what have they done,
What borne, to prove them other than we are?
What right have they to scorn us—glass-case saints,
Dianas under lock and key—what right
More than the well-fed helpless barn-door fowl
To scorn the larcenous wild-birds?

Pshaw, let be!

Scorn or no scorn, what matter for their scorn?

I have outfaced my own—that's harder work.
Aye, let their virtuous malice dribble on—
Mock snowstorms on the stage—I'm proof long since:
I have looked coolly on my what and why,
And I accept myself.

Oh I'll endorse
The shamefullest revilings mouthed at me,
Cry 'True! Oh perfect picture! Yes, that's I!'
And add a telling blackness here and there,
And then dare swear you, every nine of ten,
My judges and accusers, I'd not change
My conscience against yours, you who tread out
Your devil's pilgrimage along the roads
That take in church and chapel, and arrange
A roundabout and decent way to hell.

Well, mine's a short way and a merry one:
So says my pious hash of ohs and ahs,
Choice texts and choicer threats, appropriate names,
(Rahabs and Jezebels) some fierce Tartuffe
Hurled at me through the post. We had rare fun
Over that tract digested with champagne.
Where is it? where's my rich repertory
Of insults Biblical? '*I prey on souls*'—
Only my men have oftenest none I think:
'*I snare the simple ones*'—but in these days
There seem to be none simple and none snared
And most men have their favourite sinnings planned
To do them civilly and sensibly:
'*I braid my hair*'—but braids are out of date:
'*I paint my cheeks*'—I always wear them pale:
'*I—*'

Pshaw! the trash is savourless to-day:
One cannot laugh alone. There, let it burn.
What, does the windy dullard think one needs
His wisdom dove-tailed on to Solomon's,
His threats out-threatening God's, to teach the news
That those who need not sin have safer souls?
We know it, but we've bodies to save too;
And so we earn our living.

Well lit, tract!
At least you've made me a good leaping blaze.
Up, up, how the flame shoots! and now 'tis dead.
Oh proper finish, preaching to the last—
No such bad omen either; sudden end,
And no sad withering horrible old age.

How one would clutch at youth to hold it tight!
And then to know it gone, to see it gone,
Be taught its absence by harsh careless looks,
To live forgotten, solitary, old—
The cruellest word that ever woman learns.
Old—that's to be nothing, or to be at best
A blurred memorial that in better days
There was a woman once with such a name.
No, no, I could not bear it: death itself
Shows kinder promise . . . even death itself,
Since it must come one day—

Oh this grey gloom!
This rain, rain, rain, what wretched thoughts it brings!
Death: I'll not think of it.

Will no one come?
'Tis dreary work alone.

Why did I read
That silly diary? Now, sing-song, ding-dong,
Come the old vexing echoes back again,
Church bells and nursery good-books, back again
Upon my shrinking ears that had forgotten—
I hate the useless memories: 'tis fools' work
Singing the hacknied dirge of 'better days':
Best take Now kindly, give the past good-bye,
Whether it were a better or a worse.

Yes, yes, I listened to the echoes once,
The echoes and the thoughts from the old days.
The worse for me: I lost my richest friend,
And that was all the difference. For the world,
I would not have that flight known. How they'd roar:
'What! Eulalie, when she refused us all,
"Ill" and "away," was doing Magdalene,
Tears, ashes, and her Bible, and then off
To hide her in a Refuge . . . for a week!'

A wild whim that, to fancy I could change
My new self for my old because I wished!
Since then, when in my languid days there comes
That craving, like homesickness, to go back
To the good days, the dear old stupid days,
To the quiet and the innocence, I know
'Tis a sick fancy and try palliatives.

What is it? You go back to the old home,
And 'tis not *your* home, has no place for you,
And, if it had, you could not fit you in it.

And could I fit me to my former self?
If I had had the wit, like some of us,
To sow my wild-oats into three per cents,
Could I not find me shelter in the peace
Of some far nook where none of them would come,
Nor whisper travel from this scurrilous world
(That gloats, and moralizes through its leers)
To blast me with my fashionable shame?
There I might—oh my castle in the clouds!
And where's its rent?—but there, were there a there,
I might again live the grave blameless life
Among such simple pleasures, simple cares:
But could they be my pleasures, be my cares?
The blameless life, but never the content—
Never. How could I henceforth be content
With any life but one that sets the brain
In a hot merry fever with its stir?
What would there be in quiet rustic days,
Each like the other, full of time to think,
To keep one bold enough to live at all?
Quiet is hell, I say—as if a woman
Could bear to sit alone, quiet all day,
And loathe herself and sicken on her thoughts.

They tried it at the Refuge, and I failed:
I could not bear it. Dreary hideous room,
Coarse pittance, prison rules, one might bear these
And keep one's purpose; but so much alone,
And then made faint and weak and fanciful
By change from pampering to half-famishing—
Good God, what thoughts come! Only one week more
And 'twould have ended: but in one day more
I must have killed myself. And I loathe death,
The dreadful foul corruption with who knows
What future after it.

Well, I came back,
Back to my slough. Who says I had my choice?
Could I stay there to die of some mad death?
And if I rambled out into the world
Sinless but penniless, what else were that
But slower death, slow pining shivering death
By misery and hunger? Choice! what choice
Of living well or ill? could I have that?
And who would give it me? I think indeed
If some kind hand, a woman's—I hate men—
Had stretched itself to help me to firm ground,
Taken a chance and risked my falling back,

I could have gone my way not falling back:
But, let her be all brave, all charitable,
How could she do it? Such a trifling boon—
A little work to live by, 'tis not much—
And I might have found will enough to last:
But where's the work? More sempstresses than shirts;
And defter hands at white work than are mine
Drop starved at last: dressmakers, milliners,
Too many too they say; and then their trades
Need skill, apprenticeship. And who so bold
As hire me for their humblest drudgery?
Not even for scullery slut; not even, I think,
For governess although they'd get me cheap.
And after all it would be something hard,
With the marts for decent women overfull,
If I could elbow in and snatch a chance
And oust some good girl so, who then perforce
Must come and snatch her chance among our crowd.

Why, if the worthy men who think all's done
If we'll but come where we can hear them preach,
Could bring us all, or any half of us,
Into their fold, teach all us wandering sheep,
Or only half of us, to stand in rows
And baa them hymns and moral songs, good lack,
What would they do with us? what could they do?
Just think! with were't but half of us on hand
To find work for . . . or husbands. Would they try
To ship us to the colonies for wives?

Well, well, I know the wise ones talk and talk:
'Here's cause, here's cure:' 'No, here it is, and here:'
And find society to blame, or law,
The Church, the men, the women, too few schools,
Too many schools, too much, too little taught:
Somewhere or somehow someone is to blame:
But I say all the fault's with God himself
Who puts too many women in the world.
We ought to die off reasonably and leave
As many as the men want, none to waste.
Here's cause; the woman's superfluity:
And for the cure, why, if it were the law,
Say, every year, in due percentages,
Balancing them with males as the times need,
To kill off female infants, 'twould make room;
And some of us would not have lost too much,
Losing life ere we know what it *can* mean.

The other day I saw a woman weep
Beside her dead child's bed: the little thing
Lay smiling, and the mother wailed half mad,
Shrieking to God to give it back again.
I could have laughed aloud: the little girl
Living had but her mother's life to live;
There she lay smiling, and her mother wept
To know her gone!

My mother would have wept.

Oh, mother, mother, did you ever dream,
You good grave simple mother, you pure soul
No evil could come nigh, did you once dream
In all your dying cares for your lone girl
Left to fight out her fortune helplessly
That there would be *this* danger?—for *your* girl,
Taught by you, lapped in a sweet ignorance,
Scarcely more wise of what things sin could be
Than some young child a summer six months old,
Where in the north the summer makes a day,
Of what is darkness . . . darkness that will come
To-morrow suddenly. Thank God at least
For this much of my life, that when you died,
That when you kissed me dying, not a thought
Of this made sorrow for you, that I too
Was pure of even fear.

Oh yes, I thought,
Still new in my insipid treadmill life,
(My father so late dead), and hopeful still,
There might be something pleasant somewhere in it,
Some sudden fairy come, no doubt, to turn
My pumpkin to a chariot, I thought then
That I might plod and plod and drum the sounds
Of useless facts into unwilling ears,
Tease children with dull questions half the day
Then con dull answers in my room at night
Ready for next day's questions, mend quill pens
And cut my fingers, add up sums done wrong
And never get them right; teach, teach, and teach—
What I half knew, or not at all—teach, teach
For years, a lifetime—*I!*

And yet, who knows?
It might have been, for I was patient once,
And willing, and meant well; it might have been
Had I but still clung on in my first place—
A safe dull place, where mostly there were smiles
But never merry-makings; where all days

Jogged on sedately busy, with no haste;
Where all seemed measured out, but margins broad:
A dull home but a peaceful, where I felt
My pupils would be dear young sisters soon,
And felt their mother take me to her heart,
Motherly to all lonely harmless things.
But I must have a conscience, must blurt out
My great discovery of my ignorance!
And who required it of me? And who gained?
What did it matter for a more or less
The girls learnt in their schoolbooks, to forget
In their first season? We did well together:
They loved me and I them: but I went off
To housemaid's pay, six crossgrained brats to teach,
Wrangles and jangles, doubts, disgráce . . . then this;
And they had a perfection found for them,
Who has all ladies' learning in her head
Abridged and scheduled, speaks five languages,
Knows botany and conchology and globes,
Draws, paints, plays, sings, embroiders, teaches all
On a patent method never known to fail:
And now they're finished and, I hear, poor things,
Are the worst dancers and worst dressers out.
And where's their profit of those prison years
All gone to make them wise in lesson-books?
Who wants his wife to know weeds' Latin names?
Who ever chose a girl for saying dates?
Or asked if she had learned to trace a map?

Well, well, the silly rules this silly world
Makes about women! This is one of them.
Why must there be pretence of teaching them
What no one ever cares that they should know,
What, grown out of the schoolroom, they cast off
Like the schoolroom pinafore, no better fit
For any use of real grown-up life,
For any use to her who seeks or waits
The husband and the home, for any use,
For any shallowest pretence of use,
To her who has them? Do I not know this,
I, like my betters, that a woman's life,
Her natural life, her good life, her one life,
Is in her husband, God on earth to her,
And what she knows and what she can and is
Is only good as it brings good to him?

Oh God, do I not know it? I the thing
Of shame and rottenness, the animal

That feed men's lusts and prey on them, I, I,
Who should not dare to take the name of wife
On my polluted lips, who in the word
Hear but my own reviling, I know that.
I could have lived by that rule, how content:
My pleasure to make him some pleasure, pride
To be as he would have me, duty, care,
To fit all to his taste, rule my small sphere
To his intention; then to lean on him,
Be guided, tutored, loved—no not that word,
That *loved* which between men and women means
All selfishness, all cloying talk, all lust,
All vanity, all idiocy—not loved,
But cared for. I've been loved myself, I think,
Some once or twice since my poor mother died,
But *cared for*, never:—that's a word for homes,
Kind homes, good homes, where simple children come
And ask their mother is this right or wrong,
Because they know she's perfect, cannot err;
Their father told them so, and he knows all,
Being so wise and good and wonderful,
Even enough to scold even her at times
And tell her everything she does not know.
Ah the sweet nursery logic!

Fool! thrice fool!
Do I hanker after that too? Fancy me
Infallible nursery saint, live code of law!
Me preaching! teaching innocence to be good!—
A mother!

Yet the baby thing that woke
And wailed an hour or two, and then was dead,
Was mine, and had he lived . . . why then my name
Would have been mother. But 'twas well he died:
I could have been no mother, I, lost then
Beyond his saving. Had he come before
And lived, come to me in the doubtful days
When shame and boldness had not grown one sense,
For his sake, with the courage come of him,
I might have struggled back.

But how? But how?
His father would not then have let me go:
His time had not yet come to make an end
Of my 'for ever' with a hireling's fee
And civil light dismissal. None but him
To claim a bit of bread of if I went,

Child or no child: would he have given it me?
He! no; he had not done with me. No help,
No help, no help. Some ways can be trodden back,
But never our way, we who one wild day
Have given goodbye to what in our deep hearts
The lowest woman still holds best in life,
Good name—good name though given by the world
That mouths and garbles with its decent prate,
And wraps it in respectable grave shams,
And patches conscience partly by the rule
Of what one's neighbour thinks, but something more
By what his eyes are sharp enough to see.
How I could scorn it with its Pharisees,
If it could not scorn me: but yet, but yet—
Oh God, if I could look it in the face!

Oh I am wild, am ill, I think, to-night:
Will no one come and laugh with me? No feast,
No merriment to-night. So long alone!
Will no one come?

At least there's a new dress
To try, and grumble at—they never fit
To one's ideal. Yes, a new rich dress,
With lace like this too, that's a soothing balm
For any fretting woman, cannot fail;
I've heard men say it . . . and they know so well
What's in all women's hearts, especially
Women like me.

No help! no help! no help!
How could it be? It was too late long since—
Even at the first too late. Whose blame is that?
There are some kindly people in the world,
But what can *they* do? If one hurls oneself
Into a quicksand, what can be the end,
But that one sinks and sinks? Cry out for help?
Ah yes, and, if it came, who is so strong
To strain from the firm ground and lift one out?
And how, so firmly clutching the stretched hand
As death's pursuing terror bids, even so,
How can one reach firm land, having to foot
The treacherous crumbling soil that slides and gives
And sucks one in again? Impossible path!
No, why waste struggles, I or any one?
What is must be. What then? I where I am,
Sinking and sinking; let the wise pass by
And keep their wisdom for an apter use,
Let me sink merrily as I best may.

Only, I think my brother—I forgot;
He stopped his brotherhood some years ago—
But if he had been just so much less good
As to remember mercy. Did he think
How once I was his sister, prizing him
As sisters do, content to learn for him
The lesson girls with brothers all must learn,
To do without?

I have heard girls lament
That doing so without all things one would,
But I saw never aught to murmur at,
For men must be made ready for their work
And women all have more or less their chance
Of husbands to work for them, keep them safe
Like summer roses in soft greenhouse air
That never guess 'tis winter out of doors:
No, I saw never aught to murmur at,
Content with stinted fare and shabby clothes
And cloistered silent life to save expense,
Teaching myself out of my borrowed books,
While he for some one pastime, (needful, true,
To keep him of his rank; 'twas not his fault)
Spent in a month what could have given me
My teachers for a year.

'Twas no one's fault:
For could he be launched forth on the rude sea
Of this contentious world and left to find
Oars and the boatman's skill by some good chance?
'Twas no one's fault: yet still he might have thought
Of our so different youths and owned at least
'Tis pitiful when a mere nerveless girl
Untutored must put forth upon that sea,
Not in the woman's true place, the wife's place,
To trust a husband and be borne along,
But impotent blind pilot to herself.

Merciless, merciless—like the prudent world
That will not have the flawed soul prank itself
With a hoped second virtue, will not have
The woman fallen once lift up herself...
Lest she should fall again. Oh how his taunts,
His loathing fierce reproaches, scarred and seared
Like branding iron hissing in a wound!
And it was true—*that* killed me: and I felt
A hideous hopeless shame burn out my heart,
And knew myself for ever that he said,
That which I was—Oh it was true, true, true.

No, not true then. I was not all that then.
Oh, I have drifted on before mad winds
And made ignoble shipwreck; not to-day
Could any breeze of heaven prosper me
Into the track again, nor any hand
Snatch me out of the whirlpool I have reached;
But then?

Nay, he judged very well: he knew
Repentance was too dear a luxury
For a beggar's buying, knew it earns no bread—
And knew me a too base and nerveless thing
To bear my first fault's sequel and just die.
And how could he have helped me? Held my hand,
Owned me for his, fronted the angry world
Clothed with my ignominy? Or maybe
Taken me to his home to damn him worse?
What did I look for? for what less would serve
That he could do, a man without a purse?
He meant me well, he sent me that five pounds,
Much to him then; and, if he bade me work
And never vex him more with news of me,
We both knew him too poor for pensioners.
I see he did his best; I could wish now
Sending it back I had professed some thanks.

But there! I was too wretched to be meek:
It seemed to me as if he, every one,
The whole great world, were guilty of my guilt,
Abettors and avengers: in my heart
I gibed them back their gibings; I was wild.

I see clear now and know one has one's life
In hand at first to spend or spare or give
Like any other coin; spend it, or give,
Or drop it in the mire, can the world see
You get your value for it, or bar off
The hurrying of its marts to grope it up
And give it back to you for better use?
And if you spend or give, that is your choice;
And if you let it slip, that's your choice too,
You should have held it firmer. Yours the blame,
And not another's, not the indifferent world's
Which goes on steadily, statistically,
And count by censuses not separate souls—
And if it somehow needs to its worst use
So many lives of women, useless else,
It buys us of ourselves; we could hold back,

Free all of us to starve, and some of us,
(Those who have done no ill, and are in luck)
To slave their lives out and have food and clothes
Until they grow unserviceably old.

Oh, I blame no one—scarcely even myself.
It was to be: the very good in me
Has always turned to hurt; all I thought right
At the hot moment, judged of afterwards,
Shows reckless.

Why, look at it, had I taken
The pay my dead child's father offered me
For having been its mother, I could then
Have kept life in me—many have to do it,
That swarm in the back alleys, on no more,
Cold sometimes, mostly hungry, but they live—
I could have gained a respite trying it,
And maybe found at last some humble work
To eke the pittance out. Not I, forsooth,
I must have spirit, must have womanly pride,
Must dash back his contemptuous wages, I
Who had not scorned to earn them, dash them back
The fiercer that he dared to count our boy
In my appraising: and yet now I think
I might have taken it for my dead boy's sake;
It would have been *his* gift.

But I went forth
With my fine scorn, and whither did it lead?
Money's the root of evil do they say?
Money is virtue, strength: money to me
Would then have been repentance: could I live
Upon my idiot's pride?

Well, it fell soon.
I had prayed Clement might believe me dead,
And yet I begged of him—That's like me too,
Beg of him and then send him back his alms!
What if he gave as to a whining wretch
That holds her hand and lies? I am less to him
Than such a one; her rags do him no wrong,
But I, I wrong him merely that I live,
Being his sister. Could I not at least
Have still let him forget me? But 'tis past:
And naturally he may hope I am long dead.

Good God! to think that we were what we were
One to the other . . . and now!

He has done well;
Married a sort of heiress, I have heard,
A dapper little madam dimple cheeked
And dimple brained, who makes him a good wife—
No doubt she'd never own but just to him,
And in a whisper, she can even suspect
That we exist, we other women things:
What would she say if she could learn one day
She has a sister-in-law? So he and I
Must stand apart till doomsday.

But the jest,
To think how she would look!—Her fright, poor thing!
The notion!—I could laugh outright . . . or else,
For I feel near it, roll on the ground and sob.

Well, after all, there's not much difference
Between the two sometimes.

Was that the bell?
Someone at last, thank goodness. There's a voice,
And that's a pleasure. Whose though? Ah, I know.
Why did she come alone, the cackling goose?
Why not have brought her sister?—she tells more
And titters less. No matter; half a loaf
Is better than no bread.

Oh, is it you?
Most welcome, dear: one gets so moped alone.

(1870)

275 Mother and Daughter, *VI*

SOMETIMES, as young things will, she vexes me,
Wayward, or too unheeding, or too blind.
Like aimless birds that, flying on a wind,
Strike slant against their own familiar tree;
Like venturous children pacing with the sea,
That turn but when the breaker spurts behind
Outreaching them with spray: she in such kind
Is borne against some fault, or does not flee.

And so, may be, I blame her for her wrong,
And she will frown and lightly plead her part,
And then I bid her go. But 'tis not long:
Then comes she lip to ear and heart to heart.
And thus forgiven her love seems newly strong,
And, oh my penitent, how dear thou art!

(1895)

276 Mother and Daughter, *VII*

HER father lessons me I at times am hard,
Chiding a moment's fault as too grave ill,
And let some little blot my vision fill,
Scanning her with a narrow near regard.
True. Love's unresting gaze is self-debarred
From all sweet ignorance, and learns a skill,
Not painless, of such signs as hurt love's will,
That would not have its prize one tittle marred.

Alas! Who rears and loves a dawning rose
Starts at a speck upon one petal's rim:
Who sees a dusk creep in the shrined pearl's glows,
Is ruined at once: 'My jewel growing dim!'
I watch one bud that on my bosom blows,
I watch one treasured pearl for me and him.

(1895)

277 Mother and Daughter, *IX*

OH weary hearts! Poor mothers that look back!
So outcasts from the vale where they were born
Turn on their road and, with a joy forlorn,
See the far roofs below their arid track:
So in chill buffets while the sea grows black
And windy skies, once blue, are tost and torn,
We are not yet forgetful of the morn,
And praise anew the sunshine that we lack.

Oh, sadder than pale sufferers by a tomb
That say 'My dead is happier, and is more,'
Are they who dare no 'is' but tell what's o'er—
Thus the frank childhood, those the lovable ways—
Stirring the ashes of remembered days
For yet some sparks to warm the livelong gloom.

(1895)

278 Mother and Daughter, *XII*

SHE has made me wayside posies: here they stand,
Bringing fresh memories of where they grew.
As new-come travellers from a world we knew
Wake every while some image of their land,
So these whose buds our woodland breezes fanned

Bring to my room the meadow where they blew,
The brook-side cliff, the elms where wood-doves coo—
And every flower is dearer for her hand.

Oh blossoms of the paths she loves to tread,
Some grace of her is in all thoughts you bear:
For in my memories of your homes that were
The old sweet loneliness they kept is fled,
And would I think it back I find instead
A presence of my darling mingling there.

(1895)

279 Mother and Daughter, *XIII*

My darling scarce thinks music sweet save mine:
'Tis that she does but love me more than hear.
She'll not believe my voice to stranger ear
Is merely measure to the note and line;
'Not so,' she says; 'Thou hast a secret thine:
The others' singing 's only rich, or clear,
But something in thy tones brings music near;
As though thy song could search me and divine.'

Oh voice of mine that in some day not far
Time, the strong creditor, will call his debt,
Will dull—and even to her—will rasp and mar,
Sing Time asleep because of her regret,
Be twice thy life the thing her fancies are,
Thou echo to the self she knows not yet.

(1895)

280 Mother and Daughter, *XIV*

To love her as to-day is so great bliss
I needs must think of morrows almost loth,
Morrows wherein the flower's unclosing growth
Shall make my darling other than she is.
The breathing rose excels the bud I wis,
Yet bud that will be rose is sweet for both;
And by-and-by seems like some later troth
Named in the moment of a lover's kiss.

Yes, I am jealous, as of one now strange
That shall instead of her possess my thought,
Of her own self made new by any change,
Of her to be by ripening morrows brought.
My rose of women under later skies!
Yet, ah! my child with the child's trustful eyes!

(1895)

281 Mother and Daughter, *XV*

THAT some day Death who has us all for jest
Shall hide me in the dark and voiceless mould,
And him whose living hand has mine in hold,
Where loving comes not nor the looks that rest,
Shall make us nought where we are known the best,
Forgotten things that leave their track untold
As in the August night the sky's dropped gold—
This seems no strangeness, but Death's natural hest.

But looking on the dawn that is her face
To know she too is Death's seems misbelief;
She should not find decay, but, as the sun
Moves mightier from the veil that hides his place,
Keep ceaseless radiance. Life is Death begun:
But Death and her! That's strangeness passing grief.

(1895)

282 Mother and Daughter, *XVI*

SHE will not have it that my day wanes low,
Poor of the fire its drooping sun denies,
That on my brow the thin lines write good-byes
Which soon may be read plain for all to know,
Telling that I have done with youth's brave show;
Alas! and done with youth in heart and eyes,
With wonder and with far expectancies,
Save but to say 'I knew such long ago.'

She will not have it. Loverlike to me,
She with her happy gaze finds all that's best,
She sees this fair and that unfretted still,
And her own sunshine over all the rest:
So she half keeps me as she'd have me be,
And I forget to age, through her sweet will.

(1895)

283 Mother and Daughter, *XVII*

AND how could I grow old while she's so young?
  Methinks her heart sets time for mine to beat,
  We are so near; her new thoughts, incomplete,
Find their shaped wording happen on my tongue;
Like bloom on last year's winterings newly sprung
  My youth upflowers with hers, and must repeat
  Old joyaunces in me nigh obsolete.
Could I grow older while my child's so young?

And there are tales how youthful blood instilled
  Thawing frore Age's veins gave life new course,
And quavering limbs and eyes made indolent
  Grew freshly eager with beginning force:
She so breathes impulse. Were my years twice spent,
Not burdening Age, with her, could make me chilled.

(1895)

CHARLOTTE ELLIOT ('FLORENZ') (1839–1880)

A SCOTTISH poet, she was the daughter of Charlotte (née Lysons) and Sir James Carnegie. She was twice married, firstly to Thomas Fotheringham in 1860, who died four years later, and then to a barrister and earl's son, Frederick Boileau Elliot in 1868.

Elliot's first book of poetry, *Stella and Other Poems* (1867) was published under the pseudonym, 'Florenz'. The poem for which she was to become best known, 'The Pythoness', was included in this volume and then reprinted in her next collection, *Medusa and Other Poems* (1878), which was published under her own name and dedicated to her husband. A few days before her death, she gave her brother, the Earl of Southesk, a collection of manuscript poems with the request that he select a number of these for publication. Fifty copies of *Mary Magdalene and Other Poems* were privately printed by him in 1880 for distribution among friends. The British Library copy of this book is inscribed to a 'Mrs Oliphant', which suggests that she may well have been a friend of the novelist, Margaret Oliphant.

284 *The Pythoness*

'BIND up her loose hair in the fillet, and wipe the cold dew from her cheek,
For the force of the spirit has left her outwearied, and nerveless, and weak.'
So murmured the pitying maidens, and soothed me, and laid me to rest,
And lightly the leopard-skin mantle drew over my shivering breast;
Then bent their warm faces to kiss me, with tenderness mingled with awe,
Revering the god in his priestess, whose word is obeyed as a law
By the tyrant, the terror of nations. A word from my lips, and the land
Shall have rest, and the weapon uplifted shall fall from the threatening hand;
Though gifts may be heaped on the altar, rich goblet and gold-embossed shield,
The gods give no promise of favour, and keep what they will unrevealed.
Shall I glory in this, that decreeing the close or beginning of strife,
I, who speak what I know not, am chosen controller of death and of life?
Nay; I, who was voiceless, am fated to be as a flute which is blown
By the powerful breath of immortals, to music which is not its own:
Soon, soon, strained to tones superhuman, unfitted for use or delight,
The tremulous flute will lie shattered, cast out from remembrance and sight.
My maidens have left me to slumber; but tears scorch my eyelids instead—
Tears, bitter with passionate envy of those either living or dead;
Not as I, who exist in illusion, with body and soul rent apart,
Possessed by a terrible spirit, pierced through by a fiery dart,
Caught up by a whirlwind, tormented with light too intense for my brain,
Till the vision is past, and I waken remembering nought but the pain.
O mighty and cruel Apollo, thy gift is despair and the grave!
My life, like a wreck on the ocean, is tossed to and fro by the wave.

O fair, pleasant home of my childhood!—dear valley, thy shadows are cool;
All pale in the languor of noontide the lily bends over the pool,
The laurel and cistus are fettered by tangles of blossoming weeds,
The rose leans her cheek to the ivy, the asphodel shines through the reeds;

Wild bees, with low rapturous murmurs, drink deep at the
hyacinth's heart,
And over the mystical lotus bright legions of dragon-flies dart.
And there dwelt my woodland companions, my tender-voiced
soft-breasted dove,
Which perched on my shoulder, with flutterings and murmurs of
pleasure and love;
And my gentle white fawn, the fleet-footed, whose breath was so
wondrously sweet,
For he fed upon rose-leaves, and ever he lay on the moss at my feet,
And his wild, wistful eyes shone like jewels, as if he delighted to
hear
The dream-woven songs which I fashioned and sang when no other
was near.

I pine for the breeze of the forest, I thirst for the spring cold as ice,
Instead of these fumes of rich incense, this draught mixed with
dream-giving spice;
I long for my infancy's slumber, untroubled by phantoms of dread;
I long for cool dews of the morning, to drop on my fever-hot head;
I long—how I long—to be cradled once more in the valley's soft
breast,
And, lulled by my childhood's lost music, to sink like a babe into
rest.

* * *

The day died in flames on the mountains, and stealthily, hiding the
skies
With a film of thick-gathering darkness, night fell on the earth by
surprise;
But flashes of wild summer lightning played over the tops of the
pines,
And glanced on the streams—which meandered in slender and
silvery lines,
'Mid alder, and willow, and hazel—and shone in my face, as I fled
Alone through the depths of the forest, all panting and trembling
with dread.
Astray in the darkness, I threaded the briery paths of the wood,
Then burst through the thicket. Before me, terrific and glorious,
stood—
Oh horror! the oak of Apollo—the haunted, the fearful, the vast;
Whose roots search the earth's deep foundations, whose limbs are
as steel in the blast:
Pale visions that may not be uttered, dwell under its branches at
night,
And strike the beholder with madness, and wither his limbs and his
sight.

The hand of the god was upon me, the power that is mighty to form
My life at his will, as the cloud-wreaths are shaped by the power of the storm;
And my heart fainted in me for terror, since nowhere unmarked could I flee
From the doom that pursued me. Then, dimly, I saw in the shade of the tree
The priest of the temple; and onward he came, and drew near, and his gaze
Sought me out and subdued and enthralled me, and pierced me with glittering rays,
Which drew forth my soul from my body, with force that I could not resist,
Then grew into flames, and enwound me in meshes of fiery mist;
My eyelids drooped under the pressure, a shock of unbearable pain
Thrilled through me, as keen as a sword-thrust; then darkness fell over my brain.

* * *

Great Delphi! in desolate grandeur thy cliffs stand all bare to the sky,
As barren of beauty and freshness, as lonely and mournful as I.
The scream of the wandering eagle rings over thy echoing rocks;
The vultures flock hitherward, scenting the flesh of the sacrificed ox;
But the murmurous voice of the woodland shall never more breathe in my ear,
Nor Philomel's passionate music melt stones into tenderness here;
My soul has resigned its communion with all that it cherished and loved;
From dreams of a happier future, for ever and ever removed.
No love-lay shall thrill with my praises the balmy and sensitive air,
No hand shall twine garlands of jasmine to star the deep night of my hair,
No eye shall grow soft at my presence, nor watch me with rapturous glance,
Amid the bright circle of maidens move swift through the rhythmical dance,—
No bridegroom shall woo me, no taper of marriage be lighted for me,
No children with flower-like faces shall smile away care at my knee.

But surely the night will bring slumber, and surely the grave will bring rest,
And my spirit be lapped in Elysium in balm-breathing isles of the blest;

And as summer, and sunshine, and beauty are born of the elements' strife,
My life, which brought death, be transmuted at last into death which brings life.
For luminous visions surround me, and exquisite forms hover near,
Caress me with soft spirit-touches, and murmur strange words in my ear:
Through air which seems empty to others, bright spirit-shapes cluster and throng:—
Already I mix with their essence, already I join in their song.

(1867 *1878*)

HARRIET ELEANOR HAMILTON KING (1840–1920)

FEW Victorian women poets wrote as extensively on patriotism and nationalism as Harriet Eleanor Hamilton King. She was the daughter of Lady Harriet Hamilton and Admiral William Alexander Baillie Hamilton. Her interest in the struggle for Italian emancipation began early in life. At the age of 11, she read Samuel Rogers' *Italy* (1822–28). A few years later, she avidly consumed Leonard Sismondi's *Républiques Italiennes*. By this time, Mazzini had captured her imagination as the ideal patriot, hero, and saint. The convulsive political upheavals in Italy in the early 1850s prompted her to begin drafting her apologia for Felice Orsini. It took eighteen months to complete. This remarkable poem, which King always felt remained her finest work, was first issued privately by the publisher and banker, Henry S. King (whom she married in 1862, and with whom she parented seven children). 'The Execution of Felice Orsini' reappeared in *Aspromonte and Other Poems* (1869). Thereafter, King enjoyed a rising reputation for those poems that dramatized aspects of the Italian national struggle. Her correspondence with Mazzini began in 1862; and she became closely acquainted with him in later years. In 1876, she undertook her first and only visit to Italy.

Some of King's best work on the Revolution in Italy was collected in *The Disciples* (1873), which quickly passed into numerous editions. King acknowledged that this collection led to her conversion to Rome. On reading the volume, Cardinal Manning wrote enthusiastically to King, and some of her later work was written in his honour. Highly accomplished poems of a more lyrical and personal nature appeared ten years later in *A Book of Dreams*. In 1889, she published *Ballads of the North and Other Poems*, which includes the impressive political poem, 'The Irish Famine. Bantry, 1847.' Her religious poems were gathered together in *The Prophecy of Westminster* (1895). Although biographical information on this gifted poet is quite scant, she provides significant insights into her own life in *Letters and Recollections of Mazzini* (1912). This document makes it clear that she suffered from sustained periods of serious illness.

285 *The Execution of Felice Orsini, March 13th, 1858*

[*Felice Orsini, the Italian revolutionary, was arrested and executed after making an unsuccessful attempt to assassinate Louis Napoleon III and the Empress Eugénie while they were making their way to the opera in Paris. Eds.*]

Fuor se' dell'erte vie, fuor se' dell'arte.
Dante

PART I The Streets of Paris.

A DAY to be much remembered,
  Sad and sublime;
Written in letters of red
  In the book of Time.
Not a coronation morning,
  With its light of purple and gold,
And floods of mighty music
  In hallelujahs rolled:
Not a young bride led home
  From royal halls afar,
All pallid and pearl-glittering,
  A sweet and tremulous Star:
Not a conqueror's State entry,
  With his armies marching back
Under triumphal arches,
  A glittering scarlet track,
When the wide streets glare in sunshine,
  And the bells ring out all day,
And the people shout together,
  Knowing not what they say:—
Only a winter's morning,
  Crowds standing silent by,
A prison and a scaffold,
  And a man brought out to die.

In the cold, damp darkness,
  Between the night and day,
With nerv'd and solemn heart,
  Forth we take our way
To follow to thy martyrdom—
  Last homage we can pay;
To watch with our own eyes
  The setting of this star;
To bear thee faithful company
  Down this dark road, as far
As where the soul and God
  Alone together are.
Paris is all astir;

Another day for her
　Of tragedy.
Sunrise is not for long,
Yet onward pours along
The ever-thickening throng
　Continually.
Fresh streams from every street
A ceaseless press of feet,
In quick and countless beat;
　All one way they fare.
The darkness seems alive—
　A breathing, moving thing.
With a strange awe we strive:
　This hollow murmuring
　In the damp, leaden air,
This vague and heaving sea
　Of shadows undefin'd,
Hurrying confusedly,
　Seems every sense to bind
In nightmare weight of gloom;
For silently they come:
A horror-quiet broods
Over the multitudes;—
No wild cries—no word
Above their breath is heard:
The air is only stirred
　By a vague whispering hum.

Sudden and startling comes
A long, loud roll of drums;
　And the echo clear
Of bugle notes afar
Winds down the Boulevards:
　Be ready—the hour is near!
Through the darkness and the damp,
On comes the clatter and tramp
　Of the squadrons down the street:
A shock—a rushing past;
Furiously and fast
　The heavy, hurrying feet
Over the stones are sped.
'To guard the scaffold', said
　A voice beside us, low.
Did ye not mark it when
　They pass'd the lamp below—
　How cold and blue the steel
　Flash'd out?—Did ye not feel

A sudden shrinking then?
  And the ring of spurs and reins
  Came like the clank of chains.
  Heaven help us all this day!
  Would we were far away.
Already, in foreshadowing,
  Our spirits sink and cower;
Yet *he* has given up all things
  To suffer death this hour.

The light becomes more clear;
The daybreak draweth near,
Yet brings no warmth to cheer,
  Nor sunrise glow.
No sun will shine to-day;
The dark fogs drift away;
The skies are leaden grey,
  Sullen and low;
White and ghostly sheets
Of mist hang o'er the streets,
  Wet with trodden snow.
Dismaller and drearer
Ever as we draw nearer
  Seems the way to grow.
To the great burial garden
  Onward now it turns;
Past long lines of tombstones,
  And cold funeral urns;
Where the living have made
Of the dead a trade.
Bare, bleach'd crosses stand
Stiff on either hand,
Showing dismal white
In the chill half-light.
  All things black and dolorous:—
  Coffins with sable pall;
Dark plumes and hearse-trappings,
  Heavy on every wall;
A horror of the charnel-house
  Overshadowing all—
Only the pallid Immortelles
    Some brighter thoughts recall;
Fresh and fair, yet never a wreath
  But tears thereon shall fall.
And if the way were clear,
  As three hours hence 'twill be,
The cypress at the gates

Before us we might see,
Guarding that sad harvest field,
Sown darkly in decay,
Where twenty generations
Are mouldering to clay.
But we will leave them, lying
In their desolate array—
Not of the Dead, but the Dying,
Our hearts are full to-day.

Now we are close at hand:
Before us outlined dimly
La Roquette rises grimly,
Black as death and sorrow—
Holy ground to-morrow.
Countless thousands stand
Already crowded there,
Filling the open square,
And stretching every side
Far up the streetways wide,
Till, lost in gloom and haze,
The vague, dim, human tide
With shadowy motion sways;
Who motionless and still,
While even he has slept,
Through the night-frosts have kept
Their vigils faint and chill.
They gather'd yester-eve,
When the snow began to fall;
The long, dark hours toll'd heavily,
Standing they counted all,
And the day dawns on pale faces
Waiting to see him fall.
Nor these perhaps alone
This night has wakeful known.
The lamps burn on the altars
In the churches all night long;
Surely some pious souls
Have stay'd since evensong
To pray for the passing soul—
Christ, shrive him from his wrong!—
O! all good souls and true,
Spare him a prayer or two,—
'Tis but little while ye may;
Grudge not of tears a few,
He gives his blood for you,
He is dying to-day.

The light that flash'd all Europe through
  Is vanishing away—
The arm that like the lightning flew
Wherever there was work to do,
Braving all pain and peril anew.—
O God! Thou know'st his heart was true
    Even in this offence!
  Then watch for one hour longer,
    One hour yet more intense,
  In this dark mid-lent season,
    For him who goeth hence;—
  The haughty hero-spirit,
    Parting in penitence.

While in the Tuileries,
Sleepless and ill at ease,
Silent as Fate's decrees,
  As morn came on;
Waiting till all was o'er,
Through hall and corridor
Restless the Emperor
  Pac'd up and down;
Thinking we know not what;
If sorrow, utter'd not.—
Emperor! have you forgot,
Thinking of him, one day
Long ago, years away,
  Nearer the morning skies,
When under one command
He and you took your stand
Comrades, and, hand in hand,
  Look'd in each other's eyes;—
At your own peril, both
Utter'd the same high oath,
Self-doom'd for broken troth,
  Then parted from each other?
Since then, through chance and change,
Each by rough ways and strange,
Ye to the goal have past
Separate; and now, at last,
Once more your fates are cast
  In the world's eye together.
Each doom'd, by fortune's stress,
By each, yet not the less
Too great for bitterness;
Still that bond feels unrent,
Through all between that went,

By that old sacrament,
  He is your brother.
Those days when truth seem'd true,
One vow was on you two;
He has kept his—and you?
  Now, past recall
He goes; when next you meet
At the same Judge's feet,
Your work will be complete;—
  Hear you no call?

There, on the farther side,
  Before the prison gates,
The scaffold yet undy'd,
  The sacrifice awaits;
All the eyes around
Thereon are strain'd and bound,
  Where the hideous frame
    Rises gaunt and tall,
Its cords wound up for working,
    Dull red painted all;
The hard block ready laid,
The overhanging blade,
  Horrible they loom
  Through the thinning gloom.
    Who now feels heart among us
  To tempt this visible doom?
    A wide-swept space around
    Of clear'd and open ground,
    By guards on three sides bound;
  Deep files on either hand,
  Flank'd by the horsemen stand,
    An iron wall;
Rein'd steeds in close lines drawn,
Naked swords upright borne,
Helmets on fierce brows worn,
    Motionless all.
  Driven back by armed stress,
  Surging, the people press;
From every house in Paris
    Every man has come—
Some as to a spectacle,
    As to an altar some;
Careless and free of speech,
    Or stricken stiff and dumb.
Ah! many a crowd has gathered here
    In the grey morning light,

And many an erring spirit
    Has taken hence its flight;
But never morning dim
    So full of awe drew nigh,
And never man like him
    Stood here before to die.

These were the words that went,
With low, quick breathings blent,
From one to another sent,
    Among the crowds:
'Saw ye not at the trial
    The look that was in his eye,
When he turn'd to his false comrades,
    And said, "I pardon ye?"
Have ye read that last message
    Unto his people sent?—
The letter written yestereve,
    His dying testament;
As an emperor to an emperor,
    And yet no scorn nor pride!
Hard task to sign the death-warrant,
    With that sheet spread beside!
Ah! feelings strange and dim
Plead in our hearts for him
  More than we dare say.—
  If he had had his way,
  We might have stood to-day
    Like men, and spoken out.—
Nor law nor priest has might
To give unerring light
Whereby to read aright
    His just award:—no doubt,
Murder is deadly sin;
Yet there was therein
Nothing for him to win
Save what is here;—
And as it draws so near,
Terrible and clear,
Does it not strange appear
  That one of high estate,
  So gifted and so great,
Without constraint or call,
Should have forsaken all
    Honour'd, and sweet, and dear,
With purpose firm to go
To shame, and death, and woe,

And none to thank or cheer?
Has he not given his name
Unto reproach and shame,
Good men's sorrow, proud men's blame;
From history to claim
Only a murderer's fame?
Yea; has he not besides,
In a whole people's cause,
At his own cost defied
Divine and human laws;
The guilt of innocent blood
For ever on his head,
To stand before his God,
His hands yet reeking red?
Strange mystery, any heart
Could choose such awful part!
Was it madness?—who can tell?
Or was it something else
We know not of?—Ah! well;
What is it is stronger than fear,—
Stronger than Death and Hell?'

Not with the beat of rolling drum,
Or wild fifes wailing, dost thou come,
Tyrannicide, unto thy doom;
Nothing of sound or light
The spirit to excite
To the stern delight
Of martyrdom.
The lamps are going out,
The stars died long ago;—
The death-knell from the chapel,
Dull, and deep, and slow,—
A sick heart-throb in every stroke,—
Tolls heavily to and fro.
In the glimmer and gloom of dawning,
In the winter's mist and chill,
In the people's shiver and shudder,
Far off, and ghastly still:—
In the serried steel-clad circle,
Whose grim and glaring eyes
In hungry glee are fix'd to see
How the assassin dies;—
With never the face of an old friend
Standing by thee brave and true;—
God and thy own heroic heart
Alone to bear thee through.

PART II The Prison

CANDLELIGHT and morning gloom
Struggling in the prison-room,
That dim and desolate chamber, where
The doomed for their fate prepare.
A hush'd and solemn company
To-day is gathered there;
Some standing passionless,
With faces stern and still,
At their appointed post,
Hirelings for good or ill;
Some with clasp'd, quivering hands,
Now fever-flushed, now pale,
Cold sweat upon their brows,
Limbs that faint and fail.
Three black and hateful-brow'd,
Of rude and iron limb,
With cool and practised hands,
About their labour grim;
Felon's or martyr's blood,
It comes alike to them.
Two with deep pious eyes,
Mild with consolation,
That will unshrinking stand,
Strong in Christ, cross in hand,
Lighting the way.
And in that silent ring
One wild and fluttering—
One with the face of a king
On his crowning day.

Standing amidst them all,
In that accursed hall,
Fetter'd in helpless thrall,
Vile hands upon thee laid,
In robes of scorn array'd,
How grand thou art!
Those cold and curious eyes,
Thine aspect stranger-wise
Nor shrinks from nor defies,
But stands apart;
In unapproached strength,
Resolv'd and fix'd at length.
There is no human eye,
Nor human aid, intrudes
Into that solitude's
Heroic agony.

All clos'd and still,—and yet
The anguish thou hast met
One awful seal has set
    Too visibly.
Since we saw thee last,
What wild change has past,
As the furnace-blast,
    Over thy brow!
In one week that white hair!—
Witness perforce is there
What thou hast had to bear
Of pangs nigh to despair,—
    All over now.
Upon that glorious face
There is little trace
    Of conflicts that have been;
Calm thou standest now,
With grave, majestic brow;
Passive and marble-still;
Through thy frame no thrill
    Nor tremor seen;
No quick flashes rise
From thy deep dark eyes,—
Fathomless there lies
    A veiled soul therein.
This was all thy face betray'd
  Unto the eyes of men;
What more our hearts may read
  We cannot tell again.

Yet though thus tranc'd thou seem,
Past thee, as in a dream,
What crowding pictures gleam
    Out from the past.
All over, and so soon,—
Not forty years are done,[1]
  And life for ever gone,—
    The one die cast!
How fair and sunny shines
That home amid the vines,
    Far off in Imola;[2]
How soft the day declines
Over the Apennines,
    Purple afar.
Fearless and full of truth,

[1] Orsini was born in 1819.
[2] From nine to thirty years of age Orsini's home was at Imola.

What joy it was in youth
To feel at every breath
The dawn of manhood breaking,
With passionate dreams awaking,
And deep thoughts purpose taking
For life and death.
That young, full-hearted vow[3]
Of thy whole self, which thou,
Fulfill'd and seal'd, wilt now
Deliver back to God.
Thy first steps on the way
Which, straight on, till to-day
Thou in firm faith hast trod;
Those Roman prison-dens accurst,
Where thou, all slowly withering
In darkness and in chains, didst first
Measure thy power with suffering,
And felt it equal to the worst,—
Yea, even to the doom[4]
Of terror and despair that fell
Upon thy youth a freezing knell—
Young Life, and Love, and Hope, farewell!
Long torture till Death come.
God give patience to the end,
Or some swift succour send,
Or soon call home!
Deliverance at last;—
When two long years are past,
The act of grace has come.

1849

Then arose that dawn sublime,
That short, glowing, glorious time,
The third Rome in her bridal prime;
When Mazzini's words of fire
Rang through the halls of Rome,
And the tricolor wav'd out
Over St Peter's dome;
Hark! the clash of the bells above,
The people's shouts below
For Rome and the Republic!
Life is worth having now.
Then, chosen by the people,

[3] 'At the age of twenty-two I was admitted a member of secret societies.'

[4] At the age of twenty-five, Orisini was condemned to the galleys for life. The amnesty granted in 1846, by Pius IX, prevented the execution of his sentence.

Thy eloquent voice was heard
Thrilling throughout the Capitol,
Till hearts beneath it stirr'd,
And men rose up to follow thee,
And thou didst lead them on
Where there was danger to be dar'd,
Or glory to be won.[5]
Where the dead thickest
Strew'd the red ground;
Where rattled fastest
The sharp musket sound,
Where the battle hottest
Thunder'd around—
Fiercest and foremost
There wast thou found.
And when the golden time was rent
With lawless deeds and violent,
And others vainly aid had sent,
Thy strong, and just, and fearless hand
Gave peace and safety to the land.[6]
And at the blood-red setting
Of that scarce hailed star,
When three great armies gather'd,
Like vultures from afar;
And all around the city bound
With narrowing rings of war,
That fiery baptism-tide,
Ye, Romans, side by side,
Did at your posts abide
Stedfast through all.
How it comes back again,
That night before the fall!
When the solemn, lighted city
Up unto God did call;
When the lightning and the thunder
Burst through the battle's brawl;
When the streets were shaking under
The hail of bomb and ball,
Till down, in storm asunder,
Crash'd the defended wall;
When the one look of Mazzini
Still'd the tumultuous Hall,

[5] In June 1849, Orsini led five hundred men to the relief of Ascoli, besieged by the Neapolitan army.

[6] Ancona was kept in a state of terror by brigands and assassins, who committed open robbery and murder. Mazzini sent several commissioners to repress them, who failed to do so. He then sent Orsini, who immediately restored security.

And the eyes of Garibaldi
  Were shining over all.

1849 TO 1856

All over! It was nobly striven;
What use against all earth and heaven?
So, into bitter exile driven,
  The strife begins again.[7]
All that story, yet half-told,
Of danger strange and manifold,
Thirst and hunger, heat and cold,
Wanderings wild by field and flood,
Deeds of daring, wounds and blood,
  In peril and in pain.
Often into prisons cast,
Yet no bonds could hold thee fast;
From their hands escap'd and past,
  And forward once again.
Through the snares set in thy path,
Baffling all an empire's wrath;
From city unto city forth,
Calling men to rise and arm,
By the mighty power and charm
Of thy presence and thy name,
Keeping still the spark aflame,
Stirring life where'er they came.
And high hope upbore thee still,
Thy great mission to fulfil;
Nothing might dismay or chill,
Till that bitterest stroke of fate
  Thy honour and thy love betray'd—
  The foul and faithless wrong that made
Thy heart and home so desolate.[8]—
Lifelong shadow o'er thee thrown,
  A wound that will not heal:—
Heartsick and reckless, thou art gone
On desperate errand all alone—
Unto none thy purpose shown—
  None bidding thee farewell.
Thou, the hunted and the bann'd,
Into the heart of the strange land,

[7] On the fall of the Roman republic, Orsini retired to France. For several years he resided there at intervals; most of his time being spent in organizing insurrections in Lombardy and Tuscany. Once during this period he was obliged to take refuge in England.

[8] 'I had been robbed of my happiness, and was yet unrevenged on the destroyer. I shall find him yet.' 'The hope before I die to stand face to face with the traitor who has so foully wronged me' (*Orsini's Memoirs*).

Darest, with wild purpose plann'd,
To raise it with thy single hand.[9]
Taken at last! and by a foe
Never with life will let thee go:
Too deep and deadly debt they owe;
Thou knowest what to look for now.
All thy sufferings ever told,
Heap'd upon thee hundredfold:
Fever, famine, freezing cold,
Their utmost malice wreak'd on thee,
Entreated so despitefully,
The very gaolers wept to see
Thy patience and thy misery.[10]
And thou, as darker clos'd thy fate,
Rising more glorious and great:
Standing before thy judges,
  No friend or witness nigh,
Pallid and feverstricken,
  But the proud light in thine eye—
'Ye have your chains and tortures,
  And I have heart to die'.
The heavy chains, the damp, dark cell,
In the Mantua citadel;
The weary waiting for thy doom,
Alone within that living tomb;
The hope that flash'd on thy despair,
The deed that only thou couldst dare,
That terrible midnight, that wild tale
That froze our cheeks long after pale,
The dizzy height, the balance frail;
Our hearts within us shrink and quail,
Only thine might never fail;
It reads not like the deeds of men;
God and the angels were with thee then![11]

1856 TO 1858

Bread of exile once more thine,
Full of bitterness and brine;
Damp, downward-pressing skies,
Cold looks from stranger eyes;
Passionate pleadings thrown away,

[9] Orsini, in December 1854, travelled alone through Hungary, Austria, and Transylvania, on a revolutionary mission whose import he never fully revealed.

[10] Orsini was arrested at Hermanstadt, in Transylvania. For the terrible sufferings which followed, and which nearly cost him his life, see his *Austrian Dungeons.*

[11] See Orsini's account of his marvellous escape from Mantua, March 1856, where he remained till December 1857, endeavouring in vain to excite the Government and the public to interfere on behalf of his country.

Homesick pining day by day,
Strong health fretting to decay;
Till overwearied, overwrought,
How or whence we know not brought,
In fatal hour flash'd this thought,
  Thy strained sense before.
Then the strife, the fever pain,
Fire and frenzy of the brain—
Thank God, that worst pain is o'er!
Hatred shall be nevermore.
Thy last perilous journey past,[12]
Thy terrible secret ripening fast;
Mid the giddy whirl and press
  Of this fair city, heard without,
In thy chamber's loneliness,
  By day, with nerved hand and stout,
Working on, and violent death
Hanging over every breath:[13]
Mid the laughter and the light
Of the glittering streets by night,
Moving, as in a dream, apart,
With one stern purpose in thy heart;
The outward calm, the inward fire,
The dark hour drawing nigh and nigher.—
The night of horrors,[14] the wild cry
That through the darkness rent the sky:
On that hour we cannot dwell,
It is too near and terrible.
It is over—let it be,
And all those after days to thee,
Of madness and of agony.
Over, too, with all its glow,
  That last triumphal hour,
When multitudes once more stood hush'd
  Beneath thy spirit's power.[15]
Back to thy cell, whence thou
Wilt come but once more now,
There all alone to hear
Death's footsteps coming near,
Hour by hour more clear.

[12] Orsini left London for Paris, on his last attempt, December 1857.

[13] The preparation of the bombs used by Orsini was attended with great danger. He undertook the task alone, and was obliged to work with a thermometer always in his hand, to prevent an explosion.

[14] January 14, 1858. Orsini himself was terribly wounded; he was dangerously ill afterwards, of fever, brought on by his bodily and mental sufferings.

[15] See Orsini's magnificent speech at his trial, February 25, 1858.

Death-doom'd, and with the brand
Of murder on thy hand,
To go before God's throne,
  And all those innocent souls
But just before thee gone,
Crying for vengeance there,
Drowning in blood thy prayer,
  Barring thy way.
Mortal anguish, spirit's groan,
All that God and thou alone,
Here within these walls, have known.
  And the parting yesterday;
Children's arms, so soft and small,
Round thy neck in passionate thrall,
Where the sharp axe next must fall.
  Ah, let it be!—Not now
Thoughts such as these must must wake
The settled strength to shake
  From that majestic brow.

No man stirred or spake,
None durst the silence break,
  Fall'n on the room.
Thou takest little heed,
As at their work they speed,
  To clothe thee for thy doom;
No sign by which to read
  Thy spirit's light or gloom.
Thou dost not start to feel
The cold touch of the steel,
  As round thy neck the locks
    Are shorn away,
  That the other steel may find
    No hindrance in its way.
Never a motion, never
  A wandering of thine eyes;
The minutes steal away,
And thou hast nought to say:
  How cold and still it is.
Nearer we may not draw;
Hush'd we stand in awe,
  With lingering passionate eyes
Gazing for the last time
Upon that presence sublime,
That in its power and prime
  Is passing away for ever.
The world has seem'd of late

So noble and so great,
All rapt and consecrate
  Unto thy name:
Thou, who the air hast fill'd
  With thy great fame,
Who day by day hast thrill'd
  With words of flame,
For whom in midnights still'd
  Our wild prayers came;
Who even now hast power
To make this fearful hour
  Unutterably dear:—
Too soon it will be past,
We shall have looked our last;
Gulfs unsounded cast
  'Twixt thee and us to-morrow.
    Ah! rather have thee near
    In all this woe and fear,
    Than be without thee here,
  Alone in sorrow.

He who was join'd with thee,
  And played thee such ill part,
And now thy doom must share,
May not an aspect wear
So lofty in despair,
  But spurreth feverishly
    His sinking heart.
Wild words upon his tongue,
  Cold drops upon his brow;
Thou hast some thought to spare
  For others, even now.
Thou, the slander'd and betray'd,
To the weaker and afraid
Turnest with thy holy aid.
In the depth of thy own struggle and woe
The pardon was given long ago:[16]
Passion is over, scorn is past,
And overflowing love at last
  Has all thy soul possest.
'Twas thy last prayer yestereven
His life might be forgiven;
'My blood alone be given!'[17]
  And now to him addrest,
With an o'ermastering charm,

[16] See Orsini's speech given at his trial, February 25.
[17] See Orsini's second letter to the Emperor.

On his strain'd ear descend
The grand, grave words, 'Be calm,
Be calm, my friend!'[18]

Now it is ordered all,
As the law commands:
The shoes are off thy feet,
The cords are on thy hands;
The long robes o'er thee cast,
And on thy head at last
Plac'd the black veil and hood.
Then one lightning streak
Flash'd over eye and cheek.[19]
Up in a fervent flood
Rush'd the proud Roman blood:
Before us crown'd he stood
In the glory and the flush
Of the martyr aureole,
And his dark eyes lighted up
At the kindling of his soul;
And on the stedfast lip
Broke forth a smile divine:—
Upon our hearts for ever
That moment's look will shine.

Sorrowful around thee
Together now they crowd;
Thou, their dying prisoner,
All their hearts hast bow'd.[20]
In accents low and broken
The farewell words were spoken;
The farewell back was given
In accents low and still;
Perhaps the thought that moment
Came with a sudden thrill:
'Better to be as he is
Than doing a tyrant's will.'

We are ready—all is done;
The hour is all but run;
Beating one by one,

[18] Pierri talked incessantly, with feverish excitement. He was interrupted by Orsini with the words, 'Be calm, my friend, be calm'.

[19] 'When the hood was placed over his head, his face, which hitherto had been calm and impassive, became flushed for a moment, and his eye lighted up' (*The Times*).

[20] 'Orsini spoke little; but when the governor of the prison and some of the officers approached him, he bade them, in a low tone of voice, farewell. The turnkey of his cell announced to him in a tone of great regret that his last moment was come. Orsini thanked him for his sympathy!'

Loudly the seconds pass.
No heart-sick lingering or delay,
Short and stern is the work to-day.
Thou, full conscious of thy doom,
Hast brav'd Death—and he is come.
Neither doubtful nor afar,
Only the door ajar
Few moments more will bar
The scaffold from thy gaze.

PART III The Scaffold

SEVEN strokes toll out the hour,
Chim'd harsh and slow;
Now courage! and God help us all!
It is time to go.[21]
Ere the last sound has died,
With sudden motion glide
The prison doors aside;[22]
Look upward now!
It rises gaunt and grim
Athwart the shadows dim,
Looming in ghastly shape;
No rescue nor escape.
Forward! It must be fac'd,
It is not over yet:
Well that thou hast a hero's heart,
Or how could this be met?
Over the flinty courtyard
The dark procession go,
Lighted tapers flickering,
Funeral shadows throw;
The death-knell tolling, tolling,
Ever more sad and slow;
And a faint hymn chanted
Quivering and low;
'Mourir pour la patrie!'
It is even so.

On to the slaughter led,
Headsman and priest between;
Hands bound behind his back,
Long penance shroud of black,
Bare feet and veiled head,
And a conqueror's proud tread

[21] 'The moment of moving now came, and the Abbé Hugon cried out, "Courage!"'
[22] 'The prison clock struck seven: the last sound died away, the door leading to the scaffold opened as of itself.'

Up the steps fifteen.
Via Dolorosa!
A rude rough way;
Yet mid the mockeries
Of this dire array
There is a glory on thee
They cannot take away.
Now most of all we feel,
O Hero! we would kneel
In homage unto thee.—
One went up for this world's weal
In shame to Calvary.
It seems thou wouldst implore
Leave to speak once more
In all men's hearing free.[23]
Thou turnest, we can see,
Towards them wistfully,
Those throngs of gazers there,
Who now must witness bear
For thee to history.
But they are driven back
Too far for this to be;
Too mighty mastery lies
In thy voice, in thine eyes;
Not for enslaved ear
Patriot's last charge to hear:
So thou must have denial.
Yet fear not, O full heart,
Unread from earth to part;
Love can those words divine,
Needeth nor voice nor sign;
All our hearts beat with thine
Through this last trial.
Farewell! farewell! The cry
Ariseth far and nigh;
From the land across the sea,
From thine own Italy,
From souls in slavery
Whom thou didst seek to free,
All the world holds of sympathy
Is round thee now.
All the world waits to-day
For the tidings that will say,

[23] 'When Orisini appeared on the platform, it could be seen, from the movement of his body and of his head, that he was looking out for the crowd, and probably intended addressing them, but they were too far off.'

Thou art pass'd away.
In many a distant home,
  Thou know'st not it may be
Many a tear ere night
  Will fall for thee.
Yes, as thou standest there,
Nations in despair
Lift their eyes to thee,
Wailing passionately
  'Oh, that it should be thou!
For thy love to us
Perishing, and thus;—
  Who will save us now?'
What a deadly stillness,
  What an awful pause![24]
Closer and closer o'er us
  The black cloud draws.
In one shuddering silence
  Thousands are bound;
What a horror of darkness
  Gathers around!
Dizzy our eyes and dim—
  The earth reels to and fro;
With wildly rattling pulses
  The gasped moments go.
A dark and fearful passage
  We are entering with thee;
But thy calm aspect lighteth it
  Gloriously.

Thou hast reach'd the place of death—
  Here we must part;
We may go no further
  With thee, noble heart.
So now blessings, and adieu!
Only One can take thee through;
Nothing more we can do,
  Save, mid the breathless shiver
Of the death-agony,
Pray our last prayer for thee,
Felice Orsini,
  Once ere we sever:
'God give thee now good speed,
Help in this last great need,

[24] 'The prisoners remained upon the platform while the usher read the decree of the Court, condemning them to the death of parricides' (*Gazette des Tribunaux*).

Glory and martyr's meed
  Now and for ever!'

'Miserere, Agnus Dei!'
  The crucifix he kiss'd;
'Thanks, and farewell!'[25] One moment
  The priest's hand he press'd;
Then turn'd and stood in fixed mood,
  To his last work addrest.

Then the veil they rais'd;
But the face on which they gaz'd
  Was calm and glorious still.
Brows that darken'd not nor pal'd,
Eyes that neither quiver'd nor quail'd
  When the first stroke fell.[26]
On to the block with steady tread,
Though before him the newly dead,
And comrade's blood gush'd red
  And warm across his way.
Vive la France! then he said,
  Viva l'Italia!
Down sunk that noble head;
Shudderings and silence dread;—
  Angels, make way!

Stand still, great world, a moment!
  Fold your hands and pray:
'O God, let all tyranny
  From earth pass away!
Thy kingdom come! and never
  Let there again be need
  Of such o'erwhelming deed,
  Or of such vengeful meed,
    Earth to deliver!'

Over!—Through all these weeks,
  Hallowing their gloom and pain,
The shadow of thine agony
  Over the world has lain,—
A haunting, passionate presence,
  Beneath whose fixed strain,
We who kept watch with thee have pass'd
  Through fires of heart and brain.

[25] 'Orsini and Pierri embraced their spiritual attendants, and pressed their lips to the crucific offered to them.'

[26] 'Pierri was executed first. Orsini was then taken in hand. His veil was raised, and his countenance strill betrayed no emotion. Before he was fastened to the plank, he turned in the direction of the distant crowd and, it is said, cried "Vive la France" "Vive l'Italia".'

Now we draw breath, and say,
'Thank God—Well done!'
And out of this Gethsemane
At last thy crown is won;
Safe mid the stars for ever,
Thou brave, long suffering one!

Thus was thy victory won;
And when the deed was done,
Out went the fiery sun[27]
In wrath and fear;
Shadow and tremor fell,
Like the echo of a knell,
By hands invisible
Toll'd through the upper air.
All faces in our sight
Pal'd in that awful light
Neither of day nor night:—
And all abroad,
Over the land at noon,
Darkly th' eclipse came on—
For a great soul had gone
Back unto God.
They laid thee in the prison-yard,
Coldly and silently;
But the palaces of heaven
Were hung with black for thee,
And the planets strew'd the pall
Above thee for thy funeral.

So we take leave of thee,
Felice Orsini:
Thy like we shall not see
On earth again;
Never one century
Gave two such men.
From thy grave we part
With hush'd and reverent heart,
And comfort in our pain,
Feeling that not in vain
Such life and death could be;
With hope a coming year
Will yet make all things clear
By glorious consequence;[28]

[27] The great eclipse of the sun at noon, March 15, 1858, two days after Orsini's execution.

[28] The writer holds in firm faith that the Emperor's sudden change of policy, whence the war in Italy and all the late and present glorious event have sprung, was immediately caused

And we shall wholly see
Through this dark mystery
  Of Providence:
Why one who had stood fast
 In lifelong constancy,
Who had so nobly past
 Through all adversity,
Should have been tried at last
 So strangely, fearfully.
None, knowing thee, can doubt
Thy heart was pure throughout;
  None can thy steps have track'd,
And not felt from the first
The martyrdom the worst
  To thee lay in the act.
None hath known, or could know,
The conflict and the woe
Through which thy soul did go
  Ere it gave way.
With brain tost to and fro,
Seething in ebb and flow,
Throbbing and turning so,
Aright thou couldst not tell
Whether from heaven or hell
Those voices round thee fell,
  Ceasing not night or day;
And in that agony,
None helping thee, didst cry,
  As we may deem—
'O, save me from this hour!
Is there no other power
  My nation to redeem?
Flesh and spirit both
Abhor it, faint and loth;
Far gladlier would I go
To death by tortures slow,
To dungeons earth below,
All men can make of woe;—
Their utmost power I know.
Yet, seeing it is so,
And I am call'd thereto,
I may not shrink nor flee
From this now laid on me.

by Orsini's dying letters; and from the moment of his martyrdom believed that the salvation of his country would be wrought thereby, though without knowing how. That Orsini's last hours were cheered by the same faith, we have good reasons for believing. 1860.

O Mother Italy,
Life, name, and liberty,
And soul, if needs must be,
Were all vow'd unto thee.
    And I have kept that vow
With single heart and true,
All good and evil through,
    As I will keep it now.
For when young life was shining,
And heart with heart entwining,
I chose without repining
    A dark and cheerless road:
Therein these many years,
Through all that nature fears,
In loss, and pain, and tears,
    Straight forward I have trod;
Till unto me remain'd
Only a name unstain'd;
Now, that must perish too;—
There will be still a few
    To judge me tenderly.—
It must be: all I ask,
Is strength for this stern task;
And for the rest, my God,
    I trust my soul to Thee.
If, in Thy charity,
There is no room for me;—
If it must be indeed
Thy laws eternal need
That for this loathed deed
    I perish utterly:—
If Thou wilt cast me out,
  I that have clung to Thee
In anguish and in doubt,
  And wrestled fearfully
To know Thy truth;—yet still,
  Millions for rescue call;
  It must be,—one for all;
Here am I,—do Thy will!'

So thy resolve was taken,
And thou, revil'd, forsaken,
Didst bear that cross unshaken
  On through the gates of death.
And past them, at God's feet,
We know that thou didst meet
Award more just and tender

Than any we could render:
  Who knew thy worth as He?
Upon His mercy cast,
Toil and travail past,
Thou hast found thy home at last,
  And all is well with thee.
The *crime* by death is expiate,
Thou hast bow'd unto thy fate,
Thy place on earth is desolate,
  And it was just:
But the exalted faith,
The hope that triumpheth,
The love prov'd unto death
Tender, and true, and pure,
These cannot but endure;
And in God's love secure,
Through sorrow-clouds obscure,
  Humbly we trust;
Thankful that He has given
Another Star to Heaven,
Another name of worth,
To the memories of Earth.

Thou the crown of thorn
With stedfast brows hast worn,—
The world's reproach and scorn,
A heart by wild thoughts torn,
Dungeon depths forlorn,
And this dread judgment-morn:
The utmost thou hast borne,
  And it is o'er:
A name far down to shine,
Rest in the Life Divine,
The red rose crown is thine
  For evermore.

(1869)

MATHILDE BLIND
(1841–1896)

BORN in Mannheim, Germany, in 1841, Mathilde Blind came from a Jewish banking family by the name of Cohen. It was after her father's death that she and her brother, Ferdinand, were adopted by her mother's second husband, the famous revolutionary, Karl Blind, who was ejected from Paris on charges of conspiracy in 1849. Her stepfather found asylum first in Belgium, where she began her schooling, and then in London, as did several other German exiles, the most famous of whom was Karl Marx. The poet's identity was distinctly European. Mathilde Blind had mastery of many languages, and her English was said to be inflected with a German accent. All her published writing is in English.

Her upbringing was unorthodox. The highly respected Karl Blind was a prolific writer for the major periodicals of the day, such as the liberal-minded *Fortnightly Review*. Staunchly republican, he infuriated the Prussian government, who pressed for charges against him under English law for having libelled the King of Prussia in 1866. Mathilde Blind, understandably, grew up in a politically active and intellectually stimulating climate. Tragically, Ferdinand committed suicide at the age of 17 because he had failed in his assassination attempt on Bismarck's life. In his informative *Autobiography* (1904), Moncure Daniel Conway refers to the Blind's London home as a 'sort of *salon*'. A letter by one of Mathilde Blind's friends, the poet Algernon Charles Swinburne, reveals that she had been on bad terms with her stepfather for many years. (Swinburne reproved her for not returning to the name of Cohen; he was none the less one of Karl Blind's greatest admirers.) Among Karl Blind's many correspondents were famous European revolutionaries, including Garibaldi and Mazzini, both of whom had been important friends to Mathilde Blind. Her recollections of Mazzini were published in the *Fortnightly Review* in 1891.

The poet received, both at home and at a number of established schools, a remarkable education. Expelled from school in 1859 as an atheist, having read the geological account of the earth's formation against the view of human history put forward in the Bible, Blind's intellectual development followed a pattern strongly committed to late nineteenth-century positivism. The impact of evolutionary thinking is to be found in much of her prose and poetry. Her writing career began in 1873 with a translation of David Friedrich Strauss's *The Old Faith and the New*. In undertaking this work, Blind was following in the footsteps of George Eliot, whose translation of Strauss's celebrated *Life of Jesus* in 1845 drew attention to the German 'Higher Criticism' of the Bible, and hence made a significant contribution to Victorian loss of faith. Blind was the first biographer of Eliot (1883). Besides editing selections of Byron and Shelley, her other publications include a life of Madame Roland (1886) and *Tarantella: A Romance* (1885).

From the 1860s onwards, the poet was involved in the emerging Victorian women's movement. Her article on Mary Wollstonecraft appeared in the *New Quarterly Magazine* in 1878. More important still was her translation from the French of *The Journal of Marie Bashkirtseff* (1890), which would prove an inspiration to Katherine Mansfield many years later. Among her closest acquaintances was Mona Caird, the 'New Woman' novelist and campaigner for 'free unions' as alternatives to marriage. Details of the social and literary circles she moved within are to be found in Ford Madox (Hueffer) Ford's *Ford Madox Brown* (1896). During the 1880s she lived in Manchester, to be close to Brown and his wife. Equipped with sufficient income to support herself, she established her own household when she was thirty, and, with the aid of the occasional legacy, she left in her will a bequest to one of the recent educational establishments for women, Newnham College, Cambridge. Travelling widely throughout Europe and Egypt, Blind remained, for practically all of her life, an independent woman.

Blind's first book of poetry was published in 1867 under the pseudonym, Claude Lake. *The Prophecy of St Oran*, on ecclesiastical legend and historical questions relating to religious faith, went out on sale in 1881. Her next two collections tackled similarly complex themes. *The Heather on Fire* (published 1886) gives 'voice to the general indignation against the reckless clearance of Highland estates' (Richard Garnett's 'Memoir' in Miles, 1901), and contains some extraordinary descriptions of the eviction of peasant families. More ambitious still is *The Ascent of Man* (1889), which is the first poem in English to provide a comprehensive account of Darwinian theory. *Dramas in Miniature* (which include 'The Russian Student's Tale') came out in 1891. Collections of more lyrical pieces were published in 1893 and 1895. Her complete poetical works, edited by Arthur Symons, became available in 1900. In 1896, when she died, an invalid in south London, her close acquaintance, Theodore Watts-Dunton, wrote in the *Athenaeum*: 'I do not remember that she ever talked with me upon any subject that was not connected with poetry or with art or with science or with those great issues of the human story about which she thought so deeply and felt so keenly.'

286 *The Street-Children's Dance*

NOW the earth in fields and hills
Stirs with pulses of the Spring,
Nest-embowering hedges ring
With interminable trills;
Sunlight runs a race with rain,
All the world grows young again.

Young as at the hour of birth:
From the grass the daisies rise
With the dew upon their eyes,
Sun-awakened eyes of earth;
Fields are set with cups of gold;
Can this budding world grow old?

Can the world grow old and sere,
Now when ruddy-tasselled trees
Stoop to every passing breeze,
Rustling in their silken gear;
Now when blossoms pink and white
Have their own terrestrial light?

Brooding light falls soft and warm,
Where in many a wind-rocked nest,
Curled up 'neath the she-bird's breast,
Clustering eggs are hid from harm;
While the mellow-throated thrush
Warbles in the purpling bush.

Misty purple bathes the Spring:
Swallows flashing here and there
Float and dive on waves of air,
And make love upon the wing;
Crocus-buds in sheaths of gold
Burst like sunbeams from the mould.

Chesnuts leaflets burst their buds.
Perching tiptoe on each spray,
Springing toward the radiant day.
As the bland, pacific floods
Of the generative sun
All the teeming earth o'errun.

Can this earth run o'er with beauty,
Laugh through leaf and flower and grain,
While in close-pent court and lane.
In the air so thick and sooty,
Little ones pace to and fro,
Weighted with their parents' woe?

Woe-predestined little ones!
Putting forth their buds of life
In an atmosphere of strife,
And crime breeding ignorance;
Where the bitter surge of care
Freezes to a dull despair.

Dull despair and misery
Lie about them from their birth;
Ugly curses, uglier mirth,
Are their earliest lullaby;
Fathers have they without name,
Mothers crushed by want and shame.

Brutish, overburthened mothers,
With their hungry children cast
Half-nude to the nipping blast;
Little sisters with their brothers
Dragging in their arms all day
Children nigh as big as they.

Children mothered by the street:
Shouting, flouting, roaring after
Passers-by with gibes and laughter,
Diving between horses' feet,
In and out of drays and barrows,
Recklessly, like London sparrows.

Mudlarks of our slums and alleys,
All unconscious of the blooming
World behind those housetops looming,
Of the happy fields and valleys,
Of the miracle of Spring
With its boundless blossoming.

Blossoms of humanity!
Poor soiled blossoms in the dust!
Through the thick defiling crust
Of soul-stifling poverty,
In your features may be traced
Childhood's beauty half effaced—

Childhood, stunted in the shadow
Of the light-debarring walls;
Not for you the cuckoo calls
O'er the silver-threaded meadow;
Not for you the lark on high
Pours his music from the sky.

Ah! you have your music too!
And come flocking round that player
Grinding at his organ there,
Summer-eyed and swart of hue,
Rattling off his well-worn tune
On this April afternoon.

Lovely April nights of pleasure
Flit o'er want-beclouded features
Of these little outcast creatures,
As they swing with rhythmic measure,
In the courage of their rags,
Lightly o'er the slippery flags.

Little footfalls, lightly glancing
In a luxury of motion,
Supple as the waves of ocean
In your elemental dancing,
How you fly, and wheel, and spin,
For your hearts too dance within.

Dance along with mirth and laughter.
Buoyant, fearless, and elate,
Dancing in the teeth of fate,
Ignorant of your hereafter
That with all its tragic glooms
Blindly on your future looms.

Past and future, hence away!
Joy, diffused throughout the earth,
Centre in this moment's mirth
Of ecstatic holiday:
Once in all their lives' dark story.
Touch them, Fate! with April glory.

(1881)

287 *Chaunts of Life (from* The Ascent of Man*)*

I

STRUCK out of dim fluctuant forces and shock of electrical vapour,
Repelled and attracted the atoms flashed mingling in union primeval,
And over the face of the waters far heaving in limitless twilight
Auroral pulsations thrilled faintly, and, striking the blank heaving surface,
The measureless speed of their motion now leaped into light on the waters.
And lo, from the womb of the waters, upheaved in volcanic convulsion,
Ribbed and ravaged and rent there rose bald peaks and the rocky
Heights of confederate mountains compelling the fugitive vapours
To take a form as they passed them and float as clouds through the azure;
Mountains, the broad-bosomed mothers of torrents and rivers perennial,
Feeding the rivers and plains with patient persistence, till slowly,
In the swift passage of aeons recorded in stone by Time's graver,
There germ grey films of the lichen and mosses and palm-ferns gigantic,
And jungle of tropical forest fantastical branches entwining,
And limitless deserts of sand and wildernesses primeval.

II

Lo, moving o'er chaotic waters,
  Love dawned upon the seething waste,
Transformed in ever new avatars
  It moved without or pause or haste:
Like sap that moulds the leaves of May
It wrought within the ductile clay.

And vaguely in the pregnant deep,
  Clasped by the glowing arms of light
From an eternity of sleep
  Within unfathomed gulfs of night
A pulse stirred in the plastic slime
Responsive to the rhythm of Time.

Enkindled in the mystic dark
  Life built herself a myriad forms,
And, flashing its electric spark
  Through films and cells and pulps and worms,
Flew shuttlewise above, beneath,
Weaving the web of life and death.

And multiplying in the ocean,
  Amorphous, rude, colossal things
Lolled on the ooze in lazy motion,
  Armed with grim jaws or uncouth wings;
Helpless to lift their cumbering bulk
They lurch like some dismasted hulk.

And virgin forest, verdant plain,
  The briny sea, the balmy air,
Each blade of grass and globe of rain,
  And glimmering cave and gloomy lair,
Began to swarm with beasts and birds,
With floating fish and fleet-foot herds.

The lust of life's delirious fires
  Burned like a fever in their blood,
Now pricked them on with fierce desires,
  Now drove them famishing for food,
To seize coy females in the fray,
Or hotly hunted hunt for prey.

And amorously urged them on
  In wood or wild to court their mate,
Proudly displaying in the sun
  With antics strange and looks elate,
The vigour of their mighty thews
Or charm of million-coloured hues.

There crouching 'mid the scarlet bloom,
  Voluptuously the leopard lies,
And through the tropic forest gloom
  The flaming of his feline eyes
Stirs with intoxicating stress
The pulses of the leopardess.

Or two swart bulls of self-same age
  Meet furiously with thunderous roar,
And lash together, blind with rage,
  And clanging horns that fain would gore
Their rival, and so win the prize
Of those impassive female eyes.

Or in the nuptial days of spring,
  When April kindles bush and brier,
Like rainbows that have taken wing,
  Or palpitating gems of fire,
Bright butterflies in one brief day
Live but to love and pass away.

And herds of horses scour the plains,
  The thickets scream with bird and beast;
The love of life burns in their veins,
  And from the mightiest to the least
Each preys upon the other's life
In inextinguishable strife.

War rages on the teeming earth;
  The hot and sanguinary fight
Begins with each new creature's birth:
  A dreadful war where might is right;
Where still the strongest slay and win,
Where weakness is the only sin.

There is no truce to this drawn battle,
  Which ends but to begin again;
The drip of blood, the hoarse death-rattle,
  The roar of rage, the shriek of pain,
Are rife in fairest grove and dell,
Turning earth's flowery haunts to hell.

A hell of hunger, hatred, lust,
  Which goads all creatures here below,
Or blindworm wriggling in the dust,
  Or penguin in the Polar snow:
A hell where there is none to save,
Where life is life's insatiate grave.

And in the long portentous strife,
  Where types are tried even as by fire,
Where life is whetted upon life
  And step by panting step mounts higher,
Apes lifting hairy arms now stand
And free the wonder-working hand.

They raise a light, aërial house
  On shafts of widely branching trees,
Where, harboured warily, each spouse
  May feed her little ape in peace,
Green cradled in his heaven-roofed bed,
Leaves rustling lullabies o'erhead.

And lo, 'mid reeking swarms of earth
  Grim struggling in the primal wood,
A new strange creature hath its birth:
  Wild—stammering—nameless—shameless—nude;
Spurred on by want, held in by fear,
He hides his head in caverns drear.

Most unprotected of earth's kin,
  His fight for life that seems so vain
Sharpens his senses, till within
  The twilight mazes of his brain,
Like embryos within the womb,
Thought pushes feelers through the gloom.

And slowly in the fateful race
  It grows unconscious, till at length
The helpless savage dares to face
  The cave-bear in his grisly strength
For stronger than its bulky thews
He feels a force that grows with use.

From age to dumb unnumbered age,
  By dim gradations long and slow,
He reaches on from stage to stage,
  Through fear and famine, weal and woe
And, compassed round with danger, still
Prolongs his life by craft and skill.

With cunning hand he shapes the flint
  He carves the horn with strange device,
He splits the rebel block by dint
  Of effort—till one day there flies
A spark of fire from out the stone:
Fire which shall make the world his own.

(1889)

288 *The Russian Student's Tale*

THE midnight sun with phantom glare
Shone on the soundless thoroughfare
Whose shuttered houses, closed and still,
Seemed bodies without heart or will;
Yea, all the stony city lay
Impassive in that phantom day.
As amid livid wastes of sand
The sphinxes of the desert stand.

* * *

And we, we two, turned night to day.
As, whistling many a student's lay,
We sped along each ghostly street,
With girls whose lightly tripping feet
Well matched our longer, stronger stride,
In hurrying to the water-side.
We took a boat; each seized an oar,
And put his will into each stroke,
Until on either hand the shore
Slipped backwards, as our voices woke
Far echoes, mingling like a dream
With swirl and tumult of the stream.
On—on—away, beneath the ray
Of midnight in the mask of day;
By great wharves where the masts at peace
Look like the ocean's barren trees;
Past palaces and glimmering towers,
And gardens fairy-like with flowers,
And parks of twilight green and closes,
The very Paradise of roses.
The waters flow; on, on we row,
Now laughing loud, now whispering low;
And through the splendour of the white
Electrically glowing night,
Wind-wafted from some perfumed dell,
Tumultuously there loudly rose
Above the Neva's surge and swell.
With amorous ecstasies and throes,
And lyric spasms of wildest wail,
The love-song of a nightingale.

* * *

I see her still beside me. Yea,
As if it were but yesterday,
I see her—see her as she smiled:

Her face that of a little child
For innocent sweetness undefiled;
And that pathetic flower like blue
Of eyes which, as they looked at you,
Seemed yet to stab your bosom through.
I rowed, she steered; oars dipped and flashed,
The broadening river roared and splashed,
So that we hardly seemed to hear
Our comrades' voices, though so near;
Their faces seeming far away,
As still beneath that phantom day
I looked at her, she smiled at me!
And then we landed—I and she.

* * *

There's an old Café in the wood;
A student's haunt on summer eyes,
Round which responsive popular leaves
Quiver to each æolian mood
Like some wild harp a poet smites
On visionary summer nights.
I ordered supper, took a room
Green-curtained by the tremulous gloom
Of those fraternal poplar trees
Shaking together in the breeze;
My pulse, too, like a poplar tree,
Shook wildly as she smiled at me.
Eye in eye, and hand in hand,
Awake amid the slumberous land,
I told her all my love that night—
How I had loved her at first sight;
How I was hers, and seemed to be
Her own to all eternity.
And through the splendour of the white
Electrically glowing night,
Wind-wafted from some perfumed dell,
Tumultuously there loudly rose
Above the Neva's surge and swell,
With amorous ecstasies and throes,
And lyric spasms of wildest wail,
The love-song of a nightingale.

* * *

I see her still beside me. Yea,
As if it were but yesterday,
I hear her tell with cheek aflame
Her ineradicable shame—
So sweet a flower in such vile hands!
Oh, loved and lost beyond recall!

Like one who hardly understands,
I heard the story of her fall,
The odious barter of her youth,
Of beauty, innocence, and truth,
Of all that honest women hold
Most sacred—for the sake of gold.
A weary seamstress, half a child,
Left unprotected in the street,
Where, when so hungry, you would meet
All sorts of tempters that beguiled.
Oh, infamous and senseless clods,
Basely to taint so pure a heart.
And make a maid fit for the gods
A creature of the common mart!
She spoke quite simply of things vile—
Of devils with an angel's face;
It seemed the sunshine of her smile
Must purify the foulest place.
She told me all—she would be true—
Told me of things too sad, too bad:
And, looking in her eyes' clear blue
My passion nearly drove me mad!
I tried to speak, but tried in vain;
A sob rose to my throat as dry
As ashes—for between us twain
A murdered virgin seemed to lie.
And through the splendour of the white
Electrically glowing night,
Wind-wafted from some perfumed dell,
Tumultuously there loudly rose,
Above the Neva's surge and swell,
With amorous ecstasies and throes,
And lyric spasms of wildest wail,
The love-song of a nightingale.

* * *

Poor craven creature! What was I,
To sit in judgment on her life,
Who dared not make this child my wife,
And lift her up to love's own sky?
This poor lost child we all—yes, all—
Had helped to hurry to her fall,
Making a social leper of
God's creature consecrate to love.
I looked at her—she smiled no more;
She understood it all before
A syllable had passed my lips;

And like a horrible eclipse,
Which blots the sunlight from the skies,
A blankness overspread her eyes—
The blankness as of one who dies.
I knew how much she loved me—knew
How pure and passionately true
Her love for me, which made her tell
What scorched her like the flames of hell.
And I, I loved her too, so much,
So dearly, that I dared not touch
Her lips that had been kissed in sin;
But with a reverential thrill
I took her work-worn hand and thin,
And kissed her fingers, showing still
Where needle-pricks had marred the skin.
And, ere I knew, a hot tear fell,
Scalding the place which I had kissed,
As between clenching teeth I hissed
Our irretrievable farewell.
And through the smouldering glow of night,
Mixed with the shining morning light
Wind-wafted from some perfumed dell,
Above the Neva's surge and swell,
With lyric spasms, as from a throat
Which dying breathes a faltering note.
There faded o'er the silent vale
The last sob of a nightingale.

(1891)

289 *On a Torso of Cupid*

PEACH trees and Judas trees,
  Poppies and roses,
Purple anemones
  In garden closes!
Lost in the limpid sky,
Shrills a gay lark on high;
Lost in the covert's hush,
Gurgles a wooing thrush.

Look, where the ivy weaves,
  Closely embracing,
Tendrils of clinging leaves
  Round him enlacing,
With Nature's sacredness

Clothing the nakedness,
Clothing the marble of
This poor, dismembered love.

Gone are the hands whose skill
  Aimed the light arrow,
Strong once to cure or kill,
  Pierce to the marrow;
Gone are the lips whose kiss
Held hives of honeyed bliss;
Gone too the little feet,
Overfond, overfleet.

O helpless god of old,
  Maimed mid the tender
Blossoming white and gold
  Of April splendour!
Shall we not make thy grave
Where the long grasses wave;
Hide thee, O headless god,
Deep in the daisied sod?

Here thou mayst rest at last
  After life's fever;
After love's fret is past
  Rest thee for ever.
Nay, broken God of Love,
Still must thou bide above
While left for woe or weal
Thou hast a heart to feel.

(1895)

VIOLET FANE (MARY MONTGOMERIE LAMB, LATER SINGLETON, LATER CURRIE) (1843–1905)

VIOLET FANE was the pseudonym adopted by Mary Montgomerie Lamb after a female character in Benjamin Disraeli's *Vivian Grey* (1826–27). Born near Littlehampton in Sussex, she was brought up in a highly respectable family that appears not to have encouraged her literary endeavours. Her parents were Charles J.H. Lamb and Anna Charlotte (née Gray). Details about her early life are scant. But from her writing, it is clear that she read widely and developed considerable social skills. In early 1864, she married her first husband, Henry Sydenham Singleton, an Irish landowner, with whom she had five children. Her first marriage lasted until Singleton died in 1893. The following year, she married her second husband, Sir Philip Henry Currie, who had a distinguished diplomatic career. Until 1898, they resided together in Constantinople. The remainder of her days was spent at Hawley in Hampshire. She died of heart failure while visiting the Grand Hotel at Harrogate in 1905.

Renowned as a beauty in her youth, Fane was also remembered for her formidable conversational wit. Such was her presence among the cultured élite of the day that she features as Mrs Sinclair in W. H. Mallock's Tory-minded satire, *The New Republic* (1877). One of the most teasing exchanges in Mallock's volume takes place between Dr Jenkinson (alias the Oxford don, Benjamin Jowett) and Mrs Sinclair on the subject of the Greek Anthology, where she wishes to know why some of the poems prove so hard to translate. Are they, she asks the Doctor, not so much 'hard' as 'corrupt'?

Fane's poetry frequently reflects a sharply critical eye on the sexual orthodoxies of the time, as well displaying the wealthy upper-class environment in which she prospered. Between 1872 and 1900, she published six books of poetry. The most celebrated of these volumes is her sensational verse-novel, *Denzil Place* (1875), that charts the course of an adulterous love affair, one that met with criticism among a number of reviewers. In some respects, this finely paced work emulates the ambitions of Elizabeth Barrett Browning's *Aurora Leigh* (1856). Her extensive publications include several novels and volumes of essays, as well as a translation of the *Memoirs of Marguerite de Valois* (1892).

290 *Lancelot and Guinevere*

'Oh! read to me some other lay,'
  She cried to one about to read;
'I love to hear of tourney gay,
  Of feats of arms and daring deed,

'Yet read to-day some simple rhyme,
  Or else some tender ballad sing,
And let me hear another time
  The Idylls of the blameless king.'

Her husband did not seem to hear,
  Or, if he heard, he heeded not,
And so he read of Guinevere
  And of her love for Lancelot.

He read how first the rumour grew,
  Unheared by him it harm'd the most,
And how the courtiers link'd their two
  Unwedded names in song and toast;

And how, 'love-loyal' to her will,
  The great knight sought within her eyes
Her wishes when her lips were still,
  Ere striving for the diamond prize,

And how he did not read them right—
  The lady sadden'd at each word:
'Alas,' she sigh'd, 'how true the knight!
  How fair the queen! how great her lord!'

She turn'd away and sigh'd anew
  As in each act his love was seen,
And thought, 'Ah! I had loved him too
  Were he my knight, were I his queen.'

But when the poet told of how
  His guilty love had darken'd o'er,
And marr'd the beauty of his brow
  (Such love makes some men smile the more),

And how he did not lightly wear
  The prize of which he made no boast,
'Twas then she deem'd him doubly fair,
  'Twas then she felt she loved him most.

And when she heard of fair Elaine,
  'Alas! it seemeth hard,' she sigh'd,
'That he should let her love in vain
  The hopeless love whereof she died.

'But ah! how loyal to his queen!
  How warm the heart that seem'd so cold!
Hath ever knight so faithful been
  Since he of whom the poet told?'

And when she heard how Elaine died,
  And floated to him on her bier,
She turn'd away her head to hide
  The falling of a passing tear.

But when Sir Lancelot had sought
  The little reedy river cove,
And, all remorseful, sigh'd and thought
  The *maiden's* was the tend'rer love;

Then throbb'd the heart of her who heard,
  As though the spirit of the queen
Within her bosom lived and stirr'd,
  And made of her what *she* had been:

And wildly to herself she said,
  'The *woman's* love! the queen's! my own!
Ah! could he covet in its stead
  What but a love-sick girl has shown?

'The sneering word, the tarnish'd name,
  The galling mask for him she bore;
She heeded not her loss of fame,
  And risk'd the queenly crown she wore:

'For him she did not scorn to lie
  To one whose very life was truth;
She put her robes and sceptre by,
  And crown'd him king of all her youth.

'That simple maiden could but prove
  The love she bore him by her death;
Give me to *live* for him I love,
  To yield him heart and soul and breath!

'Give me the risk, the shame, the sin,
  The love that can have nought to gain,
Save the fond hope one day to win
  A dearer link to clasp the chain!

'But read no more!' she cried aloud;
  Her cheek was flush'd and wild her eye,
Whilst on her brow the gath'ring cloud
  Told of the tempest passing by.

'Ah! read no more,' she said again,
  'My ears are weary of the sound!'
And half in anger, half in pain,
  She flung the book upon the ground.

'Alas, for lawless love!' she sigh'd,
  'I share the cross of Guinevere;
Like her my guilty secret hide,
  Like her I earn the doom I fear.

'To see one day his passion fade,
  Or hear him say *mine* pales beside
The love of some such lily maid
  As she who floated down the tide.

'For *me* to steel my heart at need,
  Nor let that live that makes love's curse,
Then can I all unheeding read
  The tender tales of poet's verse.'

She bent her head and seem'd to pray,
  Then, starting, listen'd to a sound,
Push'd back her hair, and dash'd away
  The tears in which her eyes were drown'd.

With mantling cheeks and lips apart,
She waits and strains her anxious sight;
And all the pulses of her heart
Seem quicken'd by some near delight.

Her lord stepp'd down upon the grass
And vanish'd in the twilight dim;
Her guardian angel moan'd 'Alas!
Alas for her! alas for him!'

Alas! for erring woman's pray'r!
Reader and book alike forgot;
She trembles, hearing on the stair
The coming step of Lancelot.

(1872)

291 *The Irish 'Patriots'. (To Wilfrid Scawen Blunt)*

THINK you these men seek truly Ireland's ease
From England's yoke;—her front exalted, free,
Amongst the nations ruled by just decree
Of King or Council? . . . Dare you hope that these,—
The things they crave to-day,—could wholly please
Such fretful spirits;—that their eyes could see
The calm that would engulf them; or, maybe,
Two sister-flags,—afloat o'er friendly seas?
Nay! for above the boasted love they bear
Their native Isle;—ay, over and above
The hate they bear the Saxon,—flowers fair,
In genial soil,—another kind of love,—
The love they bear themselves; that this may thrive
It is expedient that they strut and strive!

(1889)

292 *At Christie's*

THEY scowl and simper here in rows,
Or seem to look with pleading eyes
Upon the crowd that comes and goes,
And talks and stares, and bids and buys;

Brave knights and squires, and belted earls,
  In boots and spurs, and coats-of-mail;
And ladies fair, in lace and pearls,
  And ruff, and coiff, and farthingale.

The founders of a noble race,
  Whose blood in righteous cause was shed,
Find here a brief abiding-place,
  Exiled and disinherited.

Kinsman and kinswoman are they,
  Brother and sister, bride and groom,
All waiting here in brave array
  To meet their unexpected doom;

For they that did so long abide
  Beneath one roof, by right of birth,
Must now dissever and divide,
  And be as wand'rers on the earth.

In what hot haste they came to town
  From their long sojourn in the shires!
And as they sped by dale and down,
  And flash'd past rivers, fields, and spires,

I wonder, did they, in amaze
  At such swift progress, call to mind
Those good old jog-trot pillion-days
  That seem to lie so far behind?

And (for they all have human eyes
  That from these walls look sadly down)
I wonder, did they realise
  The purport of this trip to town?

Or merely deem some lucky chance
  Released them from their dull abode,
And sent them forth to dine and dance,
  And see the plays, and learn the mode?

In mouldy vault, 'neath sculptured tomb,
  They sleep who bore these forms in life,
Kinsman and comrade, bride and groom,
  Brother and sister, man and wife.

But since their bones are brown and bare,
  And worms have spun across their eyes,
And holland sarks are what they wear
  In lieu of all these braveries,

And since they turn not in their graves
For very horror and dismay,
To see themselves, like negro slaves,
Set up for auction here to-day,

Whilst these, their sad-eyed portraits, gaze
With looks of passionate appeal,
As though regretful of the days
When arm could smite and heart could feel,

I hold these for the truer men,
More keen of soul, more clear of sight,
In closer touch with human ken
Of what is wrong and what is right.

(1896)

MARGARET VELEY
(1843–1887)

MARGARET VELEY was the second of four children born to Augustus Charles Veley, a solicitor at Braintree, Essex, and Sophia (née Ludbey). Together with her three sisters, she received her education from a number of home tutors. She did, however, complete one term at Queen's College, Tufnell Park. Most of her life was spent with the members of her immediate family at Braintree. There were many domestic difficulties, caused particularly by the infirmity of two of her sisters, whom she nursed over many years. After the death of her father, she decided to leave Braintree with her mother, and they settled in London. In his biographical Introduction to Veley's poetical works, Leslie Stephen notes that it proved difficult for her to break into London literary life, not least because of her constitutional shyness. On the basis of the extracts that Stephen took from her correspondence, one forms a picture of a devoted daughter who bore grief and disappointment with considerable stoicism. Veley, it appears, quietly dissented from the High Church principles with which she had grown up. Her political inclinations were towards Liberalism.

Veley's interest in writing poetry began at an early age, and by the time she moved to London she had begun to place notable poems in leading journals. Her first success was 'Michaelmas Daisies', published in the *Spectator* in 1870. 'A Japanese Fan' appeared in the *Cornhill Magazine* in 1876. Her distinguished poems were gathered in the posthumous collection, *A Marriage of Shadows* (1888). Many of these technically assured works concern spiritual struggles and love-lorn affairs. A special feature of the poem that titles her collection is its eerie exploration of the world of dreams, in which strange forms of 'wedlock' occur. In addition to her poetry, Veley produced a large number of stories that were accepted for publication in leading journals. In 1870, 'Milly's First Love' featured in *Blackwood's*. The *Cornhill* printed several of her fictions in the 1870s, including *For Percival*, which was published as single volume in 1878. In the later years of her life, further stories appeared in *Macmillan's* and the *Hourglass*. She died in late 1887 of a chill that led to serious infection.

293 *A Japanese Fan*

HOW time flies! Have we been talking
For an hour?
Have we been so long imprisoned
By the shower
In this old oak-panelled parlour?
Is it noon?
Don't you think the rain is over
Rather soon?

Since the heavy drops surprised us,
And we fled
Here for shelter, while it darkened
Overhead;
Since we leaned against the window,
Saw the flash
Of the lightning, heard the rolling
Thunder crash;
You have looked at all the treasures
Gathered here,
Out of other days and countries
Far and near;
At those glasses, thin as bubbles,
Opal bright—
At the carved and slender chessmen
Red and white—
At the long array of china
Cups and plates—
(Do you really understand them?
Names and dates?)
At the tapestry, where dingy
Shepherds stand,
Holding grim and faded damsels
By the hand,
All the while my thoughts were busy
With the fan
Lying here—bamboo and paper
From Japan.
It is nothing—very common—
Be it so;
Do you wonder why I prize it?
Care to know?
Shall I teach you all the meaning,
The romance

Of the picture you are scorning
With a glance?

From Japan! I let my fancy
Swiftly fly;
Now if we set sail to-morrow,
You and I,
If the waves were liquid silver,
Fair the breeze,
If we reached that wondrous island
O'er the seas,
Should we find that every woman
Was so white,
And had slender upward eyebrows
Black as night?
Should we then perhaps discover
Why, out there,
People spread a mat to rest on
In mid air?

Here's a lady, small of feature,
Narrow-eyed,
With her hair of ebon straightness
Queerly tied;
In her hand are trailing flowers
Rosy sweet,
And her silken robe is muffled
Round her feet.
She looks backward with a conscious
Kind of grace,
As she steps from off the carpet
Into space;
Though she plants her foot on nothing
Does not fall,
And in fact appears to heed it
Not at all.
See how calmly she confronts us
Standing there—
Will you say she is not lovely?
Do you dare?
I will not! I honour beauty
Where I can,
Here's a woman one might die for!
—In Japan.

Read the passion of her lover—
All his soul
Hotly poured in this fantastic

Little scroll.
See him swear his love, and vengeance
Read his fate—
You don't understand the language?
I'll translate.

'Long ago,' he says, 'when summer
Filled the earth
With its beauty, with the brightness
Of its mirth;
When the leafy boughs were woven
Far above;
In the noonday I beheld her,
Her—my love!
Oftentimes I met her, often
Saw her pass,
With her dusky raiment trailing
On the grass.
I would follow, would approach her,
Dare to speak,
Till at last the sudden colour
Flushed her cheek.
Through the sultry heat we lingered
In the shade;
And the fan of pictured paper
That she swayed
Seemed to mark the summer's pulses,
Soft and slow,
And to thrill me as it wavered
To and fro.
For I loved her, loved her, loved her,
And its beat
Set my passion to a music
Strangely sweet.
Sunset came, and after sunset
When the dusk
Filled the quiet house with shadows;
And the musk
From the dim and dewy garden
Where it grows,
Mixed its perfume with the jasmine
And the rose;
When the western splendour faded,
And the breeze
Went its way, with good-night whispers
Through the trees,
Leaning out we watched the dying

Of the light,
Till the bats came forth with sudden
Ghostly flight.
They were shadows, wheeling, flitting
Round my joy,
While she spoke and while her slender
Hands would toy
With her fan, which as she swayed it
Might have been
Fairy wand, or fitting sceptre
For a queen.
When she smiled at me, half pausing
In her play,
All the gloom of gathering twilight
Turned to day!

Though to talk too much of heaven
Is not well—
Though agreeable people never
Mention hell—
Yet the woman who betrayed me—
Whom I kissed—
In that bygone summer taught me
Both exist.
I was ardent, she was always
Wisely cool,
So my lady played the traitor,
I—the fool'——
Oh, your pardon! But remember,
If you please,
I'm translating—this is only
Japanese.

'Japanese?' you say, and eye me
Half in doubt;
Let us have the lurking question
Spoken out.
Is all this about the lady
Really said
In that little square of writing
Near her head?
I will answer, on my honour,
As I can,
Every syllable is written
On the fan.
Yes, and you could learn the language
Very soon—
Shall I teach you on some August
Afternoon?

You are wearied. There is little
Left to say;
For the disappointed hero
Goes his way,
And such pain and rapture never
More will know.
But he smiles—all this was over
Long ago.
I am not a blighted being—
Scarcely grieve—
I can laugh, make love, do most things
But believe!

Yet the old days come back strangely
As I stand
With the fan she swayed so softly
In my hand.
I can almost see her, touch her,
Hear her voice,
Till, afraid of my own madness,
I rejoice
That beyond my help or harming
Is her fate—
Past the reach of passion—is it
Love—or hate?

This is tragic! Are you laughing?
So am I!
Let us go—the clouds have vanished
From the sky.
Yes, and you'll forget this folly?
Time it ceased,
For you do not understand me
In the least.
You have smiled and sighed politely
Quite at ease,—
And my story might as well be
Japanese!

(1876 *1888*)

294 *A Game of Piquet*

SEE, as you turn a page
Of Holbein's Dance of Death,
Across the narrow stage,
Drawing a hurried breath,

The sons of men go by,
Like a bewildered dream,
Beneath a changeless sky
An ever-changing stream.
Swiftly as driven clouds
They pass in love and strife,
And all the shifting crowds
Are busy with their life,
Eager, intent, and much
Perplexed.
Then comes the deadly touch—

What next?
We do not paint Death now,
As did those men of old,
(And, truly, I allow
They make my blood run cold,)
Yet the old fancy lives
In spite of growth and change,
And to our sorrow gives
Its humour grim and strange.
The bitter wine that when
We meet our mocking chance
Is stamped from souls of men
In Death's fantastic dance.
As when the cry of Love,
Or Hate,
Rings to the heaven above
Too late.

We need not paint the scene,
The skull, the grasping hand,
For that which once has been
Our hearts will understand.
A flower may be the sign
That calls your vision back,
Or just a pencil line
In some old almanac.
A pack of cards for me,
Where smiling queen and knave
Can bid me turn and see
A shadow and a grave,
Nor to my dying day
Forget
How once I used to play
Piquet.

Once, in a quaint old place!
My dreamy thoughts recall

Its somewhat faded grace
Of painting on the wall,
Pink roses ribbon-tied.
And pairs of snowy doves
Tall vases side by side,
And lightly flying Loves,
Such as our poets sing,
Or sang, some time ago,
Dan Cupid on the wing
With quiver, shafts, and bow—
But Love had there no need
Of darts,
He simply gave the lead
In Hearts.

Into the sunlit room
To break the half-played game,
With heavy stroke of doom,
The grief of parting came.
Strong in my happy love
I faced the bitter pain,
And swore by heaven above
We two would meet again.
Silent I saw her stand,
Pallid, in trouble sore,
While from her hanging hand
Slipped downward to the floor
Black cards, whose ominous
Array
Fate had not suffered us
To play.

I bade a brave farewell
Without a thought of fear,
Ah God! I could not tell
That evil day was near,
When Life's glad music sank
To sobs, and died away,
When Earth's high mountains shrank
To one low heap of clay.
When I, aghast and sad,
Stood silent and apart,
When all Creation had
A sepulchre for heart.
No love the unknown land
Invades,
And Death played out the hand
Of Spades.

(1888)

L. S. BEVINGTON (LATER GUGGENBERGER)
(1845–1895)

Born and raised in London, Louisa S. Bevington was the eldest of eight children. Her father, Alexander Bevington, came from a line devoted to progressive causes; one of his ancestors, he claimed, had suffered confinement with George Fox in Nottingham Gaol. Although her father encouraged her in the pursuit of poetry, it was not until 1871 that she began to publish her work. Three sonnets appeared, under her initials only, in one of the earliest numbers of the *Friends' Quarterly Examiner*, suggesting that she must have had close connections with the Society of Friends. Thereafter, she published three volumes of poetry, the first of which was brought out for private circulation under the pseudonym, Arbor Leigh. Four of the poems on evolutionary topics made such an impression on Herbert Spencer that he arranged for them to be repinted in the American journal, *Popular Science Monthly* (1876), under the title, 'Teachings of a Day'. *Key-Notes* (1879) and *Poems, Lyrics, and Sonnets* (1882) were published under her own name. Many of the works included in these technically accomplished collections are highly critical of religious and social orthodoxies. Prefacing a selection of her works in 1891, Alfred H. Miles remarks that he is not surprised that Bevington 'should have broken the spell which for fifteen years had confined Darwin to the world of prose'. 'Her part', he adds, 'is emphatically that of the poetess of evolutionary science.' Her contributions to the periodical press draw many of these concerns with progressive evolutionary thinking into sharp focus. In her two-part essay, 'Modern Atheism and Mr Mallock' (1879), which appeared in the *Nineteenth Century*, Bevington takes a principled stand in opposition to W. H. Mallock's slurs against the morality of evolutionary theory. Similar in tone is 'The Moral Colour of Rationalism' (1881), which appeared in the *Fortnightly Review*. There she argues against Goldwin Smith's identification of evolutionary theory as the political ideology supporting colonial exploitation. She prefers, instead, to understand contemporary rationalist thought (including evolutionary thought) to be inclined towards 'national generosity and humane principle', laying the blame for imperial oppression firmly upon the Christian church: 'orthodoxy is naturally bent chiefly on its own propagation, and that of British rule as conducive to its own propagation, among the weak tribes into whose midst it carries at one arms and Bibles.' Two further essays, 'Determinism and Duty' and 'The Personal Aspects of Responsibility', were published by *Mind* at this time.

Before her short-lived marriage to the Munich artist, Ignatz Guggenberger, in 1883, Bevington spent periods of time in Germany. Thereafter, she moved between Meran and London. She continued to write articles for magazines, and contributed the chapter on evolution to an enlarged edition of *Religious Systems of the World*, published by the Ethical Society in 1891. In the years leading up to her death, Bevington became involved with anarchist groups based in London, lecturing in 1893 on Christianity and atheism at the Autonomie Club. Her final collection of poems, *Liberty Lyrics*, was published by James Tochatti's Liberty Press in 1895. In the same year, Tochatti's journal, *Liberty*, featured her essay, 'Why I Am an Expropriationist', revealing her sympathies with Pierre-Joseph Proudhon's attack on property-ownership.

295 *Love and Pride*

I COULD have striven for you, dear,
To save your spirit strife;
I could have suffered, aye! and died
If you had needed life:
But since you ask no boon of me
I'll love you very quietly.

I could have been a saint, for you,
Or stooped to meanest fame;
The stair to heaven or path to hell,
With you, were all the same:
But since you do not beckon, dear,
My life shall wait, unprovèd, here.

'Tis very hard to give no gift,
To yearn, and yet to bide;
The keenest pain that lovers know
Is love's own patient pride;
But since no service, dear, you ask,
My heart accepts the sterner task.

(1879)

296 *Bees in Clover.*

A SONG

UP the dewy slopes of morning
Follow me;
Every smoky spy-glass scorning,
Look and see, look and see
How the simple sun is rising,
Not approving nor despising
You and me.
Hear not those who bid you wait
Till they find the sun's birth-date,
Preaching children, savage sages,
To their mouldy, blood-stuck pages
And the quarrelling of ages,
Leave them all; and come and see
Just the little honied clover,
As the winging music-bees
Come in busy twos and threes
Humming over!
All without a theory

Quite successfully, you see;
Little priests that wed the flowers,
Little preachers in their way,
Through the sunny working day
With their quite unconscious powers
How they say their simple say.

What? a church-bell in the valley?
What? a wife-shriek in the alley?
Tune the bell a little better,
Help the woman bear her fetter,
All in time! all in time!
If you will but take your fill
Of the dawn-light on the hill,
And behold the dew-gems glisten,—
If you turn your soul to listen
To the bees among the thyme,
There may chance a notion to you
To encourage and renew you,
For the doing and the speaking,
Ere the jarring of the chime,
And the mad despair of shrieking
Call you downward to the mending
Of a folly, and the ending
Of a crime.

On the dewy hill at morning
Do you ask?—do you ask?
How to tune the bells that jangle?
How to still the hearts that wrangle?—
For a task?
When the bell shall suit the ears
Of the strong man's hopes and fears,
As the bee-wing suits the clover
And the clover suits the bee,
Then the din shall all be over,
And the woman shall be free,
And the bell ring melody,
Do you see?—do you see?
There are bees upon the hill,
And the sun is climbing still,
To his noon;
Shall it not be pretty soon
That the wife she shall be well,
And the jarring of the bell
Falls in tune?

(1882)

297 *The Unpardonable Sin*

I SPEAK to women—woman I;
  I speak to one more heart beside;
  Whatever sin may e'er betide,
But one sin damneth utterly.

If you are pledged to love a soul
  By every pledge of love and law,
  But all too late you find a flaw
That bids your heart annul the whole;—

If hold to him you never can,
  Low as you are and all untrue,
  E'en this may be forgiven you;
You sin against a son of man.

But if, or pledged or free of troth
  (It matters not to savoured salt),
  If passion, pride, or any fault
Plead on the side of bliss for both;—

If when your will is evil most
  He strive to hold you to the right,
  If then you turn from him in spite,
You sin against a holy ghost.

Be very far this sin from me,
  Dear saint, whom I have loved so well;
  'Twould be the very hell of hell
To fail you for your sanctity.

(1882)

298 *Hated*

YOU ask me where love fails me?—what I hate?
I cannot blame, for all, I hold, is fate;
Yet there are hateful, unblameworthy things
That sap life's nobler mercies at their springs;—
All deathward, pious-voiced uncleannesses;
All cold, conceited, mouthing meannesses.
Time-serving pietists who lie for fame
Sooner than hear no echo of their name;
Souls readier to limit all we hallow
By their own shallow thoughts, than deem these shallow.
Perfidious power that no compunction knows;
'Cute cleverness that makes convenient shows;

The devil-hearted insolence of sin
That to its end through broken faith doth win;
False woman who will fawn upon the neck
Of wife whose hearth she warms her by to wreck;
Some sneaking lover who for alien lust
Will mock his home and soil his social trust;
The sour, uncandid treasurer of offence,
Who sneers down generous gift with common sense;
All cold, conceited, mouthing meannesses,
All deathward, decent-garbed uncleannesses;—
These and the like keep very far from me,
For all are lies, and all unsympathy.
Love cannot move them though it suffocate,
I do not blame—I absolutely hate;
Such things of folly, perfidy, and fiction
Must be; but they shall have my malediction.

(1882)

299 *Revolution*

Ah yes! You must meet it, and brave it;
Too laggard—too purblind to save;
Who recks of your doubting and fearing
Phrase-bound 'Evolution'?
Do you not hear the sea sounding it?
Do you not feel the fates founding it?
Do you not know it is nearing?
Its name—Revolution.

What! stem it, and stay it, and spare it?
Or will you defy it, and dare it?
Then this way or that you must change you
For swift restitutions.
Do you not see men deserving it?
Do you not hear women nerving it?
Down with old Mammon! and range you
To aid Revolution!

The last hour has struck of our waiting,
The last of your bloodless debating,
The wild-fire of spirit is speeding
Us on to solution.
Do you not thrill at the uttering?
Do you not breathe the breeze fluttering
Round the brave flag of our pleading?
The world's Revolution!

(1895)

E. H. HICKEY
(1845–1924)

BORN at Macmine Castle, County Wexford, Emily Hickey was the daughter of an Irish parson. As a young woman, she lived at Goresbridge, County Carlow, and attended a number of schools as a day-boarder. While still at school she placed several poems with notable journals, including the *Cornhill* and *Macmillan's Magazine*. In her late teens, she moved to London, where she undertook secretarial work and private teaching. She spent some time employed as a governess. Her friendship with Louisa Brough encouraged her active involvement in campaigns for the higher education of women. Having obtained her Cambridge Certificate, she served for eighteen years as a lecturer in English literature at the North London Collegiate School for girls.

Her first volume of poetry, *A Sculptor and Other Poems*, which appeared in 1881, arguably contains her finest work. Its success introduced her to the London literary circle that featured the main devotees of the poet, Robert Browning. Her contact with the literary antiquarian, F. J. Furnivall, and the scholar, Alexandra Sutherland Orr (author of the influential *Handbook* to Browning's poetry), led to the creation of the Browning Society in 1881, where she served as the first honorary secretary. In 1884, she edited *Strafford*, Browning's drama of the English Civil War. Her second volume, *Verse-Tales, Lyrics, and Translations*, was published in 1891. This collection was followed by *Michael Villers—Idealist, and Other Poems* in 1891, which in part tackles the question of Irish Home Rule. Her final collection, *Poems* (1896), evinces her increasing interest in religious matters. A friend of the poet and Roman Catholic convert, Harriet Eleanor Hamilton King, Hickey joined the Church of Rome in 1901. The Catholic Truth Society published her *Thoughts for Creedless Women*. Her novel, *Lois*, appeared in the Catholic journal, *The Month*. These later works indicate the considerable degree to which Hickey rejected those women's causes to which she had committed herself at the start of her professional career.

300 *A Sculptor*

'A SCULPTOR!' 'He left no work to see!'
'A genius!' 'Wherein might his genius be?'
'A dead man!' 'Reverence for the dead
Must never blind to the truth,' ye said.

* * *

There was That within him which was divine;
But his soul was its prison, not its shrine;
And the fetter'd Thought could never, free,
Go forth in its strength and symmetry,

Though its prison-walls at its yearning cry
Trembled and shook exceedingly.—
Alas for the man whom God bids live,
And keep what he fain would die to give.

Ever with patient hand he sought
To give its due to his lovely Thought;
And day after day, the story tells,
He workt as one whom a god impels.

One watcht him ever, with eyes so deep
For love that no slumber knew nor sleep:
Fair in body and fair in mind,
True and patient and strong and kind.

The self-same arms had rockt their rest;
Their lips had drunk from the self-same breast;
And her mother, dying, had pray'd that she
Would her foster-brother's keeper be.

The woman her life's delight had deem'd
To work for him while the waiting seem'd
So long and dreary; and, ere 'twas o'er,
The wolf might be standing at the door:
So, having him thus in her heart, she said
The sister should be in the mother's stead.

But, seeing that she was fair and young,
And knowing the stranger's busy tongue,
She pray'd it would please him to confer
The shield of a husband's name on her.

And three days after the burial,
Through a dull rain driving slow and small,
Wet ground underfoot, grey sky overhead,
They walkt to the church and there were wed.

Man and wife, through the chilling rain,
They walkt to the sculptor's house again;
And the sculptor went upon his way
Just with the heart of yesterday,

As though, in a kind of somnambulism,
A priest had toucht with the sacred chrism
The lady given of God to be
Supreme in her grace and royalty,
And, waking, his brain refus'd to keep
The thought of what he had done in sleep.

Many a year had past away
Since Cecco and Lotta us'd to play
Together 'neath that blue sky of theirs,
And blest and were blest in their lovely pray'rs:—

I think you never would recognise
The baby lovers in any wise
In the quiet woman who goes to-day
Deep-soul'd, deep-eyed, on her daily way,
And the thin, dark man who, people say,
Is that strange Francesco da Fiesole,

Poor fool, who aspires to the artist's meed
But none has seen or shall see, indeed,
The fruit of the travail of his brain—
Thinking and toiling all in vain.

Fair was the woman's face, and sweet
Her voice, and swift were her noiseless feet,
And kind her hands; but her husband knew
Full little of her the fair and true.

To work when the dawn brake golden-fair;
At work when the stars of night shone there:
Forwatcht, forwearied at night and worn,
Yet eager to meet his work at morn.

Sometimes she whisper'd, half in fear,
'Rest for a little while, my dear.'
But he—'For the soul that God has blest
Only in perfect work is rest.'

'Yet rest is the truest work sometimes!
Out of the silence grow new rimes;
Out of the cool where shadows brood
Leaps up the soul in its strength renew'd.'
Then he smil'd, and the smile said wordlessly,
'*Woman, what have I to do with thee?*'

Hours, days, years, swept on, it may be,—
Which he knew not and car'd not, he,—
Art knows not Time but Eternity—
When a wonderful vision, great and sweet,
Came in the silence his soul to greet,
And, daz'd by the glory's sharp excess,
He fell in a deep unconsciousness,
With a cry that struck on her ear alone:
And the woman found him lying prone,
With his head at the base of a block of stone,
A shapeless, loveless thing he wrought,
A cenotaph of his wondrous thought.

She lifted him into the outside air,
And its breeze crept in and out of his hair,
Touching his face with a light caress,
As he lay enwrapt in the silentness.

And, just as the day had kiss'd the night,
He woke, and, with wide eyes full of light,
Lookt up to her face and murmur'd he,
'Thank God that at last through the mists I see
The star of my life arise on me.'

Oh, then the delight of sweet surprise
Glow'd in the depths of her tender eyes;
And something fairer than laughter lit
Her face with a smile most exquisite.

But not for her is that gladness deep,
And not for her are the words that leap
From his spirit's depths—'My glorious Art,
Who hast shrin'd thyself within my heart,

Pardon the weakness of earth that shrank
When the fiery draught of thy life I drank,
And teach my spirit to bear the stress
And awe of thy terrible loveliness:
As when, in the earth-sprung bush there glow'd,
And yet consum'd not its frail abode,
The awful light of the living God.'

He rose with a fresh-nerv'd energy,
And a new-born life within his eye—
'Oh, deep in my heart of hearts is writ
"Though the vision tarry, wait for it."'

So, when she brought him a wine-fill'd cup,
With flashing eyes he rais'd it up,
And dasht the red wine upon the floor,
For the strength of his hope sustain'd him more.

And, laughing, he said, 'the gods will bless
My work with an infinite success;
For the wine I have here pour'd out shall be
Libation paid unto them by me.'

But a tear was in the woman's eye,
And the thought swept over her mournfully,
As she lookt where the red stream slowly flow'd,
That its antitype was his heart's best blood.

She watcht outside the door all night,
Nor went away till the dawn of light;
And ceaselessly on her ear there broke
The ring of her husband's chisel-stroke.

And at dawn when, weary in heart and limb,
She carried the morning meal to him,
The ground was strewn with fragments white,
Where his hand had hewn at the block all night,
The block that seem'd to her eyes to grow
More shapeless and loveless at every blow.

But she saw his eyes as the eyes of a seer,
And he spoke, and her heart stood still to hear,
'It grows and grows beneath my touch—
O Art, thank God that I love thee much!

Not in the dull coarse clay will I shrine
The thought new-born from this soul of mine—
The stately marble's purity
At once shall its glorious temple be.

The beautiful wonder grows and grows—
I carve her as on my sight she rose,
Perfection and light the ministers
To wait on each motion and look of hers.

Ah, no mere lady of perfect mould
In her shall the gazer's eye behold;
The Godhead's splendour shall surely shine
In the lightest curve and the faintest line;
And my chisel shall loftily cxpress
That Beauty is one with Holiness.'

Oh, full on his face, as the woman went,
There glow'd the light of supreme content;
And silent she left him as, sharp and clear,
His chisel clasht on her heart and ear.

With quick, lithe step she climb'd the stair
To her room that was very bleak and bare,
Save that a rich fair robe was spread
In mocking splendour upon the bed,
Wrought with a delicate broidery
Of flower and leaf full daintily.

Many and many a weary hour
The woman had toil'd over leaf and flow'r,
For winner she of the daily bread
Wherewith her beloved one was fed.

She did not look on the broidery bright
That strain'd her eyes far into the night,
(Yet Love had made the task seem light)
But, panting as if in struggle fierce,
She tore off that sombre dress of hers,
And once, after years, was fain to free
The storm of her passionate agony.

But the early light of the morning fair
Smote full on a little mirror square,
And the woman's eye was caught, and lo!
She could not but see the lovely show:

The stately throat and the golden hair
That fell on the gleaming shoulders bare,
And the eyes that glisten'd with all the rush
Of tears, and the cheeks with their crimson flush.

She lookt and started amaz'd because
She saw how exceeding fair she was,
And cried with a cry of great despair,
'Alas! in vain am I made so fair,

For his life is utterly perishing
At the feet of that dreadful, shapeless thing
Which never can rise, in face or limb
To smile back the strength of his love on him.

O love, my love, who never wilt know
That I, thy wife, have lov'd thee so,
I would lie death-doom'd at thy sacred feet
To hear thee say but, *I love thee, Sweet*,

Wilt thou not open thine eyes to see
How good perfection can never be
If Nature and Art, which are its source,
Be torn from each other in grim divorce?'

Then sudden, with one great, gasping strain,
The woman regain'd her calm again,
And, when she laid down her work that night,
Her eyes were still and her cheek was white,
And never a face in the universe
More passion-free than that face of hers.

And, strong in the love whose wish and want
Is good for its darling, not to vaunt
Itself as that good's sole ministrant,
'Pray God that my husband see,' she said,
'The joy of his work accomplished.'

But sometimes the woman would sorely grieve,
As one who cannot, but would, believe:
As one who, in seeking, cannot find,
And dares to hope 'tis that he is blind.

And sometimes she brooded in dull unrest
O'er the knowledge hidden within her breast,
How some in visible form have wrought
The passion and glory of their thought,
While some in their souls, unseen must hold
What never in form can be shown or told.

* * *

The studio's door is open'd wide,
And he stands at a veiled statue's side:
The door is open'd wide and free,
For all may enter who choose and see.

As one unto whom the time doth bring
The joyful calm of the finishing,
He stands by the side of the unseen thing;
Stands calm and still with his face uprais'd,
As if on some light unseen he gaz'd.

His wife in silence holds her place
Close, close to him, with that marble face
As fair as the vision of perfectness
His soul has sobb'd and moan'd to express.

Marble-cold and marble-fair;
Is she the woman who wrestled there
Last night in the agony of prayer?
Marble-cold, and marble-pale,
She waiteth the loosing of the veil.

The veil is loost, and the sculptor's eye
Looks round in that moment's ecstasy,
With a dumb appeal for sympathy.
For, as pain dies down when hearts are there
To take and eat of the bitter fare,
So joy is half pain if none may share.

Still are they all for a little space,
And each one gazeth on other's face,
Then back to the thing that stands alone,
A thought—a work—or a block of stone.

A hush—and then, in the murmurs low,
She knows what it needeth not she know—
A march for the dead beat soft and slow;
For the great dead hope and the man who lies
With death on his heart and in his eyes.

What does it matter, silence or speech?
For there, on the height he never might reach,
His Thought, unshrin'd in the failure grim,
In terrible pathos looks at him.

* * *

The house is silent, the critics thence
Have past with pity and reverence,
And the woman is left alone to keep
Her watch by the man that God lets sleep.

Only once do his lips unclose
As he lies on her breast in deep repose:
Only the murmur'd name, the dear
Pet-name unheard for many a year,

Lotta!—the dying man to-day
Is Ceccolino again, at play
With his little comrade among the flow'rs
And hopes and joys of the long-ago hours.

* * *

'What is the moral?' ye ask me—this
I offer, tell me whether it is.
The earth all quick with the diamond's soul
In its throes oft bears but the formless coal,
So close of kin to the perfect gem
That is meet for a kingly diadem.

This is no moral! why fail'd the man?
Ay, tell me that, if ye only can.
Why and wherefore I know not, I,
Nor take upon me the mystery
Of things, as if I were God's spy.

Think ye God answers *no* or *yes*
To men as they idly guess and guess,
'If he had lov'd or if—'?—that *If*
Is God's undecipher'd hieroglyph.

(1881)

301 *A Weak-Minded Woman's Comparisons*

WELL, with whom shall I compare you, seeing, O my lief and dear,
How to one (weak-minded!) woman you are just without a peer?
Nay, there is no need to tell me; for I know you deprecate,
Proving thus at least your greatness, anyone should call you great.
What, sir? 'tis the sheerest nonsense, well I know?
I'll not contradict your worship! Be it so!

Only I have caught you now, and do not mean to let you stir
Till I've told you things that, maybe, you will laugh at, frown at, sir.
Ay, comparisons are odious! so, in very sooth, they are!
You shall be compared with—whom then? no one in particular!
Just another—quite impersonal, you know—
For convenience, any other; be it so!

I would rather have your tempest than another's radiant calm;
I would rather you should wound me than another bring me balm;
I would rather take your blame than praise from any other one;
Rather go in the dark with you than with another in the sun.
It's the very height of foolishness, I know;
But (consider I'm weak-minded!) it is so.

I would rather have your weakness than their strength men call the strong:
Let them do their rightest right, and I would rather have your wrong:
Wrong or right, my soul's beloved, yea, whatever you may do,
All my faith is clasped around you, and my whole soul loveth you.
That's the height of immorality, I know;
All the same, and notwithstanding, it is so!

But away with over-earnest; let us back to dainty jest!
Is the jest, or is the earnest, tell me, dear my lord, the best?
Is it very gracious fooling, or the way of love to me,
Who am no enfranchised woman of the twentieth century,
But a poor weak-minded creature, and, you know,
'Tis no more, as some one says, *no more but so*.

(1891)

LUCY KNOX
(1845–1884)

CLAIMED as an Irish poet (possibly second generation Irish), Lucy Knox was the daughter of Ellen (neé Frere) and the Honourable Edmond Spring Rice. In 1866 she married Octavius Henry Knox.

Her first book of poetry, *Sonnets and Other Poems* (1872), was privately printed and sold by the author through Foynes of Ireland. Another edition was published in 1876. This was followed by her only other volume, *Four Pictures from a Life and Other Poems*, in 1884, which was dedicated to her 'friend and sister', Alice Spring Rice, and includes some poetry translated from Italian and German.

302 *Sonnet. A Cry to Men*

SAY to men, women starve, and will they heed?
Say to them women drudge and faint and die
And sin, discrowning womanhood for aye;
Beseech men piteously to mind their need
Of wisdom, who must little children feed;
Implore them for her sake who stands on high
Enthroned, yet nestled in each heart, to try
If those (her sisters) may be saved indeed;
Saved from starvation, saved from overstrain,
Bloom ere they fade, not wither incomplete,
So low, so fall'n, such dust beneath the feet!
Say this to man, and wilt thou speak in vain?
Time, like a mist, thine answer from thee veils,
Yet cry, weak voice; cry while thy strength avails!

(1872)

303 *Sonnet. Lament of the Loyal Irish, 1869*

ENGLAND, that once with hard averted eyes
Strode on her way with Ireland chained behind,
Now throws towards her sister glances kind,
And turns an unreluctant ear to cries
Which, strengthening with her strength, from Ireland rise:
For chains she proffers ties that better bind,
And her remorse breeds Ireland's better mind.
Something is gained—how much beyond there lies!
O Ireland! wert thou moderate and wise,
Prompt to join England, give her honour due,

And as her acts are, were thy feelings new—
What gain were this? A clamorous few disguise
Your sentiments; before the world you stand
A Fool who dares not do the folly planned.

(1872)

EMILY LAWLESS
(1845–1913)

BORN in Gomshall, Surrey, Emily Lawless would become a poet noted for her work on Irish history. She was the eldest of eight children born into an aristocratic family. Her father was Edward Lawless, third Baron of Cloncurry. Her mother, Elizabeth Kirwan, was a noted society beauty. There was considerable domestic unhappiness. In 1859, her father committed suicide, with two of her sisters rapidly doing the same. Much of her early life was spent on the family estates, at her mother's, Castlehacket in County Galway, and at her father's in County Kildare. It was in the 1880s that she began to publish fiction. Her first two novels, *A Chelsea Householder* (1882) and *A Millionaire's Cousin* (1885), were brought out anonymously. Success came with later novels on Irish themes, such as *Hurrish* (1886), which was acclaimed by Gladstone for its insights into the struggle for Home Rule. Her most popular work was *Grania* (1892), set on Aran. Lawless found favour with two notable conservative women novelists of the period, Margaret Oliphant and Mrs Humphry Ward. In 1887, she published a history of Ireland, which was well received. Later, in 1904, she completed a life of the Irish novelist, Maria Edgeworth. Her achievements were acknowledged by the University of Dublin, which awarded her an honorary doctorate in 1905.

Lawless produced several volumes of poetry, including *With the Wild Geese* (1892) and *The Inalienable Heritage*, published posthumously in 1914. Having become disenchanted with Irish politics at the turn of the century, she spent her declining years in Surrey, with her companion, Lady Sarah Spencer.

304 *After Aughrim*

SHE said, 'They gave me of their best,
They lived, they gave their lives for me;
I tossed them to the howling waste,
And flung them to the foaming sea.'

She said, 'I never gave them aught,
Not mine the power, if mine the will;
I let them starve, I let them bleed,—
They bled and starved, and loved me still.'

She said, 'Ten times they fought for me,
Ten times they strove with might and main,
Ten times I saw them beaten down,
Ten times they rose, and fought again.'

She said, 'I stayed alone at home,
A dreary woman, grey and cold;
I never asked them how they fared,
Yet still they loved me as of old.'

She said, 'I never called them sons,
I almost ceased to breathe their name,
Then caught it echoing down the wind,
Blown backwards from the lips of Fame.'

She said, 'Not mine, not mine that fame;
Far over sea, far over land,
Cast forth like rubbish from my shores,
They won it yonder, sword in hand.'

She said, 'God knows they owe me nought,
I tossed them to the foaming sea,
I tossed them to the howling waste,
Yet still their love comes home to me.'

(1902)

MICHAEL FIELD
(KATHERINE HARRIS BRADLEY, 1846–1914, AND EDITH EMMA COOPER, 1862–1913)

NEITHER a pseudonym nor a mask, Michael Field was the name under which two writers collaborated on an extensive body of poetry and drama. They were aunt and niece. Born in Birmingham, Katherine Bradley was the daughter of a tobacco manufacturer. In 1861, she and her mother joined her married elder sister, Emma Cooper, at Kenilworth, Warwickshire. Emma became seriously unwell during her second pregnancy, remaining an invalid after the birth of her daughter, Amy. Thereafter, Katherine was devoted to the elder daughter Edith, passing on her considerable learning to her niece. Educated at Newnham College, Cambridge, in 1868, and later at the Collège de France in Paris, Bradley for some years kept up an ultimately turbulent correspondence with John Ruskin; in 1875, she subscribed to his Guild of St George, only to discover that he disapproved of the campaign of women's suffrage and her declared atheism. At this time, she encouraged Edith in the pursuit of higher education when the family moved to Stoke Bishop, Bristol, in 1878. There they attended classes in classics and philosophy at the University College, where they were actively involved in the debating society, arguing strongly in favour of votes for women. Bradley was prominent in the local Anti-Vivisection Society until 1887. During this period, they began to publish poetry, much of which reflects their scholarly interests.

Bradley's first volume, *The New Minnesinger*, was by her own hand alone, and published under the name of Arran Leigh in 1875. Their first joint volume, *Bellerophôn*, came out in 1881, this time under the names of Arran and Isla Leigh. It was only with *Calirrhoë, and Fair Rosamund* (1884) that Michael Field first made his name in public, and well over twenty volumes were completed before he passed away with them. Their most intensive period of writing occurred after 1888, when they moved to Reigate, cutting themselves off from many friends and family. Having independent means, they travelled widely, meeting Robert Browning in his last years at Asolo, Italy. In addition, they came to know a number of prominent members of the literary establishment, including Arthur Symons. Significant acquaintances were George Meredith, Herbert Spencer, and Oscar Wilde. Such contacts informed their writing, which was increasingly associated with literary aestheticism in the 1880s and then with the mood of literary decadence. Since *Stephania* (1892), *Sight and Song* (1892), *A Question of Memory* (1893), and *Attila, My Attila!* (1896) were issued by Elkin Mathews and John Lane, they belonged to a publisher's list that included some of the major poets of the Victorian *fin de siècle*. One powerful influence on their writing was the critic and essayist, Walter Pater, whom they heard lecture in 1889. But they were sufficiently displeased with the sensual nature of *The Yellow Book*, an avant-garde periodical published by John Lane's Bodley Head, that they were moved to withdraw a poem by Michael Field that it had accepted in 1894. Their friendship with the artist, Charles Ricketts, began in 1892, and he decorated several of their later volumes. It was Ricketts who encouraged them to move from Reigate to Richmond in 1899, where they remained until the time of their deaths.

Although Michael Field's earliest work was celebrated for its pagan quality, bearing some comparison with Algernon Charles Swinburne's use of classical myth, Bradley and Cooper converted to Roman Catholicism in the spring of 1907, under the influence of Father John Gray. Much of their late work is religious. But it is for their earlier volumes, such as *Underneath the Bough* (1893), that Michael Field is valued. The most significant collection, in this respect, is *Long Ago* (1889), which rewrites the legend of Sappho. Michael Field was influenced by Henry Thornton Wharton's controversial translation of the classical poet's fragments, which for the first time indicated that Sappho's love was directed at women as well as men. A selection from their copious journals, kept from 1888 to 1914, was edited by T. Sturge Moore in 1933. The complete manuscript of their journals is held by the British Library, and researchers have in recent years examined its contents to consider the question of Sapphic eroticism in their life and writings.

305 Long Ago, *XVII*

Πλήρης μεν ἐφυινεϵ́ ά σελάννα,
αὶ ὄώζ περί βῶμον εστύθησαν[1]

A. *Παρθενια, παρθενια, ποί με λιποισ οίχυ*
B. *Ούκίτι ἥξω πρὸζ σι, οὐκέτι ἥξω*[2]

THE moon rose full: the women stood
As though within a sacred wood
Around an altar—thus with awe
The perfect, virgin orb they saw
Supreme above them; and its light
Fell on their limbs and garments white.
Then with pale, lifted brows they stirred
Their fearful steps at Sappho's word,
And in a circle moved around,
Responsive to her music's sound,
That through the silent air stole on,
Until their breathless dread was gone,
And they could dance with lightsome feet,
And lift the song with voices sweet.
Then once again the silence came:
Their lips were blanched as if with shame
That they in maidenhood were bold
Its sacred worship to unfold;
And Sappho touched the lyre alone,
Until she made the bright strings moan.
She called to Artemis aloud—
Alas, the moon was wrapt in cloud!—
'Oh, whither art thou gone from me?
Come back again, virginity!
For maidenhood still do I long,
The freedom and the joyance strong
Of that most blessèd, secret state
That makes the tenderest maiden great.
O moon, be fair to me as these,
And my regretful passion ease,
Restore to me my only good,
My maidenhood, my maidenhood!'
She sang: and through the clouded night
An answer came of cruel might—

[1] 'The moon was shining full, and they [feminine] stood as round an altar', Sappho fr. 53. Lobel, E. and Page, D., *Poetarum Lesbiorum Fragmenta*, fr. 154, 2nd edn (Oxford, 1963). Eds.

[2] A. 'Maidenhead, maidenhead, whither are thou gone from me?' B. 'I shall nevermore come to thee, I shall nevermore come.' Sappho fr. 109. Label, E. and Page, D., *Poetarum Lesbiorum Fragmenta*, fr. 114, 2nd edn (Oxford, 1963). Eds.

'To thee I never come again.'
O Sappho, bitter was thy pain!
Then did thy heavy steps retire,
And leave, moon-bathed, the virgin quire.

(1889)

306 Long Ago, *XXXV*

'Αλλα, μὴ μεγαλύνεο δακτυλίω πέρι[1]

COME, Gorgo, put the rug in place,
  And passionate recline;
I love to see thee in thy grace,
  Dark, virulent, divine.
But wherefore thus thy proud eyes fix
  Upon a jewelled band?
Art thou so glad the sardonyx
  Becomes thy shapely hand?

Bethink thee! 'Tis for such as thou
  Zeus leaves his lofty seat;
'Tis at thy beauty's bidding how
  Man's mortal life shall fleet;
Those fairest hands—dost thou forget
  Their power to thrill and cling?
O foolish woman, dost thou set
  Thy pride upon a ring?

(1889)

307 Long Ago, *LIV*

...Τάδε νῦν ἐταίραιζ
τῖζ ἔμαισι τέρπνα κάλωζ ἀείσω'[2]

ADOWN the Lesbian vales,
When spring first flashes out,
I watch the lovely rout
Of maidens flitting 'mid the honey-bees
For thyme and heath,
Cistus, and trails

[1] 'But do not put on airs for the sake of a ring', Sappho fr. 35. Lobel, E. and Page, D., *Poetarum Lesbiorum Fragmenta*, fr. 5. 1, 2nd edn (Oxford, 1963). Eds.

[2] 'I shall now sing these pleasing things well for my [female] companions', Sappho fr. 11. Lobel, E. and Page, D., *Poetarum Lesbiorum Fragmenta*, fr. 160, 2nd edn (Oxford, 1963). Eds.

Of myrtle-wreath:
They bring me these
My passionate, unsated sense to please.

In turn, to please my maids,
Most deftly will I sing
Of their soft cherishing
In apple-orchards with cool waters by,
Where slumber streams
From quivering shades,
And Cypris seems
To bend and sigh,
Her golden calyx offering amorously.

What praises would be best
Wherewith to crown my girls?
The rose when she unfurls
Her balmy, lighted buds is not so good,
So fresh as they
When on my breast
They lean, and say
All that they would,
Opening their glorious, candid maidenhood.

To that pure band alone
I sing of marriage-loves;
As Aphrodite's doves
Glance in the sun their colour comes and goes:
No girls let fall
Their maiden zone
At Hymen's call
Serene as those
Taught by a poet why sweet Hesper glows.

(1889)

308 *Spring. Sandro Botticelli. The Accademia of Florence*

VENUS is sad among the wanton powers,
That make delicious tempest in the hours
Of April or are reckless with their flowers:
Through umbrageous orange-trees
Sweeps, mid azure swirl, the Breeze,
That with clipping arms would seize
Eôs, wind-inspired and mad,
In wind-tightened muslin clad,

With one tress for stormy wreath
And a bine between her teeth.
Flora foots it near in frilled,
Vagrant skirt, with roses filled,
Pinks and gentians spot her robe
And the curled acanthus-lobe
Edges intricate her sleeve;
Rosy briars a girdle weave,
Blooms are brooches in her hair:
Though a vision debonair,
Thriftless, venturesome, a grace
Disingenuous lights her face;
Curst she is, uncertain-lipped,
Riggishly her dress is whipped
By little gusts fantastic. Will she deign
To toss her double-roses, or refrain?

These riot by the left side of the queen;
Before her face another group is seen:
In ordered and harmonic nobleness,
Three maidens circle o'er the turf—each dress
Blown round the tiptoe shape in lovely folds
Of air-invaded white; one comrade holds
Her fellow's hand on high, the foremost links
Their other hands in chain that lifts and sinks.
Their auburn tresses ripple, coil or sweep;
Gems, amulets and fine ball-fringes keep
Their raiment from austereness. With reserve
The dancers in a garland slowly curve.
They are the Graces in their virgin youth;
And does it touch their Deity with ruth
That they must fade when Eros speeds his dart?
Is this the grief and forethought of her heart?

For she is sad, although fresh myrtles near
Her figure chequer with their leaves the drear,
Grey chinks that through the orange-trees appear:
Clothed in spring-time's white and red,
She is tender with some dread,
As she turns a musing head
Sideways mid her veil demure;
Her wide eyes have no allure,
Dark and heavy with their pain.
She would bless, and yet in vain
Is her troubled blessing: Love,
Blind and tyrannous above,
Shoots his childish flame to mar
Those without defect, who are

Yet unspent and cold with peace;
While, her sorrow to increase,
Hermes, leader of her troop—
His short cutlass on the loop
Of a crimson cloak, his eye
Clear in its fatality—
Rather seems the guide of ghosts
To the dead, Plutonian coasts,
Than herald of Spring's immature, gay band:
He plucks a ripened orange with his hand.

The tumult and the mystery of earth,
When woods are bleak and flowers have sudden birth,
When love is cruel, follow to their end
The God that teaches Shadows to descend,
But pauses now awhile, with solemn lip
And left hand laid victorious on his hip.
The triumph of the year without avail
Is blown to Hades by blue Zephyr's gale.
Across the seedling herbage coltsfoot grows
Between the tulip, heartsease, strawberry-rose,
Fringed pinks and dull grape-hyacinth. Alas,
At play together, through the speckled grass
Trip Youth and April: Venus, looking on,
Beholds the mead with all the dancers gone.

(1892)

309 *The Rescue. Tintoretto. The Dresden Gallery*

GREY tower, green sea, dark armour and clear curves
Of shining flesh; the tower built far into the sea
And the dark armour that of one coming to set her free
Who, white against the chamfered base,
From fetters that her noble limbs enlace
Bows to confer
Herself on her deliverer:
He, dazzled by the splendid gift,
Steadies himself against his oar, ere he is strong to lift
And strain her to his breast:
Her powerful arms lie in such heavy rest
Across his shoulder, though he swerves
And staggers with her weight, though the wave buoys,
Then slants the vessel, she maintains his form in poise.

Her sister-captive, seated on the side
Of the swayed gondola, her arched, broad back in strain,
Strikes her right ankle, eager to discumber it of chain,
  Intent upon her work, as though
  It were full liberty ungyved to go.
    She will not halt,
  But spring delighted to the salt,
When fetterless her ample form
Can beat the refluence of the waves back to their crested storm.
  Has she indeed caught sight
Of that blithe tossing pinnace on the white
  Scum of the full, up-bearing tide?
The rose-frocked rower-boy, in absent fit
Or modesty, surveys his toe and smiles at it.

Her bondage irks not; *she* has very truth
Of freedom who within her lover's face can seek
For answer to her eyes, her breath, the blood within her cheek—
  A soul so resolute to bless
  She has forgot her shining nakedness
    And to her peer
  Presents immunity from fear:
As one half-overcome, half-braced,
The man's hand searches as he grips her undulating waist:
  So these pure twain espouse
And without ravishment, mistrust, or vows
  Of constancy fulfil their youth;
In the rough niches of the wall behind
Their meeting heads, how close the trails of ivy wind!

(1892)

310 *Saint Sebastian. Antonello da Messina. The Dresden Gallery*

YOUNG Sebastian stands beside a lofty tree,
Rigid by the rigid trunk that branchlessly
  Lifts its column on the blue
  Of a heaven that takes
    Hyacinthine hue
  From a storm that wellnigh breaks.

Shadiness and thunder dout the zenith's light,
Yet a wide horizon still extends as bright
  As the lapis-lazuli;
  Poignant sunshine streams
    Over land and sky,
  With tempestuous, sunken beams.

He who was a soldier late is standing now
Stript and fastened to the tree that has no bough,
In the centre of a court,
That is bound by walls
Fancifully wrought,
Over which the daylight falls.

Arch and chimney rise aloft into the air:
On the balconies are hung forth carpets rare
Of an Eastern, vivid red;
Idle women lean
Where the rugs are spread,
Each with an indifferent mien.

On the marble of the courtyard, fast asleep,
Lies a brutish churl, his body in a heap;
Two hard-hearted comrades prate
Where a portal shows
Distance blue and great,
Stretching onward in repose.

And between the shafts of sandy-coloured tone
Slips a mother with her child: but all alone
Stays Sebastian in his grief.
What soul pities him!
Who shall bring relief
From the darts that pierce each limb?

Naked, almost firm as sculpture, is his form,
Nobly set below the burthen of the storm;
Shadow, circling chin and cheek,
Their ellipse defines,
Then the shade grows weak
And his face with noonday shines—

Shines as olive marble that reflects the mere
Radiance it receives upon a surface clear;
For we see no blessedness
On his visage pale,
Turned in its distress
Toward the heaven, without avail.

Massive is his mouth; the upper lip is set
In a pained, protesting curve: his eyes have met
God within the darkening sky
And dispute His will,
Dark, remorselessly
Fervent to dispute it still.

The whole brow is hidden by the chestnut hair,
That behind the back flows down in locks and there
Changes to a deeper grain.
Though his feet were strong,
They are swoln with strain,
For he has been standing long.

Captive, stricken through by darts, yet armed with power
That resents the coming on of its last hour,
Sound in muscle is the boy,
Whom his manhood fills
With an acrid joy,
Whom its violent pressure thrills.

But this force implanted in him must be lost
And its natural validity be crossed
By a chill, disabling fate;
He must stand at peace
While his hopes abate,
While his youth and vigour cease.

At his feet a mighty pillar lies reversed;
So the virtue of his sex is shattered, cursed:
Here is martyrdom and not
In the arrows' sting;
This the bitter lot
His soul is questioning.

He, with body fresh for use, for pleasure fit,
With its energies and needs together knit
In an able exigence,
Must endure the strife,
Final and intense,
Of necessity with life.

Yet throughout this bold rebellion of the saint
Noonday's brilliant air has carried no complaint.
Lo, across the solitude
Of the storm two white,
Little clouds obtrude
Storm-accentuating light!

(1892)

311 *A Pen-Drawing of Leda. Sodoma. The Grand Duke's Palace at Weimar*

'TIS Leda lovely, wild and free,
Drawing her gracious Swan down through the grass to see
Certain round eggs without a speck:
One hand plunged in the reeds and one dinting the downy neck,
Although his hectoring bill
Gapes toward her tresses,
She draws the fondled creature to her will.

She joys to bend in the live light
Her glistening body toward her love, how much more bright!
Though on her breast the sunshine lies
And spreads its affluence on the wide curves of her waist and thighs,
To her meek, smitten gaze
Where her hand presses
The Swan's white neck sink Heaven's concentred rays.

(1892)

312 *The Sleeping Venus. Giorgione. The Dresden Gallery*

HERE is Venus by our homes
And resting on the verdant swell
Of a soft country flanked with mountain domes:
She has left her archèd shell,
Has left the barren wave that foams,
Amid earth's fruitful tilths to dwell.
Nobly lighted while she sleeps
As sward-lands or the corn-field sweeps,
Pure as are the things that man
Needs for life and using can
Never violate nor spot—
Thus she slumbers in no grot.
But on open ground,
With the great hill-sides around.

And her body has the curves,
The same extensive smoothness seen
In yonder breadths of pasture, in the swerves
Of the grassy mountain-green
That for her propping pillow serves:
There is a sympathy between

Her and Earth of largest reach,
For the sex that forms them each
Is a bond, a holiness,
That unconsciously must bless
And unite them, as they lie
Shameless underneath the sky
A long, opal cloud
Doth in noontide haze enshroud.

O'er her head her right arm bends;
And from the elbow raised aloft
Down to the crossing knees a line descends
Unimpeachable and soft
As the adjacent slope that ends
In chequered plain of hedge and croft.
Circular as lovely knolls,
Up to which a landscape rolls
With desirous sway, each breast
Rises from the level chest,
One in contour, one in round—
Either exquisite, low mound
Firm in shape and given
To the August warmth of heaven.

With bold freedom of incline,
With an uttermost repose,
From hip to herbage-cushioned foot the line
Of her left leg stretching shows
Against the turf direct and fine,
Dissimilar in grace to those
Little bays that in and out
By the ankle wind about;
Or that shallow bend, the right
Curled-up knee has brought to sight
Underneath its bossy rise,
Where the loveliest shadow lies!
Charmèd umbrage rests
On her neck and by her breasts.

Her left arm remains beside
The plastic body's lower heaves,
Controlled by them, as when a river-side
With its sandy margin weaves
Deflections in a lenient tide;
Her hand the thigh's tense surface leaves,
Falling inward. Not even sleep
Dare invalidate the deep,
Universal pleasure sex

Must unto itself annex—
Even the stillest sleep; at peace,
More profound with rest's increase,
She enjoys the good
Of delicious womanhood.

Cheek and eyebrow touch the fold
Of the raised arm that frames her hair,
Her braided hair in colour like to old
Copper glinting here and there:
While through her skin of olive-gold
The scarce carnations mount and share
Faultlessly the oval space
Of her temperate, grave face.
Eyelids underneath the day
Wrinkle as full buds that stay,
Through the tranquil, summer hours,
Closed although they might be flowers;
The red lips shut in
Gracious secrets that begin.

On white drapery she sleeps,
That fold by fold is stained with shade;
Her mantle's ruddy pomegranate in heaps
For a cushion she has laid
Beneath her; and the glow that steeps
Its grain of richer depth is made
By an overswelling bank,
Tufted with dun grasses rank.
From this hillock's outer heaves
One small bush defines its leaves
Broadly on the sober blue
The pale cloud-bank rises to,
Whilst it sinks in bland
Sunshine on the distant land.

Near her resting-place are spread,
In deep or greener-lighted brown,
Wolds, that half-withered by the heat o'erhead,
Press up to a little town
Of castle, archway, roof and shed,
Then slope in grave continuance down:
On their border, in a group,
Trees of brooding foliage droop
Sidelong; and a single tree
Springs with bright simplicity,
Central from the sunlit plain.
Of a blue no flowers attain,

On the fair, vague sky
Adamantine summits lie.

And her resting is so strong
That while we gaze it seems as though
She had lain thus the solemn glebes among
In the ages far ago
And would continue, till the long,
Last evening of Earth's summer glow
In communion with the sweet
Life that ripens at her feet:
We can never fear that she
From Italian fields will flee,
For she does not come from far,
She is of the things that are;
And she will not pass
While the sun strikes on the grass.

(1892)

ALICE MEYNELL
(1847–1922)

Alice Meynell's reputation as a poet was so considerable during her lifetime that she was nominated twice, in 1895 and in 1913, for the post of Poet Laureate. She grew up with her parents and her sister Elizabeth in privileged circumstances, and received a quite scholastic education from their father, Thomas Thompson. Her mother was Christiana Weller. By the terms of his inheritance, Thomas Thompson was prohibited from undertaking paid employment. Strongly interested in the arts, the Thompson family travelled widely in France, Italy, and Switzerland. In England, Meynell spent some of her childhood at Prestbury, near Cheltenham, and later at Bonchurch, on the Isle of Wight. Her family moved to London in 1864. At this time, Meynell became particularly concerned with questions of conscience, and with the pressing issue of useful work for middle-class women. Her earliest poetry dates from these years. In her diary for 1865, she noted: 'Whatever I write will be melancholy and self-conscious as all women's poems are.'

By her late teens, while searching for a moral code to guide her in life, Meynell decided to follow her mother into the Roman Catholic church. Much of her subsequent career would be put into the service of fostering a Roman Catholic literary community through her extensive editorial work on several periodicals. As a young woman, her artistic endeavours—like those of her sister—were obviously not inhibited by her unusual family environment. While Alice Thompson was developing her work as a poet, Elizabeth Thompson was gaining a considerable reputation as a war artist. Later known as Lady Butler, this artist attracted attention with her well-known painting, *Roll Call*, exhibited at the Royal Academy in 1874. Three years later, as A. C. Thompson, the poet published her first collection, *Preludes*, illustrated by her sister. This volume drew the praise of Aubrey De Vere, John Ruskin, and Alfred Tennyson; it contained several lyrics and monologues that Meynell later decided not to reprint.

In 1877, through her marriage to Wilfrid Meynell, she embarked on a demanding professional and personal life. The Meynells' first joint editorial venture was *Pen: A Journal of Literature*, which ran to only seven issues in 1880. Far more successful were the *Weekly Register* (1881–99) and the literary magazine, *Merry England*, established in 1883. Throughout the 1870s, she moved in influential Roman Catholic circles, meeting society hostesses such as Lady Londonderry, Lady Herbert of Lea, and Lady Georgiana Fullerton. Two significant, if difficult, friendships developed with Catholic poets of high standing. One was with the elderly Coventry Patmore, who became close to her in 1892. Since several years later they were no longer communicating, it is possible that his enthusiasm for her was perhaps more than she could bear. At around the same time, she and her spouse came to the rescue of Francis Thompson (remembered for 'The Hound of Heaven'), whose opium addiction had almost destroyed his life. Among her most cherished friends was the poet and novelist, Katharine Tynan.

Although bearing seven children between 1878 and 1891, Meynell worked solidly as a professional author. The quantity of work she produced during the course of he marriage was phenomenal. She was an indefatigable writer of essays and reviews, which regularly appeared in leading journals, including the *National Observer*, the *Pall Mall Gazette*, and the *Spectator*. In 1897, she became President of the Society of Women Journalists. During the 1890s, she published a rapid stream of essays and monographs, including *The Rhythm of Life* (1893), *William Holman Hunt: His Life and Work* (with William Farrar, 1893), *The Colours of Life* (1896), *The Spirit of Place* (1898), and *John Ruskin* (1899). Domestic and professional obligations had prevented Alice Meynell and Wilfrid Meynell from enjoying time to themselves. In 1900, they took their first holiday together, in Italy. In coming years, she was able to travel widely, returning to parts of Europe she had first visited as a child. For several months in 1901–2, she undertook a lecture tour of the United States. After 1911, Meynell became involved in the non-militant wing of the suffrage movement.

Until her death in 1922, Meynell's output never ceased to flow, and her reputation as an essayist was exceptionally high. *Ceres' Runaway and Other Essays* appeared in 1909, selected *Essays* in 1914, and *The Second Person Singular* in 1921. Although always esteemed as a poet, the number of collections she brought out was relatively sparse. Eighteen years passed after *Preludes* (1875) until her second volume, *Poems*, was published. *Other Poems* followed in 1896, and *Later Poems* in 1902. During the First World War, Meynell's pacifism emerged clearly in her poetry, the most notable being the title poem in *A Father of Women* (1917). Her later years were spent at the family home at Greatham, near Storrington, Sussex. *Last Poems* was issued posthumously in 1923.

313 *In Autumn*

In ramo più non può foglia tenersi.
Lorenzo de'Medici

Alors je te plaindrai, pauvre âme.
Victor Hugo

THE leaves are many under my feet,
  And drift one way.
Their scent of death is weary and sweet.
  A flight of them is in the grey
Where sky and forest meet.

The low winds moan for dead sweet years;
  The birds sing all for pain,
Of a common thing, to weary ears,—
  Only a summer's fate of rain,
And a woman's fate of tears.

I walk to love and life alone
  Over these mournful places,
Across the summer overthrown,
  The dead joys of these silent faces,
To claim my own.

I know his heart has beat to bright
  Sweet loves gone by.
I know the leaves that die to-night
  Once budded to the sky,
And I shall die to his delight.

O leaves, so quietly ending now,
  You have heard cuckoos sing.
And I will grow upon my bough
  If only for a Spring,
And fall when the rain is on my brow.

O tell me, tell me ere you die,
  Is it worth the pain?
You bloomed so fair, you waved so high;
  Now that the sad days wane,
Are you repenting where you lie?

I lie amongst you, and I kiss
  Your fragrance mouldering.
O dead delights, is it such bliss,
  That tuneful Spring?
Is love so sweet, that comes to this?

O dying blisses of the year,
 I hear the young lamb bleat,
The clamouring birds i' the copse I hear,
 I hear the waving wheat,
Together laid on a dead-leaf bier.

Kiss me again as I kiss you;
 Kiss me again;
For all your tuneful nights of dew,
 In this your time of rain,
For all your kisses when Spring was new.

You will not, broken hearts; let be.
 I pass across your death
To a golden summer you shall not see,
 And in your dying breath
There is no benison for me.

There is an Autumn yet to wane,
 There are leaves yet to fall,
Which when I kiss, may kiss again,
 And, pitied, pity me all for all,
And love me in mist and rain.

(1875)

314 *A Letter from a Girl to Her Own Old Age*

Lete vedrai
Dante

LISTEN, and when thy hand this paper presses,
O time-worn woman, think of her who blesses
What thy thin fingers touch, with her caresses.

O mother, for a weight of years do break thee!
O daughter, for slow time must yet awake thee,
And from the changes of my heart must make thee.

O fainting traveller, morn is grey in heaven.
Dost thou remember how the clouds were driven?
And are they calm about the fall of even?

Pause near the ending of thy long migration,
For this one sudden hour of desolation
Appeals to one hour of thy meditation.

Suffer, O silent one, that I remind thee
Of the great hills that storm the sky behind thee,
Of the wild winds of power that have resigned thee.

Know that the mournful plain where thou must wander,
Is but a grey and silent world, but ponder
The misty mountains of the morning yonder.

Listen; the mountain winds with rain were fretting,
And sudden gleams the mountain-tops besetting.
I cannot let thee fade to death, forgetting.

What part of this wild heart of mine I know not
Will follow with thee where the great winds blow not,
And where the young flowers of the mountain grow not.

Yet let my letter with thy lost thoughts in it
Tell what the way was when thou didst begin it,
And win with thee the goal when thou shalt win it.

Oh, in some hour of thine my thoughts shall guide thee.
Suddenly, though time, darkness, silence hide thee,
This wind from thy lost country flits beside thee;

Telling thee: all thy memories moved the maiden,
With thy regrets was morning over-shaden,
With sorrow thou hast left, her life was laden.

But whither shall my thoughts turn to pursue thee?
Life changes, and the years and days renew thee.
Oh, Nature brings my straying heart unto thee.

Her winds will join us, with their constant kisses
Upon the evening as the morning tresses,
Her summers breathe the same unchanging blisses.

And we, so altered in our shifting phases,
Track one another 'mid the many mazes
By the eternal child-breath of the daisies.

I have not writ this letter of divining
To make a glory of thy silent pining.
A triumph of thy mute and strange declining.

Only one youth, and the bright life was shrouded.
Only one morning, and the day was clouded.
And one old age with all regrets is crowded.

Oh, hush; oh, hush! Thy tears my words are steeping.
Oh, hush, hush, hush! So full, the fount of weeping?
Poor eyes, so quickly moved, so near to sleeping?

Pardon the girl; such strange desires beset her.
Poor woman, lay aside the mournful letter
That breaks thy heart; the one that wrote, forget her.

The one that now thy faded features guesses,
With filial fingers thy grey hair caresses,
With morning tears thy mournful twilight blesses.

(1875)

315 *'Soeur Monique'. A Rondeau by Couperin*

QUIET form of silent nun,
What has given you to my inward eyes?
What has marked you, unknown one,
In the throngs of centuries
That mine ears do listen through?
This old master's melody
That expresses you,
This admired simplicity,
Tender, with a serious wit,
And two words, the name of it,
'Soeur Monique'.

And if sad the music is,
It is sad with mysteries
Of a small immortal thing
That the passing ages sing,—
Simple music making mirth
Of the dying and the birth
Of the people of the earth.

No, not sad; we are beguiled,
Sad with living as we are;
Ours the sorrow, outpouring
Sad self on a selfless thing,
As our eyes and hearts are mild
With our sympathy for Spring,
With a pity sweet and wild
For the innocent and far,
With our sadness in a star,
Or our sadness in a child.

But two words, and this sweet air.
        Soeur Monique,
Had he more, who set you there?
Was his music-dream of you
Of some perfect nun he knew,
Or of some ideal, as true?

And I see you where you stand
With your life held in your hand
As a rosary of days.
And your thoughts in calm arrays,
And your innocent prayers are told
On your rosary of days.
And the young days and the old
With their quiet prayers did meet
When the chaplet was complete.

Did it vex you, the surmise
Of this wind of words, this storm of cries.
  Though you kept the silence so
  In the storms of long ago,
  And you keep it, like a star?
  —Of the evils triumphing,
Strong, for all your perfect conquering,
  Silenced conqueror that you are?
And I wonder at your peace, I wonder.
Would it trouble you to know,
O sweet soul, the world and sin
By your calm feet trodden under
          Long ago,
Living now, mighty to win?
And your feet are vanished like the snow.

Vanished; but the poet, he
In whose dream your face appears,
He who ranges unknown years
With your music in his heart,
Speaks to you familiarly
Where you keep apart,
And invents you as you were.
And your picture, oh, my nun,
Is a strangely easy one,
For the holy weed you wear,
For your hidden eyes and hidden hair,
And in picturing you I may
Scarcely go astray.

Oh, the vague reality!
The mysterious certainty!
Oh, strange truth of these my guesses
In the wide thought-wildernesses!
—Truth of one divined of many flowers;
Of one raindrop in the showers
Of the longago swift rain;
Of one tear of many tears

In some world-renownéd pain;
Of one daisy 'mid the centuries of sun;
Of a little living nun
In the garden of the years.

Yes, I am not far astray;
But I guess you as might one
Pausing when young March is grey,
In a violet-peopled day;
All his thoughts go out to places that he knew,
To his child-home in the sun,
To the fields of his regret,
To one place i' the innocent March air,
By one olive, and invent
The familiar form and scent
Safely; a white violet
Certainly is there.

Soeur Monique, remember me.
'Tis not in the past alone
I am picturing you to be;
But my little friend, my own,
In my moment, pray for me.
For another dream is mine,
And another dream is true,
Sweeter even,
Of the little ones that shine
Lost within the light divine,—
Of some meekest flower, or you,
In the fields of Heaven.

(1875)

L. ORMISTON CHANT
(1848–1923)

REMEMBERED for her work in the National Vigilance Association, Laura Ormiston Chant was a notable public figure in late-Victorian England. She came to prominence in 1894 when she launched her vociferous and much satirized campaign against the Empire Theatre. The Empire, she believed, should not have had its licence renewed since it took no precautions against the soliciting by female prostitutes in the Promenade adjacent to the main auditorium.

Born in Chepstow, she was educated at home in Kensington. In her early adult life, she became an associate of arts at Apothecaries Hall. Thereafter, she worked as a schoolteacher, before taking up a position as a nurse at the London Hospital. For some years, she ran a private asylum for the mentally ill. In 1876, she married Thomas Chant. Much of her time was then devoted to the work of the NVA, particularly editing its journal, the *Vigilance Record*. She become well known for the power of her public speaking on behalf of a number of different causes. Not only vocal about temperance and purity, Chant was also at the forefront of the Women's Liberal Federation and the Ladies National Organization. In 1888, the *Women's Penny Paper* referred to her as 'the most popular of our lady speakers'. Not everyone agreed. Lucy Bland, a historian who has documented Chant's activities in detail, notes how the *Adult*, a journal published by the anarchist Legitimation League, was 'less polite': 'Mrs Ormiston Chant ... is a middle-aged lady, of strong sympathies with oppressed women, considerable powers of eloquent speech, limited range of intellect, and a plentiful lack of imagination, humour and perspective'. Chant succeeded in encouraging the London County Council to propose a ban against the sale of alcohol at the Empire. Her widely publicized campaign created an uproar, not least in the *Daily Telegraph* where 170 letters on the topic appeared. Very promptly, Chant was stigmatized as a 'prude on the prowl'. But one should not assume that she was a public moralist who sought to condemn all prostitutes. She made her home the refuge for women sex workers who wished to abandon streetwalking. Her sole book of poetry, *Verona and Other Poems* (1887), reflects the mood of many of her political concerns. She was buried in Banbury, Oxfordshire, after a long life of political activism.

316 *Hope's Song*

WE are standing on the threshold, sisters,
  Of the new and brighter day,
And the hideous night of savage customs
  Passes, with the dark, away.

Pale your faces are with weeping, sisters.
  Haggard with your weary watch,
And your voices fainter grow and weaker,
  Till we scarce your tones can catch.

But the rose light of the dawning, sisters,
  Flushing up the golden skies,
Will such rapture bring to you and beauty,
  Heaven will nestle in your eyes.

And your hearts grow young again, rejoicing
  In the warm life-giving power
Of the reign of love, and truth, and justice,
  And the gladness of the hour.

You have borne the burden, O my sisters,
  Through long dynasties of pain,
Of the scoff and scorn of being women,
  That shall ne'er return again.

'Twas the winter of the world, my sisters,
  Spring was coming, spring has come,
And the patient anguish of the women
  Sowed the seed for Harvest Home.

Still the east winds blow of hate and scorning,
  Still the savage mars the man,
Still these human brutes, or men, or women,
  Crush and ruin where they can.

But their numbers lessen surely, sisters,
  Sink the east wind's blighting chills,
In the glorious prophecy of summer
  Coming o'er the eternal hills.

I am singing to you, O my sisters,
  In the early morn of spring,
And the coldness of the gloomy shadows
  Makes me tremble as I sing.

But from where I with my song am soaring,
  High above the earth below,
I can hear the singing of the angels,
  And their psalm ye soon shall know.

Song of fruits celestial from the flowers
  Of goodwill for evermore;
And a tranquil reign of peace and beauty,
  Summer light on sea and shore.

Man and woman in one aim united,
  Dual force of unity;
Equal glory, equal progress blended
  In their one humanity.

Deepest love and kindest, in the union
  Of two equals, strong and free;
Highest hope and loftiest aim, the impress
  Of the race that soon shall be.

All the nerve-force of the human storehouse
  For the world's work and the age;
And no longer half by custom wasted
  In an endless tutelage.

Oh, take comfort, dear and honoured sisters,
  Patriots ye for country, home;
With the angels welcome ye the morning,
  Heaven in earth, the kingdom come

(1887)

ELIZABETH RACHEL CHAPMAN
(1850–post–1897)

ALL that is known about Elizabeth Rachel Chapman's life is that she was born in Woodford, the daughter of a Yorkshireman and great grand-daughter of Elizabeth Fry.

She began her writing career with a two-volume novel, *Master of All* (1881), and later published two books of poetry, the first of which, *The New Purgatory, and Other Poems*, came out in 1887. The first edition of her *A Little Child's Wreath* (1894), written to commemorate the death of her young nephew, contains a preface by the poet, Alice Meynell.

Many of her essays and articles were reprinted, in book form, from journals. *The New Godiva and Other Studies in Social Questions* (1885) engages with the distinction between vice and crime, and was dedicated to the feminist, Josephine Butler. It should be noted, however, that the essayist was not a feminist. In the Foreword to her last book of essays, *Marriage Questions in Modern Fiction, and Other Essays on Kindred Subjects* (1897), Chapman condemns the 'New Woman' and approves what she calls the 'Best Woman', who is reverential towards the 'marriage-tie': an idea she expands upon in the essay, 'Why We should Oppose Divorce'. The Foreword also expresses her vehement distrust of the concept of 'realist' fiction, as that which flaunts 'a sickly and one-sided pessimism' and is inclined to 'pornographic' representation. Her earlier *A Comtist Lover and Other Studies* (1886) contains the work for which she was best known: '*In Memoriam—Arguments*'. Alfred Tennyson highly approved of her commentary upon his poem and also enthusiastically concurred with her thoughts on Comtism (a mode of philosophical positivism). The favourable reception of this piece led to its being republished in England and America as *A Companion to 'In Memoriam'* in 1880.

317 *Hereafter*

Froebel speaks of negro slaves in the United States believing that in the next world they shall be white men and free, nor is there anything strange in their cherishing a hope so prevalent among their kindred in West Africa.

Tylor, 'Primitive Culture'

'WHITE *men and free!*' Is this the highest bliss,
   O dark-skinned slaves, your troubled fancy paints?
Turn verily your dumb desires to this,
   When earthly hope 'neath wrong and anguish faints?

Is this your heaven to come? Oh, if it be,
   Your faith yields food to us for questioning thought,
A voice it seems to us, 'white men and free',
   Scarce human, yet with infinite meaning fraught.

The thoughts are pitying which it wakens first,
For we must needs believe the weight of grief
Immense, and very torturing the thirst,
Which contemplate our state as a relief,

And call the white man blest. Ah, did they know—
Those sufferers—how our spirits echo back
Their longings, how their ignorance, their woe
Are shared by all that wail along life's track;

Did they but know their thraldom wholly ours,
Our need for 'bodies glorified' as strong
As theirs for whiteness, know how sin devours,
And grief disfigures us, it were not long

Before they sent an altered cry to heaven,
And joined with less distinctness in the prayer
For some beatitude to come, which riven
And hungry hearts still offer everywhere.

Yet with an equal fervour. That we know
As little where may be our final rest
As Job where he to find his God should go,
We do not less desire the Father's breast.

Gone, is it, gone, that sweet old dream of yore,
The fable of an earthly paradise?
And heaven and hell, are they indeed no more
Than symbols of the virtuous and the wise—

The evil, foolish? . . . God! Is this life all?
Is the Hereafter nought? . . . Ah me! ah me!
Let the earth gape! the merciful mountains fall . . .
Yet—though Thou slay me—I will trust in Thee.

Thou Heaven-Father, Whom in long-past years,
Our far fore-fathers worshipped,[1] let Thy will
Be done, nor less by reason of our tears,
Our darkness, let us in Thy hands lie still.

(1887)

318 *A Woman's Strength*

YOU ought to be stronger than I, dear,
You, who are a man—
And yet I am stronger than you, dear,—
Who proves it? I can.

[1] 'The primæval Aryan prayer—Heaven-Father.' (Max Müller).

You know how to walk upon thorns, dear,
Quite placid the while;
But I, who have tenderer feet, dear,
Can do it, and smile.

You watch the red stream as it runs, dear,
You know whence it flows,
And say, 'It is only my heart's blood,'
Or, 'Thus the world goes.'

But I, when I see my blood running,
Exclaim with delight,
'Look, look at the beautiful colour!'
I laugh at the sight.

You feel the earth opening beside you,
You stand on the brink,
And wait with all stoical calmness,
Preparing to sink.

I stretch out my arms to the chasm,
I hug the abyss;
Its fathomless depth and its darkness,
I hail with a kiss.

I stoop to pick flowers on the edge, dear!
The people around—
Who guess it is not so with you—think
I stand on firm ground.

Who says you are stronger than I, dear,
You, who are a man?
I think I shall bear off the palm, dear,
Gainsay it who can.

Hold! Hold! Do not move! Do not cancel
The effort of years!
My strength, do you see? if you touched me,
Might melt into tears.

(1887)

319 *Hope*

SOME men would tell us Hope was only given
To man to make life possible. The power
Unknown, they say, which hath bid pain devour
Our little life, refuses us the heaven
A self-sought death would bring to hearts so riven
With anguish, urging us each day and hour

To hope, persisting 'though the clouds may lower,
Light is beyond'. Oh! foolish, to have striven
To make us think so excellent a thing
Could be the slave of a mere merciless
Mad law! Hope, sweetest spirit that hath trod
With angel-feet our earth, soft whispering
Of peace, must be divine—the loveliness
Of Hope alone necessitates a God.

(1887)

320 A Little Child's Wreath, XXX

KIND little lad, with dark, disordered hair,
Who friendly-wise, forsake your half-built fort
To make me in the sand a high-backed chair,
So kind, so keen to join the livelier sport—

Haste to your trenches! Fly! To arms! to arms!
The foe prepares to storm your citadel.
Your comrades sound excursions and alarms,
And those stout hands must fight that build so well.

Laugh, happy soul!—nor dream you brought me tears.
His beauty had you not—for that the earth
Holds not his equal—but you had his years,
Almost his eyes, and something of his mirth;

And one stray lock on your bare neck that curled
Made sudden twilight of the summer world.

(1894)

ANNIE MATHESON
(1853–1924)

THE daughter of a Congregationalist minister, James Matheson, and of Elizabeth (née Cripps), Annie Matheson was born in London, though her first home was in Oswestry, Shropshire. She began writing poetry when only a child and was to publish her first volume of verse in 1890: '*The Religion of Humanity' and Other Poems*. *Love's Music and Other Poems* (1894), defined by her as 'a handful of lyrics', was followed by *Love Triumphant and Other New Poems* (1898), which includes a number of sonnets. Her selected poems were published a year later and reproduced, with a revised title, in 1918. The fourteen new lyrics included in this selection are said by her to 'have been evoked by hopes and sorrows of the Great War', and they conclude with two sonnets written in 1918 'pleading for a League of Nations'.

Many of her poems were first published in magazines, such as the *Spectator* and the *Oxford Magazine*. She also contributed essays on social issues to journals, and these were collected in book form in 1912 as *Leaves of Prose*. Her other publications include editions of George Eliot's *Silas Marner* and *Scenes from Clerical Life* (both in 1903), books for children, and a biography of Florence Nightingale (1913)

321 *A Song for Women*

WITHIN a dreary narrow room
That looks upon a noisome street,
Half fainting with the stifling heat
A starving girl works out her doom.
Yet not the less in God's sweet air
The little birds sing free of care,
And hawthorns blossom everywhere.

Swift ceaseless toil scarce wins her bread:
From early dawn till twilight falls,
Shut in by four dull ugly walls,
The hours crawl round with murderous tread.
And all the while, in some still place,
Where intertwining boughs embrace,
The blackbirds build, time flies apace.

With envy of the folk who die,
Who may at last their leisure take,
Whose longed-for sleep none roughly wake,
Tired hands the restless needle ply.
But far and wide in meadows green
The golden buttercups are seen,
And reddening sorrel nods between.

Too pure and proud to soil her soul,
Or stoop to basely gotten gain,
By days of changeless want and pain
The seamstress earns a prisoner's dole.
While in the peaceful fields the sheep
Feed, quiet; and through heaven's blue deep
The silent cloud-wings stainless sweep.

And if she be alive or dead
That weary woman scarcely knows,
But back and forth her needle goes
In tune with throbbing heart and head.
Lo, where the leaning alders part,
White-bosomed swallows, blithe of heart,
Above still waters skim and dart.

O God in heaven! shall I, who share
That dying woman's womanhood,
Taste all the summer's bounteous good
Unburdened by her weight of care?
The white moon-daisies star the grass,
The lengthening shadows o'er them pass:
The meadow pool is smooth as glass.

(1890)

TORU DUTT
(1856–1877)

TORU DUTT stands among the most distinguished nineteenth-century Indo-Anglian writers. The youngest of three children, she was the daughter of the poet and civil servant, Govin Chunder Dutt. Together with her sister, Aru, Dutt was taken by her father to Europe in 1869 to gain proficiency in English and French. For some time she studied in Nice, later attending lectures for women at Cambridge. Her competence in both languages was astounding, since she soon began work on her finely crafted translations of French poetry into English. The fruits of her labours, amounting to some one hundred translations, were published as *A Sheaf Gleaned in French Fields* by the Saptahiksambad Press in 1876. A review copy of this volume was sent to England, and it fell to the eminent literary critic, Edmund Gosse, to pass judgement on it. Gosse was deeply impressed by the quality of Dutt's work, and he was instrumental in arranging for the publication of a British edition. In his preface to the posthumous collection, *Ancient Ballads and Legends of Hindustan* (1882), from which the lyrics we have reprinted are taken, Gosse argues that her original poems in English 'constitute Toru's chief legacy to posterity'.

There is no doubt that Dutt had a dazzling literary career ahead of her. On returning to Bengal in 1873, she spent almost four years in seclusion learning Sanskrit. Her essays on Leconte de Lisle and Joséphin Soulary appeared in the *Bengal Magazine* when she was 18. During this period, she was at work on a translation into English of Clarisse Bader's study of women in ancient Indian society. But illness overcame her. She died at the age of 21. Her *Life and Letters*, edited by Harihar Das, appeared in 1921.

322 *On the Fly-Leaf of Erckmann-Chatrian's Novel Entitled 'Madame Thérèse'*

WAVERED the foremost soldiers,—then fell back,
Fallen was their leader, and loomed right before
The sullen Prussian cannon, grim and black,
With lighted matches waving. Now, once more,
Patriots and veterans!—Ah! 'Tis in vain!

Back they recoil, though bravest of the brave;
No human troops may stand that murderous rain;
But who is this—that rushes to a grave?

It is a woman,—slender, tall, and brown!
She snatches up the standard as it falls,—
In her hot haste tumbles her dark hair down,
And to the drummer-boy aloud she calls
To beat the charge; then forwards on the *pont*
They dash together;—who could bear to see
A woman and a child, thus Death confront,
Nor burn to follow them to victory?

I read the story and my heart beats fast!
Well might all Europe quail before thee, France,
Battling against oppression! Years have past,
Yet of that time men speak with moistened glance.
Va-nu-pieds! When rose high your Marseillaise
Man knew his rights to earth's remotest bound,
And tyrants trembled. Yours alone the praise!
Ah, had a Washington but then been found!

(1882)

323 *Sonnet—Baugmaree*

A SEA of foliage girds our garden round,
 But not a sea of dull unvaried green,
 Sharp contrasts of all colours here are seen;
The light-green graceful tamarinds abound
Amid the mangoe clumps of green profound,
 And palms arise, like pillars gray, between;
 And o'er the quiet pools the seemuls lean,
Red,—red, and startling like a trumpet's sound.
But nothing can be lovelier than the ranges
 Of bamboos to the eastward, when the moon
Looks through their gaps, and the white lotus changes
 Into a cup of silver. One might swoon
  Drunken with beauty then, or gaze and gaze
  On a primeval Eden, in amaze.

(1882)

MARGARET L. WOODS
(1856–1945)

MARGARET BRADLEY was the daughter of Marian (née Philpot) and George Granville Bradley, a schoolmaster at Rugby, who would later become Dean of Westminster. She was educated both at home and at Miss Gawthorp's school at Leamington. In 1879, she married Henry George Woods, President of Trinity College, Oxford, and some of her poems reflect her experiences in that city. Some of her finest poetry, which is notable for its rhetorical control, appears in *Lyrics and Ballads* (1889) and *Aëromancy and Other Poems* (1896). In addition, she published *Wild Justice: A Dramatic Poem* (1896), an ambitious narrative of a woman's attempt to protect her children from their violent father, and a later dramatic poem, *The Princess of Hanover*. *Poems: Old and New* appeared in 1907, and her *Collected Poems* was brought out in 1914. The latter contains her long meditation on Westminster Abbey, entitled 'The Builders', which is written in an innovative style of free verse. Woods was a regular contributor to journals, including the *Fortnightly Review*. Her reputation, however, mainly rested on her works of prose fiction, which began with *A Village Tragedy* (1887). Subsequent notable novels by her are *Esther Vanhomrigh* (1891) and *The Vagabond* (1894).

324 *L'Envoi*

LIKE the wreath the poet sent
   To the lady of old time,
Roses that were discontent
   With their brief unhonoured prime,
   Crown he hoped she might endow
   With the beauty of her brow;
Even so for you I blent,
Send you to my wreath of rhyme.

These alas! be blooms less bright,
   Faded buds that never blew,
Darkling thoughts that seek the light—
   Let them find it finding you.
   Bid these petals pale unfold
   On your heart their hearts of gold,
Sweetness for your sole delight,
Love for odour, tears for dew.

(1889)

325 *from Aëromancy*

I

THE watchers in the everlasting towers,
Blind watchers of bright heaven, the bells who own
No changing years, but the unchanging hours—

Listen! They strike: a sinister monotone
Deep as all time. The same sound and who hears
Could be the same, did she not hear alone.

These iron tongues have portioned out our years
Indifferently, with fateful rumours blown
About the solemn spires and aëry tiers

Of clustered pinnacles, and far unknown
Utterance that communes with the void. It fills
The valley broadening round their ancient throne,
Out to the edges of the violet hills.

. . . .

III

How in your high-walled garden has mine ear
Hung on their imminent voices, where the yew
Darkens above each grey majestic pier

Of the antique gate.
'Tis closed: none passes thro',
But in the unfooted mimic theatre
A fountain springs, scattering a lonely dew.

This was a child of music, some aver,
In olden time, and here men pressed around
Her throne of song. But one that lovèd her,

A student, who in pagan books had found
Strange lore, came once ghost-white with wrath and love,
And sat a little while upon the ground,

Hearing men whisper, seeing high above
The slim girl sing; till suddenly upright
He leapt, and shrieked out stammering words. The grove
Stood on the instant void, silence and night
Shrouded it up; nor was one left to show
How from its marble urn the fountain slight
Arose to plain the loves of long ago.

Time was this formal garden seemed our own,
So world-forgot and beautiful; the glow
Of its great flowers, the birds that as alone

Made sparkling sport upon the fountain's rim,
Its diamond drip into the pool, o'ergrown
With iris and pale reed, the skyey, slim

Poplar that still October turns to flame,
All was our own—the couchant monsters grim
Remember it: and the bells sound the same.

. . . .

VI

I hear the incantation of the bells,
And since that Hour made me her neophyte,
I know what occult power within them dwells
To mock at Time's inviolable might.

A power to make invisible things seen,
And tumult calm and morning in dull night,
To set the day with stars, and like a screen

Rolled back, the curtain of a peopled stage,
Uplift a tenuous moment's painted scene
From Life's loud pageant and mute pilgrimage.

(1896)

A. MARY F. ROBINSON (LATER DARMESTETER, LATER DUCLAUX) (1857–1944)

MARY ROBINSON was born at Leamington Spa, Warwickshire. At the time, her father was archidiachonal architect for Coventry. From 1870, she was educated in Belgium and Italy, and she proceeded to classical and literary studies at University College, London. Her parents maintained a lively cultural life at home, entertaining Robert Browning and Oscar Wilde. It is said that at the age of 21, she was given the choice between a ball, to be given in her honour, or the publication of some of her poems in a volume. She decided upon the volume, and *A Handful of Honeysuckle* was brought out by Kegan Paul in 1878.

Robinson lived in London until marrying her first husband, James Darmesteter, in 1888. Darmesteter was Professor of Persian in the Collège de France and the Écoles des Hautes Études. During the six years of her marriage (Darmesteter died in 1894), Robinson hosted a lively salon in Paris, one that created a great many Anglo-French literary connections. After Darmesteter passed away, Robinson devoted time to prefacing and translating his posthumous works. In 1904, she married Émile Duclaux, and moved to Olmet in the Cantal region.

Under her different last names—Robinson, Darmesteter, and Duclaux—she produced a highly impressive canon of poetry, noted for its lyric precision. Among her most distinguished collections are *Songs, Ballads, and a Garden Play*

(1889) and *Retrospect and Other Poems* (1893). Her *Collected Poems* appeared in 1902. Much later in life, she completed her final volume of poetry, *Images & Meditations* (1923). In addition, Robinson wrote a study of Emily Brontë, which came out in the 'Eminent Women' series, published by W. H. Allen & Co. in 1883. Also among her wide-ranging publications is a novel, *Arden*, which appeared in the same year.

326 *Tuscan Olives (Rispetti)*

I

THE colour of the olives who shall say?
  In winter on the yellow earth they're blue,
A wind can change the green to white or gray,
  But they are olives still in every hue;
But they are olives always, green or white,
As love is love in torment or delight;
But they are olives, ruffled or at rest,
As love is always love in tears or jest.

II

We walked along the terraced olive-yard,
  And talked together till we lost the way;
We met a peasant, bent with age, and hard,
  Bruising the grape-skins in the vase of clay;
Bruising the grape-skins for a second wine.
We did not drink, and left him, Love of mine;
Bruising the grapes already bruised enough:
He had his meagre wine, and we our love.

III

We climbed one morning to the sunny height
  Where chestnuts grow no more, and olives grow;
Far-off the circling mountains cinder-white,
  The yellow river and the gorge below.
'Turn round', you said, O flower of Paradise;
I did not turn, I looked upon your eyes.
'Turn round', you said, 'turn round, look at the view!'
I did not turn, my Love, I looked at you.

IV

How hot it was! Across the white-hot wall
  Pale olives stretch towards the blazing street;
You broke a branch, you never spoke at all,
  But gave it me to fan with in the heat;
You gave it me without a sign or word,
And yet, my love, I think you knew I heard.
You gave it me without a word or sign:
Under the olives first I called you mine.

V

At Lucca, for the autumn festival,
  The streets are tulip-gay; but you and I
Forgot them, seeing over church and wall
  Guinigi's tower i' the black-blue sky,
A stem of delicate rose against the blue,
And on the top two lonely olives grew,
Crowning the tower, far from the hills, alone,
As on our risen love our lives are grown.

VI

Who would have thought we should stand again together,
  Here, with the convent a frown of towers above us;
Here, mid the sere-wooded hills and wintry weather;
  Here, where the fruit-laden olives half remember
All that began in their shadow last November;
Here, where we know we must part, must part and sever;
Here where we know we shall love for aye and ever.

VII

Reach up and pluck a branch, and give it me,
  That I may hang it in my Northern room,
That I may find it there, and wake, and see
  —Not you! not you!—dead leaves and wintry gloom.
O senseless olives, wherefore should I take
Your leaves to balm a heart that can but ache?
Why should I take you hence, that can but show
How much is left behind? I do not know.

(1884)

327 *Etruscan Tombs*

I

To think the face we love shall ever die,
  And be the indifferent earth, and know us not!
To think that one of us shall live to cry
  On one long buried in a distant spot!

O wise Etruscans, faded in the night
  Yourselves, with scarce a rose-leaf on your trace,
You kept the ashes of the dead in sight,
  And shaped the vase to seem the vanished face.

But, O my Love, my life is such an urn
  That tender memories mould with constant touch,
Until the dust and earth of it they turn
  To your dead image that I love so much:

A sacred urn, filled with the sacred past,
That shall recall you while the clay shall last.

II

These cinerary urns with human head
  And human arms that dangle at their sides,
The earliest potters made them for their dead,
  To keep the mother's ashes or the bride's.

O rude attempt of some long-spent despair—
  With symbol and with emblem discontent—
To keep the dead alive and as they were,
  The actual features and the glance that went!

The anguish of your art was not in vain,
  For lo, upon these alien shelves removed
The sad immortal images remain,
  And show that once they loved and once you loved.

But oh, when I am dead may none for me
Invoke so drear an immortality!

III

Beneath the branches of the olive yard
  Are roots where cyclamen and violet grow;
Beneath the roots the earth is deep and hard,
  And there a king was buried long ago.

The peasants digging deeply in the mould
Cast up the autumn soil about the place,
And saw a gleam of unexpected gold,
And underneath the earth a living face.

With sleeping lids and rosy lips he lay
Among the wreaths and gems that mark the kind
One moment; then a little dust and clay
Fell shrivelled over wreath and urn and ring.

A carven slab recalls his name and deed,
Writ in a language no man living reads.

IV

Here lies the tablet graven in the past,
Clear-charactered and firm and fresh of line.
See, not a word is gone; and yet how fast
The secret no man living may divine!

What did he choose for witness in the grave?
A record of his glory on the earth?
The wail of friends? The Paeans of the brave?
The sacred promise of the second birth?

The tombs of ancient Greeks in Sicily
Are sown with slender discs of graven gold
Filled with the praise of Death: 'Thrice happy he
Wrapt in the milk-soft sleep of dreams untold!'

They sleep their patient sleep in altered lands,
The golden promise in their fleshless hands.

(1888)

328 *Darwinism*

WHEN first the unflowering Fern-forest
Shadowed the dim lagoons of old,
A vague, unconscious, long unrest
Swayed the great fronds of green and gold.

Until the flexible stem grew rude,
The fronds began to branch and bower,
And lo! upon the unblossoming wood
There breaks a dawn of apple-flower.

Then on the fruitful forest-boughs
For ages long the unquiet ape
Swung happy in his airy house
And plucked the apple, and sucked the grape.

Until at length in him there stirred
  The old, unchanged, remote distress,
That pierced his world of wind and bird
  With some divine unhappiness.

Not love, nor the wild fruits he sought,
  Nor the fierce battles of his clan
Could still the unborn and aching thought,
  Until the brute became the man.

Long since; and now the same unrest
  Goads to the same invisible goal,
Till some new gift, undream'd, unguess'd,
  End the new travail of the soul.

(1888)

329 *The Idea*

BENEATH this world of stars and flowers
  That rolls in visible deity,
I dream another world is ours
  And is the soul of all we see.

It hath no form, it hath no spirit;
  It is perchance the Eternal Mind;
Beyond the sense that we inherit
  I feel it dim and undefined.

How far below the depth of being,
  How wide beyond the starry bound
It rolls unconscious and unseeing,
  And is as Number or as Sound.

And through the vast fantastic visions
  Of all this actual universe,
It moves unswerved by our decisions,
  And is the play that we rehearse.

(1888)

330 *The Bookworm*

THE whole day long I sit and read
    Of days when men were men indeed
    And women knightlier far:
I fight with Joan of Arc; I fall
With Talbot; from my castle-wall
    I watch the guiding star . . .

But when at last the twilight falls
And hangs about the book-lined walls
And creeps across the page,
Then the enchantment goes, and I
Close up my volumes with a sigh
To greet a narrower age.

Home through the pearly dusk I go
And watch the London lamplight glow
Far off in wavering lines:
A pale grey world with primrose gleams,
And in the West a cloud that seems
My distant Appenines.

O Life! so full of truths to teach,
Of secrets I shall never reach,
O world of Here and Now;
Forgive, forgive me, if a voice,
A ghost, a memory be my choice
And more to me than Thou!

(1893)

331 *Liberty*

LIBERTY, fiery Goddess, dangerous Saint,
God knows I worship thee no less than they
Who fain would set thee in the common way
To battle at their sides without restraint,

Redoubtable Amazon! Who, never faint,
Climbest the barricades at break of day,
With tangled locks and blood-besmirched array,
Thy torch low-smoking through the carnage taint!

But I would set thee in a golden shrine
Above the enraptured eyes of dreaming men,
Where thou shouldst reign immutable, divine,
A hope to all generations and a sign;
Slow-guiding to the stars, through quag and fen,
The scions of thine aye-unvanquished line!

(1893)

CONSTANCE NADEN
(1858–1889)

BORN in Edgbaston, Birmingham, Constance Woodhill Naden was an only child, educated at a Unitarian day school. Between 1879 and 1881, she studied botany at the Birmingham and Midland Institute. In 1881, she became a student at Mason College, acquiring a broad knowledge of modern languages. The substantial inheritance she received from her grandmother's will in 1887 enabled her to travel widely in the Middle East and Asia. On her return to England, she bought a house in Grosvenor Square, London. For the brief remaining period of her life, she became actively involved in women's causes, helping to establish the new Hospital for Women on the Marylebone Road. Among the friends she made at this time was the noted medical doctor and suffrage campaigner, Elizabeth Garrett Anderson. Naden herself spoke at public meetings on the suffrage.

Naden published two volumes of poetry, *Songs and Sonnets of Springtime* (1881) and *A Modern Apostle, The Elixir of Life, and Other Poems* (1887). Thereafter, she gave up poetry, devoting herself to her essays and political campaigning. In 1890, Gladstone noted the power of her poems in the pages of the *Spectator*. Her *Poetical Works* were issued in 1894, and it is for her poems about the contemporary 'New Woman' that she is mainly remembered. She was a freethinker, influenced by the controversial writer on sexual morality, James Hinton, who advocated polygamous unions. *What Is Religion? A Vindication of Free Thought* appeared in 1883. It was followed by *Induction and Deduction, and Other Essays* (1890). *Further Reliques of Constance Naden* was published in 1891. She succumbed to a dangerous disease in 1889.

332 *The Lady Doctor*

SAW ye that spinster gaunt and grey,
Whose aspect stern might well dismay
   A bombardier stout-hearted?
The golden hair, the blooming face,
And all a maiden's tender grace
   Long, long from her have parted.

A Doctor she—her sole delight
To order draughts as black as night,
   Powders, and pills, and lotions;
Her very glance might cast a spell
Transmuting Sherry and Moselle
   To chill and acrid potions.

Yet if some rash presumptuous man
Her early life should dare to scan,
   Strange things he might discover;
For in the bloom of sweet seventeen
She wandered through the meadows green
   To meet a boyish lover.

She did not give him Jesuit's bark,
To brighten up his vital spark,
Nor ipecacuanha,
Nor chlorodyne, nor camomile,
But blushing looks, and many a smile,
And kisses sweet as manna.

But ah! the maiden's heart grew cold,
Perhaps she thought the youth too bold,
Perhaps his views had shocked her;
In anger, scorn, caprice, or pride,
She left her old companion's side
To be a Lady Doctor.

She threw away the faded flowers,
Gathered amid the woodland bowers,
Her lover's parting token:
If suffering bodies we relieve,
What need for wounded souls to grieve?
Why mourn, though hearts be broken?

She cared not, though with frequent moan
He wandered through the woods alone
Dreaming of past affection:
She valued at the lowest price
Men neither patients for advice
Nor subjects for dissection.

She studied hard for her degree;
At length the coveted MD
Was to her name appended;
Joy to that Doctor, young and fair,
With rosy cheeks and golden hair,
Learning with beauty blended.

Diseases man can scarce endure
A lady's glance may quickly cure,
E'en though the pains be chronic;
Where'er that maiden bright was seen
Her eye surpassed the best quinine,
Her smile became a tonic.

But soon, too soon, the hand of care
Sprinkled with snow her golden hair,
Her face grew worn and jaded;
Forgotten was each maiden wile,
She scarce remembered how to smile,
Her roses all were faded.

And now, she looks so grim and stern,
We wonder any heart could burn
For one so uninviting;
No gentle sympathy she shows,
She seems a man in woman's clothes,
All female graces slighting.

Yet blame her not, for she has known
The woe of living all alone,
In friendless, dreary sadness;
She longs for what she once disdained,
And sighs to think she might have gained
A home of love and gladness.

MORAL

Fair maid, if thine unfettered heart
Yearn for some busy, toilsome part,
Let that engross thee only;
But oh! if bound by love's light chain,
Leave not thy fond and faithful swain
Disconsolate and lonely.

(1881)

333 *Scientific Wooing*

I WAS a youth of studious mind,
Fair Science was my mistress kind,
And held me with attraction chemic;
No germs of Love attacked my heart,
Secured as by Pasteurian art
Against that fatal epidemic.

For when my daily task was o'er
I dreamed of H_2SO_4,
While stealing through my slumbers placid
Came Iodine, with violet fumes,
And Sulphur, with its yellow blooms,
And whiffs of Hydrochloric Acid.

My daily visions, thoughts, and schemes
With wildest hope illumed my dreams,
The daring dreams of trustful twenty:
I might accomplish my desire,
And set the river Thames on fire
If but Potassium were in plenty!

Alas! that yearnings so sublime
Should all be blasted in their prime
  By hazel eyes and lips vermilion!
Ye gods! restore the halcyon days
While yet I walked in Wisdom's ways,
  And knew not Mary Maud Trevylyan!

Yet nay! the sacrilegious prayer
Was not mine own, oh fairest fair!
  Thee, dear one, will I ever cherish;
Thy worshipped image shall remain
In the grey thought-cells of my brain
  Until their form and function perish.

Away with books, away with cram
For Intermediate Exam!
  Away with every college duty!
Though once Agnostic to the core,
A virgin Saint I now adore,
  And swear belief in Love and Beauty.

Yet when I meet her tranquil gaze,
I dare not plead, I dare not praise,
  Like other men with other lasses;
She's never kind, she's never coy,
She treats me simply as a boy,
  And asks me how I like my classes!

I covet not her golden dower—
Yet surely Love's attractive power
  Directly as the mass must vary—
But ah! inversely as the square
Of distance! shall I ever dare
  To cross the gulf, and gain my Mary?

So chill she seems—and yet she might
Welcome with radiant heat and light
  My courtship, if I once began it;
For is not e'en the palest star
That gleams so coldly from afar
  A sun to some revolving planet?

My Mary! be a solar sphere!
Envy no comet's mad career,
  No arid, airless lunar crescent!
Oh for a spectroscope to show
That in thy gentle eyes doth glow
  Love's vapour, pure and incandescent!

Bright fancy! can I fail to please
If with similitudes like these
  I lure the maid to sweet communion?
My suit, with Optics well begun,
By Magnetism shall be won,
  And closed at last in Chemic union!

At this I'll aim, for this I'll toil,
And this I'll reach—I will, by Boyle,
  By Avogadro, and by Davy!
When every science lends a trope
To feed my love, to fire my hope,
  Her maiden pride must cry '*Peccavi!*'

I'll sing a deep Darwinian lay
Of little birds with plumage gay,
  Who solved by courtship Life's enigma;
I'll teach her how the wild-flowers love,
And why the trembling stamens move,
  And how the anthers kiss the stigma.

Or Mathematically true
With rigorous Logic will I woo,
  And not a word I'll say at random;
Till urged by Syllogistic stress,
She falter forth a tearful 'Yes,'
  A sweet '*Quod erat demonstrandum!*'

(1887)

E. NESBIT
(1858–1924)

PROBABLY best remembered for her novel, *The Railway Children* (1906), Edith Nesbit is generally regarded as the first writer of modern fiction for children. She was a prolific writer of poetry and prose fiction, as well as one of the founder members of the Fabian Society. She was the youngest of six children whose early lives were seriously affected when their father, John Collis Nesbit, died in 1862. He was a well-known agricultural chemist who pioneered the use of artificial fertilizers such as guano. At Kennington, South London, he ran a small private agricultural college where he taught courses in new methods of farming. Several years after his death, Nesbit's mother, Sarah (née Green), found that she could no longer maintain the college. Thereafter, the family moved to continental Europe, settling in a number of places until 1870. Most of Nesbit's education was received at convent schools, in France, Germany, and finally Brighton, Sussex. In her late teens, she began to publish poetry. Her biographer, Julia Briggs, has concluded that, on present evidence, the popular journal, *Good Words*, was the first to print Nesbit's poetry. 'A Year Ago' appeared in its pages in 1876. In that year, too, the *Sunday Magazine* published one of Nesbit's stories.

In 1880, Nesbit married the socialist Hubert Bland, although he concealed their marriage from his mother for some time. As members of the Fabian Society, they came into contact with the leading socialist intellectuals of the day, including George Bernard Shaw, Beatrice Webb, and Sidney Webb. For most of their married life they settled in a succession of houses in the London region. Later, in 1899, they settled at Well Hall, at Eltham, an imposing property where they resided until the First World War. It took some time before their careers flourished. After Bland's business enterprise as a brush-maker failed in the mid-1880s, he became a journalist, editing the socialist *To-Day*. In the meantime, Nesbit devoted her energies to professional writing. She had two sons and two daughters with Bland, and raised two of his illegitimate children. Their relationship was often under pressure, not least from Bland's volatile temper. Both conducted a number of extra-marital affairs. Their infidelities and socialist sympathies contrast somewhat with their decision to join the Roman Catholic church. Bland converted in 1900, with Nesbit following a few years later. During this period, they came into contact with a number of notable Edwardian writers, in particular H. G. Wells, whom they met in 1902. Nesbit's health was affected badly after Bland's death in 1914. In the early months of the war, Nesbit found she lacked the resources for the upkeep of Well Hall. Matters were eased for her when she met Thomas Terry Tucker, a marine engineer, whom she married in 1917. She moved with Tucker to Jesson St Mary's, near Dymchurch, Kent, where she died of cancer in 1924.

Commercial success for Nesbit came with *The Story of the Treasure Seekers* (1899), which was followed by several companion novels for children. Perhaps her most highly regarded novel for adults is *The Red House* (1902). These titles count for only a small proportion of her extensive bibliography. The considerable rewards from writing fiction superseded her aspirations to be a poet, although she continued to publish volumes of poetry into the twentieth century. Among her notable collections are *Lays and Legends* (1886), *A Pomander of Verse* (1895), *Songs of Love and Empire* (1898), and *Ballads and Lyrics of Socialism, 1883–1908* (1908). The subject-matter, tone, and style of her poems range widely, from short sensual lyrics to patriotic verses, reflecting both the decadent and imperial sides to late-Victorian culture.

334 *The Wife of All Ages*

I DO not catch these subtle shades of feeling,
  Your fine distinctions are too fine for me;
This meeting, scheming, longing, trembling, dreaming,
  To me mean love, and only love, you see;
In me at least 'tis love, you will admit,
And you the only man who wakens it.

Suppose *I* yearned, and longed, and dreamed, and fluttered,
  What would you say or think, or further, do?
Why should one rule be fit for me to follow,

While there exists a different law for you?
If all these fires and fancies came my way,
Would you believe love was so far away?

On all these other women—never doubt it—
'Tis love you lavish, love you promised me!
What do I care to be the first, or fiftieth?
It is the *only one* I care to be.
Dear, I would be your sun, as mine you are,
Not the most radiant wonder of a star.

And so, good-bye! Among such sheaves of roses
You will not miss the flower I take from you;
Amid the music of so many voices
You will forget the little songs I knew—
The foolish tender words I used to say,
The little common sweets of every day.

The world, no doubt, has fairest fruits and blossoms
To give to you: but what, ah! what for me?
Nay, after all I am your slave and bondmaid,
And all my world is in my slavery.
So, as before, I welcome any part
Which you may choose to give me of your heart.

(1886)

335 *Under Convoy*

Too many the questions, too subtle
The doubts that bewilder my brain!
Too strong is the strength of old custom
For iron convention's cold reign;
Too doubtful the issue of conflict,
Too leafless the crown and too vain!

Driven blindly by wind and by current,
Too weak to be strong as I would,
Too good to be bad as my promptings,
Too bad to be valued as good,
I would do the work that I cannot—
And will not, the work that I could.

As a swimmer alone in mid-ocean
Breasts wave after green wave, until
He sees the horizon unbroken
By any coast-line—so I still
Swam blindly through life, not perceiving
The infinite stretch of life's ill.

But wave after wave crowds upon me—
  I am tired, I can face them no more—
Let me sink—or not sink—you receive me,
  And I rest in your arms as before,
Which were waiting, O Love, to receive me,
  Fulfilling the troth that you swore.

And so you are left me—what matters
  Of Freedom, or Duty, or Right?
Let my chance of a life-work be ended,
  End my chance of a soul's worthy fight!
End my chance to oppose—ah, how vainly!—
  Vast wrong with its mass and its might!

Hold me fast—kiss me close—and persuade me
  'Tis better to lean upon you
Than to play out my part unsupported,
  My share in the world's work to do.
'Tis better be safe and ignoble
  Than be free, and be wretched, and true.

And you think that you offer a haven,
  As you do, for the storm-blown and tossed,
And you know not how under your kisses
  The soul of me shrinks and is lost:
And you save me my ease as a woman,
  —And the life of a soul is the cost!

(1889)

336 *Indiscretion*

RED tulip-buds last night caressed
The sacred ivory of her breast.
She met me, eager to divine
What gold-heart bud of hope was mine.

Nor eyes nor lips were strong to part
The close-curled petals round my heart;
The joy I knew no monarch knows,
Yet not a petal would unclose.

But, ah!—the tulip-buds, unwise,
Warmed with the sunshine of her eyes,
And by her soft breath glorified,
Went mad with love and opened wide.

She saw their hearts, all golden-gay,
Laughed, frowned, and flung the flowers away.
Poor flowers, in Heaven as you were,
Why did you show your hearts to her?

(1895)

337 *The Despot*

THE garden mould was damp and chill,
Winter had had his brutal will
Since over all the year's content
His devastating legions went.

Then Spring's bright banners came: there woke
Millions of little growing folk
Who thrilled to know the winter done,
Gave thanks, and strove towards the sun.

Not so the elect; reserved, and slow
To trust a stranger-sun and grow,
They hesitated, cowered and hid
Waiting to see what others did.

Yet even they, a little, grew,
Put out prim leaves to day and dew,
And lifted level formal heads
In their appointed garden beds.

The gardener came: he coldly loved
The flowers that lived as he approved,
That duly, decorously grew
As he, the despot, meant them to.

He saw the wildlings flower more brave
And bright than any cultured slave;
Yet, since he had not set them there,
He hated them for being fair.

So he uprooted, one by one
The free things that had loved the sun,
The happy, eager, fruitful seeds
That had not known that they were weeds.

(1908)

KATHARINE TYNAN (LATER HINKSON) (1859–1931)

ALTHOUGH Tynan always claimed that she born in 1861, this Irish writer came into the world at Clondalkin, County Dublin, two years earlier, as the fifth of a large family of twelve children. Her father, Andrew Cullen Tynan, was a substantial farmer and cattle trader; an ardent Parnellite, he was devoted to the Irish nationalist movement. Tynan was from the earliest a keen admirer of Parnell, and joined the Ladies' Land League, although she was never an active member. As a child, she attended school in Dublin, and then from 1872 she apent four years a pupil at the Siena Convent in Drogheda, before being removed because an acute attack of measles. During her mid-teens, she started to publish her poetry in periodicals, first in *Young Ireland* (1875) and then in the *Graphic* (1877). Thereafter, her poetry appeared in a wide range of journals, including *United Ireland* and the *Spectator*. From 1880 until 1923, she published frequently in the *Irish Monthly*, edited by her close friend, Fr Matthew Russell. During this period, Tynan became close to Alice Meynell and Wilfred Meynell, the editors of the Roman Catholic journal, *Merry England*. It was Wilfred Meynell who arranged for Tynan to publish, at her father's expense, her first volume of poems, *Louise de la Vallière*, with Kegan Paul. The collection sold sufficiently well to pass into a second edition.

Thereafter, Tynan would publish a further seventeen volumes of poetry. All of these reflect her passionate religious and nationalist concerns, and her lyrics won admiration from many influential sources, not least W. B. Yeats, whom she met in 1885, and who in 1889 wondered if she would live with him. In 1887, he reviewed her second collection, *Shamrocks*, in *Gael*. There Yeats argues that 'Miss Tynan's very highest note is a religious one'. But a rejoinder to this review, in the same issue of the journal, by John O'Leary, disputes this view.

From 1887, her freelance career developed rapidly. After her marriage in 1893 to the barrister and novelist, Henry Hinkson, she lived in England until 1911 before he took the first two posts of magistrate in County Mayo, Ireland. After Hinkson's death in 1919, Tynan spent much of her remaining life in continental Europe.

For the best part of fifty years, Tynan produced a prolific amount of poetry, journalism, and prose fiction. Her reputation as a novelist rose quickly after the publication of the first of a very large number of romantic novels in 1895. In addition, she wrote a five-volume autobiography, published between 1913 and 1922. Her *Collected Poems* appeared in 1930, the year before her death.

338 *The Irish Hills*

I LOOK unto mine own blue hills,
   That gaze across the land,
And all their peace my hot heart stills;
   Yea, I begin to understand
How beautiful exceedingly
The everlasting hills shall be.

'The everlasting hills'—it seems
  The name to call these by;
Oh, my fair hills, as blue as dreams
  Of a passionate Italian sky;
Blue as the violet fields that spread
Girt with pale primrose overhead!

Yester eve they were silver-gray,
  Soft as a young dove's breast;
And rose and amber hues have they
  When the sun goes in the saffron west;
And all the vales are purple-black,
Below the paling day-star's track.

I know all tender shades on them,
  I love them in all moods—
Kingly robe and diadem
  Or mist that like a grey bird broods;
Their vapoury clouds that sail and glide,
The rain that clothes them like a bride.

My hills are like great angels,
  Whose wide wings sweep the stars,
And peace for their evangels
  Cried clear across earth's fumes and jars;
My hills stand all unchangingly,
While man's short days go by, go by.

And here they see the green woods stand,
  And there they gaze to sea,
Where the white ships glide from the strand,
  And the waves moan perpetually;
With *De Profundis* on their lips
For some who go to the sea in ships.

The sails drop o'er the verge o' the world,
  Like lonely birds that fly,
In the autumn days, when wings unfurled,
  Seeking Summer that will not die;
Sailing down to the Southern Star,
Where purple Summer islands are.

Sad is the sea that speaks to me
  Of parting and of pain,
Of some that go all hopefully,
  And never see their land again.
Ah me, o'er many a lonely grave,
The desolate long sea-grasses wave.

Give me mine own hills, and my woods
  That toss their branches high,
Within those dusky solitudes
  The thrushes sing all innocently;
The blackbird pipes at dawn and even,
And the lark chants at the gates of heaven.

(1887)

339 *Our Lady of Pity*

SHE stands, Our Lady of Pity,
  Over the old church porch,
Outside the walls of the city;
  The sea creeps up to the church.

She is worn and dim with the weather,
  No Baby is on her breast;
Her crown is browner than leather,
  Where swallows have made a nest.

Your Lady of marble is rarer,
  Your Lady of silver is fine,
But Our Lady of Pity is dearer,
  Stained with the rain and brine.

O, lonely she leans for ever,
  Her arms outstretched to take in
The city with woe and fever,
  The city with want and sin!

Once, the old folk aver it,
  Her hands were clasped on her heart,
Till the cry of a broken spirit
  Brought them in blessing apart.

Was a young maid wailing and crying
  In her chamber under the moon,
Of a hurt heart, hurt and undying,
  That must be hid at the noon.

Her cheeks were greyer and greyer,
  Her hands were fevered and dry;
Her lips would murmur a prayer
  But only fashioned a cry.

She was hurt past human recover,
  With a mortal pain in her side;
And she dared not think of her lover,
  Her lover was with his bride.

She said, 'I will out of the city
  Where naught of comfort is found,
And the kind, kind Lady of Pity
  Will give me staunch for my wound.'

The wind is growing, and blowing
  The snow on her silken head,
The casements no light are showing,
  For all the folk are in bed.

But she struggles on through the city,
  And out where the surges roar,
And the lonely Lady of Pity
  Is over the old church door.

She sobs her pitiful story
  To the silent Lady of stone;
The stars look down in their glory,
  The wind flies by with a moan.

The stars look down in their splendour.
  What marvel then doth betide?
The Lady of Pity so tender
  Hath opened her arms out wide.

And the heart that hath suffered and striven
  Is filled with a blessed peace.
'Is this the rapture of Heaven?'
  She cries, in her pain's surcease.

In the wild, wild morning they found her
  Dead as a frozen bird;
And the snows had drifted around her
  Like the ermine cape of a lord.

And Our Lady of Pity be praisèd!
  She leant from her place above,
Her arms outstretched and upraisèd,
  In tender pity and love.

And so she's leaning for ever,
  Her arms outstretched to take in
The city, with woe and fever,
  The city, with want and sin.

(1894)

ROSAMUND MARRIOTT WATSON (GRAHAM R. TOMSON) (1860–1912)

BORN in 1860, she was the youngest child of Benjamin Williams Ball. Little is known about her upbringing and education. Before she published anonymously her first volume of poetry, *Tares*, in 1884, she had been happily married to George Francis Armytage since 1879. But by 1885, serious disagreements had occurred, leading to a legal separation. In the autumn of 1886, she deserted the house she had been allocated by her wealthy husband to live in Cornwall with the painter, Arthur Graham Tomson. Divorce proceedings meant that she lost custody of her two children. One month after marrying Tomson in October 1887, she gave birth to another child. During this second marriage, her literary career was definitely on the ascendant, and she made friends with rising contemporaries, such as Mona Caird, Amy Levy, and Alice Meynell. Her second husband illustrated, as well as designing frontispieces for, a number of her works. In these years, she edited several substantial anthologies, including *Ballads of the North Countrie* and *Border Ballads*, both published in 1888. Between 1893 and 1894, she edited a magazine, *Sylvia's Journal*, which encouraged new writing by women. In 1895, her second marriage broke up when she became involved with H. B. Marriott Watson, a minor novelist who published in John Lane's *Yellow Book*. Her adultery with Watson resulted in a second round of divorce proceedings when, once again, she lost custody of her child. Her affair with Watson, to whom she became pregnant outside marriage, divided the London literary circles in which she moved. Particularly painful was the effect of this controversy on the poet's friendship with the feminist campaigner, Elizabeth Pennell Robins, whose husband's loyalty to Tomson resulted in a ban against any contact between the two women. Watson's associates, including the Tory poet W. E. Henley, supported him. Although she lived with Watson until her death at the age of 51, she never married him.

Throughout this period of turmoil, she produced a large and distinguished canon of poetry, and some of her most notable poems were contributed to periodicals, including the *Yellow Book* and the *Universal Review*. Both *The Bird Bride: A Volume of Ballads and Sonnets* (1889) and *A Summer Night and Other Poems* (1891) were published under the name of Graham M. Tomson. Her fourth and fifth volumes, *Vespertilia and Other Verses* and *A Summer Night and Other Poems*, appeared in 1895; on these occasions, they were brought out under the name of Rosamund Marriott Watson. Her sixth and final collection was *Sunset* (1904). John Lane's notable Bodley Head imprint issued all the poetry she published as Rosamund Marriott Watson, including her collected poems in 1912. In addition, she completed two prose works, *The Art of the House* (1897) and *The Heart of a Garden* (1905). Between 1904 and 1911, Watson followed in the steps of Augusta Webster and E. Nesbit by reviewing poetry for the influential *Athenaeum*. Recent extensive research by Linda K. Hughes, who has brought much biographical information to light, has suggested that Watson may well have remained neglected in modern literary history because of the sexual freedom she chose to exercise in the 1890s. It is certainly the case that her finest poems, notably 'Ballad of the Bird-Bride', examine marital difficulties, a topic that clearly drew on Watson's considerable creative strengths.

340 *Ballad of the Bird-Bride (Eskimo)*

THEY never come back, though I loved them well;
I watch the South in vain;
The snow-bound skies are blear and grey,
Waste and wide is the wild gull's way,
And she comes never again.

Years agone, on the flat white strand,
I won my sweet sea-girl:
Wrapped in my coat of the snow-white fur,
I watched the wild birds settle and stir,
The grey gulls gather and whirl.

One, the greatest of all the flock,
Perched on an ice-floe bare,
Called and cried as her heart were broke,
And straight they were changed, that fleet bird-folk,
To women young and fair.

Swift I sprang from my hiding-place
And held the fairest fast;
I held her fast, the sweet, strange thing:
Her comrades skirled, but they all took wing,
And smote me as they passed.

I bore her safe to my warm snow house;
Full sweetly there she smiled;
And yet, whenever the shrill winds blew,
She would beat her long white arms anew,
And her eyes glanced quick and wild.

But I took her to wife, and clothed her warm
With skins of the gleaming seal;
Her wandering glances sank to rest
When she held a babe to her fair, warm breast,
And she loved me dear and leal.

Together we tracked the fox and the seal,
And at her behest I swore
That bird and beast my bow might slay
For meat and for raiment, day by day,
But never a grey gull more.

A weariful watch I keep for aye
'Mid the snow and the changeless frost:
Woe is me for my broken word!
Woe, woe's me for my bonny bird,
My bird and the love-time lost!

Have ye forgotten the old keen life?
The hut with the skin-strewn floor?
O winged white wife, and children three,
Is there no room left in your hearts for me,
Or our home on the low sea-shore?

Once the quarry was scarce and shy,
Sharp hunger gnawed us sore,
My spoken oath was clean forgot,
My bow twanged thrice with a swift, straight shot,
And slew me sea-gulls four.

The sun hung red on the sky's dull breast,
The snow was wet and red;
Her voice shrilled out in a woeful cry,
She beat her long white arms on high,
'The hour is here,' she said.

She beat her arms, and she cried full fain
As she swayed and wavered there.
'Fetch me the feathers, my children three,
Feathers and plumes for you and me,
Bonny grey wings to wear!'

They ran to her side, our children three,
With the plumage black and grey;
Then she bent her down and drew them near,
She laid the plumes on our children dear,
'Mid the snow and the salt sea-spray.

'Babes of mine, of the wild wind's kin,
Feather ye quick, nor stay.
Oh, oho! but the wild winds blow!
Babes of mine, it is time to go:
Up, dear hearts, and away!'

And lo! the grey plumes covered them all,
Shoulder and breast and brow.
I felt the wind of their whirling flight:
Was it sea or sky? was it day or night?
It is always night-time now.

Dear, will you never relent, come back?
I loved you long and true.
O winged white wife, and our children three,
Of the wild wind's kin though ye surely be,
Are ye not of my kin too?

Ay, ye once were mine, and, till I forget,
  Ye are mine forever and aye,
Mine, wherever your wild wings go,
While shrill winds whistle across the snow
  And the skies are blear and grey.

(1889)

341 *'Eli, Eli, Lama Sabachthani?'*

STRAIGHT, slender limbs strained stark upon the cross,
  Dim anguished eyes that search the empty sky,—
All human loneliness, and pain, and loss,
  Brake forth in thine exceeding bitter cry,
Thou King of Martyrs, lifted up on high
  For men to mock at in thine agony:
Would that that last, worst cup had passed thee by!
  Would that thy God had not forsaken Thee!

The cry of each man born that loves or prays—
  Yea, be his idol human or divine,
Body or soul sinks dead in thorny ways
  Before the marsh-lit lantern of a shrine:
I, Friend, have my God—ay, and thou hast thine;
  Art, Fortune, Pleasure, Love? or Christ, may be?
Shall the cry rise from thy lips first? or mine?
  'Why hast thou, O my God, forsaken me?'

A weak soul wailing in the body's slough;
  A strong man bent beneath a leaden Fate;
Dead hopes, crushed toys, and shattered gods!—O Thou
  Whom high desires and dreams left desolate,
We cannot tread Thy narrow path and strait
  But all our pity and love go forth to Thee—
Thine is the cry of each soul soon or late:
  'Why hast thou, O my God, forsaken me?'

Grief is, and was, and evermore must be,
  Even as long waves, gathering again,
Moan to and fro between the shore and sea;
  And, as the wind wails blindly through the rain,
So all earth-voices echo—aye in vain—
  The ceaseless questioning and piteous,
The old appeal against eternal pain:
  'Why hast thou, O our God, forsaken us?'

(1889)

342 *The Story of Marpessa (As Heard in Hades)*

ALONE I strayed along the dusky mead
Musing on divers things beyond recall,
On love and constancy; and if indeed
This were reward of that, or if at all
To seize and hold Love's rolling golden ball
Were possible to folk of mortal clay—
And, as I raised mine eyes, I saw a tall
Fair woman move to meet me on the way.

And straight I knew Marpessa by her bright
Long tresses, and her shining feet, that fell
Noiseless, as onward through the dim grey light
That broods above the mead of asphodel
She came to greet me, saying, 'Is it well
With thee, good poet, and with those who yet
Are left on earth a little while to dwell
And see those happy skies I half forget?

'But come, now, tell me of that world above,
Of all the women say, and men-folk do,
And, if it may be, of thy life and love:—
Of women's fragrant raiment tell me too
If wrought the same, or fashioned aught anew,
And in high places say what men do reign?—
What sickness slew thee, or what mortal threw
The spear that joined thee to King Orcus' train?'

And now indeed I could not choose but smile
That women aye their womanhood will show!
By fair Marpessa's side I strayed awhile
Telling her all her soul desired to know,
Of this man's triumphing and that man's woe—
And then, bethinking me at last, I said,
'Tell me, Marpessa, of thy long ago,
For from my memory 'tis past and sped.'

'A foolish tale like mine is soon forgot,
Soon told, and soon forgot,' the shade replied.
'In pleasant places fell my childhood's lot,
For still my loving father's chiefest pride
Was I. But time drew on and lovers tried
To win me, and my sire Euenos cried
That no man born should win me for his wife,
But by his footstool ever must I bide.

'Bold Ides, son of King Alphareus,
Of all my suitors seemed the goodliest,
For he was comely as the sons of Zeus,
And no man living might with him contest
The crowns of parsley and wild olive; best
Was he of all the youths with bow or sword;
And oft my maidens murmured low that blest
Would be that woman who should call him lord.

'Most lordly bride gifts offered he in vain:
Ten well-wrought tripods all untouched of fire,
Twelve gleaming caldrons free from rust or stain,
And milk-white kine that lowed within his byre
(A herd that Helios' self might well desire)—
All these, with goodly store of bronze and gold,
Still fruitlessly he proffered to my sire,
Who said, "My lamb remains within my fold."

'And mine old nurse would say, "Nay, never weep,
Unthinking Haste the seed of Sorrow sows
Full oft, for grey Experience to reap;
Though now to thee a smiling face he shows,
Fair Hymen holdeth hid a world of woes;
He waits to lure thy feet through thorny ways,
(For men are aye a fickle folk, God knows!)
So live a maid unwedded all thy days."

'One morn to hear a beggar's plaint I rose,
And singing ran adown the shining stair
And through the court into the orchard-close
Abloom; no suppliant I ween was there,
But Ides clasped my knees with many a prayer,
Yet never tarried for my yea or nay—
In his strong arms he lifted me and bare
Swift to his chariot, and so sped away.

'And, as his milk-white horses onward flew,
Like driven doves, athwart the broad green plain,
Within his hand most gently mine he drew,
Saying, "Forgive my rude device to gain
What most I coveted! for all in vain
I sought thee fairly at Euenos' hands:
Not long, love, shall endure thy father's pain
When, wedded, we return from mine own lands."

'But, even as he spake, it seemed a star
Shot earthward 'twixt our horses, fair and fleet,
That cowering shrank beneath the polished car,
Nor lash nor word might urge them nor entreat:

Then on mine eyes a flaming fire there beat,
And all around me floated, fold on fold,
Close-binding every limb from face to feet,
A cloud—a wondrous mesh of misty gold.

'And then a little way along the air,
Borne by the softest wind that woos the Spring,
I floated onward in the Sun-god's snare
Unto a mead with tall trees flowering,
Where many-tinted birds on noiseless wing
Below the blossom-burdened branches flew,
And where did hang great golden fruits aswing,
While wood-nymphs' faces peered the leafage through.

'There I abode in sorrow many days,
Sore-fretting, even as a caged bird frets
Behind the golden bars, nor cares to raise
His voice in tuneful song, nor e'er forgets
His dewy home, but, dumb with vain regrets,
Sits still with ruffled plumes and clouded eye,
And museth sadly on the fowler's nets:
So sad in that green pleasaunce did I lie!

'(Now this I wist not, but thereafter knew
That Ides to my parents' house had sped
To tell them all the luckless story through,
And bid them fear not, but be comforted:
For "Far or near, by sea or sky," he said,
"My wit shall find her, and my strength retrieve.
Lament not for Marpessa as one dead—
A thing most profitless it is to grieve.")

'Now ever and anon an amber flame,
Bright as the sun and soft as ring-dove's eyes,
Lit all the meadow when Apollo came,
And sweeter, softlier than the south wind sighs,
His pleading voice would say, "Dear maid, arise
And shake this sullen sorrow from thy heart,
Refrain thy constant weeping, and be wise!"
But still I hid my face and held apart.

'And, one day, as I watched the misty morn
Steal rosy-fingered through the laurel trees,
I saw, a little way beyond the bourne
Of my fair prison, on the lower leas,
A man who strode like one who hastes to seize
Some bright lost treasure, and my heart beat loud;
But suddenly uprising to his knees,
Staying his footsteps, clung a shining cloud.

'Then Ides cried aloud upon my name
And said, "Thy father's halls forlorn of thee
Are desolate indeed, and fragrant flame
Of fair burnt-offering riseth constantly;
And, like the plaintive halcyon of the sea,
Unceasing still thy lady-mother grieves,
Nor more takes thought for wise housewifery,
Nor with her maids the purple web she weaves.

'"And all the land goes mourning for thy sake,
For fruitlessly they seek thee far and wide;
And thou, Apollo! who dost think to take
Afar for ever from her parents' side
And my strong arms this maid, my plighted bride,
Though swift thy silver arrows cleave the sky
To loose men's knees and soul from breath divide,
I fear thee not, but all thy might defy!"

'So spake he, leaning on his crooked bow,
And as a tawny lion ere he spring
Scans the rash slayer of his mate, even so
Glared mighty Ides on the fair-tressed king,
Who said (and laughing touched one silver string
Of his bright lyre), "No sorry thief am I—
A weeping woman is a woeful thing,
Nor ever joy hath anyone thereby—

'"So, maiden, if indeed thy heart incline
To this mad youth, whose reckless speech doth press
On danger's heels, or if thou wilt be mine
And dwell in more than mortal happiness
And joy beyond the skill of man to guess,
Thine either choice I bid thee now declare!"
He leaned towards me in his loveliness
And from his forehead fell his yellow hair.

'Then all my soul within my breast was stirred;
Meseemed the longing for my parents slept,
And I forgot great Ides' spoken word,
And all the tears my captive eyes had wept;
So like some fawn a snake doth charm I stept
Towards Apollo's arms a little space,
While strange bewilderment my senses kept,
Nor aught beheld I but his wondrous face.

'And then—I know not why—the magic broke:
'Twixt my slow footsteps and his presence fair,
Thin voices, shrill and sorrow-stricken, spoke
That seemed the sound of some out-worn Despair:

Pale phantoms flitted through the golden air
(As withered rose-leaves drift upon the wind),
And low the ghostly voices wailed, "Forbear!
Or fade, like us, forgotten out of mind."

'Now, as they flitted by, their forms I knew,
And all their loveliness, and all their woe:
Leucothoë, with Clytie, stern and true,
By love and vengeance made her sister's foe;
Fair Daphne with Bolina followed slow.
But all too many are those names to tell;
And each one's speech, in passing, murmured low,
Was, "Once—ah, once—Apollo loved me well."

'And from my soul uncoiled the fatal spell;
I turned, and looked on Ides where he stood
Awaiting joy—or grief unspeakable:
And earthly life once more seemed sweet and good
With all the cares of wife and motherhood:
"The gods love lightly, nor for long—may be
That men are sometimes of a constant mood—
Take me, oh Ides, and be true to me!"

'Then, through the net-like haze of golden light,
Even as a snared heron, freed at last,
Doth seek her own grey marsh-lands with delight,
Nor fears the chilly skies nor winter blast,
So, gladly, from the Sun-god's thrall I passed,
Mine eyes with too much radiance dazed and dim;
But goodly Ides seized and held me fast,
And all my heart's hid love went out to him.

'Right gladly then he bore me to my home,
And gladly to my mother's arms I sped,
Who deemed me drowned, perchance, in the sea foam,
Or with dread Scylla's victims numbered—
Thereafter soon my love and I were wed.'

'And was thy mortal lover true to thee?'
I asked—but silently the phantom fled,
Nor any answer more vouchsafed to me.

(1889 *1912*)

M. E. COLERIDGE
(1861–1907)

DESCENDING from a distinguished line of eminent literary men and women (Samuel Taylor Coleridge was her great-great-uncle, Sara Coleridge her great-aunt), Mary Coleridge grew up in an environment that fostered her artistic and educational ambitions. Her father, a man of strong Church of England principles, chose to follow the legal profession on the grounds that it would provide greater security than a life in the arts. Robert Browning, John Millais, John Ruskin, and Alfred Tennyson were visitors to her lively family home in London. In her early childhood, she displayed a voracious appetite for knowledge. By the age of 9, she was well versed in Hebrew, German, French, and Italian. Educated at home, she later learned Greek. When she was 13 years old, she met William Johnson Cory, the former Eton housemaster, shortly after he had been dismissed from his post in 1872 for his readiness to 'make favourites' among the boys. Cory, a renowned scholar and poet, guided her reading. In her early twenties, she gained a detailed knowledge of seventeenth-century drama, working on the folios of John Ford, Philip Massinger, and John Webster held by the British Museum. Although her letters and diaries suggest that she at times felt somewhat imprisoned by her scholarly pursuits, Coleridge devoted herself to passing on the fruits of her learning to a number of working women, some of whom she tutored at home. From 1895, she taught at the Women's Working College. She was also associated with King's College for Women at the University of London.

Even though Coleridge wrote poetry from an early age, her earliest publications were short prose pieces in the *Theatre*. Her first book was a novel, *The Seven Sleepers of Ephesus* (1893), and went practically unnoticed. It was her historical romance, *The King with Two Faces* (1897), that established her reputation. Among the five novels that Coleridge completed, *The Lady on the Drawingroom Floor* (1906) proved to be the most successful by far. Throughout the 1890s until the time of her death, she contributed widely to periodicals, including the *Contemporary Review*, the *Cornhill Magazine*, and the *National Review*. Among her extensive critical prose is the introduction she furnished for *The Last Poems of Richard Watson Dixon*, edited by Robert Bridges in 1905. Shortly before her death, Coleridge completed a brief life of the Pre-Raphaelite artist, William Holman Hunt, which was published posthumously in 1908.

By the age of 20, Coleridge's demanding lyrics were making their appearance in periodicals such as the *Monthly Packet* and *Merry England* (edited by Alice Meynell and Wilfrid Meynell). But it was some years before she collected her poems in a volume. Only after Bridges advised Coleridge on the revisions to her drafts did she publish *Fancy's Following* (1896), under the pseudonym 'Anodos'—the name of the hero in George Macdonald's *Phantastes* (1858). The book was issued by Daniel in Oxford. Augmented by several additional poems, this volume reappeared as *Fancy's Guerdon*, published this time by Elkin Mathews in 1897. Edith Sichel edited *Gathered Leaves from the Prose of Mary E. Coleridge* in 1910. Her poems were edited by Henry Newbolt, and brought out by Elkin Mathews a year after her death. The definitive edition of her works is edited by Theresa Whistler (Hart-Davis, 1954). Among the modern feminist critics who have drawn attention to the complexity of Coleridge's intricate short poems are Sandra Gilbert and Susan Gubar, *The Madwoman in the Attic* (Yale University

Press, 1979), and Christine Battersby, *Gender and Genius* (The Women's Press, 1989). Coleridge's collected poetry is notable for its intellectual precision.

343 *To Memory*

STRANGE Power, I know not what thou art,
Murderer or mistress of my heart.
I know I'd rather meet the blow
Of my most unrelenting foe
Than live—as now I live—to be
Slain twenty times a day by thee.

Yet, when I would command thee hence,
Thou mockest at the vain pretence,
Murmuring in mine ear a song
Once loved, alas! forgotten long;
And on my brow I feel a kiss
That I would rather die than miss.

(1896 *1908*)

344 *Gone*

ABOUT the little chambers of my heart
Friends have been coming—going—many a year.
The doors stand open there.
Some, lightly stepping, enter; some depart.

Freely they come and freely go, at will.
The walls give back their laughter; all day long
They fill the house with song.
One door alone is shut, one chamber still.

(1896 *1908*)

345 *The Other Side of a Mirror*

I SAT before my glass one day,
And conjured up a vision bare,
Unlike the aspects glad and gay,
That erst were found reflected there—
The vision of a woman, wild
With more than womanly despair.

Her hair stood back on either side
  A face bereft of loveliness.
It had no envy now to hide
  What once no man on earth could guess.
It formed the thorny aureole
  Of hard unsanctified distress.

Her lips were open—not a sound
  Came through the parted lines of red.
Whate'er it was, the hideous wound
  In silence and in secret bled.
No sigh relieved her speechless woe,
  She had no voice to speak her dread.

And in her lurid eyes there shone
  The dying flame of life's desire,
Made mad because its hope was gone,
  And kindled at the leaping fire
Of jealousy, and fierce revenge,
  And strength that could not change nor tire.

Shade of a shadow in the glass,
  O set the crystal surface free!
Pass—as the fairer visions pass—
  Nor ever more return, to be
The ghost of a distracted hour,
  That heard me whisper, 'I am she!'

(1896 *1908*)

346

Eyes

EYES, what are they? Coloured glass,
Where reflections come and pass.

Open windows—by them sit
Beauty, Learning, Love, and Wit.

Searching cross-examiners;
Comfort's holy ministers.

Starry silences of soul,
Music past the lips' control.

Fountains of unearthly light;
Prisons of the infinite.

(1896 *1908*)

347 *Mortal Combat*

It is because you were my friend,
 I fought you as the devil fights.
Whatever fortune God may send,
 For once I set the world to rights.

And that was when I thrust you down,
 And stabbed you twice and twice again,
Because you dared take off your crown,
 And be a man like other men.

(1896 *1908*)

348 *A Mother to a Baby*

Where were you, Baby?
 Where were you, dear?
Even I have known you
 Only a year.

You were born, Baby,
 When I was born.
Twelve months ago you
 Left me forlorn.

Why did you leave me,
 Heart of my heart?
Then I was all of you,
 Now you are part.

You lived while I lived,
 We two were one.
We two are two now
 While the days run.

Every maid born, love,
 Womanly, mild,
Is in herself, love,
 Mother and child.

(1908)

349 *Contradictions*

When I am dead, I know that thou wilt weep.
I that have never caused thee grief before,
I that have soothed thee, sung thy woes to sleep,
I shall have wrought thee sorrow wild and deep,
And made thy burden more.

When I am dead, I know thou wilt forget,
Thou that didst never yet forget thy friend.
'Grieve not!' I cry; 'I would not have thee fret'—
'Remember! I would live within thee yet.'
In vain, I know the end.

(1908)

350 *Mistaken*

I never thought that you could mourn
As other women do.
A blossom from your garland torn,
A jewel dropped that you had worn,
What could that be to you?

You never heard the human sound
Of wailing and despair.
Nor faithful proved nor faithless found,
You lived and moved in beauty crowned,
Content with being fair.

If I had known those eyes could weep
That used to sparkle so,
You had been mine to love, to keep,
But all too late I probed the deep
And all too late I know.

(1908)

351 *A Clever Woman*

You thought I had the strength of men,
Because with men I dared to speak,
And courted Science now and then,
And studied Latin for a week;
But woman's woman, even when
She reads her Ethics in the Greek.

You thought me wiser than my kind;
  You thought me 'more than common tall;'
You thought because I had a mind,
  That I could have no heart at all;
But woman's woman you will find,
  Whether she be great or small.

(1908)

MAY KENDALL
(1861–1943)

EMMA GOLDWORTH KENDALL was born in Bridlington, Yorkshire. Her father, James Kendall, was a Wesleyan minister. Little is known about her education. By her early twenties she was actively writing poetry and fiction. Her first published book was *That Very Mab* (1885), a collaboration with Andrew Lang that included satirical essays and verses on contemporary society. Two 'New Woman' fictions followed. Both *From a Garret* and *Such Is Life* appeared in 1889. Her final novel, *White Poppies*, went on sale four years later. It was during this period that she published most of her poetry. *Dreams to Sell* (1887) and *Songs from Dreamland* (1894) contain many exceptionally witty and incisive works that reveal her lively engagement with contemporary scientific debates. Some of her most notable poems reveal the significant impact that higher education was by this time having on women.

For most of her life, Kendall lived in York where she became actively involved in the philanthropic work of the Rowntree family. She worked as both a researcher and speech-writer for B. Seebohm Rowntree, and her input into his influential social survey, *How the Labourer Lives* (1913), was considerable. Among the materials held by the Joseph Rowntree Trust is a manuscript by Kendall on equal pay. Although never a member of the Society of Friends, she remained close to the activities of the Quakers, submitting essays and poems to both *The Friend* and the *Friends' Quarterly Examiner*. In later years, she was renowned for her eccentricity, living for many years at 10 Monkgate in a house overrun with cats. It appears that she died in poverty, since the Joseph Rowntree Trust made a grant to pay for her funeral. She is buried in an unmarked grave in York Cemetery.

352 *Lay of the Trilobite*

A MOUNTAIN'S giddy height I sought,
  Because I could not find
Sufficient vague and mighty thought
  To fill my mighty mind;
And as I wandered ill at ease,
  There chanced upon my sight
A native of Silurian seas,
  An ancient Trilobite.

So calm, so peacefully he lay,
  I watched him even with tears:
I thought of Monads far away
  In the forgotten years.
How wonderful it seemed and right,
  The providential plan,
That he should be a Trilobite,
  And I should be a Man!

And then, quite natural and free
  Out of his rocky bed,
That Trilobite he spoke to me,
  And this is what he said:
'I don't know how the thing was done,
  Although I cannot doubt it;
But Huxley—he if anyone
  Can tell you all about it;

'How all your faiths are ghosts and dreams,
  How in the silent sea
Your ancestors were Monotremes—
  Whatever these may be;
How you evolved your shining lights
  Of wisdom and perfection
From Jelly-fish and Trilobites
  By Natural Selection.

'You've Kant to make your brains go round,
  Hegel you have to clear them,
You've Mr Browning to confound,
  And Mr Punch to cheer them!
The native of an alien land
  You call a man and brother,
And greet with hymn-book in one hand
  And pistol in the other!

'You've Politics to make you fight
  As if you were possessed:
You've cannon and you've dynamite
  To give the nations rest:
The side that makes the loudest din
  Is surest to be right,
And oh, a pretty fix you're in!'
  Remarked the Trilobite.

'But gentle, stupid, free from woe
  I lived among my nation,
I didn't care—I didn't know
  That I was a Crustacean.[1]
I didn't grumble, didn't steal,
  I *never* took to rhyme:
Salt water was my frugal meal,
  And carbonate of lime.'

Reluctantly I turned away,
  No other word he said;
An ancient Trilobite, he lay
  Within his rocky bed.
I did not answer him, for that
  Would have annoyed my pride:
I merely bowed, and raised my hat,
  But in my heart I cried:—

'I wish our brains were not so good,
  I wish our skulls were thicker,
I wish that Evolution could
  Have stopped a little quicker;
For oh, it was a happy plight,
  Of liberty and ease,
To be a simple Trilobite
  In the Silurian seas!'

(1887)

353 *Education's Martyr*

He loved peculiar plants and rare,
For any plant he did not care
  That he had seen before;
Primroses by the river's brim
Dicotyledons were to him,
  And they were nothing more.

The mighty cliffs we bade him scan,
He banned them for Laurentian,
  With sad, dejected mien.
'Than all this bleak Azoic rock,'
He said, 'I'd sooner have a block—
  Ah me!—of Pleistocene!'

[1] He was not a Crustacean. He has since discovered that he was an Arachnid, or something similar. But he says it does not matter. He says they told him wrong once, and they may again.

His eyes were bent upon the sand;
He owned the *scenery* was grand,
  In a reproachful voice;
But if a centipede he found,
He'd fall before it on the ground,
  And worship and rejoice.

We spoke of Poets dead and gone,
Of that Maeonian who shone
  O'er Hellas like a star:
We talked about the King of Men,—
'Observe,' he said, 'the force of $\kappa\epsilon\nu$[1]
  And note the use of $\gamma\alpha\rho$!'[2]

Yes, all that has been or may be,
States, beauties, battles, land, and sea,
  The matin songs of larks,
With glacier, earthquake, avalanche,
To him were each a separate 'branch,'
  And stuff for scoring marks!

Ah! happier he who does not know
The power that makes the Planets go,
  The slaves of Kepler's Laws;
Who finds not glands in joy or grief,
Nor, in the blossom and the leaf,
  Seeks for the secret Cause!

(1887)

354 *Woman's Future*

COMPLACENT they tell us, hard hearts and derisive,
  In vain is our ardour: in vain are our sighs:
Our intellects, bound by a limit decisive,
  To the level of Homer's may never arise.
We heed not the falsehood, the base innuendo,
  The laws of the universe, these are our friends.
Our talents shall rise in a mighty crescendo,
  We trust Evolution to make us amends!

But ah, when I ask you for food that is mental,
  My sisters, you offer me ices and tea!
You cherish the fleeting, the mere accidental,
  At cost of the True, the Intrinsic, the Free.
Your feelings, compressed in Society's mangle,
  Are vapid and frivolous, pallid and mean.
To slander you love; but you don't care to wrangle:
  You bow to Decorum, and cherish Routine.

[1] $\kappa\epsilon\nu$ a modal particle used with verbs; it has several different functions. Eds.
[2] $\gamma\alpha\rho$ for. Eds.

Alas, is it woolwork you take for your mission,
  Or Art that your fingers so gaily attack?
Can patchwork atone for the mind's inanition?
  Can the soul, oh my sisters, be fed on a *plaque*?
Is this your vocation? My goal is another,
  And empty and vain is the end you pursue.
In antimacassars the world you may smother;
  But intellect marches o'er them and o'er you.

On Fashion's vagaries your energies strewing,
  Devoting your days to a rug or a screen,
Oh, rouse to a lifework—do something worth doing!
  Invent a new planet, a flying-machine.
Mere charms superficial, mere feminine graces,
  That fade or that flourish, no more you may prize;
But the knowledge of Newton will beam from your faces,
  The soul of a Spencer will shine in your eyes.

ENVOY

Though jealous exclusion may tremble to own us,
  Oh, wait for the time when our brains shall expand!
When once we're enthroned, you shall never dethrone us—
  The poets, the sages, the seers of the land!

(1887)

355 *An Incident in Real Life, Related by an Eye-Witness in Marble*

YOU saw him as you entered in,
  He stood at the right hand,
A terra-cotta Philistine
  Upon his wooden stand.
'Tis he who never cared a pin
  For what was really grand.

He treated us as things of nought,
  The statues calm and fair;
He said the building he had bought,
  Or we should not be there;
He owned he had the right, he thought,
  To criticise and stare.

The earliest dawn of morning crept
  Into the gallery wide;
We all, as though we had not slept,
  Stood calmly side by side:
His glimmering lyre Apollo swept,
  That in low tones replied.

It breathed a music sad and strange,
  Of living days and dead,
The echo of the years of change
  Since the old gods had fled,
In mockery of the wider range
  They had not cared to tread.

Rolled stony tears down many a face,
  Pluto was reconciled,
And sad Œnone, for a space,
  Was from her woe beguiled,
And Homer looked down from his place,
  And even Dante smiled.

It was the Philistine—ah, shame!
  Who did the fearful wrong;
Down on the mystic cadence came
  His accents harsh and strong.
He cried: 'Now Mr. What's your name,
  Give us a comic song.'

Silent the mighty harper stood,
  But with a look askance
The luckless Philistine he viewed,
  The calm, complacent glance,
The virtue of his attitude,
  His vacant countenance.

Apollo touched the mystic wand
  That was for him alone;
The statues all looked cool and bland
  As if they had not known:
A tremor shook the wooden stand—
  The Philistine was prone.

And hurrying footsteps entered in,
  Men viewed the vanquished o'er,
With yet the old superior grin,
  But crumbling more and more,
A terra-cotta Philistine
  In fragments on the floor.

(1887)

356 *The Sandblast Girl and the Acid Man*

Of all the cities far and wide,
    The city that I most prefer,
Though hardly through the fog descried,
    Is Muggy Manchester.
Of all its buildings the most dear,
    I find a stained glass factory—
Because the sandblast girl works here,
    In the same room with me!

It made a most terrific din,
    Of yore, that sandblasting machine.
I cursed the room I laboured in,
    And all the dull routine,
And the *old* sandblast girl, who broke,
    Of coloured glass, so many a sheet,
In fruitless efforts to evoke
    Tracery clear and neat.

That sandblast girl, at last she left—
    They couldn't let her blunders pass.
But Maggie's hands are slim and deft,
    They never break the glass!
From ruby, orange, or from blue,
    The letters stand out clear as pearl.
The fellows say they never knew
    So smart a sandblast girl!

I raise my eyes: I see her stand,
    A sheet of glass her arms embrace;
Out spurts the narrow stream of sand
    On each uncovered space,
Till perfectly the work is done,
    And clear again grows Maggie's brow—
Till a fresh labour is begun,
    She's merely human, now!

And sometimes when her hands are free,
    While with my acid still I work,
She'll give a hasty glance at me,
    Embossing like a Turk.
Her pretty hair so soft and brown
    Is coiled about her shapely head,
And I look up and she looks down,
    And both of us go red!

She has a dress of navy blue,
   A turn-down collar, white and clean
As though no smoke it travelled through,
   And smuts had never seen.
I've noticed that white snowdrop bells
   Have a peculiar look of her!
And nothing but her pallor tells
   Of Muggy Manchester.

Just twenty shillings every week!
   And always somebody distressed
Wants helping; and you feel a sneak
   If you don't do your best.
Suppose that I began to hoard,
   And steeled my heart, my coffer hid,
I wonder if I could afford
   To—Would she, if I did?

She has a mother to support,
   And I've a sister. Trade's not brisk,
And for a working man, in short,
   Life is a fearful risk.
The Clarion I sometimes read,
   I muse upon in winter nights,
I wonder if they'll e'er succeed
   In putting things to rights!

I'm vastly better off than some!
   I think of how the many fare
Who perish slowly, crushed and dumb,
   For leisure, food and air.
'Tis hard, in Freedom's very van,
   To live and die a luckless churl.
'Tis hard to be an acid man,
   Without a sandblast girl!

(1894)

AMY LEVY
(1861–1889)

AMY LEVY gained the distinction of being the first Jewish woman to matriculate at Newnham College, where she studied for four terms. It was at Cambridge that her first volume, *Xantippe and other verse*, was published (1881). The impressive title poem, which provides an unorthodox account of Socrates' shrewish wife, indicates that Levy's feminist politics were already well developed by the time she was 20. The remaining years of her short life were frequently spent in the company of distinguished feminist writers and campaigners of the day, including Olive Schreiner and Clementina Black. She was closely connected with the Garnett family, and Richard Garnett contributed the entry on her in the *DNB*.

Levy became relatively well known both as a novelist and poet during the 1880s. Most of *Xantippe* was incorporated in *A Minor Poet and Other Poems* (1884; second edition 1894), which displays the general influence of the Brownings' use of the monologue. Her frequent adoption of this form makes her poetry, in some respects, similar to Augusta Webster's far more extensive canon. Several of her poems are modelled on the work of the German poet, Heinrich Heine. *A London Plane-Tree and Other Verse*, containing more lyrical than dramatic pieces, appeared posthumously in 1889. On 10 September that year, having corrected the final proofs, the poet took her own life, at the age of twenty-seven, in the family home at 7 Endsleigh Gardens, London, the city where she spent most of her adult life. She died from inhaling charcoal fumes. It is possible that she was involved in some kind of suicide pact with Schreiner, although details of this matter are not at all clear. In 1892, the *Pall Mall Gazette* published the following unspecified account of Levy's relationship with Schreiner:

> Not many years ago two literary ladies—one of whom is widely famous—were spending a holiday at the seaside together, and both were indulging in very gloomy views of life. After discussing the question, they both agreed to commit suicide and the younger hurried home and but too effectively carried out her purpose. The other happily thought better of the matter, and refused to fulfil the terms of her contract. The only pity is that she did not let the other party to the agreement know in time.

On reading this, Schreiner wrote to the sexologist Havelock Ellis: 'A funny idea has struck me about the enclosed cutting, that perhaps *I* am meant ... I was always trying to cheer up Amy Levy ... I've often felt that, if I'd been more sympathetic to her melancholy mood, I might have done more for her.'

Most of Levy's fiction was published during the last two years of her life, and it was her prose writing that drew greatest public attention. Her most controversial and popular work was *Reuben Sachs* (1888), concerning avarice and promiscuousness among the London Jewish community. Many Jews felt the novel was a gross misrepresentation of their lives, the *Jewish Chronicle* receiving it badly. Oscar Wilde gave this work a favourable review in *Woman's World* (in which Levy also published), and Eleanor Marx (a close friend of Levy's) translated it into her native German. Altogether less polemical was *Miss Meredith* (1889), a governess story, written at an earlier date in the writer's career. *The Romance of a Shop* (1888) concerns the lives of three sisters who set up their own photography business in London. Two early essays were published in the *Cambridge Review* in 1882–84, one of which concerned the poetry of James Thomson ('B.V.'). Five shorter items of prose appeared in *Temple Bar* in the 1880s. These include a study of new American fiction by Henry James and William Dean Howells, whom Levy finds morally suspect and far too self-conscious: 'Some of us take a certain melancholy pleasure in reflecting that we live in a morbid and complex age; but do the most complex of us sit tense, weighing our neighbour's turn of head, noting the minute changes of complexion?' Instead, Levy advocates the emotional pleasures involved in novel-reading: 'There are certain finer ethical points which can be understood emotionally as they never could be understood intellectually.' These articles give some insight into the aesthetic choices she made in her own creative work.

Six small features (of less than half a page) on Jewish life and culture appeared in the *Jewish Chronicle* for 1886, and she contributed seven short pieces (a poem, stories, and essays) to *Woman's World* in 1888–90. Among the latter is an account of Christina Rossetti's poetry that reveals how conscious Levy was of the restrictions bearing upon women writers:

If I may be allowed a paradox, there has been no excellent woman-poet, but much woman's poetry of excellence. The name of Christina Rossetti stands high among the producers of such poetry. With unusual opportunities of culture, breathing from the first an atmosphere almost uniquely favourable to artistic production, she had never to contend with those obstacles which are apt to confront her sex at the outset of a literary career.

Shorter features appeared in other well-respected publications. The *Spectator*, Emily Faithfull's feminist *Victoria Magazine*, and the *Gentleman's Magazine* accepted contributions from her. Although her life was brief, Levy produced a substantial number of short items.

After her death, rumours about her seemingly mysterious life began to circulate in the press. Clementina Black felt compelled to bring an end to gossip by stating the following in the *Athenaeum* (October 1889):

Will you spare me a few lines in order to do justice both to the dead and the living? I have lately learnt that various reports, some exaggerated and some wholly untrue, have been made in various papers concerning the late Miss Amy Levy, and are being largely copied by the provincial press. I was a close friend of Miss Levy for many years, and my testimony is that of personal knowledge. It is not true that she ever left her father's house otherwise than on visits to friends or holiday journeys; nor that she suffered from failing eyesight, nor from the loss of her sense of humour; nor that she devoted herself to work in the East End. She did suffer for several years from slight deafness and from fits of extreme depression, not the result of unhappy circumstances or of unkind treatment, but, as those believe who knew her best, of her lack of physical robustness and of the exhaustion of strenuous brain work. Most emphatically, it is not true that her family and her personal friends among the Jewish community treated her coldly on account of the publication of 'Reuben Sachs', and thus indirectly hastened her death. Her parents were justly proud of her; it was impossible to be more uniformly indulgent, more anxious to anticipate her every wish than they were. At the time of her death they were out of town; but she had been with them only a few days before, had parted from them on the best of terms, and was expected to rejoin them the next week. Her sister was with her on the afternoon before her death, and from her also parted affectionately. I cannot imagine anything which would have caused more pain and indignation to Miss Levy than the circulation of such reports; and it is in her name that I make this protest against them.

It may or may not be the case that family and friends were attempting to cover up a scandal of some kind. Certainly, there was a growing amount of interest in her writing. Remaining facts about Levy's life, especially the charitable work conducted with her father in the philanthropic Beaumont Trust, are obscure. Her poetry remains some of the most important published in Britain during the 1880s.

357 *Xantippe*

(A FRAGMENT)

WHAT, have I waked again? I never thought
To see the rosy dawn, or ev'n this grey,
Dull, solemn stillness, ere the dawn has come.
The lamp burns low; low burns the lamp of life;
The still morn stays expectant, and my soul,
All weighted with a passive wonderment,
Waiteth and watcheth, waiteth for the dawn.
Come hither, maids; too soundly have ye slept
That should have watched me; nay, I would not chide—
Oft have I chidden, yet I would not chide
In this last hour;—now all should be at peace,
I have been dreaming in a troubled sleep
Of weary days I thought not to recall;
Of stormy days, whose storms are hushed long since;
Of gladsome days, of sunny days; alas
In dreaming, all their sunshine seem'd so sad,
As though the current of the dark To-Be
Had flow'd, prophetic, through the happy hours.
And yet, full well, I know it was not thus;
I mind me sweetly of the summer days,
When, leaning from the lattice, I have caught
The fair, far glimpses of a shining sea;
And, nearer, of tall ships which thronged the bay,
And stood out blackly from a tender sky
All flecked with sulphur, azure, and bright gold;
And in the still, clear air have heard the hum
Of distant voices; and methinks there rose
No darker fount to mar or stain the joy
Which sprang ecstatic in my maiden breast
Than just those vague desires, those hopes and fears,
Those eager longings, strong, though undefined,
Whose very sadness makes them seem so sweet.
What cared I for the merry mockeries
Of other maidens sitting at the loom?
Or for sharp voices, bidding me return
To maiden labour? Were we not apart—
I and my high thoughts, and my golden dreams,
My soul which yearned for knowledge, for a tongue
That should proclaim the stately mysteries
Of this fair world, and of the holy gods?
Then followed days of sadness, as I grew
To learn my woman-mind had gone astray,
And I was sinning in those very thoughts—

For maidens, mark, such are not woman's thoughts—
(And yet, 'tis strange, the gods who fashion us
Have given us such promptings). . . .
                                        Fled the years,
Till seventeen had found me tall and strong,
And fairer, runs it, than Athenian maids
Are wont to seem; I had not learnt it well—
My lesson of dumb patience—and I stood
At Life's great threshold with a beating heart,
And soul resolved to conquer and attain. . . .
Once, walking 'thwart the crowded market-place,
With other maidens, bearing in the twigs
White doves for Aphrodite's sacrifice,
I saw him, all ungainly and uncouth,
Yet many gathered round to hear his words,
Tall youths and stranger-maidens—Sokrates—
I saw his face and marked it, half with awe,
Half with a quick repulsion at the shape. . . .
The richest gem lies hidden furthest down,
And is the dearer for the weary search;
We grasp the shining shells which strew the shore,
Yet swift we fling them from us; but the gem
We keep for aye and cherish. So a soul,
Found after weary searching in the flesh
Which half repelled our senses, is more dear,
For that same seeking, than the sunny mind
Which lavish Nature marks with thousand hints
Upon a brow of beauty. We are prone
To overweigh such subtle hints, then deem,
In after disappointment, we are fooled. . . .
And when, at length, my father told me all,
That I should wed me with great Sokrates,
I, foolish, wept to see at once cast down
The maiden image of a future love,
Where perfect body matched the perfect soul.
But slowly, softly did I cease to weep;
Slowly I 'gan to mark the magic flash
Leap to the eyes, to watch the sudden smile
Break round the mouth, and linger in the eyes;
To listen for the voice's lightest tone—
Great voice, whose cunning modulations seemed
Like to the notes of some sweet instrument.
So did I reach and strain, until at last
I caught the soul athwart the grosser flesh.
Again of thee, sweet Hope, my spirit dreamed!
I, guided by his wisdom and his love,
Led by his words, and counselled by his care,

Should lift the shrouding veil from things which be,
And at the flowing fountain of his soul
Refresh my thirsting spirit....
And indeed,
In those long days which followed that strange day
When rites and song, and sacrifice and flow'rs,
Proclaimed that we were wedded, did I learn,
In sooth, a-many lessons; bitter ones
Which sorrow taught me, and not love inspired,
Which deeper knowledge of my kind impressed
With dark insistence on reluctant brain;—
But that great wisdom, deeper, which dispels
Narrowed conclusions of a half-grown mind,
And sees athwart the littleness of life
Nature's divineness and her harmony,
Was never poor Xantippe's....
I would pause
And would recall no more, no more of life,
Than just the incomplete, imperfect dream
Of early summers, with their light and shade,
Their blossom-hopes, whose fruit was never ripe;
But something strong within me, some sad chord
Which loudly echoes to the later life,
Me to unfold the after-misery
Urges, with plaintive wailing in my heart.
Yet, maidens, mark; I would not that ye thought
I blame my lord departed, for he meant
No evil, so I take it, to his wife.
'Twas only that the high philosopher,
Pregnant with noble theories and great thoughts,
Deigned not to stoop to touch so slight a thing
As the fine fabric of a woman's brain—
So subtle as a passionate woman's soul.
I think, if he had stooped a little, and cared,
I might have risen nearer to his height,
And not lain shattered, neither fit for use
As goodly household vessel, nor for that
Far finer thing which I had hoped to be....
Death, holding high his retrospective lamp,
Shows me those first, far years of wedded life,
Ere I had learnt to grasp the barren shape
Of what the Fates had destined for my life
Then, as all youthful spirits are, was I
Wholly incredulous that Nature meant
So little, who had promised me so much.
At first I fought my fate with gentle words,
With high endeavours after greater things;

Striving to win the soul of Sokrates,
Like some slight bird, who sings her burning love
To human master, till at length she finds
Her tender language wholly misconceived,
And that same hand whose kind caress she sought,
With fingers flippant flings the careless corn....
I do remember how, one summer's eve,
He, seated in an arbour's leafy shade,
Had bade me bring fresh wine-skins....
As I stood
Ling'ring upon the threshold, half concealed
By tender foliage, and my spirit light
With draughts of sunny weather, did I mark
An instant the gay group before mine eyes.
Deepest in shade, and facing where I stood,
Sat Plato, with his calm face and low brows
Which met above the narrow Grecian eyes,
The pale, thin lips just parted to the smile,
Which dimpled that smooth olive of his cheek.
His head a little bent, sat Sokrates,
With one swart finger raised admonishing,
And on the air were borne his changing tones.
Low lounging at his feet, one fair arm thrown
Around his knee (the other, high in air
Brandish'd a brazen amphor, which yet rained
Bright drops of ruby on the golden locks
And temples with their fillets of the vine),
Lay Alkibiades the beautiful.
And thus, with solemn tone, spake Sokrates:
'This fair Aspasia, which our Perikles
Hath brought from realms afar, and set on high
In our Athenian city, hath a mind,
I doubt not, of a strength beyond her race;
And makes employ of it, beyond the way
Of women nobly gifted: woman's frail—
Her body rarely stands the test of soul;
She grows intoxicate with knowledge; throws
The laws of custom, order, 'neath her feet,
Feasting at life's great banquet with wide throat.'
Then sudden, stepping from my leafy screen,
Holding the swelling wine-skin o'er my head,
With breast that heaved, and eyes and cheeks aflame,
Lit by a fury and a thought, I spake:
'By all great powers around us! can it be
That we poor women are empirical?
That gods who fashioned us did strive to make
Beings too fine, too subtly delicate,

With sense that thrilled response to ev'ry touch
Of nature's, and their task is not complete?
That they have sent their half-completed work
To bleed and quiver here upon the earth?
To bleed and quiver, and to weep and weep,
To beat its soul against the marble walls
Of men's cold hearts, and then at last to sin!'
I ceased, the first hot passion stayed and stemmed
And frighted by the silence: I could see,
Framed by the arbour foliage, which the sun
In setting softly gilded with rich gold,
Those upturned faces, and those placid limbs;
Saw Plato's narrow eyes and niggard mouth,
Which half did smile and half did criticise,
One hand held up, the shapely fingers framed
To gesture of entreaty—'Hush, I pray,
Do not disturb her; let us hear the rest;
Follow her mood, for here's another phase
Of your black-browed Xantippe....'
Then I saw
Young Alkibiades, with laughing lips
And half-shut eyes, contemptuous shrugging up
Soft, snowy shoulders, till he brought the gold
Of flowing ringlets round about his breasts.
But Sokrates, all slow and solemnly,
Raised, calm, his face to mine, and sudden spake:
'I thank thee for the wisdom which thy lips
Have thus let fall among us: prythee tell
From what high source, from what philosophies
Didst cull the sapient notion of thy words?'
Then stood I straight and silent for a breath,
Dumb, crushed with all that weight of cold contempt;
But swiftly in my bosom there uprose
A sudden flame, a merciful fury sent
To save me; with both angry hands I flung
The skin upon the marble, where it lay
Spouting red rills and fountains on the white;
Then, all unheeding faces, voices, eyes,
I fled across the threshold, hair unbound—
White garment stained to redness—beating heart
Flooded with all the flowing tide of hopes
Which once had gushed out golden, now sent back
Swift to their sources, never more to rise....
I think I could have borne the weary life,
The narrow life within the narrow walls,
If he had loved me; but he kept his love
For this Athenian city and her sons;

And, haply, for some stranger-woman, bold
With freedom, thought, and glib philosophy....
Ah me! the long, long weeping through the nights,
The weary watching for the pale-eyed dawn
Which only brought fresh grieving: then I grew
Fiercer, and cursed from out my inmost heart
The Fates which marked me an Athenian maid.
Then faded that vain fury; hope died out;
A huge despair was stealing on my soul,
A sort of fierce acceptance of my fate,—
He wished a household vessel—well 'twas good,
For he should have it! He should have no more
The yearning treasure of a woman's love,
But just the baser treasure which he sought.
I called my maidens, ordered out the loom,
And spun unceasing from the morn till eve;
Watching all keenly over warp and woof,
Weighing the white wool with a jealous hand.
I spun until, methinks, I spun away
The soul from out my body, the high thoughts
From out my spirit; till at last I grew
As ye have known me,—eye exact to mark
The texture of the spinning; ear all keen
For aimless talking when the moon is up,
And ye should be a-sleeping; tongue to cut
With quick incision, 'thwart the merry words
Of idle maidens....
Only yesterday
My hands did cease from spinning; I have wrought
My dreary duties, patient till the last.
The gods reward me! Nay, I will not tell
The after years of sorrow; wretched strife
With grimmest foes—sad Want and Poverty;—
Nor yet the time of horror, when they bore
My husband from the threshold; nay, nor when
The subtle weed had wrought its deadly work.
Alas! alas! I was not there to soothe
The last great moment; never any thought
Of her that loved him—save at least the charge,
All earthly, that her body should not starve....
You weep, you weep; I would not that ye wept;
Such tears are idle; with the young, such grief
Soon grows to gratulation, as, 'her love
Was withered by misfortune; mine shall grow
All nurtured by the loving,' or, 'her life
Was wrecked and shattered—mine shall smoothly sail.'
Enough, enough. In vain, in vain, in vain!

The gods forgive me! Sorely have I sinned
In all my life. A fairer fate befall
You all that stand there....
Ha! the dawn has come;
I see a rosy glimmer—nay! it grows dark;
Why stand ye so in silence? throw it wide,
The casement, quick; why tarry?—give me air—
O fling it wide, I say, and give me light!

(1879 *1884*)

358 *Magdalen*

All things I can endure, save one.
The bare, blank room where is no sun;
The parcelled hours; the pallet hard;
The dreary faces here within;
The outer women's cold regard;
The Pastor's iterated 'sin';—
These things could I endure, and count
No overstrain'd, unjust amount;
No undue payment for such bliss—
Yea, all things bear, save only this:
That you, who knew what thing would be,
Have wrought this evil unto me.
It is so strange to think on still—
That you, that *you* should do me ill!
Not as one ignorant or blind,
But seeing clearly in your mind
How this must be which now has been,
Nothing aghast at what was seen.
Now that the tale is told and done,
It is so strange to think upon.

You were so tender with me, too!
One summer's night a cold blast blew,
Closer about my throat you drew
The half-slipt shawl of dusky blue.
And once my hand, on a summer's morn,
I stretched to pluck a rose; a thorn
Struck through the flesh and made it bleed
(A little drop of blood indeed!)
Pale grew your cheek; you stoopt and bound
Your handkerchief about the wound;
Your voice came with a broken sound;
With the deep breath your breast was riven;
I wonder, did God laugh in Heaven?

How strange, that *you* should work my woe!
How strange! I wonder, do you know
How gladly, gladly I had died
(And life was very sweet that tide)
To save you from the least, light ill?
How gladly I had borne your pain.
With one great pulse we seem'd to thrill,—
Nay, but we thrill'd with pulses twain.

Even if one had told me this,
'A poison lurks within your kiss,
Gall that shall turn to night his day':
Thereon I straight had turned away—
Ay, tho' my heart had crack'd with pain—
And never kiss'd your lips again.

At night, or when the daylight nears,
I hear the other women weep;
My own heart's anguish lies too deep
For the soft rain and pain of tears.
I think my heart has turn'd to stone,
A dull, dead weight that hurts my breast;
Here, on my pallet-bed alone,
I keep apart from all the rest.
Wide-eyed I lie upon my bed,
I often cannot sleep all night;
The future and the past arc dead,
There is no thought can bring delight.
All night I lie and think and think;
If my heart were not made of stone,
But flesh and blood, it needs must shrink
Before such thoughts. Was ever known
A woman with a heart of stone?

The doctor says that I shall die.
It may be so, yet what care I?
Endless reposing from the strife?
Death do I trust no more than life.
For one thing is like one arrayed,
And there is neither false nor true;
But in a hideous masquerade
All things dance on, the ages through.
And good is evil, evil good;
Nothing is known or understood
Save only Pain. I have no faith
In God or Devil, Life or Death.

The doctor says that I shall die.
You, that I knew in days gone by,
I fain would see your face once more,
Con well its features o'er and o'er;
And touch your hand and feel your kiss,
Look in your eyes and tell you this:
That all is done, that I am free;
That you, through all eternity,
Have neither part nor lot in me.

(1884)

359 *To Lallie (Outside the British Museum)*

Up those Museum steps you came,
And straightway all my blood was flame,
O Lallie, Lallie!

The world (I had been feeling low)
In one short moment's space did grow
A happy valley.

There was a friend, my friend, with you;
A meagre dame, in peacock blue
Apparelled quaintly:

This poet-heart went pit-a-pat;
I bowed and smiled and raised my hat;
You nodded—faintly.

My heart was full as full could be;
You had not got a word for me,
Not one short greeting;

That nonchalant small nod you gave
(The tyrant's motion to the slave)
Sole mark'd our meeting.

Is it so long? Do you forget
That first and last time that we met?
The time was summer;

The trees were green; the sky was blue;
Our host presented me to you—
A tardy comer.

You look'd demure, but when you spoke
You made a little, funny joke,
Yet half pathetic.

Your gown was grey, I recollect,
I think you patronized the sect
They call 'aesthetic.'

I brought you strawberries and cream,
I plied you long about a stream
With duckweed laden;

We solemnly discussed the—heat.
I found you shy and very sweet,
A rosebud maiden.

Ah me, to-day! You passed inside
To where the marble gods abide:
Hermes, Apollo,

Sweet Aphrodite, Pan; and where,
For aye reclined, a headless fair
Beats all fairs hollow.

And I, I went upon my way,
Well—rather sadder, let us say;
The world looked flatter.

I had been sad enough before,
A little less, a little more,
What *does* it matter?

(1884)

360 *Borderland*

AM I waking, am I sleeping?
As the first faint dawn comes creeping
Thro' the pane, I am aware
Of an unseen presence hovering,
Round, above, in the dusky air:
A downy bird, with an odorous wing,
That fans my forehead, and sheds perfume,
As sweet as love, as soft as death,
Drowsy-slow through the summer-gloom.
My heart in some dream-rapture saith,
It is she. Half in a swoon,
I spread my arms in slow delight.—
O prolong, prolong the night,
For the nights are short in June!

(1889)

361 *At a Dinner Party*

WITH fruit and flowers the board is deckt,
  The wine and laughter flow;
I'll not complain—could one expect
  So dull a world to know?

You look across the fruit and flowers,
  My glance your glances find.—
It is our secret, only ours,
  Since all the world is blind.

(1889)

362 *A Ballad of Religion and Marriage*

Swept into limbo is the host
  Of heavenly angels, row on row;
The Father, Son, and Holy Ghost,
  Pale and defeated, rise and go.
The great Jehovah is laid low,
  Vanished his burning bush and rod—
Say, are we doomed to deeper woe?
  Shall marriage go the way of God?

Monogamous, still at our post,
  Reluctantly we undergo
Domestic round of boiled and roast,
  Yet deem the whole proceeding slow.
Daily the secret murmurs grow;
  We are no more content to plod
Along the beaten paths—and so
  Marriage must go the way of God.

Soon, before all men, each shall toast
  The seven strings unto his bow,
Like beacon fires along the coast,
  The flames of love shall glance and glow.
Nor let nor hindrance man shall know,
  From natal bath to funeral sod;
Perennial shall his pleasures flow
  When marriage goes the way of God.

Grant, in a million years at most,
  Folk shall be neither pairs nor odd—
Alas! we shan't be there to boast
  'Marriage has gone the way of God!'

(Composed *c.* 1889 *1915*)

LAURENCE HOPE
(ADELA FLORENCE NICOLSON)
(1865–1904)

ADELA FLORENCE CORY (later Nicolson) was born at Stoke Bishop, Gloucestershire, but was to spend most of her adult life in India. She was the daughter of a colonel in the Indian Army, Arthur Cory, and of Fanny Elizabeth (née Griffin). Having been educated in England, she then moved to India to be with her parents, and there married Colonel Malcolm Hussels Nicolson in 1889. She lived with her husband in Madras.

Both she and her novelist sister, Vivian Cory ('Victoria Crosse'), assumed pseudonyms. In the preface to her first book of poetry, *The Garden of Kama, and Other Love Lyrics from India* (1902), Laurence Hope writes that she 'produced' the volume: it is not clear whether the poems are her own or translations. The many reviewers of this first book presumed that it was written by a man. Two more volumes of poetry followed: *Stars of the Desert* (1903) and *Indian Love* (1905), which was dedicated to her husband. *Laurence Hope's Poems* appeared posthumously in 1907. These volumes were published in England and America.

Two months after the death of her husband in 1904, she committed suicide by taking perchloride of mercury.

363 *The Regret of the Ranee in the Hall of Peacocks*

THIS man has taken my Husband's life
  And laid my Brethren low,
No sister indeed, were I, no wife,
  To pardon and let him go.

Yet why does he look so young and slim
  As he weak and wounded lies?
How hard for me to be harsh to him
  With his soft, appealing eyes.

His hair is ruffled upon the stone
  And the slender wrists are bound,
So young! and yet he has overthrown
  His scores on the battle ground.

Would I were only a slave to-day,
  To whom it were right and meet
To wash the stains of the War away,
  The dust from the weary feet.

Were I but one of my serving girls
  To solace his pain to rest!
Shake out the sand from the soft loose curls,
  And hold him against my breast!

Have we such beauty about our Throne?
  Such lithe and delicate strength?
Would God that I were the senseless stone
  To support his slender length!

I hate those wounds that trouble my sight,
  Unknown! how I wish you lay,
Alone in my silken tent to-night
  While I charmed the pain away!

I would lay you down on the Royal bed,
  I would bathe your wounds with wine,
And setting your feet against my head
  Dream you were lover of mine.

My Crown is heavy upon my hair,
  The Jewels weigh on my breast,
All I would leave, with delight, to share
  Your pale and passionate rest!

But hands grow restless about their swords,
  Lips murmur below their breath,
'The Queen is silent too long!' 'My Lords,
  —Take him away to death!'

(1902)

364 *Camp Follower's Song, Gomal River*

We have left Gul Kach behind us,
    Are marching on Apozai,—
Where pleasure and rest are waiting
    To welcome us by and by.

We're falling back from the Gomal,
    Across the Gir-dao plain,
The camping ground is deserted,
    We'll never come back again.

Along the rocks and the defiles,
    The mules and the camels wind.
Good-bye to Rahimut-Ullah,
    The man who is left behind.

For some we lost in the skirmish,
And some were killed in the fight,
But he was captured by fever,
In the sentry pit, at night.

A rifle shot had been swifter,
Less trouble a sabre thrust,
But his Fate decided fever,
And each man dies as he must.

Behind us, red in the distance,
The wavering flames rise high,
The flames of our burning grass-huts,
Against the black of the sky.

We hear the sound of the river,
An ever-lessening moan,
The hearts of us all turn backwards
To where he is left alone.

We sing up a little louder,
We know that we feel bereft,
We're leaving the camp together,
And only one of us left.

The only one, out of many,
And each must come to his end,
I wish I could stop this singing,
He happened to be my friend.

We're falling back from the Gomal
We're marching on Apozai,
And pleasure and rest are waiting
To welcome us by and by.

Perhaps the feast will taste bitter,
The lips of the girls less kind,—
Because of Rahimut-Ullah,
The man who is left behind!

(1902)

ETHNA CARBERY (ANNA MACMANUS)
(1866–1902)

ETHNA CARBERY was the pen-name of the Irish poet, Anna Isabel MacManus (née Johnston). She was born in Ballymena, County Antrim, the daughter of a prosperous merchant, but was later to live in Belfast. Intensely patriotic, her poetry is said to have stimulated the early Sinn Féin movement. She began by contributing numerous poems to Irish and American periodicals (her earlier pieces being signed 'Ethna'), including *United Ireland* and the *Nation*, as well as to the journals that she set up with her friend, the poet Alice Milligan. In 1894, they founded *The Northern Patriot* in association with the Belfast National Workingmen's Club. The journal was suspended after a disagreement with the club and replaced by the two poets with the *Shan Van Vocht* (The Poor Old Woman), which ran between 1896 and 1899.

Carbery's one collection of poetry was published in the same year as her premature death, 1902: *The Four Winds of Eirinn*. She had managed to prepare two-thirds of the book for publication; the editing was completed by her husband, the poet, Seamus MacManus, whom she had married in 1901. Some of these poems were later set to music by Mrs C. Milligan Fox (Alice Milligan's sister) and Edith Wheeler. The poet, Katharine Tynan, wrote of Ethna Carbery that she had 'two songs—a song of Ireland and a song of God', and defined her as a 'prophetess' of Irish independence (*Studies. An Irish Quarterly Review*, September 1918). Another poet, Alice Furlong, similarly commended her 'passionate patriotism' (*Irish Monthly*, November 1918). Ethna Carbery was a friend of Katharine Tynan's sister, Elizabeth, and also, for some time, of Alice Furlong. Two collections of her short stories were published posthumously in 1903 and 1904, edited by her husband.

365 *Mo Chraoibhín Cno*[1]

A Sword of Light hath pierced the dark, our eyes have seen the
 star.
O Mother, leave the ways of sleep now days of promise are:
The rusty spears upon your walls are stirring to and fro,
In dreams they front uplifted shields—Then wake,
 Mo Chraoibhin Cno!

The little waves creep whispering where sedges fold you in,
And round you are the barrows of your buried kith and kin;
Oh! famine-wasted, fever-burnt, they faded like the snow
Or set their hearts to meet the steel—for you,
 Mo Chraoibhin Cno!

[1] Pr. *Mo chreeveen no*. 'My cluster of nuts' = my brown-haired girl, i.e. Ireland.

Their names are blest, their *caoine* sung, our bitter tears are dried;
We bury Sorrow in their graves, Patience we cast aside;
Within the gloom we hear a voice that once was ours to know—
'Tis Freedom—Freedom calling loud, Arise!
Mo Chraoibhin Cno!

Afar beyond that empty sea, on many a battle-place,
Your sons have stretched brave hands to death before the foeman's face—
Down the sad silence of your rest their war-notes faintly blow,
And bear an echo of your name—of yours,
Mo Chraoibhin Cno!

Then wake, *a grádh!* We yet shall win a gold crown for your head,
Strong wine to make a royal feast—the white wine and the red—
And in your oaken mether the yellow mead shall flow,
What day you rise, in all men's eyes—a Queen,
Mo Chraoibhin Cno!

The silver speech our fathers knew shall once again be heard;
The fire-lit story, crooning song, sweeter than lilt of bird;
Your quicken-tree shall break in flower, its ruddy fruit shall glow,
And the Gentle People dance beneath its shade—
Mo Chraoibhin Cno!

There shall be peace and plenty—the kindly open door;
Blessings on all who come and go—the prosperous or the poor—
The misty glens and purple hills a fairer tint shall show,
When your splendid Sun shall ride the skies again—
Mo Chraoibhin Cno!

(1902)

366 *The Well o' the World's End*

BEYOND *the four seas of Eire, beyond the sunset's rim,*
It lies half-forgot, in a valley deep and dim;
Like a star of fire from the skies' gold tire,
And whoso drinks the nine drops shall win his heart's desire—
At the Well o' the World's End.

What go ye seeking, seeking, seeking,
O girl white-bosomed, O girl fair and young?
'I seek the Well-water, the cool Well-water,
That my love may have love for me ever on his tongue.'

What go ye seeking, seeking, seeking,
O lad of the dreaming eyes, slender lad and tall?
'I seek the Well-water, the cool Well-water,
That the *cailín* I love best may love me best of all.'

What go ye seeking, seeking, seeking,
O mother, with your little babe folded on your arm?
'I seek the Well-water, the cool Well-water,
That nine drops upon his lips may shield my child from harm.'

What go ye seeking, seeking, seeking,
O gray head, long weary of the vigil that ye keep?
'I seek the Well-water, the cool Well-water,
That nigh it I may rest awhile, and after fall asleep.'

(1902)

ALICE MILLIGAN
(1866–1953)

ALICE LETITIA MILLIGAN was an Ulster Protestant, who was converted to the politics of 'Home Rule' when a teenager, and went on to become a Gaelic Leaguer, a vehement supporter of the Irish Nationalist movement and founder member of the Ulster Anti-Partition Council. There was nothing in her family background to suggest the political orientations of her own life. Born in Omagh, County Tyrone, of Methodist parents, her mother, Charlotte (née Burns) came from the heart of the 'Orange Country', and her father, Seaton Forrest Milligan, was a wealthy Irish businessman and a man of many cultural interests. Alice Milligan was educated first at a Tory and Protestant school, then at the Methodist College in Belfast, and finally at colleges in Derry and London. Increasingly aware of the bias towards English history in her schooling, she consciously remedied this by studying Irish history and later toured the country lecturing on this subject for the Gaelic League. She also learnt the Irish language.

From 1893 she was to contribute about two hundred poems to Irish periodicals (the earlier ones being signed 'Iris Olkyrn'), such as the nationalist *The United Irishman* (between 1901–1906) and *Sinn Féin* (1906–1912). Her poems also appeared in the nationalist journals that she set up with her friend, the poet Ethna Carbery (Anna MacManus). In 1894, they founded *The Northern Patriot* in association with the Belfast National Workingmen's Club. A later disagreement with the Club led to the suspension of the journal and its replacement by the two poets with the *Shan Van Vocht* (The Poor Old Woman) between 1896 and 1899.

Alice Milligan's first book of poetry, *Hero Lays*, was published in 1908, and she later wrote of it: 'Impulse and inspiration undoubtedly came from entrance into the living Gaelic movement...' ('The Scattering of the Company', *Irish Statesman*, June 1928). The collection was well received, with the poet, Thomas MacDonagh, praising it as 'the best book of national Irish poems by a single author' (*Irish Review*, September–November 1914). Even before the publication of this volume, the poet, 'AE' (George Russell), considered some of Alice Milligan's verse to be 'the best patriotic poetry written in Ireland' (Introduction to his *New Songs. A Lyric Selection*, 1904). His own selection of her lyrics, however, was intended to highlight the diversity of her poetic output. Further selections from her poetry followed within Seamus MacManus's anthology, *We Sang for Ireland* (1950) and with Henry Magan's posthumous edition of *Poems by Alice Milligan* (1954). Her other publications include poems incorporated within her father's Irish sketches, *Glimpses of Erin* (1888), words for some of the airs in her sister, Mrs C. Milligan-Fox's, *Songs of the Irish Harpers* (1910), and a number of plays. Her *The Last Feast of the Fianna* was performed by the Irish National Theatre at the outset of the Irish dramatic revival and published in the same year, 1900. She also wrote a biography of Wolf Tone (1898).

367 *A Song of Freedom*

IN Cavan of little lakes,
As I was walking with the wind,
And no one seen beside me there,
There came a song into my mind:
It came as if the whispered voice
Of one, but none of human kind,
Who walked with me in Cavan then,
And he invisible as wind.

On Urris of Inish-Owen,
As I went up the mountain side,
The brook that came leaping down
Cried to me—for joy it cried;
And when from off the summit far
I looked o'er land and water wide,
I was more joyous than the brook
That met me on the mountain side.

To Ara of Connacht's isles,
As I went sailing o'er the sea,
The wind's word, the brook's word,
The wave's word, was plain to me—
'As we are, though she is not
As we are, shall Banba be—
There is no King can rule the wind,
There is no fetter for the sea.'

(1908)

368 *When I Was a Little Girl*

WHEN I was a little girl,
In a garden playing,
A thing was often said
To chide us, delaying:

When after sunny hours,
At twilight's falling,
Down through the garden walks
Came our old nurse calling—

'Come in! for it's growing late,
And the grass will wet ye!
Come in! or when it's dark
The Fenians will get ye.'

Then, at this dreadful news,
All helter-skelter,
The panic-struck little flock
Ran home for shelter.

And round the nursery fire
Sat still to listen,
Fifty bare toes on the hearth,
Ten eyes a-glisten—

To hear of a night in March,
And loyal folk waiting
To see a great army of men
Come devastating—

An army of Papists grim,
With a green flag o'er them,
Red-coats and black police
Flying before them.

But God (Who our nurse declared
Guards British dominions)
Sent a deep fall of snow
And scattered the Fenians.

'But somewhere they're lurking yet,
Maybe they're near us,'
Four little hearts pit-a-pat
Thought 'Can they hear us?'

Then the wind-shaken pane
Sounded like drumming;
'Oh!' they cried, 'tuck us in,
The Fenians are coming!'

Four little pairs of hands,
In the cots where she led those,
Over their frightened heads
Pulled up the bedclothes.

But one little rebel there,
Watching all with laughter,
Thought 'When the Fenians come
I'll rise and go after.'

Wished she had been a boy
And a good deal older—
Able to walk for miles
With a gun on her shoulder.

Able to lift aloft
That Green Flag o'er them
(Red-coats and black police
Flying before them).

And, as she dropped asleep,
Was wondering whether
God, if they prayed to Him,
Would give fine weather.

(1908)

369 *The Dark Palace*
(The Palace of Aileach, Seat of The O'Neill)

THERE beams no light from thy hall to-night,
Oh House of Fame!
No mead-vat seethes and no smoke upwreathes
O'er the hearth's red flame;
No high bard sings for the joy of thy kings,
And no harpers play;
No hostage moans at thy dungeon-stones
As in Muircherteach's day.

Fallen! fallen to ruin all in
The covering mould;
The painted yew, and the curtain blue,
And the cups of gold;
The linen, yellow as the corn when mellow,
That the princes wore;
And the mirrors brazen for your queens to gaze in,
They are here no more.

The sea-bird's pinion thatched Gormlai's grianán;
And through windows clear,
Without crystal pane, in her Ard-righ's reign
She looked forth from here.
There were quilts of eider on her couch of cedar;

And her silken shoon
Were as green and soft as the leaves aloft
On a bough of June.

Ah, woe unbounded! where the harp once sounded
The wind now sings;
The gray grass shivers where the mead in rivers
Was out-poured for kings;
The *mín* and the mether are lost together
With the spoil of the spears;
The strong dún only has stood dark and lonely
Through a thousand years.

But I am not in woe for the wine-cup's flow,
For the banquet's cheer,
For tall princesses with their trailing tresses
And their broidered gear;
My grief and my trouble for this palace noble
With no chief to lead
'Gainst the Saxon stranger on the day of danger
Out of Aileach Neid.

(1908)

370 *Cormacan Sings (Cormacan an Eigeas, 10th Century)*

Cormacan sings—
There broods a calm upon the brow of Kings
Who sit at Tara far from sound of fight;
For memory of more than war he brings.

He harps—they hear,
Mid harp notes sighing through the banquet's cheer,
Soft voices that are sad
Of loved ones in their youthful days they had—
Of noble ladies who no more are near.

He harps again,
And now, soft tears are flowing like the rain
Down agéd unused cheeks,
And in the silence no man speaks
All, all are sobbing betwixt joy and pain.

Flann rises up,
Awards the skilful bard a royal cup—
But adds to his award
This prohibition hard,
'See that thou com'st no more where warriors sup.'

(*c.*1905–8 *1950*)

DORA SIGERSON (LATER SHORTER)
(1866–1918)

An Irish poet, Dora Sigerson (later Shorter) was born into a literary family in Dublin. Her mother, Hester (née Varian), wrote poetry and fiction, and her father, Dr George Sigerson, produced historical and scientific works, as well as being a distinguished translator of Irish poetry. Their other daughter, Hester Sigerson, contributed poetry and reviews to periodicals. After Dora Sigerson's marriage to the English critic, Clement Shorter, in 1895, she was to live in London for the rest of her life, but continued to be absorbed in Irish issues.

She contributed vast quantities of poems to English and American journals and the first of her numerous books of poetry was published in 1893. The *Collected Poems of Dora Clement Shorter* (1907) was published before she completed her poetic career, and it contains an appreciative introduction by the novelist and poet, George Meredith. Her poetry was also praised by her friend, Katharine Tynan, in *The Bookman* (December 1897). She befriended other Irish poets, such as Alice Furlong and W. B. Yeats.

Her *Love of Ireland. Poems and Ballads* (1916) includes many verses previously published in her *Collected Poems*, but also incorporates a new selection entitled 'Poems of the Irish Rebellion 1916'. She is said never to have recovered from the events of Easter 1916. After her death, an 'In Memoriam' collection of poems were written for her by Eva Gore-Booth, Alice Furlong, and Katharine Tynan (1923).

371 *With a Rose*

In the heart of a rose
  Lies the heart of a maid;
  If you be not afraid
You will wear it. Who knows?

In the pink of its bloom,
  Lay your lips to her cheek;
  Since a rose cannot speak,
And you gain the perfume.

If the dews on the leaf
  Are the tears from her eyes;
  If she withers and dies,
Why, you have the belief,

That a rose cannot speak,
  Though the heart of a maid
  In its bosom must fade,
And with fading must break.

(1897)

372 *The Wind on the Hills*

Go not to the hills of Erin
When the night winds are about,
Put up your bar and shutter,
And so keep the danger out.

For the good-folk whirl within it,
And they pull you by the hand,
And they push you on the shoulder,
Till you move to their command.

And lo! you have forgotten
What you have known of tears,
And you will not remember
That the world goes full of years;

A year there is a lifetime,
And a second but a day,
And an older world will meet you
Each morn you come away.

Your wife grows old with weeping,
And your children one by one
Grow grey with nights of watching,
Before your dance is done.

And it will chance some morning
You will come home no more,
Your wife sees but a withered leaf
In the wind about the door.

And your children will inherit
The unrest of the wind,
They shall seek some face elusive,
And some land they never find.

When the wind is loud, they sighing
Go with hearts unsatisfied,
For some joy beyond remembrance,
For some memory denied.

And all your children's children,
They cannot sleep or rest,
When the wind is out in Erin
And the sun is in the West.

(1899)

NORA HOPPER (LATER CHESSON)
(1871–1906)

ALTHOUGH she was born in Exeter and lived all her life in England, Nora Hopper (later Chesson) could claim both Irish descent through her father, Captain H. B. Hopper, and Welsh through her mother, but is more commonly identified as second generation Irish and often thought of specifically as a 'Celtic Twilight' poet.

The writer of novels and sketches, she was best known for her poetry, much of which was first published in a vast range of magazines and journals, such as the *Westminster Gazette*, the *Academy* and *Macmillan's Magazine*. Her first collection of poems, *Ballads in Prose* (1894) draws heavily, as many of her poems do, upon Irish mythology. In a letter to Katharine Tynan (20 January 1895), W. B. Yeats accused Nora Hopper of plagiarizing both his own and Katharine Tynan's poetry in this volume. However, he seems later to have become more sympathetic to her and publicly likened her poetry (by way of praise) to that of 'AE' (George Russell), also identifying the religious, later to be redefined as spiritual, dimensions of her writing ('Irish National Literature III—Contemporary Irish Poets', *The Bookman*, September 1895). She published two more books of poetry in 1896 and 1900 before her marriage to Wilfred Hugh Chesson in 1901. Her final volume, *Aquamarines* (1902), was dedicated to her husband.

373 *Finvarragh*

(To William Butler Yeats)

I AM the King of Faery:
  A thousand years ago
My elfin mother bore me
  Between the snow and snow.
My elfin mother bore me
  —Lightly, as fairies may—
To rule a doubtful country
  Between the dusk and day.

I am the King of Faery:
  And wise I am, and old,
And of my fairy wisdom
  A thousand hands take hold.
But those that seek my helping
  Are glad, for all their care.
My thousand years of wisdom
  Lie dark upon my hair.

I am the King of Faery:
And none there is so gay
Among my gentle people
That dance the dews away.
I am the King of Faery
And none there is so sad,
Though Una is my lady
And Aodh my serving-lad.

I am the King of Faery,
And I, and all my kin,
May neither weep for sorrow,
May neither serve nor sin.
But we shall fade as dewdrops
That morning sun has dried:
So serve us who have served you,
And set your kind doors wide.

(1896)

374 *Two Women*

YOU are a snowdrop, sweet; but will
You look upon this daffodil
That in a careless hand has lain
So long, it cannot drink the rain
And be renewed, or by the sun
Find that unkindly grasp undone?

You are a snowdrop: put your white
By this spoiled gold, dear heart, to-night:
Touch leaves with this less happy flower
Undone by some too happy hour.
You might have been the daffodil
If I had kissed your prudence still.

(1900)

375 *Marsh Marigolds*

HERE in the water-meadows
Marsh marigolds ablaze
Brighten the elder shadows
Lost in an autumn haze.
Drunkards of sun and summer
They keep their colours clear,
Flaming among the marshes
At waning of the year.

Thicker than bee-swung clovers
  They crowd the meadow-space;
Each to the mist that hovers
  Lifts an undaunted face.
Time, that has stripped the sunflower,
  And driven the bees away,
Hath on these golden gipsies
  No power to dismay.

Marsh marigolds together
  Their ragged banners lift
Against the darkening weather,
  Long rains and frozen drift:
They take the lessening sunshine
  Home to their hearts to keep
Against the days of darkness,
  Against the time of sleep.

(1900)

376 *Hertha*

HERTHA goes through the heaving crowd,
And the sound of the sea in men's ears grows loud.
Hertha blossoms the lily-stem
That women may dream back to Bethlehem.
Hertha strews in the trodden mud
Here a ruby and there a bud.

Hertha hides 'neath her fallen hair
Dreams too sweet for the world to bear.
Hertha's blind, but she knows and hears
The growth of grass and the dropping of tears.
Hertha's home there is no man knows:
Depth of the sea or heart of the rose.

Every pulse is a pulse of hers:
Rush of rain and the sap that stirs,
Desire of goodness, desire of sin,
Dreams that go when the day comes in—
Thrill of the thrush ere her songs begun,
Scents that the whin-bush yields the sun.

Alike in the speedwell and the skies
She has bidden the colour of faith arise:
Crocus and comet alike she knows,
And the riddling doubt with its ebbs and flows.
She has bidden the rose go down to death
With the sweetness of life in her latest breath.

From her eyes that see not is nothing hidden,
Lawful pleasure or joy forbidden.
The new grass quickening down in the sod,
And the morning star singing up to God;
The stir of the lengthening iris-spears,
And the voice of the four winds Hertha hears—

But Hertha hears, through the laughter of men,
The broken sob of the Magdalen.

(1900)

SOURCES AND NOTES

ANNA LAETITIA BARBAULD, 1743–1825 (nos. 1–10). 'Epistle to William Wilberforce Esq. On the Rejection of the Bill for Abolishing the Slave Trade, 1791', written 1791 (*the poems of Anna Laetitia Barbauld*, ed. William McCarthy and Elizabeth Kraft (Athens, GA: University of Georgia Press, 1994), 284), first published 1792 in a new and revised edition of *Poems* (1773). 'On the Expected General Rising of the French Nation in 1792' (1793), first published as 'To a Great Nation. Written by a Lady', in *Cambridge Intelligencer*, 2 November 1793 (McCarthy and Kraft, *Poems*, 291). 'To Dr. Priestley, December 29, 1792' (1793), first published in *Morning Chronicle*, 8 January 1793 (McCarthy and Kraft, *Poems*, 293). 'The Rights of Woman', first published 1825, written *c.*1793 (McCarthy and Kraft, *Poems*, 289). 'Inscription for an Ice-House', first published 1825, written *c.*1793 (McCarthy and Kraft, *Poems*, 293). 'To the Poor', written *c.*1795 (McCarthy and Kraft, *Poems*, 295). 'To a Little Invisible Being Who Is Expected Soon to Become Visible', written *c.*1795 (McCarthy and Kraft, *Poems*, 296). 'To Mr S. T. Coleridge: 1797', written *c.*1795, first published in *Monthly Magazine*, 7 (1799), pp. 231–2 (McCarthy and Kraft, *Poems*, 296). *Eighteen Hundred and Eleven; A Poem* (London: J. Johnson & Co., 1812). 'The Snowdrop', date of composition unknown, published in *Flora and Thalia; or Gems of Flowers and Poetry*, ed. 'A Lady' (London: Henry Washborne, 1835), 153. Texts for nos. 1–9 taken from *The Works of Anna Laetetia Barbauld*, with a Memoir by Lucy Aikin (2 vols, London: Longman & Co., 1825). Full point supplied in no. 9 line 176.

HANNAH MORE, 1745–1833 (nos. 11–14). 'Sensibility', first published in *Sacred Dramas: Chiefly Intended for Young Persons: The Subjects Taken from the Bible, to which Is Added, 'Sensibility', a Poem* (London: T. Cadell, 1782). 'The Black Slave Trade', first published as *Slavery, A Poem* (London: T. Cadell, 1788). 'Will Chip's *True* Rights of Man, in Opposition to the *New* Rights of Man', date of first publication unknown. Texts of nos. 11–13 taken from *Poems* (London: T. Cadell, 1816). 'The Sorrows of Yamba, or, the Negro Woman's Lamentation', date of first publication unknown (*c.* 1800?) (Newcastle: Newcastle Religious Tract Society, Edward Walker, 1823). Full point supplied in no. 14 line 162.

ANNA SEWARD, ?1747–1809 (no. 15). 'The Ghost of Cuchullin', from *The Poetical Works of Anna Seward, with Extracts from Her Literary Correspondence*, ed. Walter Scott (3 vols., Edinburgh: John Ballantyne; Longman: Longman, Hurst, Rees & Orme, 1810).

CHARLOTTE SMITH, 1749–1806 (nos. 16–20). 'Elegaic Sonnets, No. 44', first published in *Elegaic Sonnets and Other Poems* (London: J. Dodsley, 1784); text taken from *Elegaic Sonnets, with Additional Sonnets and Other Poems* (5th edn., London: T. Cadell, 1789). 'Elegaic Sonnets, No. 70', 'Elegaic Sonnets, No. 77', and 'Fragment. Descriptive of the Miseries of War; from a Poem Called "The Emigrants", Printed in 1793', from *Elegaic Sonnets, and Other Poems*, vol. ii (London: T. Cadell, and Jr., and W. Davies, 1797). 'Beachy Head', from *Beachy Head: with Other Poems Now First Published* (London: J. Johnson, 1807).

JOANNA BAILLIE, 1762–1851 (nos. 21–27). 'A Winter's Day' and 'A Summer's Day', first published in *Poems, Wherein It Is Attempted to Describe Certain Views of Nature and of Rustic Manners* (London: Joseph Johnson, 1790). 'To a Child', 'London', 'Lines to a Teapot', 'Address to a Steamvessel', and 'Volunteer's Song, Written in 1803', written post-1790 according to *Fugitive Verses* (London: Edward Moxon, 1840). Texts of nos. 21–27 from *The Dramatic and Poetical Works of Joanna Baillie* (London: Longman, Brown, Green, & Longman, 1851).

HELEN MARIA WILLIAMS, 1762–1827 (nos. 28–34). From 'Peruvian Tales'. Tale II, 'Alzira', first published as *Peru, A Poem. In Six Cantos* (London: T. Cadell, 1784). 'To Sensibility', first published in *Poems* (2 vols., London: Thomas Cadell, 1786). 'On the Bill which Was Passed In England for Regulating the Slave Trade; a Short Time before Its Abolition', first published as *A Poem on the Bill Lately Passed for Regulating the Slave Trade* (London: T. Cadell, 1788). 'The Bastille, A Vision', first published in *Julia, A Novel, interspersed with some poetical pieces* (2 vols., London: T. Cadell, 1790), vol. ii. 'Sonnet to the Strawberry' and 'Sonnet to the Curlew', first published as Nos. 4 and 5 in *Paul and Virginia: Translated from the French of Bernadine St Pierre* (London: G. G. and J. Robinson, 1795). Texts of nos. 28–33 from *Poems on Various Subjects. With Introductory Remarks on the Present State of Science and Literature in France* (London: G & W. B. Whittaker, 1823). *The Charter, Lines Addressed by Helena Maria Williams, To Her Nephew Athanase C. L. Coquerel, On His Wedding Day* (Paris: [no publisher given], 1819).

CAROLINA NAIRNE, 1766–1845 (no. 35). 'Cradle Song', from *Life and Songs of the Baroness Nairne; with a Memoir* (London: C. Griffin & Co., 1869).

AMELIA OPIE, 1769–1853 (nos. 36–45). 'The Negro Boy's Tale', 'Consumption', and 'The Despairing Wanderer', from *Poems* (London: T. M. Longman and O. Rees, 1802). 'The Warrior's Return' and 'The Mad Wanderer, A Ballad from *The Warrior's Return, and Other Poems* (London: Longman, Hurst, Reese & Orme, 1808). 'Sketches of St Michael's Mount', from *Lays for the Dead* (London: Longman, Rees, Orme, Brown, Greene & Longman, 1834).

DOROTHY WORDSWORTH, 1771–1855 (nos. 46–47). 'Thoughts on My Sick-Bed', written 1832, and '"When shall I tread your garden path?"', written 1835, first published in *The Wordsworth Circle*, 9: 1 (1978).

MARY TIGHE, 1772–1810 (nos. 48–51). *Psyche*, Cantos I, III and VI, first published in *Psyche; Or, The Legend of Love* (London: James Carpenter [privately printed], 1805). 'The Lily', first published in *Psyche, with Other Poems* (London: Longman, Hurst, Rees, Orme, & Brown, 1811). Texts of nos. 48–51 taken from this last edition.

CHARLOTTE RICHARDSON, 1775–1850? (nos. 52–53). 'Ode on Visiting the Retreat near York; a House Erected by the Society of Friends, for the Reception of Insane Persons', from *Poems Written on Different Occasions* (York: J. Todd and J. Wolstenholme; London: J. Johnson, 1806). 'The Negro, Sept. 1806', from *Poems, Chiefly Composed during the Pressure of Severe Illness* (York: Wilson & Son, W. and R. Spence, Todd & Sons, J. Wolstenholme; London: J. Johnson, Longman, Hurst, & Orme, 1809).

LUCY AIKIN, 1781–1864 (no. 54). 'Epistles on the Character and Condition of Women, In Various Ages and Nations', I, from *Epistles on Women, exemplifying their character and condition in various ages and nations. With miscellaneaous poems* (London: J. Johnson & Co., 1810).

ANN TAYLOR, 1782–1866 and JANE TAYLOR, 1783–1824 (nos. 55–57). 'The Star', from *Rhymes for the Nursery* (London: Darton & Harvey, 1806). 'A Child's Hymn of Praise', from *Hymns for Infant Minds* (2nd edn., London: J. Conder, 1810). 'The Folly of Finery', from *Original Hymns for Sunday Schools* (4th edn., London: J. Conder, 1816).

CAROLINE BOWLES (later SOUTHEY), 1786–1854 (nos. 58–63). From *Ellen Fitzarthur: A Metrical Tale*, first published as *Ellen Fitzarthur: A Metrical Tale in Five Cantos* (London: Longman, Hurst, Rees, Orme & Brown, 1820). 'The Father's Tale', first published in *Tales of the Factories: Respectfully Inscribed to Mr. Sadler* (Edinburgh: William Blackwood; London: T. Cadell, 1833). 'The Birthday', Books I, II and III and 'The Legend of Santarem', first published in *The Birthday, A Poem, in Three Parts, to which is added Occasional Verses* (Edinburgh: William Blackwood; London: Thomas Cadell, 1836). Texts of nos. 60–63 from *The Poetical Works of Caroline Bowles Southey* (Edinburgh and London: William Blackwood & Sons, 1867).

MARY RUSSELL MITFORD, 1787–1855 (no. 64). 'To a Yellow Butterfly, April 8th, 1808', from *Poems* (London: Longman, Hurst, Rees & Orme, 1810).

CHARLOTTE ELLIOTT, 1789–1871 (no. 65). '"Just as I am"', from *Selections from the Poems of Charlotte Elliott. With a memoir by E.B.* [Mrs E. Babington] (London: Religious Tract Society, 1873).

EMMA ROBERTS, *c.*1793–1840 (no. 66). 'A Scene in the Doaab', from *Oriental Scenes, Dramatic Sketches and Tales, with Other Poems* (Calcutta: Norman Grant [privately printed], 1830).

JANET HAMILTON, 1795–1873 (nos. 67–70). 'Civil War in America—Expostulation', and 'Lines Addressed to Mrs H. B. Stowe, on the Occasion of Her Visit to Glasgow, April 13, 1853' from *Poems and Essays of a Miscellaneaous Character on Subjects of General Interest* (Glasgow: Thomas Murray & Son; Edinburgh: Paton & Ritchie; London: Arthur Hall & Co., 1863). 'The Sunday Rail—I. On the Opening of the North British Railway for Running Sunday Trains, September 3, 1865' and 'A Lay of the Tambour Frame', from *Poems and Ballads, with Introductory Pages by the Rev George Gilfillan and the Rev Alexander Wallace, DD* (Glasgow: James Maclehose, 1868).

FELICIA HEMANS, 1795–1835 (nos. 71–81). 'England's Dead', first published in *The Siege of Valencia; A Dramatic Poem. The Last Constantine; with Other Poems* (London: John Murray, 1823). 'The Sword of the Tomb. A Northern Legend' and 'The Forest Sanctuary', first published in *The Forest Sanctuary; and Other Poems* (London: John Murray, 1825). 'Joan of Arc in Rheims', first published in *New Monthly Magazine and Literary Journal*, 17 (1826), 314–16. 'The Homes of England', first published in *Blackwood's Edinburgh Magazine*, 21 (1827), 392. 'Arabella Stuart', 'Properzia Rossi', 'Indian Woman's Death-Song', 'The Image in Lava', first published in *New Monthly Magazine*, 20 (1827), 255–56, first published in *Records of Woman; with Other Poems* (Edinburgh: William Blackwood; London: T. Cadell, 1828). 'Casabianca', first published in *Monthly Magazine*, n. 6. 2 (1826), 164. 'The Shadow of a Flower', first published in *Winter's Wreath* (London: Whittaker, Treacher & Co.; Liverpool: George Smith, 1830), 174–5. Texts of nos. 71–80 from *The Poetical Works of Felicia Hemans, with memoir of her life, by her sister, C. Harriet Hughes* (7 vols., Edinburgh: William Blackwood & Sons; London: Thomas Cadell, 1839).

MARIA ABDY, *c.*1797–1867 (no. 82). 'A Governess Wanted', from *Poetry* (2nd ser., London: J. Robins & Co., 1838).

MARY SEWELL, 1797–1884 (no. 83). 'The Bad Manager', from *Homely Ballads For the Working Man's Fireside* (London: Smith, Elder and Co., 1858).

LOUISA STUART COSTELLO, 1799–1870 (nos. 84–86). 'The Maid of the Cyprus Isle', and 'On Reading the Account of the Battle of Waterloo', from *The Maid of the Cyprus Isle, and Other Poems* (London: Sherwood, Neely & Jones, Sharpe, Walker, Harper & Co., R. Rees & Lloyd, 1815). No. 86 from *The Lay of the Stork* (London: William and Frederick G. Cash, 1856).

MARY HOWITT, 1799–1888 (nos. 87–88). 'The Spider and the Fly. An Apologue', from *Sketches of Natural History* (London: Effingham, Wilson, 1834); 'The Lady Magdalene. A Legend of an English Hall' (dated 1835), from *Ballads and Other Poems* (London: Longman, Brown, Green & Longman, 1847).

MARY LEMAN GRIMSTONE, ?1800–1866 (no. 89). 'The Poor Woman's Appeal to Her Husband', from *Monthly Repository*, NS 8 (1834), 351–2.

MARIA JANE JEWSBURY, 1800–1833 (nos. 90–97). 'Joan of Arc' and 'Song of the Hindoo Women, While Accompanying a Widow to the Funeral Pile of Her Husband', from *Phantasmagoria; or, Sketches of Life and Literature* (2 vols., London: Hurst, Robinson & Co.; Edinburgh: Archibald Constable & Co., 1825). 'The First Sacrifice', from *Lays of Leisure Hours* (London: J. Hatchard & Son, 1829). Texts of 'Oceanides' I, II, IV, IX, and XII from *Athenaeum*: 29 December 1832, 843; 12 January 1833, 272; 20 April 1833, 249; 12 October 1833, 682; and 28 December 1833, 896–97.

CAROLINE CLIVE ('V'), 1801–1873 (nos. 98–100). 'The Grave', 'Written in Illness' (dated 1829), and 'Former Home', from *IX Poems* (London: Saunders & Otley, 1840).

SARA COLERIDGE, 1802–1852 (nos. 101–103). '"The Sun May Speed or Loiter on His Way"', '"O Sleep, My Babe, Hear Not the Rippling Wave"', '"The Winds Were Whispering, the Waters Glistering"', first published in *Phantasmion* (London: W. Pickering, 1837); texts from *Phantasmion: A Fairy Tale*, ed. John Duke Coleridge (London: Henry S. King, 1874).

L.E.L. (LETITIA ELIZABETH LANDON), 1802–1838 (nos. 104–115). 'Different Thoughts; Suggested by a Picture by G. S. Newton, No. 16 in the British Gallery, and Representing a Girl Looking at Her Lover's Miniature', *Literary Gazette*, 22 March 1823, 189; 'The Phantom Bride', *Literary Gazette*, 18 September 1824, 604–5. 'The Haunted Lake: The Irish Minstrel's Legend', first published in *The Golden Violet, with Its Tales of Romance and Chivalry: And Other Poems* (London: Longman, Rees, Orme, Brown & Green, 1827). 'Revenge', first published in *The Venetian Bracelet, The Lost Pleiad, A History of the Lyre, and Other Poems* (London: Longman, Rees, Orme, Brown, & Green, 1829). 'The Princess Victoria', 'The Pirate's Song off the Tiger Island', and 'Hurdwar, a Place of Hindoo Pilgrimage', first published in *Fisher's Drawing Room Scrapbook* (1832), 5–6, 15–16, and 18. 'The Banquet of Aspasia and Pericles', 'Calypso Watching the Ocean', and 'A Supper of Madame de Brinvilliers', all first published as part of a group of poems, 'Subjects for Pictures,' in *New Monthly Magazine*: 47 (1836), 176–8; 48 (1836), 20–2, 24–5. 'The Factory', from *Christian Lady's Magazine*, 10 (1838), 219–22. 'The Marriage Vow', first published in *Life and Literary Remains of L.E.L.* ed. Laman Blanchard (2 vols., London: Henry Colburn, 1841). Texts of nos. 106–107 and 111–14 taken from *Poetical Works of Letitia Elizabeth Landon*, '*L.E.L.*' (London: G. Routledge, 1873).

SUSANNA STRICKLAND (later MOODIE), 1803–1885 (no. 116). 'The Spirit of Motion', from *Enthusiasm and Other Poems* (London: Smith, Elder, 1831).

SARAH FLOWER ADAMS, 1805–1848 (nos. 117–119). 'A Dream' and 'Songs of the Months.—No. 3, March. Winds and Clouds', from *Monthly Repository*, NS 6 (1832), 257–9, and N.S. 8 (1834), 203. 'Nearer, My God, To Thee' (*c.*1834), from *Memories of Some Contemporary Poets*, ed. Emily Taylor (London: Longmans, Green & Co., 1868).

MARY MARIA COLLING, 1805–? (no. 120). 'The Moon and the Cloud', from *Fables and Other Pieces in Verse*, ed. Mrs Anne Eliza Bray (London: Longman, Rees, Orme, Brown, & Green, 1831).

ELIZABETH BARRETT BROWNING, 1806–1861 (nos. 121–139). 'The Cry of the Children', first published in *Blackwood's Edinburgh Magazine*, 54 (1843), 260–2; 'Bertha in the Lane', 'To George Sand: A Desire', 'To George Sand: A Recognition', and 'L.E.L.'s Last Question', from *Poems* (2 vols., London: Edward Moxon, 1844). 'The Runaway Slave at Pilgrim's Point', first published in *The Liberty Bell* [Boston] (1848). Text of no. 126, 'Felicia Hemans', 'Sonnets from the Portuguese', nos. I, V, XII, XIV, XXIX, XLII, from *Poems*, revised and selected (2 vols., London: Chapman & Hall, 1850). *Aurora Leigh* (London: Chapman & Hall, 1856). 'A Curse for a Nation', from *Poems before Congress* (London: Chapman & Hall, 1860). 'Lord Walter's Wife' and 'A Musical Instrument', from *Last Poems* (London: Chapman & Hall, 1862).

HELEN DUFFERIN, 1807–1867 (no. 140). 'The Charming Woman', first published anonymously in London in 1835, from *Songs, Poems, & Verses by Helen, Lady Dufferin (Countess of Gifford)*, ed. with a memoir and some account of the Sheridan family, by her son the Marquess of Dufferin and Ava (London: John Murray, 1894).

ELIZA MARY HAMILTON, 1807–1851 (nos. 141–143). 'The Moon Seen by Day' (dated 1829), 'Lines Composed at Sea', and 'A Young Girl Seen in Church' (dated 1832), from *Poems* (Dublin: Hodges & Smith, 1838).

CAROLINE NORTON, 1808–1877 (nos. 144–151). Extracts from 'The Sorrows of Rosalie', II and III, from *The Sorrows of Rosalie. A Tale, with Other Poems* (London: John Ebers, 1829). Extract from 'The Undying One,' Canto II, '"As When from Dreams Awaking"', 'The Name', and 'Recollections of a Faded Beauty', from *The Undying One, and Other Poems* (London: Henry Colburn & Richard Bentley, 1830). Extract from *A Voice from the Factories in Serious Verse* (London: John Murray, 1836). 'Lines, Etc.', from *Lines to Queen Victoria* (London: Charles Reynell, 1840).

FRANCES ANNE KEMBLE, 1809–1893 (no. 152). 'Lines on a Young Woman, Who, after a Short and Wretched Marriage, Went Mad and Died', from *Poems* (London: E. Moxon & Co., 1866).

LADY JOHN SCOTT, 1810–1900 (no. 153). 'We've Lookit for Ye Lang' (dated 1873), from *Songs and Verses* (Edinburgh: David Douglas, 1904).

MARY ANN BROWNE, 1812–1844 (nos. 154–155). 'Noon by the Sea Side', from *The Cornonal; Original Poems, Sacred and Miscellaneous* (London: Hamilton, Adams and Co.; Liverpool: D. Marples, 1833). '"My Baby! My Baby! They've Told Me He is Dead"', from *The Birth-day Gift* (London: Hamilton, Adams and Co.; Liverpool: D. Marples and Co., 1834).

SARAH STICKNEY ELLIS, 1812–1872 (nos. 156–157). Extract from *The Island Queen: A Poem* (London: John Snow, 1846). Extract from *Janet: One of Many:*

A Story in Verse (London: Emily Faithfull & Co., Victoria Press (for the Employment of Women), 1862).

ANN HAWKSHAW, 1813–1885 (nos. 158–159). 'The Mother to Her Starving Child' and 'Why Am I a Slave?', from *Dionysius the Areopagite, with Other Poems* (London: Jackson & Walford; Manchester: Simms & Dinham, 1842).

GRACE AGUILAR, 1816–1847 (no. 160). 'The Vision of Jerusalem', from *The Occident and American Jewish Advocate: A Monthly Periodical Devoted to the Diffusion of Knowledge on Jewish Literature and Religion*, 1: 11 (1844), 541–2.

CHARLOTTE BRONTË, 1816–1855 (nos. 161–163). 'The Wife's Will', 'The Teacher's Monologue', and 'Evening Solace', from *Poems by Currer, Ellis, and Acton Bell* (London: Aylott & Jones, 1846).

FRANCES BROWNE, 1816–1879 (nos. 164–165). 'Words', from *The Star of Attéghéi: The Vision of Schwartz and Other Poems* (London: Edward Moxon, 1844). 'The Last Friends', from *Lyrics and Miscellaneous Poems* (Edinburgh: Sutherland & Knox, 1848).

ELIZA COOK, 1818–1889 (nos. 166–171). 'The Old Arm-Chair', first published in *Weekly Dispatch* (1837). 'Lines to the Queen of England', 'The Old Arm-Chair', 'Oh! Dear to Memory Are Those Hours', and 'The Englishman', from *Melaia; and other poems* (London: R. J. Wood, 1838). 'Song of the Red Indian' and 'Harvest Song', from *Poems of Eliza Cook* (2nd ser., London: Simpkin, Marshall & Co., 1845).

EMILY BRONTË, 1818–1848 (nos. 172–182). 'Stars', 'The Philosopher', 'Remembrance', 'Song', 'The Prisoner. A Fragment', 'To Imagination', 'Sympathy', 'Death', 'Stanzas To—', 'My Comforter', 'The Old Stoic', from *Poems by Currer, Ellis, and Acton Bell* (London: Aylott & Jones, 1846).

GEORGE ELIOT (MARY ANN EVANS), 1819–1880 (nos. 183–185). 'A Minor Prophet' (dated 1865), '"O May I Join the Choir Invisible"' (dated 1867), and 'Brother and Sister' (dated 1869), from *The Legend of Jubal and Other Poems* (Edinburgh: William Blackwood & Sons, 1874). Eliot's order retained.

ANNE BRONTË, 1820–1849 (nos. 186–188). 'The Arbour', 'If This Be All', and 'A Word to The "Elect"', from *Poems by Currer, Ellis, and Acton Bell* (London: Aylott & Jones, 1846).

ANNE EVANS, 1820–1870 (nos. 189–192). 'Over!', 'Fragments', 'Outcry', and 'Orinda: A Ballad', from *Poems and Music. With memorial preface by Anne Thackeray Ritchie* (London: Kegan Paul, 1880).

JEAN INGELOW, 1820–1897 (nos. 193–197). 'Divided' and 'The High Tide on the Coast of Lincolnshire (1571)', from *Poems* (London: Longman, Green, Longman, Roberts, & Green, 1863). 'Gladys and Her Island (On the Advantages of the Poetical Temperament), from *Poems* (2nd ser., London: Longman, Green, & Co., 1874). 'Echo and the Ferry' and 'Perdita', from *Poems* (3rd ser., London: Longman, Green, & Co., 1885).

MENELLA BUTE SMEDLEY, 1820–1877 (nos. 198–199). 'Garibaldi at Varignano', from *The Story of Queen Isabel and other verses* (London: Bell & Daldy, 1863). 'Lines on the Greek Massacre', first published as 'Lines Suggested by the Greek Massacre', in *Macmillan's Magazine*, 22 (1870), 140–41; text taken from *Two Dramatic Poems* (London: Macmillan & Co., 1874).

DORA GREENWELL, 1821–1882 (nos. 200–204). 'Christina' (dated 1851), 'Madana', 'To Elizabeth Barrett Browning in 1851', 'To Elizabeth Barrett

Browning in 1861', and 'A Scherzo (A Shy Person's Wishes)', from *Poems* (London: Alexander Strahan, 1867).

'SPERANZA' (JANE FRANCESCA WILDE), 1821–1896 (nos. 205–207). 'A Supplication', 'The Exodus', and 'The Fisherman', from *Poems* (Dublin: James Duffy, 1864).

ELIZA KEARY, *c.*1822–*c.*1889 (nos. 208–213). 'Disenchanted', 'Through the Wood', 'A Mother's Call', 'A Flower to the Moon', 'Doctor Emily', and 'Christine and Mary: A Correspondence', from *Little Seal-Skin and other poems* (London: George Bell & Sons, 1874). Closing quotation mark supplied in poem no. 212 line 48.

ANNA LETITIA WARING, 1823–1910 (no. 214). '"Father, I Know that All My Life"', from *Hymns and Meditations* (3rd edn., with additions, London: W. & F. G. Cash, 1852).

LOUISA SHORE, 1824–1895 (no. 215). 'War Music', first published in *Spectator* 27 (1854), 1230; text taken from *Poems. With a memoir by her sister Arabella Shore and an appreciation by Frederic Harrison* (London: John Lane, The Bodley Head, 1897).

ADELAIDE ANNE PROCTER, 1825–1864 (nos. 216–225). 'Now', 'The Lesson of the War (1855)', 'A Tomb in Ghent', 'A Woman's Question', and 'Envy' first published in *Household Words*, 26 November 1853, 302, 3 February 1855, 12, 29 December 1855, 515–17, 6 February 1858, 179, and 12 March 1859, 348. 'A Lost Chord', 'The Requital', and 'A Comforter', first published in *English Woman's Journal*, '5 (1860, 36 and 184–5 and 6 (1860), 177–8'. Texts of nos. 216–219 taken from *Legends and Lyrics* (London: Bell & Daldy, 1858). Texts of nos. 220–224 from *Legends and Lyrics* (2nd ser., London: Bell & Daldy, 1861). 'Homeless', first published in *A Chaplet of Verses*, published for the Benefit of the Providence Row Night Refuge for Homeless Women and Children (London: Longman, Green, Longman & Roberts, 1862).

DINAH MARIA MULOCK CRAIK, 1826–1887 (nos. 226–227). 'Only a Woman' and 'To Elizabeth Barrett Browning on Her Later Sonnets. 1856', from *Poems by the Author of 'John Halifax, Gentleman'* (London: Sampson Low, Marston, Low & Searle, 1872).

EMILY PFEIFFER, 1827–1890 (nos. 228–236). 'A Rhyme for the Time', 'Longing and Asking', and '"Peace to the Odalisque"' I and II, from *Gerard's Monument and Other Poems* (London, Trubner & Co., 1873). 'Ode to the Teuton Women', from *Poems* (London: Strahan & Co., 1876); 'Kassandra', I and II, and 'Klytemnestra', I and II, from *Quarterman's Grace and Other Poems* (London: C. Kegan Paul & Co., 1879).

'CLARIBEL' (CHARLOTTE ALINGTON, later BARNARD), 1829–1869 (no. 237). 'I Remember It' from *Fireside Thoughts, Ballads, Etc. Etc.* (London: James Nisbet & Co., 1865).

BESSIE RAYNER PARKES (MADAME BELLOC), 1829–1925 (nos. 238–239). 'To Elizabeth Barrett Browning', first published as 'To * * * * *', in *Poems* (London: John Chapman, 1852). Text of no. 238 and 'For Adelaide', from *Poems* (2nd edn., London: John Chapman, 1855).

ELIZABETH SIDDAL, 1829–1862 (nos. 240–243) 'True Love', 'Dead Love', 'He and She and Angels Three', and 'Love and Hate', from Jan Marsh, *Elizabeth*

Siddal: Pre-Raphaelite Artist, 1829–1862 (Sheffield: Sheffield City Art Galleries, 1991).

LOUISA A. HORSFIELD, 1830–?1865 (nos. 244–245). 'To My Departed Baby' and 'Lines to a Friend in Australia', from *The Cottage Lyre: Being Miscellaneous Poetry* (2nd edn., enlarged, London: Richard Davies; Leeds: John Parrott, 1862).

CHRISTINA ROSSETTI, 1830–1894 (nos. 246–258). 'Song', written 12 December 1848 (see *The Complete Poems of Christina Rossetti*, ed. R. W. Crump (3 vols, Baton Rouge, LA: Louisiana State University Press, 1979–90), i. 253); 'My Dream', written 9 March 1855 (Crump, i. 242): 'My Secret', written 23 November 1857 (Crump, i. 247); 'Winter Rain', written 31 January 1859 (Crump, i. 239); 'Goblin Market', written 27 April 1859 (Crump, i. 234); 'Up-Hill', written 29 June 1859 (Crump, i. 256). Text of nos. 246–251 taken from *Goblin Market and Other Poems* (London: Macmillan & Co., 1862). 'A Royal Princess', written 22 October 1855, first published in *Poems: An Offering to Lancashire. Printed and Published for the Art Exhibition for the Relief of Distress in the Cotton Districts* (London: Emily Faithfull, 1863 (Crump, i. 248); 'The Lowest Room', written 30 September 1856 (Crump, i. 301) first published *Macmillan's Magazine*, 9 (1864) 436–39; 'L.E.L.', written 15 February 1859, first published in *Victoria Magazine*, 1 (1863), 40–1 (Crump, i. 288); 'Under the Rose', written March 1865 (Crump, i. 292); and 'Autumn Violets', first published in *Macmillan's Magazine*, 19 (1868), 84 (Crump, i. 300). Texts of nos. 252, 254, and 255 taken from *The Prince's Progress and Other Poems* (London: Macmillan & Co., 1866). Texts of 253 and 256 taken from *Goblin Market, The Prince's Progress and Other Poems* (London: Macmillan & Co., 1875). 'Monna Innominata', date of composition unknown (Crump, ii. 370) and 'The Thread of Life', date of composition unknown (Crump, ii. 384), from *A Pageant and Other Poems* (London: Macmillan & Co., 1881). No. 248 later retitled 'Winter: My Secret'. No. 255 later retitled '"The Iniquity of the Fathers upon the Children"'.

ISA CRAIG-KNOX, 1831–1903 (no. 259). 'The Building of the City', from *Songs of Consolation* (London: Macmillan & Co., 1874).

MARIANNE FARNINGHAM (MARY ANNE HEARN), 1834–1909 (no. 260). 'It is Well', from *Poems* (London: James Clarke & Co., 1866).

M. E. BRADDON, 1835–1915 (nos. 261–262). 'Queen Guinevere', and 'To a Coquette', from *Garibaldi and Other Poems* (London: Bosworth & Harrison, 1861).

ELLEN JOHNSTON, 1835–73 (no. 263). 'The Last Sark. Written in 1859', from *Autobiography, Poems and Songs* (Glasgow: William Love, 1867).

'A FACTORY GIRL', dates not known (no. 264). Extract from 'The Cotton Famine and the Lancashire Operatives', from *The Cotton Famine and the Lancashire Operatives. A Poem* (Preston: W. & J. Dobson; London: Simpkin, Marshall and Co., 1862).

RUTH WILLS, dates not known (nos. 265–266). 'Anne Boleyn', from *Lays of Lowly Life* (London: Simpkin, Marshall, & Co.; Leicester: Winks & Son, 1861). 'A New Gospel' from *Lays of Lowly Life* (2nd edn., London: James Nisbet & Co., 1868).

FRANCES RIDLEY HAVERGAL, 1836–1878 (nos. 267–268). 'The Ministry of Song,' from *The Ministry of Song* (London: James Nisbet & Co, 1871). 'An Indian Flag', from *Under the Surface* (London: James Nisbet & Co., 1874).

ANNIE LOUISA WALKER, 1836–1907 (no. 269). 'The Night Cometh', from *Oak and Maple. English and Canadian Verses* (London: Kegan Paul & Co., 1890).

AGNES MAULE MACHAR, 1837–1927 (nos. 270–271). 'Canada to the Laureate. In Response to Tennyson's Lines' and 'Our Lads to the Front! Embarkation of the Canadian Contingent for South Africa;—Quebec, October 31, 1899', from *Lays of the 'True North' and Other Canadian Poems* (London: Elliot Stock, 1902).

AUGUSTA WEBSTER, 1837–1894 (nos. 272–283). 'Circe', 'The Happiest Girl in the World', and 'A Castaway', from *Portraits* (London: Macmillan, 1870). Sonnets nos. VI, VII, IX, XII, XIII, XIV, XV, XVI, XVII, from *Mother and Daughter: an uncompleted sonnet-sequence by the late August Webster*, with an introductory note by William Michael Rossetti (London: Macmillan & Co., 1895).

CHARLOTTE ELLIOT ('FLORENZ'), 1839–1880 (no. 284). 'The Pythoness', first published in *Stella, and Other Poems* (London: William Blackwood and Sons 1867); text taken from *Medusa and Other Poems* (London: C. Kegan Paul & Co., 1878).

HARRIET ELEANOR HAMILTON KING, 1840–1920 (no. 285). 'The Execution of Felice Orsini, March 13th, 1858', from *Aspromonte and Other Poems* (London: Macmillan & Co., 1869).

MATHILDE BLIND, 1841–1896 (nos. 286–289). 'The Street-Children's Dance', from *The Prophecy of St Oran and Other Poems* (London: Newman, 1881). Extract from *The Ascent of Man* (London: Chatto & Windus, 1889). 'The Russian Student's Tale', from *Dramas in Miniature* (London: Chatto & Windus, 1891). 'On a Torso of Cupid', from *Birds of Passage: Songs of Orient and Occident* (London: Chatto & Windus, 1895).

VIOLET FANE (MARY MONTGOMERIE LAMB, later SINGLETON, later CURRIE), 1843–1905 (nos. 290–292). 'Lancelot and Guinevere', from *From Dawn to Noon. Poems* (London: Longman, Green, & Co., 1872). 'The Irish "Patriots"'. (To Wilfred Scawen Blunt)', from *Autumn Songs* (London: Chapman & Hall, 1889). 'At Christie's', from *Under Cross and Crescent* (London: J. C. Nimmo, 1896).

MARGARET VELEY, 1843–1887 (nos. 293–294). 'A Japanese Fan', first published in *Cornhill Magazine*, 34 (1876), 379–84. Text of no. 293 and 'A Game of Piquet' from *A Marriage of Shadows and Other Poems* (London: Smith, Elder & Co., 1888).

L. S. BEVINGTON (later GUGGENBERGER). 1845–1895 (nos. 295–299). 'Love and Pride', from *Key-Notes* (London: C. Kegan Paul & Co., 1879). 'Bees in Clover. A Song', 'The Unpardonable Sin', and 'Hated', from *Poems, Lyrics, and Sonnets* (London, Elliot Stock, 1882). 'Revolution', from *Liberty Lyrics* (London: James Tochatti ['Liberty' Press], 1895).

E. H. HICKEY, 1845–1924 (nos. 300–301). 'A Sculptor', from *A Sculptor and Other Poems* (London: Kegan Paul, Trench & Co., 1881). 'A Weak-Minded Woman's Comparisons', from *Michael Villiers, Idealist and Other Poems* (London: Smith, Elder & Co., 1891).

LUCY KNOX, 1845–1884 (nos. 302–303). 'Sonnet. A Cry to Men' and 'Sonnet. Lament of the Loyal Irish, 1869', from *Sonnets and other Poems* (London: Smith, Elder & Co., 1872).

EMILY LAWLESS, 1845–1913 (no. 304). 'After Aughrim', from *Atlantic Rhymes and Rhythms. With the Wild Geese*, with an introduction by Stopford A. Brooke (London: Isbister & Co., 1902).

MICHAEL FIELD (KATHERINE HARRIS BRADLEY, 1846–1914; EDITH EMMA COOPER, 1862–1913) (nos. 305–312). Nos. XVII, XXXV, and LIV, from *Long Ago* (London: G. Bell & Sons, 1889). 'Spring', 'The Rescue', 'Saint Sebastian', 'A Pen-Drawing of Leda', and 'The Sleeping Venus', from *Sight and Song* (London: Elkin Mathews & John Lane at the Sign of the Bodley Head, 1892).

ALICE MEYNELL, 1847–1922 (nos. 313–315). 'In Autumn', 'A Letter from a Girl to Her Own Old Age', and '"Soeur Monique"', from A. C. Thompson, *Preludes, with Illustrations and Ornaments by Elizabeth Thompson* (London: Henry S. King, 1875).

L. ORMISTON CHANT, 1848–1923 (no. 316). 'Hope's Song', from *Verona and Other Poems* (London: David Stott, 1887).

ELIZABETH RACHEL CHAPMAN, 1850–post-1897 (nos. 317–320). 'Hereafter', 'A Woman's Strength', and 'Hope', from *The New Purgatory, and other poems* (London: T. Fisher Unwin, 1887). 'XXX', from *A Little Child's Wreath* (London: Elkin, Mathews & John Lane; New York: Dodd, Mead & Co., 1894).

ANNIE MATHESON, 1853–1924 (no. 321). 'A Song for Women', from *'The Religion of Humanity' and other poems* (London: Percival & Co., 1890).

TORU DUTT, 1856–1877 (nos. 322–323). 'On the Fly-Leaf of Erckmann-Chatrian's Novel Entitled "Madame Thérèse"' and 'Sonnet—Baugmaree', from *Ancient Ballads and Legends of Hindustan* (London: Kegan Paul, Trench & Co., 1882).

MARGARET L. WOODS, 1856–1945 (nos. 324–325). 'L'Envoi', from *Lyrics & Ballads* (London: Richard Bentley & Son, 1889). *Aëromancy and Other Poems*, Shilling Garland Series (London: Elkin Mathews, 1896).

A. MARY F. ROBINSON (later DARMESTETER, later DUCLAUX), 1857–1944 (nos. 326–331). 'Tuscan Olives (Rispetti)', from *The New Arcadia and Other Poems* (London: Ellis & White, 1884). 'Etruscan Tombs', 'Darwinism', and 'The Idea', from *Songs, Ballads, and a Garden Play* (London: T. Fisher Unwin, 1888). 'The Bookworm' and 'Liberty', from *Retrospect and Other Poems*, Cameo Series (London: T. Fisher Unwin, 1893).

CONSTANCE NADEN, 1858–1889 (nos. 332–333). 'The Lady Doctor', from *Songs and Sonnets of Springtime* (London: C. Kegan Paul & Co., 1881). 'Scientific Wooing', from *A Modern Apostle; The Elixir of Life; The Story of Clarice; and Other Poems* (London: Kegan Paul, Trench, & Co., 1887).

E. NESBIT, 1858–1924 (nos. 334–337). 'The Wife of All Ages', from *Lays and Legends* (Longman, Green & Co., 1886). 'Under Convoy', from *Leaves of Life* (London: Longman, Green & Co., 1889). 'Indiscretion', from *A Pomander of Verse* (London: John Lane, 1895). 'The Despot', from *Ballads and Lyrics of Socialism,* 1883–1908, Fabian Society (London: A. C. Fifield, 1908).

KATHARINE TYNAN (later HINKSON), 1859–1931 (nos. 338–339). 'The Irish Hills', from *Shamrocks* (London: Kegan Paul, Trench & Co., 1887). 'Our Lady of Pity', from *Cuckoo Songs* (London: Elkin Mathews & John Lane, 1894).

ROSAMUND MARRIOTT WATSON (GRAHAM R. TOMSON), 1860–1912 (nos. 340–342). 'Ballad of the Bird-Bride (Eskimo)', and '"Eli, Eli, Lama Sabachthani?"', from Graham R. Tomson, *The Bird-Bride: A Volume of Ballads and Sonnets* (Longman, Green, and Co., 1889). 'The Story of Marpessa (As Heard in Hades)', first published in *Universal Review*, 5 (1889), 42–49; text taken from Rosamund Marriott Watson, *The Poems of Rosamund Marriott Watson* (London: John Lane, The Bodley Head; New York: John Lane Company, 1912).

M. E. COLERIDGE, 1861–1907 (nos. 343–351). 'To Memory', 'Gone', 'The Other Side of a Mirror', 'Eyes', 'Mortal Combat', first published in *Fancy's Following* (Oxford: Daniel, 1896) 'A Mother to a Baby', 'Contradictions', 'Mistaken', and 'A Clever Woman'. Texts of 343–351 from *Poems*, ed. Henry Newbolt (London: Elkin Mathews, 1908).

MAY KENDALL, 1861–1943 (nos. 352–356). 'Lay of the Trilobite', 'Education's Martyr', 'Woman's Future', and 'An Incident in Real Life, Related by an Eye-Witness in Marble', from *Dreams to Sell* (London: Longman & Co., 1887). 'The Sandblast Girl and the Acid Man', from *Songs from Dreamland* (London: Longman & Co., 1894).

AMY LEVY, 1861–1889 (nos. 357–362). 'Xantippe', first published in *University Magazine*, 5 (1880), 592–97, and reprinted in *Xantippe and Other Verse* (Cambridge: E. Johnson, 1881). 'Magdalen', first published in *A Minor Poet and Other Verse* (London: T. Fisher Unwin, 1884). Texts of nos. 357 and 358 and 'To Lallie (Outside the British Museum)', from *A Minor Poet and Other Verse*, (London: T. Fisher Unwin, 1884). 'Borderland' and 'At a Dinner Party', from *A London Plane-Tree and Other Poems* (London: T. Fisher Unwin, 1889). 'A Ballad of Religion and Marriage' (written *c.*1889), from a privately published pamphlet, London, 1915.

LAURENCE HOPE (ADELA FLORENCE NICOLSON), 1865–1904 (nos. 363–364). 'The Regret of the Ranee in the Hall of Peacocks' and 'Camp Follower's Song, Gomal River', from *The Garden of Kama, and other love lyrics from India. Arranged in verse* (London: W. Heinemann, 1902).

ETHNA CARBERY (ANNA MACMANUS), 1866–1902 (nos. 365 366). 'Mo Chraoibhín Cno' and 'The Well o' the World's End', from *Poems* (Dublin: M. H. Gill & Son, 1902).

ALICE MILLIGAN, 1866–1953 (nos. 367–370). 'A Song of Freedom', 'When I Was a Little Girl', 'The Dark Palace (The Palace of Aileach, Seat of The O'Neill)', from *Hero Lays* (Dublin: Maunsel and Co., 1908). 'Cormacan Sings (Cormacan an Eigeas, 10th Century)' (*c.*1905–8), from *We Sang for Ireland* (Dublin: M. H. Gill & Son, 1950).

DORA SIGERSON (later SHORTER), 1866–1918 (nos. 371–372). 'With a Rose', from *The Fairy Changeling and Other Poems* (London, John Lane, The Bodley Head, 1897). 'The Wind on the Hills', from *Ballads & Poems* (London: James Bowden, 1899).

NORA HOPPER (later CHESSON), 1871–1906 (nos. 373–376). 'Finvarragh', from *Under Quicken Boughs* (London: John Lane, 1896). 'Two Women', 'Marsh Marigolds', and 'Hertha', from *Songs of the Morning* (London: Grant Richards, 1900).

SELECT BIBLIOGRAPHY

ALEXANDER, CHRISTINE, and JANE SELLARS, *The Art of the Brontës*, Cambridge: Cambridge University Press, 1995.

ARMSTRONG, ISOBEL, *Victorian Poetry: Poetry, Poetics and Politics*, London: Routledge, 1993.

ASHFIELD, ANDREW (ed.), *Women Romantic Poets, 1770–1838: An Anthology*, Manchester: Manchester University Press, 1995.

BLAIN, VIRGINIA, PATRICIA CLEMENTS, and ISOBEL GRUNDY (eds.), *The Feminist Companion to Literature in English: Women Writers from the Middle Ages to the Present* London: Batsford, 1990.

BRISTOW, JOSEPH (ed.), *Victorian Women Poets: Emily Brontë, Elizabeth Barrett Browning, Christina Rossetti*, New Casebooks, Basingstoke: Macmillan, 1995.

BROWNING, ELIZABETH BARRETT, *Aurora Leigh*, ed. Margaret Reynolds, Athens, OH: Ohio University Press, 1992.

FELDMAN, PAULA R., and THERESA M. KELLEY (eds.), *Romantic Women Writers: Voices and Countervoices*, Hanover, NH and London: University Press of New England, 1995.

HICKOK, KATHLEEN, *Representations of Women: Nineteenth-Century British Women's Poetry*, Westport, CT: Greenwood Press, 1984.

JACKSON, J. R. DE J., *Romantic Poetry by Women: A Bibliography, 1770–1835*, Oxford: Clarendon Press, 1993.

KAPLAN, CORA (ed.), *Salt and Bitter and Good: Three Centuries of English and American Women Poets*, London: Paddington Press, 1977.

——*Sea Changes: Essays on Culture and Feminism*, London: Verso, 1986.

KELLY, GARY, *Women, Writing, and Revolution, 1790–1827*, Oxford and New York: Oxford University Press, 1993.

LEIGHTON, ANGELA, *Victorian Women Poets: Writing against the Heart*, Hemel Hempstead: Harvester Wheatsheaf, 1992.

LONSDALE, ROGER (ed.), *Eighteenth-Century Women Poets: An Oxford Anthology*, Oxford: Oxford University Press, 1989.

MELLOR, ANNE, K. (ed.), *Romanticism and Feminism*, Bloomington, IN: Indiana University Press, 1988.

——*Romanticism and Gender*, New York: Routledge, 1993.

MILES, A. H. (ed.), *The Poets and Poetry of the Century*, London: Hutchinson, 1891–1897.

ROSS, MARLON B., *The Contours of Masculine Desire: Romanticism and the Rise of Women's Poetry*, New York and Oxford: Oxford University Press, 1989.

SHARP, ELIZABETH (ed.), *Women's Voices: An Anthology of the Most Characteristic Poems by English, Scotch and Irish Women*, London: Walter Scott, 1887.

——(ed.), *Women Poets of the Victorian Era*, London: Walter Scott, 1890.

SHATTOCK, JOANNE, *The Oxford Guide to British Women Writers*, Oxford and New York: Oxford University Press, 1993.

TODD, JANET (ed.), *Dictionary of British Women Writers*, London: Methuen, 1984.

INDEX OF TITLES

Note: References are to the page number on which the poem begins. The number in parentheses is the poem number.

INDEX OF FIRST LINES

Note: References are to the page number on which the poem begins. The number in parentheses is the poem number.

INDEX OF AUTHORS AND MAJOR SUBJECTS

Note: References are to page numbers. Cross-references are given only for those authors who published under or are known by more than one name. Please note that more than one poem on a page may refer to the subject in question.